1 MONTH OF
FREE
READING

at

www.ForgottenBooks.com

By purchasing this book you are eligible for one month membership to ForgottenBooks.com, giving you unlimited access to our entire collection of over 1,000,000 titles via our web site and mobile apps.

To claim your free month visit:

www.forgottenbooks.com/free963185

ISBN 978-0-260-66761-8
PIBN 10963185

This book is a reproduction of an important historical work. Forgotten Books uses
state-of-the-art technology to digitally reconstruct the work, preserving the original format
whilst repairing imperfections present in the aged copy. In rare cases, an imperfection in
the original, such as a blemish or missing page, may be replicated in our edition. We do,
however, repair the vast majority of imperfections successfully; any imperfections that
remain are intentionally left to preserve the state of such historical works.

Jan 31

34

REPORTS

OF

CASES IN LAW AND EQUITY,

DETERMINED IN THE

SUPREME COURT

OF THE

STATE OF IOWA

E. C. EBERSOLE,

REPORTER.

VOL. XIII,

BEING VOLUME LXXI OF THE SERIES.

0-12/30/21

BANKS & BROTHERS, LAW PUBLISHERS,
NEW YORK: No. 144 NASSAU STREET.
ALBANY, N. Y.: 473 AND 475 BROADWAY.
1888.

Rec. Feb. 8, 1888

JUDGES AND OFFICERS OF THE SUPREME COURT.

Hon. AUSTIN ADAMS, Dubuque, Chief Justice.
" WILLIAM H. SEEVERS, Oskaloosa,
" JOSEPH R. REED, Council Bluffs,
" JAMES H. ROTHROCK, Cedar Rapids, } JUDGES.
" JOSEPH M. BECK, Fort Madison.

CLERK—GILBERT B. PRAY, Webster City.

ATTORNEY-GENERAL—A. J. BAKER, Centerville.

REPORTER—E. C. EBERSOLE, Toledo.

JUDGES OF THE COURTS

FROM WHICH APPEALS MAY BE TAKEN TO THE SUPREME COURT.

DISTRICT COURT.

1ST DISTRICT—J. M. CASEY, Fort Madison; O. H. PHELPS, Burlington.

2D DISTRICT—H. C. TRAVERSE, Bloomfield; DELL STUART, Chariton; CHAS. D LEGGETT, Fairfield.

3D DISTRICT—JOHN W. HARVEY, Leon; R. C. HENRY, Mt. Ayr.

4TH DISTRICT—CHARLES H. LEWIS, Cherokee; GEO. W. WAKEFIELD, Sioux City; SCOTT M. LADD, Sheldon.

5TH DISTRICT—J. H. HENDERSON, Indianola; O. B. AYERS, Knoxville; A. W. WILKINSON, Winterset.

6TH DISTRICT—J. KELLEY JOHNSON, Oskaloosa; DAVID RYAN, Newton; W. R. LEWIS, Montezuma.

7TH DISTRICT—A. J. LEFFINGWELL, Lyons; C. M. WATERMAN, Davenport; W. F. BRANNAN, Muscatine.

8TH DISTRICT—S. H. FAIRALL, Iowa City.

9TH DISTRICT—JOSIAH GIVEN, W. F. CONRAD AND MARCUS KAVANAGH, JR., Des Moines.

10TH DISTRICT—C. F. COUCH, Waterloo; J. J. NEY, Independence; D. J. LINEHAN, Dubuque.

11TH DISTRICT—D. D. MIRACLE, Webster City; JOHN L. STEVENS, Ames; S. M. WEAVER, Iowa Falls.

12TH DISTRICT—JOHN B. CLELAND, Osage; GEORGE W. RUDDICK, Waverly.

13TH DISTRICT—L. O. HATCH, McGregor; C. T. GRANGER, Waukon.

14TH DISTRICT—GEORGE H. CARR, Emmetsburg; LOT THOMAS, Storm Lake.

15TH DISTRICT—A. B. THORNELL, Sidney; GEORGE CARSON, Council Bluffs; H. E. DEEMER, Red Oak; C. F. LOOFBOUROW, Atlantic.

16TH DISTRICT—J. P. CONNER, Denison; J. H. MACOMBER, Ida Grove.

17TH DISTRICT—L. G. KINNE, Toledo.

19TH DISTRICT—J. D. GIFFEN, Marion; J. H. PRESTON, Cedar Rapids.

SUPERIOR COURT.

CEDAR RAPIDS—JOHN T. STONEMAN.

COUNCIL BLUFFS—E. E. AYLESWORTH.

KEOKUK—HENRY BANK, JR.

CRESTON—GEO. P. WILSON.

ERRATUM.

The case reported in 70 Iowa, page 105, is not correctly entitled. The name of the defendant should be *The Chicago, Rock Island & Pacific R'y Co.*, instead of The Chicago, Burlington & Quincy R'y Co. as it now appears.

REPORTER.

TABLE OF CASES

REPORTED IN THIS VOLUME.

REPORTS

OF

Cases in Law and Equity,

DETERMINED IN THE

SUPREME COURT

OF

THE STATE OF IOWA,

AT

DES MOINES, MARCH TERM, A. D. 1887,

IN THE FORTY-FIRST YEAR OF THE STATE.

PRESENT:

Hon. AUSTIN ADAMS, Chief Justice.
" WILLIAM H. SEEVERS,
" JOSEPH R. REED,
" JAMES H. ROTHROCK,
" JOSEPH M. BECK.

} Judges.

THE STATE v. STRUBLE.

1. **Criminal Practice**: DISMISSAL OF PART OF CHARGE DURING TRIAL. Defendant was charged in the indictment with burglary, and also with an assault with intent to murder, but the latter charge was made only for the purpose of bringing the burglary within § 3892 of the Code, and thus aggravating the offense. There was a plea of not guilty, and also of former acquittal, the latter plea having reference to the charge of assault with intent to murder. After the trial had commenced, the state filed a motion for leave to dismiss as to the charge of assault with intent to murder, and to proceed as to the charge of burglary. *Held* that the motion was properly sustained.

2. **Criminal Evidence**: IMMATERIAL: NO PREJUDICE—NO REVERSAL. This court will not reverse a judgment of conviction on account of the

admission of immaterial evidence, where it clearly appears that the defendant could not have been prejudiced thereby.

3. ———: BURGLARY: SUBSEQUENT ACTS OF CO-DEFENDANT: RES GESTÆ. Where one of three defendants, jointly indicted for burglary and the larceny of a trunk, was on trial, evidence that the other two defendants were seen on the night of the burglary, and a few hours thereafter, driving about in a buggy near the place where the stolen trunk was found by the sheriff, was admissible as tending to show, with other evidence, that they had put the trunk where it was found, which, if true, was a part of his transaction of the burglary.

4. Criminal Law: COMPULSORY EXAMINATION OF DEFENDANT'S PERSON: WHAT IS NOT. An examination of the defendant's person, while in jail, by a physician, cannot be said to have been compulsory, where the only evidence of compulsion was that the sheriff accompanied the physician, but it was not shown that he did or said anything in respect to the examination.

5. Criminal Evidence: BURGLARY: EVIDENCE AS TO CHARGE WITHDRAWN. On a trial for burglarly, where an assault with intent to murder had been charged by way of aggravation, but that charge had been withdrawn, held that evidence of a former acquittal of the defendant on that charge was properly excluded.

Appeal from Monona District Court.

THURSDAY, MARCH 3.

THE defendant, Frank Struble, was jointly indicted with Thomas Struble and John McBride. They were charged with having broken and entered the dwelling-house of one Dr. W. W. Ordway, in Monona county, and in the night time, with intent to steal and carry away from the house the goods and property of Ordway. They were also charged with having assaulted Ordway with intent to murder him. The defendant, Struble, was tried alone. He entered a plea of not guilty, and also a plea of former acquittal. After the trial had commenced, the state elected to proceed upon the charge alone of having entered the dwelling-house in the night-time, with intent to commit larceny, and filed a motion to dismiss as to the charge of assault with intent to commit murder. The court sustained the motion, and the trial proceeded, and resulted in a verdict of guilty. Judgment of

imprisonment for twelve years having been entered upon the
verdict, the defendant appeals to this court.

G. W. Cooper, for appellant.

S. M. Marsh, A. J. Baker, Attorney-general, *G. W.
McMillan* and *John S. Monk*, for the State.

ADAMS, CH. J.—I. The defendant insists that the court
erred in sustaining the motion of the state to dismiss as to a
portion of the matter charged in the indictment.

1. CRIMINAL
practice: dis-
missal of
part of
charge dur-
ing trial.

His proposition is that, after a trial has been
entered upon, no part of the indictment can be
withdrawn from consideration of the jury without the consent of the defendant. He relies upon *Com. v.
Jenks*, 1 Gray, 490; *Com. v. Tuck*, 20 Pick., 356; *Com. v.
Scott*, 121 Mass., 33; *State v. Callendine*, 8 Iowa, 288. The
former acquittal relied upon was an acquittal of an assault
with an intent to commit murder. The motion by the state
for leave to dismiss was as to that charge, leaving the charge
of burglary in the indictment without the aggravating circumstance that it was accompanied by an assault, which circumstance, if it had been properly proved in connection with
the burglary, would have justified the court in inflicting a
greater punishment. Code, § 3892. The reason which the
state had for dismissing as to the charge of assault probably
was that it was satisfied that the defendant's plea of former
acquittal as to that charge was good. The defendant's theory
is that, the trial having once commenced, it was his right to
be tried and acquitted of both charges, whereas the state, by
dismissing as to the assault with intent to commit murder,
leaves that charge undisposed of which he had once prepared
himself to meet. But the case has this peculiarity: that the
charge of assault, etc., seems to have been made merely for
the purpose of bringing the charge of burglary within the
provisions of section 3892, above cited. We think that, if
the state had become satisfied for any reason that the convic-

tion for the crime of burglary could not be had under that section, it was the right of the state to simplify the case by withdrawing the charge of assault, etc. In our opinion, the court did not err in sustaining the motion.

II. On the night of the second of January, 1885, the dwelling-house of the prosecuting witness was entered by three men, and a trunk was taken therefrom, containing promissory notes and other papers of very large value. The evidence tended to show that the trunk was taken to the residence of the defendant, Frank Struble, and a part of the contents burned; that afterwards the trunk and part of the contents were taken to a secluded place some miles distant, and left. The number of persons engaged in the commission of the crime was three. The defendants were all debtors of the prosecuting witness, being liable to him upon some of the promissory notes which were destroyed. The court allowed evidence to be given of certain acts of Thomas Struble, a brother of the defendant Frank Struble, done three or four days after the burglary. The trunk had been carried to a place near the head of a stream, called the Beaver, and left there, where it had become covered with snow, except that the ends of iron hoops with which the trunk had been bound had been partially detached, and protruded above the snow. The sheriff, in going out to search for the trunk, took Thomas Struble in his sleigh with him, and, while searching near where the trunk was, Thomas was the first one to discover the iron hoops protruding above the snow. The defendant complains of the admission in evidence of these acts of Thomas. His position is that the acts at most were the acts of an alleged conspirator, and were done long after the transaction which constituted the alleged crime. The evidence appears to have been introduced by the state for the purpose of showing that Thomas knew where the trunk was, and so was one of the three who were engaged in the burglary.

Conceding that the evidence was immaterial, it is difficult

2. CRIMINAL evidence: immaterial: no prejudice—no reversal.

to see how the defendant could have been prejudiced by it. It is not shown that Thomas Struble guided the sheriff to the place where the trunk was, or that the sheriff found the place by reason of anything which Thomas said. The most that is shown is that the sheriff had a talk with Thomas, and afterwards went to hunt for the trunk, and took Thomas with him, and, while hunting, Thomas was the first to see the iron hoops. This, without something more, had no tendency to implicate Thomas nor the defendant, and we are unable to see how the jury could have supposed that it did. There may, of course, have been something in Thomas' words or acts which the evidence does not disclose; but, so far as we can see, Thomas went with the sheriff at his request, and searched with the sheriff where the sheriff thought best to search, and happened, as any person might, to discover what he did. If this evidence could be regarded as having any significance, it would seem to tend to show Thomas' innocence, and overthrow the theory of the state in regard to a conspiracy between these brothers. We cannot reverse on account of the admission of immaterial evidence, where it clearly appears that the party objecting could not have been prejudiced.

III. The defendant assigned as error the admission of other evidence of Thomas' acts, and of the acts of John McBride. About two o'clock of the night of the burglary, Thomas Struble and McBride were seen driving about in a buggy several miles from home, and not far from the place where the trunk was found. The defendant contends that the evidence of these acts was inadmissible, because they were done after the alleged burglary. The theory of the state, of course, was that Thomas and McBride were out trying to make a disposition of the trunk in a place remote from the residence of the guilty parties. In our opinion, the fact that they were seen driving with a buggy in the neighborhood of that place at such an hour was a circumstance to be taken in connection with other evidence tending to show that Thomas and

3. ——: burglary: subsequent acts of co-defendant: res gestæ.

McBride put the trunk where it was found, for the purpose of misleading and averting suspicion. Now, if they did this, their acts on the same night about two hours after the burglary, in endeavoring to mislead and avert suspicion from the guilty parties, by depositing the trunk in a remote place, was a part of the transaction which in the burglary was committed. We think that the court did not err in admitting the evidence.

IV. Dr. Harman, a physician, was called as a witness in behalf of the state, and testified to having made an examin-

4. CRIMINAL law; compulsory examination of defendant's person: what is not.

ation of the face and neck of the defendant when in jail, and to having found several scratches. Dr. Ordway, the prosecuting witness, had already testified to having had a struggle with one of the persons who entered the house, and he thought he caught him by the face and neck. The defendant did not object to the admission of the testimony of Dr. Harman, but he insists that there was error in admitting it. He claims that the testimony was in respect to an examination to which the defendant was compelled to submit, and that such examination was in violation of the defendant's constitutional rights, and that, being such, the admission of the testimony was error, even though not objected to. Without considering the legal questions suggested, it is sufficient to say that we see no evidence that the defendant was compelled to submit to an examination. It is true, the evidence shows that, when Dr. Harman went into the jail, the sheriff accompanied him, but there is no evidence that the sheriff did or said anything in respect to the examination. We think that there was no error in admitting the evidence.

V. The defendant offered in evidence the record of the district court, showing that he had been tried upon the charge

5. CRIMINAL evidence: burglary: evidence as to charge withdrawn.

of an assault with intent to commit murder. Upon objection by the state, the court excluded the evidence. The defendant complains of the exclusion of the evidence as error. In the indictment, the defendant was charged with burglary; and while it is true that in the first place the defendant was' charged also with an assault with intent to murder, yet the same was charged only as an aggravating circumstance, so as to bring the charge of burglary within the provision of section 3892 of the Code, and this charge of assault with intent to commit murder had afterwards been withdrawn. The former acquittal, then, had nothing to do with the charge upon which he was being tried, and the court, we think, rightly excluded the evidence of the former acquittal.

We have examined all the objections argued, and have to say that we think that they are without foundation. The evidence, to our mind, was amply sufficient to sustain the verdict, and the judgment of twelve years' imprisonment, we think, is not excessive.

.AFFIRMED.

CLOUGH v. ADAMS.

1. **Pleading**: AMENDMENT DURING ARGUMENT: ALLEGATIONS NOT CONTROVERTED ADMITTED. Where the ground upon which plaintiff sought a rescission of a conveyance of real estate was that it was obtained by fraud and undue influence, and for a grossly inadequate consideration, *held* that an amendment to her petition, in which she alleged that she and her husband were of weak intellect, and were wanting in capacity to engage in important business transactions, and that, at the time of the transaction in question, they were in financial distress, was material to the case, but did not state a new cause of action or ground of relief, and that under Code, § 2689, it was properly allowed to be filed after the evidence was all in, and during the argument of the case; *also*, that the averments contained in the amendment, not being denied, were to be taken as true, under Code, § 2712, in the further consideration of the case.

2. **Contracts**: INCAPACITY AND UNDUE INFLUENCE: RELIEF IN EQUITY. The acts and contracts of persons who are of weak understanding, and who are thereby liable to imposition, will be held void in courts of, equity, if the nature of the act or contract justifies the conclusion that the party has not exercised a deliberate judgment, but that he has been imposed upon, circumvented, or overcome by cunning or artifice or undue influence; and *held* that the facts of this case (see opinion) in

which plaintiff and her husband were induced to convey their homestead for a patent right, worthless in their hands, bring it clearly
within the rule above stated.

Appeal from Clinton District Court.

THURSDAY, MARCH 3.

ACTION for the rescission of a conveyance of real estate,
on the alleged ground that it was obtained by fraud and
undue influence, and for a grossly inadequate consideration.
The district court entered judgment for plaintiff, and defendant appeals.

Robert T. T. Spense, P. J. Clausen and *W. C. Grohe,*
for appellant.

Ellis & McCoy, C. W. Chase and *A. T. Wheeler,* for
appellee.

REED, J.—The property in question consists of two lots
in the city of Lyons, on which is situated a two-story brick
dwelling house. Plaintiff conveyed the property to defendant in consideration of the assignment by him to her husband of the right to manufacture and sell a " patent
spring bed-bottom" in certain counties in Illinois. At the
time of the transaction, the real estate was worth about
$2,500. It was incumbered with a mortgage which
amounted to about $1,000, and the defendant took it subject
to that mortgage. The trade was effected by an agent in
defendant's employ, one Garland, who was also assisted to
some extent in the transaction by one Charles Upham.
Plaintiff had owned the real estate for some years, and she
and her family occupied it as a place of residence. The debt
secured by the mortgage on the premises was about to fall
due, and neither she nor her husband had the means with
which to pay it, and they had for sometime been offering the
place for sale. Upham resided in Lyons, and he knew that
plaintiff desired to sell the place. Defendant and Garland

resided at Monroe, Wisconsin. Defendant owned an interest in the "Silver patent spring bed-bottom," and Garland was employed by him to sell the right to manufacture and sell the article in the territory owned by him. The latter had been engaged exclusively in the business of buying and selling "patent-rights" for about three years, and, prior to that, had dealt to some extent in property of that character. The right owned by defendant did not sell readily for money, and the parties appear to have adopted the plan of trading it for property. It appears also that they preferred to trade for property which was incumbered, and to take it subject to the incumbrances. This preference is to be accounted for, we suppose, by the fact that one who is under financial embarrassment, and whose property is in that situation, is naturally not so careful to insist upon a full equivalent for the right therein which he parts with, as a person who is under no embarrassment would be. A day or two before the transaction in question, Garland went to Lyons for the purpose of disposing of territory, if he should be able to do so. He learned from Upham that plaintiff and her husband desired to dispose of their property, and they went together to see them, with the object of working up a trade with them, if they found them inclined to trade. A negotiation was entered into, which, in a very short time, resulted in the trade in question.

Plaintiff alleged in her original petition that she was induced to enter into the transaction, and to part with her

1. PLEADING: amendment during argument: allegations not controverted admitted. property, by certain false and fraudulent representations, made by Garland and Upham, as to the value of the right they proposed to trade her. Also that they obtained an undue influence over her, and by their importunities and persuasions overcame her will, and induced her to make the trade. Also that the right assigned to her husband was valueless, and constituted no adequate consideration for the conveyance of her property. After the evidence had all been introduced in the district court, and while the cause was being argued by counsel,

plaintiff asked and obtained leave to file an amendment to her petition, in which it was alleged that both she and her husband were of weak intellect, and were wanting in capacity to engage in important business transactions, and that, at the time of the transaction in question, they were in financial distress. Defendant moved to strike the amendment from the files, because it was filed out of time, and it introduced a new issue or cause of action, and the allegations contained in it were immaterial. This motion being overruled, defendant elected to stand on that ruling, and did not answer the amendment; and the overruling of the motion is one of the matters complained of on this appeal.

We are of the opinion that the motion was properly overruled. The amendment did not materially change the issue. No new cause of action or ground of relief was pleaded in it. As stated above, the ground upon which plaintiff sought a rescission of the conveyance was that it was obtained by fraud and undue influence, and that the consideration paid for it was grossy inadequate. The matters pleaded in the amendment were material to the case as made by the original petition and answer. The fact that plaintiff and her husband were of weak understanding, standing alone, would afford no ground for rescission, there being no claim that they were *non compos*. But when considered in connection with the other circumstances of the transaction, it may be of the highest importance in determining whether the parties are entitled to relief in equity. And the same is true as to the allegation that the parties were in financial distress at the time of the transaction. That fact alone would not have entitled them to relief; but, if true, it might be an important circumstance in the case. Under Code, § 2689, the insertion, by way of amendment, at any time, of allegations material to the case, is allowable. The question whether an amendment shall be allowed is addressed largely to the discretion of the lower court; and, in the present case, we are very clear that there was no abuse of that discretion.

The allegations contained in the amendment, not having been controverted by any subsequent pleading, are, for the purposes of the case, to be deemed true. Code, § 2712. We start out, then, in the consideration of the merits of the case, with two important facts admitted by the pleadings, viz.: That plaintiffs are persons of weak understanding, and that they were under financial embarrassment at the time of the transaction. But if the transaction was fair, and the conveyance was supported by an adequate consideration, a court of equity, as we have already said, could not rescind the conveyance because of those facts. We will, therefore, proceed to consider the other material facts of the transaction. As already stated, Garland is a dealer in patent-rights. He is presumed to have had some success in the business from the fact that, from being an occasional dealer in that character of property, he had come to devote all of his time and energies to the business of buying and selling it. It is also to be presumed, from the fact that his employer pays him a large salary for his services, that he possesses the enterprise and peculiar skill which is essential to success in the business. Upham had also had some experience as a dealer in patent-rights. At the time of the transaction he was the owner of a large extent of territory under the same patent. He had also sold some territory, and he was then engaged in manufacturing and selling the patented article at Lyons.

There is great conflict between the testimony of plaintiff and her husband, and that of these parties, as to what took place during the negotiation. We are satisfied, however, that the advantages which would be likely to accrue to plaintiff and her husband from the purchase of the territory were depicted in very glowing terms. Stories were told of great profits which had been realized by persons who had engaged in the manufacture and sale of the articles. Other statements were made of large profits accruing to the owner of territory, as royalty on the manufacture of the article. Garland repre-

2, CONTRACTS: Incapacity and undue influence : relief in equity.

sented that he was the owner of two eastern states, and that he had received $2,500 as royalty for the manufacture of the articles in those states. There may have been a grain of truth in some of these statements. Others, we believe, were wholly and positively false. They were all made for the purpose of kindling in the heart of plaintiff and that of her husband a hope of gain which the parties who made them must have known would never be realized, and of inducing them to part with their property for something which it must have been apparent would in their hands be without value. The patented article is doubtless not without merit; but, on the market, it comes in competition with a great number of others of the same character, many of which are of equal merit, and some of which are now patented, so that the profits which accrue from the manufacture and sale of the article are too small to justify paying anything for the privilege of manufacturing it. Something might be realized, perhaps, by a shrewd and enterpising speculator like Garland from the sale of the territory; but plaintiff's husband is not of that character. It was perfectly apparent that he did not possess the enterprise nor skill that would enable him to realize anything by selling it. He unfortunately belongs to the class of " weaklings " who are always found on the wrong side of the final deal in patent-right territory. Plaintiff and her husband readily fell into the scheme. They were led to believe, by the glowing picture that was held up before them, that the purchase of the right would afford them, not only speedy deliverance from their financial distress, but the means of acquiring great wealth. Their weak judgments were subjugated by the strong natures with which they were dealing. They had neither the will to resist the spell that was about them, nor the judgment to see the absurdity and folly of the act they were being led to commit. They were given no opportunity for deliberation or consultation with friends or between themselves. The moment they consented to make the trade, an officer was sent for, and the conveyances were executed and delivered. Garland and Upham were careful to secure the entire consummation of the trade before giving them any opportunity for cool thought or consultation.

We think it clear that the case is one for equitable relief. The doctrine applicable to cases of this character is stated by Story, in his work on Equity Jurisprudence, as follows: "The acts and contracts of persons who are of weak understanding, and who are thereby liable to imposition, will be held void in courts of equity, if the nature of the act or contract justifies the conclusion that the party has not exercised a deliberate judgment, but that he has been imposed upon, circumvented, or overcome by cunning or artifice or undue influence." Section 238. See, also, *Tracey v. Sacket*, 1 Ohio' St., 54; *Freeland v. Eldridge*, 19 Mo., 325; *Earl of Chesterfield v. Janssen*, 2 Ves. Sr., 124; *Dunnage v. White*, 1 Swanst., 137. The pleadings and evidence in the present case bring it clearly within the operation of this rule.

The judgment of the district court will be

AFFIRMED.

DESMOND v. THE INDEPENDENT DIST. OF GLENWOOD.

1. **Superintendent of Public Instruction:** POWER TO CORRECT DECISIONS. The superintendent of public instruction, in the discharge of his judicial duties has the power, possessed by all courts and judicial officers, to correct mistakes in his decisions; and if, through mistake, he should announce a decision differing from the one actually rendered, or render a wrong decision, he could, before rights have been acquired under it, and within a proper time, upon discovering his mistake, recall it and decide rightly, and in such case the second decision would be the one governing the case.

Appeal from Mills Circuit Court.

FRIDAY, MARCH 4.

ACTION to recover compensation for services rendered by plaintiff to defendant as a teacher of its grammar school. A demurrer to defendant's answer was overruled. Plaintiff, standing on her demurrer, appealed.

Kelly Bros. and *John Y. Stone*, for appellant.

E. B. Woodruff, for appellee.

BECK, J.—I. The amount in controversy being less than $100, the cause is sent here upon the following certificate: "It is hereby certified that there are questions of law involved in this case upon which it is desirable to have the opinion of the supreme court, to-wit; The paintiff was a school-teacher, employed by the defendant, or the directors of the school-district, to teach for five and three-fourths months, under written contract, two months of which time was unexpired. The directors made an order discharging her. She appealed to the county superintendent from the order. The county superintendent sustained the action of the board of directors. She then appealed to the state superintendent of public instruction. Both parties appeared by their attorneys before that officer at Des Moines, and fully argued and submitted the case, and returned to their homes in Mills county, the state superintendent having taken the case under advisement. After several weeks, the state superintendent signed and forwarded his written opinion in the case to the county superintendent of Mills county, to be filed, sustaining the action of the board of directors and the county superintendent. 'Afterwards, and without any request for a rehearing having been made by either party in the case, and without any notice being given to either party by the state superintendent, [*and before said written opinion had been filed by the county superintendent of Mills county,*] the state superintendent recalled his said decision, [*as being incorrect and erroneous,*] and rendered another decision in the case, reversing the action of the board of directors and the county superintendent, and sent the same to the county superintendent of Mills county, to be filed as the decision in the case. (1) Did the state superintendent have the power to recall the first decision, and make the second one? (2) Is the *first decision* of the state superintendent, under the facts, the final order governing the case, in view of the second decision? (3) Is the *second decision* of the state superintendent the final order governing the cause? (4) Has this court power or authority to decide whether the state superintendent adopted a proper method of procedure in recalling the first decision?"

Defendant files an amended abstract, showing that the words inclosed in brackets in the foregoing certificate do not appear in the record. This amendment is not denied, and must therefore be regarded as correct. The certificate will be regarded as though the words in the brackets did not appear therein.

II. The superintendent of public instruction, in the discharge of his judicial duties, has the power to correct mistakes in rendering judgments in a case before him possessed by all courts and judicial officers. If, through mistake, he should announce a decision differing from the decision actually rendered, he possesses the power to recall such an announcement, and publish the decision correctly; or if, mistakenly, he should render a decision, he could, before rights had been acquired under it, and within a proper time, upon discovering his mistake, recall it, and decide rightly. The certificate does not show why or within what time the first decision was recalled. In the absence of any showing on the subject, we will presume it was done for a proper cause, and within a proper time, and that no rights had been acquired under the first judgment. The second decision is to be regarded as the final judgment rendered by him. These views sufficiently answer the first, second and third questions certified by the judge of the district court.

III. The fourth question we cannot answer, for the reason that the certificate fails to show what " method of procedure," if any, the superintendent adopted in recalling his first decision.

In our opinion, the district court erred in holding that the first decision was the final judgment of the superintendent.

REVERSED.

POLK & HUBBELL v. FOSTER ET AL.

1. **Appeal to Supreme Court:** ACTION AGAINST COUNTY SUPERVISORS: NOTICE. In a proceeding in *certiorari* to test the legality of the action of a board of supervisors in establishing a public road, where the county was not a party, nor liable for costs, *held* that the county auditor was not a proper person upon whom to serve notice of an appeal to bind the defendants; the action in such case not being against the county, (Code, § 2610,) and he not being the agent of the supervisors. (Code, § 3178.)

Appeal from Dickinson Circuit Court.

FRIDAY, MARCH 4.

THIS is a proceeding in *certiorari*, to test the legality of the action of the board of supervisors of Dickinson county in establishing a public road across land owned by the plaintiffs. The court below affirmed the action of the board, and the plaintiffs appeal.

O. Rice and *J. S. Polk*, for appellants.

J. W. Cory, for appellees.

ADAMS, CH. J.—The appellees raise upon the threshold a a question of jurisdiction. They insist that no appeal has been taken to this court. The fact appears to be that notice of appeal was served upon the clerk of the court and upon the county auditor, but not upon the defendants, unless service upon the county auditor was service upon them. Section 3178 of the Code provides that service may be made upon the agent of a party, and the plaintiffs' position is that the county auditor is agent of the board of supervisors. They rely upon the fact that he keeps the records of the board, (Code, § 320;) that, in the location of a highway, he is charged with specific duties, (Code, §§ 924, 934, 944, 949, 961;) and that, in suits against the county, it is expressly provided that service of notice may be made upon him. But, in our opinion, he cannot properly be considered as the agent of the board, either in keeping the records, or in discharging the duties imposed upon him by statute in the establishment of a highway. In whatever he does, he acts as a public officer. He is not appointed by the board, nor discharged by it, nor is he subject to its control in the performance of his duties. The express provision made in section 2610 of the Code, that, in an action against a county, service upon the county may be made by service upon the auditor, does not aid the plaintiffs, unless these proceedings can be regarded as an action against the county, and, in our opinion, they cannot. The papers do not show that any one is made defendant but the members of the board. It is not the county that is charged with having acted illegally, nor has the county become liable even for costs. Having reached this conclusion, it is not important nor proper that we should express an opinion upon the merits of the case. We might be allowed to say that we reach the conclusion that the appeal must be dismissed with less regret, because a majority of the court are inclined strongly to think that the matters complained of are mere irregularities, and not of such a character as to entitle the plaintiffs to a judgment in their favor, annulling the action of the board.

The appeal must be

DISMISSED.

COURSON ET AL. v. THE CHICAGO, MILWAUKEE & ST. PAUL
    R'Y Co.

1. **Railroads**: KILLING COW ON CROSSING: SPEED OF TRAIN: QUESTION
   FOR JURY. Where there was a conflict in the evidence as to the speed
   of the train which killed plaintiffs' cow at a highway crossing, and as
   to the distance from the crossing at which the cow could have been seen
   by the engineer, and there was a sharp curve in the track as the train,
   which was a wild one, approached the crossing, *held* that it was a question for the jury whether the train was run at a dangerous rate of speed.

2. ——: ——: CONTRIBUTORY NEGLIGENCE: QUESTION FOR JURY.
   Where plaintiffs' cow was killed by a wild train at a highway crossing,
   and it appeared that plaintiffs lived near the track, and knew of the
   crossing, and of the time when regular trains passed, and more than an
   hour before the time for the first regular train they turned the cow into
   the highway, intending soon to follow her and drive her to a pasture
   which lay beyond the track, but she was shortly afterwards killed by the
   passing wild train, *held* that it could not be said, as a matter of law,
   that plaintiffs were guilty of contributory negligence, but that it was a
   question for the jury.

Appeal from Allamakee Circuit Court.

FRIDAY, MARCH 4.

ACTION to recover the value of a cow killed at a highway
crossing by a train on defendant's railway, on the ground of
the faulty construction of the crossing, and that the train
was running at a dangerous speed. Trial by jury. Judgment for the plaintiffs, and defendant appeals.

Noble & Updegraff, for appellant.

F. S. Burling, for appellees.

SEEVERS, J.—I. The defendant asked the court to instruct
the jury that "counsel for plaintiffs has argued to the jury
*   *   *   that the fact that the fireman did not see
the cow as soon as he could, if he had looked, was negligence on the part of the defendant. You are instructed that
you should give no attention to that argument. There is
no evidence before you that the fireman was negligent."

This instruction was refused, and we cannot say that the court erred in this respect, for the reason that it does not appear that counsel for the plaintiffs made any such argument or claim to the jury.

II. There was a conflict in the evidence as to the speed of the train, and also as to the distance from the crossing the cow could have been seen by the engineer. There

1. RAIL-
ROADS: kill-
ing cow on
crossing;
speed of
train: ques-
tion for jury.

is a sharp curve in the railway as trains approach the crossing from the west. The train in question was a wild train. The court instructed the jury that there was no evidence tending to show that the engineer was not watchful, or did not do all he could to stop the train after he saw the cow, and also that the right of the plaintiffs to recover depended on the question whether the defendant was negligent in running the train at the speed it did, under all the circumstances, and the jury found specially that it was so run. We think it was for the jury to say whether the train was run at a dangerous rate of speed, when approaching the crossing around the curve, and therefore the court correctly instructed the jury in this respect. *Kuhn v. Chicago, R. I. & P. R'y Co.*, 42 Iowa, 420.

III. The plaintiffs lived near the track, had full knowledge of the crossing, and, we think, of the time at which reg-

2. ——: ——:
contributory
negligence:
question for
jury.

ular trains, or some of them, passed. One such train passed the crossing about 9 o'clock in the morning. The train in question passed before 8 o'clock. Prior to that time, the cow had been milked and turned in the highway to go to pasture, which was across the track. No one was in charge of the cow. She crossed one crossing, but did not go into the pasture as she might have done, but passed along the highway a short distance to another crossing, and was standing thereon at the time of the accident. It was not the plaintiffs' habit to so turn their cattle on the highway, with no one in charge of them; but they did so on the morning in question for a sufficient reason, as they claim, intending to follow them soon, and before any train of which they had any knowledge passed along. The court submitted the question to the jury whether, under the circumstances, the plaintiffs were negligent, and refused an instruction asked by the defendant that the plaintiffs were, as a matter of law, guilty of contributory negligence, and therefore could not recover. We think the action of the court was correct. *Krebs v. Railroad Co.*, 64 Iowa, 670; *Hammond v. Same*, 49 Id., 450. It is true, the plaintiffs turned the cow into the highway, as they had the perfect right to do, for the purpose above stated; but we cannot say, as a matter of law, that they were immediately to follow her, some time, at least could be allowed. When turned out, the cow did not pass immediately on the track, and we think it was for the jury to say whether the plaintiffs were negligent or not.

We cannot disturb the verdict on the ground that it is not supported by the evidence.   AFFIRMED.

HUEBNER v. THE FARMERS' INS. CO.

1. **Judgment**: ON PREMATURE DEFAULT: SET ASIDE. In the absence of a rule of the court to the contrary, a default taken before noon of the second day of the term is premature, (Code, § 2635,) and should be set aside on motion made before that time.

2. ——: ——: ——: AFFIDAVIT OF MERITS. A verified answer, filed with a motion to set aside a default, and which the defendant asks to be considered as an affidavit of merits, may properly be so considered by the court.

3. **Practice on Appeal**: JUDICIAL NOTICE OF RULES OF DISTRICT COURT. While this court is required to take judicial notice of the rules of the district court, yet, where the non-existence of a rule as to appearance day is implied in a motion to set aside a default as being premature, and opposing counsel do not in any way, in this court, call attention to any such rule, it will be assumed that none existed.

Appeal from Sac District Court.

FRIDAY, MARCH 4.

THIS is an action upon a policy of insurance against loss by fire. A default and judgment were entered against the defendant on the first day of the term to which the suit was brought. On the second day of the term, the defendant appeared, and moved the court to set aside the default and judgment. The motion was sustained. Plaintiff appeals.

Goldsmith & Hart, for appellant.

Ed. R. Duffie and *Frank Hormel*, for appellee.

ROTHROCK, J.—One ground of the motion to set aside the default was that the same was entered on the first day of the term, and that there was no authority in law for entering a default on that day. In the absence of a rule of court designating a different time for pleading, the defendant is not required to appear and answer or demur to a petition before noon of the second day of the term. Code, § 2635. The record in the case does not show that there was any rule of the court on the subject. It is true, this court is required to take judicial notice of any such rule; but, as the question that the default was premature is distinctly made in the motion and the argument of appellee, and as counsel for appellant do not even in argument call our attention to any rule of court on the subject, we will assume that there is none, and that the court set aside the default because it was prematurely entered. And it does not appear at what time on the second day of the term the defendant appeared and moved to set aside the default. If it was before noon, it is apparent that the motion was properly sustained. The record shows that defendant, when it made the motion, tendered a verified answer, which, if true, is a complete defense to the action, and asked that the answer might be accepted and taken by the court as an affidavit of merits. Counsel for appellant contends that an affidavit of merits should have been actually filed in order to authorize an order setting aside the default. We think the answer was proper to be considered by the court as an affidavit of merits, and we will presume, as it was tendered with the motion, that it was examined by the court.

There were other reasons presented in the motion to set aside the default, which are discussed by counsel; but, as we think the ruling of the court should be sustained upon the ground above considered, it is unnecessary to further elaborate the case. **AFFIRMED.**

THE STATE v. KREIGER ET AL.

1. **Criminal Law**: TWO ON TRIAL: CONFESSION BY ONE. · K. and B. were tried together for larceny, and there was evidence of confessions made by K., tending also to implicate B. to a slight extent. The court instructed the jury that "the confessions of the defendants, or either of them, unless made in open court, will not warrant a conviction, unless accompanied with other proof that the offense was committed, and such confessions, to have any weight, must have been freely and voluntarily made." *Held* that the jury could not have inferred from this instruction that any confessions made by K. were in any manner to prejudice B.

Appeal from Iowa District Court.

FRIDAY, MARCH 4.

INDICTMENT charging the defendants Kreiger and Beal with the larceny of "one set double harness." Trial by jury. Verdict and judgment. The defendant Beal appeals.

J. T. Beem, for appellant.

A. J. Baker, Attorney-general, for the State.

SEEVERS, J.—This case has been submitted on a transcript, without argument, and we have examined, as is our duty, the entire record. We are not advised as to the grounds upon which the appellant relies to obtain a reversal of the judgment; but we infer that it is claimed that the court erred in giving the fifth paragraph of the charge to the jury, for the reason that this is the sole ground upon which a new trial was asked. That instruction is as follows: "You are instructed that the confessions of the defendants, or either of them, unless made in open court, will not warrant a conviction, unless accompanied with other proof that the offense was committed; and such confessions, in order to have any weight, must have been freely and voluntarily made." This instruction, as an abstract proposition, is undoubtedly correct; but we assume that it is claimed to be erroneous upon the ground that there is no evidence tending to show that appellant made any confessions. Kreiger, however, did, and, as to him, there was evidence upon which the instruction can be properly based. It is possibly true that the court should have said to the jury that the confessions of one defendant should not prejudice his co-defendant; but we are not prepared to say that the appellant was prejudiced by the failure of the court in this respect. We think the jury must have understood the instruction to mean that the confession of one defendant was insufficient to warrant *his* conviction, unless made in open court, etc. To hold otherwise, we should be compelled to assume that the jury did not possess ordinary intelligence. The confessions made by Kreiger tend to implicate the appellant to a slight extent; but no objections were made thereto at any time by the appellant. For some satisfactory reason, it must be assumed, his counsel deemed it best that such evidence should be admitted, and therefore we cannot say that the court erred.

Upon the whole record, we are not prepared to say that the court committed any prejudicial error during the trial of this case.

AFFIRMED.

McArthur v. Garman.

1. **Garnishment:** DISPUTED FUND: HUSBAND AND WIFE. A wife was the owner of certain horses which her husband entered, in his own name, but with his wife's money, for premiums at a county fair. These entrance fees were returnable by the rules of the society, but the society did not know that the horses belonged to, and that the fees were paid by, the wife. *Held* that the society might have discharged its obligations by paying these fees to the husband, but that, while they remained unpaid, they could not be appropriated by garnishment on execution against the husband, against the objections of the wife as an intervenor.

2. **Chattel Mortgage:** OF HORSE AND EARNINGS: FUTURE EARNINGS. A chattel mortgage upon a horse, which provided: "This mortgage to cover all earnings of the horse, whether by premiums or otherwise," *held* not to include premiums earned after the execution of the mortgage. (*Lormer v. Allyn*, 64 Iowa, 725, followed in principle.)

Appeal from Des Moines Circuit Court.

FRIDAY, MARCH 4.

THE plaintiff, being the owner of a judgment against D. K. Garman, caused an execution to issue thereon, and the Des Moines Agricultural Society was garnished as a supposed debtor of Garman. The garnishee answered that it was indebted in the sum of $117. Sarah Garman, the appellant herein, intervened in the proceeding, claiming that the indebtedness from the society was due to her, and not to the defendant in execution. The cause was submitted to the circuit court upon an agreed statement of facts, and it was found that the plaintiff was entitled to the fund in dispute, and a judgment was entered in accord with the finding. Sarah H. Garman appeals.

Hull & Huston, for appellant.

Hedge & Blythe, for appellee.

ROTHROCK, J.—I. It appears from the agreed statement of facts that, in September, 1884, and prior to the seven-

1. GARNISH-
MENT: dis-
puted fund:
husband and
wife.

teenth day of that month, D. K. Garman entered certain horses in his own name, as contestants for premiums offered by said agricultural society. All of the horses, except one known as

"Barney," were .the property of the intervenor, Sarah H. Garman; but they were entered for premiums in D. K. Garman's name by her consent, but without the knowledge of the agricultural society as to her ownership. The rules of the society did not require horses to be entered in the name of the real owner. "She paid the entrance money for said horses out of her own funds furnished by her to D. K. Garman, but this was not known to the society." On the fifteenth day of September, 1884, D. K. Garman bought of the intervenor, who is his wife, the said horse "Barney," and executed to her a chattel mortgage upon the horse to secure the whole of the purchase money. The mortgage contained the following provision: "This mortgage to cover all earnings of the horse, whether by premiums or otherwise." The notes secured by the mortgage did not become due until December 15, 1884. The mortgage was filed for record on the seventeenth day of September, 1884. The sum of $101 of the amount owing by the garnishee was premiums earned by the horse "Barney" at the meeting of said society in September, 1884, subsequent to the execution of the mortgage; and the balance due from the society, being $16.40, was due for the amount of entrance money paid for entering the other horses owned by the intervenor, and which sum is returnable under the rules of said society.

We think that the plaintiff should not have had the judgment for the $16.40 entrance money. The agreed statement of facts shows that the money belonged to Mrs. Garman, and was paid for the purpose of entering her horses as competitors for premiums. The fact that her husband entered the horses in his own name did not preclude her from claiming that repayment should be made to her. Of course, as the horses were entered in the husband's name, if the society had refunded the entrance fees to him without notice of the wife's ownership of it, she could not recover of the society. But the money is not paid, and it should be refunded to the party actually entitled thereto. It is conceded that it was the wife's money paid for the entrance of her horses; and it seems to us there is no escape from the conclusion that she should recover in that amount.

II. The horse known as " Barney " was not the property of the intervenor when he earned the premiums amounting to $101. If she is entitled to the premiums, it is by reason of her chattel mortgage upon the horse. This depends upon whether the clause in the mortgage, that it shall " cover all earnings of the horse, whether by premiums or otherwise," should be held to include premiums earned after the mortgage was executed.

2. CHATTEL mortgage: of horse and earnings: future earnings.

In the case of *Lormer v. Allyn*, 64 Iowa, 725, a chattel mortgage was executed upon a stock of groceries. The mortgage purported to cover " all books of account and rights of credit arising out of said business." It was held that the mortgage did not include " rights of credit arising out of the business " after the execution of the mortgage, but such only as had accrued before that time. That holding was based upon the rule " that a chattel mortgage will not be deemed to cover after-acquired property, unless the intention that it should is clearly expressed."

In our opinion the mortgage in the case at bar must be held subject to the same rule. There is no reference therein to the future earnings of the horse; and, in the absence of such a provision, such earnings cannot be held to be included in the mortgage. The judgment of the circuit court in favor of the plaintiff for premiums earned was therefore correct. But the intervenor should have been awarded the sum of $16.40, being the money paid by her for the entrance of her own horses.

MODIFIED AND AFFIRMED.

POOLE, GILLIAM & CO. v. CARHART ET AL.

1. **Assignment:** EFFECT OF UNACCEPTED ORDER. An order drawn upon a third person cannot, until accepted, be the basis of an action by the payee against the drawee. (*Roberts v. Corbin*, 26 Iowa, 315, where the action was based on a bankers draft, distinguished.)

2. **Chattel Mortgage:** RECOVERY OF PROCEEDS: PROOF OF BALANCE DUE. Where an intervenor in a garnishment proceeding claimed the attached fund as the proceeds of the sale of chattel property on which he held a mortgage, but he failed to prove for how much the mortgage was given, and it appeared that $700 had been paid on it, *held* that he could not recover, because it did not appear that the mortgage was not fully paid.

Appeal from Franklin District Court.

FRIDAY, MARCH 4.

THE plaintiffs, judgment creditors of John Seney, garnished the defendant L. B. Carhart as the debtor of Seney. J. M. Hemingway intervened, claiming the funds sought to be reached by the garnishment. The court rendered judgment against the garnishee in favor of the plaintiffs. The intervenor, Hemingway, appeals.

J. M. Hemingway, for himself.

Taylor & Evans, for appellee.

ADAMS, CH. J.—The answer of the garnishee, Carhart, showed that he had in his hands a fund amounting to $281.39, arising from the sale of certain grain and feed belonging to the plaintiff's execution debtor, John Seney. The court rendered judgment for that amount in the plaintiffs' favor. Hemingway, the intervenor, claims the fund as having belonged to Charles Seney, and as having been assigned by Charles Seney to him. The fact is that John Seney mortgaged the grain to Carhart. Afterwards he and Carhart caused it to be ground and sold, and Carhart was allowed to retain the amount due him, and a balance of $281.39 was left in his hands. Hem-

ingway claims that Charles Seney had a junior mortgage
upon the same grain, and that, when the grain was converted
into money, his mortgage rested upon the proceeds, subject only to Carhart's claim, and that, after Carhart's claim
was satisfied out of the proceeds, Charles Seney became the
owner of the balance.

Several interesting questions have been presented in this
case. One is as to whether Charles Seney's mortgage was so
drawn as to cover the grain in question. The court below thought it was not. Another question is as to whether,
if Charles Seney's mortgage did cover the grain in question,
it covered the proceeds resulting from the sale of the grain.
The appellees contend that it did not, and rely upon *Waters
v. Cass Co. Bank*, 65 Iowa, 234. Another question presented
is as to whether the intervenor, who claims as assignee of
Charles Seney, has proven the alleged assignment. The
plaintiffs denied the assignment; and, if the intervenor has
failed to prove it, he cannot be allowed to recover. For
the purpose of proving the assignment, a paper was introduced, which is in the following words:

"Pay to J. M. Hemingway cash now in your hands belonging to me, proceeds of fees, etc.   CHARLES SENEY.

"*To L. B. Carhart.*"

No evidence was introduced in proof of the genuineness of the signature, nor is the instrument referred to in the
intervenor's petition in such a way as to render proof of the
signature unnecessary. This alone would seem to be sufficient to defeat the intervenor's recovery. But that objection
has not been raised in argument, and we prefer to rest our
decision upon a different ground. The paper introduced was
1. ASSIGN-   nothing but an order; and there is no pretense
MENT: effect
of unaccepted that it was ever accepted by Carhart, or even
order.   presented to him. We do not think, then, that
any contract arose between Carhart and Hemingway upon
which the latter can maintain an action. It is true that, in

Roberts v. Corbin, 26 Iowa, 315, it was held that a draft drawn by a banker in Dubuque on the defendants, as bankers in New York city, with whom the Dubuque banker kept his deposits in New York to enable him to sell exchange on New York, constituted an assignment of so much of the deposit as the draft called for, and that the purchase of the draft by Roberts gave him a right of action against the defendants; but the ruling was based upon the ground that the defendants, at the time of the receipt of the deposits, contracted to pay the same out on the Dubuque banker's drafts, and that Roberts, by the purchase of the draft in question, became a party to that contract.   Carhart, in the case at bar, had received no money from Charles Seney, nor made any contract with him.   We have to say, then, that the mere drawing and delivery of the order by Charles Seney to Hemingway did not, in our opinion, give the latter a right of action against Carhart.

There is another reason why the intervenor cannot recover.

2. CHATTEL mortgage: recovery of proceeds: proof of balance due.

He bases his right upon Charles Seney's mortgage and has failed to prove how much if anything, is due on the mortgage.   There is no evidence as to how much the mortgage was given for, and there is evidence that $700 has been paid on it.

We think that the judgment must be

AFFIRMED.

THE STATE v. KREIGER ET AL.

1. **Criminal Evidence**: TWO ON TRIAL: DECLARATIONS OF ONE. Where K. and B. were together on trial for larceny, the declarations of K., made in a conversation with the witness, implicating both himself and B. in the crime, were admissible as against himself, but not as against B., and the court should have excluded so much of the evidence as related to B., or, if that could not have been done without excluding the evidence entirely, the jury should have been told at the time, and also in the written charge, not to consider the evidence as against B.

Appeal from Iowa District Court.

FRIDAY, MARCH 4.

INDICTMENT charging the defendants, Levi Kreiger and Andrew A. Beal, with the larceny of "one Defiance corn plow," and other property. Trial by jury. Judgment for the plaintiff, and the defendant Beal appeals.

J. T. Beem, for appellant.

A. J. Baker, Attorney-general, for the State.

SEEVERS, J.—This cause has been submitted on a transcript, without argument. We have examined the whole record, and find, among the grounds upon which a new trial was asked by appellant, the following: "The court erred in admitting. as against the defendant, that part of witness Wilson's testimony of his conversation with defendant Kreiger which related to this defendant." It appears from the record that the witness was asked to state a conversation he had had with Kreiger in relation to the property charged to have been stolen, whereupon counsel for the appellant objected to any declaration or statement Kreiger may have made in relation to the appellant's connection with the larceny. The objection was overruled, and thereupon the witness stated what Kreiger stated to him, and such evidence tended strongly to show that the appellant stole or aided in stealing the property described in the indictment. Of course, the

statements of Kreiger were competent evidence against himself, but not against the appellant; and the court should
either have excluded so much of the evidence as related to
the appellant, or, if this could not have been done without
excluding the evidence entirely, then the court should at the
time have said to the jury that they were not to consider the
statements of Kreiger in relation to the appellant, and also
have so said to them in the written charge. This the court
failed to do. We think it quite clear that the court erred in
admitting the evidence above referred to, for the reason, as
we understand the record, that the witness could have stated
what Kreiger said, so far as the same related to himself, without any reference to what he said in relation to the appellant.
It will not even be claimed that the appellant was bound, or
should be in any respect prejudiced, by the statements made
by Kreiger. Such evidence is purely hearsay, and its admission cannot be justified.

Upon the ground above stated, the court should have
granted a new trial.

REVERSED.

KNAPP v. THE SIOUX CITY & PACIFIC R'Y Co.

71
88

1. **Measure of Damages**: INJURY TO LOCOMOTIVE ENGINEER. Where
a sober, prudent and trusty locomotive engineer, less than forty years
old, who was earning more than $100 per month, was permanently
injured through the negligence of the company for which he was working, so that he could no longer follow his occupation, and could not
earn one-third as much as before, *held* that a verdict of damages in
the sum of $9,500 was not excessive.

71
120
120
71
127

2. **Railroads**: INJURY TO ENGINEER: PROXIMATE CAUSE. Where
defendant's negligence in failing to keep its track in repair caused the
engine in charge of plaintiff to leave the track, and required plaintiff
to reverse the lever in order to arrest the movement of the engine, *held*
that, if this was done in the exercise of due care under the circumstances, and injury resulted from his arm or hand being caught in
the latch of the lever, the proximate cause of the injury was defendant's
negligence, for which it was liable. (Same case, 65 Iowa, 91, followed.)

71
d131

3. ——: ——: "MEDICAL ATTENDANCE :" WHAT INCLUDED IN. In an action based on a personal injury, plaintiff sought to recover also for "nursing and medical attendance." *Held* that under this claim he was entitled to recover all expenses which, as shown by the evidence, he incurred in procuring medical assistance *and medicines;* and that the jury was properly so instructed. (See opinion for cases distinguished.)

4. ——: RISKS ASSUMED BY ENGINEER: INSTRUCTION. A sentence in an instruction must be read in the light of the rest of the instruction: and an instruction which, when so read, holds, in substance, that a locomotive engineer assumes all the ordinary risks of his employment, but that he does not assume risks arising from the negligence of the company or its employes in failing to keep its road bed in good repair, is approved.

5. **Railroads**: INJURY TO ENGINEER: PROXIMATE CAUSE: QUESTION OF LAW. In an action by a locomotive engineer for a personal injury, *held* that, if the evidence showed that the injury to plaintiff was received by him in the reversing of the engine; that the reversing of his engine at that particular time was rendered necessary or prudent by the fact that part of the train was leaving the track; and that the train, or part of it, was leaving the track on account of the negligence of defendant in keeping the track in repair, then the proximate cause of the injury was defendant's negligence, and that the court properly so instructed as matter of law.

6. ——: ——: CONTRIBUTORY NEGLIGENCE: RISKS ASSUMED. In such case, an instruction which, in effect, directed the jury that, if plaintiff acted with reasonable skill and prudence in reversing the lever, in view of the haste and sudden emergency in which he was required to act, he did not contribute to the injury, *held* correct, against the objection that he assumed such risks as belonging to his employment.

7. ——: ——: CARE IN INSPECTION OF TRACK. A frequent inspection of the track, and the repairing of it whenever there is an apparent necessity, by the employes charged with such work, is not all the care that a railroad company owes to a locomotive engineer in that respect. There must be proper care as well as frequency in making the inspections, and such repairs must be made as, in the exercise of such care, appear to be necessary.

8. **Damages**: PERSONAL INJURY: LIFE TABLES. In an action for injuries received through negligence, and which are of a permanent nature, life tables are admissible to show the plaintiff's expectancy of life, in order to determine the measure of his damages. (*McDonald v. Chicago & N. W. R'y Co.*, 26 Iowa, 124, followed, and *Nelson v. Chicago, R. I. & P. R'y Co.*, 38 Id., 564, overruled.)

9. **Railroads**: INJURY TO ENGINEER: DEFECTIVE TRACK: INCOMPETENT EVIDENCE OF REPAIRS. In an action for an injury to a locomotive

engineer caused by a defective track, evidence of repairs to the track, which did not tend to show that the repairs had been made at the place of the accident, was properly excluded.

Appeal from Pottawattamie District Court.

FRIDAY, MARCH 4.

ACTION to recover for personal injuries sustained by plaintiff while in defendant's employment as a locomotive engineer. There was a judgment upon a verdict for plaintiff. Defendant appeals. This case has before been in this court. See 65 Iowa, 91.

Wright, Baldwin & Haldane and *Joy, Wright & Hudson*, for appellant.

Sapp & Pusey, for appellee.

BECK, J.—I. The plaintiff claims to recover for injuries sustained by him while exercising proper care in the discharge of his duty as engineer. The petition alleges that the injuries were caused by defective and rotten ties, by reason of which the engine operated by plaintiff was thrown from the track. The allegations of the petition are denied by defendant's answer. Other matters found in the pleadings need not be more particularly referred to here. We will consider the grounds of objection to the judgment in the order they are discussed by defendant's counsel.

II. It is first insisted that the verdict is excessive. It is for $9,500. The injury caused a permanent disability of

1. MEASURE of plaintiff's right arm. While the disability is
damages:
injury to not total, plaintiff being able to use his arm for
locomotive
engineer. some light work, he is incapable of following his business of an engineer, and cannot work on a farm, at which he was employed before he commenced working upon railroads. He has not sufficient education to teach school, and the condition of his arm is such that he cannot write, so that he can engage in no clerical occupation. The evidence fails

to show that, with his disability, he can engage in any business in which he could earn a living. His case is simply that of a man of less than forty years of age, who is qualified to perform manual labor requiring skill and experience, commanding compensation of more than $100 per month, permanently thrown out of employment through the negligence of defendant, and required to seek other employment which can be followed by one having a disabled right arm, and which will yield but inconsiderable compensation compared with his earnings before the injury. He is prevented by defendant's negligence from pursuing the life business he had chosen; his plans and purposes are defeated; he cannot now earn one-third the sum he received for his services before his injury; he must go through life a *cripple*, with blighted hopes and disappointed ambition. His employment as an engineer shows that he is sober, prudent and trusty, and therefore a good citizen. Surely the usefulness of such a citizen ought not to be lightly esteemed, and his sufferings already endured, and the life of humiliation before him, ought not to be forgotten in determining the compensation he should receive. We think the sum awarded by the verdict of the jury is not excessive.

III. It is next insisted that the verdict is unsupported by the evidence. This claim is based upon the position that
2. RAIL-
ROADS:
Injury to
engineer:
proximate
cause.
the injury to plantiff resulted from his arm or hand being caught in the latch of the lever, when he reversed it quickly in order to stop the train after it had left the track, and not from his arm or elbow coming in contact with the side or end of the cab, when making the movement, as claimed by plaintiff in his testimony. We need not inquire which of these theories is correct. There was evidence to support plaintiff's theory, and the jury may well have found it to be correct. But if it be assumed that defendant's theory as to the cause of the injury be correct, the direct cause was defendant's negligence in failing to keep the track in proper condition, which

caused the engine to leave the rails, and required plaintiff to reverse the lever in order to arrest the movement of the engine. If this was done in the exercise of due care, and injury resulted, the proximate cause was defendant's negligence which demanded the reversal of the lever in the manner in which it was done by plaintiff. This conclusion was reached by us when the case was here before, and is announced and supported by satisfactory arguments in our. opinion then filed. 65 Iowa, 91. The evidence clearly supports the conclusion, which the jury evidently reached, that the track was not in proper repair, which caused the engine to leave it. We are well satisfied that the verdict is sufficiently supported by the evidence.

IV. The court, in the eighth instruction, directed the jury that plaintiff was authorized to recover for the sums

3. ——: ——: which "he expended in procuring medical assist-
' medical
attendance :" ance and medicines." It is insisted that plaint-
whatincluded
in. iff makes no claim in his petition for medicines, and cannot recover therefor. But in his petition he seeks to recover for "nursing and medical attendance;" and he testifies to the amount of his expenses incurred in visiting three or four cities for medical treatment, including physicians' bills. He also testifies to the expense incurred by the treatment he received from the physician first employed by him. In our opinion, the claim in the petition for expenses incurred for "medical attendance" covers expenditures for medicine used by the physician in giving such medical attendance. The evidence shows that plaintiff incurred such expenses. In one instance, the expense for treatment, which includes medicine, is distinctly proved. In others, such expenses are included with outlays for travel, etc., in visiting the physicians treating the plaintiff. We think the instruction complained of was applicable to this evidence, and the jury could well have allowed plaintiff all the expenses which, as shown by the evidence, he incurred for "medical assistance and medicine." *Gardner v. Burlington, C. R. & N.*

R'y Co., 68 Iowa, 588; *Stafford v. City of Oskaloosa*, 57 Id., 748; and *Reed v. Chicago, R. I. & P. R'y Co.*, Id., 23, —cited by defendant's counsel, are not applicable to the question involved in this point, for the reason that, in each, there was an entire absence of evidence showing expenses for medicine and attendance of physicians which the jury were authorized by instructions to allow in each case. These instructions were held to be erroneous, for the reason that there was no evidence to which they were applicable.

V. An instruction in the following language was given to the jury: "(2) When plaintiff entered the service

4. ——: risks assumed by engineer: instruction. of defendant as a locomotive engineer, he assumed all the risks which are incident to the prosecution of that employment in the usual and ordinary way, and under the circumstances usually surrounding the running of a locomotive engine in the operation of a railway; and he cannot recover for any injury which may have come to him in the usual and ordinary prosecution of that business. But the plaintiff, when he entered such employment, had a right to assume that defendant would use all reasonable care in the keeping of its road and appliances in good order and repair; and if any injury came to him by reason of any negligence of the defendant or its employes, other than his own negligence, this would not be a risk which he assumed as one incident to his employment." A criticism of this instruction is made by defendant's counsel, on the ground that the last sentence holds defendant liable for damages resulting from all negligence of defendant's employes. The whole instruction must be read together, and especially must the last sentence be interpreted by the consideration of all its parts. It plainly means that defendant was required to use reasonable care in order to keep its road bed in good repair, and was liable for " any " [all] negligence in this regard. It is surely unfair criticism to insist that the negligence referred to in the last sentence is other than the absence of care in keeping the road in good order referred to in the preceding part of the sentence. The instruction is correct.

VI. An instruction (the fifth) contains the following language: "If the evidence shows that the injury to plaintiff was received by him in the reversing of the

5. RAILROADS: injury to engineer: proximate cause: question of law.

engine; that the reversing of his engine at that particular time was rendered necessary or prudent by the fact that part of the train was leaving the track; and that the train, or part of it, was leaving the track on account of the negligence of defendant in keeping the track in repair,—this showing would trace the cause of the injury directly to the negligence of defendant. But unless this train of connection is shown by the evidence, as above stated, it will not be shown that the negligence of defendant was the proximate cause of the injury; and if there is a failure on this point, the plaintiff cannot recover, even though the defendant may have been negligent in the maintaining of its track." This instruction is in harmony with the doctrine recognized by this court in the opinion in this case when it was here before. 65 Iowa, 91. Counsel insist that the question involving the proximate cause of the injury sustained by plaintiff should have been left for determination by the jury, and, in support of this position, declare that the cause, when here before, was reversed for the reason that the court did not submit the question to the jury. The question is clearly one of law, and is so recognized in our prior decision in this case. The cause was reversed for the reason that the court below held that the negligence of the defendant was not the proximate cause of the injury, and not because the question of proximate cause was not submitted to the jury.

VII. The sixth instruction, in effect, directs the jury that, if plaintiff acted with reasonable skill and prudence in

6. ——: ——: contributory negligence: risks assumed.

reversing the lever, in view of the haste and sudden emergency in which he was required to act, he did not contribute to the injury. Counsel insist that, as his employment required him to act in haste in such sudden emergencies, he assumed all risk thereof. This may, for the purposes of the case, be admitted. But then he did not assume the risk from the negligence of defendant in failing to keep the road bed in good order, which required prompt action, and which, as we have seen, was the proximate cause of the injury. Counsel insist that this instruction directs the jury as to the weight to be given evidence introduced by defendant tending to show that plaintiff's act in reversing the engine was not prudent. We think the instruction has no such effect. Counsel's objection is therefore groundless.

VIII. The refusal of an instruction in the following language is made the ground of another complaint of defend-

7. —: —: ant's counsel: "(3) If the jury find from the
care in in-
spection of testimony that the officers of the defendant
truck.
employed skillful and competent men to look after and keep in repair its track, and furnished the requisite men and material to do the work and keep the track in good repair, and if you further find from the testimony that the track was frequently inspected by them, and that the old ties were taken out and replaced by new ties as often as there was any apparent necessity for so doing, you cannot find that the defendant was negligent in keeping and maintaining its track." The instruction was rightly refused, for the reason that it fails to present the thought that defendant's employes used proper care in the inspection of the road, and, in the exercise of such care, there was "an apparent necessity" discovered by them to make the repairs required.

IX. The Carlyle tables were admitted in evidence, to show plaintiff's expectancy of life. Plaintiff's injury was

8 DAMAGES: permanent, and rendered him incapable of earn-
personal in-
jury: life ing compensation which he would have received
tables.
had he escaped the injury. The damage is continuing, and will end only with his life, or with his ability to labor on account of age. It is very plain that his expectancy of life must be considered in order to determine the

actual damages he sustained. The decisions of this court upon this point are conflicting. The evidence is held admissible in *McDonald v. Chicago & N. W. R'y Co.*, 26 Iowa, 124, after due consideration of the question. In *Nelson v. Chicago, R. I. & P. R'y Co.*, 38 Iowa, 564, a contrary doctrine is announced, but no reference is made to the prior case, and no attempt is made to support the decision announced upon principle or precedent. It was evidently reached without consideration. We follow the first case, deeming it in accord with sound reason and justice. See *Simonson v. Chicago, R. I. & P. R'y Co.*, 49 Iowa, 87.

X. Defendant complains that a witness was permitted to testify to the condition of the ties at places along the road other than at the place where the accident occurred. An amended abstract, which is not denied by defendant, shows that the witness testified as to the condition of the ties at the place of the accident. Defendant's objection is not based upon facts.

XI. A witness, who was the section foreman, and had charge of the road at the place of the accident, testified that

2. RAILROADS: injury to engineer: defective track: incompetent evidence of repairs.

he put in new ties not long before plaintiff was injured. He was then asked several questions touching his report to the road master as to this work, which he was not permitted to answer. There is no error in this ruling of the court below, for the reason that the evidence sought to be elicited would not tend to show that the repairs had been made at the place of the accident. The evidence, to be competent, should have that effect.

We have considered all objections urged in argument by defendant's counsel, and reach the conclusion that the judgment of the court below ought to be

AFFIRMED.

COTTRELL V. SOUTHWICK ET AL.

1. **Practice on Appeal**: EVIDENCE TO SUPPORT VERDICT. Although the testimony of a party as to a material question is uncontradicted by any direct evidence, yet where circumstances are proved which tend to cast suspicion on such testimony, there is a conflict of evidence, and this court will not interfere with the verdict of a jury based thereon.

2. **Usury**: NOTE FOR MONEY TO PAY USURIOUS NOTES. A note is not usurious because given for money advanced by the payee for the maker in payment of usurious notes made to a third party.

Appeal from Cedar Circuit Court.

· FRIDAY, MARCH 4.

ACTION on a promissory note. Defendant S. P. Southwick answered that the only consideration of the note was usurious interest, which plaintiff charged and computed on certain other promissory notes which he held against defendant. The other defendant answered that he signed the note as surety for his co-defendant, and that it was agreed between him and plaintiff at the time he signed the note that plaintiff would obtain the signature of one Gearhart thereto as a co-surety, and that it was not to become binding on defendant until Gearhart's signature was obtained. The verdict and judgment were for defendants. Plaintiff appeals.

Piatt & Carr, for appellant.

J. W. Jamison, for appellees.

REED, J.—We find it necessary to consider only those questions which arise under the plea of usury. In 1874 the defendants executed a promissory note to one S. S. Whitmore, for $400. This note afterwards came into plaintiff's possession, and afterwards defendant S. P. Southwick received from him a sum of money as a loan, and for the amount of such loan, and in renewal of the $400 note, the defendant gave two promissory notes, which amounted in the aggregate to $683. These notes by their terms were made payable to Louis G. Cottrell, who is plaintiff's father. Subsequently those notes were taken up, and a single note for the same amount was given, which was also made payable to Louis G. Cottrell. The parties afterwards made a computation to ascertain the amount due on the note, which was found to be something over $900, and defendant paid to plaintiff $745, and gave the note sued on, which is for $191, and took up said note. The note in suit by its terms is payable to plaintiff.

Defendant claims that in these several transactions interest was computed on the notes at the rate of eighteen per cent per annum, and that he paid interest at that rate on the notes which were given for the borrowed money, and in renewal of the $400 note. Also that, in the transaction in which the note in suit was given, interest was computed at the same rate on the $683 note, and that the note in suit was given wholly for such usurious interest. This claim as to the rate at which the interest was computed is not denied by plaintiff. His claim, however, is that the money which was originally loaned to defendant belonged to Louis G. Cottrell, and that, while he had the said $400 note, and those given in renewal of that and for the borrowed money, also the $683 note, in his possession, they all belonged to Louis G. Cottrell, and that the payments of usurious interest which were made by defendant before the transaction in which the note in suit was given were made to him, or for his benefit. He also claims that, in the final transaction, he advanced the sum of $191 to defendant to enable him to pay the amount which was found under the computation to be due said Louis G. Cottrell on the $683 note, and that the note in suit was given for the money so advanced. And on the trial he testified that those were the facts of the several transactions.

I. The first point urged by counsel is that the verdict is not supported by the evidence. There was no direct evidence

1. PRACTICE on appeal: evidence to support verdict. as to the ownership of the several notes prior to the one in suit, except that given by plaintiff. Defendant, however, contended that said notes were in fact the property of plaintiff, and that, in the several

transactions, he acted for himself. He also testified positively that the note in suit was given for a balance which
was found due on the $683 note, after deducting the cash
payment made by him. He also denied that, in the transaction, there was a loan by plaintiff to him of $191, or any
other sum. If we could say, as matter of law, that the jury
were bound to accept plaintiff's statement as to the ownership of the other notes as the truth, it would follow, probably,
that the verdict should be set aside, as lacking the support
of evidence. But we think we cannot say that. While
plaintiff's testimony as to that question is uncontradicted by
any direct evidence, there were some circumstances proven
which tended to cast suspicion on his story. As stated above,
the money borrowed by defendant was obtained from him.
While the note which was given for the amount was made
payable to L. G. Cottrell, no suggestion was made during the
negotiation that the money belonged to him. All of the
transactions were had with plaintiff in person, and in none
of them did he make the claim that he was acting for his
father, and defendant understood, during all of the transactions, that he was dealing with plaintiff in his own right.
Notes were given at other times for the interest found due,
and some of these notes were made payable to him or to
his firm. We think the question fairly arose as to the
credence which should be given to his testimony. The jury
might fairly conclude, from all of the circumstances, that the
manner in which the business was transacted was but a
device resorted to by him to avoid the statute against usury.
The rule has long prevailed here that we will not disturb the
verdict of a jury when there is a fair conflict in the evidence.
And it is equally well settled that, when the jury have determined a question as to the credit which should be given to
the testimony of a particular witness, when such question
fairly arose in the case, their finding will not be set aside.

II.   The circuit court gave the following instruction, to

which exception is taken by plaintiff: "It is conceded that

1. USURY: S. P. Southwick signed said note, and delivered
note for
money to pay the same to plaintiff, and he is liable thereon,
usurious
notes. unless you find that said note was given for balance on previous notes, and that said notes were usurious;
and if you so find, then the note in suit is tainted with usury;
but if you find that the note was given to plaintiff for money
to be applied in payment of other notes which were usurious,
then it would not be usurious, and such defense would fail."
Counsel for appellant contend that this instruction warranted
the jury in finding that the note was tainted with usury, notwithstanding they may have found that plaintiff was not a
party to the usurious contract, but that it existed between
defendant and L. G. Cottrell, and the note was given
for money advanced by plaintiff to be paid on that contract.
But we think the instruction is not fairly capable of that
construction. By the last clause of the instruction the jury
were told that the defense of usury is not sustained, if the
evidence shows that the note was given for money advanced
by plaintiff, to be applied in payment of other notes which
were usurious. That clause fairly submits plaintiff's claim
as to the character of the transaction in which the note was
given to the jury for determination.

We discover no error in the record, and the judgment
will be

AFFIRMED.

54   SUPREME COURT OF IOWA,

The State, ex rel. Littleton, v. Leach et al.

THE STATE, EX REL. LITTLETON, v. LEACH ET AL.

1. **Practice**: SAVING EXCEPTIONS: METHOD AND TIME: An exception
can be preserved only by having it embodied in a bill of exceptions, or
by having it noted in the record of the decision to which it relates.
(Code, §§ 2831, 2833.) And a party who would save his exceptions by
the first method must have his bill of exceptions signed and filed during
the term at which the decision objected to was made, or within such
time thereafter as the court may fix; and where the court did not fix
any such time, *held* that a bill of exceptions signed and filed at the next
term must be disregarded on appeal, even though it embodies the several
rulings of the court, and recites that appellant excepted to each of them.

2. **New Trial**: MOTION FOR: CAUSE DECIDED ON DEMURRER: Where,
pending the trial, plaintiff amended his petition, and a demurrer to the
petition as amended was sustained, and judgment was rendered thereon, a motion for a retrial, based on the ground that, upon the facts
proved, the judgment should have been for plaintiff, was properly overruled, because the judgment was not based on any facts proved.

Appeal from Polk Circuit Court.

FRIDAY, MARCH 4.

THE defendant Leach obtained from the board of supervisors of Polk county a permit to buy and sell intoxicating
liquors for the purposes for which such liquors may be sold
under the statute. He also gave a bond, in the form prescribed by the statute, with the other defendants as sureties.
This action was brought for the recovery of the penalties
prescribed by the statute for certain alleged breaches of the
bond. It was charged in the original petition that Leach
did not, on the last Saturday of each of certain named
months, or within five days thereafter, file with the county
auditor a report in writing showing the kind and quantities
of liquors purchased by him since the date of his last report,
the price paid, and the amount of freights paid on the same;
also the kind and quantities of liquors sold by him since the
date of his last report, to whom sold, for what purpose, and
for what price sold, and the kind and quantity of liquors
remaining on hand. The answer of the defendant to this

petition was a general denial of its allegations. During the progress of the trial, plaintiff filed an amendment to the petition, in which it was alleged that the breaches of the bond relied on were that defendant did not, in any one of the returns alluded to, state the kinds and quantities of liquors purchased by him during the periods covered by the returns, and the price paid for the same; but in each of said returns he stated the price paid as having been from a greater to a lesser sum for a given number of gallons per gallon, so that the returns do not intelligibly state what price was paid for any one purchase, either in detail or in the aggregate. Thereupon defendant demurred to the petition as amended, on the ground that it neither alleged a failure to file a report within the time provided by the statute, nor the filing of a false report. The circuit court sustained this demurrer, and, the plaintiff declining to plead further, an order was entered dismissing the action, and taxing the costs to the relator. Afterwards, counsel for plaintiff filed in the case a paper, denominated a motion for a rehearing, which was subsequently overruled by the court, and plaintiff appealed.

M. D. McHenry, for appellant.

Cummins & Wright, for appellee.

REED, J.—I. The first assignment of error is that "the court erred in sustaining the demurrer to the petition as amended;" and the question arising under this assignment is the one mainly relied on by counsel for the plaintiff for the reversal of the judgment. But we cannot on the record in the case consider that question. The ruling on the demurrer was made on the twenty-first day of March, and the order dismissing the action was made on the same day. Counsel for plaintiff did not cause an exception to these rulings to be noted in the record at the time they were made,

1. PRACTICE: saving exceptions: method and time.

or within three days thereafter. On the twenty-second of
March he filed his motion for a rehearing, and it was submitted on the same day, and taken under advisement by the
judge; but the order overruling it was not made until the
next term of the court, which was in May following. After
the order overruling that motion was entered, the judge
signed a "bill of exceptions," which embodies the various
rulings of the court in the cause, including those sustaining
the demurrer and dismissing the action. It is recited in
this "bill of exceptions" that plaintiff excepted to each of
said rulings. This is the only record of an exception by
plaintiff to the ruling on the demurrer; and it is very clear,
we think, that it does not save the question for review on
this appeal. It has so frequently been held that, in ordinary
actions, we could review only such rulings of the lower court
as were excepted to, and the exception properly made a matter of record, that it cannot now be necessary to refer to the
cases in which the ruling has been made. The statute is
clear and explicit as to the time at which exceptions may be
taken, and the manner in which they must be preserved.
Section 2831 of the Code is as follows: "An exception is
an objection to a decision of the court on matter of law.
The party objecting to the decision must do so at the time
the same is made, (but if the decision is on motion, demurrer, or judgment, exception may be taken within three days.)
and embody his objection in a bill of exceptions, to be filed
during the term, or within such time thereafter as the court
may fix. * * * "   And section 2833 is as follows:
"When the decision objected to is entered on the record, and
the grounds of the exception appear in the entry, or when
any error appears of record, the exception may be taken by
the party causing to be noted, at the end of the decision or
in connection therewith, that he excepts." It is clear that,
under these provisions, an exception can be preserved only
by having it embodied in a "bill of exceptions," or by having it noted in the record of the decision to which it relates.

And a party who would save his exception by the first method mentioned, must have his "bill of exceptions" signed and filed within the time prescribed by the first provision quoted; that is, during the term at which the decision objected to was made, or within such time thereafter as the court may fix. As stated above, the bill of exceptions in this case was signed during the next term after the one at which the ruling in question was made. But the court did not fix a time after that term within which it should be signed and filed. There was no authority, then, for signing a bill of exceptions at that time for the preservation of that question, and we must disregard it.

II. Error is assigned on the judgment of the court taxing the costs to the relator. But, as to this question, the record is in the same condition. The only record **THE SAME.** of any exception to the ruling is contained in the bill of exceptions, which, as stated above, was not signed until the next term after that at which the ruling was made, and no time after the term was fixed within which it should be signed. The exception was therefore not properly preserved, and we cannot consider the question attempted to be raised by the assignment of error.

III. The final action of the court in overruling the motion for a rehearing, or a new trial, is also assigned as error. 2. NEW trial: The following are the grounds of that motion: motion for: cause decided "(1) Because the court erred as to the finding on demurrer. of the facts of the case. (2) The court erred as to the law of the case on the facts. (3) On the law and facts, as submitted to the court, the plaintiff was entitled to judgment." The amendment to the petition, it will be borne in mind, was filed after an issue had been joined and the parties had entered upon the trial, and the demurrer was to the petition as amended. In submitting this motion, counsel appear to have proceeded on the theory that there had been a determination of the case on the facts. Each of the grounds of the motion is, in effect, that, upon the facts

proven, the judgment should have been for plaintiff. But
the judgment was not based upon evidence. The court
determined that the petition, as amended, was not sufficient
to entitle the plaintiff to relief, and that was the ground
upon which the judgment was rendered. The motion did
not assail that ruling; nor did it call for a review of it. It
was manifestly filed through a misconception of the record
in the case, or a misunderstanding as to the action which
had been taken by the court, and it was properly overruled.
The judgment must be

AFFIRMED.

VIMONT v. THE CHICAGO & NORTHWESTERN R'Y CO.

58
465

1. **Railroads**: REQUIREMENT OF PASSENGER TO LEAVE MOVING TRAIN:
FACTS NOT AMOUNTING TO: EVIDENCE. Action to recover for injuries
received in alighting from a moving train under the alleged command of
the conductor; but, upon consideration of the facts and circumstances
as shown by the evidence, (see opinion,) *held* that the facts proved did
not amount to a command by the conductor, and that the court erred in
assuming in an instruction given that there was evidence of any such
command.

Appeal from Polk Circuit Court.

FRIDAY, MARCH 4.

THE plaintiff, as assignee of one Oscar Johnson, brings
this action to recover for a personal injury to Johnson.
There was a trial to a jury, and verdict and judgment were
rendered for the plaintiff. The defendant appeals.

Hubbard, Clark & Dawley, for appellant.

Nourse, Kauffman & Guernsey, for appellee.

ADAMS, CH. J.—Johnson took passage on the defendant's
train at Marshalltown, having purchased a ticket either for
Moingona or Ogden, the next station west of Moingona.
Soon after the train left Moingona, and while it was in

motion, he got off, and, in doing so, he fell into a culvert several feet deep, and received an injury. The accident occurred between three and four o'clock in the morning of a very dark night. The culvert was 513 feet west of the Moingona station. The train, according to the strong preponderance of the evidence, had acquired a very considerable speed, probably at the rate of about twelve miles an hour. Johnson intended, when he left Marshalltown, to get off at Ogden, and did not conclude to get off at Moingona until after the train had left that station. The plaintiff averred that the conductor required Johnson to leave the train, and that he jumped off when and where he did in obedience to the conductor's requirement. The defendant denied that the conductor made such requirement.

The court instructed the jury in these words: " Whether Johnson had a right to travel on the train to Odgen or not, if the conductor required him to leave it a time and place and under circumstances that rendered it dangerous to do so, then it was negligence in the conductor to so require. You will first determine whether the conductor did require Johnson to leave the train at the time and place he did leave it. To constitute such requirement, it must appear that the conductor intended to be, and was, understood by Johnson as requiring that he should leave the train." The defendant assigns the giving of this instruction as error. The objection made is that there was no evidence that the conductor required Johnson to leave the train at the time he did. It is undisputed that, after Johnson started from his seat to leave the train, something was said to him by the conductor. As to what precisely was said the witnesses differed somewhat. According to the testimony of a passenger who appears to be entirely disinterested, the conductor said: " Don't try to get off, the train is going too fast." The conductor's testimony, though differing a little in the words used, was to the same effect. According to the testimony of Johnson, what the conductor said

was, "Jump off quick, if you are going to." Now, while
there is some difference, it is manifest, so far as the testimony alone is concerned, that the conductor might have said
both what the passenger and what Johnson testified that he
did. He might have advised him not to get off, but, if he
was going to do it, to be quick about it. Such advice would
not have been unreasonable, as the train was leaving the station, and was probably gaining in speed. But Johnson testified in rebuttal of the testimony of the conductor and of
the passenger, and denies that he was advised by
the conductor not to get off. Now, while there is no
question about the preponderance of evidence, so far as it
appears from the record, it is not for us to pass on such
question; and we must assume, for the purposes of the opinion, that the conductor said what Johnson testified that he
did, and that he did not advise him not to get off. We have,
then, the question as to whether the words, "jump off
quick, if you are going to," constituted a requirement to
leave the train. It appears to us they did not. It was still nothing but advice, and good advice at that. Doubtless, the conductor might have given him better advice, and that is not
to attempt to get off; but Johnson was a young man about
twenty years of age, in the full possession of his powers,
and the defendant is not liable if the conductor merely
allowed him to get off.

Thus far, in considering whether Johnson's act was purely
voluntary, we have looked merely at the words, "jump off
quick, if you are going to." We ought, perhaps, to say in
this connection that Johnson testified in his examination in
chief that the conductor said, "jump off quick." If upon
his cross-examination he had adhered to this as being what
the conductor said, the case might be different; but he did
not adhere to it, but showed very clearly that the conductor
did not require him to leave the cars. We ought, perhaps,
to say further in this connection that there had been one or
two previous conversations between Johnson and the conduc-

tor, and while the train was standing at the station. There was one conversation, we think, before the train reached the station. We infer from the argument of the plaintiff's counsel that what was said at those times is relied upon largely as constituting a requirement to leave the train.

Before proceeding to consider precisely what was said, and the circumstances under which it was said, we desire to say that a requirement to leave a train when standing at a station could hardly be deemed a requirement to leave it after it had hauled out, and was fairly under way, as this was. It is undisputed that Johnson had abundant time to leave the train at the station. The train stopped three or four minutes. He knew the station. His attention was expressly called to it. The evidence is conclusive that, while the train was standing at the station, he concluded to remain upon it, and go further, and changed his mind only after the train had commenced to move out. Whatever, then, was said by the conductor previous to the starting of the train must be construed with reference to the circumstances. But we do not think that, in any view, what was said at the station could be construed as a requirement to leave the train. There was no altercation, and no question about Johnson's right to go further if he pleased. The fact was simply this: Johnson wanted to get off at Ogden, the next station, from which he expected to walk a short distance into the country. He happened to get upon a train that did not stop at Ogden. The next station west of Ogden was not as near Ogden as Moingona was. The testimony relied upon as showing a requirement of the conductor that Johnson should get off at Moingona is the testimony of Johnson, and in these words: "He [the conductor] said he would not stop at Ogden, and I would have to get off at Moingona." Johnson also testified that the conducter picked up his satchel and handed it to him. But there is not the slightest reason for supposing that what the conductor said he said in the exercise of authority. It was Johnson's right to ride just as long as he would pay the company for carrying him, and no question of payment had been raised. We are aware that there is some evidence that Johnson had bought a ticket to Ogden, and insisted upon being carried to Ogden, and let off there; but that was a mere question of contract, and has nothing to do with the tort sued for. If the company broke its contract, such breach had no tendency to excuse Johnson in remaining in his seat when at the station, and in attempting to leave when the train had moved out and had acquired considerable speed. He could not be allowed to enhance his damages by jumping in the dark into a culvert 500 feet from the station.

The plaintiff's counsel claimed that Johnson left the train under a pressure of circumstances, and that the plaintiff is not precluded from recovering, even though it should appear that Johnson's act was purely voluntary. It may be conceded that a right of recovery sometimes accrues where the injury is received by reason of the voluntary act of the injured party in leaving a train. This may be so, where the time allowed to get off is insufficient. *Filer v. New York Cent. R. Co.*, 49 N. Y., 47. A passenger is not necessarily guilty of contributory negligence because he voluntarily incurs some risk in getting off to prevent being carried by a station where he desires to stop. But Johnson had ample time to get off before the train started; and, furthermore, whether he had or not, the instruction cannot be approved. That proceeds upon the theory that there was evidence that Johnson's act was not purely voluntary, but was done in obedience to the requirement of the conductor, and we have to say that we do not think that there was any such evidence.

REVERSED.

MALLORY v. RUSSELL ET AL.

1. **Dower**: PARTNERSHIP LAND: TITLE IN TRUSTEE. Where two persons entered into a contract, which was, in effect, a contract of partnership for the purchase and sale of real estate, and the contract provided
that the real estate purchased and sold should be conveyed to and by a
certain person as trustee, and contemplated a conversion of all lands
into cash before a settlement of the partnership, and not a division of
any lands between the partners, *held* that lands so purchased were to be
regarded as personal property belonging to the firm, and that a purchaser
of such land from the trustee held the same free from any claim of
dower made by the wife of one of the partners. (Compare *Hewitt v.
Rankin*, 41 Iowa, 35.)

Appeal from Des Moines Circuit Court.

FRIDAY, MARCH 4.

THIS action involves a controversy as to the right of the
defendant Cornelia Thayer to a dower interest in certain real
estate owned by the plaintiff. The cause was submitted to
the court below upon an agreed statement of facts, and it
was held that the plaintiff owned the land free and clear of
any claim for dower. Defendant appeals.

W. L. Cooper, for appellant.

J. W. Blythe, for the other defendants.

Thomas Hedge, Jr., and *Jas. I. Gilbert*, for appellee.

ROTHROCK, J.—The defendant Cornelia Thayer is the
widow of N. Thayer, deceased. In the month of September,
1871, said N. Thayer and one J. M. Forbes entered into a
written contract, of which the following is a copy:

" By this agreement the undersigned, Jno. M. Forbes and
Nathaniel Thayer, of Boston, Massachusetts, have formed an
association for the purpose of buying and selling land in the
state of Iowa, and principally on the line of the branch of
the Burlington & Missouri River Railroad. This association
shall be called the ' Russell Trust.' Each subscriber agrees

to pay over to the agent of said association the sum of six thousand four hundred and forty-five and 12-100 dollars, or as much thereof as may be required by the trustee herein-after provided for, for the purchase of land for the association; which money shall be paid for in such installments as may be called for by the trustee. The legal title of the land purchased shall be placed in H. S. Russell, as trustee, to be held, managed and sold by him in trust for the benefit of all the parties subscribers hereto, each of said parties having an interest in all the properties and rights which may be acquired in proportion to the amount of his payments to the agent of the association. Said trustee and his successors shall have the right to bargain, sell and convey any and all the property of the association; which sale and business shall be done through and by Charles E. Perkins, of Burlington, Iowa, who shall act as the authorized agent or attorney in fact of said trustee. The death of any of the said parties subscribed shall not in anyway affect the action of said trustee; but he shall become trustee for the legal representatives of such deceased party. The transactions and property of the association shall be wound up and closed within ten years from date, by auction sale or otherwise, unless all the parties subscribers hereto agree in writing to extend the time. It is understood that the trustee, as long as the details of the business are actually done by an agent, is not to charge for his services, nor is he to be responsible for anything but ordinary care in transacting the business of the trust. It is further agreed that the said association and said trustee shall not contract or incur any indebtedness for or against the association aforesaid, but all property shall be purchased for cash in hand. The trustee shall keep a book, showing in detail the business of the association, describing the land bought and sold, the prices paid and received, taxes and all charges and expenses paid and incurred, and all other matters connected with the business of the association, which shall be open to the inspection .all the parties hereto. In case of the death, resignation, incapacity, or refusal of said trustee to act, the members of the association may appoint his successor, by written agreement to that effect. A distribution of the receipts from land sales or otherwise shall, from time to time, be made by the trustee to the parties hereto, or to their heirs or assigns, in proportion to their respective interests.

" Witness our hands this first day of September, 1871.

[Signed] " J. M. FORBES.

" N. THAYER."

H. S. Russell accepted the trust created by said written contract. Business under the contract was carried on by the purchase and sale of lands; and in January, 1872, the said Russell, trustee, sold to the plaintiff the property in controversy, and executed to the plaintiff his warranty deed therefor, which deed was duly acknowledged and recorded. Prior to the sale to plaintiff, the trustee was in possession of the land under a warranty deed to him, and in receiving and conveying the title he acted under the trust created by the written contract. The plaintiff purchased the property in good faith, for a valuable and full consideration, without any notice of any trust affecting the title, except such notice, if any, as would be implied by the fact that in the conveyance to plaintiff the name of the grantor, Russell, was followed by the word "trustee." The business of the association in the " Russell Trust " has not been wound up; but the trustee is continuing to buy and sell land thereunder, by and with the written consent of all the beneficiaries thereof. Said beneficiaries do not desire the affairs of said trust to be wound up, but to continue, and do not ask or desire an accounting between themselves, or between them and the trustee. The associates in the " Russell Trust " authorized and consented to the sale and conveyance to the plaintiff by said trustee, and said trustee has fully accounted to each party interested for his share of the purchase money, and the association has no creditor except those persons to whom Russell, trustee, has sold lands, and executed his warranty deeds pursuant to the articles of association.

The foregoing is the substance of the agreed statement of facts. The circuit court held that the lands purchased by the partnership or association became personal property, so far as any rights therein might accrue to the individual members of the association. Appellant claims that the wife of a partner or associate became seized of an inchoate interest in the undivided estate, and that she could not be divested of this right, except by her own deed. It is true that, under section 2440 of the Code, a wife is endowable in all " legal or equitable estates in real property possessed by the husband, at any time during the marriage, which have not been sold on execution or any other judicial sale, and to which the wife has made no relinquishment of her right." We think, however, that the defendant's husband was not possessed of any estate in the lands in question. The enterprise was a partnership, the object of which was to buy and sell real estate; and the interest of the individual members of the partnership was the proceeds of the sales of the land. The written contract expressly provides that the trustee shall be invested with the legal title of the land purchased, and the same shall be sold and conveyed by him, and a distribution of receipts from the land sales shall, from time to time, be made to the members of the association, in proportion to their respective interests. It was not contemplated that there should at any time be any partition or division of the lands among the members of the partnership; but the contract plainly provides that the lands shall be sold by the trustee, and the proceeds divided among the several partners. Being partnership land, it must be treated as personal assets, not only so far as the rights of creditors of the partnership are involved, but, so far as necessary, for the purpose of carrying out the provisions of the partnership contract. It is plain to be seen that, if the claim of plaintiff be well founded, a husband could not become a member of a partnership of this character, without associating his wife with him as a member of the firm. It is not claimed that the contract of partnership is void. Contracts of partnership for buying and selling real estate as a business are as valid and binding upon the parties as any other legal contracts. The parties to this contract expressly provided that the title to the land should be held by a trustee, and that he should sell and convey a clear and absolute title. The contract itself rebuts the idea that persons who paid their money in aid of the enterprise became seized of any estate in the land. Their relation to the enterprise was very much like the relation of a stockholders in a corporation to the property of the corporation.

We are very clearly of the opinion that the defendant is not entitled to any interest in the land. See *Hewitt v. Rankin,* 41 Iowa, 35.

AFFIRMED.

SULLIVAN SAVINGS INSTITUTION v. COPELAND ET AL.

71
81

1. **Usury**: WHO MAY PLEAD: GRANTEE OF MORTGAGOR. The grantee of a mortgagor who assumes the payment of the mortgage cannot plead usury as a defense to the mortgage. (See cases cited in opinion.)

71
128

2. **Practice on Appeal**: AMENDED ABSTRACT NOT DENIED. An amendment to appellant's abstract filed by appellee, and not denied, is deemed to be true.

3. **Practice**: PLEA FILED AFTER SUBMISSION WITHOUT LEAVE. An answer which presents new issues, and which is filed after the submission of the cause without leave of the court, is properly stricken from the files.

Appeal from Fremont Circuit Court.

SATURDAY, MARCH 5.

ACTION in chancery to foreclose a mortgage. There was a a decree for plaintiff. Defendants appeal.

A. R. Brewer and *Geo. E. Draper,* for appellants.

Stow & Day and *J. M. Hammond,* for appellee.

BECK, J.——I. The action was originally brought against
Copeland, the mortgagor, and Brewer, to whom he had sold
1. USURY: and conveyed the land. The defendants united
who may
plead:grantee in an answer, setting up as a defense usury in
of mortgagor. the note and mortgage. When the cause was
called for hearing, it was dismissed as to defendant Copeland,
the mortgagor. Thereafter the answer in the case was in
fact the answer of Brewer alone, as there was no other defendant in the case; and the defense of usury was therefore
pleaded by him alone, the mortgagor being out of the case.
It is the settled rule recognized by this court that the debtor
can alone plead the defense of usury to an action on a contract. The grantee of a mortgagor, who assumes the payment of the mortgage, cannot set up the defense of usury.
See *Miller v. Clarke*, 37 Iowa, 325; *National Life Ins. Co.
v. Olmsted*, 52 Iowa, 354; *Burlington Mut. Loan Ass'n v.
Heider*, 55 Iowa, 424, and cases cited therein. Brewer,
therefore, could not avail himself of the defense of usury.

II. Counsel complain of the refusal of the court below
to sustain a motion made by defendants for a decree on the
2. PRACTICE pleadings. But the amended abstract, which is
on appeal:
amended ab- not denied, shows that no such motion was
stract not de-
nied. made.

III. Complaint is also made of the ruling of the court in
striking out an answer filed by Brewer, setting up that he
3. PRACTICE: and Copeland had agreed at the time of the con-
plea filed af-
ter submis- veyance of the land that Brewer should have the
sion without
leave. right and authority to set up the defense of
usury to proceedings to enforce the mortgage. We need not
determine whether this agreement would confer upon Brewer
the right to plead the usury in this action, for the reason
that the record, as disclosed by the amended abstract, shows
that the answer, which presents new issues, was filed after the
cause was fully submitted, and without leave of the court.
This answer was rightly stricken from the files.

These views dispose of all questions in the case. The
decree of the circuit court is   AFFIRMED.

RUSSELL v. THE CEDAR RAPIDS INS. Co.

1. **Fire Insurance**: CHANGE OF INCUMBRANCE ON PROPERTY: EFFECT: QUESTION OF FACT. Where a fire insurance policy provided that it should be void "if the assured hereafter mortgage or incumber the property," and the land on which the property was situated was mortgaged when the policy was issued, and the assured, by the sale of a portion of the land and the purchase of other land adjacent, paid off the original mortgage and made a new one, *held* that, whether this avoided the policy or not depended upon whether the hazard was increased; that is, whether the incumbrance on the insured property was proportionately increased by the change; and that that was a question for the jury.

Appeal from Humboldt Circuit Court.

SATURDAY, MARCH 5.

ACTION upon a policy of insurance. The cause was tried to a jury, and, upon the close of plaintiff's evidence, the circuit court directed a verdict for defendant. Plaintiff appeals.

A. E. Clarke, for appellant.

Deacon & Smith, for appellee.

BECK, J.—I. The policy insures plaintiff against loss by fire in the sum of $700 on a barn, and $300 "on hay in barn or in stack on cultivated premises." The property insured is described as being situated upon 280 acres of land owned by plaintiff in a section specified in the policy. A condition of the policy is to the effect that it shall be void "if the assured hereafter mortgage or incumber the property" without consent of defendant. The evidence introduced by plaintiff shows that, when the policy was issued, there were mortgages amounting to $1,600 upon the 280 acres of land described in the policy, being the land upon which the property insured was situated; and that afterwards the plaintiff sold 200 acres of the land, and bought another tract of forty

acres adjacent to the land she did not sell. She also bought
other land near by, but the precise quantity does not clearly
appear. She paid the original mortgage, and, in order to
raise $1,000 of the sum required, she executed a mortgage
upon the eighty acres remaining unsold. Her farm, it thus
appears, after this transaction, had incumbrances upon it less
in amount by $600 than when the policy was issued. The
case, then, is one of change of incumbrances, reducing the
amount thereof, as well as the quantity of land incumbered.
The land was incumbered when the policy was issued, and
remained incumbered after the new mortgage was taken.
The renewal or change of the incumbrance was not necessarily a breach of the condition of the policy. If the incumbrance remaining upon the land unsold should be less in proportion to the quantity than was upon the land when the
policy was issued, there was surely no breach of the condition against incumbrances. Or if for any reason the hazard
should not be increased by the change, so that no higher rate
of premium would be demanded, there would arise no violation of the condition. The question, then, in order to determine whether there has been a breach of the condition, is
this: Was the risk increased, or was defendant's security
decreased by the change of the incumbrances? This is a
question of fact, and should have been left to the jury. The
evidence by no means establishes beyond dispute that there
was an increase of hazard, and a demand for a higher rate of
premium. Indeed, the evidence as to the tracts of land covered by the mortgages in question is inadequate and uncertain. We cannot say that, without dispute or conflict, it
appears that the hazard was increased. That question should
have been submitted to the jury under proper instructions.

II.   It appeared from the evidence introduced by plaintiff
that she executed a chattel mortgage upon the hay insured
after the policy was executed. There was evidence tending
to show that the mortgage was executed by the plaintiff's
husband in his name, and that it was without consideration,

and did not in fact cover the hay insured. These matters, of course; should have been submitted to the jury, to be determined by their verdict. In our opinion, the circuit court erred in directing a verdict for defendant. The judgment is reversed, and the cause is remanded for a new trial.

REVERSED.

KIRK v. LITTERST.

1. **Practice on Appeal**: INSTRUCTION NOT EXCEPTED TO. An instruction not excepted to will not be reviewed.

2. ———: SUBMISSION TO JURY NOT EXCEPTED TO. Appellant cannot be heard to complain that the court submitted the case to the jury without any evidence to sustain the petition, where it does not appear that he excepted to such submission at the time, or asked the court to direct a verdict in his favor.

3. **Practice**: MOTION IN ARREST OF JUDGMENT: OFFICE OF. A motion in arrest of judgment is provided where the facts stated in the petition do not entitle the plaintiff to any relief; (Code, § 2650;) but such a motion is properly overruled when based on the ground of want of evidence to sustain the verdict. A motion for a new trial is the proper remedy in that case.

4. **Assignment of Error**: NOT SUFFICIENTLY SPECIFIC. An assignment of error that the court erred in overruling a motion for a new trial, where the motion was based upon eight grounds, is not sufficiently specific to be considered.

5. ———: JUDGMENT ON VERDICT. An assignment of error that the court erred in rendering judgment against defendant upon the verdict, in the absence of necessary evidence, raises no question for consideration, where the verdict is not assailed; for judgment follows, of course, if the verdict stands.

Appeal from Cass District Court.

SATURDAY, MARCH 5.

THIS action was brought under section 1539 of the Code to recover, in behalf of the school fund, a statutory penalty for selling intoxicating liquors to minors. A verdict and

judgment were rendered for the plaintiff for $200. The
defendant appeals.

L. L. DeLano, for appellant.

John Hudspeth and *Temple & Phelps*, for appellee.

ADAMS, CH. J.—The plaintiff averred that he was a citizen and resident of Cass county. The defendant pleaded a
general denial, except as to the ownership of a certain lot.
No evidence of citizenship was offered.

I. The defendant assigns as error that the court erred in
instructing the jury that the plaintiff was entitled to recover

1. PRACTICE
on appeal:
instruction
not excepted
to.

in the absence of testimony showing that the
plaintiff was a citizen of Cass county, Iowa.
But the instruction does not appear to have been
excepted to. We cannot review an instruction not excepted
to.

II. The defendant assigned as error that the court erred
in submitting the cause to the jury upon the testimony

2. ——: submission to
jury not excepted to.

adduced upon the trial, because there was no
evidence sustaining the allegation of the plaintiff's petition that the plaintiff was a citizen of
Cass county, Iowa. But the defendant did not at the time
except to the action of the court in this respect. If the
plaintiff had really failed to show himself entitled to recover,
the defendant should, we think, have moved the court to
direct a verdict in his favor, or should have asked an instruction to that effect; and if the court overruled him he should
have excepted.

III. The defendant assigned as error that the court erred
in refusing to sustain his motion in arrest of judgment,

3. PRACTICE:
motion in
arrest of
judgment:
office of.

based upon a lack of proof of citizenship. If
there was a lack of evidence to sustain the verdict, the defendant's remedy was to move for a
new trial. He in fact made such motion, and the court
ruled upon the question of the sufficiency of the evidence in

ruling upon the motion for a new trial.   A motion in arrest
of judgment is provided where the facts stated in the petition do not entitle the plaintiff to any relief.   Code, § 2650.
We see no error in overruling the motion in arrest.

IV.   The defendant assigned as error that the court erred
in overruling the defendant's motion for a new trial.   But
4. ASSIGN- the motion for a new trial was based upon eight
MENT of
error: not grounds.   The assignment is not sufficiently
sufficiently
specific. specific.   It is manifest that, under such an
assignment, as many different errors might be argued as
there were stated grounds for a new trial.   Such an assignment has been repeatedly held to be defective.

V.   The defendant assigned as error that the court erred
in entering a judgment against the defendant upon the ver-
5. ——: dict in the absence of proof of the plaintiff's
judgment on
verdict. citizenship.   But the entry of judgment followed,
of course, if the verdict was to stand.   The error, if any,
was in not granting a new trial on the ground of a lack of
evidence; but, as we have seen, such error was not specifically assigned.   Some of the members of the court do
not think that the allegation of the plaintiff's citizenship
was properly put in issue by a mere general denial.   Possibly we should have reached an affirmance upon that ground,
if we had thought it necessary to examine the question; but
we did not so think.

The judgment must be

AFFIRMED.

KING v. WILLIAMS.

1. **Contract**: FRAUD: PECULIAR KNOWLEDGE OF ONE PARTY: EVI-
DENCE. Plaintiff assigned to defendant a contract for the purchase of
land, which he knew had been forfeited. Defendant, failing to get the
land, had a settlement with plaintiff, wherein plaintiff gave defendant
his promissory note. Plaintiff now seeks to recover of defendant on
the ground that defendant deceived him by false statements as to what
it would be necessary to pay to secure the land and avoid the forfeiture;
and that defendant was possessed of knowledge in the matter not possessed by him. *Held* that plaintiff's knowledge of the forfeiture was
a complete answer to all his allegations of fraud, and that he could not
recover.

Appeal from Page District Court.

SATURDAY, MARCH 5.

THE plaintiff seeks by this action to recover of the defendant a certain sum of money, of which he claims he was
defrauded in a settlement made between the parties, growing
out of the assignment of certain land contracts by the plaintiff to the defendant. The defendant set up a counter-claim,
which consisted of a promissory note executed by plaintiff
to defendant. At the conclusion of the introduction of the
evidence, the court, on its own motion, instructed the jury
that the plaintiff had failed to make a case against the
defendant, and the jury were directed to return a verdict for
the defendant for the amount of the note set up in the counter-claim. A verdict was returned in accord with the instruction, and a judgment was rendered thereon. Plaintiff
appeals.

K. A. Pence and *James McCabe*, for appellant.

Stockton & Keenan, for appellee.

ROTHROCK, J.—It is claimed by the appellant in his petition that the settlement in question was procured by duress
and fraud upon the part of the defendant. We determined
in a former appeal that there was no duress in the trans-

action. (See 65 Iowa.) In the present appeal plaintiff appears to have abandoned his claim to recover on the ground of duress; but he still insists that he has a right of action against the defendant for fraud. The facts which made a settlement necessary between the parties are as follows: The plaintiff held two contracts for the purchase of land from the Burlington & Missouri River Railroad Company in Nebraska. They were long-time contracts, and they required annual payments of interest, and small amounts of principal. They were liable to forfeiture for non-payment of principal and interest according to their terms. It is not disputed by the parties hereto that the railroad company had the right to declare an absolute forfeiture of the contracts for any failure of the purchaser to make payments as they became due. The plaintiff had paid up nearly all that was owing on one of the contracts, but, upon the other, he had paid but a small amount, and he was in default thereon. He had purchased a farm from the defendant, and was indebted to him therefor. A contract was made between the parties, by which the plaintiff assigned the land contracts to the defendant for about $825. This amount extinguished the debt on the farm which plaintiff bought of defendant, and left a balance due the plaintiff of about $178, for which the defendant gave plaintiff his promissory note. This was on the seventh day of July, 1882. The defendant was to make all the payments yet to be made on the land, including all overdue payments. The plaintiff claims that the defendant agreed to make payment in three days after the assignment of the contract was made. The proof shows that an attempt to pay would have been unavailing, because the contract upon which this payment was due had been forfeited long before the assignment. The settlement of which complaint is made was concluded in September following the assignment of the contracts.

The plaintiff claims that the defendant deceived him by false statements as to what it would be necessary to pay to

the railroad company to secure the land, and avoid the forfeiture; that he was possessed of knowledge in the matter not
possessed by the plaintiff.   It appears to us that the fact that
plaintiff knew that the contract had been forfeited when he
made the settlement is a complete answer to all his allegations of fraud.   He not only knew the contract had been
forfeited at that time, but it was in fact forfeited long before
he assigned it to the defendant, and he had good reason to
believe that it was forfeited when he made the assignment.
He had been advised in March, 1882, that, unless payment
was made by April 10, 1882, the contract would be forfeited,
and the land restored to market, and the forfeiture was actually made on the twenty-fifth day of April, 1882.   These
facts, and the terms upon which the land could again be purchased from the company, were as accessible to the plaintiff
as they were to the defendant.

Without further elaboration, we may say that it is very
clear that the evidence failed to show that the plaintiff was a
victim of fraud, and we think the court did not err in directing a verdict for the defendant.

AFFIRMED.

ARMSTRONG v. THE TOWN OF ACKLEY.

1. **Personal Injury:** EXAMINATION BY PHYSICIAN: TESTIMONY OF
   PHYSICIAN AND PATIENT: HEARSAY.   In an action to recover for a personal injury, a physician called upon to examine the plaintiff may state
   as a witness the complaint made by plaintiff at the time, (*Gray v. Mc-
   Laughlin,* 26 Iowa. 279,) and may also give an opinion, based on such
   examination, as to the extent and probable consequences of the injury,
   and what caused it; but the testimony of the plaintiff as to what the
   physician said at the examination is mere hearsay, and should be excluded.

2. ———: EVIDENCE: CONTEMPORARY STATEMENTS OF ONE PRESENT:
   HEARSAY.   The statements made by one present at the time to a person injured on a defective sidewalk, when offered to be shown by the
   person injured, in an action against the town, are mere hearsay, and
   are inadmissible, unless, possibly, in rebuttal, to contradict the testimony of such person as a witness for the defendant.

3. ——: ——: TESTIMONY OF PATIENT AS TO SUBSEQUENT ILL HEALTH. In an action to recover for a personal injury, the plaintiff may testify as to the condition of his health, and in relation to the pain suffered after receiving the injury; it being for the jury to say whether the impaired health and pain were caused by the alleged injury.

4. **Evidence:** CONDITIONAL MATERIALITY: ADMISSIBILITY. . Where the materiality of certain evidence depends upon the establishment of a certain theory of the case, it should be admitted when the evidence is in conflict as to such theory.

5. **Cities and Towns:** INJURY ON SIDEWALK: NOTICE OF DEFECT: EVIDENCE. If a walk is continuously unsafe for sixty feet, and an injury occurs to a pedestrian at one end of such distance, evidence of the condition of the walk for the whole distance may be introduced, in an action against the town by the person injured, for the purpose of showing that the defendant should have known of its condition. (*Ruggles v. Town of Nevada*, 63 Iowa, 185, distinguished)

6. ——: ——: ACTION TO RECOVER: DEFECTS MUST BE PROVED AS ALLEGED. In an action to recover for an injury occasioned by a defective sidewalk, it is not sufficient to prove that the walk was unsafe at the place of the accident, but plaintiff must prove the specific defects alleged in the petition.

Appeal from Hardin District Court.

SATURDAY, MARCH 5.

THE plaintiff claims that when walking along a sidewalk in the town of Ackley, owing to the defective and unsafe condition of the walk, she fell and was greatly injured. Trial by jury, judgment for the plaintiff, and defendant appeals.

J. H. Scales, for appellant.

Huff & Pillsbury, for appellee.

SEEVERS, J.—I. The plaintiff was a witness in her own behalf, and testified that, several days after she fell on the

1. PERSONAL injury: examination by physician: testimony of physician and patient: hearsay.

sidewalk and was injured, Dr. Kelso was called to make an examination as to her condition, and prescribe for her, and she was asked: "What, if any, statement did you make to Dr. Kelso on his first visit, as to where and how you received the injury?

And where you were suffering, if any?" And the plaintiff was further asked: "Did Dr. Kelso, on his first visit after the statement made by you, make an examination of your person to determine the cause of your complaint or affliction? If so, what did he say to you at the time was the cause of your ailment or affliction from such examination?" There were other questions of like import. This, and the previous question, were objected to; but the objections were overruled, and to the latter question the witness answered, "Yes, he examined me, and he said my liver was terribly bruised, and I was bruised inwardly; and he said he could not tell just where it would locate itself. I mean that he could not tell where it would be the worst, or where it was going to settle; I was bruised so bad." It was not material what Dr. Kelso said, but what the fact was. Dr. Kelso was not under oath, and the evidence of the plaintiff above stated was simply hearsay, and, in our opinion, inadmissible. Dr. Kelso was examined as a witness; and he described the condition in which he found the plaintiff; but, so far from using the language above stated, his description of her condition and symptoms was materially different, and therefore it cannot be said that the admission of the foregoing evidence was not prejudicial. That it is proper and competent for a physician, when called upon to make an examination of a person injured as the plaintiff claimed to be, to inquire and state the complaint made by such person, we think, is true. Such evidence, coming from that source, we think is clearly admissible. It was so held in *Gray v. McLaughlin*, 26 Iowa, 279. Also, we think, a physician may give an opinion, after making such examination, as to the extent and consequences likely to follow the injury, and also what caused it. This is said in relation to certain objections made to the admission of other evidence. There are a great many such objections relied on by counsel, which we do not deem it essential to notice.

II.   The plaintiff being unable to attend court, her deposition was taken, and she was asked: "Have you a knowledge of seeing and talking with Mrs. John Scanlon immediately after you arose from your fall, August 1, 1881? If so, what was said between you at the time?"—and other questions of similar import were also asked. These questions were objected to, but the objections were overruled. It is immaterial what Mrs. Scanlon said, and clearly it was hearsay and inadmissible. But counsel for the appellee justify the admission on the ground that it was known that Mrs. Scanlon would be a witness for the defendant, and, as the plaintiff could not attend court, her statement of what was said at that time could only be obtained by her deposition taken in advance of the trial. If the object was to contradict Mrs. Scanlon, the evidence should not have been introduced until she had testified; but it in fact was introduced, not in rebuttal, but in chief, and at least was clearly inadmissible at that time.

2. ——: evidence: contemporary statement of one present: hearsay.

III. The plaintiff was asked and testified, against the objection of the defendant, what several physicians said was the matter with her at the time they severally made examinations as to her condition and afflictions. This was hearsay evidence, and should have been excluded. The doctors were not then under oath. Counsel for the defendant, as we understand, insist that the plaintiff should not have been permitted to testify as to the condition of her health, and in relation to the pain suffered since she received the injury; but in this proposition we do not concur. It was for the jury to say whether the pain suffered and the impaired health of the plaintiff was caused by her fall on the sidewalk.

3. ——: ——: testimony of patient as to subsequent ill-health.

IV. The material questions in the case we understand to be whether the walk was defective and unsafe, in the manner stated in the petition, and at the place where the accident occurred; and also whether the defendant had knowledge, or should have known, of such unsafe condition. There is a conflict in the evidence

4. EVIDENCE: conditional materiality: admissibility.

as to where the accident occurred, or what caused it. The plaintiff claims, and there is evidence tending to show, that the accident was caused by a loose board upon one end of which the plaintiff's husband stepped, thereby causing the other end to suddenly tip up, against which the plaintiff tripped and fell to the ground. The plaintiff claims that this occurred on the walk in front of the lot owned by O'Brecht, or near where it joined the Scanlon lot. The defendant claims that the accident was about sixty feet west of such place, and where it is not shown the walk was seriously out of repair, or in any respect known to be defective. Because of such conflict, the plaintiff had the right to have the case submitted to the jury on the theory her evidence tended to sustain. Therefore she had the right to introduce evidence tending to show that the walk was unsafe and defective at the place where she claims the accident occurred, and that it had been in such condition for such a length of time prior thereto that the defendant should be presumed to have known it.

There was evidence tending to show that the walk in front of a portion of the O'Brecht lot was unsafe and defective, 5. CITIES and and had been so for some time; but it is not towns: injury on sidewalk: certain that such was the condition of the walk notice of defect: evidence. at the western side of said property, where the defendant claims the accident occurred. There is some evidence, to which appellant seriously objects, tending to show that the walk along the whole of the O'Brecht lot was unsafe. Such evidence, we think, was admissible, and does not conflict with the rule established in the *Ruggles Case*, 63 Iowa, 185. In this case, however, as well as that, the accident was caused by a loose board; but in the cited case it reasonably appears that the walk was not continuously unsafe, but that there was a single loose board; and the evidence held inadmissible in that case had reference to the walk from twenty-five to fifty feet distant therefrom. If, however, a walk is continuously unsafe for say sixty feet, and an accident occurs at the western end of such distance, it seems to us that evidence of the condition of the walk for the whole distance may be introduced for the purpose of showing that the defendant should have known of its condition. The defendant claimed that the walk was not unsafe at the place where the accident occurred, or, at least, that it had not been known generally to be in that condition. It was a question for the jury to say which theory was true. Unless it was in that condition, and the accident was caused not only by its being unsafe, but also because of the unsafe condition stated in the petition, then the plaintiff was not

6. ——: ——: action to recover: defects must be proved as alleged.

entitled to recover. The ground upon which a recovery is asked in the petition is that the walk was out of repair; the stringers were decayed; the boards thereon were loose, liable to become misplaced, and were liable to tip up by persons walking thereon. There was some evidence tending to sustain such allegations. The court, instead of instructing the jury that these specific grounds of negligence must be sustained by the evidence, instructed the jury that, if the walk was defective and unsafe, and the defendant should have so known, the plaintiff was entitled to recover. While we are not prepared to say that the defendant was prejudiced by the general statement in the instructions as to the unsafe condition of the walk under the evidence, still it is possible that it may have been. At least, on another trial, we think the jury should be instructed that, in order to entitle the plaintiff to recover, the specific grounds of negligence stated in the petition must be found to have been established by the evidence.

We have deemed it proper to say this much without referring to each error briefly discussed by counsel. To do so would require much time and space, and, as many of such errors are not deemed prejudicial or not well taken, we have said all we deem material or proper to say in view of a retrial.

REVERSED.

EIKENBERRY & Co. v. EDWARDS.

1. **Change of Venue**: DISCRETION OF JUDGE: CHAP. 94, LAWS OF 1884: APPLICATION TO PENDING ACTIONS. Chapther 94, Laws of 1884, permitting affidavits to be filed in resistance of a motion for a change of venue on account of the prejudice of the judge, and vesting the court with a discretion in the matter, applies to actions which were pending when the statute was enacted, as well as to those since begun. Section 45, subd. 1, does not prevent such application.

2. **Former Adjudication**: SEPARATE TRIALS FOR SEVERAL DEFENDANTS. Where several alleged makers of a promissory note were made defendants in an action on the note, and one of them procured a separate trial for himself, *held* that nothing in the record of the trial as to the others could be relied on as *res adjudicata* on the separate trial of such defendant.

3. **Attorney's Fees**: CHAP. 185, LAWS OF 1880: AFFIDAVIT IN CASE OF EXISTING CONTRACTS. Chapter 185, Laws of 1880, regulating and limiting the amount of attorney's fees that may be taxed on written contracts stipulating for attorney's fees, applies wholly to contracts made after the passage of the act, and it is not necessary to file the affidavit required by § 3 of the act, in order to recover attorney's fees on a contract antedating the act itself.

4. **Pleading**: CONFESSION AND AVOIDANCE: PLEADING ESTOPPEL IS NOT. Where in an action on a promissory note defendant pleaded that his signature to the note was a forgery, and plaintiffs replied, averring that defendant's signature was genuine, and that he was by his acts and conduct estopped from denying it, *held* that this reply was not in the nature of a confession and avoidance of the answer, and did not change the issue as to the genuineness of defendant's signature.

Appeal from Appanoose District Court.

SATURDAY, MARCH 5.

ACTION upon a promissory note. There was a trial by jury, which resulted in a verdict and judgment for the plaintiffs. Defendant appeals.

Geo. D. Porter and *Henry L. Dashiell,* for appellant.

T. B. Perry, Tannehill & Fee and *T. M. Stuart,* for appellees.

ROTHROOK, J.—I. The following is a copy of the note upon which this action is founded:

"ALBIA, IA., July 18, 1878.

"Two years after date, for value received, we jointly and severally, as principals, promise to pay to the order of the Monroe County Bank twenty-five hundred dollars, with interest payable semi-annually, and if not paid when due, the note shall become due and collectable at once, and we also agree to pay reasonable attorney's fee if this note is collected by suit.   "T. S. THARP & Co.

"D. M. MILLER.

"LOUIS MILLER.

"T. S. THARP.

"HENRY MILLER.

"J. A. EDWARDS."

The defendants T. S. Tharp & Co., and the defendant Edwards, filed separate answers in the case, denying the execution of the note, and claiming that the same was a forgery. T. S. Tharp & Co. was a partnership, and the firm also pleaded that the partnership was dissolved before the date of the note, and no one at that time had authority to bind the firm by a note. The issues having thus been made up, the defendant Edwards made an application to the court for a separate trial as to him. The application or motion was granted. The case against T. S. Tharp & Co. was first tried, and there was a verdict and judgment for the partnership. This verdict was based upon one of two grounds,— either that the note was a forgery as to the partnership, or that it was executed after the firm had dissolved, without proper authority, and therefore did not bind the firm. Afterwards the case was separately tried as to the defendant Edwards, and a verdict and judgment rendered against him. From this judgment he appealed to this court, and the judgment was reversed. See 67 Iowa, 14. The case was again tried, and there was a second verdict and judgment against Edwards, from which he now appeals.

After the cause had been remanded from this court for a new trial, the defendant made a motion for a change of venue, based upon the alleged prejudice of the judge of the district court. The motion was over-ruled, and complaint is made of this ruling. The defendant supported his application by affi-davits, and the plaintiffs filed counter-affidavits, and the court, upon the showing thus presented, overruled the motion. It was provided by section 2590 of the Code that, where either party to an action filed an affidavit, verified by himself and three disinterested persons not related to him nor in his employ as servant, agent, or otherwise, that the judge is so prejudiced against him that he cannot obtain a fair trial, the place of trial shall be changed. By the law, as it then was, the court was required to change the place of trial upon the filing of such affidavits. But, by chapter 94 of the acts of 1884, the Code was amended, so that the other party may file counter-affidavits, and the court or judge is required to decide whether a change shall be granted. It is not claimed by appellant that the court made an erroneous decision upon the question; but it is contended that, as this action was commenced before the statute was amended, the defendant had a vested or accrued right to have a change of venue upon filing the affidavits required by statute when the action was commenced.

1. CHANGE of venue: dis-cretion of judge: chap. 94, laws of 1884: applica-tion to pend-ing actions.

It is true, section 45 of the Code provides that the repeal of a statute does not affect any proceeding commenced under or by virtue of the statute repealed. It will be observed that the statute authorizing changes of the place of trial of actions is not repealed by chapter 94 of the acts of 1884. It is a mere amendment to the statute, prescribing that the party opposed to a change of venue may submit counter-affi-davits, and requiring the court to decide the question. It does not affect a vested right, and has no direct effect upon any pending suit. It is simply a new rule of practice, appli-cable to pending actions as well as those commenced after the passage of the amendment. The amendment of the law requiring the court to determine the question according to the right of it, after permitting the other party to be heard, cannot be said to impair any right, or to prejudice the defendant in any respect.

II. The defendant offered in evidence the pleadings, one of the instructions of the court to the jury, the verdict of the jury, the judgment, and the evidence of jurors in the trial against T. S. Tharp & Co., as to their liability on the note in suit. All of this evidence was excluded. It is claimed that it should have been admitted, because it would have shown that the question as to the genuineness of the signature of the defendant to the note was 'adjudicated on that trial. It is very clear that the offered evidence was properly excluded. It would be a novelty in the law of former adjudication if a defendant in an action can procure a separate trial as to the issues between him and the plaintiff and then claim that the trial between the plaintiff and another defendant was an adjudication as to him. It is wholly immaterial what the instructions to the jury in the other trial were. The record shows affirmatively that the individual liability of the defendant was not, and under the order for a separate trial it could not have been, determined in the trial between the plaintiff and Tharp & Co.

III. It will be observed that the note provides that the defendants agree to pay a reasonable attorney's fee if collection is made by suit. The court permitted the plaintiffs to introduce evidence showing what would be a reasonable attorney's fee. The defendant claimed that the evidence was erroneously admitted, because no affidavit had been filed, as required by chapter 185, Laws 1880. That is an act regulating and limiting the amount of attorney's fees that may be taxed in suits on written contracts stipulating for the payment of attorney's fees. That act does not attempt to affect existing contracts.

(marginalia: 2. FORMER adjudication: separate trials for several defendants.)

(marginalia: 3. ATTORNEY'S fees: chap. 185, laws of 1880: affidavit in case of existing contracts.)

On the contrary, it expressly provides in the first and second
sections, which fix the amount of the fee, that it shall apply
to written contracts made after the taking effect of the act.
It is true that, in section 3, which provides for the filing of
an affidavit, it is not declared that the affidavits shall be
required only in suits on contracts made after the taking
effect of the act; but the whole scope of the act shows that
none of its provisions were intended to be applicable to prior
contracts. We think the court did not err in submitting to
the jury the evidence in question.

IV. As we have said, the defendant denied that he signed
the note, and claimed that it was a forgery. The plaintiffs
filed a reply, in which it was averred that, by the

4. PLEADING.
confession
and avoid-
ance: plead-
ing estoppel is
not.

acts and conduct of the defendant, he was
estopped from denying his signature to the note.
In this reply the allegation of the petition that
defendant signed the note was reiterated. The court instructed the jury that, in order for the plaintiffs to recover,
they must find as a fact that the signature of the defendant
was genuine. Counsel for the defendant insist that the reply
was in the nature of a confession and avoidance; that it in
effect admitted that the note was a forgery, and sought a
recovery upon the ground of estoppel. It is urged that the
execution of the note was not in issue, and that the court
should have based the right to a recovery upon the estoppel,
that being the issue between the parties. The real issue
between the parties was the genuineness of defendant's signature. The matter pleaded as an estoppel was not an admission that the signature was a forgery. The defendant may
have signed the note, and also his acts may have been such
as to preclude him from maintaining a denial of the signature. The two propositions are not inconsistent. It may be
that the acts were not such, and did not induce the plaintiffs
to so act, as to constitute a technical estoppel; but the defendant's conduct may have been such in directing suit to be
brought on the note, and in admitting that it was a valid

instrument, and the like, as to completely defeat his defense of forgery. By section 2666 of the Code, the plaintiff in an action is authorized to set up in a reply "any new matter, not inconsistent with the petition, constituting a defense to the matters alleged in the answer."

V. Numerous other objections are made to rulings of the court upon the admission and exclusion of evidence pending the trial. We have examined these objections, and, without setting them out in detail, will say that they do not appear to us to be well taken. They relate to matters of minor consideration in the case, and in no way involve questions affecting the merits of the controversy, and most of them are so extremely technical as to require no consideration.

In our opinion, there is no good reason for disturbing the judgment of the district court.

AFFIRMED.

THE STATE, EX REL., ETC., V. BOTKIN.

1. **Criminal Law:** INTERPRETATION OF ORDINANCE: VISITING DISORDERLY HOUSE. A city ordinance which provides that "any person who shall be found in or frequenting any disorderly house shall be subject to a fine," is not void on the ground that it fails to use the word "unlawfully," and makes it an offense to visit a disorderly house for a lawful purpose; for the reason and the spirit of the ordinance plainly show that the offense, and not the act, is prohibited, and a defendant prosecuted under it should be charged with being unlawfully in the disorderly house; and he may show as a defense that he was lawfully there.

2. ———: DEFECTIVE INFORMATION: JUDGMENT NOT VOID. A judgment of conviction in a criminal case is not rendered void by the fact that the information on which it is based is defective.

3. **Cities and Towns:** RESTRAINING DISORDERLY HOUSES. Under the power, given by § 456 of the Code, to "repress and distrain disorderly houses," a city has authority by ordinance to make it an offense to visit such houses.

Appeal from Polk District Court.

SATURDAY, MARCH 5.

THIS is a proceeding by *habeas corpus.* The petitioner,
T. J. Reynolds, should have been designated in the title of
the case as plaintiff. Upon a trial before the district court,
the petitioner was discharged. Defendant appeals.

James H. Detrick and *Hugh Brennan,* for appellant.

No appearance for appellee.

BECK, J.—I. An ordinance of the city of Des Moines
declares that, if the keeper of any store, grocery, saloon, etc.,
or other place, permit games of cards, dice, or
other games of chance, to be played therein, he
shall be deemed the keeper of a disorderly house,
and shall be subject to fine. Another section of
the ordinance is in these words: "Any person who shall be
found in or frequenting any disorderly house, shall be subject
to a fine." The police court of the city, upon an information
filed therein charging the petitioner, Reynolds, with the
offense of being found in a disorderly house, found him
guilty, and fined him, and committed him in default of payment of the fine. This imprisonment, he alleges in his petition, is illegal, and that he is therefore unlawfully restrained
of his liberty. The district court held that the ordinance
was void, and that petitioner was therefore illegally restrained
of his liberty.

II. The petitioner alleges in his petition that the city
council had no legal authority to pass the ordinance. It
appears that the district court did not pass upon the question of the authority of the city to enact a proper ordinance
to punish persons who were found in disorderly houses for
unlawful purposes, but held that the section of this ordinance
was void for the reason that it fails to prescribe that, to render one guilty of the offense prohibited, he should be unlaw-

1. CRIMINAL law: inter- pretation of ordinance: visiting dis- orderly house.

fully in the house when found there, and that, under the language of the ordinance, one found in a disorderly house is guilty, though he be there for a lawful or innocent purpose. This position of the court below is clearly unsound, and in violation of familiar rules of construction and interpretation of statutes. The subject-matter, effect and consequence, and the reason and spirit, of a statute, must be considered, as well as its words, in interpreting and construing it. A statute intending to prohibit an offense will, under these rules, never be applied to an innocent and lawful act. The offense is prohibited, and not the lawful act. Hence, if an act is done which is prohibited by the words of the statute, it may be shown to be lawfully or innocently done. The illustration of the application of these rules given by Blackstone are most apt, and are familiar to the profession. See Introduction to Commentaries, § 2, pp. 59–62. We need not consume time to repeat them. In support of these views, see, also, 1 Bl. Comm., 59, 62, 87, *et seq.* and Potter's Dwar. St., 208 *et seq.*

The court below thought that, as the ordinance imposes upon the accused the burden of showing his lawful presence in a disorderly house, it is void. But it is competent for the legislature to prescribe that an offense may be presumed from an act done. The ordinance in question, as we have seen, is intended to forbid unlawful presence in a disorderly house, and is to be so interpreted. The presence should be charged in the information as unlawful. As a defense, the person charged may show that he was lawfully or innocently in the house. These rules are of constant application in the administration of the criminal law.

III. The court below, in the decision, criticises the information, and holds that it does not allege that defendant was found in the house when unlawfully there.

2. ——:
defective
information:
judgment not
void.

That it was the obvious purpose of the information to so charge there can be no doubt; and we think, under a fair construction, it must be so understood.

But even if the information be defective, it is not a matter that will render the judgment of the police court void.

IV.   The city is clothed with authority to "repress and restrain disorderly houses." Code, § 456. No more effi-

3. CITIES and towns: restraining disorderly houses. cient manner of exercising this power can be devised than to prohibit persons to enter such houses, or to be found there. The ordinance was clearly enacted in the exercise of lawful authority.

We reach the conclusion that the district court erred in discharging the petitioner from custody.

Reversed.

90|
35|

SMALLEY v. MILLER.

1. **Garnishment:** PROPERTY IN CONSTRUCTIVE POSSESSION OF GARNISHEE: LIABILITY. In order that a garnishee may be holden for property belonging to the debtor, he must have the property in his possession, so that he can surrender it, if the court so directs, in exoneration of his liability as garnishee. If he has only a right of possession, or constructive possession, he may possibly be required to make a demand for the property, but he cannot be required to commence an action to recover it; and an action to recover property, on the sole ground that the plaintiff has been garnished in a suit against the owner of it, cannot be maintained.

Appeal from Bremer District Court.

MONDAY, MARCH 7.

ACTION to recover possession of specific personal property. There was a demurrer to the petition, which was sustained, and plaintiff appeals.

E. L. Smalley, for appellant.

A. F. Brown, for appellee.

SEEVERS, J.—The petition states that the plaintiff, as agent of William Britt, under and by virtue of a chattel mortgage executed by L. W. Hutchinson, took possession of the personal property in controversy, and that he, on the twenty-sixth day of January, 1886, delivered the same to Priscilla Hutchinson, to be redelivered to him upon demand; that on the same day he was garnished as the supposed debtor of L. W. Hutchinson, in an action wherein William Britt was plaintiff; that he has demanded possession of said property of said Priscilla Hutchinson, and that the defendant wrongfully detains the same, under the claim that she has a chattel mortgage thereon. The petition also states that the mortgage under which the plaintiff took possession of the property was paid off and discharged after he was garnished. The plaintiff claims to recover the possession of the property on the sole ground that he is liable in the garnishment proceeding, and is entitled to such possession as a protection from personal liability therein.

It will be observed that the plaintiff was not in the actual possession of the property when he was garnished, and we do not believe that a mere right to such possession would render him liable in such proceeding. The statute provides that a garnishee "must retain possession of all property * * * then or thereafter being in his custody, or under his control." Code, § 2975. The possession and control referred to is something more than constructive possession and control. Suppose Mrs. Hutchinson had destroyed the property, or had so disposed of it that it could not be found; clearly the plaintiff would not be liable as garnishee. In order to make him responsible, he must have the property in his possession, so that he can surrender it, if the court so directs, in exoneration of his liability as garnishee. If out of possession, and he can obtain it upon demand, it will be conceded, for the purposes of this case, that he is bound to make such demand. But nothing more can be required. He cannot be required to commence an action, and incur costs and expenses, and possible hazard, in order to relieve himself from liability.

AFFIRMED.

HOWE & CO. ET AL. v. JONES ET AL.

1. **Practice on Procedendo:** ENTERING JUDGMENT OF SUPREME COURT: NOTICE: CHANGE OF VENUE. Where in a cause on *procedendo* the judge was charged simply with the duty of rendering a judgment against a receiver, the amount of the judgment being fixed by the decision of this court and the receiver's report, which was a part of the record, *held* that, as there was nothing to try, and nothing left to the discretion of the judge, the receiver could not complain because the case was docketed and disposed of, without notice to him, after it had been announced that no civil causes would be tried at that term, nor because the judge who entered the judgment had been of counsel in the case, and did not order a change of venue.

2. **Interest:** ON MONEY WITHHELD AFTER TITLE ADJUDICATED. Where the holder of a fund refuses to pay it after the title thereto has been adjudicated, he must pay interest from the date of such adjudication.

Appeal from Marshall District Court.

MONDAY, MARCH 7.

THE court below entered an order requiring Boardman, the receiver, to pay to the clerk of the district court $555.39, and $136.09 interest thereon, which he held as a reciever in this case, and also directing the clerk to pay this money to Caswell and Meeker, intervenors. From this order Boardman, the receiver, appeals.

H. E. J. Boardman, appellant, *pro se.*

Caswell & Meeker, appellees, *pro se.*

BECK, J.—I. This is the fourth time this case has been in this court. See 57 Iowa, 130; 60 Id., 70; 66 Id., 156; Its history, and the facts and questions of law involved in it, may be learned from the several decisions of this court referred to, as well as from the records before us. In the last appeal we held that (1) the court below erroneously allowed the receiver certain credits, and thereupon the cause was reversed and remanded to the district court for further proceedings, where an order was made for the payment of the money in the receiver's hands, with interest, to the clerk, and by him to be paid to the intervenors. The questions of fact and law upon which this order was based had been settled by the prior decisions of this court, and by the reports of the receiver. The court below had nothing to do but to ascertain therefrom the amount of money in the receiver's hands, and enter the order accordingly, which was correctly done.

II. The receiver complains that the order was made after an announcement that no civil cases would be tried during the term, and that it was made on the last day

1. PRACTICE
on proce-
dendo: enter-
ing judgment
of supreme
court : notice:
change of
venue.

of the term, without the case being on the docket, and without trial, and without giving the receiver time to examine papers and pleadings, and to make issues. He also complains that the court below did not order a change of venue for the reason that the judge had been of counsel in the cause. All of these complaints are readily disposed of upon the following consideration: The matter, so far as the receiver is concerned, was not a case for issue and trial usual in actions. The court was called upon to enforce the performance of duty by one of its officers, by requiring him to pay over money in his hands; his liability therefor having been determined by prior adjudications, and the amount thereof fixed in the same manner and by his own reports. There was nothing for trial, for there was no disputed question of fact or law under these adjudications. The court below was left with no discretion. The judge was charged simply with the duty to render the order; the amount of money to be paid being fixed by the decision of this court and the receiver's reports. In this state of facts, the receiver could have suffered no prejudice from the matters he complains of. If it be admitted that the judge had been of counsel in the case, (but it is not shown that he appeared for intervenors,) as his duty was prescribed in the manner we have pointed out, the receiver could have suffered no prejudice from his acting in the case.

III. The receiver complains that interest was allowed by

the order of the court below upon the money he was ordered to

2. INTEREST: pay over. It was determined by the prior adjudi-
on money
withheld after cation that the intervenors were entitled to this
title adjudi-
cated. money. Since that adjudication he has retained
the money, and resisted all efforts to obtain it by the intervenors. In law and in good conscience he ought to pay
interest from the time the intervenors established their right
to the money, and no more was allowed by the order of the
court.

It becomes unnecessary to consider the motion made by·
the intervenors to dismiss the appeal. The judgment of the
district court is

AFFIRMED.

487|

BARRETT v. DOLAN.

1. **Animals:** TRESPASSING: ASSESSMENT OF DAMAGES BY TOWNSHIP
TRUSTEES: ALL MUST BE NOTIFIED. When power is conferred on three
or more persons to do an act, and notice to such persons is required, all
must be notified, if possible, although, when duly notified, a majority
may act. (See cases cited in opinion.) Accordingly, *held* that an
appraisement by two of the township trustees, of the damages done by
trespassing animals, under Code, § 1454, was void, where no attempt
was made to notify the other trustee.

2. **Fences:** DIVISION FENCE: OBLIGATION TO MAINTAIN: HERD LAW.
Where at defendant's solicitation, after the herd law had been adopted,
the township trustees were called together and apportioned the division
fence between him and plaintiff, and both parties acquiesced in the
apportionment and erected the fence accordingly, *held* that defendant
could not afterwards, of his own motion, relieve himself of the obligation to keep his portion of the fence in repair.

Appeal from Cass District Court.

MONDAY, MARCH 7.

ACTION to recover possession of specific personal property
consisting of certain cattle. The defendant justified the taking on the ground that the cattle were trespassing on his
premises, that he had distrained them, that he had had his

damages assessed by the proper authorities, and was entitled to the possession of the cattle until such damages were paid. Trial by jury, judgment for the plaintiff, and defendant appeals.

L. L. DeLano, for appellant.

Willard & Fletcher, for appellee.

SEEVERS, J.—I. The theory of the defendant is that certain cattle, belonging to an unknown owner, were trespassing on his premises, that he distrained or took them into his possession, and caused his damages to be assessed by the township trustees. Upon the objection of the plaintiff, the court refused to permit evidence as to what the trustees did to be introduced as evidence, on the ground that they had not been legally convoked or called together. It is provided by statute that, when stock has been distrained, the person doing so " shall, within twenty-four hours thereafter, notify the township trustees to be and appear upon the premises to view and assess the damages. * * * And when two or more trustees have assembled they shall proceed to view and assess the damages, and the amount to be paid for keeping said stock." Code, § 1454. There were three trustees, and one of them was not notified of the meeting, although he was at his residence in the township, and he took no part in the assessment of the damages. Such assessment was made by the other two trustees; and we are required to determine whether it was legally made or void. The statute in express terms requires the trustees to be notified of the meeting. This means all, not a part of them. Such a notice is of a jurisdictional character. ' Until it is given, there is no power to act. It is well settled, we think, both on principle and authority, that, when power is conferred on three or more persons to do an act, and notice to such persons is required, all must be notified, although, when

1. ANIMALS: trespassing: assessment of damages by township trustees: all must be notified.

duly notified, a majority may act. *People v. Batchelor*, 22
N. Y., 128; *Harding v. Vandewater*, 40 Cal., 77; *Wiggin
v. Freewill Baptist Church*, 8 Metc., 301; *Smyth v. Darley*,
2 II. L. Cas., 769. It may be that, when one of such persons is absent so that he cannot be notified, a different rule
may prevail. The court did not err in refusing to admit as
evidence the assessment of damages made as above stated.

II. The plaintiff and defendant occupied adjoining farms.
In 1874 the herd law was adopted, and has been in force
since that time. In 1877, at the request of the
defendant, the township trustees met and apportioned the division fence between him and the
plaintiff, and a fence was erected in accordance
with such apportionment. In 1884 the fence had become
dilapidated, and needed repairing. The trustees were called
together at the instance of the plaintiff, as we understand, to
make some order as to repairing it. The defendant declined
to repair that part of the fence which had been previously
assigned to him, and caused the plaintiff to be notified that
he did not want such a fence, and that the plaintiff could
repair it if he desired to do so. To some extent the plaintiff
did so. The theory of the plaintiff is that the cattle were
lawfully upon his own premises, and escaped therefrom
because that portion of the division fence which it was the
defendant's duty to erect and keep in repair, as directed by
the trustees in 1877, was out of repair, and therefore the
defendant could not lawfully distrain the cattle. The court,
in substance, so instructed the jury, and we are required to
determine whether it erred in this respect. The apportionment was made after the adoption of the herd law at the
instance of the defendant, and both parties acquiesced
therein and erected the fence. The defendant cannot now,
upon his own motion, relieve himself from the obligation
thus imposed. Until so relieved by the plaintiff, or possibly
by the action of the trustees, it is his duty to maintain the
portion of the fence so allotted to him. The fact that the

2. FENCES:
division
fence: obliga-
tion to main-
tain: herd
law.

plaintiff voluntarily to some extent did what the defendant. was obligated to do, cannot have the effect to relieve the latter. We think the instructions of the court are right, and that the judgment must be

AFFIRMED.

LEWIS v. THE BURLINGTON INS. CO.

1. **Evidence:** DAMAGE TO HOUSE BY TORNADO: NON-EXPERT. Where a farmer testified what in his opinion it would cost to repair his house, which had been damaged by a tornado, but on his cross-examination he stated that he was no mechanic, could not tell how badly the house was damaged, nor how much repairing would be necessary, *held* that his estimate should have been excluded on motion.

2. **Insurance:** FORFEITURE: PREMIUM NOTE UNPAID: COPY OF NOTE NOT ATTACHED TO POLICY. Where a past due premium note was set up to defeat a policy of insurance, *held* that it could not have that effect, since a copy of it was not attached to the policy, as required by statute.

Appeal from Mitchell Circuit Court.

MONDAY, MARCH 7.

ACTION upon a policy of insurance. There was a trial to the court, without a jury, and judgment was rendered for the plaintiff. The defendant appeals.

F. F. Coffin and *L. M. Ryce*, for appellant.

W. L. Eaton and *J. H. Sweeney*, for appellee.

ADAMS, CH. J.—This action was brought to recover on an alleged contract of insurance against tornadoes. It seems to be conceded that, on the fourteenth day of June, 1885, the plaintiff had such contract of insurance in the defendant company, whereby he was insured against loss by tordadoes upon his dwelling-house, barn and cattle; and the undisputed evidence shows that on that day a tornado occurred, and that the property insured was considerably injured.

I. The plaintiff was introduced as a witness in his own behalf, and was allowed to testify, against the objection of 1. EVIDENCE: the defendants, that in his opinion it would take damage to house by between $300 and $400 to put the house in as tornado: non-expert. good condition as it was before the injury. The evidence shows that the house had not been greatly moved, but had been wrenched by the wind, and the plastering had been cracked, and that some of the walls had been thrown a little out of a perpendicular line. On cross-examination the witness testified in these words: "I can't tell how bad the house is damaged. I am not mechanic enough to tell that. Don't know how many days it would take a man to repair the house, nor the amount of repairing that would be necessary. I have never done any such job. I don't know anything about it." After this statement, upon cross-examination of the witness, and some other statements showing his ignorance of the cost of repairing the house, the defendant moved to strike out his testimony respecting the amount of damage to the house, but its motion was overruled. We are not prepared to say that a farmer might not be allowed to testify in respect to the value of an ordinary farm house. While his opinion would not be as good as that of a carpenter, it would not, perhaps, be entirely unreliable. But the cost of repairing a house which had been wrenched by a tornado is manifestly not as easily estimated. If, as the witness testified, he did not know anything about it, we think that his estimate should have been excluded; and this appears especially so, as the only mechanic called estimated the damage at only about one-half what the plaintiff did.

II. The policy provided, in substance, that it should be void if any premium note should be overdue and unpaid at 2. INSURANCE: the time of the loss. The defendant pleaded forfeiture: premium note unpaid: copy of note not attached to policy. that, at the time of the loss, one note given for the premium was overdue and unpaid. The note claimed to be overdue and unpaid was executed upon the day of the date of the policy, and was for forty-nine dollars and eighty cents. The plaintiff, however, claimed that this note was not given for the premium on the policy in question, but for the premium upon another policy, in which the plaintiff was insured upon the same property against loss by fire and lightning. Upon this point we have to say that the policies are so drawn that the question is not free from difficulty. But we do not need to determine it. The appellee insists that the appellant is not entitled to take advantage of the plaintiff's default, if he made one, because a copy of the note, as provided by statute, was not attached to the policy sued on. In our opinion, the appellee's position must be sustained.

III. The plaintiff in his application stated that the incumbrances upon the property amounted to $2,500. The amount standing apparently against the property, as shown by judgment records, was largely in excess of that amount. Some evidence, however, was introduced in respect to payments made upon the judgments. While there is no especial conflict in this evidence, much of it is vague and unsatisfactory. The defendant's counsel claim that the proven payments would not reduce the amount of the judgments below $4,000, while the plaintiff's counsel claim that the proven payments would reduce the amount below $2,500. We are not prepared to say that all the evidence relied upon by the plaintiff could be considered; but as there must be another trial, it seems probable that the plaintiff will come much better prepared to prove his payments than he was before, and that no question in regard to the incumbrances will again be presented to this court.

For the error pointed out, the judgment must be

REVERSED.

KIRBY v. GATES & BOWMAN.

1. **Affidavit:** AFFIANT'S NAME IN JURAT. An affidavit stated, "I, Frank Pierce, do on oath say," etc., and was signed "Frank Pierce." The jurat was as follows: "Subscribed and sworn to by ——, before me," etc. "J. Compton, Notary Public." *Held* sufficient to show that the affidavit was sworn to by Frank Pierce.

2. **Practice and Procedure:** STRIKING OUT ORDER GRANTING LEAVE TO ANSWER: EFFECT. A default and judgment thereon were set aside on motion, and leave was g'ven defendant to answer. After defendant had answered, the court, on plaintiff's motion, set aside the former order, so far as it set aside the default and gave defendant leave to answer. *Held* that the effect of the last ruling was to lay the answer out of the case, and with it all issues raised thereby.

3. ——: SETTING ORDER ASIDE. A court may, for good reasons shown, set aside a previous order made at the same term.

Appeal from Polk Circuit Court.

MONDAY, MARCH 7.

ACTION for damages alleged to have been sustained by reason of the conversion of certain personal property. There was a judgment for the plaintiff. The defendants appeal.

Cole, McVey & Clark, for appellants.

Goode & Phillips, for appellee.

ADAMS, CH. J.—Judgment was rendered against the defendants by default. Afterwards they appeared, and filed a motion to set aside the judgment and the default, and for leave to answer; which motion the court sustained. Afterwards the plaintiff filed a motion to cancel the order setting aside the default and judgment. This motion the court sustained in part. It allowed the order setting aside the judgment to stand; but the order setting aside the default, and granting leave to answer, it canceled. The plaintiff was then directed to call his witnesses and prove his claim, and the defendants were allowed to cross-examine, and the trial thus had resulted in the rendition of a judgment for the same amount as before. The defendants claim to be aggrieved by the reinstatement of the default, which resulted in a trial upon the plaintiff's evidence alone.

In the first place, it is claimed that there was no proper evidence that the defendants were served with the original notice. The notice purports to have been served by one Pierce, who was not an officer. The return is in due form, and underneath the same is an affidavit in the following words:

1. AFFIDAVIT: affiant's name in jurat.

" I, Frank Pierce, do on oath say that I served the annexed notice on the defendants, Gates & Bowman, C. H. Gates and A. C. Bowman, therein named, at the time and place and in the manner mentioned in my return thereof.

[Signed] " FRANK PIERCE.

" Subscribed and sworn to by ———, before me, this fourteenth day of November, A. D. 1885.

" J. COMPTON, Notary Public in and for Polk County, Iowa."

The proof of service is said to be deficient in that the jurat does not contain the name of the affiant; but the jurat shows that what was written for an affidavit was subscribed and sworn to by some one, although the name is not given. It purports, however, to have been subscribed by Frank Pierce, and no one else. If Frank Pierce's name had been written by some one without authority, the words written for an affidavit could not in any proper sense be said to be subscribed. We think, then, it is expressly shown that they were subscribed by Frank Pierce, and the fair inference is that they were sworn to by the same person. In the absence of a statute expressly requiring the jurat to contain the name of the affiant, we think that we must hold the jurat in question sufficient.

It is next urged that the answer which had been filed was

Robinson v. Chicago, Rock Island & Pacific R'y Co.

not stricken from the files; that there was therefore an issue,

2. PRACTICE and proced- ure: striking out order granting leave to answer: effect. and the defendants had a right to introduce evidence, and submit the case to a jury; but the entry made by the court shows that it sustained the plaintiff's "motion, so far as the former order sets aside the default and gives the defendant leave to answer." The leave then to. answer was withdrawn, and that, we think, was equivalent, under the circumstance, to

3. ——: set- ting order aside. striking the answer from the files. It is insisted that the court had no jurisdiction to set aside the order by which the default had been set aside. But a court may, for good reason shown, set aside at the same term a previous order. We see no error.

AFFIRMED.

ROBINSON v. CHICAGO, ROCK ISLAND & PACIFIC R'Y Co.

1. **Railroads:** NEGLIGENCE: PROPER DISTANCE BETWEEN CATTLE GUARD AND SWITCH: EVIDENCE. In an action for a personal injury based on the alleged negligence of the defendant in building a switch too near to a cattle-guard, *held* that the mere fact that another switch at the same station was farther from the cattle-guard did not tend to prove that there was negligence in building and maintaining the first one so near.

Appeal from Polk Circuit Court.

MONDAY, MARCH 7.

ACTION to recover for a personal injury. There was a trial to a jury, and a verdict and judgment were rendered for the plaintiff. The defendant appeals.

T. S. Wright, for appellant.

Baylies & Baylies and *D. Donovan*, for appellee.

ADAMS, CH. J.—This case is before us upon a second appeal. See 67 Iowa, 292. The plaintiff, while acting as a brakeman on the defendant's road, and while engaged in the duty of uncoupling cars, stepped into a cattle-guard, and received the injury of which he complains. Since the former trial, the plaintiff has filed an amended and substituted petition, in which he avers, in substance, that the defendant was using a dangerous switch-yard at the place in question; that a switch connected with the main track less than fifty feet east of a trestle work cattle-guard, which was across its main line; that, while obeying orders in attempting to uncouple cars to be switched upon a side track, he was walking along the main track, in the night, between the cars, and stepped into the cattle-guard; that the defendant had negligently constructed and maintained said side track and switch and cattle-guard in too close proximity to each other.

The court gave an instruction in these words: "Under the law and the uncontroverted testimony, the defendant had the right to maintain the cattle guard and switch mentioned as they were being maintained. If, however, brakemen were authorized or required to uncouple cars for the purpose of switching outside of the switches, and the proximity of the switch and cattle-guard rendered that service more than ordinarily dangerous, then it was the duty of the defendant to inform them thereof before requiring them to uncouple at that place, unless the danger was already known to them, or defendant had some good reason to believe that it was so known. If the defendant knew, or by the exercise of ordinary care and vigilance would have known, that it was unusually dangerous to uncouple on the main track outside of the switch, and if the plaintiff was ignorant of such unusual danger, and the conductor giving the order did not have sufficient reason to believe that the plaintiff knew thereof, then it would be negligence for the conductor to have ordered the plaintiff to uncouple at that place, without first informing him of such unusual danger." The giving of this instruction is assigned as error. The instruction held that "the defendant had a right to maintain the cattle-guard and switch as they were being maintained." The plaintiff's counsel,

notwithstanding this ruling, insist that the cattle-guard and
switch were unnecessarily near together, or, at least, that
there was evidence which would have justified a jury in
so finding; but, in considering the objection to the instruction urged by the defendant, we must assume that the
instruction in regard to the right of the company to maintain the cattle-guard and switch so near together is correct.
The company, then, was not in fault in so maintaining them.
The circumstances of the case required it. This excludes all
negligence on the part of the company prior to the time the
conductor ordered the plaintiff to uncouple the cars. The
order was given, unaccompanied with information that the
cattle-guard and switch were only about forty-three feet
apart. The court thought that the negligence of the company, if any, consisted in giving the order unaccompanied
with such information, and it submitted the case to the
jury upon the theory that they might find a verdict for the
plaintiff on the ground of the want of such information,
and not otherwise; and it made the question as to the conductor's obligation to give the information depend upon the
question as to whether the order, by reason of the proximity
of the cattle-guard and switch to each other, involved an
unusual danger. The defendant objected to the instruction
upon two grounds: In the first place, it is insisted that the
permanent, necessary and visible construction of the switch
and cattle-guard and things of that nature, necessarily affecting the safety of the brakemen in the performance of their
ordinary work, are things which they must learn by the exercise of observation, and not wait to be told by the conductor,
whose knowledge, if he had it, must have been acquired in
in the same way. In the second place, it is said that there
is no evidence that the order as given involved an unusual
danger. It will be sufficient for the purpose of the opinion
to consider whether this last objection is valid.

The plaintiff contends that there was some evidence that
the order as given involved an unusual danger; and, in the

second place, if it did not, that the court was justified in giving the instruction, because the burden was on the defendant to prove that the order as given did not involve an unusual danger. There was very little evidence as to the distance between switches and cattle-guards on the defendant's road, and none whatever as to such distance upon other roads. All that the evidence showed was that, at the station where the accident occurred, there was, besides the switch in question, another eighty-one feet from a cattle-guard. The plaintiff insists that this was some evidence that the distance between the switch and cattle-guard in question was unusually small; but, in our opinion, this position cannot be sustained. We do not think that the evidence which shows nothing more than that one of two things is smaller than the other can be regarded as any evidence that the smaller is unusually small. When a thing is said to be ùnusually small, it is meant that it is small as compared with the *class* to which it belongs; and the comparison involved is essentially different from that which can be made between merely two things of the class.

The position taken by the plaintiff, that the burden was upon the defendant to prove that the order as given did not involve an unusual danger, is based upon what the plaintiff regards the issue as tendered by the defendant's answer. It is said that the defendant assumed this burden by an allegation in its answer. The allegation relied upon is that the cattle-guards were numerous, and located without regularity in regard to their distance from each other or any other given point or object. But this is not an allegation that the distance between the cattle-guard and switch in question was not unusually small. The allegation appears to have been made upon the theory that, there being no regularity, no specific place or yard could be relied upon in the absence of specific knowledge.

In our opinion there was nothing in the evidence, or in the issues as made by the pleadings, upon which the instruction could properly be based. REVERSED.

DILLOW v. WARFEL.

1. **Subrogation**: LAND SOLD ON TIME CONTRACT: PAYMENT OF PURCHASE
MONEY BY ASSIGNEE. D. and wife owned two forty acre tracts of land
under contracts of purchase. D., acting for himself, and as agent for
his wife, but without her authority, sold the land and assigned the contracts to W., who went into possession. In an action by the vendors to
foreclose the contracts, there was judgment against D. and wife for the
purchase money, but W. intervened, and it was ordered, among other
things, that he pay into court a certain sum, and that upon payment of
the same the vendors execute to him a warranty deed for the land. D.'s
wife was, for certain reasons, not bound by the judgment and decree.
Held that she was the owner of the undivided one-half of the land during all the time that W. was in possession, and entitled to rents and
profits accordingly; that from the time W. paid his money into court
under the decree he was entitled to be subrogated to all the rights of
the vendors as against D.'s wife, and that his relation to her was that of
a mortgagee in possession, and that a judgment and decree of foreclosure were properly entered against her in favor of W. for one-half of
the judgment and costs in the former action, less her share of the rents
and profits during the time W. had been in possession.

Appeal from Union District Court.

MONDAY, MARCH 7.

THIS is an action in equity, involving conflicting claims
of the parties to certain real estate. After the issues were
made up, the cause was referred to a referee. The referee
heard the evidence, and reported the facts and his conclusions of law to the court. Both parties filed exceptions to
the report. The court modified the report and entered a
decree. The plaintiff appeals.

Higbee & Hanna, for appellant.

James G. Ball, for appellee.

ROTHROCK, J.—The case is very much involved in its facts,
and it appears to be necessary to an understanding of the
controversy to set out the report of the referee. It is as follows:

"On May 29, 1879, R. H. and R. A. Dillow, who were
then husband and wife, and living together as such, purchased

of T. J. Potter and O. M. Levy the N. W. ¼ of N. E. ¼, and
N. E. ¼ of N. W. ¼, of section 22, and the S. W. ¼ of the S. E. ¼
of section 15, all in township 73, range 30, Union county, Iowa,
at which time the real estate contract herewith returned was
executed and delivered by the parties. In making this purchase, R. H. Dillow acted for himself, and as the agent of
his wife. In the following spring the Dillows took possession of said real estate under and by virtue of said contract
of purchase.

"II. On the thirteenth day of June, 1880, the Dillows,
by R. H. Dillow, acting for himself and as the agent of his
wife, R. A. Dillow, sold the N. E. ¼ of the N. W. ¼ of section 22, above described, to W. A. Maxwell, and assigned
and conveyed to him in writing all their interest in said
tract, which they held under the Potter-Levy contract.

"III. On the fourth day of February, 1882, the Dillows,
who had ceased to live together as husband and wife, sold the
remaining eighty acres of said land to Amzey Courter, and
conveyed the same to him by an assignment in writing of
the Potter-Levy contract, which assignment was executed
personally by each of the Dillows.

"IV. Owing to the failure of said Courter to comply
with his contract of purchase with the Dillows, the above
contract was rescinded by the parties, and said Courter, on
the eleventh day of February, 1882, reassigned said contract to R. H. Dillow. Said assignment, as originally drawn,
seems to have been made to Reuben H. Dillow and R. A. Dillow, but the latter name has been erased from the instrument,
and I am unable to say from the evidence whether or not this
erasure was made before or after its execution; but I find, as a
matter of fact, that it was intended as a rescission of the contract mentioned in number three, and it, in effect, places the
title to the land in the same position it was in before the making of the contract mentioned in number three.

"V. On the reverse side of the Courter assignment there
appears an assignment of said contract from R. H. Dillow

to R. A. Dillow, dated February 11, 1882; but I find that this assignment was not based on any consideration, and no delivery of the same was ever made, and the same is without any legal force or effect.

"VI. From the above, after making these various assignments, I find that the interest in said land conveyed by the Potter-Levy contract was owned as follows: The N. E. $\frac{1}{4}$ of the N. W. $\frac{1}{4}$ of section 22, by W. A. Maxwell; and the remaining eighty acres was owned jointly by R. H. and R. A. Dillow.

"VII. On August 3, 1882, Potter and Levy commenced an action in the circuit court of Union county, being case numbered 3,249, in which R. H. and R. A. Dillow were the only defendants. In said action plaintiffs ask for judgment for the amount due on their contract, and the foreclosure of the same, etc. The Dillows, being served by personal service, appeared by J. H. Copenheffer, attorney, and filed their answer in said cause. The appearance of said attorney for R. A. Dillon, she claims, was wholly unauthorized, and, further, that it has already been adjudicated by the circuit court that such appearance was unauthorized; and I find as a matter of fact that this latter claim is established by the evidence.

"VIII. On September 18, 1882, W. A. Maxwell appears by J. H. Copenheffer, attorney, and files in said cause his petition of intervention, setting up his claim to the forty-acre tract of said land, purchased by him of the Dillows; and the cause was continued to the March, 1883, term of court.

"IX. On March 5, 1883, the Dillows, by R. H. for himself, and claiming to act as the agent of R. A., assigned the said contract, and sold the eighty acres held by them under the same to the defendant Warfel, for the agreed price of $2,500; said Warfel assuming to pay, as a part of the consideration, the amount due Potter and Levy on said contract. As to this conveyance, R. A. Dillow insists that she never

received any part of the purchase price, nor ever authorized
R. H. Dillow to make said contract and sale for her; and I
find, as a matter of fact, that R. H. Dillow had no authority
from R. A. Dillow to make this contract or sale of her interest in said land, and that she received no part of the consideration therefor, except what was paid by defendant to Potter and Levy.

"X. On the same day W. A Maxwell sold the forty acres
of said land held by him to defendant Warfel, and executed
the proper assignment of his contract and interest in the
same to defendant.

"XI. On March 12, 1883, defendant Warfel, by J. H.
Copenheffer, attorney, filed his petition of intervention in
the circuit court in the Potter-Levy foreclosure case, setting
up his purchases and assignments from the Dillows and
Maxwell, and offering to pay into court the amount due Potter and Levy, and asking that they be required to execute to
him a deed for the premises upon his payment of said
amount.

"XII. On the same day, a judgment and decree were
rendered in said cause, which gave the plaintiffs judgment
against R. H. and R. A. Dillow, for the sum of $1,789, the
amount due on said real estate contract, and the further sum
of $150, attorneys' fees, and, among other things in said
decree, was the following: 'And it is further ordered that
the plaintiffs have judgment against the intervenors, W. A.
Maxwell and A. M. Warfel, for costs of their proceedings in
intervention, and that plaintiffs have a foreclosure of said
real estate contract against all defendants and intervenors
impleaded in this cause; and it is further ordered that the
intervenor A. M. Warfel pay into this court the sum of
$1,887.89, according to the prayer of his said petition of
intervention, which said sum shall be applied on and in satisfaction of the above judgment; that on the payment of the
said sum of money, as aforesaid, to the clerk of this court,
for the use and benefit of plaintiffs, it is further ordered that

the plaintiffs make, execute and deliver to the said clerk for
the intervenor A. M. Warfel a warranty deed for the real
estate described in the contract, set forth in the intervenor
Warfel's petition; that, should the plaintiffs fail or refuse to
make, execute and deliver said deed of conveyance as above
designated within five days after the said money shall have
been paid into court, then B. T. Nix, the clerk of this court,
is hereby authorized to execute said conveyance as a commissioner of this court, and deliver the same to A. M. Warfel;
that, on the failure of said intervenor Warfel to pay the said
sum, plaintiffs to have special execution,' etc.

"XIII.   In accordance with the provisions in said decree,
defendant Warfel paid the amount of judgment into court,
and, on the twentieth day of March, 1883, received a warranty deed from Potter and Levy for the land, and immediately entered into the possession of the same, and has occupied and used the same as a farm ever since.

"XIV.   On July 17, 1883, R. A. Dillow filed in the circuit court her motion to reform said decree, and served
notice of the filing of said motion on Patterson & Ball, attorneys for plaintiffs in said cause; and said motion was tried
upon evidence introduced before the circuit court. On
the twenty-second day of September, 1883, Jas. G. Ball
appearing for plaintiffs, and Higbee & Hanna for defendant, R. A. Dillow, said motion was sustained by the court,
which in substance expunged from said decree the portion thereof set out in number twelve above, and modified the same so as to give plaintiffs judgment against R. A.
Dillow for $1,731.87, and the further sum of $150, attorney's fee, and costs of suit taxed at ——— dollars, and that
said judgment draw interest at the rate of ten per cent per
annum from March 12, 1883; and further decreeing the foreclosure of said real estate contract, and ordering the sale of
the premises under special execution to satisfy the judgment,
and expressly declaring that the decree heretofore entered
should not be held to in any manner affect defendant R. A.

Dillow's equity of redemption in and to said property; and that all that portion of the decree set out in number twelve should in no manner affect the defendant R. A. Dillow.

"XV. Subsequent to the modification of said decree by the circuit court, plaintiffs Potter and Levy filed their motion to modify the modified decree, and the same was submitted to the court, and by him taken under advisement, and over-ruled on the thirtieth day of December, 1884.

"XVI. This action was commenced on the tenth day of April, 1884; but the pleadings have been properly amended from time to time, in harmony with the ruling of the circuit court, on motion to modify the decree.

"XVII. I find that defendant Warfel acted in good faith in paying his money into court under the original decree, and receiving the deed to said lands.

"XVIII. Defendant, on the twentieth day of May, 1885, filed an amendment to his answer, asking in his prayer, among other things, to be subrogated to all the rights of Potter and Levy in the land in controversy, as against plaintiff.

XIX. That the rental value of the whole of said real estate is $225 per annum; and defendants have occupied and used the same for the years 1883, 1884 and 1885.

"From the foregoing facts I find the following conclusions of law: (1) That, at the time of the rendition of the judgment and decree, originally in favor of Potter and Levy, plaintiff R. A. Dillow was the owner of the undivided half of the N. W. $\frac{1}{4}$ of the N. E. $\frac{1}{4}$ of section 22, and the S. W. $\frac{1}{4}$ of the S. E. $\frac{1}{4}$ of section 15, all in township 73, range 30, by contract of purchase from Potter and Levy; (2) that since that time she has been the owner of an equity of redemption in said described land, and entitled to the rents, issues and profits thereof; (3) that from the time defendant paid his money into court under the original decree, he is entitled to be subrogated to all the rights of Potter and Levy in said land, as against the plaintiff, and that his relation to the same since taking the possession thereof has been that of a

mortgagee in possession, and that he should account to plaintiff for the rents and profits of an undivided one-half of the
land described in number one, last above, which, assuming
the land to be of the same general character and rental value,
would be $75 per annum, aggregating $225 for the three
years which he has been in possession. I recommend judgment and decree be entered by the district court accordingly.

"All of which is respectfully submitted.

"THOS. L. MAXWELL, Referee."

The plaintiff moved the court to correct the report as to
the facts by finding that the alleged sale of the forty acres to
Maxwell was adjudicated against him in the case of *Potter
and Levy v. Dillow et al.*, and to modify the report throughout in such way as that R. H. and R. A. Dillow be held to
be the joint owners of the whole 120 acres, and to compel
Warfel to account for the rents and profits of all the land,
instead of only two-thirds thereof. The court overruled this
motion, and we think the ruling was correct. We do not
understand that it was at any time adjudged that Maxwell
did not purchase the forty acres from the plaintiff and her
husband. It is true, the court entered judgments against the
intervenors Maxwell and Warfel for the costs of intervention; but, in the same decree, Warfel was authorized to pay
the whole debt, and receive a deed of the land from Potter
and Levy. It is true that this decree was afterwards modified on motion; but Warfel was not made a party to that proceeding. He paid the money required to be paid both for
the eighty acres he claimed and for the forty acres claimed
by Maxwell, to whose rights he succeeded by assignment.
He became the assignee of Maxwell before the decree; and
the decree authorizing him to pay the purchase money and
receive the deed was in pursuance of his offer to make payment as assignee of the Dillows and Maxwell. That decree
has never been modified in any proceeding to which Warfel
was a party.

On the motion of the defendant, the court modified the report of the referee so that the plaintiff should be required to pay one-half of the judgment rendered against her, and one-half of the costs of the former action, and an account of the rents and profits of the land was made, and a judgment rendered in favor of Warfel for the balance, and a decree of foreclosure was entered, and the land ordered sold to satisfy the judgment, interest and costs. It appears to us that the decree thus entered is a fair and equitable adjustment of the rights of the parties, for the reason that, when Warfel paid for the land, he became the equitable assignee of Potter and Levy, and was entitled to all the rights possessed by them. He has an undoubted right to insist on a foreclosure for the purchase money, and this is just what the court decreed.

AFFIRMED.

RISSER & Co. v. RATHBURN ET AL.

SPERRY, WATT & GARVER v. THE SAME.

1. **Practice on Appeal**: EVIDENCE TO SUPPORT VERDICT. A verdict founded upon conflicting evidence will not be disturbed on appeal for want of support in the evidence.

2. **Fraudulent Conveyance**: EVIDENCE: CONVERSATION BETWEEN PARTIES. Where it was sought to charge a garnishee with the value of goods alleged to have been transferred to him by the principal defendant in fraud of creditors, *held* that it was proper to allow the defendant to testify to a conversation had between him and the garnishee showing their fraudulent purpose.

3. ———: SALE BY FRAUDULENT VENDEE: LIABILITY ON GARNISHMENT. A fraudulent vendee of goods may sell the same to an innocent third party and give a good title, but he may nevertheless be held liable for the proceeds on garnishment, in a suit against his vendor by the creditors sought to be defeated by the fraudulent transfer.

4. ———: ———: ———: INTEREST ON PROCEEDS. In such case the garnishee is liable for interest on the proceeds of the goods from the date of their sale by him.

Appeal from Pocahontas District Court.

MONDAY, MARCH 7.

ACTION by attachment against defendant Rathburn, in which Bothwell was garnished. An issue upon the answer of the garnishee, denying indebtedness to defendant, was in each case tried to a jury. A judgment for plaintiff was in each case rendered against the garnishee upon special findings for plaintiff. The garnishee appeals. The cases were submitted together upon the same abstract and argument.

Robinson & Milchrist, for appellant.

Henry S. Wilcox, for appellee.

BECK, J.—I. The garnishee, Bothwell, in his answer denies that he is indebted to the defendant, or has in his possession or under his control any property rights or credits of the defendant. He admits that he purchased of defendant a stock of merchandise, but alleges that defendant was indebted to him in the sum of $500 for goods sold and money loaned, and alleges that, in payment of the debt, he took the stock of merchandise, with the agreement that, if he could sell it for more than the debt, such overplus, after deducting expenses incurred in handling the goods, should go to defendant. He shows in his answer that he sold the goods for $600; that the expense of handling them was $25; and that he is ready to account for the balance remaining in his hands. He afterwards paid into court $40, which he admits is due from him to defendant. The answer of the garnishee is denied by proper pleadings filed by plaintiff, in which it is averred that the stock of goods alleged to have been sold by defendant to the garnishee was of the value of $1,200, for which the garnishee paid $530, leaving a balance due defendant of $670. In another count of their pleadings, plaintiffs allege that the sale of the goods by defendant to the gar-

nishee was made with the purpose and intention on the part
of both to defraud plaintiffs and other creditors of defendant,
and is therefore void, and that, at the time of the service of
the garnishee process, the garnishee was in possession of the
goods, which he has converted to his own use. It is alleged
that the goods were of the reasonable value of $1,200. Un-
der an agreement of the parties, the two causes were tried
together, and are submitted in the same manner in this
court.

The district court directed the jury to return special findings in response to the following question submitted to them.
Their findings are indicated by the answers following the
questions:

"Submitted by the court on its own motion: (1) What
was the actual value of the goods at the time of sale to
Bothwell? *Answer.* $1,030. (2) What was the reason-
able value of the expenses and services of Bothwell in taking
and negotiating a sale of the goods? *A.* $25. (3) How
much was the entire consideration to be paid by Bothwell
for the goods under the contract of purchase? *A.* $1,000.
(4) Under the contract of purchase, was the garnishee to
pay the defendant anything above $541.74, which defendant
was owing the garnishee? *A.* Yes. (5) If you answer the
foregoing interrogatory by 'yes,' then state how much the
garnishee was to pay for the goods above the sum of
$541.74? *A.* $488.26.

"Submitted at the request of plaintiffs, Sperry, Watt &
Garver and Chas. E. Risser & Co.: (1) Was the garnishee
indebted to defendant on the twelfth day of May, 1884, at
the time of the service of the notice of garnishment in the
case of *Risser & Co. v. Rathburn?* If so, state the amount
Answer. $488.26. (2) Was the garnishee, Bothwell, in-
debted to defendant on the nineteenth day of May, 1884, at
the service of notice of garnishment in the case of *Sperry,
Watt & Garver v. Rathburn?* If so, state the amount.
A. $463.26. (3) What was the fair market value of the

property conveyed to the garnishee by the defendant on the
tenth day of May, 1884, at the time of sale? *A*. $1,030.
(4) Was the sale by defendant to Bothwell on the tenth day
of May, 1884, made by defendant with an intent to defraud
his other creditors? *A*. Yes. (5) If you answer 'yes' to
question No. 4, state whether said garnishee knew of such
intent at the time of sale. *A*. Yes. (6) Was there a secret
agreement or understanding between the defendant and the
garnishee that said garnishee should invoice the property
sold him by said defendant, and pay the said defendant the
amount said goods should invoice over and above the amount
said defendant owed said garnishee? *A*. Yes. (7) Was
there a secret agreement or understanding between the defendant and said garnishee that the said garnishee should
sell said stock of goods, and pay to defendant the amount
realized from said sale, after deducting reasonable compensation for his service and expenses in making the same, and
the indebtedness of said defendant to said garnishee? *A*.
Yes.

"Submitted at the request of the garnishee: (1) Did the
garnishee have any fraudulent purpose in purchasing the
goods of Rathburn? *Answer*. Yes. (2) Was the purpose
of Bothwell, in purchasing the goods in controversy, to secure payment for his own claim against Rathburn only? *A*.
No."

Upon these special findings the district court rendered
judgment against the garnishee in favor of Risser & Co.,
for $359.90, and costs of the garnishment proceedings, and
a like judgment in favor of Sperry, Watt & Garver for
$723.20, and costs. It appears that interest upon the value
of the goods as found by the jury was included in the judgment.

II. The special findings are for plaintiffs upon both
counts of their pleadings, denying the garnishee's answer.
The findings upon the second count are in response to questions asked upon the motion of Sperry, Watt & Garver.

We presume that, as they were the second attaching creditors, they thought it important that the issues raised by the
second count should be determined in order to recover their
claim as against the garnishee. We shall find it necessary
to consider only the findings under the second count.

III. It is first insisted that the evidence does not sufficiently support the special findings, which, therefore, should

**1. PRACTICE
on appeal:
evidence to
support ver-
dict.**
have been set aside. All that can be said upon
this point is that the evidence was conflicting.
Upon the question of fraud the verdict was supported by the direct testimony of Rathburn, and a number
of circumstances established by other evidence. Against it
was the equally direct and positive evidence of the garnishee, corroborated to some extent by other witnesses. The
jury believed the testimony for plaintiffs, and discarded the
evidence on the other side. There is no ground to hold that
in doing so they did not intelligently and honestly exercise
the discretion imposed upon them by law. The same
remarks are applicable to the question of the value of the
goods. Counsel for the garnishee make earnest complaint
upon this point. It may be that the preponderance of the
evidence shows that the goods were of less value than was
found by the jury; but there is not such a lack of evidence
on this point as authorizes us to reverse the judgment.
Complaint is made that the deposit of $40 was not consid-
ered by the court in rendering judgment; but, if there be
an error in this regard, it is cured by an agreement of record
in this case, under which that sum is credited upon the
judgment in favor of Risser & Co.

IV. Rathburn, the defendant, was, against the garnishee's objection, rightly permitted to testify to a conversation had between the two, clearly showing their

**2. FRAUDU-
LENT convey-
ance: evi-
dence: con-
versation be-
tween parties.**
fraudulent purpose. Counsel insist that, if the
sale was valid, it could not be rendered invalid
by any misrepresentations as to its character.
This position may be admitted; but, if the conversation was

actually had, it shows the fraudulent purpose of both parties, and was not a " misrepresentation." And if the testimony showing the conversation be believed, the sale must
be held void for fraud.

V. Counsel insist that, as the sale was not void as between the parties thereto, Brewer, the purchaser from Both-
3. ——: sale well, acquired a good title; and, if he acquired
by fraudulent
vendee: lia- a good title, Bothwell must have had a good
bility on gar-
nishment. title. But it does not follow that, because Brewer
acquired a good title, Bothwell, by disposing of these goods
while they were so subject to plaintiffs' debts, did not become liable to plaintiffs for their value, who rightly pursued
their remedy against him by garnishment. These views
sufficiently answer counsel's position that Bothwell cannot
be held liable for the goods by reason of the fact that he
had disposed of them when the process of garnishment was
served upon him.

VI. Counsel for the garnishee insist that two of the
special findings are conflicting, in that one finds that the
consideration paid by Bothwell for the goods was $1,000,
and the other that he was to pay $1,030. The first finding cor-
rectly states the consideration to be paid under the contract
of purchase by Bothwell. The second is doubtless based
upon the value of the goods for which Bothwell was liable
without regard to the contract.

VII. Counsel also complain that the court added to the
value of the goods interest, which was included in the judg-
4. ——: ——; ment. This was correct. The goods were sub-
——:inter-
est on pro- ject to plaintiffs' debt. The garnishee fraudu-
ceeds. lently appropriated them to his own use. He
was lawfully charged with interest from the day of the
appropriation.

The foregoing discussion disposes of all questions in the
case. The judgment of the circuit court must be

                                        AFFIRMED.

HICKS v. THE FARMERS' INS. Co.

1. **Fire Insurance**: CONDITION AGAINST INCUMBRANCE: VIOLATION.
A condition in a fire-insurance policy, issued to a firm, that the property
should not afterwards be in any manner incumbered, was violated by
the execution of a mortgage by one of the partners on his undivided
one-third interest in the property, and by a judgment against him which
became a lien on his said interest.

Appeal from Monroe Circuit Court.

MONDAY, MARCH 7.

ACTION upon a policy of insurance. A demurrer to the
defendant's answer to the petition was overruled. Plaintiff
standing on his demurrer, judgment was rendered for defendant. Plaintiff appeals.

Gleason & Haskell and *H. L. Dashiell*, for appellant.

Frank C. Hormel, for appellee.

BECK, J.—The policy in suit contains a condition that it
shall become void "if the property insured be sold, or any
change take place in the title thereof, or if the property or
any part thereof, hereafter in any manner whatever incumbered." The answer alleges that plaintiff, after the execution of the policy, and before the fire, incumbered the property insured by executing on his interest therein, which was
one-third, a mortgage, etc., and that it was incumbered during the same time by a judgment against plaintiff, which
became and has remained a lien on the property. It is
shown by the pleadings that the policy was issued to a firm
of which plaintiff is a partner, and that the policy, after the
loss, was assigned to him. The plaintiff demurs to the
answer, on the ground that the mortgage and judgment,
having been executed and rendered while plaintiff was one

of the partners to whom the policy was issued, do not constitute a breach of the condition of the policy. The property insured was an office building and furniture therein.
The answer alleges that plaintiff held a one-third interest
therein, and that it was incumbered by the mortgage and
judgment. Surely, under these allegations, defendant would
be permitted to show both a mortgage and judgment incumbrance upon plaintiff's interest in the property. And that
the mortgage and judgment, as they are set out in the ·
answer, would incumber plaintiff's interest in the property,
there can be no doubt. The petition alleges that plaintiff owned
one-third of the property, and that the mortgage was executed
upon that interest, and the judgment was rendered while he
owned it. That liens were created as against the realty is
very plain. Their extent or the manner of their enforcement need not be a subject of inquiry.

The case, in our opinion, was rightly decided by the court
below.

AFFIRMED.

THE NATIONAL BANK OF GALENA v. CHASE ET AL.

1. **Garnishment:** SURPLUS PROCEEDS OF COLLATERAL SECURITY.
Where a bank received from C. certain notes as collateral security for a
loan, and collected the notes and paid the loan out of the proceeds, and
had money left, and the bank was garnished as the debtor of C., and
there was no proof by an intervenor claiming the money of an assignment
to him, *held* that it was error to discharge the garnishee on motion of
the intervenor.

Appeal from Plymouth Circuit Court.

MONDAY, MARCH 7.

THIS is a proceeding in attachment by garnishment. The
defendant Chase is the judgment debtor. The First National

Bank of Le Mars is the garnishee. The subject of the garnishment is money in the possession of the garnishee, the proceeds
of a promissory note which the bank collected. C. A. Robbe
appeared as an intervenor, and claimed that the note was
purchased by him of Chase, while in the possession of the
bank, and before the garnishment, and that he is entitled to
the proceeds of the note. At the May term, 1885, certain
depositions taken in behalf of Robbe, the intervenor, were
suppressed, on motion of the plaintiff, and the cause was
continued to the December term, 1885. During the vacation, the intervenor sued out another commission, and took
the depositions again; and, at the December term, they were
again suppressed, on motion of plaintiff. At the same time
the cashier of the Bank of Le Mars, garnishee, appeared,
and was examined in open court, and his answers, as garnishee, were reduced to writing. The garnishee and the
intervenor moved that the garnishee be discharged, on the
ground that the evidence did not show an unpaid judgment
against Chase, and the answers of the garnishee did not show
that the garnishee had any money rights or credits of the
defendant Chase in its possession. The motion was sustained
and the garnishee discharged, to which ruling the plaintiff
excepted. Afterwards, and at the same term, the plaintiff
filed a motion to dismiss the petition of the intervenor, on
the ground that, as the garnishee had been discharged, the
court had lost all jurisdiction over the garnishee, as well as
over the garnished property. This motion was overruled, to
which ruling the plaintiff excepted. At the same term the
court called the case "for trial as to the intervenor's intervention," and the intervenor offered in evidence the depositions which had been suppressed, and attempted to show by
oral testimony that the depositions were taken in accordance
with the laws of New Hampshire, where they were taken.
The plaintiff objected to all the evidence. The court sustained the objection, and the intervenor excepted. Thereupon the court, upon its own motion, and against the objec-

tions and exceptions of both parties, continued the cause until the next term.   Both parties appeal.

J. H. Struble, for the plaintiff.

Curtis & Durley, for the defendant Chase and for the garnishee and the intervenor.

ROTHROCK, J.—It will be observed from the above statement of facts that there has been some remarkable practice in this case.   There has been no final judgment in the court below.   The last step that appears to have been taken was a continuance of the cause against the objection of both parties.   Our first impression, after an examination of the record, was that no appeal would lie, because the court below might yet correct any of the errors complained of.   We are still of the opinion that the intervenor has no right to appeal.   Indeed, we do not understand that he claims that his depositions were properly taken; and, as the cause was continued, there was nothing to prevent him from again taking depositions.   But, on reflection, we think the plaintiff has the right to appeal from the order discharging the garnishee.   That order appears to have been adhered to throughout all the subsequent proceedings.   It was an order which affected the substantial rights of the parties.   It is very plain that the order should not have been made.   The answer of the garnishee showed that Chase, the judgment debtor, deposited two notes with the garnishee, as collateral security for a loan by the bank and a loan by another party.   The notes were executed by one Blades, payable to the order of Chase, and, when deposited as collateral, were not due.   Blades resided in Dakota; and, when the notes became due, the bank sent them to Dakota for collection.   Blades paid the notes.   The proceeds of the first note paid the loans for which both notes were collateral, and the bank held the proceeds of the second note for Chase, or his assignee.   If Chase made no assignment of the note or proceeds before the garnishment, the proceeds were attachable for his debts. When the answer of the garnishee showed this state of facts, Robbe, the intervenor, should have set himself about proving the allegations of his petition of intervention, instead of moving to discharge the garnishee. It is true, he also claimed in his motion that plaintiff did not prove that the judgment had not been paid; but we are not prepared to believe that the court sustained the motion on this ground. The execution was introduced in evidence, and, if it had been necessary to prove that the judgment was not paid, this proof was sufficient. The fact that the garnishee had been discharged no doubt led to the subsequent somewhat anomalous proceedings in the case. The record shows that the plaintiff was permitted to appear afterwards in the case, although it had no interest therein. The discharge of the garnishee effectually disposed of all it claimed in the case. The discharge was an adjudication that the plaintiff had no right to the money in the custody of the garnishee. But the plaintiff did appear afterwards, and, when the intervenor attempted to resurrect the defunct depositions, plaintiff objected, and the objection was sustained. The intervenor was then left without proof of the assignment, and the court doubtless thought that the best way out of the dilemma was to continue the case, which was done.

We think the motion to discharge the garnishee should have been overruled, and that the parties should take up the case at that point, and try it in a regular and orderly manner. The cause will be reversed on the plaintiff's appeal.

AULMAN v. AULMAN ET AL. (TWO cases.)

GUELICH v. THE SAME.

1. **Assignment for Benefit of Creditors**: WHAT IS NOT: PREFER-
RING CREDITORS. The transfer by an insolvent of all his property, in
parcels, by deeds and mortgages, to several of his creditors, in satisfaction or security of their claims, does not constitute an assignment for
the benefit of creditors, though all done at one time and as one transaction; and such conveyance cannot be set aside as being in violation of
§ 2115 of the Code. (See opinion for cases followed and distinguished.)

2. **Fraudulent Conveyance**: EVIDENCE: RIGHT OF CREDITOR TO
SECURE PREFERENCE. A creditor has a right to secure his own claim,
even though he knows that there will be nothing left to secure or satisfy other creditors; and, there being no other evidence of a fraudulent
intent in the conveyances herein assailed, *held* that they could not be set
aside as being in fraud of creditors.

Appeals from Polk Circuit Court.

MONDAY, MARCH 7.

THESE are actions for the foreclosure of mortgages given
by Lorenz Aulman and George Aulman to the plaintiffs.
Certain creditors of the mortgagors became parties to the
suits by intervention, and they filed cross-bills, in which they
claimed that the mortgages were void as to the creditors of
the mortgagors. The mortgagees and plaintiffs herein were
also creditors of Lorenz and George Aulman; and the suits
involve the conflicting claims of creditors to the assets of an
insolvent partnership. There were decrees in the court below
declaring the mortgages to be void. Plaintiffs appeal.

Goode & Phillips, for appellants.

Cummins & Wright and *Barcroft & Bowen*, for appellees.

ROTHROCK, J.—I. Lorenz Aulman and George Aulman
were engaged for several years in the foundry business, under

1. ASSIGN-
MENT for ben-
efit of credi-
tors: what is
not: prefer-
ring creditors.

the name of the Aulman Engine Works. About
the first of December, 1885, they found
that they were financially embarrassed and
unable to meet the demands of their creditors,
and, unless relieved in some way from their embarrassment,

they would be compelled to suspend business. They conceived the plan of organizing a joint-stock company and inducing their brother William, and one Schwester, to take stock in the venture, and advance money sufficient to continue the business. This was not accomplished. Lorenz Aulman was the active business manager of the firm, and; knowing that he could not discharge the liabilities, there were given to certain of the creditors of the firm the following instruments: To the plaintiff Theodore Aulman a chattel mortgage upon all the personal property of the grantors, including books of account and notes, and another mortgage to the same party upon certain real estate; one mortgage to Theodore Guelich upon certain real estate; a deed to Lena Rompano of certain real estate, and an assignment to William Aulman of a certain chattel mortgage held by the partnership against another party. These instruments covered all of the property of the partnership, and all the property of the individual members of the firm which was subject to execution or attachment. The instruments above enumerated were all executed on the eleventh day of December, 1885, and filed for record two days afterwards. They were all prepared by the same person, and signed at the same time; and the evidence shows quite satisfactorily that they were all parts of a general design to secure the creditors to whom they were given. The defendants contend that these several instruments constituted a general assignment, and were void because they gave preference to certain of the creditors of the partnership.

It is provided by section 2115 of the Code that "no general assignment of property by an insolvent, or in contemplation of insolvency, for the benefit of creditors, shall be valid, unless it be made for the benefit of all his creditors in proportion to the amount of their respective claims." It is not denied that an insolvent debtor may lawfully make such a disposition of his property as to entitle one or more creditors to a preference over others. This he may do by mortgage, or sale, or conveyance; and the fact that such mortgages, sales and conveyances embrace all of his property does not necessarily constitute the transaction a general assignment.

In *Van Patten v. Burr*, 52 Iowa, 518, it was held that a number of mortgages to creditors and an assignment may be taken as one transaction, and as constituting a general assignment. That case was determined upon a demurrer to the petition, in which it was alleged that the mortgages and the assignment were all parts of the same transaction, and were intended by the insolvent to operate as a general assign- ment for the benefit of creditors.

• In *Fromme v. Jones*, 13 Iowa, 474; *Lampson v. Arnold*, 19 Id., 479; *Farwell v. Howard*, 26 Id., 381; *Kohn v. Clem- ent*, 58 Id., 589, and *Gage v. Parry*, 69 Id., 605, and other cases, this court has held that the execution of mortgages by insolvent debtors, with the *bona fide* intention of securing par- ticular creditors, does not operate as a general assignment for the benefit of creditors; and some of the cited cases hold that the execution of a general assignment for the benefit of cred- itors, within a very short time after the execution of the mortgages, cannot be considered part of the same transaction.

In the case of *Burrows v. Lehndorff*, 8 Iowa, 96, where several mortgages and deeds of trust were executed by a party in a state of insolvency, and covering all of his prop- erty, by which certain creditors were preferred to others, each instrument conveying the same property and reciting that it was subject to the prior conveyance, and all filed for record on the same day, five minutes time intervening between the filing of each, it was held that the transaction consti- tuted, in legal effect, a general assignment, and was void. But in that case the mortgages and deeds of trust were exe- cuted by the insolvent without the knowledge of the credit- ors secured thereby, and it was not shown that the insolvent had creditors who were not secured in the manner above stated. One of the creditors repudiated the mortgage made to him, and attached the property of the insolvent. It requires two or more parties to make a lawful contract; and it appears that, in the cited case, the insolvent executed the mortgages and deeds of trust, and put them on record, without consultation with the creditors he intended to secure. Their relation to the transaction was the same as they would have had to a general assignment. It might well be held, upon such a state of facts, that the transaction was a general assignment.

The facts in the case at bar are quite different. The creditors secured by the mortgages and deeds were *bona fide* creditors. The evidence shows that from the time their debts were contracted it had been contemplated by the parties that they were to be secured. It is true that Lorenz Aulman, one of the insolvent partners, sought out the creditors, and offered the security. This was done by a personal interview with one of them, and by mail with another, and by telegraph with another. All of them assented to the arrangement, and accepted the security offered. The transaction is conclusively shown by the evidence to have been intended by the debtors as security to their creditors, and, as is said in *Gage v. Parry, supra,* "they had the legal right to pay or secure any one or more of their creditors; and their right in this respect was not at all affected by the fact that they were insolvent. Nor does the fact that the whole of their assets was devoted to the payment or security of but a portion of the debts they were owing afford any ground of complaint to those creditors whose debts were unsecured." We think it is quite clear that the transaction cannot be held to be a general assignment.

II.   It was further claimed by the defendant creditors that the mortgages and the deed were void, because they were made for the purpose of hindering, delaying and defrauding the unsecured creditors. It is stated in argument that the circuit court held the instruments to be void on this ground. We have examined all of the evidence with that care which is requi-

2. FRAUDU-
LENT con-
veyance: evi-
dence : right
of creditor to
secure prefer-
ence.

site where a question of fact is triable anew in this court, and our conclusion is that, if the decree of the court below was based upon this ground, it cannot be sustained. The evidence shows that the debts secured by the instruments were valid obligations of long standing. The principal creditor secured was the mother of the partners. She was an invalid old lady, incapable of transacting business, and depended upon her son Lorenz Aulman as her business agent. Theodore Guelich was a relative of the insolvents, and resided at Burlington, in this State, and Mrs. Rompano, another relative, resided in the city of New York. When Lorenz Aulman determined to secure these claims, he called upon Mr. Phillips, an attorney, and upon his advice he communicated to the creditors the fact that it was his purpose to secure their debts. As soon as he received their assent, the securities were made and put upon record by Mr. Phillips for the creditors secured. We need not discuss the purpose or intention of the debtors in securing these creditors. It is enough to say that there is no evidence that the creditors secured had any unlawful or fraudulent motive in taking security for their debts. If they had known that the security taken by them would defeat other creditors in securing their claims, their acts would not be fraudulent. A creditor has the right to secure his own claim, although he may know that by so doing other creditors will lose their claims. Any other rule would preclude a creditor from securing a debt, because of his knowledge that his debtor was not able to pay or secure all of his creditors. There is no evidence that the plaintiffs received the mortgages with any intent to hold the property for the benefit of the insolvents. On the contrary, the mortgages were given without time, and to secure notes made payable one day after date. It is useless to further discuss this question. It appears to us that there is no evidence whatever that the instruments in question were fraudulent. Indeed, if it had been shown that these secured creditors entered into all of the purposes and acts of the debtors, and were moved by the same intent, we question very much whether a decree holding the instruments to be fraudulent ought to be sustained.

REVERSED.

| 71 1
79

BRADFORD v. McCORMICK ET AL.

71
112
| 71 1
|119 1

1. **Statute of Limitations**: WHEN IT BEGINS TO RUN: FRAUDULENT CONCEALMENT. When the party against whom a cause of action in favor of another has accrued, by fraud or actual fraudulent concealment prevents him from obtaining knowledge thereof, the statute of limitations will commence to run only from the time the right of action is discovered, or might, by the use of due diligence, have been discovered. (*Dist. Twp. of Boomer v. French*, 40 Iowa. 601, and *Findley v. Stewart*, •46 Id., 655, followed)

2. ———: ———: ———: APPLICATION OF RULE TO JUSTICE OF PEACE AND SURETIES. Accordingly, where a justice of the peace had collected a judgment upon his docket in favor of the plaintiff, and, when plaintiff inquired of him from time to time whether anything had been collected thereon, the justice falsely answered that nothing had been collected, *held* that the statute of limitations did not begin; to run against plaintiff's right of action against the justice and his sureties to recover the money so collected, until he had discovered the fraud, notwithstanding the collection was entered on the justice's docket, and plaintiff might have learned of it by consulting the docket.

3. ———: LIABILITY OF SURETY. Ordinarily, if the principal is bound, so is the surety; and, in this case, *held* that, where the fraudulent concealment of a justice of the peace prevented the statute of limitations from running in his favor, it also prevented it from running in favor of his sureties.

Appeal from Franklin Circuit Court.

TUESDAY, MARCH 8.

THE defendant McCormick was elected and qualified as justice of the peace. The other defendants are sureties on his official bond, on which this action was brought to recover money collected by him as such justice on a judgment upon his docket. The money was received by the justice on the twenty-fourth day of January, 1882, and this action was commenced on the sixth day of July, 1885, and the term of office of the justice expired on the first day of January, 1883. The petition states that McCormick "fraudulently concealed the fact from the plaintiff that any amount had been collected on said judgment, and retained said money, and converted the same to his own use, * * * and, by such fraudulent concealment, prevented the plaintiff from obtaining any knowledge of the payment of said money until about the month of February, 1885." The defendant sureties pleaded the statute of limitations. Trial to the court, judgment for the defendants, and the plaintiff appeals.

Taylor & Evans, for appellant.

Henley & Hemingway, for appellees.

SEEVERS, J.—It is insisted by counsel for the appellees that a right of action accrued upon the payment of the money to the justice, and, as more than three years had elapsed when the action was commenced, it is therefore barred under section 2529 of the Code. Counsel for the plaintiff concede that the action is barred under that section, unless it appears that the justice fraudulently concealed from the plaintiff the fact that the money had been received. Counsel for the appellant further concede that the action is not saved by Code, § 2530, but that the rule contended for exists independent of the statute, and it was so held in *District Township of Boomer v. French*, 40 Iowa, 601, in which case the rule is thus stated: "That, when the party against whom a cause of action existed in favor of another, by fraud or actual fraudulent concealment prevented another from obtaining knowledge thereof, the statute would only commence to run from the time the right of action was discovered, or might, by the use of due diligence, have been discovered." Many authorities are cited in support of this rule, and it "applies when the cause of action does not grow out of the fraud alleged, but exists independently of it, and is governed by the general statute of limitations." In *Findley v. Stewart*, 46 Iowa, 655, it is also said, by DAY, J., speaking for the court: "Now, while it is true that mere ignorance of their right upon the part of those entitled to the land would not prevent the statute of limitations from running, yet that effect is produced when this ignorance arises through the fraudulent acts of him in whose aid the statute is invoked." It is true, the statute in this case is pleaded by the sureties, and they have not been guilty of any fraud; but they, without doubt, we think, are bound by the fraudulent conduct of the principal defendant. The liability of a surety is dependent upon the liability of the principal. The ordinary rule is, if the principal is bound, so is the surety. *Charles v. Haskins*, 14 Iowa, 471; *Boone Co. v. Jones*, 54 Id., 699.

The plaintiff testified that in July, 1882, and afterwards, in 1883, he made inquiry of the justice whether anything had been paid on said judgment, and he was told there had not. The justice so wrote the plaintiff on more than one occasion. There is no evidence contradictory to that of the plaintiff. This, we think, is a fraudulent concealment of a material fact. The money had been paid, and the justice so knew, and he was bound, upon inquiry being made by plaintiff, to so state. Instead of so doing, he told a willful and deliberate falsehood, and thereby the plaintiff was deceived. It is true that when the money was paid the justice made an appropriate entry of such fact on his docket, and if the plaintiff had inspected it he would have discovered such fact. It is also true that such docket is a book which all persons, interested at least, have the right to examine, and therefore it is insisted that, because the plaintiff failed to do so, the action is barred for the reason that he "might, by the use of diligence," have discovered that the money had been paid to the justice. We, however, think that the plaintiff had the right to rely on what the justice told him. Ordinarily, this is all that any one would do. The most careful business man, we think, would ordinarily rely on such information.

It is insisted that fraud is not sufficiently pleaded; but we think otherwise. Conceding, then, that the cause of action accrued when the money was received by the justice, we do not think it is barred under section 2529 of the Code, and that the court erred in so holding.

REVERSED.

KOON v. TRAMEL ET AL.

1. **Mortgage:** FORECLOSURE: NOTICE OF EQUITY: EVIDENCE CONFINED TO ISSUES. In an action to foreclose a mortgage, a general averment that plaintiff's mortgage was superior to a mortgage held by one of the defendants was but a legal conclusion, and did not warrant the admission of evidence to show that the defendant, when he took his mortgage, had actual notice of plaintiff's equity. Such notice should have been pleaded if plaintiff intended to rely upon it.

2. ———: POSSESSION OF LAND BY MORTGAGEE'S VENDOR: NOTICE OF EQUITIES. The rule that the possession of real estate is notice to all the world of the equities of the possessor, does not apply to the vendor in possession after he has conveyed the land to another and the conveyance has been recorded. So *held*, where the vendor in possession sought to have a mortgage for purchase money, made some time after the recording of the deed, declared superior to an intervening mortgage made by the vendee while the vendor was still in possession. (See opinion for cases cited.)

3. ———: FOR PRE-EXISTING DEBT: SUBSEQUENT MORTGAGE FOR PURCHASE MONEY: PRIORITY. A mortgage for a pre-existing debt, without any additional consideration, is inferior in equity to a subsequent mortgage taken for the purchase money of the land; (*Phelps v. Fockler*, 61 Iowa, 340;) but where the time of payment of the pre-existing debt is extended for a definite period, and the mortgage is taken to secure the debt as thus extended, a new consideration enters in, which gives the mortgage priority according to its date. (Compare *Port v. Embree*, 54 Iowa, 14.)

Appeal from Jasper District Court.

TUESDAY, MARCH 8.

THIS is an action in equity, and involves the question as to the priority of two mortgages upon certain real estate, the plaintiff being the owner of one mortgage, and the defendant, the First National Bank of Newton, being the owner of the other. The court below held the plaintiff's mortgage to be the first lien on the land, and the defendants appeal.

Winslow & Varnum, for appellants.

S. C. Cook, for appellee.

ROTHROCK, J.—I. At some time previous to April 1, 1884, the plaintiff was the owner of an eighty acre farm, and the defendant Tramel was the owner of a farm of fifty acres, and they agreed to exchange farms. It does not appear that the agreement was reduced to writing; and the terms of the trade or exchange are not very clearly shown by the evidence. The fifty acre farm was incumbered by a mortgage to one Smith, which mortgage Tramel was to discharge and pay. The eighty acre farm was mortgaged to the school fund for $150, and Tramel was also to pay this mortgage. The evidence is very indefinite as to whether this was all that was to be paid by Tramel as the difference between the agreed value of the farms. The plaintiff testified on the trial that Tramel was to pay him $350 in cash by May 1, 1884. This testimony is not contradicted by any witness, unless it be in what we regard as loose and random statements by some of the witnesses, that the difference. between the two farms was the two mortgages which were to be paid by Tramel, and amounting to $500. Both parties were to retain possession of their respective farms during .the farming season of 1884. Counsel for appellants make a claim in argument that Koon leased the fifty acre farm of Tramel for that year, and that Tramel failed to plow and grub part of the land, and that the damages for this failure to perform the contract of lease forms part of the considera-- tion for plaintiff's mortgage. This claim, however, is not supported by any evidence.

On the first day of April, 1884, Koon, the plaintiff, conveyed the eighty acre farm to Tramel by a deed, with cove-

nants of general warranty, excepting the school fund mort
gage for $150; and on the same day Tramel conveyed the
fifty acre farm to Koon. There was a mistake made in the
last named deed, and a corrected deed was made on the second day of May, 1884. The deed from the plaintiff to
Tramel was filed for record on the eleventh day of April,
1884. Some time before this, Tramel had borrowed $1,000
from the defendant bank, for which he gave his note, with
personal security. He forged the names of the sureties to
the note. Both parties to this controversy claim that Tramel
was insolvent, and the record shows that he was largely in
debt, and, besides being a felon, he was utterly worthless.
When the bank ascertained that the names of the sureties to
the note were forged, its officers set themselves about securing the debt. They discovered that the eighty acre farm
had been conveyed to Tramel, and they went to his house,
some fifteen miles from Newton, and took a mortgage on
the land to secure the bank debt. This mortgage was taken
on the morning of May 2, 1884, and filed for record at 10
o'clock and 10 minutes A. M. of that day. Afterwards, and
on the same day, the plaintiff took a mortgage on the same
land to secure $650. This mortgage was filed for record at
4 o'clock and 47 minutes P. M. of the same day.

It will be observed that, so far as the execution and recording of the mortgage is material to the rights of the parties,
the bank mortgage is superior in point of time. The plaintiff claims, however, that his mortgage is the superior lien,
because it was given to secure part of the purchase money
for the land, and that he was at the time both mortgages
were executed, and is now, in possession of the mortgaged
premises. The defendant bank filed an answer and cross-
bill, in which it was claimed that its mortgage was superior,
and that plaintiff had notice of defendant's mortgage before
plaintiff's mortgage was executed. The plaintiff replied by
reiterating the superiority of his mortgage, and by averring
specially that his mortgage was made for part of the pur-

chase money, in pursuance of an agreement with Tramel that he would make such a mortgage.

The first question presented by counsel for appellant is one of pleading. It is urged that all of the evidence intro-

1. MORTGAGE: foreclosure: notice of equity : evidence confined to issues. duced by plaintiff, tending to show the priority of his mortgage, was inadmissible, because the issues between the parties did not entitle the plaintiff to introduce the evidence. The evidence objected to tended to prove that the plaintiff was in possession of the land; that it was agreed between him and Tramel that the latter was to mortgage the land to the plaintiff to secure his unpaid obligations in the way of purchase money, and that the bank, by its president, had actual notice that the plaintiff was to have a mortgage from Tramel. As to all these questions, excepting that of actual notice to the president of the bank, the evidence was clearly admissible under the pleadings; and all this evidence was objected to when it was offered. It will be seen by the above statement of the pleadings that the possession, the agreement of Tramel to make a mortgage, and that the mortgage was for purchase money, were all specially pleaded. The fact that the president of the bank had actual notice of plaintiff's claim when the bank mortgage was taken was not pleaded, and was not in issue, unless made so by the general averment of the superiority of plaintiff's mortgage. This averment is made both in the petition and in the reply.

The general averment of the priority of plaintiff's mortgage was not the pleading of any fact. It was the mere assertion of a legal conclusion. And the plaintiff in his pleadings gives the reasons why his mortgage is superior, which are, the possession of the land, the previous agreement to give the mortgage, and that it was given for purchase money. We think it is very plain that proof of actual notice was not competent under the issues. As we regard the questions involved, actual notice was a most vital consideration in the case. But we cannot sustain the practice of omitting vital issues from the pleadings, and determining causes upon questions not in the case. If we did so in a case of supposed hardship, which this appears to be, we might as well abolish the fundamental rule that the evidence must be confined to the issues made by the pleadings.

II.   We come now to consider the other questions made in the case; and the one which lies at the foundation of all the others is, was the plaintiff's possession of the land constructive notice to the bank of the rights which he now claims? Counsel for appellee cite a large number of cases, in this court and other courts, which hold that a party purchasing real estate is bound to take notice of the equities of any one in possession. These authorities merely announce a general rule, and we think they are all cases where the equities of the parties in possession are independent of, or adverse to, the legal title of record.   In this case the record showed that the plaintiff had made an absolute conveyance of the land, and the conveyance was put upon record.   An examination of adjudged cases will show that the great weight of authority is to the effect that possession by the grantor, after a full conveyance, is not constructive notice to subsequent purchasers of any right reserved in the land of the grantor. *Eylar v. Eylar*, 60 Tex., 315; *Dawson v. Danbury Bank*, 15 Mich., 489; *Bloomer v. Henderson*, 8 Id., 395; *Newhall v. Pierce*, 5 Pick., 450; *Cook v. Travis*, 20 N. Y., 400; *Van Keuren v. Central R'y Co.*, 38 N. J. Law, 165; *Scott v. Gallasher*, 14 Serg. & R., 333.

In *Eylar v. Eylar*, it is said that, " by the deed in question, the parties who now assert a claim through a secret agreement declared in the most solemn form that the land in controversy was the property of Eylar [the grantee.]   They permitted that declaration to be placed on record for the very purpose of giving information to all persons as to the true ownership."   In some of the cited cases the rule is placed upon the ground that a subsequent purchaser may well rely

[margin note: 2. ——— : possession of land by mortgagee's vendor: notice of equities.]

upon the fact that the possession retained after a conveyance may be presumed to be a mere holding over at will until it becomes convenient to remove from the land. There appears to us to be much force in the thought. A party ought not to be allowed to contradict the force and effect of a full conveyance by the mere fact of possession after the deed is recorded.

III. But counsel for the plaintiff contends that the rule above announced has no application except to purchasers of the land, and that a mortgage for a pre-existing debt, without any additional consideration, is junior to a subsequent mortgage, taken for the purchase money of the land. This rule is correct, and this court has so held. *Phelps v. Fockler*, 61 Iowa, 340. The facts in this case, however, showed that the bank, when it took the mortgage from Tramel, took a new note, and extended the time of payment for one year; and the mortgage was taken as security. The law is settled in this state that a mortgagee of real estate is regarded as a purchaser. *Porter v. Greene*, 4 Iowa, 571. And it is also well settled "that the giving of further time for the payment of an existing debt by a valid agreement for any period, however short, is a valuable consideration, and is sufficient to support a mortgage as a purchase for a valuable consideration." 1 Jones, Mortg., § 459, and authorities there cited. See, also, *Port v. Embree*, 54 Iowa, 14. It is no answer to this position to claim that the original debt to the bank was a forgery, and that Tramel was insolvent. The original note was a valid obligation as against Tramel, and his financial standing is wholly immaterial, for the fact remains that the extension of time was a sufficient consideration to constitute the bank a purchaser.

IV. The foregoing discussion practically disposes of this case against the appellee, because, if the possession of the land was not constructive notice to the bank of plaintiff's rights, and the bank procured the mortgage upon a sufficient

3. ——— : for pre-existing debt: subsequent mortgage for purchase money : priority.

consideration, and without actual notice of the plaintiff's claim, the fact that an agreement had been entered into between Koon and Tramel that the latter was to make a mortgage to the plaintiff is wholly immaterial, the bank having had no actual notice of such an agreement. When the two propositions, that the possession of plaintiff was not constructive notice to the bank, and that the bank is a purchaser upon a sufficient consideration, are established, it is an end of the case.

REVERSED.

McLEOD v. THE HUMESTON & SHENANDOAH R'Y CO.

1. **New Trial**: CONSIDERATION BY JURY OF EXTRANEOUS EVIDENCE. Where a paper containing evidence material and pertinent to the issues, and capable of influencing the minds of the jurors, but which had not been introduced as evidence in the case, was, by inadvertence, given to the jury with the proper papers in the case, and the same was read by the jurors, *held* that the court properly set aside the verdict and granted a new trial, even after it had denied a new trial on the ground that the verdict was not supported by the evidence. (See opinion for cases cited.)

Appeal from Page Circuit Court.

TUESDAY, MARCH 8.

PLAINTIFF brings this action to recover for personal injuries sustained by him while in the employment of defendant as a fireman of a locomotive running upon defendant's road. The petition alleges that the injuries were caused by the negligence of defendant in failing to keep its track at the place of the accident in a safe condition, whereby the locomotive upon which plaintiff was employed was thrown from the track, and precipitated down an embankment. There was a verdict for defendant, which was set aside upon motion of plaintiff, based upon the misconduct of the jury.

Defendant appeals from the order of the court setting aside the verdict.

W. W. Morsman, for appellant.

McCabe & Hill, for appellee.

BECK, J.—I. The engineer in charge of the locomotive was killed by the accident, and a coroner's inquest was held upon his body. The evidence taken at the inquest, by some means which are unexplained, was taken by the jury when they retired to consider the case, and was read by many, if not all, of the jurors. No fault can be attached to counsel on either side for the evidence coming into possession of the jury. It was in the possession of one of the counsel during the trial, and, it appears, was left by him upon the table where he sat. It was given to the jury with other papers when they retired to consider the verdict. The evidence had not been offered or admitted in evidence, and was, in violation of law, wrongfully taken and read by the jurors. It gave a particular and, in some respects, a minute description and statement of matters pertaining to the accident, some of which tended to show that it was caused by the felonious act of some unknown person; spikes fastening the rails having been pulled out, and the rails thus displaced. The evidence was thus material and pertinent to the issues in the case, and capable of influencing, adversely to plaintiff, the minds of the jurors who read and considered it. Some of the jurors declare in affidavits filed in support of the motion that the evidence was considered by the jury in determining the verdict; others, in affidavits filed by defendant, declare that it was not; but all who speak upon that point admit that it was read by many jurors.

II. The evidence in question being capable of influencing the jury, and unlawfully before them, there can be no assurance that their verdict was the result of the consideration alone of the lawful evidence in the case. The jury were exposed to unlawful influence; it cannot be said that none of them yielded thereto. The law requires, to the end that a correct and pure administration of justice be attained, that the verdict be regarded as tainted with the misbehavior of the jury in taking and reading the evidence, and be set aside. This is the only course of safety. No other rule will secure the jury from attempts to introduce for their consideration evidence of this character, or other matters which have not come to them through the hands of the court,—the only channel through which lawful evidence can reach them. These views are based upon familiar elementary principles. See *Coffin v. Gephart*, 18 Iowa, 256; *Stewart v. Burlington & M. R. R'y Co.*, 11 Id., 62; *Wright v. Illinois & M. Tel. Co.*, 20 Id., 195; *Kruidenier v. Shields*, 70 Id., 428; *Perry v. Cottingham*, 63 Id., 41.

III. Counsel for defendant think that, as the court held that a motion could not be sustained on the ground that the verdict was not supported by the evidence, it was thus held that the verdict was in accord with the evidence lawfully before the jury, and therefore no prejudice was wrought by the evidence before the coroner's jury, and the verdict should have been permitted to stand. But the circuit court did not hold that the verdict was in accord with the evidence. Nothing further was held than that the verdict was not so wanting of support in the evidence that the court below, under familiar rules, was authorized to disturb it. The circuit court, doubtless, concluded that, if the unlawful evidence had not been before the jury, the verdict might have been the other way. The decision, we must presume, was based upon these grounds, thus harmonizing with the law.

These conclusions dispose of all questions in the case. The decision of the circuit court is

AFFIRMED.

THE MOLINE PLOW CO. v. BRADEN.

1. **Sale:** CONDITIONAL: MORTGAGE TO THIRD PARTY WITHOUT NOTICE: CODE, § 1922. Where one had possession of personal property under a conditional sale to him, whereby the title remained in the vendor until payment was made, and the contract under which he held was not acknowledged or recorded, (Code, § 1922,) and he mortgaged the property to a third party who had no actual notice of the condition of the title, *held* that the mortgagee's title was superior to that of the vendor.

2. ———: ———: ———: WHAT IS NOTICE. In such case, if the mortgagee had such notice as to put him on inquiry, then he had actual notice. If he did not have such notice, negligence on his part in failing to make inquiry was immaterial, unless, possibly, it amounted to fraud.

3. **Evidence:** NOT RELEVANT TO ISSUES. It is error to admit evidence on a point not put in issue by the pleadings.

Appeal from Polk Circuit Court.

TUESDAY, MARCH 8.

ACTION to recover specific personal property. Trial to a jury, who, under direction of the court, and by consent of the parties, found a special verdict. On such finding the plaintiff moved the court for judgment, and the intervenor moved the court to set aside a part of the special findings, because the same were immaterial and against the evidence. The former motion was sustained, the latter overruled, and judgment rendered for the plaintiff. The intervenor appeals.

W. S. Sickmon, for appellants.

Macy, Sweeney & Sherman, for appellee.

SEEVERS, J.—This action was commenced against the defendant, Braden, and the petition and amendment thereto state that the plaintiff is the absolute and unqualified owner of the property therein described, and is entitled to the possession thereof; that the alleged cause of detention is that the defendant purchased the property of the plaintiff, which the latter denies, and it is stated "that a portion of the

property was left with defendant, subject to the order of the
plaintiff, and that the balance of said goods were left with
the defendant for sale under and by virtue of the certain
contract of the plaintiff and defendant, and hereto attached,
marked "Exhibit A." The contract referred to is in the
' form of an order, signed by the defendant, and accepted by
the plaintiff, by the terms of which the plaintiff, in substance, is directed to ship certain goods, consisting of agricultural implements, to the defendant, upon certain named
terms as to the price; one-fourth of which was to be paid
on July 1, 1882, and the balance at certain named times
thereafter. The defendant agreed in the contract to turn
over to the plaintiff "farmers' notes due not later than
October 1, 1882, and January 1, 1883, as collateral security
to his notes." It is further provided in the contract "that
the ownership of all goods furnished on this contract, or
their proceeds, shall be vested in Moline Plow Company
until final settlement and payment shall be made for the
same."

The intervenor, claiming to be interested in the subject-
matter of the controversy against both plaintiff and defendant, pleaded that in January, 1883, the defendant was in the
full and undisputed possession of the property, and, being
indebted to the intervenor, executed a mortgage thereon to
secure such indebtedness; that at that time the intervenor
had no notice, actual or constructive, of said contract, and
that the same had never been acknowledged and recorded.
The defendant adopted the intervenor's petition as his
answer.

I.   Under the pleadings, it becomes material to inquire
and determine what are the rights of the parties under the

1. SALE: con- contract, and what is the character and legal
ditional:
mortgage to   effect of such instrument. It is and must be
third party
without no-   regarded as a conditional sale of at least a large
tice: Code, §
1922.   portion of the property in controversy; the condition being that the ownership of the property should not

vest in the defendant until it was paid for. Until then the contract provides the property shall belong to the plaintiff. But, as between the plaintiff and intervenor, this portion of the contract is inoperative, and must be disregarded, because it is provided by statute that "no sale, contract, or lease, wherein the transfer of title or ownership of personal property is made to depend upon any condition, shall be valid against any creditor or purchaser of the vendee or lessee in actual possession, obtained in pursuance thereof, without notice, unless the same be in writing, executed by the vendor or lessor, acknowledged and recorded the same as chattel mortgages." Code, § 1922. As the defendant had possession of the property under a contract or conditional sale, which was not acknowledged and recorded, and as the jury found the intervenor had no notice of such contract and sale, the same, as to the intervenor, must be regarded as invalid; and therefore the court erred in rendering judgment on the special findings for the plaintiff. *Singer S. M. Co. v. Holcomb*, 40 Iowa, 33; *Pash v. Weston*, 52 Id., 675; *Thorpe v. Fowler*, 57 Id., 541.

II. The intervenor moved the court to set aside the special finding that it could have obtained knowledge of the contract by the exercise of due diligence. This
2. ——: ——:
——: what
is notice.
motion should have been sustained. Under the statute, there must be either actual or constructive notice. In *Warner v. Jameson*, 52 Iowa, 70, there was actual notice. When the instrument is duly recorded, there is constructive notice of its contents. The .statute does not require any person whose rights may be affected to make inquiry, or to use diligence to ascertain what the fact is. If there is neither actual nor constructive notice, the sale is invalid as to creditors or purchasers of the party in possession of the property. If the creditor has such notice as to put him on inquiry, then he has actual notice. If he does not have actual notice, negligence on his part in failing to make inquiry is immaterial, unless, possibly, it amounts to fraud.

III.   Evidence was introduced, against the objection of the intervenor, tending to show that the defendant held pos-

3. EVIDENCE: not relevant to issues. session of the property under some other right than under the contract.   In so holding the court erred, for the reason that there was no such issue.   As we understand the pleadings, it should, under the statements in the petition, have been regarded as a conceded fact that defendant was in possession of a large portion of the property under and by virtue of the contract therein referred to.

The judgment of the circuit court is

REVERSED.

AUSPACH v. FERGUSON.

1. **Appearance:** WHAT CONSTITUTES: AGREEMENT FOR CONTINUANCE. A request or an agreement for the continuance of a cause, whether it be made orally by the party or by his counsel, or by a writing filed in the case, involves an appearance in the case, notwithstanding the record for the first time formally recites the appearance of the party on the day to which the case is so continued.

2. **Justices' Courts:** TERRITORIAL JURISDICTION: CONSENT. Where the plaintiff resided in one township of the county, and the defendant in another, in which notice was served on him, but the suit was brought before a justice of the peace in still another township, held that, while the justice did not obtain jurisdiction of the person of defendant by such service, (Code, §§ 3509, 3510,) yet, when defendant appeared and, without objecting to the jurisdiction, consented to an order for a continuance, he thereby conferred jurisdiction upon the court.

Appeal from Ida Circuit Court.

TUESDAY, MARCH 8.

THIS action was brought before a justice of the peace, and a recovery had.   The defendant appealed, and on his motion the circuit court dismissed the case on the ground that no jurisdiction had been acquired.   From this order.the plaintiff appeals.

Kiner & Riddle and *H. S. Bradshaw*, for appellant.

Rollins & Frink, for appellee.

ADAMS, CH. J.—This case, involving less than $100, comes to us upon a certificate.   The first question certified is in these words: "As shown by the records, the parties lived in Ida county, Iowa, but in townships adjoining the township in which the suit was commenced; and the notice was served personally in the township of the defendant's residence.   The defendant appeared upon the return-day, and, without filing any plea, agreed with the plaintiff to a continuance of the cause to a subsequent day, and the cause was continued accordingly.   Did such appearance and continuance without plea confer jurisdiction upon the justice of the peace?"

1. APPEAR-ANCE : what constitutes: agreement for continuance.

While, as is seen from the above, the court finds that the defendant appeared and agreed to a continuance, it is contended by the defendant that he did not appear previous to the continuance, and that, when he did appear, he pleaded to the jurisdiction.   According to his view of the facts, as shown by the record, the precise question certified did not arise.   Where a case comes to us upon a certificate, it is proper for us to look into the record far enough to determine whether the question certified arose in the case.   The record in question to which we look to determine the facts in .dispute is the justice's transcript.   In that we find the following: "January 9, 1886, by agreement of parties this cause is continued until January 14, 1886, at ten o'clock in the forenoon."   The defendant contends that this does not show an appearance by him.   But, where an order of court is obtained upon an agreement of parties, there is a virtual request made for the order by both parties.   Now, we are not able to see how a party can make a request of a court which shall be of such a character as shall justify the court in acting upon it, unless the party is to be regarded as in some way making an appearance. The party invokes the action of the court. If he does it orally, he must, of course, be actually in court, either personally or by his authorized representative. If he does it by writing, the writing must have been filed, either by himself personally, or by his authorized representative, and that would constitute an appearance. If the defendant had filed a motion and affidavit for continuance, no one would doubt that the act constituted an appearance. The case before us is not different in principle. The defendant relies in part upon a fact which remains to be stated. The transcript of the justice expressly recites that, on the fourteenth day of January, the day to which the cause was continued, the defendant appears. His view seems to be that strictly there can be but one appearance in a case by the same party, and that, if the defendant entered appearance on the fourteenth day of January, he had not entered appearance earlier. But it is quite common, we believe, in making up a record, to recite the appearance of the parties at the trial, notwithstanding they may have appeared before; and, even if it were not, we could not give the force to the recital in question which the defendant contends for. We think that the court properly found that the parties appeared at the time the agreement for a continuance was communicated to the court, with a virtual request that it should act on it. We come, then, to the question certified: "Did such appearance and continuance, without plea, confer jurisdiction upon the justice?"

Suits may, in all cases, be brought in the township where the plaintiff or defendant, or one of several defendants, resides. Code, § 3509. They may also be brought in any other township of the same county, if actual service on one or more of the defendants is made in such township. Code, § 3510. The justice in the case before us had jurisdiction of the subject-

2. JUSTICES' courts: territorial jurisdiction: consent.

matter of the controversy, and had only to acquire jurisdiction of the person of the defendant. Service of notice upon the defendant in the defendant's township, it may be conceded, did not give the court jurisdiction of him; but it was ·competent for him to waive service, and give the court jurisdiction by appearance. This, we think, he did do when he virtually invoked the jurisdiction of the court to make an order.

Several other questions are certified; but the conclusion which we have expressed renders it unnecessary to consider the other questions.

We think that the court erred in holding that the action should be dismissed on the ground that the justice did not acquire jurisdiction.

REVERSED.

71 1
79

71
112

MILLER v. LESSER.

1. **Statute of Limitation:** ACTION BY SURETY AGAINST PRINCIPAL. An action by a surety against a principal, for money paid as such surety, is based on an implied promise, and is barred in five years from the date of the payment. (Code, § 2529, par. 4.)

2. ———: RESIDENCE IN IOWA UNDER ASSUMED NAME: INABILITY TO TO DISCOVER RESIDENCE. An action upo n an unwritten contract against one who had removed to Iowa, and had lived here for five years after the cause of action had accrued, *held* barred by the statute of limitations, notwithstanding the defendant had lived here under an assumed name, and plaintiff, by the exercise of diligence, was not able sooner to discover his place of residence.

Appeal from Scott Circuit Court.

TUESDAY, MARCH 8.

PLAINTIFF brought this action to recover an amount of money which he was compelled to pay as surety on a bond on which defendant was principal, and which was given by him in a proceeding in bankruptcy. The defendant pleaded as a defense that the action was barred by the statute of limitations. The judgment was for the defendant, and plaintiff appealed.

Davison & Lane, for appellant.

George E. Hubbell, for appellee.

REED, J.—When the bond was signed, which was in 1871, the parties were both residents of the state of Ohio. It was given as security for the costs in a bankruptcy proceeding, which had been instituted by defendant. In 1873 defendant removed to Davenport, in this state, and he has since resided there continuously. In 1879 plaintiff was compelled to pay the costs which accrued in the proceeding in which the bond was given. This action was commenced in March, 1886. When defendant settled in Davenport, he assumed the name of M. Levy, and he has been known in the community by that name ever since. He is a married man, and his family came with him when he removed to this state; and continuously since his settlement at Davenport he has carried on business in his assumed name. Plaintiff's cause of action arose when

1. STATUTE of limitations: action by surety against principal.

he paid the costs in the bankruptcy proceeding. It arose upon the promise by defendant, which is implied from the relation in which the parties stood to each other, that he would indemnify plaintiff against his liability on the bond. The action being upon an unwritten contract, the period within which it might be brought was five years. Code, § 2529, subd. 4.

When the cause of action accrued, defendant was a resident of this state. The statute, therefore, began to run at

2. ——: residence in Iowa under assumed name: inability to discover residence.

once, unless some fact existed which suspended its operation. In addition to the fact that defendant was living under an assumed name, it was shown that his place of residence was unknown to plaintiff, and that he had made diligent inquiry to ascertain where he lived. Did these facts prevent the

running of the statute? We think not. The provision of
the statute is explicit that the actions enumerated in it may
be brought within the period specified after their causes
accrue, "and not afterwards, except when otherwise specially
declared." Section 2529, *supra*. This language is explicit,
and there can be no doubt as to its meaning. The only
exceptions to the general rule created by the statute are those
which are specially declared. It is provided by section 2530
that, when relief is sought on the ground of fraud or mistake,
or when the action is for trespass to property, the period of
the statute shall not begin to run until the discovery of the
fraud, mistake, or trespass; and section 2533 provides that
the time during which a defendant is a non-resident of the
state shall not be included in computing any of the periods
of limitation. Other sections create exceptions in favor of
minors, and in cases in which the persons in whose favor
causes of action have accrued have died during the period of
limitation. But no provision can be found which creates an
exception in favor of a creditor, upon the ground that he has
been unable for any reason to discover the place of residence
of his debtor within the period prescribed by the statute
within which the action may be brought.

Plaintiff's action, then, falls within the general rule of the
statute. It does not belong to either of the classes of actions
enumerated in section 2530. Nor were either of the parties
under any of the disabilities which, by the other provisions,
make certain cases exceptional.

AFFIRMED.

MCGREW v. THE TOWN OF LETTSVILLE ET AL.

REISCH v. THE SAME.

1. **Cities and Towns**: VACATION OF PLAT: WHO MAY VACATE: "PRO-
   PRIETORS:" CODE, §§ 563, 564. Under the provisions of §§ 563 and
   564 of the Code, not only the original proprietors of a town plat may
   vacate the same, or a portion thereof, but persons who have acquired
   title from such original proprietors may exercise the power conferred by
   the statute. (Compare *Lorenzen v. Preston*, 53 Iowa, 580, and *Conner
   v. Iowa City*, 66 Id., 419.)

2. ——: ——: EFFECT ON CORPORATION BOUNDARIES. The vacation
   of a portion of a town plat does not have the effect to take the vacated
   portion out of the corporation,

Appeals from Louisa Circuit Court.

WEDNESDAY, MARCH 9.

ACTION in chancery to restrain defendants, the town of
Lettsville and its officers, from opening certain streets and
alleys, which plaintiffs aver have been vacated. A motion to
dissolve a temporary injunction allowed in the case, made
after answer, and after an agreed statement of facts was filed
by the parties, was overruled, and thereupon defendants
appeal. The causes being alike as to the facts and pleadings,
are submitted together.

E. W. Tatlock and *Brannan, Jayne & Hoffman*, for
appellants.

R. Caldwell, for appellee.

BECK J.—I. The record before us shows that plaintiffs
owned separately certain lots and blocks in the town of

1. CITIES and
towns: vaca-
tion of plat:
who may
vacate: "pro-
prietors:"
Code, §§ 563,
564.

Lettsville, which were used, with other lands
they owned adjacent thereto, for agricultural
purposes; no streets or alleys ever having been
opened through them. They united in a written
instrument, prescribed by Code, § 563, for the
purpose of vacating that part of the town plat covering the
blocks, lots and streets in question. We think the record

shows that plaintiffs are the separate owners of the lots in question in this suit. The statute just referred to authorizes the vacation of the whole of a town plat by the proprietors, at any time before sale of any of the lots, by an instrument of the character of the one executed by plaintiffs. Section 564 provides that "any part of a plat may be vacated, under the provisions, and subject to the condition, of this chapter, provided such vacating does not abridge or destoy any of the rights and privileges of other proprietors in said plat, and providing, further, that nothing contained in this section shall authorize the closing or obstructing of any public highway laid out according to law."

We are of the opinion that the term "proprietors," used in the chapter in which these sections are found, indicates the owners of the land, and not alone the persons who originally plat the land; and that owners who have acquired title from such original proprietors may exercise the power conferred by the chapter. The section just quoted contemplates the case of separate proprietors, having distinct and separate interests; and the same is true of sections 565 and 567, which confer upon them the powers to vacate part of a town plat. This court has recognized this rule in *Lorenzen v. Preston*, 53 Iowa, 580, and *Conner v. Iowa City*, 66 Id., 419.

II. Counsel for defendants insist that the instrument executed by plaintiffs is insufficient, for the reason that it does not describe by lots and blocks the part of the plat vacated. It is sufficient to say, in reply to this objection, that it so refers to and describes the lots and blocks that it can be understood with absolute certainty what part of the plat is vacated. This is sufficient.

III. It will be remembered that the authority conferred upon the owners to vacate a part of a plat, where exercised,

2. —: —: does not have the effect to limit the boundaries
effect on corporation : of an incorporated town, and to take that part
boundaries. of which the plat is vacated out of the corporation. It, therefore, does not affect the authority of the cor-

poration over the lands covered by the part of the plat which
is vacated.

IV. The record before us shows that, as the streets and
alleys were never opened, the vacation does not abridge or
destroy any of the rights of any owner of land within the
town. Code, § 564. The vacation was therefore lawfully
made.

We reach the conclusion that the circuit court did not err
in overruling the motion to dissolve the temporary injunction.

AFFIRMED.

THE FORT DODGE COAL CO. v. WILLIS.

1. **Venue**: ACTION IN WRONG COUNTY: MOTION TO CHANGE: PLEADING.
   In an action brought in Webster county, against a citizen of Butler
   county, for coal delivered on the track in Webster county, under a contract contained in letters between the parties, plaintiff's petition alleged
   that, by the terms of the contract, the coal was to be delivered and paid
   for in Webster county. Certain of the letters between the parties were
   attached as exhibits to the petition, and from these it appeared that the
   coal was to be *delivered* in Webster county, but it did not expressly
   appear therefrom, as was necessary to maintain the action in Webster
   county, (see Code, § 2581,) that *payment* was to be made in that county.
   The petition, however, further averred that certain other letters were
   lost, in which Webster county was expressly stated as the place of both
   delivery and payment. *Held* that these averments, which must for the
   purpose be taken as true, showed a right of action in Webster county,
   under § 2581 of the Code, and that a motion for a transfer of the cause
   to the county of defendant's residence, under § 2589 of the Code, was
   properly overruled.

Appeal from Webster District Court.

WEDNESDAY, MARCH 9.

ACTION to recover the value of certain coal which plaintiff claims to have sold and delivered to defendant. Defendant resides in Butler county, and he filed a motion in the
district court for the removal of the cause to that county,
and, that motion being overruled, he declined to plead, and

a default was entered against him, and judgment rendered thereon for the amount of the claim, from which he appeals.

Courtright & Edwards, for appellant.

J. F. Duncombe, for appellee.

REED, J.—The coal, the value of which plaintiff seeks to recover, is alleged to have been sold and delivered in car-lots on the second, fourth and eighth of October, 1883. It is alleged that the sales were made under a written contract, and that such contract was contained in the letters which passed between the parties, some of which are attached as exhibits to the petition. The first of these in point of time is a letter from plaintiff to defendant, and which purports to be an answer to one written by him, in which they advised him that the lowest price at which they could sell coal was $2.50 per ton on track at Fort Dodge. The next is one written by defendant, some ten days later, in which he inquires whether they would bill a car-load to Parkersburg if he should order the same, and asking them to give him the price of nut coal. The next is in answer to this by plaintiff, in which they inform him that they would fill his order for a car to Parkersburg if he made it, and that the price of nut coal was $1.75 per ton on track at the mines. The only other letter set out is one from defendant, of a later date, in which he stated that he had ordered one car of lump coal, and one of nut, but that he had not received them, and in which he directed them to ship to him a car of lump coal as soon as possible. It is alleged in the petition that one of the letters written a short time prior to the delivery of said coal cannot be found, but that the same was an order by defendant for the delivery of lump coal, and that the answer thereto stated the price of said coal and the place where the delivery was to be made, and the place of payment therefor. The petition also contains the following allegation: "That by the terms of said written contracts contained in said let-

ters, and by the answers thereto, and by the terms of said
several written agreements therein contained, the coal was to
be delivered in Webster county, and the payment therefor was
to be made in said county."

The question to be determined is whether it is shown by
the petition that, by the terms of the contract, payment for.
the coal was to be made in Webster county. If that is
shown, the action was properly brought in that county; but,
if not, the venue should have been changed to the county of
defendant's residence. Code, §§ 2581, 2589. It is expressly
averred in the portion of the petition quoted above that the
property was sold upon an agreement that it should be delivered and paid for in Webster county. But, so far as the contract between the parties is evidenced by the letters which
are exhibited, its terms are to be gathered from their language, rather than from the general averments of the petition; and, if they were to be considered alone, it could be
determined from them only that the coal was to be delivered.
on track at Fort Dodge, or at the mines, (which are in Webster county,) at the prices designated. In the absence of
any stipulation as to the time and place of payment, the law
would imply an undertaking by defendant to pay at the time
and place of delivery. But, to entitle plaintiff to prosecute
the action in that county, the payment must have been
required to be there made by the *terms of the contract*, (section 2581, *supra;*) that is, the parties must have expressly
stipulated that that should be the place of payment. But
the letters exhibited do not contain any express stipulation
as to the time and place of payment.

But it is averred that one of the letters written by defendant, and in which he ordered coal, has been lost, and is not
exhibited; also that in the answer which plaintiff wrote to it
the place both of delivery and payment was stated. This
letter in answer is not exhibited, and the averment as to its
contents must be taken as true. The language quoted above
from the petition has reference to this, as well as the other

letters which passed between the parties. By it the pleader undertook to state the contract of the parties as contained in the whole correspondence. The allegation is that, by the terms of the contract as contained in the letters, payment for the property was to be made in that county. That allegation must be taken as true; and, if true, the action was properly brought in Webster county.

AFFIRMED.

BRAYLEY v. ELLIS ET AL.

71 155
93 575

1. **Mortgage**: PAYMENT TO MORTGAGEE AFTER TRANSFER OF NOTES: SALE OF MORTGAGED PREMISES: LIABILITY. Where the mortgagee of land transferred the secured notes before maturity, but did not assign the mortgage, and afterwards fraudulently, and without the knowledge of his assignee, received from the mortgagor, who was led to believe that he still owned the notes, a partial payment thereon, taking only a receipt therefor, and the mortgagor afterwards sold the land to another, *held*, in an action by the assignee to foreclose the mortgage, that he was entitled to recover, as against the mortgagor and the land, the whole amount of the notes, regardless of the partial payment so negligently made by the mortgagor.

Appeal from Humboldt Circuit Court.

WEDNESDAY, MARCH 9.

ACTION to foreclose a mortgage on real estate. Judgment for the plaintiff, and defendants appeal.

A. E. Clarke, for appellants.

M. D. O'Connell, for appellee.

SEEVERS, J.—The conceded facts are that the defendant Ellis, in February, 1882, executed a mortgage to the defendant Colby to secure two negotiable promissory notes. The notes were sold and assigned by Colby to the plaintiff before maturity, but no assignment of the mortgage was made of record or otherwise. The defendant Fuller purchased the property of Ellis. The defendants claim that Ellis paid

Colby $150 in part payment of the notes, without knowledge of the transfer to the plaintiff, and under the belief that Colby still owned both the notes and mortgage. They claim that Colby so stated and represented at the time the payment was made; but the fact is that the notes, prior to that time, had been assigned to the plaintiff. The evidence as to such payment is exceedingly conflicting, and the plaintiff claims that the preponderance is with him; but, if mistaken in this, he insists that he is still entitled to recover.

The appellants insist, if it be conceded that the payment was made as above stated, that this case comes within the rule established in *Bank of the State of Indiana v. Anderson*, 14 Iowa, 544; *McClure v. Burris*, 16 Id., 591; *Cornog v. Fuller*, 30 Id., 212; and *Bowling v. Cook*, 39 Id., 200. In these cases the mortgagee released the mortgage of record; and it was held that a subsequent purchaser or incumbrancer could well rely on the record, and govern himself accordingly. In this case we are asked to go a step further, and hold that a mere payment to the mortgagee extinguishes the mortgage to that extent. Ordinarily, the maker of a note, when he makes a partial payment thereon, sees that it is properly indorsed on the note. When this is done, it amounts to a partial satisfaction of the note and mortgage. In this case no such indorsement was made, and the mortgage remained wholly unsatisfied of record when the defendant Fuller purchased the real estate of Ellis. That Colby had the power to wholly or partially release the mortgage of record when the payment was made will be conceded; but he did not do so, nor was he asked to either credit the amount paid on the notes, or release the mortgage to that extent of record. Ellis, when he made the payment, relied on the statement of Colby that he owned the notes. Instead of having the amount paid credited on the notes, he claims he took a receipt for the money, stating that it was paid on one of the notes secured by the mortgage. If he had insisted on having it credited, Colby could not have done so, for the reason that the note was not in his possession. We feel constrained to hold that the defendants must suffer the loss, if one in fact it is, because of the negligence of Ellis. If he had taken ordinary care, and insisted on what he was entitled to at the time he made the payment, his own rights would have been fully protected, and also those of the plaintiff, who it is conceded is an innocent holder for value. When Fuller purchased the real estate, the mortgage was in full force, and had not been canceled or satisfied, in whole or in part, of record. She had the power to protect herself fully by having the mortgage partially satisfied of record, or declining the purchase.

We think the judgment is right, and must be

AFFIRMED.

71
79

POSTEL v. PALMER.

1. **Evidence:** SECONDARY: CONTENTS OF DEED: FOUNDATION. Where the grantee in a deed and the custodian thereof testified positively that it had been lost, *held* that this was sufficient foundation for the introduction of parol testimony as to its contents, without showing that search had been made for it. (*Horseman v. Todhunter*, 12 Iowa, 230, and *Howe Machine Co. v. Stiles*, 53 Id., 424, distinguished.)

2. **Real Estate:** QUITCLAIM DEED: OUTSTANDING EQUITIES. The grantee in a mere quitclaim deed can acquire no rights thereby against outstanding equities which are valid against the grantor. (*Watson v. Phelps*, 40 Iowa, 482, and other cited cases, followed.)

Appeal from Buchanan Circuit Court.

WEDNESDAY, MARCH 9.

PLAINTIFF brought an action for the possession of a tract of land. Defendant denied that plaintiff was the owner or entitled to the possession of the property, and in a cross-petition he set up title thereto in himself, and asked to have the title quieted in him. The circuit court entered judgment dismissing plaintiff's petition, and quieting the title to the land in defendant. Plaintiff appeals.

Woodward & Cook, for appellant.

Lake & Harmon, for appellee.

REED, J.—Both parties' claim title under one Edward R. Norton, who became the owner of the premises on the seventeenth of October, 1873. He conveyed to plaintiff, by quitclaim, on the thirty-first of March, 1884. On the twentieth of February, 1884, one Isaac Brown executed a conveyance of the premises to defendant. The claim alleged by defendant is that Norton sold and conveyed the land to Brown in November, 1873. But no conveyance between these parties was of record when plaintiff bought of Norton. It is claimed, however, that a conveyance was in fact executed and delivered, but that the same has been lost or destroyed. Both Norton and Brown were examined as witnesses on the trial. The former testified that he sold the timber growing on the premises to Brown, but that no other interest in the premises was included in the sale, and he denied that he ever executed any conveyance of the property to him. Brown testified that his purchase was of the land, and that a conveyance thereof (a quitclaim) was executed by Norton, and delivered to him, but the same had been lost, and could not be produced as evidence. Plaintiff objected to the parol evidence as to the execution and contents of this deed, (assuming that one had in fact been executed,) on the ground that the absence of the instrument was not sufficiently accounted for, and it was not shown that search had been made for it. The rule is elementary that secondary evidence is not admissible until it is shown that it is out of the party's power to produce the primary. We think, however, that this was done in the present case.

The witness testified positively that the deed had been

marginal note: 1. EVIDENCE: secondary: contents of deed: foundation.

lost, and that he conld not produce it. He was not examined as to the manner of the loss, but his answers implied
that the fact that the instrument had been lost was within
his knowledge. As he was the custodian of the instrument,
this was all defendant was required to establish to entitle
him to introduce the secondary evidence. There would be
no reason for requiring him to show that a search had been
made, for it already appeared that a search would be unavailing. The case is very different in its facts from *Horseman v. Todhunter*, 12 Iowa, 230, *Howe Machine Co. v.
Stiles*, 53 Id., 424, and other cases cited and relied on by
plaintiff in support of the objection.

Coming to the question whether a sale and conveyance of
the property was made by Norton to Brown, we have to say
2. REAL estate: that we think the claim made by defendant with
quitclaim
deed: out- reference to the transaction is clearly established
standing
equities. by the proof. It is shown that Norton frequently stated that he had sold the land to Brown. These
statements were made soon after the sale is alleged to have
been made. They were also made to parties who applied to
him to purchase the land. He exercised no acts of ownership or dominion over the property after that time. He
removed from the state nearly ten years before he gave the
conveyance to plaintiff, and during all that time he neither
paid the taxes on the land nor made any claim that he was
the owner of it. His conduct during all the time was inconsistent with the claim that he continued to be the owner of
the property. Having found that Nelson sold and conveyed·
the property to Brown, it follows that plaintiff acquired no
interest or right by the conveyance from Norton to him.
That conveyance, as we have stated, was a mere quitclaim,
and by it plaintiff could acquire no right against outstanding
equities which were valid as against Norton. *Watson v.
Phelps*, 40 Iowa, 482; *Smith v. Dunton*, 42 Id., 48; *Besore
v. Dosh*, 43 Id., 211.

AFFIRMED.

NICHOLS, SHEPARD & CO. v. WYMAN ET AL.

160
125

160
661
664

1. **Sale**: WRITTEN WARRANTY: EVIDENCE OF ADDITIONAL PAROL WAR-
RANTY. Where there is a written contract of sale, an oral warranty of
the thing sold cannot be shown; and when there is a written warranty,
the vendee cannot show an additional parol warranty. (*Mast v. Pearce*,
58 Iowa, 579, and *Shepherd v. Gilroy*, 46 Id., 193, followed.)

2. ———: CONDITIONAL WARRANTY: FAILURE TO COMPLY. Where the
contract of the sale of machinery required the purchaser, in case it
failed to satisfy the warranty, to give written notice thereof to the vendors and their agent, and he failed to do so, *held* that he could not set
up a failure of the warranty in defense to an action for the purchase
money.

Appeal from Warren Circuit Court.

WEDNESDAY, MARCH 9.

ACTION in chancery to foreclose a mortgage. There was a
decree for defendants. Plaintiffs appeal.

Smith & Morris, for appellants.

H. McNeil, for appellees.

BECK, J.—I. The notes secured by the mortgage in
suit were executed by defendant John H. Wyman in the

1. SALE: writ-
ten warranty:
evidence of
additional
parol war-
ranty.

purchase of a steam-engine, and a separator to
be propelled by the engine, and fixtures accompanying each. The defendants in their answer
allege that plaintiffs orally warranted the machinery to be perfect, and capable of doing good work, and that
the engine would haul the separator, tank, water, and one-
half ton of coal, through stubble and over plowed fields, and
over all the territory wherein defendant was to use the
machines, and to perform other conditions of the warranty.
It is further alleged that the machinery failed to comply
with the terms of the warranty. The plaintiffs in their
reply deny the oral warranty pleaded by defendant, and
allege that the machinery was sold upon a written warranty,
and no other, which is set out as an exhibit.

II. The preponderance of the evidence shows that there was no oral warranty. Defendant Wyman testifies that there was, but one of the plaintiffs, and the agent who made the sale for them, testify to the contrary.

III. The written warranty is introduced in evidence, and it is shown that the sale was made under it, being embraced in the order which defendant gave for the machinery. It is a well-settled rule, recognized by more than one decision of this court, that where there is a written contract of sale an oral warranty of the thing sold cannot be shown, and when there is a written warranty the vendee cannot show an additional parol warranty. *Mast v. Pearce*, 58 Iowa, 579; *Shepherd v. Gilroy*, 46 Id., 193. The evidence fails to show that the agent who defendant testifies warranted the machinery had authority to make such a contract.

IV. We think the evidence fails to show that the machinery did not comply with the terms of the written warranty. The principal ground of complaint made by defendant is that the engine did not possess sufficient power to draw the separator, tank, etc. But the written contract contains no warranty to the effect that it could do so. Defendant also claims that it did not possess sufficient power to run the separator. The evidence hardly supports this claim.

V. But the defendant is not in a position to enforce the warranty, even should we find that the machinery did not comply therewith. The contract of sale requires him, in case the machinery failed to satisfy the warranty, to give written notice thereof to the plaintiffs, and their agent of whom he made the purchase. This he did not do.

2. ——: conditional warranty: failure to comply.

These views dispose of the case, and lead to the conclusion that plaintiffs are entitled to the relief prayed for in the petition. The judgment of the circuit court is reversed, and the cause remanded for such a decree; or, at the option of plaintiffs, it may be rendered in this court.

REVERSED.

EAST v. PUGH ET AL.

1. **Real Estate**: VENDEE OF INNOCENT PURCHASER TAKES GOOD TITLE. One who, as an innocent purchaser of land for value, has good title against an outstanding equity, may transmit such good title to subsequent purchasers, even though they have notice of such equity. (See authorities cited in opinion.)

2. **Acknowledgment**: LEGALIZING ACT: EFFECT OF. Chapter 160, Laws of 1870, legalizing acknowledgments of conveyances made in other states in accordance with the laws thereof, caused a deed so acknowledged, and recorded before said act became a law by publication, to have the same effect as if it had been properly acknowledged according to the laws of Iowa.

Appeal from Adair Circuit Court.

WEDNESDAY, MARCH 9.

ACTION to foreclose a mortgage. After trial upon the merits, plaintiff's petition was dismissed. He now appeals to this court.

John Hudspeth, Temple & Phelps and *Harry E. Don Carlos,* for appellant.

Gow & Hager, for appellees.

BECK, J.—I. The mortgage in suit was executed and acknowledged March 22, 1879, in the state of Indiana, in conformity to the laws of that state. The mort-

1. REAL es-
tate: vendee
of innocent
purchaser
takes good
title.

gagee, the plaintiff, on the same day and at the same place, conveyed the land to the mortgagor by a warranty deed, executed and acknowledged in the same form and manner as the mortgage, which was given to secure a part of the purchase money for the land. The deed was filed for record March 24, 1870, and the mortgage on the sixteenth day of April of the same year. On the twenty-fourth day of March, 1870, the mortgagor, Pugh, conveyed the land by deed of warranty, for a sufficient consideration to John Taylor; the deed being filed for record the same day.   The defendant Myers acquired title to the land through Taylor and his grantees, by sufficient deeds.   The certificates showing the acknowledgment of the deed and mortgage executed by plaintiff and Pugh, respectively, do not conform with the requirements of the statute then in force in this state.

II.   The controlling question in the case is this: Is the title acquired by defendant Myers paramount to the mortgage in suit, which was not recorded when the deed to Taylor was executed upon which Myers' title is based?   Leaving out of view questions arising upon the defective acknowledgments, we answer the question affirmatively.   Taylor was a purchaser for value, and without notice, constructive or actual, of plaintiff's mortgage.   He therefore acquired a valid title, superior to plaintiff's mortgage.   It is a rule that the holder of a good title clothes his grantee with the same rights, and conveys to him the same title, which he holds himself.   It is not necessary for Myers to show that the grantees intervening between him and Taylor purchased without notice of the mortgage, and paid value for the land. We will not be expected to cite authorities in support of this familiar rule.   See, however, *Nolan v. Grant*, 53 Iowa, 392, cited by plaintiff's counsel; *Chambers v. Hubbard*, 40 Id., 432; and *Ashcraft v. De Armond*, 44 Id., 229.

III.   We will now inquire as to the effect of the defective acknowledgment of the deed and mortgage.   Chapter 160, Acts
2. ACKNOWL-   of the Thirteenth General Assembly, provides that
EDGMENT: all deeds and conveyances of land situated in
legalizing act:
effect of.   this state, which have been acknowledged or proved in another state in accord with the laws thereof, and which have been recorded in this state, are "confirmed and declared effectual and valid in law, to all intents and purposes, as though the said deeds or conveyances so acknowledged or proved and recorded had, prior to being recorded, been acknowledged or proved within this state."   Statutes to the same effect were subsequently enacted.   Chapter 110, Acts

Fourteenth General Assembly. See Miller's Code, (Ed. 1880) §§ 1966–1968, p. 533. Under these statutes the deed of plaintiff to Pugh is to be regarded as having the same effect from the day of its record as it would have had if it had been properly acknowledged. Pugh's title, then, is based upon a valid deed, and the whole world must be regarded as having notice thereof from the time it was filed for record; and Myers, and those under whom he claims, including Porter, were not put upon inquiry, as may have been the case if the law would permit us to regard plaintiff's deed to Pugh as unrecorded because it was not lawfully acknowledged.

We reach the conclusion that Myers' title is superior to the lien of plaintiff's mortgage.

The decree of the circuit court dismissing plaintiff's petition is

AFFIRMED.

THE OTTUMWA, CEDAR FALLS & ST. PAUL R'Y CO. v. MC-
WILLIAMS ET AL.

1. **Specific Performance**: CONTRACT TO CONVEY RIGHT OF WAY: SUF-
FICIENCY OF DESCRIPTION. Plaintiff had surveyed and marked by stakes two lines for its proposed railway across defendant's farm, and the road was afterwards built on one of these lines. Before the build-ing of the road was begun, defendant agreed in writing to convey to plaintiff, by metes and bounds, for its right of way, a strip of ground not less than than fifty feet in width on each side of the center of the track of said railway, over and through the land owned by him " in sections 22 and 28, Tp. 79, R. 13, Poweshiek county, Ia." In an action for specific performance, defendant insisted that the contract was too indef-inite and uncertain, as to the description of the land to be conveyed, to be enforced by an action for specific performance; and especially that the letters and figures " Tp. 79, R. 13, Poweshiek county, Ia.," did not locate the land anywhere. But *held* that this position could not be sus-tained,—" Tp." being universally understood to mean " township," and " R.," " range," and their location being made otherwise definite by naming the county.

2. ——: ——: INSUFFICIENT DESCRIPTION CURED. Even if the de-scription in such case were liable to the objection made, it ought to be

regarded as cured by defendant's putting plaintiff in possession of the land intended to be conveyed.

3. ——: ——: ADEQUACY OF CONSIDERATION. Even though the land taken under said contract, which provided for the necessary width for embankments, excavations, slopes, spoil-banks and borrowing-pits, greatly exceeded in value the money consideration named in the contract, yet, since the benefits to be derived from the construction of the road were named in the contract as a part of the consideration, *held* that a specific performance could not be avoided on the ground of inadequacy of consideration.

4. ——: ——: WAY THROUGH HOMESTEAD: CONTRACT NOT SIGNED BY WIFE. Although part of the land through which defendant agreed to convey the right of way was his homestead, and his wife did not sign the contract, yet, since a right of way is but an easement, (*Chicago & S. W. R'y Co. v. Swinney*, 38 Iowa, 182,) and since the right of way in this case did not destroy the homestead or defeat its occupancy as such, *held* that the homestead character of the premises would not defeat a specific performance.

5. ——: ——: CONTRACT FOR FEE-SIMPLE: DECREE FOR RIGHT OF WAY. In such case, where the contract in one place provided for a deed in fee simple, but the whole object of the contract was to procure a right of way only, *held* that the court properly granted a decree for a right of way deed only.

Appeal from Poweshiek District Court.

WEDNESDAY, MARCH 9.

THIS is an action in equity, in which the plaintiff demands the specific performance of a written contract entered into by the defendant Robert McWilliams, by which he bound himself to convey to the plaintiff the right of way for a railroad over certain land owned by him. There was a decree in the district court for the plaintiff, and defendants appeal.

Thos. A. Cheshire, for appellants.

Hubbard, Clarke & Dawley, for appellee.

ROTHROCK, J.—I. The written contract upon which the action is founded is as follows:
"$120.00.

"In consideration of one dollar in hand paid, and a further consideration of $120.00, to be paid before work is com-
1 SPECIFIC
performance:
contract to
convey right
of way: suf-
ficiency of
description.
menced, and of the location and construction of the Ottumwa, Cedar Falls & St. Paul Railroad, and the benefits to be derived therefrom, I do hereby release to said railroad company the right of way through the land owned by me in sections 22 and 28, Tp. 79, R. 13, Poweshiek county, Ia., together with all necessary width for embankment, excavations, slopes, spoil-banks and borrowing-pits; and I, for myself, and for my heirs, executors and assigns, do hereby covenant and agree to and with said railroad company to convey, by metes and bounds, at any time the said railroad company shall call for the same, by deed in fee-simple, a strip of ground not less than fifty feet in width on each side of the center of the track of said railroad, over and through the above-described land.

"Witness my hand this twentieth day of August, 1883.

[Signed| "ROBERT McWILLIAMS."

The defendants answered the petition by setting up a number of defenses, some of which are not necessary to be considered, for the reason that counsel for appellants, in his argument, confines himself to three grounds upon which he demands a reversal of the decree of the district court.

The first ground is that the contract is too indefinite and uncertain to be enforced by an action for specific performance. It is true, the agreement does not describe the land to be conveyed by metes and bounds. But the evidence shows that the railroad was not constructed when the contract was entered into. The construction of the road had not then been commenced, but the plaintiff had surveyed two lines across the defendants' land, and staked out the center of the lines so surveyed. These lines were nearly over the same ground, being not more than fifteen or twenty feet apart. The road was afterwards constructed over the land upon one of these lines. It became necessary to make a cut for part of the way through defendant's land, and at

that point the plaintiff appropriated more than one hundred
feet in width.   It was doubtless to provide for this very con-
tingency that the contract was not made definite in this
respect.   Contracts are to be construed in the light of the
facts surrounding the transaction, and known to the parties.
The defendants knew, by the surveys and stakes, where the
road was to be constructed; and, not knowing the exact
width required, they contracted for so much as would be
necessary for a right of way.

We do not understand, however, that counsel makes a
specific claim that the contract was too uncertain in the
description of the quantity of lands by metes and bounds.
His contention, in the main, is that the description of the land
owned by defendants, and through which the road was constructed, was too indefinite and uncertain, as to section,
township and range, to authorize a decree for specific performance.   He claims that the description, "sections 22 and
28, Tp. 79, R. 13, Poweshiek county, Iowa," does not
describe any land, because "$Tp.$ 79, $R.$ 13," does not locate the
land anywhere.   It appears to us that there is no uncertainty
or indefiniteness in these contractions of words.   They are
in almost universal use in this state in describing lands, and
everybody understands that they mean "township" and
"range."   It is true, the contract does not state whether the
range is east or west, but that was wholly unnecessary, as
the land was described as in Poweshiek county, and the
courts of this state take judicial notice that all the land in
that county is in range west.   Besides, the land is described
as owned by the defendant Robert McWilliams, and the
plaintiff took possession of the very land described and
intended by the parties as the right of way for the railroad.
It appears to us that, if we were to hold this description to
be too vague, indefinite and uncertain to authorize a decree
for specific performance, we would be without the support
of any adjudged case.   On the other hand, there are many
cases where descriptions of land, even more vague than this

one, have been sustained. See *Pursley v. Hayes*, 22 Iowa, 11;
Beal v. Blair, 33 Id., 318; *Barlow v. Chicago, R. I. & P. R'y
Co.*, 29 Id., 276; *Spangler v. Danforth*, 65 Ill., 153; *Mead
v. Parker*, 115 Mass., 413; *Hurley v. Brown*, 98 Id., 545.

But, even if the description of the land in the case at bar
should be thought liable to the objection under consideration,

2 ——: ——:
insufficient
description
cured.

the defective description ought to be regarded as
cured by the fact that the defendant put the
plaintiff in possession of the land intended to be
conveyed.

II. Next it is urged that the consideration named in the
contract is so inadequate that to compel a specific perform-

3. ——: ——:
adequacy of
consideration.

ance would be inequitable and unconscionable.
It is true, the evidence shows that the number
of acres taken and appropriated by the plaintiff far exceed
in value the sum agreed to be paid. But the defendant
thought, when he made his contract, that "the location and
construction of the road, and the benefits to be derived therefrom," would be of value to him, and these facts are recited
in the contract as part of the consideration; and the record
shows that he now has a railroad station within two miles of
of his home, and that, before the plaintiff's railroad was constructed, the nearest station was nine miles and a half away.
It is notorious that many of the railroads in this state were
constructed, in part, at least, by donations of right of way
and money by subscription, as well as by taxation. There
is nothing in the facts of this case to cause a court of equity
to hesitate to decree a specific performance, as that the contract is inequitable, unconscionable, or founded in fraud.

III. One forty acre tract through which the railroad is
constructed is the homestead of the defendants. The defend-

4. ——: ——:
way through
homestead:
contract not
signed by
wife.

ant Margaret McWilliams did not sign the contract. She is the wife of Robert McWilliams,
and she claims that the contract is void because
it is an obligation to convey a part of the homestead in fee-simple, and she did not concur in or sign the con-

tract. It is provided by section 1990 of the Code that a conveyance or incumbrance of the homestead is of no validity, unless the husband and wife concur in and sign the same joint instrument. But it was held in the case of *Chicago, & S. W. R'y Co. v. Swinney*, 38 Iowa, 182, that the husband can convey a right of way over the homestead without the concurrence and signature of his wife to the deed, when such conveyance will not defeat the substantial enjoyment of the homestead as such. It is insisted, however, that in the case at bar the substantial enjoyment of the homestead is defeated because the railroad is in a deep cut, through the homestead forty acres, and is so near to the dwelling house as to be a great annoyance and damage, and the land actually taken by plaintiff is greatly in excess of 100 feet in width; and other inconveniences and damages are enumerated as resulting from the construction and operation of the road. In the cited case it is said that " the right of way is but an easement, and does not pass the title;" and that, "if the homestead was a single lot, and the right of way occupied it all, so as to destroy the homestead, or defeat its occupancy, the case would be very different." In the case at bar, the defendants still occupy and possess their homestead. It is true, their home would perhaps be more desirable if the railroad had been built further away from the house. The edge of the railroad cut is about 95 feet, and the track about 144 feet, from the dwelling house. It ought not to be claimed that this is either a destruction of the homestead, or defeats its occupancy as such.

The contract recites that the land to be conveyed is for a right of way for a railroad. It also provides that the right

5. ——: ——:
contract for
fee-simple: of way is to be conveyed by deed in fee-simple.
decree for
right of way. The learned judge before whom the case was tried granted a decree for a right of way deed, and not a deed in fee-simple. This appears to be in accord with the case of *Barlow v. Chicago, R. I. & P. R'y Co., supra*. The purposes for which the land was to be used, and

the object of the plaintiff in securing the contract, was to
procure a right of way, and not a fee-simple title to the
land.

The decree of the court below is

AFFIRMED.

AMISH ET AL. v. GELNAUS ET AL.

1. **Religious Society:** ROMAN CATHOLIC CONGREGATION: SPECIAL
FUND FOR BUILDING CHURCH: TITLE TO. If it be conceded that, under
the laws and rules of the Roman Catholic church, the bishop of the diocese, and the priest of the parish under the direction of the bishop, are
invested with the absolute control of the general funds and property of
the church, yet a special fund raised by a congregation for the purpose of
building a church does not belong to the bishop and priest, but to the congregation itself. And although such fund was placed in the hands of the
priest for safe keeping, and the bishop afterwards joined the congregation, without its consent, to the congregation and parish at R.,
and requested the property to be delivered to the priest at R., and
ordered the priest to go to R., which he did, and a part of the congregation went also, but a majority refused to go, and continued to worship,
but without a priest, at the old place, *held* that the money so raised still
belonged to the congregation, and that trustees appointed by the congregation were entitled to recover it from trustees, previously named by
the congregation, to whom it had been committed by the priest when
he left the congregation.

Appeal from Johnson District Court.

WEDNESDAY, MARCH 9.

THE plaintiffs claim that they are members of the congregation of St. Stanislaus, a parish or congregation of the
Roman Catholic faith, of Liberty township, Johnson county,
and that in February, 1883, at a meeting of said congregation, they were appointed trustees to receive from defendants
a certain trust fund belonging to said congregation; that
defendants had received said trust fund as former trustees of
said congregation, but had been removed from their trust for
good and sufficient reasons, and the plaintiffs appointed

trustees in their stead.   There was a trial by the court without
a jury, and judgment was rendered for the plaintiffs.
Defendants appeal.

Gannon & McQuirk and *Remley & Remley*, for appellants.

S. H. Fairall and *Boal & Jackson*, for appellees.

ROTHROCK, J.—I.   The learned judge of the district court
before whom the case was tried reduced his findings of fact
and conclusions of law to writing.   They are as follows:

"(1) That prior to the year 1880 there existed in Liberty
township, Johnson county, Iowa, a parish or congregation of
the Roman Catholic faith, known as the congregation of St.
Stanislaus, and that said congregation still exists.

"(2) That, about the years 1880–81, said congregation
determined to erect a new church building on the site of
the old one,—said old one having gone into decay to some
extent; and for that purpose said congregation raised by subscription and fairs about $3,000.

"(3) That at said date said congregation had a priest duly
set over them, and that plaintiffs Adam Amish, Gregory
Gruss and Nicholas Doll were, in 1880, and have been ever
since, members of said congregation of St. Stanislaus; that
about 1881, in the fall, there was held a meeting of said congregation, at which nearly all the congregation were present;
that the defendants, Benedict Gelhaus, Rochus Knebel and
Joseph Schumm, were members of said congregation at that
date; that they were then selected by said congregation as a
committee to take charge of the moneys raised to build said
church.

"(4) That after the money had been so raised by fairs, etc.,
held by said congregation, the bishop ordered the congregation not to build said church at St. Stanislaus, and ordered the
congregation to celebrate or attend mass at Riverside, four
or five miles distant; that about $825 of said money was

placed in the hands of said committee, and held by said committee; that no church building was erected, as contemplated,
with said moneys; that they were not used for any purpose;
that $567.58 of said moneys still remain in the hands of
said committee, as appointed by said congregation in 1881,
or in the hands and under the control of Rochus Knebel and
B. Gelhaus; that since that time Joseph Schumm, one of
said committee, left Iowa, and located in Nebraska, where he
now resides; that the other members of said committee, viz.,
Rochus Knebel and Benedict Gelhaus, went to Riverside to
attend church, and left the congregation of St. Stanislaus,
and the priest of St. Stanislaus also went there,—that is, to
Riverside; that he was ordered there by the bishop of the
diocese in which Riverside and St. Stanislaus are situated.

"(5) That about February 1, 1883, said congregation of
St. Stanislaus called a meeting of its members, and a meeting was held, at which a majority of its members were present; that, at said meeting then held, plaintiffs were
appointed and chosen as a committee to receive and demand
said money from defendants; that they subsequently, and
before the bringing of this suit, demanded of said first committee said money, which was refused; that said congregation also, at said meeting, authorized plaintiffs to sue, if
necessary, therefor.

"(6) That said St. Stanislaus congregation continued to
worship at their church at St. Stanislaus after the bishop
ordered them to Riverside, and still worship there; that the
priest was ordered to Riverside by the bishop, and they have
not had a priest since.

"(7) That in February, 1882, through Vicar-general H.
Cosgrove, the bishop of the Roman Catholic Church
expressed a desire that St. Stanislaus congregation attend
mass at Riverside, and join the Riverside congregation;
that all the articles belonging to St. Stanislaus, whatever
they might be, be given into the custody of Father Brom-
menschenkel, the priest at Riverside; that the bishop, without

the consent of the St. Stanislaus congregation and parish,
joined St. Stanislaus congregation with the Riverside parish,
making the two one, and calling it Riverside parish.

" (8) That, although requested to do so, the plaintiffs
refused to join the Riverside congregation and worship there;
but the majority of the St. Stanislaus congregation refused to go
to Riverside; that said St. Stanislaus congregation continued,
and still continues, to worship at the St. Stanislaus church—
that is, to hold prayer meetings, etc.,—but were without a
priest, and were deprived of mass, unless they went to Riverside; that the church property at St. Stanislaus consisted
of the church, together with forty acres of land, on which was
the church and cemetery of St. Stanislaus congregation,
where they have always buried and still bury their dead; that
the title to said property is in the bishop of the Roman
Catholic Church of the diocese, and does not belong to the
congregation."

The court found the following conclusions of law: "(1)
The money aforesaid was held by said first committee in trust
for said congregation, and never was the property of the Roman
Catholic Church, and was never under the control of the
bishop or priest. (2) The second committee, the plaintiffs
herein, are duly authorized and lawfully entitled to recover
the same from said first committee, the defendants, or from
Rochus Knebel and B. Gelhaus, the members of said committee served in this action."

Counsel for appellants attack the findings of fact as not
supported by the evidence. They also insist that the court
erred in rulings upon the admission and exclusion of evidence.
In our opinion, the judgment should be affirmed upon the conceded facts in the case, regardless of the alleged errors. Those
conceded, or rather undisputed, facts are as follows: ·

(1) The money in dispute is the residue of a fund raised
for the special purpose of building a church at St. Stanislaus.

(2) When the priest who officiated at that church was
removed to Riverside, he called a meeting of the St. Stan-

islaus congregation, and requested the meeting to name a committee of three of the congregation, to take charge of the fund. The defendants were selected as such a committee. It ought to be stated, perhaps, that the priest testified on the trial that he merely requested the congregation to give him the names of three persons in whom they had confidence, and, the names being given, he appointed them. All of the other evidence in the case tends to show that the appointment was made by the congregation. But, even if the formal appointment was made by the priest after the defendants were selected by the congregation, the fact that the priest requested the congregation to name the committee was a recognition of the right of the congregation to have the money remain at St. Stanislaus, and not to be taken elsewhere. The priest, who was then in possession of the money, paid it over to the committee.

(3) After the removal of the priest to Riverside, two of the committee-men attended service at that place, and the other removed from the state.

(4) A number of families refused to assume church relations at Riverside or elsewhere. They remained as a voluntary association of persons, and, until within a short time before the trial in the court below, they assembled together for the purpose of religious worship.

(5) The congregation, or, rather, those that remained, held a meeting about February 1, 1883, and appointed the plaintiffs as a committee to receive and demand the money in question from the defendants.

Counsel for appellants insist that, under the laws and rules of the Roman Catholic Church, the bishop of the diocese, and the priest of the parish under the direction of the bishop, are invested with the absolute control of the funds and the property of the church, and the laity have no right to interfere with such control. If this fund had been raised for the general purposes of the church, and paid to the priest without any obligation upon him to apply it to a specific

purpose, the position of counsel might be correct.   But it is
conceded that the money was raised for a special purpose.   This
being so, it passed into the hands of the priest as a trust
· fund.   It did not vest absolutely in either bishop or priest
to be disposed of as they might think for the best interest
of the church.   The priest doubtless recognized this fact
when he ·left the money at St. Stanislaus in the hands of
the defendants.   In regard to the action of the congregation
in appointing the plaintiffs trustees instead of the defendants
it is sufficient to say that the defendants were liable at any
time to be removed.   They did not hold their trust in per-
petuity.   They were the mere agents of the congregation,
liable to be discharged at any time by the power that
appointed them, and, when their successors were appointed,
they should·have surrendered the funds in their hands to the
plaintiffs.

AFFIRMED.

KOEVENIG v. SCHMITZ ET AL.

1. **Mortgage**: PRIORITY: EQUAL EQUITIES: SIMULTANEOUS DELIVERY
   AND FILING: PAYMENT PRO RATA.   S. bought land of W. for $600,
   paying $300 in cash, and agreeing to secure the residue by a note and
   mortgage on the property.   But he borrowed of T. the $300 with
   which to make the cash payment, and agreed to secure T. by a mortgage on the property.   Both mortgages were executed on the day of the
   sale, but neither was delivered until some days afterwards, when S. took
   them to the recorder's office and delivered them to the recorder to be
   recorded.   He first handed the recorder the mortgage to T., and immediately thereafter the mortgage to W., intending to give priority to the
   one so first delivered, but not expressing any such intention, and the
   recorder marked them as filed at the same time.   In the mortgage to
   W. the land was described as being in the wrong county.   In an action
   to foreclose, *held*—

   (1) That S.'s secret intention to give priority to the mortgage to
   T. could not have that effect.

   (2) That the mere act of handing one mortgage to the recorder an
   instant before the other did not give it priority.

   (3) That the fact that W. waived his vendor's lien by taking the

71
86

mortgage, while T. had no prior interest in the property, did not give to W.'s mortgage any superiority in equity.

(4) That the clerical error in the description of the land in W.'s mortgage did not render it inferior in equity to the other, since there was no question of notice in the case.

(5) That both mortgages were entitled to be paid *pro rata* out of the proceeds of the sale of the land.

Appeal from Winneshiek District Court.

WEDNESDAY, MARCH 9.

THE controversy in this case is between plaintiff and the defendants Dornewick and Theodore Wiltgen. The material facts of the case are as follows: On the thirteenth of April, 1876, the defendant J. J. Schmitz bought of the Wiltgens the undivided one-third of three lots in the town of Ossian, in Winneshiek county, for the consideration of $600, one-half of which he paid in cash, and for the balance he gave his promissory note, and to secure the same gave a mortgage on the property. The Wiltgens purchased the property from one Hennessy, who, by their direction, conveyed to Schmitz. Schmitz borrowed the money with which to make the cash payment from Theodore Wictor. This loan was made on the agreement that it should be secured by mortgage on the property. Schmitz gave his note for the amount. He also executed a mortgage on the property securing the same. This note and mortgage were executed on the same day on which he gave the note and mortgage to the Wiltgens, viz., the thirteenth of April, 1876. Neither of the mortgages was delivered, however, until the third of May following. On that day Schmitz took the two instruments to the county recorder's office, and delivered them to the recorder to be recorded. He testified that he intended that the Wictor mortgage should have priority, and that he delivered it first. It was first recorded, but the certificates of the recorder indorsed on the instruments show that they were filed for record at the same time. By a mistake of the scrivener who drew the Wiltgen mortgage, the real estate was described as being situated in Howard county. Plaintiff is the owner of the Wictor note and mortgage, and she brought this action for the enforcement of the same. The question of controversy is as to which of the mortgages is the superior lien on the premises. The district court adjudged that defendants' mortgage was prior to plaintiff's. Plaintiff appeals.

F. S. Burling, for appellant.

M. J. Carter, for appellees.

REED, J.—The mortgages become effective on delivery, and delivery was accomplished when Schmitz delivered them to the recorder. It is immaterial, therefore, which was first executed. Neither of the mortgagees, when he agreed to accept a mortgage on the property as security for his debt, knew, or had any notice, of the contract between Schmitz and the other. It is therefore not material which of the contracts was first entered into. If one of the mortgages is superior to the other, it must be either because there existed when it was executed some equity in favor of the party to whom it was given which has the effect to give it superiority, or because priority was given to it by the acts of the parties·

I. Is priority given to either by any equity existing at the time of their execution? It is contended that, as defendants surrendered their vendor's lien on the property for the unpaid purchase money when they accepted their mortgage, and as Wictor had no prior interest or right in the property, and surrendered nothing when he accepted the mortgage, they should be given priority over him. It is true, perhaps, that defendants, if they had not accepted the mortgage, would have had an equitable lien on the property for the unpaid purchase money, and that they waived that lien by accepting it. The mortgage created a new and distinct lien on the property. It did not have the effect to continue or preserve the vendor's lien, but that lien ceased when the parties accepted the mortgage. The vendor's lien arises by implication of law. But a mortgage lien is created and measured by the contract of the parties. When a party accepts a mortgage, he acquires the rights and interest simply which accrue under the contract. The law neither adds to nor detracts from them. The defendants have no advantage, then, from the fact that their mortgage was given to secure the purchase money.

II. Was priority given to either by the acts of the parties? When the mortgagees agreed to accept a mortgage on the property, each expected, no doubt, that he would receive a first mortgage. But neither of them contracted expressly for a first mortgage. What is relied on as creating priority in favor of plaintiff's mortgage are the acts and purposes of Schmitz at the time of delivery. He claims to have first delivered that mortgage to the recorder, and that he did that for the purpose of giving it priority over the other. What he did do, as we are satisfied by the evidence, was to take the instruments to the recorder's office, and there first hand to the recorder the mortgage to Wictor, and immediately thereafter the one to defendants. They were both delivered by substantially the same act. The question as to which has priority cannot be affected by the fact that one instrument was handed over to the officer an instant before the other was passed to him. Neither is the intention with which the act was done important. Schmitz could have given priority to the one by an expression to that effect in the instruments, and perhaps he could have accomplished the same result by an express declaration at the time of delivery. But, clearly, he could not, by his mere secret intention, give character and effect to the instruments.

III. A claim was made by plaintiff that Schmitz subsequently sold his interest in the property to defendants, the Wiltgens, and that they agreed, as part of the consideration of the purchase, that they would pay her note. But this claim is not established by the evidence. The mistake in the mortgage to defendants, as to the county in which the property is situated, does not affect the rights of the parties. There is no question as to what property was intended. As between the mortgagor and morgagee, it is a valid mortgage on the property in question.

If plaintiff had been a subsequent mortgagee, a question might have arisen as to whether the record of defendants' mortgage imparted constructive notice to her. But she was not a subsequent mortgagee. Her rights and interests accrued at the same instant as those of defendants. The mortgages, as we hold, were delivered at the same time, and the rights of the parties could not be affected by any question of notice.

As the liens created by the mortgages accrued at the same instant, neither of the parties has any rights in the property superior to those of the other, and equity will dispose of it for the benefit of both.

So much of the judgment of the district court as adjudges that the debt due the defendants shall be first satisfied out of the proceeds of the property will be reversed, and a judgment will be entered directing the application of such proceeds *pro rata* to the satisfaction of the debts due plaintiff and defendants.

The judgment will be entered either in this or the district court, as the parties may elect.

REVERSED.

SCOTT v. LASELL ET AL.

1. **Highway:** ESTABLISHMENT: ALLOWANCE OF DAMAGES: APPEAL: WHEN TRIABLE. Where a claimant of damages caused by the establishment of a highway gives notice, twenty-one days prior to the next term of the circuit court, of an appeal from the allowance made by the supervisors, the appeal is triable at that term, and he cannot delay such trial by neglecting to file notice of the appeal in the auditor's office for so long a time that the auditor, taking the ten days allowed him by statute to prepare a transcript, does not get it on file in the clerk's office until after the opening of the term.

2. ——: ——: ——: ——: PAYMENT OF FILING FEE. In such case, the appellant must pay to the clerk the fee for filing the transcript and docketing the case, although the costs of the appeal must, in the end, be paid by the petitioner for the road, or by the county. (Code, § 963.)

3. ——: ——: ——: ——: FAILURE TO HAVE CASE DOCKETED. Such an appeal is a "civil case" within the meaning of a rule of practice which provides that in appeals from justices' courts, or other inferior tribunals, in civil cases, if the appellant fails to pay the filing fee and to have the appeal docketed by noon of the first day of the term, the appellee may pay the fee and have it docketed, and may thereupon have the judgment below affirmed.

4. ——: ——: ——: ——: WAIVER OF FILING FEE. In such case, where the appellee's right to an affirmance had already accrued, it was of no avail to show that appellant caused the transcript to be filed on the third day of the term, and that the clerk then waived the payment of the filing fee.

Appeal from Shelby Circuit Court.

WEDNESDAY, MARCH 9.

THE plaintiff is a claimant of damages caused by the establishment of a highway through his land. The board of supervisors allowed him $260. From the order he appealed to the circuit court, but did not pay the filing fee by noon of the first day of the next succeeding term, and, on motion of the defendant, the court affirmed the order of allowance, and from that ruling the plaintiff appeals.

Smith & Cullison, for appellant.

Beard & Myerly, for appellees.

ADAMS, CH. J.—The rule of practice under which the motion was sustained is in these words: "In appeals from justices' courts or other inferior tribunals, in civil cases, the appellant shall cause the case to be docketed, and the docketing and filing fee to be paid by noon of the first day of the term to which the case is returnable, and, in case of his failure so to do, the appellee may pay such filing fee, and have the case docketed, and will thereupon be entitled to have the judgment below affirmed, or to have the case set down for trial on its merits, as he may elect."

I. The notice of appeal in this case, it appears, was served on the twenty-ninth day of September, 1885. The next term of court commenced October 20, 1885. The first question presented is as to whether the case was returnable, within the meaning of the rule, to that term. The plaintiff insists that it was not. There does not appear to be any express provision as to the time which should elapse between the service of notice of appeal and the first day of the term at which the case should be deemed triable. But, following such analogies as we have, we think it should be at least ten days. In this case the time was twenty-one days. Notice of appeal, however, was not filed in the auditor's office until October 10th, and by statute he had ten days after that in which to make out and file in the clerk's office a transcript. The last day of the time within which he should file the transcript was the first day of the term, and the appellant's position is that, where the transcript is not due from the auditor, and is not in fact filed, as in this case, until after the commencement of the term, the case could not be deemed triable at that term. But, in our opinion, the appellant's position cannot be sustained. The notice of appeal might have been filed with the auditor several days sooner than it was. The appellees, when they were served with notice of appeal, were bound to assume that the case would be ready for trial at the next term, and govern themselves accordingly. They ought not to be affected by the appellant's neglect. If his position were correct, he would have the power to post-

1. HIGHWAY: establish-
ment: allow-
ance of dam-
ages: appeal:
when triable.

Scott v. Lasell et al.

pone the trial of the case indefinitely, and the appellees
would be obliged to hold themselves in readiness in the
meantime. Having served the notice of appeal in time for
trial at the next term, it was the duty of the appellant to
file the notice with the auditor in time to allow a transcript
to be filed for that term.

II. It is said, however, that the court erred in affirming
the order of allowance for want of payment of the filing fee,

2. ——: ——: because the appellant in such proceedings is not
——: ——: chargeable with the costs of an appeal. It is
payment of
filing fee. true that the statute provides that the cost occasioned by an appeal in such proceedings must be paid by
the petitioner for the highway of the county. Code, § 963.
But neither the petitioner nor county can be made to pay
the cost until the appeal has been determined, and the cost
has been adjudged. The clerk in the meantime is, we think,
entitled to be paid. We think that the filing fee should be
advanced by the appellant, and that it is enough for him that,
under the statute, he is entitled to be reimbursed.

III. Another position taken by the appellant is that the
rule of practice is not applicable, because the board of

3. ——: ——: supervisors, from whose order of allowance an
——: ——: appeal was taken, is not a tribunal, and because
failure to
have case
docketed. the proceedings in which the appeal was taken
cannot properly be denominated a "civil case," within the
meaning of the rule. But the order of allowance was made
in the exercise of a judicial function, and it appears to us
that the board of supervisors, in exercising such function,
may properly enough be called a "tribunal." We think,
also, that the proceedings, though of a special character, are
a civil case, within the meaning of the rule.

IV. Finally, it is said that the evidence shows that the
payment of the filing fee was waived. The plaintiff's attor-

4. ——: ——: ney filed an affidavit showing that, when he filed
——: ——: the transcript on the third day of the term, he
waiver of fil-
ing fee. told the clerk to docket the case, and he would

pay the filing fee, and that the clerk said, "all right." But the appellees' right to an affirmance had already accrued, and they were not under obligation to watch the case longer.

We think that the motion for an affirmance was properly sustained.

AFFIRMED.

JUDGE v. KRIBS ET AL.

THE SAME v. KOHL ET AL.

THE SAME v. HERRITY ET AL.

THE SAME v. CHRISTENSEN.

71
d108

71
115

1. **Nuisance:** INTOXICATING LIQUORS: INJUNCTION: REFORMATION BEFORE HEARING. Where it appeared from the evidence that defendants had been engaged in selling intoxicating liquors contrary to law, and had kept and maintained buildings for that purpose, thus creating and maintaining nuisances, *held* that temporary injunctions should have been granted, notwithstanding defendants testified that, after notice of the hearing for the allowance of temporary injunctions had been served on them, they had reformed and quit the business. (See opinion for authorities cited.)

Appeals from Clinton Circuit Court.

WEDNESDAY, MARCH 9.

ACTION in equity to restrain nuisances caused by the selling and keeping for sale of intoxicating liquors: Temporary injunctions were asked, which were denied, and the plaintiff appeals.

Henry Rickel, for appellant.

Ellis & McCoy, A. Howat and *W. C. Grohe,* for appellees.

SEEVERS, J.—The petitions are substantially alike, and state that the several defendants were engaged in using, keeping and maintaining, and are intending to use, keep and

maintain, certain described premises, situate in Clinton
county, for the purpose of unlawfully selling as a beverage
therein certain intoxicating liquors, the sale of which as a
beverage is prohibited by law;   *   *   *   and
that the several defendants are now engaged in unlawfully
selling, and keeping with intent to sell, such intoxicating
liquors upon said premises, thereby creating and continuing
a public and common nuisance.   The relief asked is that a
preliminary injunction issue restraining the defendants from
keeping and maintaining the nuisance, and that the same, at
the final hearing, be made perpetual, and the nuisance
abated, as provided by law.   The defendants filed answers,
and denied each and every allegation in the petition.

I.   The only question to be determined is whether the
circuit court erred in refusing to grant temporary injunctions restraining the nuisances until the final hearing.   We
are required to examine the evidence and determine such
question as if the application had been made to this court in
the first instance.   We have examined the evidence in each
case.   It is brief, readily understood, and it sufficiently
appears that, prior to the day fixed for hearing the application for a temporary injunction, the defendants had been
engaged in selling, in a place maintained for that purpose,
intoxicating liquors as a beverage, contrary to law, and
therefore were engaged in maintaining nuisances as provided
by statute.   The evidence is so clear, direct and certain as
to leave no room for reasonable doubt.   It is not deemed
necessary to set out the evidence, or state the reasons for the
conclusions reached.

II.   The several defendants were witnesses in their own
behalf, and severally testified, with more or less directness,
that they, after notice of the hearing for the allowance of a
temporary injunction was served on them, had quit the business, and, as one of them stated, he had "reformed."   In all
instances, we believe, such reformation occurred a day or
two before the hearing.   It is upon this ground, we pre-

same, that the court refused to grant an injunction. If the nuisance is abated, there is nothing to enjoin, nor would the defendants be in any respect prejudiced if one was granted. But where it is ascertained that a person has violated the rights of another, or of the public, by erecting and maintaining a nuisance, does it necessarily follow, because he asserts that the nuisance has been abated, that a temporary injunction cannot issue? Suppose there is a small-pox hospital established and maintained in the populous part of a city, and that it is furnished with all the appliances used for properly and judiciously taking care of the patients, and that an application is made to enjoin such use, and abate the nuisance; and, upon the hearing for an injunction, the proprietor should testify that he had quit the business, and removed the patients a day or two prior to the hearing,— would the court be bound for this reason to refuse the injunction? We think not, but, on the contrary, the court, in its discretion, could restrain the party from so using the building in the future. So here it appears from the evidence that the defendants were engaged in selling intoxicating liquors contrary to law, and kept and maintained a building for that purpose. Upon being advised that an effort was about to be made to vindicate the law, they suddenly reformed and quit the business.

It appears to us that there is great reason to suppose such a reformation is not in good faith. There is also reason to believe that it was adopted as a temporary expedient. The evidence, we think, tends to so show, or, if not, this court does not feel disposed to accept the evidence of the defendants that they have ceased the unlawful sale of intoxicating liquors as conclusive evidence of such fact. Much less do we feel disposed to do so as to the future. Having been engaged in violating the law, it is not by any means certain that they will not do so in the future. The disposition to do so clearly appears, and there are heavy doubts as to the good faith of the reformation.

In principle, the applicability of the following adjudged cases cannot, we think, be questioned: *Goodyear v. Berry*, 2 Bond, 189; *Rumford Chemical Works v. Vice*, 14 Blatchf, 179; *Jenkins v. Greenwald*, 2 Fish. Pat. Cas., 37; *White v. Heath*, 10 Fed. Rep., 291. In all of these cases injunctions were asked restraining the use of a patented article, and the defendants in each case claimed that they had ceased to do so, and therefore an injunction should not issue. But it was held that this fact was immaterial, and that the plaintiff "was not obliged to rest its interest on the mere assertion of the defendant (made under oath) that he would not repeat the act of infringement."

We therefore think the circuit court erred in refusing to grant a temporary injunction, and the causes will be remanded, with directions to the court below to grant such injunctions.

REVERSED.

JUDGE v. ARLEN ET AL.

THE SAME v. CARSTENSEN ET AL.

THE SAME v. FEDDERSON ET AL.

1. **Nuisance:** INTOXICATING LIQUORS: ABATEMENT: VESTED RIGHTS: REMOVAL OF CAUSES TO FEDERAL COURTS. Plaintiff sought to abate as nuisances certain places kept for the unlawful sale of intoxicating liquors. Defendants, by proper petitions, sought to have the causes removed to the federal courts on the ground that, long prior to the passage of the statute under the provisions of which the actions were brought, they had purchased the real estate described in the petitions for the purpose of selling beer thereon, and had procured fixtures and furniture for said business, and placed them on the real estate, and that the same were not fitted for any other business, and would be rendered practically valueless if they should be enjoined from carrying on said business, and thus they would be deprived of their property without compensation and without due process of law. *Held* that no federal question was involved, and that it was error to grant the petitions for removal. (*McLane v. Leicht*, 69 Iowa, 401, followed.)

2. **Removal to Federal Courts:** APPEAL: BETTER PRACTICE. Where the petition for the removal of a cause to the federal courts has been

granted, and the plaintiff desires to contest the legality of such removal, it is the better practice to move in the federal court to have the case remanded, rather than to appeal to this court, since the decisions of the state courts in such cases are not binding on the federal court.

Appeal from Clinton Circuit Court.

WEDNESDAY, MARCH 9. ·

ACTION IN EQUITY. The relief asked was denied, and the plaintiff appeals.

Henry Rickel, for appellant.

Ellis & McCoy, W. C. Grohe and *A. Howat*, for appellees.

SEEVERS, J.—The petitions in the above-named cases are substantially alike, and state that the defendants are engaged

1. NUISANCE: intoxicating liquors: abatement : vested rights; removal of causes to federal courts.

in selling, keeping and maintaining a place for the sale of intoxicating liquors, thereby creating a nuisance; and the relief asked is that the nuisance be enjoined and abated. The defendants severally answered the petitions, denied the allegations thereof, and asked that the causes be removed to the federal court upon the ground that a federal question was involved. A proper and sufficient petition was filed asking such removal, in which the federal question was, in substance, stated to be that, long prior to the passage of the statute under the provisions of which the action was brought, the defendant had purchased the real estate described in the petition for the purpose of selling beer thereon; and procured fixtures and furniture for such business, and placed them on the real estate; and that the same were not fitted for any other business, and would be rendered practically valueless if they should be enjoined from carrying on said business, in which they had been lawfully engaged for many years. We understand the federal question stated in the petition to be that, if the statute is enforced, as the plaintiff claims it should be, the effect will be to deprive the defendants

of their property without compensation and due process of
law, and therefore the statute conflicts with the constitution
of the United States. The application for the injunction
was made to the judge of the circuit court in vacation, and,
upon filing the petition for removal, he held that a federal
question was involved, and refused to proceed any further
with the hearing. In so holding we are of the opinion that
he erred.

It is to be regretted that the state courts are called upon
to determine questions in relation to the removal of causes
to the federal courts. Such decisions are not
binding on the federal courts, and may be reviewed therein; and, as the supreme court
of the United States is of necessity the court of last
resort in such cases, to prevent unseemly conflicts of
jurisdiction, the state courts must regard the decision of the
federal court as to such questions as final and conclusive on
them. It would therefore seem to be the better practice,
when a petition for removal is presented to the state court,
and a decision is made, or if the court entertains the petition, but refuses to proceed and try the case, to remove the
record to the federal court, and move to remand before
appealing to this court. But, as this course has not been
adopted, it becomes our duty to determine whether the judge
or court below erred in holding that a federal question
was involved. To enable us to do this, it is necessary to look
into the petition for removal. This we think we are authorized to do, and that such is our duty.

The question presented by the record before us is not a
new one, and we understand it to have been determined in
McLane v. Leicht, 69 Iowa, 401, adversely to the holding
below. It is not deemed necessary to add anything to what
is said in that case. Counsel for the appellees cite and rely
on *State v. Walruff*, 26 Fed. Rep., 178. The facts in that
case are materially different, and the decision, we think, is
clearly distinguishable.   REVERSED.

2. REMOVAL to federal courts: appeal: better practice.

CLARK V. RALLS ET AL.

1. **Practice on Appeal**: ERROR WITHOUT PREJUDICE. Where on account of certain special findings of the jury, which could not have been the result of errors in the admission of evidence or in the instructions, the judgment appealed from could not lawfully have been different, *held* that a reversal could not be had on account of such errors.

2. **Practice**: SPECIAL INTERROGATORIES: PRIOR SUBMISSION TO ADVERSE COUNSEL. The requirement of § 2808 of the Code, that before special interrogatories shall be submitted to the jury they must be submitted to the counsel of the adverse party, does not apply to special interrogatories submitted to the jury on the court's own motion. BECK, J., dissenting.

Appeal from Poweshiek Circuit Court,

WEDNESDAY, MARCH 9.

THIS is an action to recover damages for alleged false and fraudulent representations as to the character of a stream of water, and its capacity for water-power, whereon was situated a mill purchased by the plaintiff from the defendants, the purchase having been made on the faith of said representations. There was a trial to a jury, and a verdict and judgment for the defendants. Plaintiff appeals.

Caswell & Meeker, for appellant.

Brown & Carney, for appellees.

ROTHROCK, J.—This is the third appeal in this case. See 50 Iowa, 275; 58 Id., 201. Upon the first submission of the present appeal an opinion was filed reversing the judgment. A petition for rehearing was presented, and a rehearing was granted, and the cause has again been argued and submitted.

It is unnecessary to set out the facts of the case,—they fully appear in the opinions on the former appeals; and we may say, further, that, in view of the investigation this court has made of the case in all these appeals and on this rehearing, we think it unnecessary to elaborate the case further

than to briefly announce our views, and the conclusion which
we have reached.

The appellant claims a reversal upon rulings of the court
upon the admission and exclusion of evidence, and for alleged
errors in the instructions of the court to the
jury. We now think that the case must be
affirmed by reason of certain special findings of
the jury which could not have been the result of any of the
alleged errors. These special findings are as follows: "*Interrogatory*. Did Willits himself make any false and fraudulent representations to the Clarks, or either of them, in
reference to the water-power of the mill?" Answer by the
jury: "No." "*Int*. 2. Before the sale was completed, did
Willits direct Ralls to negotiate for the sale, and include, in
the trade with the Clarks, Willits' share of the mill property
in question?" Answer by the jury: "No." "*Int*. 3. Before
such directions by Willits, had Ralls, by himself, or by Howe, as
his agent, made false and fraudulent representations, as alleged,
to the Clarks, or either of them, as to the capacity or permanency
of the water power?" Answer by the jury: "No." "*Int*.
4. Did Ralls, by himself, or Howe, as agent, make any such
false and fraudulent representation to the plaintiff or J. W.
Clark, after such direction by Willits, and before the sale?"
Answer by the jury: "No." "*Int*. 5. If you have answered
that Ralls made no such false and fraudulent representations
after such directions by Willits, if you find that Willits gave
such direction, but that Ralls did make such representations
before that time, when, if ever before suit was commenced,
did Willits have knowledge thereof?" Answer by the jury:
"No." "*Int*. 6. By whom was the sale of Willits' share of
the property to the Clarks negotiated?" Answer by the
jury: "By Willits." "*Int*. 7. If you have answered that
Willits negotiated his own sale, did he at the time have
knowledge that Ralls, by himself, or Howe, as agent, had
made false and fraudulent representations to the Clarks, or
either of them, as to the capacity or permanency of the water-

1. PRACTICE
on appeal:
error
without prej-
udice.

power?" Answer by the jury: "No." "*Int.* 8. If you have answered that Ralls, by himself, or by himself and the assistance of Howe as his agent, negotiated the sale of the entire mill property, including Willits' share, did Willits at the time know of and premit such negotiations for the purpose of adopting it, if an advantageous sale should be brought about?" Answer by the jury: "No." "*Int.* 9. Did Willits adopt the sale negotiated by Ralls, or Ralls and Howe as Ralls' agent, (jury answered, 'No,') or did Willits negotiate and make his own sale?" Answer by the jury: "Yes."

The foregoing interrogatories were submitted to the jury by the court on its own motion. ·Appellant insists that they were improperly submitted to the jury because they were not submitted to the attorneys of the adverse party before the argument to the jury was commenced, and we are cited to section 2808 of the Code, which is as follows: "In all actions the jury, in their discretion, may render a general or special verdict; and, in any case in which they render a general verdict, they may be required by the court, and must be so required on the request of any party to the action, to find specially upon any particular questions of fact to be stated to them in writing, which questions of fact shall be submitted to the attorneys of the adverse party before the argument to the jury is commenced."

2. PRACTICE: special interrogatories: prior submission to adverse counsel.

We think it is apparent that the requirement to submit the questions to the attorneys of the adverse party is limited to such questions as are requested by the parties. When the court, on its own motion, submits questions of fact to the jury, they are not in the interest of either party, and there cannot be any party adverse to the questions submitted, and there is no more reason for submitting them to one party than to the other. It will be observed, from the questions and answers, that the jury found that neither Ralls nor Willits made any false representations as to the character and capacity of the stream as a water-power. The question, then, as to Willits' liability

for false representations, made by Ralls, is eliminated from
the case, for the very good reason that Willits could not be
held liable for Ralls' representations, unless such representations were made. The plaintiff was defeated in the very
threshold of the case by the findings that no false representations were made by any one.

Now, if the court correctly instructed the jury as to what
constituted actionable false representations, if there were
erroneous instructions as to Willits' liability for Ralls' misrepresentations, or as to other questions in the case not relating to what constituted false representations, it is very plain
that such errors were without prejudice. They could in no
way influence the jury upon the question of whether any false
representations were made. As to the instructions pertaining to the false representations, we deem it sufficient to say
that we find no error in them. The same may said of the
alleged errors in the rulings on the admission and exclusion
of evidence.

It is said that the case has been five times tried to a jury.
Previous to the last trial it had been twice appealed to this
court. The last trial was had in the light of all that had
preceded it, and our judgment is that there is nothing in the
record, as now presented, requiring us to interfere with the
judgment of the circuit court.

AFFIRMED.

BECK, J., dissenting.

THE CITY OF WATERLOO v. THE WATERLOO STREET R'Y CO.

1. **Injunction**: GRANTED ONLY IN ABSENCE OF LEGAL REMEDY: ILLUS-
TRATION. Injunction is an extraordinary remedy, and it will be
granted only when the party is likely to suffer some irreparable injury
against which he has no other speedy or adequate remedy. Accordingly, where plaintiff had granted to defendant the privilege to construct and maintain a street railway on its streets and alleys, providing
that the track should conform to the established grade, but with no provision in regard to the kind of rail to be used, or the guage of the road,
held that it was not entitled to an injunction to restrain the defendant
from using a certain kind of rail, or from building its road upon a certain guage, on the ground that thereby the defendant would cause its
track to be a nuisance; because the plaintiff did not part with its lawful
authority over its streets, and, in the exercise of such authority, it had
full power to make and enforce all necessary and reasonable regulations
as to the manner in which the track should be constructed and maintained, and it had no need of the interference of equity.

Appeal from Black Hawk District Court.

·　WEDNESDAY, MARCH 9.

THIS is an action in equity to restrain the defendants from
laying down a street railway track in one of the streets of
the plaintiff city. Defendant appealed from an order overruling a motion to vacate a temporary injunction.

L. W. Reynolds and *Platt & Hoff*, for appellant.

C. W. Mullan, for appellee.

REED, J.—The city counsel of plaintiff passed an ordinance granting to defendant the exclusive privilege of constructing in the streets and alleys of the city the necessary
tracks for a street railway. The privilege granted extended
to all the streets and alleys of the city, and was to continue
for thirty years. Defendant accepted the grant, and proceeded to construct and operate its railway in a number of
streets. It afterwards commenced the work of constructing
a track in Jefferson street, when the council passed an ordi-

nance which, by its terms, repealed the former grant, but
granted the same privilege as to the streets then occupied by
defendant.   The city thereupon commenced this action,
alleging in its petition that, in constructing its track in Jefferson street, the defendant was acting without authority or
right.   The petition was presented to the judge of the district court, who, without any notice of the hearing having
been served on defendant, granted a temporary writ of injunction, restraining defendant from prosecuting the work on that
street.   After this writ had been served, defendant appeared,
and filed an answer, setting up the grant under which it
claimed to be acting, and denying that it was acting without
authority.   Plaintiff thereupon filed an amendment to its
petition, in which it alleged that defendant was using in the
construction of the track what is known as the "T" rail,
which was a different rail from that ordinarily used in street
railways; also that it was constructing the track on an unusual
gauge, and that, if it was permitted to construct the track
with that rail, and on that gauge, it would constitute a nuisance, and would greatly obstruct and interfere with the use
of the street for ordinary purposes.   Defendant answered
this amendment, admitting that it was using the "T" rail,
but denying that said rail was not ordinarily used in street
railways, or that the gauge on which it was constructing its
track was an unusual gauge, or that the track would constitute a nuisance.   It also moved to vacate the injunction on
the grounds, among others, that the order granting the writ
was made without notice to it, and that, the material allegations of the petition being denied, the writ ought not to be
continued.   The present appeal is from the order overruling
that motion.

The grounds upon which the motion was denied were set
out in the decision.   The court held that, as the grant had
been accepted by defendant, and partially performed, it constituted a contract between the parties, the terms of which
could not be impaired or changed by the subsequent action

of either of them. It held, further, that the question whether the track, as defendant proposed to construct it, would constitute a nuisance, could only be determined upon a full hearing of the evidence, and that the injunction should be continued until such hearing was had; also that notice of the hearing of the application for the temporary writ was not essential.

Counsel for the city did not claim in this court that the city could repeal the grant after it had been accepted and performed in part by defendant, if its original action in making it was valid. In our consideration of the case, we will assume that the grant, if the city had power to make it, constituted, after the acceptance, a contract between the parties, the obligation of which could not be impaired by the action of one of them.

Counsel contended, however, that the grant was invalid for the reason that the city had no power to give to defendant an exclusive privilege to use the street. But, if these premises were conceded, it would follow only that the city, notwithstanding the grant to defendant, might lawfully confer the same privileges upon others, and not that the grant of the privilege to it did not confer upon it the right to use the street for the purpose intended.

Coming, then, to the ground upon which the court placed its ruling, we deem it unnecessary to enter upon any discussion of the question whether an injunction should be granted against a mere threatened nuisance; for the record discloses a state of facts which, to our minds, afford a very conclusive reason why plaintiff ought not to be permitted to maintain the action. The ordinance making the grant was attached as an exhibit to the pleadings, and is set out in the abstract. It is simply a grant of the privilege to construct and maintain a street railway in the streets and alleys of the city. It provides that the track of the railway shall be made to conform to the established grade of the streets, and that it shall be planked at the crossings. There are no provisions as to the rail which shall be used on the track, or the gauge upon which it shall be constructed. Now, the council of the city is vested by law with the power to determine the condition of repair in which the streets shall be kept. They have full control over the streets, and they may make any reasonable and necessary regulation as to. the manner in which they shall be used. It does not appear to us that their powers in this respect are at all affected by the contract with defendant. The city may require defendant to so exercise the privileges conferred upon it by the grant as that the use of the street for ordinary purposes will not be unreasonably interfered with. It has the power to make all necessary and reasonable regulations as to the manner in which the track shall be constructed, and the condition in which it shall be maintained. It has the power, also, to enforce its regulations. Having these powers in its possession, it does not need the aid of a court of equity. Injunction is an extraordinary remedy, and it will be granted only when the party is likely to suffer some irreparable injury against which he has no other speedy or adequate remedy. Clearly, plaintiff is not in that condition. We find it unnecessary to consider whether the writ should have been dissolved because no notice of the application was given to defendant.

REVERSED.

WINSLOW ET AL. v. THE CENTRAL IOWA R'Y CO. ET AL.

1. **Champerty:** WHAT IS NOT: CONTINGENT FEE. A contract between an attorney and his client that the former shall have for his compensation one-third of the amount that may ultimately be recovered in an action, the attorney to pay no costs or expenses, except his own personal expenses, is not champertous. (*McDonald v. Railroad Co.*, 2J Iowa, 174, and *Jewel v. Neidy*, 61 Id., 299, followed.)

2. **Attorneys' Fees:** NOTICE OF LIEN ENTERED ON JUDGMENT DOCKET: EFFECT OF: REVERSAL OF JUDGMENT. Where, after a judgment has been procured for the plaintiff in an action, his attorneys enter upon the judgment docket notice of their claim for a lien for their fees in the case, such notice creates a lien not only upon the judgment, but upon any money due the plaintiff from the defendant in that action. And so, even where the judgment is reversed on appeal, the defendant may not settle with plaintiff and pay him the amount agreed on, and thus defeat the lien of his attorneys. And in this case, where a defendant did so settle and pay, *held* that it was still liable to the attorneys for their fees.

Appeal from Mahaska Circuit Court.

WEDNESDAY, MARCH 9.

THIS is an action to recover attorneys' fees which plaintiffs claim to be due them from defendants. There was a trial to the court without a jury, and a judgment rendered for the plaintiffs. Defendants appeal.

A. C. Daly and *J. H. Blair*, for appellants.

Wm. R. Lacey, for appellees.

ROTHROCK, J.—In the year 1882 the defendant Bucklew commenced an action against the Central Iowa Railroad Com-

1. CHAMPER- pany to recover damages for a personal injury
TY: what is
not: contin- received while in the employment of said com-
gent fee. pany. The action was brought in Mahaska county, and a change of venue was taken to Jasper county, where a trial was had, which resulted in a verdict and judgment against the railroad company for $6,000. Before commencing the action, Bucklew entered into a written contract

with the plaintiff Lacey, which contract was in these words:

"I agree to pay to John F. Lacey, as a contingent fee in the above case, a sum equal to one-third of the amount that may be ultimately collected therein. Said Lacey is not to pay any costs or expenses except his own personal expenses.

"WM. BUCKLEW."

When the cause was removed to Jasper county, Lacey, with the knowledge and consent of Bucklew, procured the plaintiff Winslow to assist him in the trial. After the judgment was entered on the judgment docket of the district court of Jasper county, the plaintiffs entered upon said docket a notice of a lien in the following words:

"We hereby give notice that we claim an attorneys' lien on this judgment for the sum of $2,000, for services rendered the plaintiff in this cause, and as compensation for service so rendered him in their professional capacity, and in the course of their professional employment.

"JOHN F. LACEY.
"H. S. WINSLOW."

The case was appealed by the railroad company to this court, and the judgment was reversed. See 64 Iowa, 603. After the cause had been remanded for a new trial, and on the eighth day of July, 1885, Bucklew and the railroad company settled the suit by a written stipulation, in which it was agreed that the company should pay Bucklew $1,650 in full and complete satisfaction and discharge of all claims for damages for the injuries complained of. It was also agreed that Bucklew should pay his attorneys in said suit, and he received from the company $150 for that purpose, which sum was included in the $1,650 for which the suit was settled. The plaintiffs claim by this action that they are entitled to recover of the defendants the one-third of the amount received by Bucklew in this settlement. The claim is based upon the notice entered upon the judgment docket.

The defendants set up several defenses to the action. One

of these defenses was that the plaintiffs' services were of no value to Bucklew in the trial of the action. This defense is without support in the evidence. Another defense was that the written contract made by Bucklew with Lacey was "champertous, against public policy, and void." We think this defense is without merit. The contract is an agreement for a contingent fee. It has long been settled in this state that such a contract is not unlawful. *McDonald v. Railroad Co.*, 29 Iowa, 174; *Jewel v. Neily*, 61 Iowa, 299.

There are other minor questions in the case, including objections to an order of the court authorizing the approval of an attachment bond, and striking out a counter-claim filed by the defendant Bucklew. These orders are so manifestly correct that we do not deem it necessary to more than mention the fact that objections were made to them.

II.   We come now to the only real question in the case, which is, did the plaintiff acquire a valid and continuing lien upon the claim against the railroad company by the writing entered upon the judgment docket?

2. ATTOR-
NEYS' fees:
notice of lien
entered on
judgment
docket: effect
of: reversal of
judgment.

It appears to be conceded that, if the judgment had not been reversed, the lien would have been valid. But counsel for the defendants strenuously contend that the lien was on the *judgment*, and when that was reversed the lien was lost. The third subdivision of section 215 of the Code provides that an attorney has a lien upon "money due his client, in the hands of the adverse party, or attorney of such party, in an action or proceeding in which the attorney claiming the lien was employed, from the time of giving notice in writing to such adverse party, or attorney of such party, if the money is in possession or under the control of such attorney, which notice shall state the amount claimed, and, in general terms, for what services." And the fourth sub-division of said section provides that, "after a judgment in any court of record, such notice may be given, and the lien made effective against the judgment

debtor, by entering the same in the judgment docket opposite the entry of the judgment."

Counsel for appellant contend that the lien entered of record was on the *judgment*, and not upon money in the possession of the adverse party due the plaintiff in the action.
It is true that the entry made upon the judgment docket
states that a lien is claimed on the judgment. We think,
however, that the plaintiffs had no right to make any claim
other than that provided by statute, and the section of the
Code above cited does not provide for a lien on the *judgment*,
as such. It expressly provides for a lien on money in the
hands of the adverse party or his attorney.

It is further claimed that, as the statute provides, where
notice of the lien is placed upon the judgment docket, and
thus made effective against the judgment debtor, the notice
ceased or expired when the judgment was reversed, because
there was then no "judgment debtor." We think, however, that
the words "judgment debtor," as used in the fourth sub-division of the section above quoted, are merely descriptive of
the person against whom the lien may be enforced. It will
be observed that notice of the lien upon money in the hands
of the adverse party is not required to be personally
served after judgment. The adverse party is charged with
notice by the entry on the judgment docket. From the
time of such entry he cannot prejudice the rights of the
attorney claiming the lien by a settlement with his client;
and as the law does not place the lien upon the *judgment*,
but upon the claim against the adverse party, or the money
in his hands, we think the notice remained binding upon the
defendant as long as the money remained in its hands. If
the plaintiffs had merely stated in tne entry upon the judg.
ment docket their lien upon the money claimed of the rail.
road company, and in its hands, due to Bucklew for the
injury of which he complained, the notice would have been
in strict conformity with the statute, and would have been
binding on the railroad company through all the further

progress of the case, and up to the actual payment of the demand. We do not think the fact that the word "judgment" was used in the entry instead of "suit," "action," or "claim," or some other equivalent word, was a matter of any consequence in fixing the rights of the parties.

In our opinion, the judgment of the circuit court should be

AFFIRMED.

PALO ALTO COUNTY v. BURLINGAME ET AL.

1. **Clerk of Courts:** SALARY AND FEES OF. An officer is entitled to charge and receive only such fees as the statute provides as compensation for the services he may perform. Accordingly, the fees of the clerk of the courts are defined and limited by § 3781 of the Code, and reporter's and jury fees and marriage license fees, collected by him, not being included in said section, are no part of his compensation; neither is he entitled to extra compensation for a necessary rearrangement of the papers and records of his office, nor for issuing jurors' certificates to the auditor for the fees of jurors.

2. **County:** SETTLEMENT WITH CLERK: ESTOPPEL. The fact that the board of supervisors, in making settlement with the clerk, failed to compel the latter to account for certain fees collected by him and belonging to the county, did not estop the county from afterwards demanding and recovering such fees.

3. ———: ACTS OF SUPERVISORS NOT IN SESSION. A county is not bound by statements made by its supervisors when not in session.

Appeal from Kossuth District Court.

THURSDAY, MARCH 10.

THE defendant Burlingame was elected and duly qualified as clerk of the district and circuit courts, and this action was brought on his official bond, to recover certain moneys received by him by virtue of his office, which he failed to pay over to the plaintiff. Trial by jury. Judgment for the plaintiff, and the defendants appeal.

Harrison & Jenswold, for appellant.

Soper, Crawford & Carr, for appellee.

SEEVERS, J.—I.   There is no dispute as to the facts, and,
under the direction of the court, the jury found for the
1. CLERK of   plaintiff.   In January, 1884, the board of super-
courts: salary
and fees of.   visors fixed the salary of the clerk at $250, and
fees of his office.   During that year there came into the
clerk's hands certain jury, reporter's, and marriage license
fees, contemplated in sections 3777, 3787, and 3812 of the
Code, and the court held that the jury and reporter's fees
belonged to the county.   It is conceded that the clerk is
entitled to the fees allowed him by statute, in addition to
such salary as may be fixed by the board, and also that he is
entitled to such fees, although the board may not allow him
any addition thereto as salary or extra compensation.   But
counsel for the appellee contend that such fees are defined
and fixed by section 3781 of the Code, which provides that
"the clerk of the district or circuit court shall be entitled to
charge and receive the following fees."   Then follows an
enumeration of the fees to which the clerk is so entitled.
And this, we think, is the proper construction of the several
sections of the Code in relation thereto.   The clerk is not
entitled to the fees provided in sections 3787 and 3812, simply for the reason that the statute does not so provide.   An
officer is entitled to charge and receive only such fees as the
statute provides he is entitled to as compensation for services
he may perform.   Counsel for the appellant, as we understand, do not claim the rule to be otherwise.   Their contention is that the board contracted that the clerk might retain
the fees in question as additional compensation.   That the
salary was such is conceded, but it is denied that the jury
and reporter's fees are fees appertaining or belonging to the
clerk's office; and we think this is so.   All the clerk has to
do with such fees is to receive them when paid by the party
liable therefor.   He renders no other service, nor does he
earn such fees.   The service is performed, and the statutory
compensation is earned, by others; and such fees do not
"belong" to his office any more than do the fees of witnesses

or district attorney, which are taxed as a part of the costs, and paid to the clerk. The court held that the marriage license fees did belong to the clerk's office, on the ground, we may suppose, that he performed the service, and therefore earned the fees.

II. In January, 1883, the board fixed the salary of the clerk "at $250, [for that year,] to be paid at the close of each month," and the court held that the clerk THE SAME. was not thereunder entitled to the marriage license fees received by him during such period. Unless the board otherwise directs and allows, the clerk is only entitled to the fees and compensation provided in section 3781 of the Code. The marriage license fees are simply paid to the clerk, and he is directed to pay the same "into the county treasury." Code, § 3787. This clearly shows that he is not entitled to them as a matter of right.

III. The defendant pleaded that, when the clerk entered upon the duties of his office, the records thereof, without his fault, were "so defective, incomplete, inconsistent, THE SAME. ent, misleading and disarranged, that it was absolutely necessary to the proper discharge of the duties of said office, and for the public benefit, to complete, correct and rearrange them," and that he did so. For such services he sought to recover compensation from the plaintiff. The court held that he was not entitled thereto; and this ruling is correct, for the reason that the statute does not fix or prescribe any compensation for such services.

IV. The defendants also pleaded that the clerk issued a large number of jurors' certificates, directed to the auditor, THE SAME. showing the amount of fees each of the jurors was entitled to for his services. Such certificate was made under section 3811 of the Code, but no fee is provided therefor, and therefore the clerk is not entitled to any compensation for such service.

V. In 1883, and prior thereto, settlements were made by

the board with the clerk, and at such settlements, as we

2. COUNTY: settlement with clerk: estoppel. understand, the clerk did not account for the jury and reporter's fees received by him prior thereto, and the board acquiesced therein, or failed to exact the same of the clerk. This is immaterial, and does not constitute a defense to this action. If the board failed at one time to insist on the legal rights of the county, this cannot have the effect of creating an estoppel.

VI. The defendants claim that, at the January meeting of the board in 1883, there were negotiations between the

3. ——: acts of supervisors not in session. clerk and the board in relation to his salary, and that the individual members of the board agreed and informed the clerk that his salary and compensation had been fixed materially different from what in fact was done, as shown by the recorded action of the board. We do not understand that the members of the board, when in session, took any action, or proposed to take any, different from what they did, and caused to be entered of record. All that is claimed is that the members, when not in session, expressed views which the clerk understood to be different from the recorded action. This is not binding on the county. *Rice v. Plymouth Co.*, 43 Iowa, 136.

The judgment of the district court is   **AFFIRMED.**

COOPER v. WILSON ET AL.

1. **Practice:** DISMISSAL AS TO PART OF CAUSES OF ACTION. Where plaintiff brought an action in three counts upon as many promissory notes, and sought a decree foreclosing a mortgage securing the notes, it was his privilege to dismiss as to two of the counts.

2. **Practice on Appeal:** LESS THAN $100. Where a plaintiff has dismissed as to some of his causes of action, and less than $100 is left in controversy, and judgment is rendered therefor, the defendant cannot appeal to this court without the certificate of the trial judge.

Appeal from Linn Circuit Court.

THURSDAY, MARCH 10.

THIS is an appeal from a judgment and a decree for the foreclosure of a mortgage upon certain real estate.

Geo. W. Wilson, for appellants.

Frank G. Clark, for appellee.

ROTHROCK, J.—The plaintiff filed a petition in equity in three counts upon three separate promissory notes, and he demanded a decree for the foreclosure. of a mortgage to secure the same. As to the first note, the defendant pleaded a tender of what he admitted to be due, and the difference between the tender and the amount claimed in that count of the petition was but a few dollars. The plaintiff dismissed his action as to the other notes, and the court rendered judgment against defendants on the first note for some eight or ten dollars more than the tender. Counsel for appellants appear to be dissatisfied because the plaintiff was permitted to dismiss his action as to the two last notes. We cannot understand why a plaintiff may not at any time withdraw or dismiss one or more of the causes of action in his petition. After the dismissal the amount in controversy, as shown by the pleadings, was less than $100, and appellants present this appeal without the certificate of the trial judge, as required by statute. In such case, the certificate is requisite to confer jurisdiction on the court. We cannot entertain the appeal.

DISMISSED.

BUTLER v. THE CHICAGO & NORTHWESTERN R'Y Co.

1. **Railroads:** COW KILLED ON TRACK: DEFECTIVE GATE: NEGLIGENCE: QUESTION FOR JURY. In an action to recover for a cow which escaped from a pasture, through a gate in defendant's fence, and got on the track, and was killed, *held* that the fact that the fastening of the gate was on the side toward the pasture was proper to be considered by the jury, with other evidence, in determining whether the gate was negligently constructed; but that the mere fact that the fastening was on that side would not warrant a verdict for plaintiff, unless there was evidence tending to show that the gate became open by reason of that fact.

2. **Instructions:** PROVINCE OF JURY: WEIGHING PROBABILITIES. It is the duty of the jury to determine, as best they can, which theory of the case is supported by the evidence, and not which is the more probable; and an instruction directing them to consider the probabilities of the case was properly refused.

Appeal from Carroll Circuit Court.

THURSDAY, MARCH 10.

ACTION to recover double the value of a cow killed by a train on the defendant's road. Trial by jury. Judgment for the plaintiff, and the defendant appeals.

Hubbard, Clark & Dawley, for appellant.

F. M. Powers, for appellee.

SEEVERS, J.—The railway was fenced, but there was a gate which constituted a part of the fence through which the cow escaped from a pasture. It is not claimed that the gate was defectively constructed, except in two particulars. The first is that it was so constructed as to be fastened on the side next to the pasture, and the second that the fastening provided was insufficient. The fastening consisted of an iron staple and latch, with a hook which passed through the staple. The amount in controversy being less than $100, we are only required to determine such questions as have been properly certified, and which have been insisted upon in argument by counsel.

I. We are asked whether the fact that the fastening was on the pasture side of the gate constitutes "any evidence warranting the jury to find for the plaintiff." This we understand to mean whether such fastening constitutes evidence tending to show that the gate was negligently constructed. We do not think that, as a matter of law, we can say that the fastening should have been on the gate next to the railway or pasture. We are of the opinion that this was a question for the jury. It is difficult to say, as a matter of law, that any fastening is or is not sufficient; and it is more difficult to affirm on which side of the gate it should be placed. This must depend upon the lay of the ground, the kind of gate, and possibly other circumstances. What would be proper in one case might not be in another. The fact, therefore, that the fastening was so placed was a proper matter to be considered by the jury, and whether it alone was sufficient to warrant the verdict, we are not called on in this connection to determine. The question asked must be answered in the affirmative.

1. RAILROADS: cow killed on track: defective gate: negligence: question for jury.

II. The defendant asked the court to instruct the jury as follows: "The mere fact that the fastening of the gate was on the side of the gate towards the cow is not evidence warranting you to find for the plaintiff." While the thought of this instruction may not be as clearly expressed as it should be, we think it means that, if there was no other evidence tending to show negligence, then the plaintiff could not recover. In other words, the thought of the instruction is that, if it be conceded that the placing of the fastening on the side of the gate next to the pasture is evidence tending to show negligence, this alone is not sufficient to entitle the plaintiff to recover. There was evidence tending to show that the plaintiff passed through the gate a comparatively short time prior to the escape of the cow from the pasture, and that he closed it; but whether he fastened it by putting the latch in place, and the hook in the

THE SAME.

staple, is doubtful. If he did, then how the gate was opened does not certainly appear. We understand the theory of the plaintiff to be that it was opened by the cow rubbing against the latch and hook. It may be conceded that, if the fastening was such that it could be opened by the cow, it was negligently constructed; but the defendant's theory is that the fastening was in every respect sufficient, and it had the right to have such theory, under proper instructions, submitted to the jury. The burden was on the plaintiff to show that the gate became open by reason of the defendant's fault. *Johnson v. Chicago, R. I. & P. R'y Co.*, 55 Iowa, 707. The mere fact that the gate was defectively constructed, unless it became open by reason of such construction, is not sufficient to entitle the plaintiff to recover; and it was for the jury to say whether this was so or not. We therefore are of the opinion that the court erred in refusing the instruction asked, and that the third question propounded to us must be answered in the affirmative.

III. There was a special finding of the jury, and we are asked whether the court erred in refusing to enter judgment thereon, notwithstanding the general verdict. We are unable to see that there is any such inconsistency or conflict between the general and special verdicts as counsel for the appellant claim, and deem it sufficient to say that the court did not err in this respect, and therefore the fourth question asked must be answered in the negative.

IV. The defendant asked an instruction which contains the thought that, if it was "equally probable that the gate was left open by the plaintiff as was the other theory, then he could not recover." This instruction was correctly refused. We do not understand that it is the province of the court to direct the jury to consider what is or is not probable. It is the duty of the jury to determine as best they can which theory is supported by a preponderance of the evidence, and not which is probably true. Of course, if there is no preponderance,

2. INSTRUC-
TIONS: prov-
ince of jury:
weighing
probabilities.

the party on whom the burden rests must fail, but the jury must so find, and not that this is probably so.   The fifth question must be answered in the negative.

For the error in refusing to give the instruction referred to in the third paragraph of this opinion, the judgment of the circuit court is

REVERSED.

SLATER v. THE BURLINGTON, CEDAR RAPIDS & NORTHERN R'Y CO.

1. **Railroads:** INJURY TO PERSON CROSSING TRACK: CONTRIBUTORY NEGLIGENCE. The plaintiff, a boy of about twelve years, was riding with his mother in a carriage driven by his mother's servant. While attempting to cross the defendant's track, the carriage was struck by a passing locomotive, and plaintiff was seriously injured. The driver was careless in not stopping at a proper place and looking for an approaching train, and the mother was careless in not requiring the driver so to stop and look. *Held* that this carelessness must be imputed to the plaintiff, and that a judgment in his favor must be reversed.

Appeal from Johnson District Court.

THURSDAY, MARCH 10.

ACTION at law to recover for personal injuries sustained by plaintiff, resulting from a locomotive, operated upon defendant's road, striking a carriage wherein plaintiff and others were riding; the driver having attempted to cross the railroad track before the engine.   There was a judgment upon a verdict for plaintiff.   Defendant appeals.

S. K. Tracy and *Boal & Jackson*, for appellant.

S. H. Fairall, *C. S. Ranck* and *H. F. Bonordon*, for appellee.

BECK, J.—I.   The plaintiff, a boy of about twelve years of age, with a brother probably younger than himself, his

VOL. LXXI—14

mother, a young woman, and a driver, were riding for pleasure in a carriage through the streets of Iowa City, in the night-time. They drove along a street which runs parallel with, and about 100 feet from, the street upon which defendant's railroad is constructed, until they approached the point where the Chicago, Rock Island & Pacific Railroad crosses over defendant's road by a bridge. Here they left the street, following a track down the descent to defendant's road, which it was the purpose of the driver to cross. When attempting to do so, a locomotive running upon defendant's road struck the carriage, and all were more or less injured, the plaintiff very severely, his arm being so torn and crushed as to render amputation necessary, and his skull fractured. The evidence probably shows that defendant was negligent in running the engine at a high rate of speed, in failing to give signals of its approach, and in having no watchman at the crossing of the street over its road. But of these matters we need not inquire, in the view we take of the case.

II. In our opinion, the evidence shows, without conflict, that the driver was negligent in attempting to cross the railroad track without making an effort to discover whether there was a train approaching; and the mother shared in this negligence, in that she failed to require the driver, at a proper place, to stop, and watch and listen for the approaching train. No question is raised upon the point that the negligence of the driver and mother, in whose charge the plaintiff was at the time, would defeat recovery under the rule of contributory negligence recognized by this court. We need not, therefore, examine or consider the doctrine regarding it, as it is not in dispute, but recognized by counsel as the law of this case.

The evidence of the mother, young woman, and driver, show that, before they had made the descent to the defendant's road, the carriage was stopped for the purpose of discovering what course a train on the other road would take. They probably all unite in stating that they then listened

and watched for a train on defendant's road.   But there can
be no question that from their position no such train could
have been discovered.   The driver says that he stopped again,
before he reached defendant's road, to watch and listen, but
the other witnesses do not support him in this statement.
We are inclined to think that he is mistaken in the statement.
But certain it is that, if he did stop, it was at a place from
which the view was cut off by an embankment of the other
road and the abutments of the bridge, or that he did not
look with attention.   He know of the existence of the
embankment and abutments, and the exercise of the smallest
degree of attention would have revealed to him the fact that
they cut off the view.   He therefore did not look in the direction the train was approaching, or, if he did, it was with
such want of attention and thought as to amount to culpable
heedlessness, and to render him chargeable with gross negligence.   In the exercise of a moderate degree of care, and a
low degree of intelligence, the driver, by stopping and lis-
tening at a proper point, could have discovered the danger
into which he was heedlessly taking those in his charge, and
the exercise of this same degree of intelligence and care
would have enabled him to determine the point at which he
should have stopped.

In our opinion, the district court should have sustained the
motion of defendant's counsel for direction to the jury to
return a verdict for defendant.   As this conclusion is decisive of the case, other questions discussed by counsel need
not be considered.

REVERSED.

MORGAN v. WILFLEY ET AL.

1. **Evidence:** PAROL TO AID MINUTES OF SCHOOL BOARD. · Where the record of the proceedings of a school board showed that a motion was passed, but failed to show what the motion was, it was competent to prove by the secretary who made the record what the motion was.

2. ———: CUMULATIVE: EXCLUSION OF: ERROR WITHOUT PREJUDICE. The exclusion of evidence on a point which has been sufficiently established by other testimony is not prejudicial to the party offering it, and hence is no ground for reversal.

3. **Practice on Appeal:** CERTIFICATION OF EVIDENCE. The certificate of the judge, printed in the abstract, to the effect that the bill of exceptions contains all the evidence, is not sufficient to show that the abstract contains all the evidence.

Appeal from Page District Court.

THURSDAY, MARCH 10.

MANDAMUS to compel the defendant to remove a school-house from sub-district No. 1 to sub-district No. 9, in obedience to the action of the board of directors, or to erect the necessary school-house in sub-district No. 9. There was a judgment in accord with the prayer of plaintiff's petition. Defendants appeal.

William Orr, for appellants.

No appearance for appellee.

BECK, J.—I.   The plaintiff at the trial introduced in evidence the minutes of the proceedings of the board of direc-

1. EVIDENCE: parol to aid minutes of school board.

tors of the district township of East River.   It showed that a certain motion was adopted, but failed to show what the motion was.   Plaintiff was permitted to show, against defendants' objection, by the witness who was secretary when the motion was adopted, that it was to the effect that a new school-house be built in district No. 1, and the old house be removed to district No.

9. The admission of this evidence is now complained of by defendants. We think the court below ruled correctly. There was an apparent omission in the minutes, which was supplied by the evidence. The oral evidence did not impeach, contradict, or vary the contents of the minutes. It simply supplied an evident omission, and thereby applied it to its proper subject,—the record of the vote of the directors.

II. The defendants offered to prove that the directors had not complied with the vote to remove the school-house, for

2. ——: cumulative: exclusion of: error without prejudice. the reason that they had intended, pursuant to a petition presented to them, to redistrict the district township. The evidence was rejected. The facts proposed to be proved were testified to by other witnesses, except as to the petition. The material fact, the purpose which constituted their reason for failing to act, was testified to by other witnesses, and was before the court. Defendants were not prejudiced, therefore, by the ruling, so far as that fact was concerned. The other fact, the presentation of a petition, would not affect their determination to make new districts. We conclude that defendants suffered no prejudice from the ruling.

III. No other objections are urged against the judgment, except that it is not sufficiently supported by the evidence.

3. PRACTICE on appeal: certification of evidence. But the abstract fails to show that we have before us all the testimony. It is nowhere so stated. The certificate of the judge, or a part of the bill of exceptions, is printed as a part of the abstract. It shows that the bill of exceptions contains all the evidence. We have often held that this is not sufficient to show that the abstract contains all the evidence.

The judgment of the district court is

AFFIRMED.

MORLAN v. RUSSELL & Co.

1. **Procedure**: WHEN JURY DISREGARDS INSTRUCTIONS. Where the court instructed the jury that, under the evidence, they could not find more than nominal damages for the plaintiff, but they found substantial damages for him; it would have been competent for the court, on its own motion, to set aside the verdict and award a new trial; (*Allen v. Wheeler*, 54 Iowa, 628;) or it might have reduced the amount of the verdict to a nominal sum, and rendered judgment accordingly. But it was error to enter an order that the verdict should be reduced to a nominal sum and judgment rendered therefor, *unless* the plaintiff should elect to take a new trial, and to then grant a new trial upon his election.

Appeal from Carroll District Court.

THURSDAY, MARCH 10.

DEFENDANT appealed from an order of the district court setting aside the verdict of the jury, and awarding plaintiff a new trial.

Wright, Baldwin & Haldane, for appellant.

M. W. Beach and *E. M. Betzer*, for appellee.

REED, J.—The action was brought for the recovery of damages for an alleged breach of the warranty made by defendant in the sale of a threshing-machine to plaintiff. The district court instructed the jury that, upon the evidence before them, they could not award the plaintiff more than nominal damages. The jury, however, returned a verdict for plaintiff for substantial damages. The district court, thereupon, on its own motion, made the following order, viz: "It is ordered and adjudged that the verdict of the jury herein be reduced to the sum of one dollar, to conform to the instructions of the court herein, and that judgment be rendered on the verdict for one dollar and costs, unless plaintiff elect to take a new trial, in which event a new trial will be ordered, at the costs of plaintiff." Plaintiff did elect to take a new trial on the terms imposed, and an order was accordingly entered setting the verdict aside, and granting a new trial.

As the jury disregarded the instruction of the court as to the amount of damages that could be awarded plaintiff under the evidence, it would have been competent for the court, on its own motion, perhaps, to set aside the verdict entirely, and award a new trial. The power of the court to do this was affirmed by this court in *Allen v. Wheeler*, 54 Iowa, 628. In the exercise of the same power, the court, after it received the verdict as returned by the jury, and before discharging them, might have directed them to reduce the amount of the verdict to a nominal sum; or it might do just what it did do,—reduce the amount of the award by its own order. Now, the question in the case is whether the court had the power, on its own motion, after having amended or reformed the verdict on its own motion, to set it aside, and grant a new trial, on the ground merely that the jury had disregarded the instruction. Clearly, we think, not. The verdict, as modified, stood as the verdict of the jury. It was then entirely consistent with the instructions of the court, which we must assume were correct. The cause was in the same position after the modification of the verdict was made as it would have occupied if the jury had obeyed the instructions, and returned a verdict in that form. There was no conflict between it and the instructions, and it was the verdict that plaintiff had shown himself entitled to, and neither he nor defendant was making any complaint with reference to it. Clearly, there was no ground for disturbing it.

The judgment of the district court will be reversed, and the cause remanded, with directions to enter a judgment for plaintiff on the verdict as modified by the court.

REVERSED.

THE STATE v. ARLEN ET AL.

1. **Intoxicating Liquors:** CONDEMNATION: VALUE: JURISDICTION OF JUSTICE OF THE PEACE. An action for the condemnation and destruction of intoxicating liquors kept for illegal sale is a criminal action, (see cases cited in opinion,) and is not affected by the constitutional provision limiting the jurisdiction of justices of the peace in civil cases. Accordingly. *held* that such an action, brought before a justice of the peace, under §§ 1544–1547 of the Code, is within the jurisdiction of the justice, regardless of the value of the liquors involved therein.

Appeal from Clinton District Court.

THURSDAY, MARCH 10.

THIS is a proceeding before a justice of the peace, under Code, §§ 1544–1547, providing for the seizure, condemnation and destruction of intoxicating liquors kept for sale in violation of law. The justice rendered a judgment for the destruction of the liquors. Upon appeal, the district court dismissed the proceeding, the court holding that the justice had no jurisdiction of the case, for the reason that the liquors exceeded in value $400.

A. J. Baker, Attorney-general, for the State.

Ellis & McCoy, A. Howat and *W. C. Grohe,* for appellees.

BECK, J.—I. The defendants, by their answer, showed that the value of the liquors exceed $400, and pleaded that the justice had therefore no jurisdiction of the case. A demurrer to the answer was overruled, and judgment was entered dismissing the case; the state standing upon its demurrer.

II. The proceeding is a criminal action. *State v. Intoxicating Liquors,* 40 Iowa, 95; *Santo v. State,* 2 Id., 165; *State v. Bryan,* 4 Id., 349. It is not, therefore, within the provision of the constitution limiting the jurisdiction of justices of the peace in civil cases.

III.　There is no provision of the statute limiting the jurisdiction of justices of the peace to proceedings in cases where the liquors seized are of a specified value. The authority of the justices extends to all cases, without regard to value. There is therefore no limitation upon its exercise.

IV.　But, it is said, liquors of great value may be destroyed by the judgments of a justice of the peace, who is an inferior judicial officer. This is true; but the law has so ordered. The law presumes that justice will be rightly administered by these officers; and, if the parties claiming to own the liquors think they are not subject to condemnation, an appeal may be taken to a higher court. Code, § 1546. There is no occasion for the fears expressed, that property of great value may be destroyed when not subject thereto under the law. Criminal proceedings before justices and other magistrates are authorized, under our statutes, wherein property, without regard to its value, is the subject of adjudication, and its possession and custody is disposed of; and no complaint has ever been made of injustice done under these provisions. A justice of the peace may issue a search warrant for property alleged to be stolen or embezzled. Upon the return of the warrant, the right to the possession of the property may be determined, and it may be delivered accordingly. Code, §§ 4654–4659.

Sullivan v. City of Oneida, 61 Ill., 242, contains arguments which we do not approve, in conflict with these views.

The judgment of the district court is

REVERSED.

* BOWERS V. HALLOCK ET AL.

1. **Tax Sale and Deed**: NO NOTICE TO REDEEM: NOT VOID BUT VOID-
   ABLE. A tax deed issued without service of the notice to redeem, as
   required by the statute, or without filing in the treasurer's office the
   statutory proof of such service, is not void, but it conveys the title to
   the land subject to the right to redeem when lawfully established.

2. ———: WHO MAY QUESTION: PROOF OF TITLE. One cannot question the
   validity of a tax title unless he, or the person under whom he claims,
   had title to the land at the time of the tax sale. (Code, § 897.) But
   such title is not shown by proof that *Porter* C. M. had title from the
   government, and by the introduction of the record of a deed to such
   person made by P. C. M., and acknowledged by *Peter* C. M.; nor by the
   introduction of the record of the deed alone, without the acknowledgment, for then there would be no proof of the execution of the deed by
   P. C. M.

Appeal from Audubon Circuit Court.

THURSDAY, MARCH 10.

ACTION in equity to establish plaintiff's right to redeem a
quarter section of land, and to quiet in him the title thereto.
The circuit court entered judgment for defendants, and
plaintiff appeals.

H. E. Long, for appellant.

H. F. Andrews and *Willard & Fletcher*, for appellees.

REED, J.—The land in question was sold by the county
treasurer, at the annual tax sale in 1873. The treasurer executed a deed of the land to the defendant Van Gorder, who
was the holder of the certificate of purchase, and he, on the
same day, sold and conveyed it to defendant Hallock, who at
once took possession, and continued in actual occupation
when this suit was instituted, which was in September, 1884.
The ground upon which plaintiff claims the right to redeem
from the sale is that the notice of the expiration of the time
for redemption required by the statute was not served on the
person in whose name the land was taxed, and there was no

legal evidence of the service of such notice on file in the office of the treasurer when the deed to Van Gorder was executed. The answer denies that plaintiff has any interest in the land, or any right to redeem from the sale. Counsel for plaintiff contend in argument that it was not essential to plaintiff's right to redeem the land that he show a perfect title in himself, but that he would be entitled to that right on proof that he was possessed of any interest in it.

The statute (Code, § 897) provides "that no person shall be permitted to question the title acquired by a treasurer's deed without first showing that he, or the person

1. TAX sale and deed: no notice to re-deem: not void, but voidable.

under whom he claims title, had title to the property at the time of the sale." Another provision of the same section is that the treasurer's deed, when executed in the form prescribed, and duly recorded, shall vest in the purchasers all the right, title, interest and estate of the former owner in and to the land conveyed. There can be no question, in view of this latter provision, that Van Gorder acquired the title to the land by the treasurer's deed. If, however, the notice to redeem required by the statute was not served, or if the proof of the service of the notice required by law was not on file in the treasurer's office when the deed was executed, the land remained subject to redemption. The deed, however, is not void. It conveys the title to the purchaser, who holds it subject, however, to be defeated by the redemption of the land when the right of redemption is established and exercised in the manner provided by law. It is equally clear, also, that plaintiff is questioning the title acquired under the treasurer's deed. He is seeking to defeat it by redeeming from the sale. Under the first provision quoted, then, he is required to show that either

2. ——: who may question: proof of title.

he, or the person under whom he claims, had title at the time of the sale. He claims to be the owner of the land. It is not necessary to inquire whether he would be entitled to redeem on proof that he held an interest less than an absolute estate under the one who held

the title at the time of the sale. To establish his ownership
of the property, he introduced the record of the conveyances
which he claims constitute the chain of title from the government
of the United States to himself. These convey-
ances show that John E. Brooks became the owner of the
property by proper conveyance in 1858, and that he conveyed
it, on the twentieth of May, 1860. The first question which
arises with reference to plaintiff's proof of title is as to the
name of the grantee from Brooks. Plaintiff claims the
name to be " Porter C. McLane," while defendants contend
that it is Porter C. M. Lane. There is no evidence on the
subject except that afforded by the record of the conveyance,
and it is conceded that an inspection of the record leaves it
reasonably in doubt as to which is the true name of the
grantee. It may be conceded, however, that the plaintiff's
claim is correct, and that the name of the grantee is Porter
C. McLane. The next conveyance in the chain appears to
have been executed on the fifth of March, 1868. The record
shows that this conveyance was signed by P. C. McLane.
The certificate of the notary public who took the acknowledgment, however, shows that, on the day named, *Peter* C.
McLane, who was personally known to him to be the identical person whose name is affixed to the deed, appeared before
him, and acknowledged the same to be his voluntary act, etc.
It was the record of this deed, also, that was introduced in
evidence, and it may be that the recorder made a mistake in
recording the instrument. But we have no evidence of that
fact, and we must accept the record as it is.

It is shown, then, that the conveyance was executed by
Peter C. McLane, while the grantee in the conveyance from
Brooks was *Porter* C. McLane. There is no proof, then,
that the person to whom Brooks conveyed the land has ever
conveyed it. We cannot assume that the Peter C. McLane
who executed the conveyance on the fifth of March, 1868, is
the person to whom Brooks conveyed the land on the
twentieth of May, 1860. Plaintiff's proof of title, therefore,

fails at this point. It does not show that either he, or those under whom he claims, had title at the time of the sale.

He claims, however, that he introduced in evidence only the record of the deed dated March 5, 1868, and that his offer did not include the record of the certificate of acknowledgment, and that, as the body of the deed shows that it was executed by P. C. McLane, we should assume that this was the Porter C. McLane who is named as grantee in the conveyance from Brooks. But if this claim, as to the extent of his offer, should be conceded, he would be in no better position; for, in that case, there would be no evidence of the execution of the deed, and it could not be considered. Having failed to establish title, he cannot question the title acquired under the treasurer's deed.

AFFIRMED.

EVERITT v. EVERITT.

1. **Dower:** IN EQUITABLE ESTATE: ILLUSTRATION. Where a husband enters into an oral contract for the purchase of land, and takes possession thereunder, and subsequently pays the whole amount of the purchase price, he is the equitable owner of the land, and he cannot, by causing the vendor to execute a deed to his son by a former wife, deprive a wife who survives him of her dower interest in the land, but she may recover the same in an action against the son. (*Beck v. Beck*, 64 Iowa, 155, distinguished.)

Appeal from Hamilton Circuit Court.

THURSDAY, MARCH 10.

PLAINTIFF is the widow of George M. Everitt, deceased. The said George M. Everitt at one time was the owner of a quarter section of land. Before his marriage with plaintiff, he conveyed this land to K. Young. After the marriage of the parties, Young conveyed the land to defendant, who is the son of George M. Everitt by a former marriage, and his only heir at law. Plaintiff alleges that the conveyance to

Young was intended as a mortgage for the security of an indebtedness which Everitt was owing Young, and that Everitt continued to be the equitable owner of the property while the title was in Young, and that the debt secured by the mortgage was satisfied before the conveyance to defendant was executed; and prays that this conveyance be set-aside, and that one-third in value of the property be admeasured and set off to her in fee-simple as her widow's share therein. The circuit court granted the relief demanded, and defendant appeals.

W. J. Covil, for appellant.

Kamrar & Boeye, for appellee.

REED, J.—Before George M. Everitt conveyed the land to Young, he was indebted to him in an amount fully equal to two-thirds of the value of the property. The greater part of this indebtedness was secured by mortgage on the property, but a portion of it was not secured. The evidence shows, without any doubt, we think, that the conveyance was given in satisfaction of the indebtedness, and was not intended as a mortgage. An understanding was subsequently entered into, however, between the parties, by which it was agreed that Young would reconvey the property to Everitt upon the payment of the amount of the indebtedness. In pursuance of this understanding, Everitt made a number of payments to Young. The latter also received some rents for the premises. He also received $150 from a railroad company for a right of way over the land; and for these amounts he gave Everitt credit. When the conveyance to defendant was made, Young had received from all these sources an amount equal to the original indebtedness, with interest thereon. This conveyance was made to defendant by the direction of his father, such direction being given at the time of the execution of the conveyance. Soon after the agreement between Young and Everitt was entered into, the latter took possession of the land, and erected a dwelling-house and other buildings thereon. He moved into this dwelling-house, and continued to live there with his family until his death, which occurred soon after the conveyance of the land by Young to defendant.

Counsel for defendant contended that the facts of the case brought it within the holding in *Beck v. Beck*, 64 Iowa, 155. But there is a clear distinction between the two cases. In that case the husband purchased real estate which he caused to be conveyed to his son. He paid for the property with money which he had derived from the sale of other real estate, in which his wife had had a dower interest, but which she had relinquished at the time of the sale. He purchased the property for his son, and paid for it at the time of the purchase, and he had no intention of taking or acquiring any interest in it himself; and we held that the wife was not endowed of the land. But in the present case the contract between Everitt and Young was entered into by the former in his own interest, and for his own benefit. He contracted for the purchase of the land, not for his son, but for himself. The interest and right which accrued in the land under the contract accrued in his favor. When he procured the conveyance to be made to his son, he simply caused those rights to be transferred to him. In the *Beck Case* the interests in the real estate acquired by the purchase accrued at once to the son. In this case they accrued to the father and were subsequently transferred to the son. But, if the interest so acquired was of such a nature as to give the wife a dower right in the property, it is clear that she would not be divested of that right by the conveyance to the son. The statute (Code, § 2440) provides that "one-third in value of the legal or equitable estates in real property possessed by the husband at any time during the marriage, which have not been sold on execution or any other judicial sale, and to which the wife has made no relinquishment of her right, shall be set apart as her property in fee-simple if she survive him."

Under this provision, the question whether plaintiff has a dower right in the property depends upon whether the husband acquired a legal or equitable estate therein under the agreement with Young. The contract was by parol, but Everitt took possession under it, and made valuable improvements upon the property, and he continued in possession up to the time of his death. At the time he directed the conveyance to be made to defendant, the full amount of the consideration had been paid. At least, that is the fair inference from the evidence. That he was the equitable owner of the property at that time cannot be doubted. All that was required to be done in order to vest him with absolute ownership was the passing of the naked legal title to him; and that he was entitled to have done.

It is entirely clear that plaintiff is entitled, under the statute, to have one-third in value of the property set off to her.

AFFIRMED.

ROBINSON v. LINN COUNTY.

1. **Practice on Appeal:** NO RULING EXCEPTED TO: JUDGMENT AFFIRMED. Where the action was begun by ordinary proceedings, but, after trial was begun, the court ordered that plaintiff could proceed no further without amending his petition, and plaintiff amended, asking for the reformation of a contract, and the issue thereon was tried by the court, and a decree entered thereon for defendant, and the cause was then transferred back to the law docket, and, upon the trial of the law issues, the court instructed the jury to find for the defendant, which was done, and judgment entered accordingly, and no exception was taken except to the final judgment, and this was more than three days after the said instructions had been given, *held* that there was nothing for this court to try, and that the judgment should be affirmed.

Appeal from Linn Circuit Court.

THURSDAY, MARCH 10.

THE plaintiff seeks by this proceeding to recover of the

defendant $175 for certain work done upon a public highway.
An action at law was first brought, a jury was impaneled to
try the case, and, after the trial had proceeded for some time
the court ordered that plaintiff could proceed no further without amending his petition. Thereupon plaintiff amended
his petition, in which he asked a reformation of a certain
written contract which was involved in the controversy, and
the jury was discharged. The amendment of the petition presented an equitable issue, and this issue was tried, and a decree
was entered for the defendant, and the abstract recites that
" the cause was transferred back to the law side of the docket
by the court." The plaintiff then filed an amended and substituted petition. Issue was taken by answer, and a trial was
had to a jury, which resulted in a verdict and judgment for
the defendant. Plaintiff appeals.

Charles W. Kepler and *G. W. Wilson*, for appellant.

Davis & Brooks, for appellee.

ROTHROCK, J.—When the court determined, at the first
trial, that the plaintiff could not recover without a reformation of the written contract, the plaintiff made no objection
to the ruling, but acquiesced therein by filing a petition in
equity; and, when the equity cause was determined against
him, he made no objection to that decision, but filed another
petition at law. When the evidence was closed at the last
trial, and counsel had argued the case to the jury, the court
on its own motion instructed the jury to return a verdict for
the defendant. This instruction was given, and the verdict
returned, on the fourth day of the month. The plaintiff did
not except to the instruction at the time it was given, nor at
any other time. Judgment was entered on the verdict on the
tenth day of the same month. The first and only exception
made to any of the above rulings and orders of the court
was a general exception entered to the final judgment rendered by the court.

It is very plain that the plaintiff, by acquiescing in the rulings of the court by which three trials were had for the same claim, precluded himself from appealing from such orders; and it is equally clear that his failure to except to the instruction given by the court to the jury precludes him from now complaining of that ruling of the court. Exceptions to instructions to the jury must be taken at the time the jury is charged, or within three days after the verdict. Code, § 2789; *Harrison v. Charlton*, 42 Iowa, 573. As the alleged error of the court in giving the instruction complained of lies at the threshold of an examination of the case in this court, the judgment of the circuit court must be

AFFIRMED.

Stewart v. The Waterloo Turn Verein.

1. **Corporations**: LIABILITY AS NATURAL PERSONS: SALE OF INTOXICATING LIQUORS. Corporations are to be considered as persons, when the circumstances in which they are placed are identical with those of natural persons expressly included in a statute, (*Wales v. City of Muscatine*, 4 Iowa, 302.) Accordingly, *held* that a corporation which, by a committee, sold beer to a person in the habit of becoming intoxicated, at a ball given under its supervision, was liable, under § 1539 of the Code, the same as a natural person, for the penalty thereby provided to be collected for the benefit of the school fund.

Appeal from Black Hawk Circuit Court.

THURSDAY, MARCH 10.

THE plaintiff, a citizen of Black Hawk county, seeks by this action to recover of the defendant, for the use of the school fund, the sum of $100 for unlawfully selling beer to one Heizer, who is a person in the habit of becoming intoxicated. The defendant alleges that it is a corporation, and not liable to prosecution for the act complained of. There was a trial by jury. The plaintiff offered and introduced

his evidence, whereupon the court, on motion of the defendant, instructed the jury to return a verdict for the defendant,
which was accordingly done. From a judgment upon the
verdict plaintiff appeals.

C. W. Mullan, for appellant.

M. T. Owens and *J. L. Husted*, for appellee.

ROTHROCK, J.—The cause involves less than $100, and the
appeal comes to us upon a certificate of the trial judge,
from which it appears that the defendant is a corporation
organized under the provisions of chapter 2, tit. 9, of the
Code, which provides for the organization of "corporations
other than those for pecuniary profit." The objects of the
corporation are declared in the articles of incorporation to be
"the intellectual and physical improvement of the members,
by forming and keeping up a library, by establishing a school
for instruction in gymnastic exercises, under such laws, rules
and regulations as are now and shall be hereafter prescribed
by said Waterloo Turn Verein, not in conflict with the
constitution and laws of the state of Iowa." Another
provision of said articles of incorporation is as follows:
"The said corporation may sue and be sued by and
under its corporate name, and may purchase and hold both
real and personal property, and sell and dispose of the same
in and by its corporate name, and have and exercise all the
powers and privileges which an individual person possesses
and exercises, in the transaction of business, etc., under and
by virtue of the laws of the state of Iowa." The business
of the corporation is conducted by a speaker, a vice-speaker,
treasurer, secretary, financial secretary, two teachers of gym-
nastics, librarian, and three trustees.

At a regular meeting of said corporation, held February
14, 1884, it was resolved "to have a masquerade ball," and
five members of the corporation were appointed a committee
to provide for and take charge of said entertainment. The

speaker of the corporation was one of this committee. The masquerade ball was held at Waterloo on the twenty-sixth day of February, 1884, at which ball two of said committee sold beer to a number of persons, and the sales were made with the knowledge of the speaker. The money received from the sale of the beer, with the other proceeds of the entertainment, was reported by the committee to the corporation at a subsequent meeting, and turned over to the treasurer of the corporation. No mention was made in the report of said committee, or otherwise, that any part of the proceeds so reported was derived from the sale of beer.

The questions certified as arising upon the foregoing facts are as follows: "(1) Whether the sale of beer by the members of said committee, at the entertainment aforesaid, to a person in the habit of becoming intoxicated, subjects the defendant to the penalty provided in section 1539 of the Code. (2) Is the defendant corporation a person within the meaning of said section 1539?"

Section 4326 of the Code contemplates that there are some offenses for which a corporation may be indicted and punished. It provides for process upon an indictment against a corporation, and it appears to be well settled that a corporation may be indicted and punished for a public nuisance, such as the obstruction of a public highway, a navigable stream, and the like. Wood, Nuis., 783. The case at bar is not a criminal action prosecuted by indictment. It is in form a civil action for a penalty, and jurisdiction of the defendant is obtained by the service of an original notice as in a civil action. The penalty is a judgment for money. It does not involve imprisonment. There is therefore no obstacle in the way of the prosecution of an action against a corporation, the same as against a natural person. It is provided by subdivision 12 of section 45 of the Code that "the word 'person' may be extended to bodies corporate.", This is laid down as a rule to be observed in the construction of the statutes of this state. It is apparent, however,

that this rule cannot be of universal application, especially
in the construction of criminal statutes, for the reason that
there are some crimes for which a corporation cannot be punished. For example, if all the members of a corporation
should be guilty of a criminal homicide in pursuance of a
resolution of the corporation, the corporation would not be
liable to indictment for the murder. The true rule is
that corporations are to be considered as persons when the
circumstances in which they are placed are identical with
those of natural persons expressly included in a statute.
Wales v. City of Muscatine, 4 Iowa, 302; *South Carolina
R. Co. v. McDonald*, 5 Ga., 531.

Applying this rule to the case at bar, it is clear that a corporation is a person within the meaning of section 1539 of
the Code.   There is nothing therein which may not be applied
as well to a corporation as to a natural person, and there is
no more reason for claiming that a private corporation is not
included within its provisions than there is in holding that
such a corporation is a person within the meaning of the law
authorizing attachment by garnishment, or any other provision of the statute equally applicable to natural and artificial
persons.

It appears from the facts certified in this case that the corporation "ordered the ball."   Its principal officer was one of
the managing committee, and knew of the violation of the
law; and the money arising from the sale of the beer was
received by the corporation.   Under these circumstances, the
evidence as to the participation of the corporation in violating the law was abundant.   It was not necessary to prove
that the beer was ordered and sold by an order of the defendant made in its corporate capacity.   When a railroad company is indicted for a nuisance in obstructing a public highway in this state, (a prosecution which is of frequent occurrence,) it has never been thought necessary to prove that the
obstruction was placed in the highway in pursuance of some
resolution of the board of directors of the corporation.   The

corporation is liable for the acts of its agents and employes in such cases.

In regard to the liability of private corporations for violations of criminal laws, Mr. Morawetz, in his work on Private Corporations, employs this language, (volume 2, §§ 732, 733): "It follows, therefore, that a corporation cannot be charged criminally with a crime involving malice, or the intention of the offense. Even though the corporators themselves should unanimously join, with malice aforethought, in committing a crime as a corporate act, yet the malice would be that of the several members of the company, and not actually one malicious intention of the whole company. There, are, however, certain classes of crimes which do not depend upon the intention of the offender, and are not distinguishable from simple torts, except by the fact that in the one case an individual sues for damages on account of a private tort, and in the other case the state sues for a penalty on account of a public wrong. In these cases the crime consists of the act alone, without regard to the intention with which it was committed; and there is no difficulty in attributing an offense of this character to a corporation, since it may be committed entirely through the company's agents. Accordingly, it has been held that a corporation may be indicted for causing a public nuisance, for not performing a duty cast upon it by law, or for doing any act which is made indictable, without regard to the intention of the offender." The author cites many authorities in support of the text, and it appears to us that the principles therein laid down are so plainly correct as to command the approval of every legal mind.

Applying these principles to the case at bar, the conclusion is inevitable that the defendant is liable. The persons who sold the beer, and the officers and members of the corporation who stood by and acquiesced in the sales, were not actuated by malice. They doubtless believed that the beer gave zest to the ball, and added to the enjoyment of the entertainment. They had "malice towards none, but charity for all," and thought it no crime to dispense to the festive throng that which they believed to be exhilarating but not intoxicating.

We think both of the questions certified should be answered in the affirmative.

REVERSED.

OHLQUEST v. FARWELL & CO. ET AL.

1. **Attorney and Client:** LIMIT OF ATTORNEY'S AUTHORITY. While an attorney cannot consent to a judgment against his client, nor waive any cause of action or defense in the case, nor settle or compromise it, without his special authority, yet he is authorized by his general employment to do all acts necessary or incidental to the prosecution or defense, which pertain to the *remedy* pursued. And, in the application of this rule, *held* that, where a client was a party to two suits involving substantially the same question, it was competent for his attorney to bind him by an agreement that only one of the cases should be tried, and that the judgment resulting from such trial should determine the kind of judgment to be entered in the other case.

Appeal from Linn District Court.

THURSDAY, MARCH 10.

A MOTION by defendant Becker to vacate and set aside a judgment in this case against him, as well as the other defendants, was, by order of the district court, overruled. From that order he now appeals to this court.

J. S. Stacy and *J. C. Davis*, for appellants.

Tenny, Bashford & Tenny and *Herrick & Doxsee*, for appellees.

BECK, J.—I. The facts involved in this case are as follows: J. V. Farwell & Co., G. Becker, and another firm, brought actions by attachment in the district court of Jones county against A. & P. Ohlquest. Two other actions by other firms were brought in the same court by attachment against Ohlquest Bros. The defendants in all of these actions were the same. They were doing business under the firm name of Ohlquest Bros., in both Jones and Linn counties. Writs of attachment were issued in the cases to the sheriffs of Jones and Linn counties, and levied upon separate stocks of goods found in each county; Farwell & Co.'s attachments being levied first in each county, Becker's second in Jones county, and last in Linn. Judgments were rendered in all of these actions, and such proceedings were had, after considerable litigation and delay, that Farwell & Co.'s and Becker's judgments were satisfied in full from the avails of the property attached.

N. A. Sunburg, claiming to own the goods seized in Jones county, brought an action against the sheriff to recover the value thereof. Farwell & Co. were finally substituted as defendants. N. A. Sunburg and F. B. Ohlquest, who claimed to own the goods seized in Linn county, brought an action for their value against the sheriff of that county, in which Farwell & Co., Becker, and other attaching creditors, were substituted as defendants. It thus appears that separate suits, one in Jones and the other in Linn county, having different parties both as defendants and plaintiffs, were pending for the recovery of the value of the goods which had been seized and sold upon the attachments, and the avails thereof appropriated to the satisfaction of Farwell & Co.'s and Becker's judgments. The issues in these cases involved the question whether the goods were the property of the Ohlquests, and whether the sales by them to the plaintiffs in these suits were valid or fraudulent, and therefore void. Herrick & Doxsee and E. Keeler were the attorneys for Farwell & Co., Becker, and some other attaching creditors, both in the attachment suits and in the actions against the parties brought to recover the value of the goods. The litigation in the suits last named was protracted and strongly contested on both sides. A written agreement was finally entered into between the attorneys just mentioned, representing the parties we have named, and the attorneys on the other side, to the effect that the Jones county cases should be tried, and judgment should be entered in the Linn county case for plaintiff or defendant in accord with the verdict and judgment in the Jones county case; thus settling both cases by one trial. The judgment in Linn county, in case plaintiff recovered, was to be in proportion to the amount realized by the sale of the goods seized in that county. The trial was had in Jones county, and judgment was rendered for plaintiffs, which was affirmed in the supreme court. Thereupon the attorneys of the parties united in a stipulation authorizing judgment in the Linn county case pursuant to the agreement just referred to, which was accordingly entered. The defendant Becker filed his motion to set aside this judgment, on the ground that the agreement therefor by the attorneys representing him was made without his authority or consent. The motion was overruled. The correctness of this action is brought in question upon this appeal.

II. It is undoubtedly true that an attorney cannot consent to a judgment against his client, or waive any cause of action or defense in the case; neither can he settle or compromise it without special authority. But he is, by his general employment, authorized to do all acts necessary or incidental to the prosecution or defense which pertain to the remedy pursued. The choice of proceedings, the manner of trial, and the like, are all within the sphere of his general authority, and, as to these matters, his client is bound by his action. These rules are conceded by counsel in this case. It cannot be doubted that under them counsel for parties in several suits, involving the same issues, may, in the exercise of their general authority, consent to the consolidation of all for trial, or stipulate that the trial of one shall determine the others. This pertains to the remedy pursued,—to the manner of trial,—and is not an agreement for judgment or

a compromise. The parties are not deprived of a trial, nor
is judgment rendered by consent. The counsel simply
assent to a trial in a particular manner; that one trial shall
settle the same issues in several cases. This is just what
was done by counsel for Becker in this case. The form of
the agreement is that judgment in his case should follow a
trial in another action. This is not an agreement for a
judgment, but in effect an agreement for a manner of trial.
No question is presented in the case involving the skill, diligence, or good faith of Becker's attorneys in assenting to one
trial in the several cases. The authority to do so is alone
brought in question.

We need pursue the case no further. The familiar and
undisputed principles we have stated, applied to the admitted
facts in the case, demand that the judgment of the district
court be

AFFIRMED.

THE CHARLES CITY PLOW & MANF'G CO. v. JONES & CO. ET AL.

1. **Attachment:** ACTION ON BOND: EVIDENCE. Where an attachment
was issued on the ground that defendants were about to dispose of their
property with intent to defraud their creditors, and defendants sought
to recover on the bond for the wrongful suing out of the attachment,
held that the testimony of one of them that they had no such intent
was irrelevant to the issue. (*Selz v. Belden*, 48 Iowa, 451, followed)

2. ————: RETURN OF SHERIFF: WHAT IT IS EVIDENCE OF. A sheriff's
return upon a writ of attachment is evidence only of such of his acts as
he may lawfully do under and by virtue of the writ. And so, where
the sheriff returned not only that he had seized certain chattels under
the writ, but that he had also, at plaintiff's direction, seized, closed up
and held possession of the houses in which the chattels were stored,
which was not necessary for the preservation of the chattels, *held*, in an
action on the attachment bond, that the return was not evidence of
such seizure of the buildings, nor of the attachment plaintiff's direction
so to seize them.

3. ————: WRONGFUL SUING OUT: ADVICE OF COUNSEL WHO ARE STOCK-
HOLDERS OF THE PLAINTIFF. In an action on an attachment bond for

the wrongful suing out of the attachment, the attachment plaintiff m iy show, for the purpose of rebutting the charge of malice, that it sought the advice of counsel, and acted under such advice, in suing out the attachment, even though the counsel consulted were stockholders or officers of the attachment plaintiff, which was a corporation.

4. ——: ——: ——: EVIDENCE OF CONVERSATION WITH COUNSEL. In such case, evidence should have been admitted of the conversation between the attachment plaintiff's business manager and its attorneys, relative to the suing out of the attachment.

5. ——: ——: ADVICE OF LAWYER NOT IN PRACTICE. In such case, the attachment plaintiff may show that it consulted an attorney by profession, but not in actual practice, and that he advised the suing out of the attachment.

6. **Damages:** MEASURE OF: LIMITED BY PLEADINGS: ERRONEOUS INSTRUCTION. Where some of the evidence tended to show that defendants' damages were greater than claimed in their counterclaim, it was error for the court to instruct the jury that if they found for the defendants they should award them such damages as the *evidence* showed them to be entitled to.

7. ——: ——: USE OF STORE FOR ATTACHED PROPERTY. Where certain articles in a stock of goods were levied on by attachment, and the building also was seized, but the attached property was left in the possession of one of the attachment defendants, (who were partners,) and his receipts taken for the same, and the key of the building was also left with him, and he was the person who had charge of the store and stock of goods, and he had the privilege from the sheriff to carry on the business at the store, but he voluntarily relinquished the charge of the store and surrendered the keys to the sheriff, who locked up the building for a time, *held* that defendants' measure of damages for the seizure of the building was not the value of its use from the date of the levy to the date of the release, but only the value of the storage of so much of the attached property as was in the building.

Appeal from Floyd Circuit Court.

THURSDAY, MARCH 10.

PLAINTIFF brought an action against defendants on a money demand, and sued out a writ of attachment, on which certain personal property belonging to defendants was seized. There was no controversy as to plaintiff's demand, but defendants pleaded a counter-claim for damages on the attachment bond for the wrongful suing out of the attachment. On the trial, defendants recovered on the counter-claim, and plaintiff appeals.

Ellis & Ellis, for appellant.

Starr & Harrison and *J. C. Cook*, for appellees.

REED, J.—I. The grounds on which the attachment was sued out were "that defendants are about to dispose of their property with intent to defraud their creditors, and that defendants have property or rights in action which they conceal." On the trial a member of defendants' firm was examined as a witness on behalf of his firm, and was asked whether the firm, before the attachment was issued, was about to dispose of its property with intent to defraud its creditors, or whether there was any talk or intimation or intent on their part of doing so in the future. It was alleged, in an amended abstract filed by appellees, that these questions were not objected to, and, this allegation being denied by appellant in an additional abstract, we were required, in determining the controversy, to examine the transcript. We find, upon an examination of the bill of exceptions, that the questions were objected to on the ground of incompetency. Under the rule laid down in *Selz v. Belden*, 48 Iowa, 451, the objection should have been sustained.

1. ATTACH-MENT: action on bond; evidence.

II. The writ of attachment was directed to the sheriff of Kossuth county, and was levied on property in that county; the levy being made by the deputy-sheriff, who certified in his return that he had seized, on the writ, eighty-five plows, two churns, a ledger and day-book, one safe, two buggies, five corn-planters and five horses, and had garnished certain persons as supposed debtors of the defendants. Before the writ was returned, however, all of the property except the eighty-nve plows was released, and the fact of such release was shown by the certificate of the sheriff indorsed on the writ. The

2. ———: return of sheriff: what it is evidence of.

plows, when the levy was made, were situated in a building which is described in the return as the east warehouse, while the other property (except the five horses) was in the business house in which defendants carried on business. At the term at which the cause was tried, the sheriff filed what is denominated an amendment to the return, in which he certified that, when the levy was made, by direction of plaintiff, he seized and locked up both buildings in which the property was situated, and that he kept possession of the storeroom or building in which defendants carried on business for one month, when he released it, and restored it to defendants, and that he continued to hold possession of the warehouse in which the plows were situated.

One of the matters complained of by defendants, and for which they claimed damages, was that they were deprived of the use of these buildings. On the trial they offered the amendment to the return in evidence, and it was admitted by the court, over the objection of plaintiff. There is no claim that the writ was levied on either of the buildings, or that the officer had any intention of seizing them. Neither is it shown by the return that it was necessary to retain possession of the store-room as a place of deposit for the articles which were in it when the levy was made and were seized by the officer. We have, therefore, no occasion to inquire whether the sheriff might occupy it as a place of deposit for the goods, to the exclusion of defendants, and without their consent. It is clear, however, that, unless he occupied it for some purpose which was connected with the execution of the writ, his act was a trespass; and it may be conceded that, if plaintiff directed him to commit the act, it is liable therefor. But whether their liability therefor would be on the attachment bond we do not determine, as that question was not raised by the objection. But it does not appear by the return that the act was committed in the execution of the writ. It appears simply that he levied on the property; and that, by direction of the plaintiff, he locked up the building, and that he retained possession of it for one month.

The sheriff is required by the statute (Code, § 3010) to return upon every attachment what he has done under it. The return should show what property was attached, and the disposition made of it, and all acts done by the officer in the execution of the writ, and his return is evidence against the parties as to the acts done by him in executing it, which are required by law to be shown by the return. But, under the ruling of the circuit court, the return was received as evidence of the locking up and retention of the building by the sheriff, and that this was done by plaintiff's direction. We are of the opinion that it was not competent evidence against it of those facts. If the sheriff had returned that in making the levy he had committed an assault on defendant, and that in committing that act he acted under the direction of the plaintiff, it would hardly be contended that in an action against the plaintiff for the assault the return would be admissible in evidence to prove either the commission of the assault, or that it was committed by its direction. Yet, upon the facts shown by the return, there is no difference in principle between this case and that. The return recites, in effect, that the officer, by plaintiff's direction, committed a trespass against defendant's property, while in the supposed case the act would be a trespass against his person.

III. Plaintiff claimed that, before it sued out the writ, it made a statement of the facts to counsel, who advised it that upon the facts there was probable ground

3. ——:
wrongful su-
ing out: ad-
vice of coun-
sel who are
stockholders
of the plaint-
iff.

for the action, and that in suing out the writ it acted on that advice. The proof showed that the advice was given by a firm of attorneys, both members of which held stock in the corporation, (plaintiff being a corporation,) and one of whom was an officer of the corporation; and the circuit court instructed the jury to disregard the evidence given in sup-

port of the defense.   By this ruling the court in effect held
as matter of law, that, owing to the relations which the
attorneys bore to the corporation, it could not show that it
acted on their advice in suing out the writ, in rebuttal of
the presumption of malice which might arise from the fact
that no probable cause for the action existed.   This is erroneous.   The question was one of fact.   The counsel were
not necessarily incapable of giving a correct opinion on the
fact because of their pecuniary interest in the result.   The
question in every such case is whether the party has honestly sought the advice of competent and trustworthy counsel, and acted in good faith on the advice given him; and
that question is for the jury, and should be determined by
them, like any other question of fact, from all the circumstances of the case.   *Center v. Spring*, 2 Iowa, 393.

IV.   The petition was sworn to by plaintiff's business
manager.   The president of the corporation was examined

4. ——: ——: as a witness, and testified that he was present at
——: evi-
dence of con- the consultation with the attorneys when it was
versation
with counsel. determined that the writ should be sued out.
He was asked to state the conversation between the business
manager and the attorneys, but, on defendants' objection,
the question was excluded.   It should have been allowed.
Plaintiff was required to prove that the advice of the counsel, on which it claims to have acted, was given upon a full
and fair statement of the facts of the case, and the evidence
sought to be elicited related to that matter.   The witness
also testified that he is a lawyer by profession, although he

5. ——: ——: was not then engaged in the practice; and he
advice of law-
yer not in was asked whether a statement of the facts of
practice. the case had not been made to him, and whether
he had not, on that statement, advised the suing out of the
writ; but the court sustained an objection by defendants to
this question.   We think these rulings were wrong.   As we
have said, the question whether plaintiff, in suing out the
writ, acted in good faith, on the advice of counsel, was one

of fact. It could no't be determined, as matter of law, that it did not so act, merely because the advice upon which it acted was given by one who, although learned in the law, was not engaged in the active practice of his profession.

V. The defendants in their counter-claim set out the different items of damages which they sought to recover.

6. DAMAGES: measure of: limited by pleadings: erroneous instruction.

In some instances the evidence tended to prove that their damage was greater than the amount claimed in the pleading. The court instructed the jury that if they found for defendants they should award them such sum as the evidence showed would be a just compensation for the injury sustained by them in consequence of the suing out of the writ, and the seizure of their property thereon. Under the instructions and evidence the jury would be warranted in awarding them, in some instances, an amount greater than was claimed in their pleading. The jury should have been told that they could not award a greater sum than was claimed in the pleadings. This error was doubtless committed through inadvertence, but it was clearly prejudicial.

VI. When the levy was made, the property was left in the possession of one member of defendants' firm, who gave

7. —: —: use of store for attached property.

his receipt therefor. He was left in possession of the store, and the key was left with him. As we understand the evidence, there was an exten-sive stock of goods in the store, and but a few articles of the stock were levied upon. The member of the firm who was left in possession was in charge of the business; the other partners being absent. He had the privilege of continuing the business, and even of selling any portion of the attached property; being required, however, to pay over to the sher-iff the proceeds of any such sales. He remained in posses-sion but a few days after the levy, when he stated to the sheriff that he would no longer be responsible for the prop-erty, and surrendered to him the keys to the store. Under the rulings of the circuit court on the trial, defendants were allowed to recover, as part of their damages, the value of the use of the store from the date of the levy to the time of the release by the sheriff of the property in it. As they had the privilege of using the building themselves during that time, and voluntarily relinquished that privilege, they are not entitled to recover the value of its use. If they are entitled to recover any amount on that claim, the measure of their recovery is the value of the storage of such of the attached property as was in the building.

Many other assignments of error have been argued by counsel. Some of the rulings complained of are clearly right, but they do not present any question which we deem of sufficient importance to demand special notice in this opinion; others are perhaps technically erroneous, but are not prejudicial; while others relate merely to the conduct of the trial, and will not probably arise again.

For the errors pointed out, the judgment will be reversed, and the cause remanded for a new trial.

REVERSED.

SAYLES v. SMITH.

1. **Appeal:** CERTIFICATE TO EVIDENCE: DATE OF: TOO LATE. The certificate of the judge to the evidence in this case was headed "May term, 1885," that being the term when the case was tried and submitted: but at the end, just before the judge's signature, was the date, "September 15, 1886." *Held* that the certificate must be regarded as made at the date last named, and that, being more than six months subsequent to the date of the decree appealed from, it was too late, and the appeal (the case being in equity) must be dismissed.

Appeal from Guthrie Circuit Court.

THURSDAY, MARCH 10.

ACTION TO QUIET TITLE. There was a decree for the defendant. The plaintiff appeals.

Lyman Porter, for appellant.

C. S. Fogg, for appellee.

ADAMS, CH. J.—The appellee insists that the judge's certificate to the evidence was not made within the time allowed for an appeal. The case was heard at the May term, 1885, and was then taken under advisement, and a decree rendered December 16, 1885. The evidence appears to have been certified September 15, 1886. The appellee's abstract and transcript show the judge's certificate to be in these words:

"*E. R. Sayles v. J. F. Smith.*

"IN THE CIRCUIT COURT OF GUTHRIE COUNTY, IOWA, MAY TERM, 1885.

"I hereby certify that the foregoing transcript, together with the exhibits, records, and depositions therein referred to, contain all the evidence offered and objections made on the trial of the above-entitled cause.

"*September*, 15, 1886.   S. A. CALLVERT, Judge.

The appellant insists that the certificate appears to have been made at the May term, 1885; but we think otherwise. We think that term was mentioned merely as the term at which the case was tried and submitted. The date at the bottom of the certificate was evidently intended to show the time when it was made. The certificate, then, was not made within the time allowed for an appeal, and the case must be

DISMISSED.

THE AMERICAN INSURANCE CO. v. GARRETT.

1. **Fire Insurance**: SURRENDER OF POLICY: LIABILITY FOR OVERDUE PREMIUMS. The holder of a policy of fire insurance cannot avoid liability on a premium note, for an installment already past due, by surrendering the policy to the company.

Appeal from Buchanan Circuit Court.

THURSDAY, MARCH 10.

THIS is an action upon a promissory note, brought by a fire insurance company. There was a trial by jury, and a verdict and judgment for the defendant. Plaintiff appeals.

Chas. E. Ransier, E. M. Thompson and *Geo. W. Wilson,* for appellant.

L. F. Springer and *J. H. Williamson,* for appellee.

ROTHROOK, J.—The note in suit is in these words:

"$50.

"For value received in policy No. 176,619, dated the twenty-ninth day of June, 1874, issued by the American Insurance Company, of Chicago, Illinois, I promise to pay the said company twelve dollars and fifty cents on the first day of June, 1875, and twelve dollars and fifty cents on the first day of June, 1876, and twelve dollars and fifty cents on the first day of June, 1877, and twelve dollars and fifty cents on the first day of June, 1878, without interest.

"R. P. GARRETT."

The amount in controversy being less than $100, the appeal comes to us upon the following certificate of the trial judge:

"The amount in controversy in this cause, as shown by the pleadings, does not exceed one hundred dollars. The cause involves the determination of a question of law upon which it is desirable to have the opinion of the supreme court, as follows: *First.* Is it a complete defense to an action on an installment promissory note, due in four equal annual installments, given for the premium on an insurance policy, the execution of which note is admitted by the answer, to show that the assured, more than a year after said note was given, mailed the policy to the insurance company, plaintiff, and in the letter accompanying said policy requested cancellation thereof, the assured neither paying, nor offering to pay, any part of the premium note,—there being at that time one installment of the note past due and unpaid, and three installments not mature, there having been two notes given for the premium on said policy, the first of which was paid when it became due, upon notice from the company, and no notice of non-acceptance and of cancellation of policy, as requested by defendant, was ever received by the defendant, and no notice to pay the further installments due on said note as they became due, no notice having afterwards been received by the defendant to pay said note, and there being no evidence of the condition of the policy of insurance? *Second.* Under the facts being shown on the trial in the foregoing question, was it error in the court to overrule plaintiff's motion to direct a verdict for plaintiff ? *Third.* Under the facts being shown on the trial as stated in the first question, was it error on the part of the court, on its own motion, to direct a verdict for the defendant? This certificate is made by the court at the time of overruling plaintiff's motion for a new trial, and at the time judgment is rendered in said action against the plaintiff, on this October 16, 1885. W. H. UTT, Circuit Judge."

It will be observed that the note in suit names the consideration thereof to be the policy of insurance. It was a contract of insurance, and the defendant claims that he rescinded the contract by returning the policy to the plaintiff. But the certificate shows that this rescission was not made until after the first installment of the notes became due. The defendant was surely liable to pay all dues up to the time that he chose to rescind the contract. In order to absolve himself from further liability to the plaintiff, he should have paid the installment then due. We think that, under the facts, the jury should not have·been directed to return a verdict for the defendant.

REVERSED.

SLYFIELD v. BARNUM ET AL.

CLARK v. THE SAME.

71 245
97 269
71 24:
105 11
71 24:
112 331
112 334
71 24,
117 6

1. **Tax Sale and Deed:** NOTICE TO REDEEM TO WRONG PERSON: STATUTE OF LIMITATIONS. Where the notice to redeem from a tax sale is directed to a person other than the one to whom the land is taxed, it is no notice at all, and does not cut off the right of redemption as against one who takes a tax deed under the sale; and in such case the period of limitation (Code, § 902,) does not begin to run from the date of the tax deed. (*Trulock v. Bentley,* 67 Iowa, 602, distinguished.)

2. ——: REDEMPTION: TERMS OF: FILING DUPLICATE TAX RECEIPTS. Section 889 of the Code, requiring one who pays taxes on lands purchased at tax sale to file a duplicate tax receipt with the county auditor, has nothing to do with the amount which the holder of the patent title must pay to redeem, when redemption is effected by a suit in equity; but in such case the redemptioner is required to pay the interest and penalty provided by § 890 of the Code on each installment of taxes which has been paid by the purchaser.

Appeal from Palo Alto District Court.

FRIDAY, MARCH 11.

THESE are actions to redeem lands from tax sales after treasurer's deeds had been executed to the purchasers. The district court entered judgments denying to plaintiffs the right of redemption, and they appealed.

A. F. Call and *George E Clark,* for appellants.

Soper, Crawford & Carr, for appellees.

REED, J.—The treasurer's deeds under which defendants

claim were executed more than five years before these suits
were instituted. No person was then in possession of either of the tracts, but that involved in
one of the cases was taxed for the year in which
the deed was executed to J. Graham, and that
involved in the other case to J. W. Van Myers. After the
expiration of two years and nine months from the sales, the
owners of the certificates of purchase caused notices of the
expiration of the period for redemption to be published in a
newspaper, but the notice in each case was directed to C. C.
Smeltzer and the "unknown owners" of the land. The only
evidence of the service of the notices which was on file in
the treasurer's office when the deeds were executed was the
affidavits of the publisher of the newspaper in which they
were published, showing the fact of the publications and the
dates thereof. The first question which arises in the case is
whether plaintiffs' right of action is barred by the statute of
limitations.

1. TAX sale
and deed:
notice to
redeem to
wrong per-
son: statute
of limitations.

　We held in *Trulock v. Bentley*, 67 Iowa, 602, when the
notice required by the statute had in fact been given to the
person in whose name the land was taxed, but the proof of
the service of such notice on file when the deed was executed
was defective, that the period of limitation provided by section 902 of the Code commenced to run from the date of the
execution and recording of the deed. The ground of that
holding is that, as the notice required by the statute was in
fact given to the person who was entitled to redeem from the
sale, the deed was not void because of the defective or irregular manner in which the service of the notice had been
proven, but that this was a mere defect in the proceeding,
which could be taken advantage of only within the five years,
which is the period within which an action may be brought,
under the statute, for the recovery of the property.

　But these cases do not come within that holding. True,
the proof of the service of such notice as was given was
defective, but the notice itself was not directed to the per-

son who was required by the statute to be notified. Published notices directed to C. C. Smeltzer and the unknown owners of the lands were in no sense notices to J. Graham and J. W. Van Myers, the persons to whom the lands were taxed. It was not a case of defective proof of service of notice, but of no notice whatever. Now, the requirement of the statute, when the land is taxed to a particular person, is that the notice shall be served on that person. Code, § 894. Under that and the following section the power of the treasurer, in such cases, to execute a deed, is dependent on the giving of the notice. Unless the notice has been served on the person in whose name the land is taxed, he is not authorized to execute a deed. The deeds in question, then, were executed without authority. They are not absolutely void, it is true, for they operated to transfer the title to the lands to the grantees. But they did not have the effect to terminate the right of redemption, and the title conveyed by them was subject to be defeated by the exercise of that right; (*Bowers v. Hallock, ante* 218;) and, as long as a right to redeem the lands exists, there is no completed sale; and the settled rule is that until there is a completed sale the period of limitation presented by the statute does not begin to run. *Eldridge v. Kuehl,* 27 Iowa, 160; *Henderson v. Oliver,* 28 Id., 20; *McCready v. Sexton,* 29 Id., 356.

As we reach the conclusion that plaintiffs are entitled to redeem from the sales, a question arises as to the amount

2. ——: ——: they are required to pay in making the redemp-

redemption: terms of: filing duplicate tax receipts. tion. Defendants have paid the taxes on the lands for all of the years since the sale. For the taxes paid by them after the sale, and before the execution of the deeds, they filed duplicate receipts with the county auditor, as required by section 889 of the Code; but for the years subsequent to the execution of the deeds no such receipts were filed with the auditor. Plaintiff's contend that they should be permitted to redeem by paying the amount paid by defendants for the years for which the duplicate receipts were filed, with the interest and penalties thereon provided by section 890, together with the amount of the taxes for the subsequent years, with six per cent interest. Section 889 provides that the purchaser, when he pays taxes on the property subsequent to the sale, shall receive from the treasurer two receipts therefor, one of which he shall present to the county auditor. It also provides that, if he neglects or fails to file such duplicate receipt with the auditor before redemption, the taxes shall not be a lien upon the land, and he shall not be entitled to recover the same of the owner of the property. The provisions of this section apply to cases in which redemption is made by paying the amount necessary therefor to the auditor. They amount simply to this: that, when the person entitled to redeem has paid to the auditor the amount necessary to effect a redemption, as shown by the duplicate receipts on file in the auditor's office, the redemption is complete, and no further claim can be asserted, either against him or the land, for taxes which have been paid by the purchaser on the property. But these provisions have no application to cases in which redemption is effected by a suit in equity; but, when redemption is effected in that manner, the redemptioner is required to pay the interest and penalty provided by section 890 on each install-ment of taxes which has been paid by the purchaser.

The judgment of the district court will be reversed, and that court will be directed to enter a judgment establishing the right of plaintiffs to redeem the property by paying the amounts which we have indicated are necessary to effect the redemption.

REVERSED.

THE ESTATE OF PACKER v. CORLETT.

1. **Estates of Decedents**: FEES OF CLERK. Under § 3787 of the Code, the clerk is entitled to only three dollars for all services performed by him in the settlement of an estate which does not exceed three thousand dollars in value; all fees taxed by him in excess of that sum in such a case are illegal.

Appeal from Clayton Circuit Court.

FRIDAY, MARCH 11.

THIS case involves the question as to the legality of certain fees taxed by the defendant, who is clerk of the circuit court of Clayton county, said fees having been taxed in the course of the settlement of the estate of O. Packer, deceased. The circuit court held that the fees were illegal, and the defendant appeals.

J. Larkin, for appellant.

A. Chapin, for appellee.

ROTHROCK, J.—The value of the estate did not exceed $3,000, and the clerk taxed the costs for the settlement thereof at $9.40. The amount was made up of several items, including a fee for the order appointing the administrator, another fee for filing and approving the administrator's bond, another item for the commission issued to the administrator, and fees for an application to sell real estate, etc. The administrator contends that all these items of fees are unauthorized by law, and the circuit court so held. The amount in controversy involves less than $100, and we acquire jurisdiction of the appeal by the following certificate of the trial judge: "In an estate of which the value does not exceed $3,000, and no complete record has been made, in which a will has been duly admitted to probate, the certificate of the clerk and the seal of the court as to said probate duly attached, an administrator duly appointed, whose bond was duly filed with said clerk, approved and recorded, a commission of appointment issued to said administrator, an order for publication of notice of appointment of administrator made, an application of said administrator to sell realty duly filed in said court, an order made that said application should be heard at McGregor, and that notice of said hearing should be given, and said application was once continued by said administrator without affidavit, and said administrator duly filed with the clerk of said court a final report and petition for discharge,—is the clerk of said court authorized to charge or tax as costs a greater sum than $3 for all of said services, including the further services of approving the report, and granting the discharge of the administrator?"

Section 3787 of the Code provides as follows: "There shall be paid to the clerk of the circuit court the following fees: *   *   *   For all services performed in the settlement of the estate of any decedent, except where actions are brought by the administrator or against him, or as may be otherwise provided herein, when the value of the estate does not exceed three thousand dollars, three dollars.   *   *   *"

It appears to us that this statute is so plain as to leave no room for doubt or construction. It fixes the clerk's charges or fees for all services in the settlement of an estate at a gross sum. It is useless to speculate as to what the legislature meant by such fees "as may be otherwise provided herein;" for, if this clause may be so enlarged as to refer to the whole Code, there is nothing therein authorizing the charging of the fees in question. It is true, section 3781 provides for fees for the clerks of the district and circuit courts for issuing and entering rules or orders, for approving bonds, etc., but it has no reference to the settlement of estates in the circuit court; and the best reason for so holding is that section 3787 makes special provision for fees in that behalf. The argument that the compensation provided by law is not sufficient for the service performed can have no weight, because the rule is that public officers are entitled to such fees only as are specially authorized by law.

We think the circuit court correctly held that the fees for the settlement of the estate could not exceed three dollars.

AFFIRMED.

WHITNEY & CO. v. BROWNEWELL ET AL.

PEREGOY & MOORE v. THE SAME.

SWEENEY & CO. v. THE SAME.

1. **Practice**: COURT NOT BOUND BY ITS OWN RULING: ILLUSTRATION. In this case, plaintiffs moved for a continuance on the ground of ,the absence of a witness, and the court erroneously held that the facts which it was alleged the witness would swear to were material to the issues. Defendants, however, offered to allow the affidavit for a continuance to be read as evidence of what the witness would swear to if present, and the trial proceeded. Afterwards, when plaintiffs offered to read the affidavit, defendants objected on the ground that the facts therein stated were not material, and the courts sustained the objection. *Held* no error, as the court was not bound to adhere to its erroneous ruling.

2. **Evidence**: ADMISSIONS OF ONE OF TWO DEFENDANTS. Evidence that one of two defendants made an admission derogatory to their defense cannot be admitted where the witness is unable to state which one of the defendants made the admission, since it could not bind the other.

3. ———: EXCLUSION: ERROR WITHOUT PREJUDICE. Where, in an action on an attachment bond, the jury found only nominal damages, it was at most error without prejudice to exclude evidence offered in mitigation of damages.

4. **Attachment**: ACTION ON BOND: ATTORNEYS' FEES. Where the whole defense in an attachment case tended to show the wrongfulness of the attachment, it was proper, in an action on the bond, to allow attorneys' fees for services in defending the entire case.

5. **Practice**: RIGHT TO OPEN AND CLOSE. Where, upon the pleadings, the plaintiffs had the burden of proof, but by failing to introduce evidence, they shifted the burden upon defendant, the latter had the right to open and close.

6. **Instruction**: ERROR WITHOUT PREJUDICE. An erroneous instruction is no ground for the reversal of a judgment which could not have been otherwise had the instruction not been given.

Appeal from Plymouth Circuit Court.

FRIDAY, MARCH 11.

THESE cases are submitted together as involving substantially the same question. The plaintiffs in the respective actions sold goods to the defendant George W. Brownewell, and the actions are brought to recover for the goods. Mrs. D. E. Brownewell, wife of George W. Brownewell, and Mrs. T. E. Murphy, mother of Mrs. Brownewell, are made defendants, and are sought to be made liable, upon the ground that they were silent partners with George W. Brownewell, or, if not, that they conspired with him to defraud the plaintiffs in the purchase of the goods. Writs of attachments were issued and levied upon the stock of goods which had been held by George W. Brownewell in trade, and also upon the lot and store building used in trade. Previous to the levy, George W. had conveyed the stock to Mrs. Murphy, and the lot and store building to Mrs. Brownewell, and Mrs. Murphy had conveyed the stock to Mrs. Brownewell in exchange for the lot and store building. Mrs. Murphy and Mrs. Brownewell denied all liability for the goods purchased, and claimed damages for the wrongful issuance and levy of the attachment. George W. Brownewell made default. As against Mrs. Murphy and Mrs. Brownewell, there was a trial to a jury, and judgment was rendered in their favor for one dollar as damages for the wrongful issuance and levy of the attachment. Judgment was rendered in their favor for attorney's fees. The plaintiffs appeal.

G. A. Girard and *Ira T. Martin*, for appellants.

T. B. S. O'Dea and *Argo & Kelly*, for appellees.

ADAMS, CH. J.—I. The plaintiffs assign several errors pertaining to the alleged liability of Mrs. Murphy and Mrs. Brownewell for the goods. We do not need to consider them. There was no evidence introduced or offered tending to show such liability, and the plaintiffs were not prejudiced by the alleged errors, if they were made.

II. The plaintiffs, by way of answer to the claim of Mrs. Murphy and Mrs. Brownewell for damages for the wrongful issuance and levy of the attachment, averred that the property levied upon had been conveyed to Mrs. Murphy and Mrs. Brownewell to defraud his creditors.

1. PRACTICE: court not bound by its own ruling: illustration.

To prove the fraud in the conveyance, the plaintiffs had relied upon one Richards as a witness, but they were unable to procure his attendance at the trial. They accordingly made an affidavit for a continuance on account of his absence. The court held the affidavit to be sufficient, but, the defendants offering to allow the affidavit to be read as showing what the testimony of Richards would be if present, the trial was allowed to proceed. Afterwards, when the plaintiffs offered to read the affidavit in evidence, the defendants objected, and the court sustained the objection, remarking, as the abstract shows, that the facts set forth in the affidavit as to what the witness, if present, would swear to, did not appear to be material. The refusal to allow the affidavit to be read in evidence is assigned as error. If the affidavit was sufficient to entitle the plaintiffs to a continuance, as the court held, they should have been allowed to read it in evidence. But the court was not bound to allow it to be read because of the former ruling. The court might examine the affidavit again; and, if it appeared from the second examination that the facts shown as to what the witness would swear to were not material, it was the duty of the court to exclude it, notwithstanding the former ruling. The question presented, then, is simply as to whether the facts shown were material. The alleged facts were that, after the sale and conveyance of the goods by George W. Brownewell to Mrs. Murphy, and of the lot and store building to Mrs. Brownewell, the witness Richards heard Brownewell talk about the transaction in the presence either of Mrs. Brownewell or Mrs. Murphy, and heard him state, in substance, that the sales were

2. EVIDENCE: admissions of one of two defendants.

fraudulent, and heard Mrs. Brownewell or Mrs. Murphy, whichever was the one present, admit the truth of what he said. Mrs. Brownewell's admission would, of course, have been competent to prove the fraudulent character of the sale made to her, and Mrs. Murphy's admission would have been competent to prove the fraudulent character of the sale made to her. But it is not shown that more than one made any admission, and it is not shown which one that was. The affidavit, then, would not have aided the jury in finding a verdict. We think that the court did not err in not admitting it.

III. The plaintiffs, J. R. Whitney & Co., in order to mitigate the damages alleged to have been sustained by the wrong-

3. ——: exclusion : error without prejudice.

ful issuance and levy of the attachment, pleaded that the goods, prior to the levy, had been seized and were being held by the sheriff on other writs of attachment against the same defendant. For the purpose of showing that J. R. Whitney & Co.'s writ was levied first, the defendants introduced Mrs. Brownewell as a witness, and she was allowed to testify that J. R. Whitney & Co.'s writ was levied first. They insist that it was error to admit parol evidence upon such a point. We have to say, however, that under the verdict we do not need to determine this question. The jury rendered a verdict for only nominal damages. If it had been conceded that J. R. Whitney & Co.'s attachment was subsequent to others, the defendants would have been entitled to nominal damages, if any.

IV. The allowance made for attorneys' fees appears to have been for their services in defending the entire case.

4. ATTACHMENT: action on bond: attorneys' fees.

The plaintiffs contend that there was error in this. But the whole defense made tended to show the wrongfulness of the attachment.

V. The plaintiffs contend that it was their right to open and close, and that the right was denied. They did have the

5. PRACTICE: right to open and close.

right to open by offering evidence tending to show the alleged liability of Mrs. Brownewell and Mrs. Murphy; but they introduced none. After that there was nothing to try but the question of damages, and as to that the burden was ou the defendants, and they had the right to open and close.

VI. In the twenty-first instruction the court instructed the jury that it was incumbent upon the plaintiffs to prove by a preponderance of evidence the existence of some one of the alleged causes of attachment. They contend that in this the court erred. But, as the plaintiffs introduced no evidence tending to show any indebtedness on the part of these appellees, the attachment, as against them, was wrongful, regardless of the statutory grounds of attachment.

6. INSTRUC-
TION: error
without preju-
dice.

VII. The plaintiffs complain that the issues were not fairly stated to the jury, but we think otherwise. We see no error.

AFFIRMED.

WENTWORTH v. BLACKMAN, EX'R, ET AL.

1. **Damages:** EXEMPLARY: WHEN NOT ALLOWABLE. In an action for the value of property alleged to have been wrongfully taken, where there was no evidence that it was taken maliciously, it was error for the court to instruct the jury that they might find exemplary damages; and where the verdict was much in excess of the value of the property, such instruction must have prejudiced defendants, and the judgment must be reversed.

2. **Evidence:** TITLE TO PERSONAL PROPERTY: INOPERATIVE CONTRACT OF SALE. In an action against B.'s executors, involving the title to certain old and unsalable castings in a foundry and machine shop, where it appeared that B. had been in possession, with the presumptive right of ownership, *held* that a contract of sale from B. to plaintiff of the real estate and machinery, but on which plaintiff had paid nothing, and under which, if he had ever taken possession, he had relinquished it again to B., was not admissible to prove plaintiff's title to the castings.

Appeal from Mitchell Circuit Court.

FRIDAY, MARCH 11.

THIS suit involves the question of the ownership of certain

personal property, consisting of iron castings and other articles which were for many years in an old, dilapidated and unused foundry and machine-shop. The plaintiff alleges that he was the owner of the property, and in possession thereof, and that defendants forcibly, unlawfully, willfully and maliciously broke open said building, and removed the property therefrom. He demanded judgment for the alleged value of the property, and for $100 exemplary damages. The defendants, who are the executors of the estate of George Briggs, deceased, claim that said property belongs to said estate. There was a trial by jury, and a verdict and judgment for the plaintiff. Defendants appeal.

F. F. Coffin and *Foreman & Marsh*, for appellants.

M. M. Browne, *L. M. Ryce* and *J. M. Moody*, for appellee.

ROTHROCK, J.—I. The evidence shows that Briggs was the owner of the foundry and machine shop, and that about

1. DAMAGES: exemplary: when not allowable.

the year 1873 he and the plaintiff formed a partnership, and carried on the business from that time to some time in the year 1875, when the partnership ceased, and Briggs carried on the business for a few months, and quit. The plaintiff afterwards ran the business for a time—in the years 1878 and 1879. During the time of the partnership, nearly all of the property in dispute accumulated in the foundry. It was manufactured by the firm, and possibly some of it was purchased by the firm. There has been no business done in the establishment since 1879. It has been practically closed since that time. Both of the partners were residents of Mitchell county, and in the year 1879 the plaintiff left this state, and went east, and remained there until after the death of Briggs, which occurred in the summer of 1883. The executors of Briggs, believing that these old castings and other property belonged to the estate, removed the same from the building. This is the·

ground of plaintiff's action and claim for vindictive damages. There is no evidence in the case authorizing any court or jury to find that the removal of the property was a malicious act. We do not propose to set out the evidence bearing upon the motives which prompted the act of removal. It is sufficient to say that it does not tend in the remotest degree to show malice, and the jury should not have been instructed that they might find exemplary damages. Such an instruction was given, and the amount of the verdict leads us to think that the jury must have found exemplary damages, because, as we view the evidence, the verdict was much in excess of the value of the old, rusty, dilapidated and unsalable property in controversy.

II. The property in dispute originally belonged to the partnership. There is no direct evidence that there was at any time a settlement of the partnership and a division of the partnership property. But it is conceded that, when the plaintiff quit the partnership, he went out, and left this property in the possession of Briggs, his late partner. Possession is presumptive evidence of ownership, and, without more, the inference would be that the property belonged to Briggs. It is true, the plaintiff testified generally that he owned the property when the defendants removed it from the building. But there is no evidence of when or where he purchased it of Briggs or of the partnership. This being the state of the case when the defendants had introduced their evidence, the plaintiff, in rebuttal, introduced a written agreement by which Briggs contracted to sell the foundry and machine-shop to the plaintiff and one Nowell, and an assignment of Nowell's interest to the plaintiff. This written agreement was dated May 1, 1878. The first payment was to be made on the first day of October, 1878, and the property agreed to be conveyed was the land and "the foundry and machine-shop thereon, with all the machinery therein, and tools therein." If this evidence was admissible for any purpose, it was to show that

2. EVIDENCE: title to personal property: inoperative contract of sale.

the plaintiff was the owner of the property in controversy. It will be observed that the property is neither machinery nor tools. It consists of manufactured articles held for sale.

But we suppose the theory of plaintiff was that it was important to prove that he bought the real estate, machinery, and tools. The defendants objected to the introduction of this evidence, and the objection was overruled. We think that it should not have been admitted, especially as there was no evidence that the plaintiff ever took and held possession of the property under it, or that he at any time paid any of the purchase money. It is true, the contract provides that for non-payment of the sums of money agreed to be paid Briggs might consider the contract at an end, and consider the plaintiff as a tenant at will, and have the right to remove him from said premises by a proceeding in forcible entry and detainer. It might seem from this that plaintiff took possession under this contract. But, if he did, we think the evidence shows he did not retain the possession. When he went east, two or three years before Briggs died, he left no one in charge of the property, and he admits in his evidence that he gave up the key of the building to Briggs, and Briggs took possession of the property, and continued in possession until he died. But the plaintiff testified that there were two keys, and that he gave but one to Briggs. We think that, under this state of proof, without any evidence that the plaintiff ever paid a dollar on the agreement, and with the evidence tending very strongly to show that Briggs resumed possession of the property, the written agreement was improperly admitted in evidence.

For the errors above discussed, the judgment is reversed, and the cause is remanded for a new trial.

REVERSED.

GARDNER V. HALSTEAD ET AL.

1. **Bill of Exceptions**: WHEN NOT NECESSARY. A bill of exceptions is not necessary to bring before this court, on appeal, a question which arises on the pleadings, since they are a part of the record without such a bill.

2. **Pleading**: ANSWER TO COUNTER-CLAIM IN INJUNCTION SUIT: TRANSFER TO LAW DOCKET. Plaintiff sued out a preliminary injunction restraining the collection of certain notes on the ground that they had been paid. Defendants answered, denying that the notes had been paid, and, upon proper averments, asking judgment thereon; and on their motion the injunction was dissolved and the cause transferred to the law calendar. *Held* that the case then stood like an action at law for the collection of the notes, and that plaintiff had a right to plead any matter of defense.

Appeal from Webster Circuit Court.

FRIDAY, MARCH 11.

THE plaintiff executed to the defendant Halstead certain promissory notes, and a chattel mortgage to secure the payment of the same. Halstead transferred the notes to the Kansas Manufacturing Company. Plaintiff commenced an action in equity against the manufacturing company to restrain it from foreclosing the mortgage, on the ground that the notes had been paid, and averring that the company took said notes with notice of plaintiff's defense to them. The defendants answered, denying that the notes had been paid, and setting the same up as a cause of action against the plaintiff, and demanding judgment thereon. A preliminary injunction was granted restraining the foreclosure of the mortgage, which injunction, on motion of the defendant, was dissolved; and the defendants moved to transfer the cause to the law calendar, upon the ground that nothing was in issue between the parties except the payment of the notes set out in the defendants' answer. The motion was sustained. After the cause was thus transferred, the plaintiff filed what he denominated an "answer" to the defendants' *cross-petition*, setting up an account due him from the defendant Halstead amounting to more than the sum due on the notes, averring that the notes were not transferred to the manufacturing company until after they became due, and demanding judgment against the company for costs, and judgment against Hal-stead for the balance of the account, after deducting the amount of the notes. The defendants moved to strike the answer to the cross-petition from the files. The motion was sustained, and plaintiff excepted to the ruling. Pending the hearing on the motion, the plaintiff withdrew and dismissed his petition in equity. After the ruling on the motion, the plaintiff withdrew his appearance, and judgment was rendered against him on the notes. Plaintiff appeals.

A. E. Clarke, for appellant.

Wright & Farrell, for appellees.

ROTHROCK, J.—I. The appellee insists that the bill of exceptions was not filed within the proper time. We have

1. BILL of ex-ceptions : when not nec-essary.

been compelled to resort to the transcript to settle this question, and it appears from the filing on the back of the original bill of exceptions that it was deposited in the clerk's office, and marked "Filed," on the thirteenth day of January, 1886, which was within the time allowed appellant for filing the same. The record is not altogether clear about this, as counsel have procured the clerk to make contradictory certificates, and two bills of exceptions are filed in this court, each claimed to be original. But the question appears to us to be immaterial, because the plaintiff's exceptions were duly made of record, and the question presented for our determination arises upon the pleadings, and nothing else, and the pleadings were of record, without a bill of exceptions.

II. The motion to strike the plaintiff's pleading is founded on seven grounds, and the appeal is presented to us upon

2. PLEADING: answer to counter-claim in in-junction suit : transfer to law docket.

twenty-one assignments of error. We must decline to enter into a discussion of all the propositions submitted by counsel. The seven grounds of the motion really amount to but one, which, stated in our own language, is that the pleading is in the nature of a reply to the answer of the defendants, and introduces new matter not contained in the petition, and inconsistent with the petition. The ready answer to this position is that there was no petition of plaintiff when the ruling was made. His petition was a petition in equity. It was disposed of when the injunction was dissolved, and the cause transferred to the law docket. It is true, the plaintiff averred in his petition that the notes had been paid. This, if true, would have entitled him to a decree canceling the notes. But, when the cause was transferred to the law calendar, he had no right to proceed at law and demand a cancellation of the notes, because that was an equitable issue. More than this, it was his right to dismiss his petition; and when he did this, as the defendant still insisted on judgment on the notes, it was his right to make any legal defense thereto. It is no matter what the defendants called their pleading. It was the first pleading in the case, and was, in effect, a petition demanding judgment on the notes; and when the petition was dismissed, if not before, it is no matter what the plaintiff denominated his defense to the notes. It was in the nature of an answer and counter-claim, and was not inconsistent with any petition then pending, for there was no petition. It had been disposed of by the transfer to the law calendar, and by being expressly dismissed.

The motion should have been

OVERRULED.

FOSTER & CO. v. ELLSWORTH.

1. **Tax Sale and Deed:** ACTION TO SET ASIDE: CROSS-PETITION TO QUIET: EVIDENCE: PRACTICE. Plaintiffs, claiming to be the patent owners, brought their action to set aside a tax deed to defendant's grantor. Defendant, in a cross-petition, to which there was no reply, sought to have his title quieted. After the introduction of the evidence and the argument, plaintiffs, having failed to show that they or their grantors had title at the time of the tax sale. (Code, § 897.) dismissed their petition. *Held* that defendant had the right to proceed with the trial of the cause made by the cross-bill, and that, upon his showing a tax deed sufficient on its face to convey the title to his grantor, he was entitled to a decree, because the court could not consider any evidence of the invalidity of the tax deed without first finding that plaintiffs were the holders of the patent title. (See *Varnum v. Shuler*, 69 Iowa, 92.)

Appeal from Wright District Court.

FRIDAY, MARCH 11.

THIS action involves the title to real estate in Wright county. The plaintiff claimed the land under the patent title, and averred that, though the same had been sold for taxes, and a treasurer's deed executed, yet the period for redemption had not expired, because no proper notice of expiration of redemption had been given. The defendant filed a cross-bill setting up title under a tax sale and deed to one Young, and a warranty deed from Young to the defendant. The prayer of the cross-bill was that the title to the land be quieted in the defendant. No reply was filed by the plaintiff. After the evidence was introduced, and after the arguments of counsel were made upon the hearing of the cause, the plaintiffs dismissed their case without prejudice, to which the defendant objected. Thereupon the defendant demanded a decree quieting his title to the land, and submitted his case upon his answer and cross-bill and evidence, and the court dismissed the cross-bill. Defendant appeals.

Nagle & Birdsall, for appellant.

W. T. R. Humphrey, for appellees.

ROTHROCK, J.—The plaintiffs doubtless dismissed their case because they failed to prove that they were the owners of the patent title. Code, § 897, provides that "no person shall be permitted to question the title acquired by a treasurer's deed without first showing that he, or the person under whom he claims title, had title to the property at the time of the sale." Plaintiffs introduced in evidence a conveyance to them from one Casper Geisart, and made no further proof of title. They therefore utterly failed to show title in themselves, or in Geisart, under whom they claimed.

The defendant introduced in evidence a tax deed which was regular upon its face, and appeared to be a conveyance of the land in due form of law to one Young, the assignee of the tax-sale certificate. He also put in evidence a warranty deed of the land from Young to himself. When the plaintiffs dismissed their action, the cause stood upon the cross-bill of the defendant, without answer or reply. The cross-bill was in proper form, with all the averments necessary for an original petition to quiet title. It is questionable whether the plaintiffs had the right to introduce any evidence, or, rather, whether they did not withdraw their evidence with the dismissal of their case. They were in default for want of an answer to the cross-bill. But this question we need not determine. It was the defendant's right to proceed with the trial of the case made in his cross-bill, notwithstanding the plaintiffs dismissed their action, (Code, § 2846;) and when he presented a treasurer's deed, which upon its face was sufficient to convey a title, the court could not consider any evidence of the invalidity of the deed without first finding that the plaintiffs were the holders of the patent title. *Varnum v. Shuler,* 69 Iowa, 92.

We think the court should have entered a decree quieting the title to the land in the defendant.

REVERSED.

SEEKEL v. NORMAN ET AL.

1. **Usury**: EVIDENCE TO DISCOVER: PAROL TO IMPEACH WRITING. The conditions, covenants and recitals of any and all instruments under which usury is hidden may be contradicted, impeached and assailed by any evidence, parol or written, in order to disclose the real facts and uncover the usury.

2. **Instruction**: REPETITION NOT REQUIRED. Instructions asked are properly refused when the thought of each is sufficiently expressed in insructions given by the court on its own motion.

3. ————: CORRECT IN THE ABSTRACT BUT NOT PROPERLY APPLIED: ESTOPPEL. It may sometimes occur that a correct abstract rule of law may mislead the jury, in the absence of directions for its application to the facts in the case. In such a case it will be error, if the court fails on its own motion to give such directions for its application that the jury will not be misled. So *held* in regard to an instruction in which the court rightly stated that, to constitute an estoppel, the party pleading it must have been prejudiced, or sustained injury, by acting upon the representations alleged as ground for the estoppel, but failed to give other necessary instructions for the application of the rule.

4. **New Trial**: MISCONDUCT OF COUNSEL: DISCRETION OF TRIAL COURT. The decision of the trial court upon a question of the misconduct of counsel in argument to the jury, where the decision was based upon conflicting affidavits and the court's own knowledge of the facts, will not be disturbed on appeal.

5. **Usury**: JUDGMENT FOR SCHOOL FUND: PROCEDURE: EVIDENCE. Where in the progress of an action on a promissory note it appears that there should be a judgment for the school fund on account of usury, (Code, § 2080,) it is competent for the court to ascertain by evidence. in addition to what is introduced on the trial, the amount of the forfeiture for which the judgment should be rendered.

Appeal from Harrison Circuit Court.

FRIDAY, MARCH 11.

ACTION upon three promissory notes executed by Norman & Williams to Winch, and by him indorsed to plaintiff. There was a judgment against plaintiff upon a verdict for defendant Norman & Williams, and a judgment against them in favor of the state for the use of the school fund. Both parties appeal.

G. W. Argo and *L. R. Bolter & Sons*, for plaintiffs.

H. H. Roadifer, S. H. Cochran and *G. T. Kelley*, for defendants.

BECK, J.—I.   While the abstract shows that Winch, the payee and indorser of the notes in suit, was joined as a defendant with the makers, it fails to show what disposition of the action was made as to him.   The other defendants, Norman & Williams, answering the petition, admit the execution and indorsement of the notes, and allege as defenses that the notes were given without consideration, and are usurious, having been given for the amount of interest accruing upon other notes at the rate of fifteen per centum per annum, and for no other consideration.   They further allege that the notes have been paid; and, as another defense, show that the notes at the time of their execution were delivered, under an agreement between the makers and payee, to another party, to be delivered, upon specified conditions, to the payee, but, in violation of their conditions, the payee, Winch, obtained possession of the notes, and wrongfully assigned them to plaintiff without consideration.   The plaintiff, in reply to the answer, denies the fraud, usury, and other matters of defense set up therein, and alleges that she is the innocent holder of the notes, under indorsement thereof made before their maturity.   She further alleges that, before the notes were transferred to her, Norman made representations, which were communicated to her before she purchased the notes, to the effect that they were all right, and would be paid at maturity, and, relying on these representations, plaintiff purchased them; wherefore she claims that defendants are estopped to deny the validity of the notes. Other matters appearing in the pleadings upon which the case was tried, and in other pleadings withdrawn, need not be further mentioned.

II.   We will be able more satisfactorily and conveniently

to dispose of the objections urged against the judgment by
considering them in the order of their discussion
by counsel. A great many objections are urged
by counsel for plaintiff to evidence permitted to
be introduced by defendants. This evidence, or a part of it,
tended to show all the transactions from which the notes in suit
originated, the amount of defendants' indebtedness, the usurious rate of interest contracted for by the parties, and that
such usurious interest constituted the consideration of the
notes in suit, and many other matters tending to show usury in
the notes, which need not be particularly stated. It appeared
that there was a written contract pertaining to some of these
matters. Counsel for plaintiff insist, as to the matters covered
by the written contract, that the parol evidence in question is
incompetent. But it may be remarked, generally, that usury,
as other frauds, may be shown by any evidence, in other
respects competent, tending to establish the real character of
the transaction. The conditions, covenants and recitals of
any and all instruments under which usury is hidden may be
contradicted, impeached and assailed by evidence, parol or
written, in order to disclose the real facts, and uncover the
usury. The law against usury would be in vain, and incapable of enforcement, except for this familiar rule of the law.
Its application sustains the circuit court's rulings upon the
admission of evidence complained of by counsel for plaintiff.
They demand no further attention.

III. Numerous papers were introduced in evidence, being
notes, deeds, mortgages and receipts pertaining to the deal-
ings between the parties. Counsel for plaintiff
complains rather of their number than their relevancy and pertinency to the case. As they all pertained to
the transactions between the parties out of which the notes
in suit, more or less remotely, had their origin, we do not
think they were incompetent. As these notes are claimed to
represent usury arising in prior transactions between the
parties, it is plain that such transactions were proper subjects

1. USURY: evi- dence to dis- cover: parol to impeach writing.

THE SAME.

of inquiry, and all papers pertaining thereto were properly received in evidence as explanatory thereof.

IV. Plaintiff requested an instruction to the effect that, if the notes were given for property purchased by defendants, they were not usurious; another to the effect that a credit price for property sold greater than a cash price is not usurious; and a third to the effect that usury arises only upon a contract for the payment of unlawful interests. They were each rightly refused, as the thought of each was sufficiently expressed in instructions given by the court on its own motion.

2. INSTRUC- TIONS: repe- tion not re- quired.

V. As applicable to the estoppel pleaded in plaintiff's reply, based upon the alleged representations of defendant Norman, to the effect that the notes were all right, and would be paid at maturity, the circuit court, in stating the doctrine of estoppel, expressed the thought that, to constitute the estoppel, among other things, the plaintiff must have been prejudiced, or sustained injury, by acting upon the representations. Counsel for plaintiff insists that the instruction is erroneous, for the reason that the effect to injure or prejudice is not an element of estoppel. Clearly, if no injury or prejudice arises to the party acting upon a representation, he can have no cause of action, and the alleged estoppel will not be enforced. Prejudice or injury is an essential element in the foundation of all claims for the enforcement of rights, or for the redress of wrongs. If neither exists, no right will be regarded as violated, or wrong suffered, of which the law will take notice. *Lucas v. Hart,* 5 Iowa, 415; *Eikenberry v. Edwards,* 67 Id., 14. We think the instruction correctly announces an abstract rule of law. But without explanation and other instructions directing its application to the facts of the case, it is probable that it led to a verdict in conflict with the rights of plaintiff and the obligations of the defendants. If plaintiff was prejudiced by relying upon defendant's declarations, above stated, an estoppel would arise.

3. ——: cor- rect in the abstract but not properly applied: estoppel.

Such prejudice did arise upon the fact, if upon no other, that plaintiff was induced by the representations to commence this suit against defendants, thus incurring costs and expenses. Relying upon the estoppel, she was justified in bringing the action. She thus acted upon defendant's declarations, and a complete estoppel arose thereon, if prejudice resulted, as it surely did, by inducing her to incur costs and expenses. The jury should have been directed by another instruction to this effect. As such instruction was absolutely essential to enable the jury to correctly apply the rule of estoppel, it was the duty of the court to give it, even in the absence of request therefor by the plaintiff. It may sometimes occur that a correct abstract rule of law may mislead the jury, in the absence of directions for the application to the facts of the case. In such an instance the trial court should be careful, on its own motion, to give such directions for its application that the jury may not be misled. In our opinion, prejudicial error was committed by the circuit court in failing to give sufficient directions to the jury as to the prejudice suffered by plaintiff as above pointed out.

VI. Plaintiff complains of misconduct of the attorneys of defendants at the trial in discussing facts and matters not shown by the evidence. The complaint is based upon an affidavit of her attorney. But counter-affidavits show that whatever was said by defendants' attorney about matters not in proof, was in reply to the argument of the attorneys of plaintiff, who departed from the record in the arguments. Plaintiff fails to establish the fact upon which her complaint is based. The court below was fully cognizant of the whole matter, and had before it the conflicting affidavits. We are required to presume that it rightly overruled the motion to set aside the verdict on the ground of the misconduct of the defendants' attorneys.

L. NEW trial: misconduct of counsel: discretion of trial court.

VII. The circuit court rendered judgment against

defendants for $330 in favor of the state for the use of the
school fund. This judgment is authorized by
Code, § 2080, which provides that, "if it shall be
ascertained in any suit brought upon any contract
that a rate of interest has been contracted for greater than is
authorized for by this chapter, either directly or indirectly,
in money or property, the same shall work a forfeiture of
ten cents on the hundred by the year, upon the amount of
such contract, to the school fund of the county in which the
suit is brought." The section directs that a judgment
accordingly shall be entered against the defendant, in favor
of the state, for the use of the school fund. The proceedings and adjudication against defendants were, of course, had
after the verdict and judgment against plaintiff. It was
competent for the court to ascertain, by evidence, in addition
to what was introduced upon the trial, the amount forfeited
to the state. The fact that there had been a contract for
usurious interest sufficiently appeared in the evidence in
the case. But that evidence, probably, does not alone support fully the conclusion of the court as to the amount of
the forfeiture. We will presume that other facts were
brought to the attention of the court which showed the true
amount of the forfeiture. The abstracts fail to show that
we have before us all the evidence upon which the judgment
was rendered against the defendants. We cannot, therefore,
review it. The cause must be reversed, upon plaintiff's
appeal, for the error pointed out in the fifth paragraph of this
opinion, and it will be remanded for a new trial, in which
the question of defendants' liability to a judgment in favor
of the state for the use of the school fund must of necessity
again arise, in view of the fact that the issues of the case
involve the question of the existence of usury. If usury
be established on the new trial, defendants may be liable to
such a judgment; if not, they will not be so liable. But it
becomes necessary in this case to pass upon the question
involved in defendants' appeal, in order to determine the

5. USURY: judgment for school fund: procedure: evidence.

question of costs involved therein. For this reason we determine it. The defendants will pay the costs upon both appeals.

Affirmed on defendants' appeal. Reversed on plaintiff's appeal.

THE FORT MADISON LUMBER CO. v. THE BATAVIAN BANK ET AL.

1. **Corporations:** TRANSFER OF STOCK: ENTRY ON BOOKS: WHEN NECESSARY. A transfer of corporation stock is not valid as against attaching creditors of the assignor without notice, unless the transfer is entered on the books of the company, as provided by § 1078 of the Code. (See opinion for a full discussion of the question on principle and authority by ADAMS, CH. J.)

Appeal from Lee Circuit Court.

FRIDAY, MARCH 11.

ACTION in equity to compel the defendants to interplead, in order that their respective claims against each other, and against the plaintiff company, may be determined. The facts appear to be that one Weston was at one time the owner of certain shares of stock in the plaintiff company, and the same stood in his name on the books of the company. In 1883 he borrowed money of the defendant, the Batavian Bank of La Crosse, Wisconsin, and assigned to it certificates of his stock as collateral security; but no transfer of the stock was made upon the books of the company. Afterwards he became insolvent. Among his creditors were the defendants D. Hammell & Co., the Clark County Bank and the Neillsville Bank. These creditors brought actions upon their respective claims in the circuit court of Lee county, Iowa, and caused writs of attachment to be issued, and levied upon the stock in question. At the time of the levy they had no knowledge of any transfer of the certificates by Weston.

Shortly after the levy the Batavian Bank procured the secretary of the plaintiff to indorse upon the stubs of the book
from which the certificates had been detached an entry or
memorandum of a transfer. This action is brought for the
purpose of procuring a determination of the question as to
whether the rights of the Batavian Bank, as pledgee, are
subject to the attachments, or the attachments subject to the
rights of the Batavian Bank. The court held that the attachments were subject to the rights of the Batavian Bank. The
defendants D. Hammell & Co., the Clark County Bank and
the Neillsville Bank appeal.

Casey & Casey, for D. Hammell & Co., appellants.

M. C. Ring, R. F. Kounts and *Casey & Casey*, for the
other appellants.

C. W. Bunn and *W. J. Knight*, for the Batavian Bank.

Van Valkenburg & Hamilton, for the other defendants.

Frank Hagerman, for plaintiff.

ADAMS, CH. J.—The question whether a transfer of stock
in an incorporated company in this state, when not entered
upon the books of the company, is valid, as against attaching creditors of the assignor without notice, is now presented
for the first time in this court. Its determination must
depend upon the view which should be taken of the meaning of the provision found in section 1078 of the Code, and
which is as follows: "The transfer of shares is not valid,
except as between the parties thereto, until it is regularly
entered on the books of the company, so as to show the name
of the person by and to whom transferred, the numbers or
other designation of shares, and the date of the transfer."

The question now presented does not arise between the
parties to the transfer. Without any question, the transferee
will hold the stock, as against the transferer, for all the purposes for which the transfer was made. The question arises

between one of the parties to the transfer and others who were not parties, and who dispute the validity of the transfer. If we give the statute a literal construction, we must hold that the transfer is not valid. To hold otherwise, we should be obliged to enlarge the exception. The rule would be that the transfer is not valid, except as between the parties, and except as between the transferee and the attaching creditors of the transferer. But ordinarily, in the construction of a statute, an exception is not to be enlarged.

The question, however, is not free from difficulty. It is urged by the appellee, the transferee, that an attachment can in no case bind more than the interest of the debtor; and, if the transfer is valid between the parties, it is said that it follows, from the necessity of the case, that the attaching creditor of the transferer acquires a lien only upon such interest as the transferer has left, if any.

That there is plausibility in this argument cannot be denied. But in our opinion it is not sound. It would carry us too far. It would make a transfer that is valid between the parties to it valid as against all persons claiming under the transferer. But no one pretends that this is so. If the transferer sells again, and to an innocent purchaser for value, who obtains a transfer upon the books, no one doubts that he would become both the legal and equitable owner; and this is true though the transferer had, in one sense, no interest in the stock which he could sell. It is entirely competent, then, for the legislature to provide arbitrarily that a given transfer shall be deemed by a court valid or invalid, according to the parties which shall be before the court. The transfer is valid if the parties before the court were the parties to the transfer, and otherwise not. This, at least, is the rule of the statute, and must be followed, unless some equitable consideration controls. If the attaching creditors of the transferer had knowledge of the transfer, it may be that a court of equity would protect the transferee's rights. It has frequently been so held, but that question is not before us.

Our conclusion thus far has been based upon what seems to be the fair meaning of the language of the provision. But we are entitled to take a broader view, and look at other provisions. It is provided in the same section that the " books of the company must be so kept as to show intelligibly the original stockholders, their respective interests, the amount paid on their shares, and all transfers thereof; and such books, or a correct copy thereof, so far as the items mentioned in this section are concerned, shall be subject to the inspection of any person desiring the same." The above, it will be seen, is a provision that the books shall show, at any given time, precisely who the stockholders are at that time. The books, too, shall be kept open for inspection by any one. Where a provision is made for a record of specific facts, and another provision that the record shall be kept open for inspection by any one, the intention must be that any one inspecting the record should be entitled to rely upon it as true; and, if a person inspecting the record expends money upon the faith of it, any other person through whose negligence the record fails to show the truth should be estopped from setting up its untruthfulness.

It is contended by the appellee that the provision for a record, designed to show who the stockholders are at any given time, is for the sole benefit of the corporation itself. But there is nothing in the provision that calls for such construction. Besides, nothing can be clearer than that the record is for the benefit of any one who may desire to inspect it, because it is expressly provided for such.

It is contended by the appellee that a mere attachment of stock should not have precedence over a prior assignment, not made of record, because the attaching creditor has expended nothing but his labor and the costs. By way of argument, it is said that an attachment does not take precedence of an unrecorded deed. But such a case differs in this: The statute expressly requires transfers of stock to be recorded; it does not require that deeds shall be.

Stock in an incorporated company is personal property. Transfers of personal property, to be valid as against attaching creditors, should be attended by a visible change of possession, or else evidence of the transfer should be spread upon a public record. We have an express provision of statute for property where a visible change of possession can be made. In the case of stock in an incorporated company, no visible change of possession can be made. Stock is a share in the interests and rights of the corporation. Certificates are mere evidence. They may never be issued. It is not essential that they should be. When issued, they are merely for convenience. The object of the imperative provision that transfers of stocks shall be recorded unquestionably is that the ownership may be made apparent.

Chief Justice SHAW, in *Fisher v. Essex Bank*, 5 Gray, 373, (380), in speaking of stock in an incorporated company, said: "It is of importance that the title be certainly and easily ascertained, that the mode of acquiring and alienating it may at any time be made available by process of law for the debts of the owner." Again, speaking of the necessity of a record of the transfers as passing title, and of a levy according to the record, he says: "The shares [otherwise] could never be attached, for the officer could have no means of obtaining possession of the certificate from a reluctant debtor adversely interested, and without it the shares might pass the next day to a purchaser without notice." Again he says: "It is necessary to fix some act, and some point of time, at which the property changes, and rests in the vendee; and it will tend to the security of all parties concerned to make that turning point consist in an act which, while it may easily be proved, does at the same time give notoriety to the transfer."

In support of the conclusion which we have reached, that the statute in question was designed in part for the benefit of attaching creditors, we will refer to another provision of the statute. The sheriff must, as nearly as the circumstances

will permit, levy upon property fifty per cent greater in value
than the amount of the debt as sworn to.   Code, § 2954.
Now, if the construction contended for by the appellee is
correct, the attaching creditor and sheriff, proceeding strictly
according to law in attaching stock, and exhausting their
ability to secure the debt by such attachment, cannot know
whether any security at all has been obtained.   The certificate holder may keep himself concealed until the very
moment when the stock is offered for sale on execution, and
it is sufficient if he then appear, and give notice of his claim.
We cannot think that the statute was designed to admit such
a result.   We may say, indeed, that the very mode of attaching stock provided by statute seems to be a legislative construction of the statute in question.

We come, now, to inquire how the question stands upon
the authority of adjudicated cases.

In Maine the statute provides that " a transfer of shares is
not valid, except between the parties thereto, until it is so
entered in the books of the corporation."   The provision is
identical with the provision of our own statute.   In *Skow-
hegan Bank v. Cutler*, 49 Me., 315, a question arose as to
whether an attachment would take precedence of an unrecorded assignment, and it was held that it would.

In Illinois it is provided that shares of stock in a corporation can be transferred only upon the books of the corporation.   In *People's Bank v. Gridley*, 91 Ill., 457, a question arose as to whether the levy of an execution would take
precedence of a transfer of shares not entered upon the
books.   It was held that it would.   The action was brought
to enjoin the sale on execution.   The point was made that
the execution creditor, who had merely levied, was not an
innocent purchaser for value, and that, not being such, the
transfer, though not entered upon the records, might be set
up against him; but the court held otherwise.   It is true,
the Illinois statute differs a little from ours.   It provides
that transfers can be made only on the books of the company.

It does not, like our statute, expressly provide that a transfer not entered upon the books will be good as between the
parties to the transfer.   But the difference, in our opinion,
is not material.   The statute is the same in effect.   It is
well settled that, under a statute like the Illinois statute, a
transfer not entered upon the books is good between the parties.   The case, then, appears to be strictly in point.

The same view was taken in *Sabin v. Bank of Woodstock*,
21 Vt., 353, and *Cheever v. Meyer*, 52 Id., 66.   In the
former case, Chief Justice REDFIELD said: "We entertain
no reasonable doubt that   *.   *   *   all persons
unaffected with notice to the contrary are at liberty to act
upon the faith of the title being where it appears upon the
books of the company to be."   In *State Ins. Co. v. Sax*, 2
Tenn. Ch., 507, Chancellor COOPER cites the case, and refers
to it approvingly.

In Wisconsin the statute pertaining to the transfer of stocks
is like ours, and in *Application of Murphy*, 51 Wis., 419,
8 N. W. Rep., 419, a construction was put upon it which
sustains the appellants in the case at bar.   The court said:
"We think that the meaning of the law is that all transfers
of shares should be entered, as here required, upon the books
of the corporation; and it is equally clear to us that all transfers of shares not so entered are invalid as to attaching or
execution creditors of the assignors, as well as to the corporation and subsequent purchasers in good faith."

In *Pinkerton v. Manchester & L. R. Co.*, 42 N. H., 424,
(462), an attachment, made without notice of a prior transfer not entered upon the books, was held to take precedence
of it.   The court said: "As to goods and chattels in possession, a substantial change of possession is by our law
essential when it can be had.   In the case of stock, the
natural and appropriate indication of ownership is the entry
upon the stock record."

In Connecticut an attachment was upheld as against a

prior assignment not entered upon the books. *Northrop v. Newton & Bridgeport Turnpike Co.*, 3 Conn., 544.

It is claimed by the appellee that in New York, New Jersey and California it has been held otherwise; and it may be conceded that this is so, though we are not prepared to say that all the statutory provisions in those states bearing upon the question are quite the same as in this.

The case of *Black v. Zacharie*, 3 How., 483, is cited by the appellee. In that case language was used which might seem to support the appellee's position, but the case was essentially different from the one at bar. The attaching creditors had notice of the assignee's rights at the time the attachment was levied.

The appellee also cites *Moore v. Walker*, 46 Iowa, 164. But the pretended attachment in that case was made before the assignment, and would unquestionably have taken precedence of it if it had been properly made; but it was not, and had no validity, regardless of any question of transfer. It was expressly held that the provision of statute now in question (section 1078, Code,) had no application to the case. The remark, then, in the opinion, in regard to the scope of that section, does not have the force of an adjudication.

There is no question in regard to the preponderance of authority. It is clearly on the side of the appellants. But we are not influenced more by this fact than what seems to be the plain language and intent of the statute, and the difficulty and uncertainty which would often attend securing debts by attachment of stock, if stock, as against attaching creditors, can be transferred by mere delivery of the certificates, and if the books provided expressly for inspection by such creditors are to serve especially the purpose of a false scent.

We think the judgment must be

REVERSED.

STEVENSON ET AL. V. POLK ET AL.

· 1. **Title Bond**: FORECLOSURE: TENDER OF DEED. No tender of a deed is necessary by the vendor of real estate in order to the maintenance of an action in equity to foreclose a title bond for the collection of the purchase money. In an action at law for the purchase money a different rule prevails. (See opinion for authorities cited.)

2. **Contract**: SIGNING AS TRUSTEE: PAROL TO DISCLOSE CAPACITY: WHO LIABLE. Where one signs a contract as trustee, and there is nothing on the face of the contract to indicate for whom he is trustee, parol evidence is not admissible to show such fact, and he is personally liable. (See cases cited in opinion.)

3. **Vendor and Vendee**: ACTION FOR PURCHASE MONEY: DEFENSE OF DEFECTIVE TITLE: BURDEN OF PROOF. Plaintiffs' intestate sold land to defendant, and gave him a bond for a deed, and put him in possession, and his right of possession had not been questioned. He also furnished him an abstract of title to the land. In an action for the purchase money and to foreclose the title bond, defendants pleaded, not that there was no title to any portion of the land, but, in general, that the title was defective, as shown by the abstract. Plaintiffs on the trial did not trace their title back to the government, by introducing in evidence deeds from their grantors, but simply showed that the land had been conveyed to the intestate, and that he had been in open, notorious and undisturbed possession for more than ten years. *Held* that this was presumptive evidence of title, and that the burden was on defendants to show wherein the title, as shown by the abstract, was defective.

4. ———: ———: ———: REMOVAL OF INCUMBRANCE. In such case, a recovery cannot be defeated on the ground that a portion of the land is encumbered, if the incumbrance is removed prior to the trial; unless there has been a rescission, or such an offer to rescind as entitled the party making it to a rescission at the time the offer was made.

5. ———: ———: ———: MORTGAGE TO CORPORATION: RELEASE. In such case it is sufficient for the plaintiff to prove that a mortgage on the premises has been paid, without proving a release of record; but where the mortgage was to a corporation, and it was satisfied of record by the secretary and treasurer of the company, *held* that this was a sufficient release, though not executed in the manner required by the articles of poration for instruments affecting the title to real estate.

6. ———: ———: ———: MERE POSSIBILITY OF LITIGATION. In such case, a mere possibility that there may be litigation over the title will not defeat a recovery, but there must be a reasonable probability that there will be such litigation. And so, where, after plaintiffs' intestate and his grantors had been in undisturbed possession for nearly forty

years, under a deed with a defective description, he brought an action to correct the defect in his title arising from such error, and notice was served by publication, and the two years allowed by statute for a motion for a new trial had not expired, *held* that the possibility of the defendants' applying for and obtaining a new trial was too remote to be considered.

7. **Judgment:** QUIETING TITLE: IRREGULARITIES: COLLATERAL ATTACK. The failure of the clerk to mark "filed" and to enter on the appearance docket an original notice showing the acceptance of service by defendants in an action to quiet title, cannot be urged, in a collateral proceeding, against the validity of the judgment, especially where the court has found that the defendants were duly and legally served.

8. **Action:** TO QUIET TITLE AGAINST MISDESCRIPTION: PARTIES. The wives and husbands of the descendants of one who has conveyed land by a wrong description are not necessary parties to an action to quiet the title against such imperfection, on the ground that they have a dower interest in the land; for they have no such interest. (Compare *Lea v. Woods*, 67 Iowa, 304.)

9. **Administrator:** CONVEYANCE OF LAND BOUGHT IN ON MORTGAGE FORECLOSURE. An administrator who buys in land upon the foreclosure of a mortgage belonging to the esta'e holds it as personal property, and he may convey it without an order of court.

10. **Vendor and Vendee:** FAILURE OF TITLE AS TO PART: RESCISSION OR COMPENSATION. Where the vendor in a bond for a deed is unable to convey a portion of the land because of a defect of title, but such portion did not constitute an inducement to the purchase, and is so situated as not to detract from the value of the whole tract, compensation, and not rescission, is the rule.

11. ——: OBJECTIONS TO TITLE: WHEN MADE. Where a purchaser of land under a contract made certain objections to the title as shown by an abstract furnished by the vendor, and thus induced the vendor to expend money in litigation in removing such objections, *held* that the vendee could not afterwards raise other objections which he knew the vendor could not remove, and then insist upon a rescission of the contract on account of such objections; but that the vendee must, in such case, present all his objections within a reasonable time after being furnished with an abstract.

12. ——: ——: INCUMBRANCE BY CONSENT OF VENDEE. Where land was purchased to be used for a town site on a proposed railway, and the persons interested in the purchase were, with one exception, the same as those interested in the railway, and the purchase was made by one who was agent for both the purchasers and the railway company, and after the oral contract for the purchase had been made, and a part of the consideration paid, but before the bond for a deed had been executed, the same agent procured from the vendor a deed for the right of way for

Stevenson et al. v. Polk et al.

the railroad over the same land, *held* that the purchasers could not set up such right of way as an incumbrance on the title, for the purpose of avoiding the contract of purchase; and especially is this so in view of the fact that a right of way through the land was necessary to render the purchase valuable for the purpose for which it was made.

13. ———: TIME AS ESSENCE OF CONTRACT: WAIVER. Time should sometimes be regarded as of the essence of a contract for the sale of land, even when it is not so expressly stated, if the object and purposes of the contract so indicate, and it has been so treated by the parties. But if time be regarded as of the essence of the contract in this case, *held* that it was waived by the vendee by giving the vendor time, after the day fixed for performance, to perfect his title.

14. ———: OBJECTIONS TO TITLE: RESCISSION OF CONTRACT: TERMS. A vendee of real estate under a bond for a deed cannot rescind the contract on account of imperfections in the title, without tendering back as good a title as the vendor had when the contract was made. In other words, he cannot further incumber or becloud the title, and then tender it back, and demand a rescission.

15. ———: ACTION FOR PURCHASE MONEY: DELAY IN PERFECTING TITLE. In an action for the purchase money of land sold under a bond for a deed, it appeared that there was a delay on the part of the vendor in perfecting his title, but no right of rescission had accrued to the vendee, and no substantial damage had resulted to him on account of the delay, and he had not been disturbed in his possession of the premises. *Held* that the vendor was entitled to recover the purchase money with the stipulated interest.

Appeal from Marion District Court.

FRIDAY, MARCH 11.

ACTION in equity. Judgment for the plaintiffs, and defendants appeal.

J. S. Polk and *J. M. St. John*, for appellants.

Bousquet & Earl, for appellees.

SEEVERS, J.—This action was commenced in September, 1883, by Andrew Stevenson, and the petition states that he sold to the defendant Polk, in July, 1881, certain described real estate for $7,850, of which sum $1,200 was paid, and that the said defendant agreed to pay the residue of the purchase money on the first day of March, 1882, with eight per cent interest; and it was agreed that said defendant might enter into possession of the real estate, and make improvements thereon; that said agreement was reduced to writing, but no copy was attached, for the reason that it was in possession of defendants; that said Polk executed to said Stevenson his promissory note for the balance of the purchase money, payable on the first day of March, 1882, and has conveyed the said real estate to the Union Land Company, and such corporation is made a defendant; that said Polk and his grantee entered into possession of the premises under the contract, and that such possession has not been in any respect disturbed. Said Stevenson expressed a willingness to fully comply with said agreement on his part, and convey the real estate by warranty deed as he had agreed. The relief asked is that the plaintiff recover judgment against defendant Polk for the purchase money due, with interest, and that a lien on said real estate in his favor be established, and the defendants' equity of redemption foreclosed, and the premises sold on special execution, and that a general execution issue for any balance of said judgment remaining unsatisfied against said defendant Polk. Afterwards the death of said Stevenson was suggested, and the action revived in the name of D. B. Stevenson, administrator of the estate, as plaintiff.

The defendant Polk filed a separate answer, denying that he entered into possession of the real estate; but he admitted that he, as trustee for the Union Land Company, had purchased such real estate under a written contract, and that said Stevenson well knew that said contract was made by him as such trustee, and not in his individual capacity. The conveyance to the Union Land Company was admitted, but Polk alleged that the same was done in order to discharge and relieve him of the trust; and he asked that the action be dismissed.

The land company answered the petition, and denied all allegations not admitted, and alleged that said Polk, as its trustee and agent, purchased of the intestate certain described

real estate, upon certain conditions, and that the contract
was reduced to writing. It is sufficient to state here that
said defendant pleaded that the intestate and plaintiffs had
failed to comply with said contract on their part. It is
admitted that said defendant entered into possession under the
contract, and is still in possession; that afterwards said Polk
fully executed his trust, and conveyed the real estate to his
co-defendant; that defendant has been at all times ready and
willing to comply with the contract, but that plaintiff's intestate, at no time prior to bringing the action, was seized of
the title to said real estate in fee-simple, unincumbered, and
that said intestate at all times has been unable to perform
the contract on his part, and that plaintiff is unable to comply therewith; that on or about March 12, 1882, said intestate furnished defendant's attorney an abstract of the title to
the real estate, which showed that the title to a large part
thereof was defective, and other portions incumbered, of
which defects the intestate was duly advised; and thereafter
the defendant waited over two years for the intestate to perfect his title, and, failing to do so, the defendant, in September,
1882, notified the intestate that it would wait no longer for a
title, and that it would insist on a rescission of the contract,
and then offered and declared the same rescinded, and offered
to restore the plaintiff to the possession of the real estate,
and to account for rents and profits, and demanded repay-
ment of the money paid on said contract, which the intestate
declined to do, but insisted that defendant should accept a
deed (though none was tendered) conveying an imperfect
title. The said defendant also pleaded that the chief inducement for the purchase of the land was for the purpose of laying out a town-site at a proposed station on the Des Moines
& St. Louis Railroad, then in process of construction, which
was well known to the intestate, and that, under a statute, no
such town could be laid off, and the plat recorded, unless
there was a perfect record title in the proprietors; and,
because of its inability to lay off and record the plat of such

town, it suffered special damage. Wherefore the said defendant asked that its answer be treated as a cross-petition, and that the contract be rescinded, and the plaintiff be required to pay the defendant $1,200, with interest, and that defendant have a lien on the real estate therefor; that an accounting of the rents and profits be had, and the damages of the defendants ascertained, and that defendant have such other relief as it may be entitled to.

The administrator filed a replication, and denied that Polk purchased the land as trustee for his co-defendant, and pleaded that the title was perfect in every respect in the intestate, except a mortgage, which had been paid; and that the intestate and his grantors have had actual, open, notorious and peaceable possession of the premises for more than ten years; and all affirmative allegations in the cross-petition were denied.

There is a discrepancy in the land as described in the petition and the answer and contract. As to this, it was pleaded in the replication that a mistake had been made in describing the land in the contract, and it was asked that the same be reformed so as to conform to the intention of the parties.

The widow and heirs at law of the intestate intervened, and were made plaintiffs, and adopted the prior pleadings filed by the intestate and administrator, and asked the same relief.

The defendants, in a subsequent pleading, denied that there was any mistake in describing the land purchased in the contract, and denied that the intervenors were the widow and heirs at law of the intestate. There were two amendments to the petition filed, which demanded the same relief as the petition. Substantially the allegations therein were denied.

The foregoing lengthy statement is deemed necessary to present, in a general way, the issues. The contention of the several parties will now be referred to in the order, or nearly so, as presented by counsel.

I. The obligation executed by the defendant Polk is in these words:

"DES MOINES, July 23, 1881.

"Know all men by these presents that I acknowledge myself indebted to Andrew Stevenson in the sum of six thousand six hundred and fifty dollars, ($6,650,) which I agree to pay the said Stevenson on or before March 1, 1882, on condition that the said Stevenson and wife shall fully comply with their title bond of even date herewith, wherein they agree to convey to me certain real estate lying and being in Marion county, Iowa. This obligation to draw interest at the rate of eight per cent per annum after maturity, provided that the said Stevenson and wife shall comply with their title bond aforesaid. In witness whereof I have hereunto set my hand the day and date first above written.

"J. S. POLK, Trustee."

The bond referred to was executed by the intestate and his wife at the same time as the foregoing, and recites that they are held and firmly bound, in a named penal sum of money, unto J. S. Polk, trustee, and it recites that the intestate and his wife have sold unto the said J. S. Polk certain described land, and contains this provision: "And if the above-bound Andrew and Maria Stevenson shall make, execute and deliver or cause to be made, executed and delivered, a good and sufficient warranty deed and abstract in fee-simple title to the above-described real estate, then this obligation shall be null and void, otherwise to remain in full force, both in law and equity; * * * and it is hereby further expressly agreed by and between said parties * * * that, the party of the second part shall have the right to enter on said land, and make changes and improvements as he may deem best for his interests."

It is provided by statute that where the vendor of real estate has given a bond to convey the same on the payment of money, he may "file his petition, asking the court to require the purchaser to perform his contract, or foreclose ·

and sell his interest in the property." The vendee shall be treated as a mortgagor, and his rights may be foreclosed in the same manner. Code, §§ 3329, 3330.

The plaintiffs contend that this action is prosecuted under and in accordance with this statute, and the contention of the defendants is that the action is for specific per-

1. TITLE bond: foreclosure: tender of deed.

formance. We are clearly of the opinion that the action is brought under the statute to recover the purchase money of real estate, and to foreclose the interest of the vendee therein, and that no tender of a conveyance is required. This, we think, is apparent, for the reason that the vendee is to be treated as a mortgagor, and his rights to the real estate foreclosed in the same manner; and it has been so held in *Winton v. Sherman*, 20 Iowa, 295, and *Montgomery v. Gibbs*, 40 Id., 652. The reason of the rule is that a court of equity can so mould the judgment or decree as to fully protect the rights of the vendee.

Appellants cite and rely on *School District No. 2 v. Rogers*, 8 Iowa, 316, and *Berryhill v. Byington*, 10 Id., 223. These were actions at law, and in such actions a different rule prevails.

II. The district court rendered a personal judgment against Mr. Polk on the obligation signed by him as trustee. It is insisted by appellants that such judgment

2. CONTRACT: signing as trustee: parol to disclose capacity: who liable.

is erroneous, and the plaintiff's claim otherwise. Counsel for the latter cite and rely on *Bryan v. Brazil*, 52 Iowa, 350; *Wing v. Glick*, 56 Id., 473, and *American Ins. Co. v. Stratton*, 59 Id., 696. There is no difference in principle between this and the two cases first cited. All are based on unnegotiable instruments or contracts, and there is nothing to indicate, on the face of either the title bond or obligation, for whom the defendant Polk was trustee; and it was held in the cited cases that parol evidence was inadmissible to show such fact.

The appellants claim, however, that it is always admissible to show by parol, where a person signs his name to an

obligation as agent, and the name of his principal is not disclosed on the face of the obligation, whose agent he is, that
he may escape personal liability to a person who has full
knowledge of the facts.   It was so held, it is said, in *Met-
calf v. Williams*, 104 U. S., 93.   If this be conceded, the
burden is on the defendant to show that the intestate had
knowledge that Mr. Polk was acting as trustee for the land
company at the time the contract was entered into.   This
should not be left in doubt, for either the land company or
Mr. Polk is personally liable on the obligation.   If the latter is discharged, the former must be bound.   The contract
was entered into by N. C. Towne, as agent for Polk, trustee.
There is a' written agreement showing the agency.   It was
executed on the first day of April, 1881.   The land company
was not incorporated until the sixth day of April, and the
incorporators are Mr. Polk and three other persons.   Mr.
Towne testifies that the intestate had knowledge that Mr.
Polk was "trustee for said several parties."   By said several
parties the witness undoubtedly meant the other persons,
besides Mr. Polk, who were interested in the company.   We
are unable to find from the evidence that the intestate, at the
time the contract was entered into, had any knowledge that
Mr. Polk was acting as trustee for the land company.   It is
immaterial what knowledge he afterwards acquired, and it is
likewise immaterial whether Mr. Polk was the trustee for
persons jointly interested with him, for the reason that there
is no such issue.

III.   The plaintiffs did not trace their title back to the
general government, by introducing in evidence deeds from

3. VENDOR   their grantors, but simply showed that the real
and vendee: estate had been conveyed to the intestate, and
action for
Purchase   that he had been in open, notorious and undis-
money: de-
fense of de-   turbed possession of the premises for more
fective title:
burden of   than ten years.   The court held that this was
proof.
presumptive evidence of title.   The defendants claim that
in so holding the court erred.   At the same time it is con-

ceded that the burden was on them to show incumbrances, but it is claimed that the burden was on the plaintiffs to show title in themselves or the intestate. The intestate agreed that he would furnish an "abstract." This we understand to mean that he would furnish an abstract of the records in the recorder's office, and of all the records showing title in himself. The object of this abstract was to enable the defendants to determine as to the sufficiency of the title, and facilitate their examination of the records. The abstract furnished showed to whom the land was conveyed by the government, and by and to whom it was afterwards conveyed. Such abstract was examined by the defendants or their attorneys, and certain objections made thereto. Certain defects were pointed out. It is not pleaded as a defense that the intestate did not have a title to any specific part of the land, but that such title was defective only. We therefore think the plaintiffs were not required to trace their title back to the government, by the introduction of deeds or other evidences of title. The title of the intestate was shown and exhibited by the abstract, and the defendants were required either to accept or reject it within a reasonable time. They were in no respect bound by it. But it amounted to an exhibition of title on the part of the intestate, and should have the same effect as if he had placed in the hands of the defendants all patents and deeds showing such a title as the defendants were entitled to under contract, which undoubtedly was a fee-simple title which would vest in them absolute ownership of the real estate free of incumbrances. It has been repeatedly held that a title by adverse possession may be acquired which has the same force and effect as a title based on a grant. *Sherman v. Kane*, 86 N. Y., 57; *Leffingwell v. Warren*, 2 Black, 599; *Heinrichs v. Terrell*, 65 Iowa, 25. Such possession must be at least presumptive evidence of title and of soizin in the person in possession. It must be remembered that the defendants were in the undisturbed possession of the premises, and made objections to the title as shown by the abstract. We therefore think, under the circumstances, that the burden was on the defendant to show wherein the title, as shown in the abstract, was in any respect defective.

IV. One parcel of the land was incumbered by a mortgage to the Ætna Insurance Company. This mortgage was
4. ——: ——: due January 1, 1883, and, as we understand,
——: removal of incumbrance. embraced other lands, which are not included in the contract. This mortgage, in fact, was paid, and, as we think, satisfaction duly made of record. But this was not done until after the institution of this action, but prior to the trial in the court below. It is sufficient if the title is perfected or incumbrances removed prior to the trial. If the court can then, by a decree, protect the rights of all parties, this is all either can justly ask, unless there has been a rescission, or an offer to rescind, and the party so offering has done all he is required to do, and was entitled thereto, at the time the offer was made. *McKinney v. Jones*, 57 Wis., 301; S. C. 15 N. W. Rep., 160; *Luckett v. Williamson*, 37 Mo., 388; *Montgomery v. Gibbs*, 40 Iowa, 622; Pom. Cont., § 421.

Whether the defendants were entitled to a rescission of the contract at the time it was claimed such an offer was
5. ——: ——: made, will be hereafter considered. What we
——: mortgage to corporation: release. have said applies to another mortgage, on a different tract of land. This mortgage was given to the Pella Manufacturing Company in 1877, and the money secured thereby was payable in 1878. It clearly appears that the mortgage is paid, and it further appears to be satisfied of record by J. B. Cotton, secretary and treasurer of said company. If Cotton had no such power, it devolved on the defendants to introduce evidence so showing. All that was done in this direction was to show by the articles of incorporation that no "instrument affecting the title to real estate should be binding unless ordered at a meeting of the official board," and such instrument must be signed by the president

and secretary. This provision has no application to the release of a mortgage given to secure a debt. We think the release of record is sufficient. Besides this, it has been held that it is not essential that such a release should be established, and that payment of the mortgage is all that can be justly required. *Curran v. Rogers*, 35 Mich., 221.

V. One parcel of the real estate was at one time owned by George Billups, and, as the plaintiffs claim, he con-

&. ——: ——: ——: mere possibility of litigation.

veyed, or intended to convey, the same to David R. Rea, in 1848, but that the description of the land is not strictly correct. It, however, clearly appears that the grantee, and those claiming under him, have been in the undisturbed possession of such real estate all the time since the execution of such conveyance. The intestate commenced an action against said Billups and others to correct the description in such conveyance, and thus remedy the defect in the title. A decree correcting the misdescription in the conveyance was rendered in such action by the district court. As there was no appearance, a default was entered against the defendants, and the court found that there had been due, legal and timely service of notice. To this decree the defendants object, because service was made on six of the defendants by publication only, and proof of the publication of notice was not marked "Filed," and entered on the appearance docket. It is said that the defendants so served may, within two years thereafter, under the statute, obtain a retrial as a matter of right. This is true, but it is exceedingly improbable, and it may, with reasonable safety, be affirmed that if they did so, they would not succeed in having the decree set aside. The long-continued adverse possession would, without more, defeat the action. A mere possibility that there will be litigation is not sufficient. There must be reasonable probability that such will be the case. Pom. Cont., §§ 203, 204. It seems to us that there is not and cannot be the slightest probability that the persons served by publication will ask a retrial.

The decree is further objected to because the original notice showing that the acceptance of service on two of the defend-

7. JUDGMENT: quieting title: irregularities: collateral attack. ants was not marked "Filed," or entered on the appearance docket. This is a collateral attack on the decree, and it appears certain to us that the failure of the clerk to file papers, and enter the same on the appearance docket, in no manner affects the jurisdiction of the court; and especially is this so when it was found by the court that notice to the defendants had been properly and legally served. Counsel cite and rely on *Nickson v. Blair*, 59 Iowa, 531, but that was a direct proceeding on appeal. We are unable to see that the failure of the clerk to so file and enter on the appearance docket any paper, in the absence of a statute so providing in express terms, can oust the court of jurisdiction, or have the effect to render the judgment void when attacked in a collateral proceeding.

It is further urged that it appears that some of the defendants in the action were married, and, as their wives or hus-

8. ACTION: to quiet title against misdescription: parties. bands were not made parties, their right of "dower" has not been extinguished. But it seems quite clear that no such right of dower attached. In legal effect, Billups conveyed to Rea the premises by the proper description. The mistake in incorrectly describing the premises intended to be conveyed is immaterial, so far as the right to dower is concerned. *Lea v. Woods*, 67 Iowa, 304.

VI. In discussing the objections made to the title to what the parties designate as the "Hutchinson" tract of land,

9. ADMINIS- TRATOR: conveyance of land bought in on mortgage foreclos- ure. it should be assumed that a fee-simple title was vested in E. R. Hutchinson, and that he contracted to and did sell the same to one Vink, who failing to comply with the terms of the sale, an action was commenced against him, in which the plaintiff recovered judgment, and the interest of Vink in the real estate was sold under a special execution. H. P. Hutchinson was administrator of the estate of E. R. Hutchinson, and he became the purchaser, and the real estate was conveyed by the sheriff to "H. P. Hutchinson, administrator." Upon what the plaintiffs claim was a proper application, the proper circuit court authorized said Hutchinson, as such administrator, to sell said real estate, and the plaintiffs claim that said proceedings were in every respect regular and sufficient; but the defendants claim otherwise. We do not deem it necessary to determine the questions thus presented. Vink was, in effect, a mortgagor, and the mortgage was foreclosed, and the real estate sold and conveyed as above stated. Such mortgage, and the indebtedness secured thereby, constituted personal assets of the estate, and as such came into the executor's hands. It was his duty to collect the same, and properly account therefor. When the mortgage was foreclosed, and the land conveyed to "Hutchinson, administrator," it was still his duty to convert the land into money, and account therefor. But he was the owner of the legal title to the land, and could sell and convey it without making any application to the court for that purpose, and the person to whom he so conveyed would take the title, and was not required to see that the purchase money was properly accounted for. *Lockman v. Reilly*, 95 N. Y., 64; *Long v. O'Fallon*, 19 How., 116.

Some objections are made to the legality of the foreclosure proceeding against Vink, but, clearly, they do not present any valid reasons why the judgment should be held to be void in a collateral attack thereon. There are also objections to other judgments or decrees in actions brought by the plaintiffs to cure certain defects of like character to those heretofore stated, to which the rules heretofore stated fully, in our opinion, apply. We deem it unnecessary to more particularly refer to them.

VII. There is a deficiency of four acres of land described in the bond for a deed. That is, there is that quantity to which it is conceded the intestate had no title. Conceding that the defendants relied on or stated this as an objection to complying with the contract when the abstract was presented to them, we think it is not a valid objection. In the first place, the

10. VENDOR and vendee: failure of title as to part: rescission or compensation.

four acres did not constitute an inducement to the purchase,
and is so situated as not to detract from the value of the whole
tract.   In such case the law is well settled that compensation
is the rule.   The whole number of acres sold was at least
314.   But we do not think the defendants are entitled to compensation for such deficiency, for the reason that we are satisfied from the evidence that the four acres never were sold
or purchased, and were described in the bond for a deed by
mistake, and therefore the district court correctly reformed it
in this respect.

VIII.   It is shown that there are certain highways on the
land which are used by the public. The fact that such was the

11. ——: ob-
jections to
title : when
made.

case was one of the inducements to the purchase,
so that the public could readily reach the town-
site proposed to be laid off.   For the purpose for
which the defendants desired to obtain a portion of the land,
such highways were absolutely essential.   We are satisfied
from the evidence that the defendants did not object to the
title for this reason when other objections were made to the
abstract and title.   They well knew that this was something
the plaintiff could not remove, and, if they regarded the
existence of highways as an objection to fulfilling their contract, they were bound to so indicate when the other objections were made.   Instead of doing this, the intestate had
reason to believe he could remove the objections made, and
perfect his title, and proceeded to do so, and thereby incurred
expense in reliance thereon.   The defendants were bound to
present all their objections to the title at the time the abstract
was presented to them, or within a reasonable time thereafter.   Besides this, a literal compliance on the part of the
intestate cannot be required, but a substantial compliance is
sufficient, if thereby the defendants obtain all that constituted the inducement to the purchase.   Wat. Spec. Perf., §§
422–427.

IX.   The bond, as we have seen, was executed in July,

1881. There was a parol contract entered into prior to that

12. ——: ——:
Incumbrance
by consent of
vendee.
time, and a small portion of the consideration paid. The exact date of such parol contract does not appear. On the sixth day of July, 1881, the intestate conveyed to the railroad company the right of way over the premises, and the road has been constructed and is daily operated. The contract was entered into between the intestate and Towne, as agent for the defendants, or one of them; and he testifies that the right of way was so conveyed as a part of the sale and purchase. There is no evidence contradictory to this, except that it may be said the defendants deny the authority of Towne in this respect, and that they had no knowledge of such fact. The railroad corporation is composed of Mr. Polk and four other persons, and the land company is composed of Mr. Polk and three persons, who are the same persons who are members of the railroad company. Mr. Towne was the agent of Mr. Polk, trustee, and of both of these corporations, and as such procured the right of way, and, as we have stated, made the contract. The object and inducement of the purchase was the location of the town-site on the railroad on the premises. We think the intestate was justified, under the circumstances, in believing Towne had authority to make the contract he did, and that the defendants are bound thereby. Besides this, the defendants knew that, unless the railroad was located and constructed over the land, the town-site would be valueless; and for this purpose and object the purchase was made. Again, no such objection was made to the abstract and title when the other objections were made, and the defendants cannot be permitted to make such objection now.

X. The defendants contend that time is of the essence of the contract, but the contract does not so provide. There is

13. ——:
time as es-
sence of con-
tract: waiver.
nothing on its face which so indicates. Their contention is that time may be, and should sometimes be, regarded as of the essence of the contract, even when it is not so expressly stated.

This will be conceded when the object and purpose
of the contract, reasonably construed, in the light of all the
circumstances, so indicate, and it has been so treated by the
parties.   The covenants in the contract are dependent, and
were to be performed on or about the first day of March,
1882.   The intestate was then to convey a good title, and the
defendants to pay the purchase money.   It was not until the
twelfth day of March, 1882, as stated in the answer, that the
intestate furnished the abstract.   No objection was made to
this delay, but, the title being defective, as the defendants
thought, the plaintiff undertook to obviate such objections.
This required time, and the defendants so knew.   Conceding
that time was of the essence of the contract, such time must
have been the day fixed for performance.   Clearly, such time
was waived, for it is not pretended that there was any offer to
rescind made then, or until eighteen months afterwards.
During that time the intestate made efforts to have his title
approved, but the defendants still thought it was defective,
and urged the plaintiff to perfect it, and he was making
efforts to do so, until finally, in September, 1883, the defendants made an offer, and elected to rescind.   It will be observed
that no time of performance was fixed after the time specified in the bond had passed.   We therefore do not think that
time was of the essence of the contract, or, if it was, there
was a waiver; and therefore the defendants are not entitled to
a rescission for this reason.

XI.   The defendants further contend that they had the
right to rescind at the time they made the offer and elected

14. ——: ob-   to do so, because of existing incumbrances on the
jections to
title: resci8-   land, and because the intestate was unable at that
sion of con-
tract: terms.   time to convey such a title as they were entitled
to.   The bond for a deed was duly acknowledged and recorded.
Mr. Polk, trustee, was therefore invested, as between him and
the intestate, with an equitable title of record to the premises.   Afterwards he conveyed such title as he had to the
land company, which was duly recorded.   Afterwards the

offer to rescind was made by tendering back to the intestate the title bond, and offering to account for rents and profits, and surrendering possession of the premises. The bond and conveyance to the land company created at least clouds upon the title, and we have been unable to discover any evidence which tends to show that the land company offered to convey to the intestate, or remove the cloud existing by reason of the deed to it.

It also appears that by some contract with the railroad company the land company had the right to locate stations, and this right had been exercised, and a station located on the land described in the contract. A railroad had been constructed over the premises, and the track laid down. This was a permanent structure. The right of way was conveyed by the intestate without any other consideration than that it constituted a part of the sale and purchase. It is therefore apparent that, when the offer to rescind was made, it was inequitable and unjust to compel the plaintiff to take the land back. There had been part performance on the part of the plaintiff by the conveyance of the right of way, or, if this be not true, there was no offer to remove the cloud caused by the conveyance to the land company. It is fundamental that, before a contract can be rescinded by one party, he must place the other party in the same position he was at the time the contract was made, or the power to do so must at least exist. *Burge v. Cedar Rapids & M. R. R. Co.,* 32 Iowa, 101; *Montgomery v. Gibbs,* 40 Id., 652. Many other authorities might be cited in support of the foregoing proposition.

XII. We are unable to find that the defendants were damaged by the delay. There is evidence tending to show, in a general way, that they were. One or more witnesses state that in their opinion the defendants were damaged, but no facts are stated upon which such an opinion could be based. It does not appear that the land has depreciated in value. A town was laid off

15. ——: action for purchase money: delay in perfecting title.

on the land, and platted, but the plat was not recorded, as the defendants claim, for the reason that they could not legally do so because of defects in the title and incumbrances on the land.   Lots in the town were advertised for sale extensively, and for considerable time, but it does not appear that a single application to purchase was made.   No substantial damage, therefore, is shown.

XIII.   The defendants being in the undisturbed possession of the premises, with the right expressly given in the title bond to "make changes and improvements" as they saw proper, and having failed to show a right to rescind, or that they have been substantially damaged, should comply with the contract; and therefore the plaintiffs are entitled to judgment for the purchase money, with interest as specified therein.

The judgment of the district court is in all respects

AFFIRMED.

EDWARDS v. COSGRO ET AL.·   (TWO CASES.)

1. **Appeal.** AMOUNT IN CONTROVERSY: TWO CASES UNITED.   A garnishee under two executions, issued upon judgments rendered by the same justice of the peace, paid to the officer enough of money to satisfy both judgments, each of which was less than $100, but which together exceeded that sum. The justice, upon receiving the money, applied it upon the judgments, and entered an order discharging the garnishee.   While the money was yet in the justice's hands, an intervenor appeared and claimed the whole of the money.   His petition was entitled in but one of the cases, but it was agreed by the parties that it should be applicable to both of them. The justice sustained a motion to strike the petition from the files. Upon a writ of error the circuit court affirmed the ruling of the justice, and the intervenor appeals to this court.   *Held* that the action by the intervenor was but a single proceeding, involving more than $100, and that a certificate of the trial judge was not necessary to give this court jurisdiction of the appeal.

2. **Justice's Court:** JURISDICTION: QUESTION NOT RAISED: APPEAL. Where a cause before a justice of the peace involved more than $100, but the question of jurisdiction was not raised, it could not be raised upon writ of error in the circuit court, nor upon an appeal from the judgment of the circuit court to this court.

3. **Garnishment:** ON EXECUTION: INTERVENTION: WHEN PERMITTED. So long as money paid into court by a garnishee on execution has not been paid over to the execution plaintiff, a third party claiming the money may intervene in the action for the purpose of asserting his claim to the money. (Code, §§ 3016, 3051.) So *held* where the garnishee had paid over the money and had been discharged, without answering, and without notice to the execution defendant, and where the money had been applied in satisfaction of the judgments on which the executions had been issued, but had not yet been paid over to the judgment creditors.

Appeal from Louisa Circuit Court.

FRIDAY, MARCH 11.

THE plaintiffs each recovered a judgment in justice's court against the defendant Cosgro. Executions were issued on these judgments, on which one John Huff was garnished as a supposed debtor of the defendant. The garnishee paid over to the officer who held the executions an amount of money sufficient to satisfy both judgments. The officer thereupon returned the writs, and certified in his return that he had garnished Huff thereon, and that he had received the money from him. He also paid the money so collected to the justice, who made a record of the payment on his docket, and entered an order in each case discharging the garnishee. The garnishee, however, had not answered, nor was any cause docketed against him, nor had notice of the garnishment been served on the defendant Cosgro. While the money remained in the hands of the justice, Tatlock filed a petition of intervention, in which he claimed that the money belonged to him, and prayed that he be adjudged to be the owner thereof. This petition was entitled in the cause of Salina Edwards, but by the written agreement of the parties it was made to apply to both cases. The plaintiff filed a motion to strike this petition from the files, which was sustained by the justice. Thereupon the intervenor removed the cause into the circuit court by writ of error, and that court, upon a final hearing, affirmed the order of the justice. Intervenor appeals.

E. W. Tatlock, for appellant.

R. Caldwell, *C. A. Carpenter* and *Arthur Springer*, for appellee.

REED, J.—I.   The point was made by counsel for appellee that this court did not have jurisdiction of the cause, for the

1. APPEAL: amount in controversy: two cases united.

reason that the amount in controversy is less than $100, and there was no certificate of the trial judge that the case involved a question of law on which the opinion of this court was desired.   Neither of the judgments against Cosgro amounted to $100, but the two aggregated more than that amount, and the amount of money paid by the garnishee was $105.   The intervenor claimed the whole of the money.   His petition was entitled in but one of the actions, but, as stated above, the parties agreed that it might be made applicable to both.   It was therefore a single proceeding, which involved a claim to the whole amount of money paid by the garnishee.

II.   It is next insisted that, if the amount in controversy exceeds $100, the justice did not have jurisdiction to deter-

2. JUSTICE'S court: jurisdiction: question not raised: appeal.

mine the claim made by the intervenor.   But no question as to his jurisdiction was raised by the motion on which he disposed of intervenor's petition, and neither he nor the circuit court could have passed upon any such a question.   The cause was removed into the circuit court for the purpose of having the ruling of the justice, in dismissing the intervenor's petition, reviewed, and that court could pass on such questions only as were raised by the motion; and the appeal to this court brings up for review only such questions as arose in the circuit court, and were there passed upon.   We cannot, therefore, on this appeal, consider the question whether the justice had jurisdiction to determine the claim alleged by the intervenor in his petition.

III.   The grounds of the motion to strike intervenor's peti-

tion from the files were that, at the time the petition was
filed, there was no action pending in which the
party could intervene, the judgments against the
defendant having been rendered long prior to
that, and the garnishee having been discharged;
also that the money had already been applied in satisfaction
of the judgments, and could not be recovered by the intervenor; also that, as the garnishee had not answered, but had
paid over the money without being required to do so by any
order of the court, the payment should be regarded as having
been made on the request of the defendant. The important
question is whether Tatlock was entitled to intervene for the
purpose of claiming the money when the proceedings had
reached the stage at which they were when he filed his petition.

Section 2683 of the Code provides " that any person who
has an interest in the matter in litigation   *   *   *
may become a party to an action between other persons,
either by joining the plaintiff in claiming what is sought by the
petition, or by uniting with the defendant in resisting the claim
of the plaintiff, or by demanding anything adversely to both
the plaintiff and defendant.   *   *   * "   It is very
clear that this provision empowers a person to become a party
by intervention, to an action or controversy between others,
only during the pendency of the action. Under it he cannot
come into the case after judgment or final order. Section
3016, however, empowers any person other than the defendant to intervene at any time before the sale of attached property, or before the proceeds thereof, or any attached debt, is
paid over to the plaintiff in the action, and make a claim to
the property or money. This section, by its terms, applies
especially to cases where the property or money has been
seized by attachment, or garnishment under attachment proceedings. But section 3051 provides that garnishments on
execution shall be effected in the manner prescribed in the
sections governing garnishment on attachment, and that in

(margin note:) 3. GARNISH-MENT: on execution: intervention: when permitted.

every particular the proceedings shall be the same as under garnishment or attachment. The effect of this section is to give third parties who claim the property or money seized on execution, or by garnishment on execution, the right to intervene, and assert their claim at the time and in the manner prescribed by section 3016, and their rights in the premises may be determined in the manner prescribed in that and other sections in the same chapter. As, therefore, the money in question had not been paid over to the plaintiffs when intervenor filed his petition, he had the right to intervene for the purpose of asserting his claim to it.

The fact that the justice had credited the amounts on the judgments in no manner affected his right; for, under the express provision, he had the right to assert his claim in that manner at any time before the money was paid over to plaintiff.

The claim that the payment by the garnishee should be regarded as having been made at the request of the defendant finds no support in the record. It appears clearly enough, from the record, that he paid over the money for the purpose of effecting his discharge as garnishee. The justice evidently regarded it in that light, for he entered an order discharging him, which was entirely unnecessary if the payment had been made in any other capacity than that of garnishee.

We think the circuit court erred in affirming the order of the justice striking the petition of intervenor from the files.

REVERSED.

RAINBOW v. BENSON ET AL.

1. **Justices' Courts**: SELECTION OF OFFICER TO SUMMON JURY IN CRIM-
INAL CASE: INQUIRY AS TO FITNESS. When a justice is about to issue
a *venire* for a jury in a criminal case to a certain peace officer, (Code, §
4673,) the prosecutor may properly file a motion, supported by affidavit,
showing that such officer is prejudiced against the prosecution, and is
likely to select jurors to the prejudice of the state, and asking that the
venire be issued to some other peace officer; and in such case it is the
duty of the justice to institute an inquiry, and investigate the truth of
. the charge, and govern his action accordingly.

2. **Libel**: PRIVILEGED COMMUNICATION: JUDICIAL PROCEEDINGS: STATE-
MENTS IN AFFIDAVIT. Whatever is said or written in good faith in the
course of judicial proceedings, and which is pertinent and material to
the matter in controversy, is privileged. So *held* as to the statements
made by a prosecutor of alleged criminals before a justice of the peace,
in an affidavit setting forth that the peace officer to whom a *venire* was
about to be issued was in collusion with the alleged criminals, and therefore an unfit person to summon a jury for their trial.

Appeal from Shelby District Court.

FRIDAY, MARCH 11.

PLAINTIFF brought an action for damages for an alleged
libelous publication. The district court sustained a demurrer
to an answer filed by the defendants, and from that order
they appeal.

Smith & Culleson and *Platt Wicks*, for appellants.

Beard & Myerly and *J. W. Di Silva*, for appellee.

REED, J.—The alleged libelous publication was contained
in an affidavit filed by the defendants in a criminal action
pending before a justice of the peace, and is as follows: " I,
F. E. Benson and John Reed, on oath state, I (John Reed)
am the party filing the information herein, and that G. S.
Rainbow, the deputy sheriff, the officer to whom it is proposed
to issue the *venire* and have to summon the jury in such
cause, and act as constable or officer therein, is prejudiced in

favor of the defendant in said cause, and is colluding with
said defendant, and men in the saloon business, for the purpose
of preventing their conviction; and to that end he, in exercising the duty of selecting and impaneling a jury to try said
cause, wherein a party is accused of the crime of selling
intoxicating liquors, takes particular pains to select men who
are opposed to the enforcement of the prohibitory law, so
called, and in hopes thereby to secure the acquittal of the
defendant then to be tried; and that, if he should be allowed
to select a jury in that cause, affiant believes and alleges that
he would, in the manner as aforesaid, select a jury in the
interest of the defense, and with an object of securing the
defendant's release. All this I verily believe."

The answer alleged that the defendants, at the time they
signed and filed the paper, were citizens of Shelby county;
that the defendant John Reed had filed an information before
a justice of the peace, accusing one Al Wicks of the crime
of selling intoxicating liquors contrary to law; that, when
said Wicks was brought before the justice for trial on said
charge, he demanded a trial by jury, and thereupon the justice was about to direct the plaintiff to prepare a list of
names from which such jury would be drawn, and to issue
to him a *venire* to summon said jurors, when the defendant
Reed made a motion orally asking the justice to designate
some other peace officer to perform said duties, on the ground
that plaintiff was prejudiced against the interests of the state
in cases of that character; that he was directed by the justice to reduce the motion to writing, and support the same
by affidavits, and that he thereupon made and filed a written
motion to that effect, and filed the affidavit in question in
support thereof; that said motion and affidavit were made
and filed in good faith, and without malice, and in the performance of a public duty; and that defendants had good
grounds for believing, and did believe, that the allegations in
the affidavit were true, and that they made the same for the

sole purpose of imparting to the justice the matters contained
therein.

The grounds of the demurrer were that the justice did not
have jurisdiction of the subject to which the publication
referred, and that, upon the facts alleged in the answer, it
was not privileged. The law undoubtedly is that whatever
is said or written in the course of a judicial proceeding, and
which is pertinent and material to the matter in controversy,
is privileged. The question in this case is whether the
answer shows that the communication in question is within
that rule. It will readily be conceded that the matters
alleged in the affidavit had no relevancy to the charges
involved in the criminal cause which was pending before the
justice, and which was about to be tried. But in our opinion that consideration is not at all material to the inquiries
before us. Whether the communication was privileged
depends upon whether the justice had the power, when Reed
objected to the designation of plaintiff for the performance
of the duty of making the jury list, to enter upon an inquiry
as to the truth of the matters alleged in the motion, and
determine therefrom whether plaintiff was a proper person
to be designated for the performance of the duty, and whether
the matters alleged in the affidavit were pertinent and material to such inquiry.

I. As to the power of the justice to entertain the motion
and make the inquiry: The statute (Code, § 4673) provides
that, "if a trial by jury be demanded, the jus-
1. JUSTICES'
courts: selec-
tion of officer
to summon
jury in crim-
inal case:
inquiry as to
fitness.
tice shall direct any peace officer of the county
to make a list in writing of the names of eighteen inhabitants of the county having the qualifications of jurors in the district court, from
which list the prosecutor and defendant may each strike out
three names." Other sections provide that the twelve jurors whose names remain upon the list shall be summoned to
appear before the justice, and that the jury for the trial of
the cause (which consists of six persons) may be selected

from this number. It will be seen that the duty of making the list of eighteen names is one of very considerable importance. The officer who performs that duty has it in his power to compel the parties to accept as triers of the cause the persons selected by him, however objectionable they may be to them. Of course, the presumption is that the officer will properly perform the duty imposed upon him; but the power might be abused, to the great detriment of the parties.

The section quoted above confers upon the justice a discretion in the selection of the officer for the performance of the duty. The language is that he "shall direct any peace officer of the county" to make the list. He is empowered by this language to designate the sheriff, or one of his deputies, or any constable in the county, for the performance of the duty, and to use his discretion in making the selection. In the exercise of this discretion, it is his duty to select such officer as he believes will act fairly and impartially as between the parties. This power to select a single individual from among a number, for the performance of the duty, necessarily includes the power to institute an inquiry as to the fitness of the one intended to be designated, when a question as to his fitness arises. The parties in interest clearly have the right to object to the designation of a particular officer on the ground of his unfitness for the performance of the duty. Monstrous wrongs might be perpetrated if the law were otherwise. Suppose the justice was about to designate an officer whom the defendant had reason to believe was the real instigator of the prosecution against him, or who was his bitter personal enemy, certainly the law would give him the privilege of objecting to the designation of that particular person. And, when such objection was made, it would clearly be the duty of the justice to institute an inquiry as to the truth of the charge. In making such inquiry, it would often become necessary for him to hear evidence in support or resistance of the objection.

And we think the informant has the same right to enter an objection to the designation of a particular officer. He is not a party to the record, it is true, but the law allows him to institute the prosecution for the reason that, as a citizen of the state, he has an interest in the faithful execution of its laws. Indeed, the duty of private individuals to institute criminal prosecutions is often among the highest duties of citizenship; and, having instituted such a prosecution, he has the right to have the cause fairly and impartially tried. The right to make the objection in question results necessarily from his relation to the case. The investigation, while it does not relate to the matters involved in the main cause, takes place in the progress of the case, and is incident to it. It is a judicial investigation in the same sense that the trial by a court of record of a challenge to a juror for cause is a judicial investigation.

II. The matters alleged in the affidavit were clearly pertinent and material to the subject of the investigation. They

2. LIBEL: privileged communication: judicial proceedings: statements in affidavit.

tended to show that the officer was the partisan of the defendant, and that he would, if intrusted with the duty of selecting the jury, exercise the power of his position with the view of securing the acquittal of the defendant, regardless of the merits of the case. If the statements of the affidavit were true, he was not a fit person to be intrusted with the power proposed to be conferred upon him. If the statements were made in good faith, and in the honest belief that they were true, they are privileged.

REVERSED.

BALL v. THE KEOKUK & NORTHWESTERN R'Y Co.

1. **Pleading:** AMENDMENT AFTER VERDICT. On an appeal from an award of damages for right of way taken by a railroad company, where the land was in township sixty-seven, and the trial and all the proceedings had reference to that land, but the land was described in the papers as being in township sixty-nine, *held* that plaintiff was properly allowed to amend, after verdict, by substituting sixty-seven for sixty-nine.

2. **Action:** OTHER ACTION PENDING: REMOVAL OF BAR. Where the pendency of a former action is relied upon as a bar, the dismissal of the former action, before the question of its pendency comes before the court for determination, removes the bar. (*Rush v. Frost,* 49 Iowa, 183, followed.)

3. **Railroads:** RIGHT OF WAY DAMAGES: EVIDENCE ON APPEAL. On an appeal from an award of damages for land taken for right of way for a railroad, it was error to allow evidence as to the damages per acre to the land from which the right of way was taken, without definite proof as to the number of acres in the several tracts. It was also error to allow evidence of damages to certain tracts indefinitely referred to by counsel, and which were not clearly shown to be crossed by the railroad or involved in the case.

Appeal from Lee Circuit Court.

FRIDAY, MARCH 11.

THE appeal is from proceedings instituted to ascertain the right of way damages due the plaintiff by reason of the taking of land for the defendant railway company. A sheriff's jury was called, and the damages assessed. From the assessment the defendant appealed to the circuit court, where a trial was had, and the damages were again assessed. From that assessment the defendant appeals to this court.

James H. Anderson, for appellant.

D. N. Sprague and *Frank Hagerman,* for appellee.

ADAMS, CH. J.—I. In the proceedings as instituted, and in the trial upon appeal in the circuit court, the land in

1. PLEADING: amendment after verdict. question was described as in township sixty-nine, whereas the land is in township sixty-seven. After the verdict the plaintiff asked leave to amend the

papers so as to describe the land as in township sixty-seven, and such amendment was allowed to be made. The defendant claims that, in allowing such amendment, the court erred.

The sheriff's jury examined the land in question in township sixty-seven, and all the witnesses who testified upon the trial upon appeal testified with reference to the same land. No one was misled by the mistake in describing the township at first as township sixty-nine. The amount of damages assessed could not have been different if the mistake had not been made. After the amendment, the papers, upon their face, applied to the land intended, and every interest of the defendant was protected. We think that the amendment was allowable in furtherance of justice, and that the defendant has no good ground of complaint.

II. The defendant filed an answer in the circuit court, in which it averred that the plaintiff had another action pending for the same damages. The fact appears to be that there was another action pending at the time these proceedings were commenced, but was dismissed before the trial on appeal. Whatever may be the rule at common law, under our practice the dismissal of the former action, before the question as to its pendency comes before the court for determination, removes the bar. *Rush v. Frost,* 49 Iowa, 183.

1. ACTION: other action pending: removal of bar.

III. The defendant has presented a large number of questions arising upon the introduction of evidence, but it will not be necessary to consider them all. The case in some respects presents itself to us as a remarkable one. The amount of land taken by the railroad company was about eight acres. No buildings seem to have been disturbed, and yet the jury assessed the plaintiff's damages at $3,259.44. How much land there was in the farm does not appear from any reliable evidence. In the petition of the plaintiff to the sheriff, asking him to summon a jury to assess the damages, the land is described

2. RAILROADS: right of way damages: evidence on appeal.

as embracing two tracts of forty acres each, and one tract of fifty-four and one-half acres, and one tract described as half of a quarter section. No one of the governmental subdivisions is described as fractional, and, taking the description as it stands, the amount should be presumed to be 214½ acres. Yet none of the witnesses speak of it as such, and a part of them, without any tangible evidence upon the subject, assume that there was more, and estimated the damages at a certain amount per acre.

The case seems to have been tried, on the part of the plaintiff, in a very loose and confused way. Some of the evidence as presented in the abstract is not intelligible. The court itself seems to have been confused by the way the plaintiff's counsel examined his witnesses. Whether the witnesses themselves had a better understanding of what was asked we do not know. Testimony was allowed in regard to an eighty-seven-acre tract, against the objection of the defendant that no such tract is described in the papers in the case. The plaintiff testified that the tract was worth forty dollars per acre before the road was built; that the road ran slantwise across it; and that the tract was damaged eighteen dollars per acre. It is certain no such tract appears to be described in the papers. There is a tract described presumably containing eighty acres, and no more. Possibly this is the tract referred to. But, according to the map introduced, the railroad does not touch the tract. Again, the defendant's counsel, after examining him in regard to what is called the eighty-seven-acre tract, proceeded as follows: "Now, then, take the next forty acres,—the forty south of the eighty-seven-acre tract." *Answer.* "Yes, sir." "What was that worth before the railroad was built?" *A.* "Worth about forty-five dollars per acre." "When they put the railroad in there, what was it worth then?" *A.* "It was worth about twenty dollars, the way I had it." Here we find an inquiry made about a forty-acre tract south of the eighty-seven-acre tract; but there is no forty-acre tract involved in these proceedings lying south of what is described as "the west half of the southeast quarter of section nine," nor does the map purport to show such forty-acre tract. If there is an eighty-seven-acre tract lying north of a forty-acre tract involved in the proceedings, it is not the W. ½ of the S. E. ¼ of section 9. We think it was error to admit evidence in regard to an eighty-seven-acre tract without any evidence that there was such tract, and especially as the witnesses generally estimated the damages at a certain amount per acre.

IV. The plaintiff's counsel then proceeded as follows: "Now, there is an eighty,—the last towards Keokuk; does the railroad run on that?" *Answer.* "It cuts off a corner." This evidence was objected to, and we think properly. A forty-acre tract had been mentioned as south of the eighty-seven-acre tract, and now an eighty-acre tract is inquired about as south of the south forty. There is certainly no such tract involved in these proceedings, and we do not think that any evidence should have been admitted concerning it. It is true that further on an objection was interposed to any evidence respecting the N. E. ¼ of section 16, and the court ruled upon the objection in the defendant's favor, the ruling being made in these words: "It is not competent to show damages as to the last eighty bought since the taking of the right of way." But this ruling did not purport to exclude the evidence which had been previously expressly admitted over the defendant's objection, when an inquiry was made about an eighty lying south of the south forty. Possibly the court intended that it should be so understood, but no jury could be properly relied upon to find its way through so much confusion of terms.

Evidence should not have been allowed as to the damages per acre, without definite proof as to the number of acres, and accurate words of description of the tracts should have been used in the examination of the witness, and all evidence as to damages to land not embraced in the proceedings, whether it might have been embraced or not, should have been excluded.

We think that the judgment must be

REVERSED.

310
417
418

BLANFORD v. THE MINNEAPOLIS & ST. LOUIS R'Y CO.

1. **Railroads:** RIGHT TO FENCE TRACK IN CITIES AND TOWNS. A railroad corporation does not have the right to fence its track in cities and towns where it is intersected by streets and alleys; and it is immaterial whether the track crosses a lot or block for a greater or less distance, or whether the lot or block is owned by one or many persons. BECK and REED, J. J., *dissenting*.

Appeal from Boone Circuit Court.

FRIDAY, MARCH 11.

ACTION to recover under the statute double the value of a cow killed by a train on the defendant's road, at a point where it had the right to fence its track. It is also stated in the petition that the train was carelessly and negligently operated. Trial to the court; judgment for the plaintiff; defendant appeals.

A. E. Clarke, for appellant.

Crooks & Jordan, for appellee.

SEEVERS, J.—Certain facts were stipulated and agreed upon, among which were the following: "The plaintiff's cow, while at large in the streets of the incorporated town of Ogden, at a point where said town was platted and laid out in blocks, streets and alleys, was struck and killed by defendant's train, where the defendant's road crosses one of the lots of said town."

The amount in controversy being less than $100, we are required to determine the following question: "Has a railroad corporation the right to fence its track and right of way when the same passes over and across a town lot or block, 264 by 574 feet, being a portion of the territory embraced in and within the corporate limits of an incorporated town which is laid out and platted in streets and blocks?"

We are unable to determine, from the facts stipulated and the foregoing question, whether the lot or block is all owned by one person, or by several, or whether the road crosses it for the distance of 574 or only 264 feet. We incline, however, to think it immaterial what the facts are in the respects mentioned. We will therefore assume that the lot in question is owned by one person, and that the road passes across it, at a right angle, for the longest distance mentioned. While this assumption is made, it is obvious that in some other case it may appear that the blocks are, say, 250 feet square, divided into lots of twenty-five feet, each of which is crossed by the road for that distance, and each lot is owned by a different person. If this makes any difference, and each case must be decided according to the facts shown in the record, then it would seem to be a question for the jury, under proper instructions from the court, as to whether the right to fence existed; that is, whether the railroad company had such right. We, however, are asked to determine the question propounded as a matter of law, and such it has been assumed to be in numerous decisions of this court, and such we believe it to be, and such question we think may be stated as follows: whether a railroad company has the right to fence its track within the corporate limits of a city or town, outside of or beyond the switches and depot grounds, but within that part of the corporate limits where the track is intersected by streets and alleys. We assume that outside or beyond where there are any streets, and where the land is used for agricultural purposes, although within the corporation, the right to fence exists. *Coyle v. Chicago, M. & St. P. R'y Co.*, 62 Iowa, 518.

Assuming, then, that the question to be determined is correctly stated, it is immaterial whether the lot or block is crossed by the road for the distance of 250 or 600 feet, and whether it is owned by one or many persons. The real legal question is whether the right to fence exists within the corporate limits, as above limited and defined. If it does, then cattle-guards must be constructed on both sides of each street and alley, for the reason that the fence would not prevent stock from getting on the track without such cattle-guards. *Mundhenk v. Central Iowa R'y Co.*, 57 Iowa, 718.

It is provided by statute that, when a person owns land on both sides of a railway, the corporation may be required to construct a cattle-guard and causeway, and the corporation also is required to construct cattle-guards where the railway enters or leaves improved or fenced land. Sections 1268, 1288, Code. Does this statute apply to lots and blocks in towns and cities? As there are no restraining words, such a construction could be placed thereon with as much propriety as the theory adopted by the circuit court in relation to the right to fence. The corporation is not required to fence, but, if it fails to do so, it is absolutely liable for stock injured or killed. Code, § 1289.

There are no exceptions, and it is immaterial where the stock is injured or killed. But it is evident that the corporation does not have the right to fence across highways. There is clearly one other exception,—it does not have the right to fence its depot grounds; and it makes no difference, we apprehend, whether such grounds are in a city or town, or not within either. *Davis v. Burlington & M. R. R'y Co.*, 26 Iowa, 549. The question under consideration was elaborately considered in the cited case, and, while the precise question under consideration was not in that case, yet it is evident that it was in the mind of the court, and was considered. Among other things, it is said in the opinion: "The fitness or propriety of fencing a road, we need hardly say, depends upon circumstances. *   *   *   The legislature had in mind, beyond question, these lines as they were constructed over our prairies, knowing that cattle were free commoners, and desiring to protect stock running at large so generally in agricultural districts of the state." The opinion, as a whole, clearly conveys the impression that it was written with the view and intended to determine two other cases then pending, in which the facts were different. Those cases are *Rogers v. Chicago & N. W. R'y Co.*, 26 Iowa, 558, and *Durand v. Same*, Id., 559. In the former, the following instruction was given: "That, if the horse was killed in the town of Oxford, but not on the depot grounds, or within the switches, and not on any street crossing, and the road was not fenced, the verdict should be for the plaintiff for double the value." And an instruction embodying the proposition that the company would not be liable, under the statute, for failure to fence within the limits of the town situated and traversed by the road, as this was, being refused, there was a verdict for the plaintiff. The court said: "In principle, this case is 'on all fours' with that immediately preceding, (*Davis v. Burlington & M. R. R'y Co.*) The argument made we will not repeat. Following the construction there given of the statute, this judgment is erroneous."

When the foregoing cases are carefully considered, we think it is evident that this court is committed to the rule that a railroad corporation does not have the right to fence its track in cities and towns where it is intersected and crossed by streets and alleys. The question we are required to determine must therefore be answered in the negative.

The circuit court saw fit to propound another question, and that, in substance, is whether the defendant is liable on the ground of negligence. Inasmuch as the court rendered judgment for double the value of the cow, this question is immaterial, and only presents for determination an abstract proposition, and therefore we are not required to consider it.

REVERSED.

BECK, J., *dissenting.*—Under the decisions in this court,

a railroad company may fence its track whenever it is "fit, proper and suitable" to do so, and the right rests upon the public convenience, the public interest, and not upon the convenience of the railway company. This rule has been applied by this court to cases wherein was involved the right to fence depot grounds and a strip of land adjacent to a railroad track, "designed to afford room for teaming and driving" on each side of the track. *Davis v. Burlington & M. R. R'y Co.*, 26 Iowa, 549; *Rogers v. Chicago & N. W. R'y Co.*, Id., 558.

This court has not held that a railroad company has not the right to fence its track within the limits of a town or city, when the public interest and convenience do not prohibit it. *Gilman v. Sioux City & P. R'y Co.*, 62 Iowa, 299, and *Coyle v. Chicago, M. & St. P. R'y Co.*, Id., 518, are claimed by counsel to so hold, but they are not to that effect.

The mere fact that a lot, containing nearly four acres, (the lot in question being that size,) is within a town or city, does not authorize the conclusion that the interest and convenience of the public does not demand that a railway running through it should not be fenced. Indeed, it may be that a fence, in such a case, is more urgently demanded by the public good than in case of farming lands away from towns and cities. It will be observed that the facts shown by the question submitted in this case disclose that the railroad runs "over and across" the town lots, not upon a street or road adjacent thereto. The foregoing opinion, while admitting that the rule it approves has not been held by this court, declares that it was in the "mind" of the court, and therefore recognized in *Davis v. Burlington & M. R. R'y Co.*, 26 Iowa, 549. We cannot fathom the "mind" of the court in order to determine the rule of law decided, nor can we consider the arguments advanced in the discussion by the court in order to determine the point decided. We look to the facts, and, if we discover that the point was not in the case, whatever is said about it is not to be regarded as a decision; it is mere *dictum*. The foregoing opinion admits what is true,—that the question before us was not in the case cited; it is therefore no authority in this case.

A doubt may well be expressed as to whether the point in controversy in this case was "in the mind" of the court in the case cited, and whether any arguments found in it support the conclusion reached in the foregoing decision.

REED, J., concurs in this dissent.

ELLITHORPE V. REIDESIL ET AL.

1. **Appeal to Supreme Court:** AMOUNT IN CONTROVERSY. Plaintiff in his petition alleged that defendants had entered upon his land and cut and carried away a portion of the crops, and laid his damages at $100. He also asked for an injunction to restrain them from cutting and carrying away the remainder of the crops. *Held* that the amount in controversy, as shown by the pleadings, exceeded $100, and that an appeal would lie to this court without the certificate of the trial judge.

2. **Execution:** GROWING CROPS CANNOT BE SOLD UNDER. Immature crops belong to the land on which they are growing, and they cannot be levied upon and sold on execution as personal property; and where such sale is attempted the purchaser acquires no right which he can assert as against one who purchases the realty from the judgment debtor before the maturity of the crops. (See opinion for cases followed and distinguished.)

Appeal from Ida Circuit Court.

SATURDAY, MARCH 12.

PLAINTIFF claimed damages for an alleged trespass committed by the defendants in entering upon certain premises belonging to him, and cutting and carrying away a portion of the crops growing thereon. He also prayed for an injunction to restrain defendants from committing further trespass on the premises. There was a verdict and judgment for defendants. Plaintiff appeals.

L. A. Berry, for appellant.

Gray, Warren & Buchanan, for appellees.

REED, J.—I.   Appellees filed a motion to dismiss the appeal, on the ground that the amount involved, as shown by the pleadings, does not exceed $100, and that no question of law was certified to this court for determination by the trial judge.   Plaintiff alleged in his petition that the trespass complained of consisted in cutting and carrying away a portion of the crops growing on the premises, and that he had sustained damages in consequence thereof in the sum of $100, for which amount he prayed judgment.   He also prayed that defendants be restrained by injunction from further trespassing upon the premises.   The defendant Leinmiller alleged in his answer that he was the owner of all the crops growing on the premises, and that he acquired title thereto by purchase at a sale on execution against the property of one M. R. Ellithorpe, and that he had no notice when he made the purchase that plaintiff had any title or interest therein.   The pleadings then put in issue the question of the ownership of that portion of the crop which remained on the premises, as well as the portion which defendants are charged with having cut and carried away.   It clearly appears that the controversy involves an amount sufficient to give this court jurisdiction. The motion will therefore be overruled.

1. APPEAL to supreme court: amount in controversy.

II.   Plaintiff acquired title to the premises on the sixth of July, 1885, by deed from the Iowa Railroad Land Company.   In 1880 that company had executed a contract for the sale of the land to W. R. Able. M. R. Ellithorpe became the owner of this contract by assignment, and he went into possession of the premises in 1884.   He cultivated the land during that year, and raised a crop thereon during that year.   He also planted the crops in question in 1885.   At some time before the date of the deed from the land company, he assigned the contract to

2. EXECUTION: growing crops cannot be sold under.

plaintiff, who paid the balance of the purchase money due thereon, and received the conveyance; but the date of that assignment was not shown. The defendant Reidesil recovered a judgment against M. R. Ellithorpe in justice's court, on which an execution was issued on the sixth of June, 1885. The constable to whom this execution was directed attempted to levy the same on the crops growing on the premises, and on the sixth of July following he offered them for sale under the execution, and they were bid in by the defendant Leinmiller. At the time of the levy and sale, the crops were all immature, some of them having been planted but a short time before the levy. Leinmiller entered upon the premises some three or four weeks after his purchase, and harvested a portion of the crop, and removed a small portion of the grain from the premises; and these are the acts of which plaintiff complains.

Plaintiff claimed that his purchase of the contract was made before the sale on execution; but, as stated above, the date of the assignment was not proven. Nor did he prove that Leinmiller had any notice of his purchase when he bid in the crops at the execution sale. The circuit court ruled that, as Leinmiller had no notice of plaintiff's ownership of the premises when he bid in the property, he acquired title to it, and was not guilty of a trespass in gathering the crops after they matured. This ruling cannot be sustained. There is no pretence that the constable had any authority or power to levy on or sell any interest in the real estate. Nor is it claimed that he did so. The whole proceeding was on the theory that the crops were personal property, and could be levied on and sold as such. But while they remained immature, and were being nurtured by the soil, they were attached to and constituted part of the realty. They could no more be levied upon and sold on execution as personalty than could the trees growing upon the premises. This doctrine is elementary, and it has frequently been declared by this court. See *Downard v. Groff*, 40 Iowa, 597; *Burleigh v. Piper*, 51

Id., 649; *Hecht v. Dettman*, 56 Id., 679; *Martin v. Knapp*, 57 Id., 336. The case is very different in its facts from *Nuckolls v. Pence*, 52 Id., 581. In that case, although the crop was immature when the plaintiff purchased the premises, it was mature when the execution against the vendor was levied upon it and it was sold; and it was held that it was then personalty; and, as the purchaser at the execution sale had no notice of the change of ownership, he acquired title by his purchase. But in the present case it pertained to the realty when the attempt to sell it was made. The purchaser, therefore, acquired nothing by his purchase. Conceding that the plaintiff had no interest in the premises before the execution of the deed from the land company, as the crops were then immature, they passed to him by the conveyance as part of the realty.

REVERSED.

PAIGE v. PAIGE ET AL.

1. **Partnership**: FIRM PROPERTY DEEDED TO PARTNERS: RESULTING TRUST: PAROL EVIDENCE: DOWER TO WIDOW OF PARTNER: RIGHTS OF ADMINISTRATOR. Where real estate is purchased by a firm, with partnership money, and for use in the partnership business, but is deeded to the partners in their individual names, *held* that the real estate still belongs to the firm; that the individual partners only hold the title in trust for the firm; and that such trust, being an implied or resulting one, may be shown by parol testimony. Also, that, after the dissolution of the firm by the death of a partner, the firm and the individual partners all being insolvent, the widow of the deceased partner cannot recover a distributive share of the realty; and that the administrator of the deceased partner cannot, while the firm creditors are unsatisfied, appropriate a share of the property to satisfy the creditors of the decedent, even though they may have become creditors on the faith that the decedent had an individual interest in the property. (See opinion for authorities cited.)

Appeal from Scott Circuit Court.

SATURDAY, MARCH 12.

THE plaintiff in this action is the widow of Simon B. Paige, deceased. She claims that her husband died seized of certain real estate in Scott county, in which she is entitled, as widow, to a distributive share or dower interest, and this suit was brought to have the same set apart to her as is provided by law. The heirs of Simon B. Paige, the administrator of his estate, and the surviving member of a partnership known as the firm of Paige, Dixon & Co., and one Henry Brown, a creditor of said firm, were all made parties defendant to the action. Answers were filed, and, upon a hearing of the cause, a decree was entered against the plaintiff, and she appeals. Charles S. Watkins, administrator of the estate of the decedent, also appeals.

Bills & Block, for appellants.

Davison & Lane, for Paige and others, appellees.

Stewart & White, for Brown, appellee.

ROTHROCK, J.—I. The property in controversy is certain real estate in the city of Davenport, upon which there is situated a saw mill, planing mill, etc. It is known as the "Davis Saw Mill Property," and was formerly the property of John L. Davis, deceased, who owned the same at the time of his death. On the second day of February, 1880, F. H. Griggs, the administrator of Davis, conveyed the real estate in controversy to said Simon B. Paige and John A. Paige. There is no question about the validity of this conveyance. By its terms it is a conveyance to the two grantees as individuals, and, if the deed alone were to be considered, it would appear that Simon B. Paige and John A. Paige each owned the undivided one-half of the property; and, as there is no dispute that the plaintiff was the lawful wife of Simon B. Paige at the time of his death, it would follow that she is entitled to dower in the undivided half of the property. But the defendants claim that the real estate was not the individual property of the grantees in the deed, and that it was part of the assets of a partnership of which said grantees were members, and that said partnership was insolvent when

Simon B. Paige died, and that all of the property of the partnership would be insufficient to pay its indebtedness.

It is not disputed that there was a partnership of which the said grantees in the deed were members, and that said partnership was insolvent when Simon B. Paige died.   The ultimate question in the case, then, is, was the real estate in question partnership property?   If it was, the plaintiff is not entitled to dower.   If it was the individual property of Simon B. Paige and John A. Paige, the plaintiff is dowerable therein.   In order to a proper consideration of this question, it is necessary to recite certain facts which appear in the record.

It appears that for a number of years prior to the purchase of the property in question Simon B. Paige and John A. Paige had been engaged in business in partnership, under the firm name of "S. B. & J. A. Paige."   For some sixteen years they were engaged in the general merchandizing business.   Afterwards they operated in pine lands, getting out timber and pine saw logs.   They were so engaged up to the time of the death of S. B. Paige, and their place of business was at Oshkosh, Wisconsin.   They purchased the property in controversy, and took the conveyance therefor, on the second day of February, 1880.   The evidence shows that at the time of the purchase a new partnership was in contemplation, which firm was to operate the saw mill, planing mill, etc., so purchased, and on the sixth day of February, 1880, written articles of partnership were executed, by which S. B. and J. A. Paige and R. F. Paige and E. W. Dixon associated themselves as partners, under the firm name of Paige, Dixon & Co.   The following is a copy of the agreement for a partnership:

"Articles of agreement made this sixth day of February, A. D. 1880, between S. B. & J. A. Paige, of the city of Oshkosh and state of Wisconsin, party of the first part, and R. F. Paige and E. W. Dixon, of the city of Davenport, state of Iowa, parties of the second part, witnesseth that both parties, having formed a copartnership under the firm name of Paige, Dixon & Co., each of the four named persons having equal interest in the profit and losses in the business to be conducted by said firm, said business being the manufacturing of lumber, timber, shingles and lath in the mill known as the ' Davis mill,' and in said city of Davenport and state aforesaid. It is hereby agreed to by the said R. F. Paige and E. W. Dixon, of the second part, together and each by himself, that in consideration of the party of the first part agreeing, and do hereby bind themselves, to sell and deliver to each of the aforesaid R. F. Paige and E. W. Dixon, by quitclaim deed, (free of encumbrance arising from any act of the said S. B. & J. A. Paige,) of an undivided one-fourth part of said Davis Mill property, when each of them separately shall have paid to the party of the first part the one-fourth part of the sum of thirty-six thousand ten and sixty-five one-hundredths dollars, ($36,010.65,) which, being for the costs of said property, $32,250, and for insurance on the same, $660.50, with expenses paid in making the purchase of said property, $100.15, making in all the said sum of $36,010.65, together with interest from the second day of February, A. D. 1880, at the rate of eight per cent per annum, interest payable annually; that they, the said R. F. Paige and E. W. Dixon, are to give their entire time and service to the business aforesaid, and for the benefit of the firm of Paige, Dixon & Co., without any compensation during the continuance of said firm. The said S. B. & J. A. Paige are to receive no compensation for any services they may render to said firm, or for expenses when making voluntary visits from Oshkosh to Davenport, but such times as working up, examining, and purchasing logs they shall be paid all expenses of travel and otherwise, and same shall be charged up to the expense account of said firm of Paige, Dixon & Co.; and the expenditure of any considerable amount of money, also the purchase of any considerable amount of logs, shall be left to the decision of the said S. B. & J. A.

Paige, as also all matters of importance; and the said R. F.
Paige and E. W. Dixon are each privileged to draw out from
the moneys and credits of said firm of Paige, Dixon & Co.,
for the purpose of expenses only, a sum not exceeding one
hundred and fifty dollars per month; and, at the expiration
of one year from said second day of February, A. D. 1880,
that the total amount so drawn out by each of said R. F.
Paige and E. W. Dixon shall be deducted from his one-fourth
interest in the net profits of the business of said firm of
Paige, Dixon & Co. for said term, and the remaining part
shall be paid to said S. B. & J. A. Paige, until each, the
said R. F. Paige and the said E. W. Dixon, shall have paid
in full his one-fourth part of the said thirty-six thousand ten
and 65-100 dollars, ($36,010.65,) together with interest as
aforesaid; and it is further agreed by both parties that said
mill shall be kept in as good repair as it is now in, and that
on or before it is set to running there shall be not less than
ten thousand dollars ($10,000) more insurance put upon the
said mill, and continued on the same, in the name of S. B. &
J. A. Paige, the expenses thereof to be paid by the said firm
of Paige, Dixon & Co., who also are to pay all taxes, and all
expenses of whatever kind and nature, during the existence
of said firm of Paige, Dixon & Co., and the same to be
charged to the expense account of said company; and at the
expiration of the insurance now upon said mill property,
the firm of Paige, Dixon & Co. are to insure the same for a
like amount, which is fifteen thousand dollars ($15,000) on
mill and contents, the insurance to be in the name of S. B.
& J. A. Paige, the expenses thereof to be paid by the firm
of Paige, Dixon & Co.; and at no time shall the insurance
be less than twenty-five thousand dollars, ($25,000,) so long
as it remains the property of said S. B. & J. A. Paige; and
also it is agreed by said R. F. Paige and E. W. Dixon that
the said firm of Paige, Dixon & Co. shall carry at all times
a good and sufficient amount of insurance upon all manufactured lumber, shingles, lath and timber, so fast as it is

made and accumulates.   All expenses of selling, of entertaining customers, and any expenditures of money for the benefit of carrying on the business, shall be charged in the expense account of Paige, Dixon & Co.

"In witness whereof we have hereunto set our hands and seals.

"S. B. & J. A. PAIGE.   [Seal.]

"R. F. PAIGE.   [Seal.]

"E. W. DIXON.   [Seal.]

, We have set out the foregoing agreement for a partnership *in extenso*, for the reason that it appears to us to have an important bearing upon the main question in the case. The resident members of this partnership took immediate possession · of the property, and operated the mills, and expended a large amount of money of said partnership in making improvements thereon.   In August, 1881, said R. F. Paige died.   An administrator was appointed, and, the personal estate of said decedent being insufficient to pay his debts, upon proper application being made to the circuit court, the administrator was ordered to sell, and did sell, to Simon B. and John A. Paige the interest owned by said decedent in said real estate under the articles of partnership above set out.   After the death of R. F. Paige, the business was conducted under the same firm name; S. B. & J. A. Paige having three-fourths interest, and E. W. Dixon a one-fourth interest, and it so continued until the death of Simon B. Paige.   The plaintiff was married to the deceased within a month or two before his death.   The partnerships of S. B. & J. A. Paige, and Paige, Dixon & Co., and all of the individual members thereof, were insolvent at the date of the death of S. B. Paige.

The parol evidence in the case shows quite conclusively that, at the time the conveyance of the property was made, S. B. Paige stated that the purchase was made by the partnership of S. B. & J. A. Paige, and the property belonged to the partnership, and he desired the deed to be made in the name of the partnership; but that, under the advice of coun-

sel, it was made in the individual names of the members of
the firm, so that, if the property should be subsequently sold,
it would not be necessary to prove who were the proper parties to join in a conveyance.

This evidence, and all of the other parol evidence tending
to show that the property was purchased and paid for by
the partnership, is objected to by counsel for the plaintiff,
upon the ground that a written conveyance of real estate
cannot be varied by parol. It is insisted that such evidence
is incompetent, under the statute, which provides that "conveyances to two or more, in their own right, create a tenancy
in common, unless a contrary intent is expressed." Code, §
1939. And the following provisions of the Code are also
relied upon: Section 1934: "Declarations or creations of
trust or power, in relation to real estate, must be executed in
the same manner as deeds of conveyance; but this provision
does not apply to trusts resulting from the operation or construction of law." Sections 3663 and 3664 provide that no
evidence of any contract for the creation or transfer of any
interest in lands (except leases for a term not exceeding one
year) shall be competent, "unless in writing, signed by the
party to be charged."

Appellant concedes that, if the property had been paid
for with partnership money, and one of the partners had
taken the title to the whole, there would be a resulting trust
for the benefit of the firm. But it is claimed that, as each
received the legal title to just the share he was equitably
entitled to, there can be no resulting trust. The evidence in
the case shows quite satisfactorily that payment for the property was made, not with the money of each individual partner, but with the undivided money of the partnership. It
seems to us it is wholly immaterial whether the conveyance
was made to one or both of the partners. The law recognizes
the partnership as a person distinct from the individual members of the firm, and, this person or partnership having paid

its money for the property, there was a resulting trust in its favor, no matter in whose name the title was taken.

In the notes to *Coles v. Coles*, 1 Amer. Lead. Cas. (Hare & W.) 487, it is said: " If land is bought with partnership funds, and is brought into the business of the firm and used for its purposes, it will be considered as partnership stock, *in whose name soever the legal title may be*, unless there be *distinct evidence of an intention to hold it separately*, such as an express agreement in the articles of co-partnership, or at the time of the purchase, or the fact that the price is charged to the partners respectively in their several accounts with the firm; for such arrangements would operate as a division and distribution of so much of the funds, and each would take his share divested of any *implied trust;* but the mere circumstances that the conveyance was to them *expressly, as tenants in common,*would not, of itself, be sufficient to rebut the trust."

In 2 Story, Eq., § 1207, it is said: " Where real estate is purchased for partnership purposes, and on partnership account, it is wholly *immaterial*, in the view of a court of equity, *in whose name or names the purchase is made* and the *conveyance taken,*—whether in the name of *one* partner, or of *all* partners; whether in the name of a stranger alone, or a stranger jointly with one partner. In all these cases, let the *legal* title be vested in whom it may, it is in equity deemed partnership property, not subject to survivorship, and the partners are deemed the *cestuis que trust* therefor."

This court has frequently held that where land is purchased with partnership funds, and intended to be used for partnership purposes, it is to be treated as personal assets of the partnership. *Evans v. Hawley*, 35 Iowa, 83; *Hewitt v. Rankin*, 41 Id., 35; and other cases. In such case the trust is not an express one, but is implied, or results from the operation or construction of the law, and is within the exception named in section 1934 of the Code, and such a trust may be shown by parol evidence. *York v. Clemens*, 41

Iowa, 95; *Cotton v. Wood*, 25 Id., 43; *Fairchild v. Fairchild*, 64 N. Y., 471.

The cases of *Hale v. Henrie*, 2 Watts., 143; *Kramer v. Arthurs*, 7 Pa. St., 165, and *Ridgway's Appeal*, 15 Id., 177, hold that, " where partners intend to bring real estate into the partnership, their intention must be manifested by deed or writing placed on record, that purchasers and creditors may not be deceived." This rule is doubtless correct, so far as the rights of innocent purchasers without notice are involved; but this court is committed to the doctrine above announced, that a purchase of real property with partnership funds, and investing the title in a person or persons other than the partnership, creates a resulting trust in favor of the partnership, and the facts necessary to establish the trust may be shown by parol.

The evidence that the property involved in this case was paid for by the firm of S. B. & J. A. Paige is clear and satisfactory. It consists of the declaration of S. B. Paige, made when the deed was executed, and the recitals in the articles of partnership entered into within a few days after the deed was made, and the subsequent acts of both of the grantees in the deed in the management and use made of the property.

II. The defendant Brown is a creditor of the firm of Paige, Dixon & Co., and attached the property in controversy in an action upon his claim. His counsel submitted an argument in the cause, the drift of which seems to be a claim that he, as a creditor of that firm, is entitled to a preference over the creditors of the firm of S. B. & J. A. Paige in the property in controversy. It would be improper to determine that question in this appeal.

III. The administrator of S. B. Paige appealed, and claims that the debts against the estate were contracted while the title to the property was in decedent, and on the faith and credit of the same. He insists that the equities of these individual creditors should not be ignored for the benefit of the firm creditors. But, as the property in controversy is assets of the partnership, it is first liable to the payment of the partnership debts, and a creditor of one of the firm has no claim thereon until such debts are paid. *Evans v. Hawley*, 35 Iowa, 83.

We unite in the conclusion that, as it is conceded that both of the partnerships and all of the surviving members thereof are insolvent, the plaintiff is not entitled to a dower interest in the property in dispute.

AFFIRMED.

GILBERT v. BAXTER ET AL.

1. **Agency**: AUTHORITY TO SELL LAND: LETTERS CONSTRUED. G., a real estate agent in Iowa, but who had never done any business for S., who resided in New York, wrote to S., asking the price of S.'s land in a certain county, and stating that he would, on learning the price, endeavor to effect a sale. S. replied that, to close out all his lands in that county, he would . sell for four dollars per acre. *Held* (1) that this did not confer upon G. authority to bind S. by a contract for the sale of the lands; and (2) that, if it were conceded that the letters did confer such authority on G., still he could sell only unconditionally for cash, and that a contract made by him for the sale of all the lands at four dollars per acre, $500 paid in cash, and the balance to be paid when an abstract of title should be furnished showing perfect title in the grantor, was not binding upon S.

2. ———: REPUDIATION OF CONTRACT: GROUNDS ASSIGNED: WAIVER. Where the principal did not know the terms of a contract which one claiming to be his agent had made for him, but he repudiated it on the ground that the person who made it was not his agent, *held* that he was not precluded afterwards from repudiating it on the ground that it was not in accordance with the terms of the letter on which the alleged agent relied for his agency.

3. **Contract**: OFFER TO SELL LAND: ACCEPTANCE. An offer by a resident in New York to sell land in Iowa for four dollars per acre, means four dollars per acre cash, paid in New York, and the offer is not accepted by an agreement to take the land at four dollars per acre payable at Des Moines upon the delivery of the deed.

71 327
101 609
71 327
107 578
71 327
111 604
71 327
112 281
71 32
116 37
71 32
121 11
71 32
127 40
71 3
133 6

Appeal from Pocahontas District Court.

SATURDAY, MARCH 12.

ACTION in equity for the specific performance of an alleged contract for the sale and conveyance of real estate. The district court denied the relief demanded, and dismissed the petition. Plaintiff appeals.

Nourse, Kauffman & Guernsey, for appellant.

Robinson & Milchrist and *Hagerman, McCrary & Hagerman,* for appellees.

REED, J.—The defendants J. & J. Stuart & Co. were the owners of about 8,000 acres of land in Pocahontas county.

1. AGENCY: authority to sell land: letters construed.

They resided and carried on business in New York city. A. O. Garlock resided in Pocahontas county, and was engaged in business as a land agent. On the second day of June, 1881, he wrote to defendants the following letter: "*Messrs. J. & J. Stuart & Co., New York*—GENTLEMEN: I have a party that has some trust funds in his hands which he wishes to invest in land in N. W. Iowa, and I think your lands in this county will suit him if the price does. If you want to sell all the lands you hold in this county at once, I think this will be a good opportunity. If you will write me, giving your price per acre, purchaser to take the entire list in this county, I will submit price to the party, and effect a sale if possible."

On the seventh of June the Stuarts wrote the following answer to this letter: "DEAR SIR: We have your favor of second inst., in relation to our lands in your county. We have been getting $5 per acre for small lots; to close out all left, would sell at $4 cash."

The person referred to by Garlock in his letter was F. M. Gilbert. After Garlock received Stuarts' letter, Gilbert made an inspection of the lands, and on the twenty-fifth of June he and Garlock entered into a written contract for the sale and purchase of the land, Garlock assuming to act as agent for the Stuarts. By this contract Gilbert agreed to pay four dollars per acre for the land, $500 of the amount to be paid in cash on the signing of the contract, and " the balance as soon as a good and sufficient deed of conveyance, with covenants, is furnished, and also abstract of title showing perfect title in the grantor in said deed of conveyance." This contract was subsequently assigned to plaintiff. On the same day Garlock sent to the Stuarts the following telegram: " I have sold your land in this county. Write you." He also wrote them the following letter: " I have closed a sale of your lands in this county to F. M. Gilbert at $4 per acre. Received $500, the balance to be paid on delivery of deed. You may make deed to F. M. Gilbert, of Polk county, Iowa; and you may send the deed to the Valley Bank of Des Moines, Iowa, to be delivered to Mr. Gilbert on payment of balance of the purchase money, and direct the bank to pay me my com. I will make an abstract of title to land, and send Mr. Gilbert. I send you telegram to-day."

On the twenty-second of June the Stuarts entered into a negotiation with defendant Kinsley for the sale of the land to him, and gave him an option to buy it at $3.25 per acre, which was to terminate on the twenty-eighth of that month. They received Garlock's telegram on the twenty-seventh, and immediately sent the following answer: " Party here has refusal for all till Tuesday; will advise then." On the twenty-eighth Kinsley appeared, and offered to take the land at $3.25 per acre, and they entered into a written contract with him by which they agreed to sell and convey it at that price. Kinsley was acting in the matter for defendant Baxter, and the land was subsequently conveyed to him in pursuance of the contract. Kinsley was informed before the contract was entered into that Stuarts had an offer of four dollars per acre for the land in Iowa, but neither he nor they knew at that time that the contract had been entered into by Garlock and Gilbert; but the suit was instituted before any but a small amount of the purchase money was paid, and when the balance was paid, and the conveyance was executed, they knew of its execution, and were fully informed of the claim made by plaintiff under it. On the same day Stuarts sent the following telegram to Garlock: "DEAR SIR: We yesterday received your message as to our lands in Pocahontas county; to which we replied by wire that party here had refusal till Tuesday, (to-day,) and we now wire you party took all lands in your county. Of course there's no more to be added on above account."

The relief demanded by plaintiff is that the parties in whom the title is now vested be required to convey the property to him. This relief is demanded on the ground (1) that the written contract executed by Garlock was binding on the Stuarts, and, as the other defendants had notice of that contract when they paid the purchase money for the property, and received the conveyance, they took it charged with the equities created by the contract; and (2) if the contract was not binding on the Stuarts, their letter of the seventh of June was a distinct offer to sell the land at four dollars per acre, which was accepted by Gilbert, and of which acceptance they were notified by Garlock's letter of the 25th, and that the two letters constitute a contract for the sale of the land at that price, which was binding from the time Garlock's letter was deposited in the mail.

In our opinion, neither of these positions can be sustained. Before plaintiff can recover on the first ground, he is required to establish that Garlock had authority from the Stuarts to execute the contract in their name, and this he has not done. Garlock had never acted for them in any transaction before the one in question, and there is no claim that he had authority to bind them by the contract, unless such authority was conferred by their letter of the seventh of June. That letter was written in answer to his communication asking for information as to the price at which they were willing to sell their land. True, he stated in his letter that he would submit the price to the party to whom he referred, and endeavor to effect a sale. But in their answer they stated merely the price at which they would sell. They simply imparted the information for which he had asked, and their letter contains no intimation that they desired or expected him to contract in their name for the sale of the property, if his customer should be willing to buy it. The authority to do that was not expressly conferred, and it cannot be implied either from the language of the letter or the circumstances under which it was written. The mere statement of the price at which they were willing to sell, clearly cannot be construed as creating an agency with power to contract for the sale of the property. The case differs very materially in its facts from *Hopwood v. Corbin*, 63 Iowa, 218, cited by appellant. In that case the authority to sell the land was expressly conferred on the agent by the letters of the defendant, and the judgment for specific performance of the contract was based on that fact, while in this no such authority was given.

But, if it should be conceded that Garlock was empowered to contract for the sale of the land, there would still be an insurmountable difficulty in plaintiff's case. If he is entitled to recover at all, his recovery must be based upon the contract executed by Garlock, and he must show that the agent had authority to bind the principal by that particular agreement. The answer of the defendants is but a general denial, it is true, but it puts in issue the allegation that the contract sued on is the contract of the Stuarts. They were not required to plead specially that the agent had exceeded his authority in making the contract, but that question arises upon their denial that the contract was their agreement. If the letter of the seventh of June can be construed as conferring authority on Garlock to contract for the sale of the land, such authority is limited by the terms of the letter in two particulars, viz: The sale must be of all of the lands owned by the Stuarts in Pocahontas county; and it must be for four dollars per acre cash. By no possible construction can it be said that the agent was empowered to contract upon any other terms or with any other conditions; yet the contract which he assumed to make provides for the payment of but a small portion of the purchase money in cash, while the balance was to be paid when an abstract of title should be furnished, showing "perfect title in the grantor." Let it be conceded that, by usage, the vendor is required to furnish an abstract of title, yet it does not follow that the agent, whose authority was to sell for cash, had authority to bind his principal by an agreement containing a provision for payment when an abstract should be furnished showing perfect title in him. The contract was not for the absolute sale of the property; for it is at least doubtful whether the buyer could be compelled to consummate the purchase, if, upon an inspection of the abstract, it should appear that the title to any of the property was defective. Neither was it a sale for cash, for by the terms of the contract the payment was dependent on the furnishing of an abstract showing "perfect title in the grantor."

It is true, the principal did not assign, as a reason for repudiating the contract, that the agent had exceeded his

2. ——: repudiation of contract: grounds assigned : waiver.

authority in making this provision a part of it. But, when they repudiated what Garlock had done, they did not know that such provision was incorporated in the contract. They had not then been informed that he had assumed to bind them by a written agreement. They proceeded on the theory that they had not empowered him to bind them by any contract for the sale of the land. They clearly did not by so doing waive the right to make the objection that he had exceeded his powers by making that condition a part of the contract, when that fact came to their knowledge. It is proper to say in this connection that Gilbert was fully informed as to the extent of Garlock's authority when he entered into the contract. He had seen the correspondence, and it is presumed that he understood the effect of the letters.

Garlock's letter of the twenty-fifth of June was not an acceptance of the offer contained in Stuarts' letter of the

3. CONTRACT:
offer to sell
land : accept-
ance

seventh, for the acceptance was upon conditions not contained in the offer. The offer was to sell for four dollars per acre, cash. Under the offer, the Stuarts were entitled to have the money paid to them in New York, where they lived. By the acceptance, the money was to be paid in Des Moines on the delivery of the deed there. The case in this respect is like *Sawyer v. Brossart*, 67 Iowa, 678.

The judgment of the district court will be

AFFIRMED.

71	333
105	552
71	383
122	166
71	
135	
135	

RUSH ET AL. v. MITCHELL ET AL.

1. **Execution Sale:** IRREGULAR REDEMPTION: ASSIGNMENT OF CERTIFICATE: SHERIFF'S DEED. Where one who was apparently the owner of a junior judgment redeemed from an execution sale of land, and procured an assignment of the certificate of purchase, *held* that, even if he was not entitled to redeem on account of his having assigned his judgment, yet, in the absence of a redemption from himself, he was entitled to a sheriff's deed as a purchaser of the certificate of purchase. (Compare *Wilson v. Conklin*, 22 Iowa, 452.)

2. ———: SHERIFF'S DEED MADE TOO LATE: INTERVENING PURCHASER: GOOD FAITH: EVIDENCE: BURDEN OF PROOF. Plaintiff, claiming title to the land in question under a sheriff's deed made more than twenty days after the expiration of the year for redemption, (Code, § 3125,) brought this action to quiet his title against M., who claimed under a deed made by the execution defendant after the expiration of the twenty days, and before the execution and recording of the sheriff's deed. The deed from the execution defendant was a mere quitclaim, made to one R., for the purpose of defrauding plaintiff. M. took by a warranty deed from R., and gave to R. notes secured by mortgage on the land for the purchase money. The petition put M.'s good faith in issue. *Held—*

    (1) That, since M. took from a fraudulent grantee, she had the burden of proof to show that she was a good faith purchaser for value.

    (2) That the mere recitals in her deed would not show that she paid value for the land. Nor would that fact be established by proof that she executed negotiable notes, secured by mortgage, for the

purchase money, unless she also showed that the notes had been negotiated by her grantor. (See opinion for authorities cited on all branches of the case.)

Appeal from Fayette Circuit Court.

SATURDAY, MARCH 12.

ACTION in chancery to quiet the title of certain lands in plaintiffs. There was a decree in the circuit court granting the relief-prayed for in plaintiffs' petition. Defendants appeal.

J. W. Rogers & Son, for appellants.

Ainsworth & Hobson, for appellees.

BECK, J.—I. The parties to this suit claim the land in controversy under conflicting titles. Plaintiffs claim as the
1. EXECUTION sale: irregular redemption: assignment of certificate: sheriff's deed.
widow and heirs of Henry Rush, who they allege acquired title under a sheriff's deed executed and recorded April 18, 1882. It appears that the title thus acquired is good, unless it be defeated by defendant's title, which is based upon the following facts: The sheriff's deed to Rush was not executed until thirty days after the expiration of the full time for redemption from the sheriff's sale. April 17, 1882, Hathway, the defendant in the judgment upon which the land was sold, conveyed it by quitclaim to Rogers. The deed was recorded April 18, 1882. On the seventeenth day of April, 1882, defendant Rogers conveyed to defendant Louisa Mitchell the land in question by deed of warranty. On the same day she executed a mortgage to Rogers to secure the payment of the purchase money, $900. The deed and mortgage were recorded on the eighteenth of April, 1882. Defendants insist that their title is paramount to plaintiffs', and base this position on two grounds, which we will proceed to consider.

II. The sheriff's deed was made to Rush upon a redemption made by him under a junior lien, being a decree of foreclosure of a junior mortgage. It is claimed that the evidence shows that he did not own this decree, having before assigned it. Upon these facts it is insisted that his redemption was void, and the sheriff's deed to him as a redemptioner is void. It is difficult to discover a ground upon which the defendant in execution, Hathway, or his grantee, can base an objection to Rush's redemption. It is not claimed or shown that Hathway was prejudiced by the redemption of Rush. If he be not prejudiced, he and his grantee ought not to object to the redemption. But, without further inquiry into the right of the defendants to show that Rush had no right to redeem, and refraining from announcing any conclusions upon the question, we are clear in the opinion that, if it be held that he had no right as the owner of the judgment to redeem, his sheriff's deed is nevertheless valid. Before it was made, the certificate issued by the sheriff upon the sale under the senior judgment was assigned to Rush. If he was not a redemptioner as the holder of the junior judgment, he was, by virtue of the assignment, the holder of the certificate of sale, and as such was entitled to the sheriff's deed, under Code, § 3101. This precise point is decided in *Wilson v. Conklin*, 22 Iowa, 452. We conclude, therefore, that the sheriff's deed to Rush is a valid instrument.

III. Defendants insist that the sheriff's deed to Rush does not defeat the title of defendant Mitchell, for the reason that

2. ——: sheriff's deed made too late: intervening purchaser: good faith: evidence: burden of proof.

she acquired it without notice of adverse rights under the sale and deed upon which plaintiffs base their title. Before considering this point, it may be remarked that, as Rogers acquired the land by a quitclaim deed, and paid nothing for it, which is shown by his own evidence, he was not a good faith purchaser, and is chargeable with notice of the rights of Rush. The evidence clearly shows that Rogers had also actual notice thereof. Mitchell, therefore, is not protected as a purchaser from one without notice. We shall soon see that, as she has failed to show that she was a *bona fide* purchaser without notice, she cannot hold the land against plaintiffs' title. Code, § 3125, provides that, for twenty days after the expiration of the time for redemption from a sale of land upon execution, the proceedings impart constructive notice of the purchase. But under this section only a *bona fide* purchaser without notice is protected. *Harrison v. Kramer*, 3 Iowa, 562. One who is not a *bona fide* purchaser is chargeable with notice. Is Mitchell to be regarded as a *bona fide* purchaser? The petition alleges that the purchase was fraudulently made for the purpose of defeating the title of Rush. Her good faith in the purchase was thus put in issue. The evidence clearly shows that Rogers had full notice of the rights of Rush, and that he acquired the quitclaim deed for the fraudulent purpose of defeating Rush. Mitchell, holding under a fraudulent purchaser, must assume the burden of proving that she purchased in good faith for a valuable consideration. *Throckmorton v. Rider*, 42 Iowa, 84; *Sillyman v. King*, 36 Id., 207; *Falconbury v. McIlravy*, Id., 488.

IV. The recitals of her deed, as to the payment of the consideration, will not show, upon the issue in this case, that she paid value for the land. *Hodgon v. Green*, 56 Iowa, 733; *Falconbury v. McIlravy* and *Sillyman v. King, supra*.

V. The execution of notes, and a mortgage securing them, if the notes, though negotiable, remained in the hands of Rogers, would not be regarded as the payment of the consideration for the land. *Kitteridge v. Chapman*, 36 Iowa, 348. It is shown that the notes and mortgage were executed by Mitchell for the land, but it is not shown that the notes passed out of the hands of Rogers. Without such showing, she cannot claim that she is a purchaser for value. It thus appears that Mitchell has failed to establish that she is a good-faith purchaser for value. She is therefore chargeable with notice of the rights and equities of Rush under the sheriff's deed.

We are brought to the conclusion that the decree of the district court quieting the title of plaintiffs is correct. It is therefore   AFFIRMED.

WELSH v. THE DES MOINES INS. CO.

71　337
96　42
96　226
98　223

71　337
107　746

71　337
108　10
f108　645

71
110
71
113

71
119　306

1. **Fire Insurance**: PROOFS OF LOSS: WHAT NECESSARY. Under § 3, chap. 211, Laws of 1880, proof of loss under a policy of insurance must be by affidavit, stating the facts as to how the loss occurred, so far as they are within the knowledge of the assured, and the extent of the loss. Therefore, *held* that an unverified certificate of a veterinary surgeon, stating how, in his opinion, a certain cow came to her death, without giving the extent of the loss, and fixing the ownership of the cow in a person other than the insured, was insufficient; and, in an action on the policy to recover the value of the cow, evidence that such certificate was sent to the company was inadmissible.

2. **Evidence**: MUST BE CONFINED TO ISSUES. In an action on a policy of fire insurance, evidence offered to show that the company had waived proper proofs of loss was inadmissible, where such waiver was not pleaded.

Appeal from Boone Circuit Court.

SATURDAY, MARCH 12.

THIS is an action upon a policy of insurance against loss by fire and lightning. There was a trial by jury, and a verdict and judgment for the plaintiff. Defendant appeals.

Cole, McVey & Clark, for appellant.

S. R. Dyer, for appellee.

ROTHROCK, J.—I. The property insured consisted of a barn, wagons, work horses and cattle. The plaintiff claimed that a valuable cow included in the insured property was struck by lightning and killed; and it was averred in the petition that the plaintiff fulfilled all of the conditions of said insurance on her part, and, before the commencement of the action, "gave to the defendant due notice and proof of said cow being struck by lightning, and loss aforesaid, and duly demanded payment of the sum of three hundred dollars." The defendant, by its answer, denied that the cow in question died or was struck by lightning, and averred that, if the same be dead,

1. FIRE Insurance: proofs of loss: what necessary.

the cause of her death was disease; and it is especially alleged in the answer that plaintiff did not at any time give to the defendant any notice nor proof of the alleged loss under said policy. The policy required that, in case of loss or damage, the assured should notify the secretary of the company within thirty days from the time the loss occurred, and the assured was also required to make proper proofs of loss.

To sustain the allegation that these requirements of the policy had been complied with, the plaintiff introduced in evidence a letter, of which the following is a copy:

"BOONE, IOWA, July 16, 1885.

"*Theo. F. Gatchell, Des Moines, Iowa:* The cow mentioned in policy No. 22,198, Mrs. H. F. Welsh, as appears from the enclosed statement, was struck by lightning on the morning of the thirteenth inst., from the effects of which she died on the fifteenth inst. Please send some one to adjust the loss at once.   W. W. NIXON, Agt."

Inclosed in the above letter there was a statement of which the following is a copy:

"*Boone, Boone Co., State of Iowa:* I, the undersigned, veterinary surgeon, do hereby certify that I was called to see Thilda Williams, a full-blooded Jersey cow, owned by George H. Welsh, on the thirteenth of July, 1885, and found upon examination of said animal that, in my opinion, she had the night previous been struck by lightning, which caused the hindmost parts, together with the bowels, to become paralyzed, which caused death on the fifteenth day of July, 1885.   C. EASTWOOD, Vt.

"We, the undersigned, having examined the animal, find from external marks that the above statement is correct.

"ALFR. L. TORNBLOM.
E. A. WARREN."

The defendant objected to these instruments on the ground that they did not show notice and proof of loss. The objection was overruled. Whatever may be said of the notice of loss as evidence, it is very plain that the instrument signed by Eastwood was in no just sense proof of loss. The policy did not require any specific mode of proof of loss. Section 3, c. 211, Laws 1880, (Miller's Code, 299,) prescribes what proof of loss shall be necessary to maintain an action upon a policy of insurance. It must be by "affidavit, stating the facts as to how the loss occurred, so far as they are within his (the assured's) knowledge, and the extent of the loss. *   *   *" The object of this statute was to simplify the proofs of loss necessary to be made, and to prevent insurance companies from availing themselves of technical defenses founded upon unreasonable requirements in making proofs of loss. In the case at bar, what is claimed to be proof of loss is not an affidavit. It is a mere certificate of a veterinary surgeon that a cow was struck by lightning, and killed. It does not give the extent of the loss, nor name the plaintiff herein as the owner of the cow, but fixes the ownership in another. We think that, under the issue made in the pleadings, this evidence should not have been admitted.

II. It is claimed that the so-called "proof of loss," in connection with certain parol evidence in the case, shows
2. EVIDENCE: must be confined to issues. that the defendant made no objection to the form of the proof of loss, or, in other words, that the defendant waived proper proofs of loss. The defendant objected to said parol evidence, and the objection was overruled. In our opinion, this evidence should have been excluded, because it did not correspond with the averments of the petition. There was no allegation therein that proper proofs of loss were waived. *Lumbert v. Palmer*, 29 Iowa, 104; *Woolsey v. Williams*, 34 Id., 413; *Edgerly v. Farmers' Ins. Co.*, 43 Id., 587; *Zinck v. Phœnix Ins. Co.*, 60 Id., 266.

REVERSED.

ATKINSON v. THE HAWKEYE INS. CO.

1. **Fire Insurance**: CONTRACT OF INSURANCE: FACTS NOT CONSTITUT-
ING. Plaintiff executed an application to the defendant company for
insurance, and delivered it, with the premium and policy fee, to one who
was only a soliciting agent of defendant, with the understanding that it
should be sent to the defendant for acceptance, and that, if not accepted,
the money should be returned. The application and premium were sent
by the agent, but were never received by the company, and no policy
was issued, and nothing further done. More than two years afterwards
the property was burned. *Held* that the facts did not create a contract
of insurance, and that defendant was not liable for the loss. (Compare
Walker v. Farmers' Ins Co., 51 Iowa, 679, and *Armstrong v. State Ins.
Co.*, 61 Id., 212.)

Appeal from Fremont District Court.

SATURDAY, MARCH 12.

This is an action upon an alleged contract for the insurance of a dwelling-house against loss or damage by fire.
The cause was submitted to the court below upon the pleadings and an agreed statement of facts. The court determined
that the defendant was not liable for the loss, and the plaintiff appeals.

W. H. Wilson and *W. P. Ferguson*, for appellant.

Draper & Thornell, for appellee.

ROTHROCK, J.—The facts essential to a proper determination of the case are as follows; One Baylor was a soliciting
agent of the defendant at Tabor, in this state. The plaintiff
made a written application to him for insurance upon his
dwelling-house by the defendant company. This application
was made upon one of the printed forms in use by the company. This printed blank form was as follows:

"Application is made by ———, of ———, county ———,
state of Iowa, for insurance against loss or damage by fire
———, to the Hawkeye Insurance Company, in the sum of

―――― dollars, for the term of ―――― years from the――――
day of ――――, 188―, by a policy with the usual conditions
of the company, on the property hereinafter mentioned, viz:
[Here follows a description of the property on which insurance is sought.] The applicant agrees that each of the foregoing answers, statements and valuations are true, and a
warranty on his part, and that the accepting of this risk, and
the issuing of a policy of insurance thereon by the company,
is to be based solely upon this application;   *   *   *
that no liability of the company shall attach until this application has been actually approved by the home office."

Upon making the application, the plaintiff paid to Baylor
the sum of $10.80, premium and policy fee, and Baylor
delivered to the plaintiff a receipt in these words:

"Received of J. H. Atkinson an application for insurance,
by the Hawkeye Insurance Company, of Des Moines, Iowa,
on property to the amount of $500, for the term of five
years from date, with $10.80, and an obligation for ――――
due and payable on the ―――― day of ――――, 188―, premium and policy fee, subject to the approval of the company. In case the company decline to issue a policy on said
application, then the obligation and premium received shall
be returned to him by mail or otherwise.

"D. R. BAYLOR, Soliciting Agent."
"*Dated August* 30, 1882.

Baylor, being a soliciting agent only, immediately upon
the receipt by him of the application and premium, deposited
them in the post office, properly directed to the home office
at Des Moines. They were never received by the defendant,
nor any of its officers. The application and receipt were
made and the premium paid upon the thirtieth day of
August, 1882. The dwelling-house of plaintiff was destroyed
by fire on the eighth day of January, 1885. No officer nor
agent of the defendant, except Baylor, had any knowledge
that an application for insurance had been made by plaintiff

until after the building was destroyed. There are other facts in the case which, in the view we take of the rights of the parties, are not necessary to be stated.

Counsel for plaintiff contend that, although Baylor was unauthorized to execute contracts of insurance, yet that the transaction became a contract as soon as the company could have an opportunity to accept the risk, and failed to do so, or return the premium. If the defendant had received the application and premium, and retained the same, and remained silent, it may be that it should be held to have approved the application. But this question is not in the case. The company had no knowledge that any application had been made and premium paid, and no contract can therefore be implied from any neglect to issue the policy founded upon the knowledge of the defendant that such an application had been made. The case is very much like *Walker v. Farmers' Ins. Co.*, 51 Iowa, 679, where it was held that the giving of an application for insurance to an agent of the company authorized to receive applications only, and the execution of a premium note, do not constitute a contract for insurance. In that case the agent of the defendant neglected to forward the application and premium note, and the company had no knowledge of their existence until after the property was destroyed by fire. In this case the agent was not negligent. We think the case is controlled by that above cited, which was followed and approved in *Armstrong v. State Ins. Co.*, 61 Iowa, 212.

. AFFIRMED.

THE STATE v. STOUT.

71
f133

1. **Adultery**: COMPLAINT BY WIFE: WHAT IS NOT. The mere fact that a wife, in obedience to a subpœna, testifies before the grand jury upon the question of her husband's adultery, does not constitute a complaint by her against her husband, within the meaning of § 4008 of the Code, which provides that no prosecution for adultery can be commenced except on the complaint of the husband or wife. (*State v. Donovan*, 61 Iowa, 278, followed.)

Appeal from Henry District Court.

SATURDAY, MARCH 12.

INDICTMENT for adultery. Trial by jury. Verdict of guilty. Judgment. The defendant appeals.

Woolson & Babb, for appellant.

A. J. Baker, Attorney-general, for the State.

SEEVERS, J.—The indictment, among other things, states or charges that this prosecution is commenced on the complaint "of the wife of the defendant." It is provided by statute that "no prosecution for adultery can be commenced but on the complaint of the husband or wife," (Code, § 4008,) and the only question we are called on to determine is whether this prosecution is so commenced.

In *Bush v. Workman*, 64 Iowa, 205, it was said that the statute is plain, easily understood, and that it forbids prosecutions for adultery except when the same are commenced on the complaint of the husband or wife.

In *State v. Henke*, 58 Iowa, 457, it was held that an averment in the indictment that the prosecution was commenced on the complaint of the wife was insufficient, and that the fact that the prosecution was so commenced was material, and must be established on the trial.

But in *State v. Donovan*, 61 Iowa, 278, it was held that such fact could be established by a preponderance of the evidence. In the same case the court instructed the jury that if the defendant's wife "appeared before the grand jury in response to a subpœna, and testified in the case, but not intending to prefer the charge of adultery against the defendant; but gave her testimony supposing she was required to do so, this would not be a complaint by her against her husband, within the meaning of the law." It was said that this instruction announces a correct rule.

In the present case, the court instructed the jury that, if the wife of the defendant went before the grand jury as a witness, even though she did so in obedience to a subpœna, and testified as a witness, this would be sufficient to sustain the averment in the indictment, in the absence of evidence to the contrary, that the prosecution was commenced on the complaint of the defendant's wife. It seems to us that this instruction conflicts with the instruction which was approved in *State v. Donovan*, above cited. Besides this, a complaint we understand to be a formal allegation or charge, preferred by some one against another, to an appropriate court or officer. Such a complaint, the statute requires, must be preferred by husband or wife. The indictment is not necessarily so preferred. Mrs. Stout no doubt testified to certain facts before the grand jury, and it will be conceded that she could not have been compelled to testify, but still she may not have believed her husband guilty, and did not intend to prefer a complaint against him. The mere fact that she testified as a witness is materially different from preferring a complaint. She in fact made no complaint, but simply responded to such questions as were asked her. We think the instruction above referred to is erroneous, and that there is no sufficient evidence showing that Mrs. Stout made a complaint as provided by statute.

REVERSED.

71
91

WILSON v. TROWBRIDGE.

1. **Former Adjudication:** WHAT IS NOT: WITHDRAWING OF INTER-
VENOR. Where the claimant of attached property appeared in the
attachment suit and took time to file a petition of intervention, but a
few days afterwards withdrew his appearance, and afterwards a judgment was rendered against the attachment defendant, with an order for
the sale of the property, *held* that such judgment did not in any way
affect the rights of the intervenor, and was not a bar to an action by
him to recover the property.

2. **Practice in Supreme Court:** INSTRUCTION: ERROR WITHOUT
PREJUDICE. This court will not review an instruction when it appears
that, even if it was erroneous, it could not have prejudiced the appellant under the facts proved.

Appeal from Shelby Circuit Court.

SATURDAY, MARCH 12.

THIS is an action of replevin for certain horses. There
was a trial by jury, which resulted in a verdict and judgment for the plaintiff. Defendant appeals.

Foss & Hellyer, for appellant.

Macy & Gammon, for appellee.

ROTHROCK, J.—I. The plaintiff claimed the possession
of the property by virtue of two chattel mortgages executed
to him by one Joseph Bucher. The defendant
is sheriff of Shelby county, and was in possession of the horses in controversy by virtue of a
writ of attachment sued out by one Quinn. It was claimed
by Quinn in his attachment proceedings that the property
was subject to a landlord's lien for the rent of certain land
leased by him to Bucher. After the attachment suit was
brought, the plaintiff herein made an appearance in that suit
by his attorneys, and took time to file a petition of intervention in the action. He filed no petition of intervention, and
within a few days thereafter his attorneys withdrew their

1. FORMER ad-
judication:
what is not:
withdrawing
of intervenor.

appearance for him. The plaintiff in that action took judgment against Bucher for the rent, and procured an order for the sale of the attached property. The action at bar was then pending, and the plaintiff's mortgages are upon the same property as that ordered sold in the attachment suit. The defendant herein pleaded these facts, and claimed that the rights of the plaintiff were adjudicated in the attachment suit. The plaintiff demurred to this defense, and the demurrer was sustained. Defendant complains of this ruling of the court. We think it was correct. Quinn did not make the plaintiff herein a party to his attachment suit. He appeared voluntarily, and announced his intention of making himself a party by intervention. But he reconsidered the matter, withdrew, filed no petition of intervention, and did not make himself a party to the suit. There was no issue between him and Quinn that could be adjudicated, and when the appearance was withdrawn the *status* of the case was the same as if he had made no appearance.

II. The court, in its instruction to the jury in reference to the property of a tenant upon which the landlord is entitled to a lien for rent, under section 2017 of the Code, held, in effect, that the lien attached to such property as was "used on the premises" in the conduct of the farm by the tenant, but not to such live-stock as may be running at large on the premises, and growing up for the market, or unfit for use. The defendant complains of this instruction as embodying an incorrect rule of law. We need not determine this question, because the evidence shows without conflict that none of the property in question was at any time upon Quinn's land. If the instruction was erroneous, it could not possibly have prejudiced the defendant, because, under the proven facts, he had no landlord's lien thereon.

2. PRACTICE in supreme court: instruction: error without prejudice.

AFFIRMED

VREELAND V. ELLSWORTH ET AL.

1. **Supreme Court:** JURISDICTION: LESS THAN $100. In appeals involving less than $100, this court has no jurisdiction to determine any question not properly certified by the trial judge.

2. **Parties to Actions:** WHO ARE NOT. Persons whose names are inserted as parties defendant in a petition, but who are not served with notice and do not appear, are not parties to the action.

3. **Mechanic's Lien:** ENFORCEMENT BY SUBCONTRACTOR: NECESSARY PARTIES. A subcontractor who holds an open, unliquidated and unsettled account against the principal contractor cannot bring his action against the owner of the building or improvement, and establish a mechanic's lien on the property, without adjudicating the claim, or attempting to adjudicate it in any way, against the principal contractor, who is the person principally liable on the account.

4. ——: SUBCONTRACTOR: ESTOPPEL. A subcontractor who stands by in silence and sees the owner of a building pay the principal contractor in full, is estopped from afterwards claiming a mechanic's lien on the property.

5. **Practice in Supreme Court:** LESS THAN $100: INSUFFICIENT CERTIFICATE. In an appeal involving less than $100, this court cannot declare the law upon the facts of the case, where the necessary facts are not all found and certified by the trial court.

Appeal from Dickinson District Court.

MONDAY, MARCH 14.

THIS is an action in equity to establish and enforce a mechanic's lien. There was a judgment and decree for the plaintiff. Defendant appeals.

J. W. Cory, for appellant.

Rice & Gridley, for appellee.

ROTHROCK, J.—I. The amount claimed by plaintiff is less than $100, and the appeal comes to us upon the following certificate of the trial judge:

"(1) Upon the trial of this case, the evidence shows that the defendant E. S. Ellsworth employed his co-defendant, E.

G. Hammond, to do certain mason work upon the house named in the plaintiff's petition, and that under this agreement he was to pay the contractor as the work progressed; that the contractor, Hammond, employed the plaintiff, L. W. Vreeland, L. J. Vreeland and Abraham Hartman, as subcontractors, to perform certain portions of the work. These subcontractors commenced their work on the sixth day of August, 1883, and continued to the eleventh of the same month, on which day they completed their work. The defendant Ellsworth saw these subcontractors performing work upon this job during the time that they were performing the same, but had no other knowledge that the contractor, Hammond, was owing them anything for the work than what would be inferred from his knowledge of their doing the work. On the day on which the work was completed by the subcontractors there was a settlement between Hammond and Ellsworth, and at that time the defendant Ellsworth paid the contractor for all the work that had been done up to that date, but withheld the sum of ten dollars, which was still required to complete the job. At the time of this settlement and payment to Hammond, there was enough money in Ellsworth's possession due upon the contract to pay the several claims of the subcontractors. On the fourteenth day of August, A. D. 1883, these subcontractors personally notified Ellsworth of their claims, and afterwards Ellsworth procured another party to complete the contract of Hammond, and paid him therefor. Statements and affidavits for the mechanic's liens were filed by the several subcontractors in the clerk's office on the thirty-first day of August, A. D. 1883.

"(2) Can a subcontractor obtain a decree foreclosing a mechanic's lien against land and buildings before such subcontractor obtains a judgment against the original contractor for claims against the contractor for work upon said land and buildings, and in a suit where said original contractor is a party, but no notice of suit served upon him, and no appearance made by him? Upon the foregoing statements of facts, is the defendant Ellsworth liable to the subcon-tractors in this case?"

Several questions are argued by counsel which do not arise

1. SUPREME court: juris-diction: less than $100.

upon the above certificate. This court has no jurisdiction to determine any questions except-ing those propounded by the trial court.

The first point arising upon the above certificate is found in the question numbered 2. It appears therefrom that

2. PARTIES to action: who are not.

Hammond, the principal contractor, was not made a party to the action. It is true, it is stated that he was a party, but this merely means that he was named in the petition as a party, because it appears from the same question that there was " no notice of suit served upon him, and no appearance made by him." Inserting his name in the petition did not make him a party. We have, then, the question whether a subcontractor, who holds an open, unliquidated and unsettled account against the princi-

3. MECHANIC'S lien: enforce-ment by sub-contractor: necessary par-ties.

pal contractor, may bring his action against the owner of the building or improvement, and establish a mechanic's lien upon the property, without adjudicating the claim, or attempting to adjudicate it in any way, against the contractor, who is the person principally liable upon the account. We think this question must be answered in the negative. If the claim were liquidated, it may be that the principal contractor would not be a necessary party. But that question we need not determine. This is an open, unliquidated account,—a mere charge against the contractor. The burden of ascer-taining whether there is any defense to the action ought not to be put upon the owner of the property. He is not pre-sumed to have any knowledge upon the subject. Further than this, if the subcontractor establishes his lien against the property, and the owner is compelled to pay it, he has recourse on the principal contractor. He ought to be fur-nished with an adjudicated claim, and not with a mere open account. The record in this case shows that there was a defect of parties, but that a personal judgment was actually rendered against Ellsworth, the owner of the building. There was no warrant for such a judgment. It may have been thought that it was necessary to adjudicate the claim as against some one, and, as Ellsworth was the only defendant, a judgment was rendered against him.

II. In interrogatory numbered 2, we are asked to determine whether Ellsworth is liable upon the statement of facts

4. ——: sub-contractor: estoppel. preceding the interrogatories. The statement of facts is not complete. An important question in the case was, whether the subcontractors were present at the settlement, and knew that Ellsworth paid Hammond in full, and made no objection to such payment. If they stood by, and by their silence permitted Ellsworth to make full payment, the law of estoppel would compel them to ever after remain silent as to any claim for a lien. Their silence was equivalent to saying to Ellsworth that they had no claim for a lien, and if any one of them was present, and made no sign, his right to a lien would be lost. If we must be required to determine the law upon a given state of ultimate

5. PRACTICE in supreme court: less than $100: insufficient certificate. facts, all of the necessary facts should be found by the trial court. It is impossible to determine from the facts, as recited, whether the court found that the subcontractors were present, and by their silence acquiesced in the settlement and payment, or were not present. For anything that appears, they may or may not have been present.

For the error in determining the cause without a necessary party defendant, judgment and decree will be

REVERSED.

WILSON v. PALO ALTO COUNTY.

1. **Contract**: CONSTRUCTION: SALE OR SECURITY. B. & G. had contracted to build a court house for the defendant county, and had purchased materials therefor of W., but had not paid for the materials, and nothing was yet due from the defendant on the contract. In order to make a payment on the materials out of the contract price of the building, B. & G. and W. made a bill of sale of the materials to defendant, whereupon defendant paid to W., to be applied on the price of the materials, (which was $1,900,) the sum of $450 of the contract price of the building. Afterwards, defendant made further payments to W. upon orders made by B. & G., but the materials were never fully paid for. *Held* that the bill of sale was not a transfer of the title of the materials from W. to the defendant, because W. had already transferred his title to B. & G., but that the effect of the writing (for the particulars of which see opinion) was only to secure the defendant for an advance of $450 of the contract price before it was due, and that W. could not recover of the defendant the unpaid portion of the price of the materials.

Appeal from Clay District Court.

MONDAY, MARCH 14.

THIS is an action at law by which the plaintiff seeks to recover of the defendant the purchase price of certain lumber and materials alleged to have been sold by the plaintiff to the defendant, to be used in the construction of a court house. The defendant denies that it purchased any of said lumber and materials of the plaintiff. There was a trial by jury, and a verdict and judgment for the plaintiff. Defendant appeals.

Soper, Crawford & Carr, for appellant.

T. W. Harrison, for appellee.

ROTHROCK, J.—This action is founded on a written contract of which the following is a copy:

"Know all men by these presents, that we, Burdick & Goble, of Palo Alto county, Iowa, and J. J. Wilson, of Kossuth county, Iowa, on the one part, in consideration of the

sum of $450 to us paid by the county of Palo Alto, state of
Iowa, party of the second part, the receipt whereof is hereby
acknowledged, do hereby sell, transfer and convey, and by
these presents have sold, transferred and conveyed, unto the
said party of the second part the following described property,
to-wit: All the lumber now in the court house square in
said county, or bought of said J. J. Wilson by said Burdick &
Goble, or either of them, and all window and door frames
and sash, either in the carpenter shop owned by said Burdick
& Goble, or on said court house square;—to have and to
hold the same forever, for the purpose of using the said lumber, sash, etc., in building and constructing the court house
now in process of construction in Emmetsburg, Palo Alto
county, Iowa, except such as may be condemned by the
proper authorities; and we hereby agree and covenant to warrant and defend the title to said property unto the said party of
the second part against the claims of all persons whomsoever.

"Witness our hands this sixteenth day of June, 1886.

"BURDICK & GOBLE.

"D. E. BURDICK & J. J. GOBLE.

"J. J. WILSON,

"By J. L. MARTIN, Agent."

Duly acknowledged before John J. Robins, notary public.

"It is hereby agreed and understood that, so far as J. J.
Wilson is concerned, the above bill of sale is not an absolute
evidence of payment by the county of the lumber bought of
him, but only for such portion as may be paid him; and it
does not preclude said Wilson from recovering from the
proper parties all amounts that may, from time to time, be
due him for lumber sold to said Burdick & Goble, or either
of them.

"Dated June 16, 1880.

"PALO ALTO COUNTY, IOWA,

"By ROBERT SHEA,

"JOHN J. ROBINS,

"Building Com."

The defendant denied that it at any time purchased the lumber and material of the plaintiff, but that the same were sold by the plaintiff to Burdick and Goble, and that the written contract upon which the suit is founded was taken by the defendant to secure it in the sum of $450 advanced by the defendant to Burdick and Goble, and by them paid to the plaintiff in part payment for the lumber mentioned in the written contract.

The cause was tried in the court below upon the theory that it was competent for the parties to introduce oral evidence as to what the real contract was. We will determine the appeal in the same manner.

It appears from the evidence that D. E. Burdick contracted with the defendant to furnish all the necessary material, and erect a court house for the defendant, according to certain plans and specifications, for the sum of $11,900. He after-wards associated J. J. Goble with him in the undertaking, and the partnership name was Burdick & Goble. They purchased lumber and other materials of the plaintiff, to be used in the building. When their purchases of the plaintiff had amounted to about $1,900, the plaintiff insisted that he should receive some payment thereon. No money was actually due from the county to Burdick & Goble, and, as an expedient to to relieve the plaintiff, the written instrument above set out was executed, and the county paid to the plaintiff $450, for which he executed a receipt in these words:

"EMMETSBURG, IOWA, June 16, 1880.

" Received of Burdick & Goble, per building committee on court house of Palo Alto County, four hundred and fifty dollars.

"J. L. MARTIN,

"For J. J. WILSON & Co."

It is proper to state that Martin was the managing agent of the plaintiff, and that he (Martin) made all the contracts and agreements which were made in the matter in controversy. When the written instrument was executed, there was no sale of the property made by Wilson to the county, for the very satisfactory reason that he was not the owner of the lumber. He had sold it to Burdick & Goble, and there is no evidence that the sale had been rescinded. There is no conflict in the evidence on this important fact in the case. It is claimed, however, that what is called the *addendum* to the contract shows that the instrument was more'than a mere security for the money advanced. It is true, it is therein recited that the "bill of sale is not an absolute evidence of payment by the county of the lumber bought of him." In view of the fact that Wilson did not own the lumber named in the bill of sale, the reference to the purchase from him can only be construed to mean the purchase theretofore made by Burdick & Goble, and the reference to his right to recover from the "*proper parties*" all amounts that may from time to time be due him, rebuts the idea that the county was one of these proper parties.

All of the building committee testified as witnesses that the contract was not a purchase of the property, but a mere security for the money advanced. It is true that the building committee afterwards paid the plaintiff considerable sums upon the indebtedness of Burdick & Goble to the plaintiff, but these payments were always made upon the orders of Burdick & Goble. There is really no conflict in the evidence upon the fact that this instrument was made as a mere security for the $450 advanced by the county. Even Martin, the agent of the plaintiff, testified that " the committee said they would advance money on the condition that they be secured on the material, and agreed with Burdick & Goble and ourselves to have the material turned over to them,—all the material we had furnished,—and took the money they advanced us then until the bill was paid;" and he again stated in his testimony that, " before paying the money over, they required this bill of sale as security for the money advanced." It is true that the witness afterwards testified as follows:

" It was understood by the building committee, at the time this *addendum* was made, that this $450 was not all the money we were to have. I know what the building committee then understood, because we talked it up, and they agreed to pay us more in the future. That was the talk between me and this building committee, and that is the reason this *addendum* was made. It was talked over between me and the building committee, and we jointly agreed to make this *addendum*, in order to show that we were to have more pay. It was to secure to Palo Alto county all of this property, and to make Palo Alto county the party responsible to us for the pay. After this contract was made, Burdick & Goble had nothing to do with the payment for this material, except to sign orders *at the request of the building committee.* The county or building committee paid all that was paid after that."

This may all be true without making the county liable to the plaintiff on this claim for a balance due. The county did pay Wilson, but it was always on the orders of Burdick & Goble. They were not bound to honor these orders, unless Burdick & Goble were entitled under their contract to the payments represented by the orders; and it is a conceded fact in the case that Burdick & Goble failed to complete their contract, left the court house unfinished, and the county paid some $5,000 to complete the building. Another fact which shows that the claim of the plaintiff is not a valid claim against the county, is that none of the material for which this suit was brought was actually used in the construction of the court house.

Counsel for the defendant claim that the verdict of the jury is without support in the evidence, and we think the claim is well made.

REVERSED.

BLAKE, ADM'R, v. KOONS ET AL.

1. **Former Adjudication**: VENDOR'S LIEN: SUBROGATION OF SURETY UPON PAYING NOTE FOR PURCHASE MONEY. The vendor of real estate sued the purchaser and his surety on a purchase-money note, and procured judgment, but the court refused to decree a vendor's lien on the premises. The surety paid the judgment. *Held* that, since he was a party to the action in which the vendor was refused a lien, he was bound by that adjudication, and that he could not afterwards claim to be entitled to such a lien by subrogation to the rights of the vendor.

2. **Mortgage**: WANT OF CONSIDERATION: RIGHTS OF SUBSEQUENT PURCHASER WITH NOTICE. A subsequent purchaser of land with notice of a prior mortgage is in no position to question the validity of the mortgage and secured notes in the hands of an assignee, even though he takes them after maturity, and subject to equities in favor of the maker. (*Crosby v. Tanner*, 40 Iowa, 136, followed.)

Appeal from Wapello Circuit Court.

MONDAY, MARCH 14.

ACTION in equity to forclose a mortgage executed by defendant B. C. Koons to M. L. Koons, to secure seven promissory notes. The mortgage and notes were assigned by M. L. Koons to plaintiff's intestate, in payment of an indebtedness, such assignment being made after the maturity of the notes. It is alleged in the petition that the defendants Harmon and Madsen assert some claim to the mortgaged property, but that their claims are junior to that of plaintiff. Harmon alleged in a cross-petition that B. C. Koons was indebted to him for borrowed money which was used by him in paying for the mortgaged premises, and that at the time the loan was made the intestate assigned to him the mortgage as collateral security therefor; and he prayed for judgment against Koons for the amount of the indebtedness, and for a foreclosure of the mortgage. Madsen answered that when Koons purchased the premises he became surety for him on a note given for a portion of the purchase price, and that judgment was subsequently obtained thereon against Koons

and himself, on which execution was issued, and the property
sold, and that he became the purchaser, and subsequently
obtained a sheriff's deed to the premises; also that the notes and
mortgage sued on were given without consideration, and in pursuance of a corrupt combination between M. L. Koons and
B. C. Koons to cheat and defraud the creditors of the latter.
The district court entered judgment in favor of Harmon on
his cross-petition, for the amount of the indebtedness from
Coons to him, and for the foreclosure of the mortgage. It also
gave plaintiff judgment for the amount of the notes, and for
the foreclosure of the mortgage, and adjudged that Madsen's
interest in the property was junior and inferior to the liens
of plaintiff and Harmon. Defendant Madsen appealed.

H. B. Hendershott, for appellant.

McNett & Tisdale, for appellees.

REED, J.—I. The note that Madsen signed as surety for
B. C. Koons was given for part of the purchase price of the

1. FORMER
adjudication:
vendor's lien:
subrogation
of surety upon
paying note
for purchase
money.

mortgaged premises, and was given before plaintiff's mortgage was executed. Judgment was
subsequently rendered on the note against both
Koons and Madsen, and that judgment was satisfied by the sale of the property to Madsen. It
is urged that the vendor had a lien on the premises for the
unpaid purchase money, and, as Madsen paid the debt, he is
now entitled, as against Koons, to be subrogated to the rights
of the vendor under that lien; and, as the intestate and Harmon had notice of that equity when they acquired the mortgage, they took subject to it. The record in the action in
which the judgment was rendered, however, affords a conclusive answer to this position. The plaintiff in the action
alleged that he was entitled to a vendor's lien on the premises, and prayed for the enforcement of such lien. Koons
answered denying that claim, and the court gave the plaintiff
a money judgment for the amount of the note, but refused

to give any further relief. The judgment determines, then, that the vendor was not entitled to a lien for the unpaid purchase money. Madsen was a party to the record, and he is bound by the adjudication. He is clearly in no position now to assert that a lien existed in favor of the vendor, and we need not inquire whether, in view of the fact that he satisfied the judgment in which he was surety by bidding in the property of the principal debtor at execution sale, he would be entititled to be subrogated to the rights of the vendor under the lien, if one had existed.

II. Appellant seeks to defeat the foreclosure of the mortgage on the ground that it was given without consideration, and for the fraudulent purpose of covering the property, and preventing the creditors of the mortgagor from appropriating it for the satisfaction of their debts. We think it unnecessary to enter into the question of fact arising under this claim. As the intestate purchased the notes after maturity, she took them subject to existing equities in favor of the maker. But appellant was not a party to the contract. He is a subsequent purchaser of the mortgaged premises, but purchased with notice of the mortgage, and the question is whether he is in a position to plead, as against an assignee of the notes, the infirmity of the contract. We think not. The case on this question falls within the rule of *Crosby v. Tanner*, 40 Iowa, 136.

2. MORTGAGE: want of consideration: rights of subsequent purchaser with notice.

AFFIRMED.

THE CHICAGO LUMBER CO. v. WOODSIDE ET AL.

1. **Mechanic's Lien:** SUBCONTRACTOR: PAYMENT TO CONTRACTOR: NOTICE. Where the owner of an improvement knows that subcontractors are furnishing labor and materials, and knows who they are, he cannot defeat them of their rights under the mechanic's lien law by paying to the contractor, or to subsequent subcontractors on his orders, the contract price of the work, in disregard of the claims of the prior subcontractors.

2. **Practice in Supreme Court:** IMMATERIAL QUESTIONS. This court will not determine which of two mechanic's liens is entitled to priority, where it appears that both are sufficiently secured and will be paid.

Appeal from Polk Circuit Court.

MONDAY, MARCH 14.

ACTION to foreclose a mechanic's lien. The defendant Joseph Rogg is the owner of the property in question. In June, 1885, he entered into a contract with the defendant Woodside for the construction of a building. Woodside contracted with the plaintiff to furnish the lumber for the building, with the exception of the doors, sashes, etc., furnished by the Capital City Planing Mill Company. The plaintiff claimed a lien for the entire balance due it, to-wit. $452.61. The court decreed that the plaintiff was not entitled to a lien for the whole of such amount, but was entitled to a third lien to the extent of a balance remaining unpaid by the owner to the principal contractor, to-wit, the sum of $235.68. The plaintiff appeals.

Berryhill & Henry, for appellant.

Mitchell & Dudley and *Parsons & Perry*, for Joseph Rogg, appellee.

Read, Hutchinson & Read, for Capital City Planing Mill Co.

Smith & Morris and *James Embree*, for other appellees.

ADAMS, CH. J.—The plaintiff commenced furnishing lumber to the contractor, Woodside, July 8, 1885, and continued

1. MECHANIC's lien: subcontractor: payment to contractor: notice. to furnish lumber until October 8, 1885, on which day it furnished the last item. Within thirty days therefrom, to-wit, October 26, 1885, it filed a statement for a lien, and served notice thereof upon the owner Rogg. The contract between Rogg and Woodside called for payments as the work progressed. Rogg proceeded to make payments, and paid upon the contract, either directly to Woodside, or to subcontractors upon his orders, about $1,600 after the plaintiff began to furnish lumber, and the balance remaining unpaid is not sufficient to secure the plaintiff. The principal question presented is as to whether the plaintiff's lien attached for the full amount due him, notwithstanding the payments made by the owner.

The plaintiff took all the steps required by statute to acquire a lien for every item of lumber from the time it was furnished. This being so, the plaintiff has a *prima facie* right to such lien. If the right did not arise under the statute thus fully complied with, it must be by reason of a fact which excused the owner in making the payments, and the burden of proving such fact rested upon the owner. He contends that he was excusable in paying Woodside, because he was ignorant of any claim on the part of the plaintiff for the lumber furnished by it to Woodside. But it was not necessary for him to know that the plaintiff had a claim. If we should hold that it was, we should go far towards frittering away the whole mechanic's lien law, so far as subcontractors are concerned. On this matter of knowledge there was some conflict in the evidence, as might be expected. According to the testimony of Woodside, Rogg knew that the plaintiff was furnishing the lumber, and was not being paid in advance, nor as each item was furnished, but that it was to be paid out of the money coming due to Woodside on the building. According to the testimony of Rogg, he simply knew that

the plaintiff was furnishing the lumber. Taking Rogg's testimony to be true, it will be seen that the case is an ordinary
one, and such as might be expected to arise every day. The
owner sees men furnishing labor or materials under the contractor, and neither sees nor hears anything more. Can he
properly proceed to pay the contractor upon the assumption
that the men furnishing the labor or materials have been
paid in advance, or contemporaneously with the furnishing
of the labor or materials? We think not. Laborers are not
usually paid in advance, nor strictly as the labor progresses.
Nor is material usually paid for in advance, nor as each item
is furnished, where, as in this case, it is furnished from time
to time during a considerable period.

In the case of *Othmer Bros. v. Clifton & United Presbyterian Church*, 69 Iowa, 656, the church was charged with a
lien in favor of subcontractors, notwithstanding the church had
paid the contractor. The fact was that one or more officers of
the church had knowledge that Othmer Bros. did painting on
the church as subcontractors, but did not know that they were
not paid in advance, nor as the work went on. This court
thought that the church was bound to take notice that the
painters might be acquiring a claim against the contractor
for which the statute gives a lien.

Where the owner knows that subcontractors are furnishing
labor or materials, and knows who they are, he should not be
excused in paying the contractor in disregard of their claims.
He would, we think, be put upon inquiry. Nothing could
be easier than the ascertainment of their claims. Nor is it
any hardship upon him to require that he shall withhold
payment during the time which the law allows the subcontractor to perfect his lien. The hardship, if any, arises after
he has once needlessly proceeded in disregard of rights which
the statute was designed to give. And, as the evidence
shows that more money became due from the owner to the
contractor after the plaintiff commenced furnishing lumber
than was necessary to pay it and others having prior liens, it

follows that in our opinion the plaintiff was entitled to a lien upon the property for the full amount due.

One other question has been presented, and that is as to priority of liens. The court held that the defendant, the

2. PRACTICE in supreme court: immaterial questions.

Capital City Planing Mill Company, had a lien for $54.61 paramount to the lien of the plaintiff. In the view which we have taken of the case, it appears that both claims are sufficiently secured, and will be paid, and, if so, the question of priority has no practical importance.

MODIFIED AND AFFIRMED.

WILLIAMS & BURGHART V. FRICK.

1. **Practice**: JUDGMENT ON SPECIAL VERDICT: ERROR CURED. Error, if any, in overruling a motion for judgment on a special verdict, notwithstanding the general verdict, is cured by afterwards sustaining a motion by the same party to set aside the general verdict and for a new trial.

Appeal from Harrison Circuit Court.

MONDAY, MARCH 14.

The facts are stated in the opinion.

L. Brown, for appellant.

F. M. Dance and *Dewell & McGavern*, for appellee.

SEEVERS, J.—There was a general and special verdict. They were inconsistent, and the defendant, in substance, moved the court to set aside the general verdict, and render judgment in his favor on the special findings. This motion was overruled, and the defendant excepted. For the purposes of the case, it will be conceded that the court erred in so ruling. Afterwards the defendant moved the court to set aside the general verdict, and for a new trial. This motion was sustained.

The error assigned and relied on is that the court erred in overruling the first motion. Conceding this, we think the defendant waived the error by moving to set aside the general verdict, asking a new trial, and obtaining it.

AFFIRMED.

71
92

CALLANAN ET AL. V. WILLIAMS ET AL.

71
105

1. **Pleading**: ANSWER: DENIAL OF AMOUNT DUE: EFFECT. A denial in an answer that defendants are indebted in the amount claimed in the petition does not present an issue of fact, and does not amount to a general denial. (*Stucksleger v. Smith*, 27 Iowa, 286, followed.)

2. **Promissory Note**: PAYMENT: DEPOSIT OF MONEY WITH ONE NOT A BANKER. Where a note is made payable at the office of one not a banker, and not the payee, the deposit of money to pay the note with such person is not a payment of the note, as the holder is not required by law to present the note at that place for payment. (Compare *Lazier v. Horan*, 55 Iowa, 75.)

Appeal from Taylor District Court.

MONDAY, MARCH 14.

ACTION on three promissory notes and to foreclose a mortgage. A demurrer to the answer was overruled, and the plaintiffs appeal.

J. J. Davis, for appellants.

Flick & Jones, for appellees.

SEEVERS, J.—The following is a copy of one of the notes upon which the action was brought:

"$180. REAL ESTATE, LOAN AND EXCHANGE OFFICE OF N. B. MOORE.

"CLARINDA, IOWA, November 1, 1880.

"One year after date I promise to pay to the order of N.

B. Moore one hundred and eighty dollars, with ten per cent interest from date, payable annually at the office of N. B. Moore, in Clarinda, Iowa, and, if not paid when due, the interest to draw the same per cent after due as the original note, and, if collected by suit, a reasonable attorney's fee. Value received.   J. T. WILLIAMS."

The other two notes are in all respects like the foregoing, except that one is payable in one and the other in two years after date. It is stated in the petition that the notes were indorsed and transferred by the payee, before maturity, to an innocent holder, from whom the plaintiffs obtained the notes. The defendants admitted the execution of the notes and mortgage, denied that they were indebted in the amount claimed in the petition, and pleaded that on the first day of October, 1881, the maker paid the note above set out to N. B. Moore, at his office, at Clarinda, Iowa; and that on the fifteenth day of April, 1882, the maker paid the full amount due on the two last described notes to N. B. Moore, at his office at Clarinda, Iowa; that said Moore has possession of said money at his said office to pay said notes when presented at said place; that, when said money was paid, Moore represented that the notes had been lost or mislaid, and he canceled the mortgage to secure the same, and then and there agreed with said Williams to take up and pay said notes in full at their maturity, or when presented at his office; and he now holds said money, but said notes have never been presented for payment at said office. A demurrer to the answer was overruled.

I.   Counsel for the appellees insist that the court did not err in overruling the demurrer, because a general denial was 1. PLEADING: answer: denial of amount due: effect· pleaded, and the demurrer was to the whole answer. A denial in an answer that the defendants are indebted in the amount claimed in the petition does not present an issue of fact, and does not amount to a general denial. *Stucksleger v. Smith*, 27 Iowa, 286.

II. It is suggested by counsel, and we assume that the demurrer was overruled on the ground, as the court thought, that this case comes within the rule recognized in *Lazier v. Horan*, 55 Iowa, 75. The decision in that case is grounded on the fact that the note was payable at a bank, in which money is ordinarily and usually deposited; and where notes are made payable at a bank the parties expect collection to be made through it. For a full discussion of the question determined, see the late case of *Adams v. Hackensack Imp. Com.* 44 N. J. Law, 638. We therefore do not feel disposed to extend the rule of the cited case. The facts of this case are materially different. The notes were made payable at the office of N. B. Moore, (or at least the interest was,) at Clarinda, Iowa, and we may assume, possibly, that it was a real estate, loan and collection office; and it seems to us that such an office is in no respect different from the office of a lawyer, merchant, or hundreds of other offices where business of a similar character is done. At least, it does not appear that money was ordinarily deposited by people generally at said office, or that notes payable there were usually sent, placed or kept there for collection or payment. The ordinary rule is that payment must be made to the holder of the note, and it is not essential to the maintenance of an action on a note payable at a particular place that it should be presented there for payment. This rule is recognized in *Lazier v. Horan*. If this payment is recognized as valid, then we are unable to see why a note payable at any office or designated place of business where notes are ordinarily or occasionally executed could not be paid at such place. This would greatly embarrass commercial transactions, and prove detrimental, we think, thereto. The court, we think, erred in overruling the demurrer.

2. PROMISSORY note: payment: deposit of money with one not a banker.

REVERSED.

ARTZ v. CULBERTSON ET AL.

1. **Practice in Supreme Court:** AGREEMENT OF COUNSEL ENFORCED. Where counsel agreed to dispense with a transcript unless one was required, and that in that case appellant should have time to file one, and it became necessary to file one on account of denials made in an amended abstract, and appellant showed by affidavit, submitted with the case, that one of the papers required for a transcript was temporarily lost from the files of the court below, *held* that the denials in the amended abstract should not be taken as true, but that appellant's motion to strike it from the files should be overruled, the submission set aside, and the cause continued with leave to appellant to file a transcript.

Appeal from Carroll Circuit Court.

MONDAY, MARCH 14.

E. M. Betzer, for appellant.

H. W. Macomber and *Geo. W. Paine,* for appellees.

BECK, J.—I. In this case no transcript has been filed. The parties entered into a stipulation to dispense with a transcript, unless the court should require one to be filed, and in that case the appellant was to be granted reasonable time to comply with the requirements.   The abstract was filed August 25, 1886.   An amended abstract was filed by defendants December 8, 1886, which denies that the evidence was reduced to writing as required by law, and that a translation of the short-hand notes has been filed in the court below.   Plaintiff filed a motion asking leave and time to file a transcript, which is supported by an affidavit showing, in effect, that the transcript of the reporter's notes of the evidence was filed in the court below, but is now mislaid, or cannot be found.   He also moves to strike defendant's amended abstract.   These motions were submitted with the case.

In our opinion, under the agreement of the parties, the plaintiff ought to have time to file a transcript, and the amended abstract ought not to be taken as true. His motion for time to file transcript is sustained. The plaintiff's motion to strike the defendant's amended abstract is overruled. The submission is set aside, and the case continued.

WILLIAMS v. MILLS COUNTY.

71 367
96 615

1. **Statute of Limitations**: ACTION FOR WILLFUL TRESPASS. An action for a willful trespass committed by entering upon plaintiff's land and, by digging a ditch thereon, interfering with his water power, accrues immediately upon the commission of the trespass, and is barred in five years thereafter. (Code, § 2529.)

Appeal from Mills District Court.

MONDAY, MARCH 14.

THE plaintiff seeks by this action to recover damages of the defendant for the alleged wrongful diversion of a stream of water away from his mill. A demurrer to the petition was sustained, and plaintiff appeals.

Kelley Bros. and *E. B. Woodruff*, for appellant.

Watkins, Williams & Wright and *L. T. Genung*, for appellee.

ROTHROCK, J.—The petition in this case is a remarkable document. It is remarkable for its great length, and for the indefiniteness of its averments as to the injury complained of. It appears therefrom that the plaintiff is the owner of a mill upon a creek or stream of water in Mills county, and that in the year 1879 a county ditch was constructed, which had its initial point at said creek. But whether the ditch intersected the stream above or below the mill it is impossible to determine from the petition. In one part of the petition it is averred that "the defendant entered upon plaintiff's land, against his protests and objections, and erected and made over and across the same the ditch and levee aforesaid, and did cut, dig and tear out, and cause to be torn out, along the bank of said stream above plaintiff's mill-dam, certain levees and embankments constructed by plaintiff to protect said mill property, and constructed in lieu thereof the ditch and levee aforesaid." It would appear from this averment that the defendant diverted the water from the stream above the mill-dam. But it is elsewhere averred in the petition that plaintiff was not injured by reason of water being diverted from the stream above the mill, but because the ditch interfered with the flow of water below the mill, and the channel, therefore, became filled up so that the water would not flow away from the mill. And; in the argument in reply, we are for the first time advised that the initial point of the ditch was between the mill and the mill-dam.

This suit was commenced more than five years after the ditch was constructed, and one ground of demurrer was that the action was barred by the statute of limitations. Accepting the averments of the petition to be true, the act complained of was a willful trespass, without authority of law, and done against the protests of the plaintiff made at the time. For this invasion of his rights he had an immediate cause of action. We do not mean that he had a cause of action against the county. That question we do not determine, because it may admit of doubt whether the county would have been liable. But there then accrued a right of action to the plaintiff for the trespass, against the trespassers, whether they were the men who constructed the ditch, the contractors, or whoever was liable therefor. The present action is founded upon the original trespass. It should have been brought within five years after the right of action accrued. Code, § 2529.

AFFIRMED.

DAVIS' SONS v. COCHRAN ET AL.

1. **Evidence**: LOST RECEIPT: EFFECT OF SECONDARY EVIDENCE. Where a written receipt made by plaintiffs to defendants became material as evidence, but defendants testified that it had been lost, an instruction to the effect that "all questions and disputes as to the language of the written receipt are to be taken strongly against defendants and the claim made by them as to the language and construction of the same," was rightly refused, in the absence of any evidence of bad faith or fault on the part of the defendants in suppressing the receipt.

2. ———: PAROL TO VARY WRITING: RULE NOT APPLICABLE. The rule that parol testimony is not admissible to vary the terms of a written contract does not apply to evidence that a contract was to be made, but which does not refer to the terms of the contract.

3. **Verdict**: EVIDENCE TO SUPPORT ON APPEAL. A verdict will not be disturbed on appeal for want of evidence, when the evidence is conflicting.

Appeal from Buena Vista District Court.

MONDAY, MARCH 14.

ACTION upon a promissory note. There was a judgment upon a verdict for defendants. Plaintiffs appeal.

M. Wakefield, for appellants.

Robinson & Milchrist, for appellees.

BECK, J.—I. The only defense pleaded to the action is to the effect that the note in suit, with other notes held by plaintiffs against the defendants, were settled by defendant Cochran giving other notes, with security, and turning over to plaintiffs two notes of other parties; and that, pursuant to this settlement, plaintiffs agreed to surrender and release the note in suit.

II. The evidence shows that, when the settlement was made, plaintiffs retained the note in suit, giving a paper or receipt to defendant pertaining to it. Plaintiffs claimed that, under this instrument, the note was to be given up and canceled if they secured the possession of two notes which were held by another

1. EVIDENCE: lost receipt: effect of secondary evidence.

VOL. LXXI—24

party, and for which defendant gave an order. Defendant
insisted that there was no condition as to the surrender of
the note, and that the agreement to do so was retained by
plaintiffs to aid them in some other transaction or suit, and,
when so used, it was given up to defendant.

The defendants testified that the receipt was lost, and
could not be found, and therefore was permitted to state its
contents. The plaintiffs asked an instruction directing the
jury, among other matters, that "all questions and disputes
as to the language of the written receipt are to be taken
strongly against defendants, and the claim made by them as
to its language and construction of the same." This
instruction was rightly refused. The loss of the writing
having been established, the law authorized evidence of its
contents, to the end that the real contract of the parties might
be known. It throws no discredit upon defendant's evidence, nor does it raise presumptions against the merits of
his claim as to the contents of the writing, thus fettering the
defendant's defense in order to defeat the truth. If the
defendant wrongfully, fraudulently, or purposely withheld
the writing, the rule of the instructions would be correct.
Upon this ground the plaintiffs insist that it ought to have
been given. But there is not a particle of evidence tending
to show that defendants withheld or suppressed the paper, or
that it was lost through their fault. Its loss is shown without any evidence tending to show fraud or fault on the part
of the defendant. There was, therefore, no evidence to
which the instruction was applicable.

III. The plaintiffs asked the court to give the following
instruction to the jury: "(2) If the jury believe from the
evidence that, at the time the witness Smith and
defendant were at the house of witness Holmes,
it was then and there agreed between the
witness Smith and the defendant that witness Smith was to
execute a receipt in writing to defendant, expressing the condition and reason why said Smith was not to surrender the

2. ——: parol
to vary writ-
ing; rule not
applicable.

possession of the note in suit, and you further find from the
evidence that said Smith did execute a writing to said
defendant, stating the terms and conditions on which said
Smith retained possession of said note, and the defendant
accepted said instrument, then you are instructed as a matter
of law that you must not consider the testimony of the witness Holmes, the law presuming that all prior parol and
verbal agreements were merged in the writing so executed by
witness Smith."

Smith was the attorney of the plaintiffs, who made the
settlement between the parties, and signed the lost receipt,
the contents of which were shown by defendant's evidence.
It was signed after the parties returned from the house of
Holmes to defendant's house. The thought of the instruction is that, as Holmes testified to a contract made at his
house, it was not competent to contradict or vary the contract set out in the receipt, for the reason that the law will
presume that it was superseded or merged into the contract
finally expressed in the receipt. The rule of law here recognized is, of course, correct, but we think it is not applicable to exclude Holmes' evidence. He testified that he was
a justice of the peace, and the defendant and his wife came
to his house to acknowledge the mortgages to plaintiffs.
They were accompanied by Smith. The witness understood
that plaintiff and defendant had a settlement, and that some
notes were to be given up, and others to be taken secured by
the mortgages; that one note was to be returned by Smith
after the conclusion of a suit; and that the witness suggested
that defendant take a receipt for it, and Smith said he would
give it if defendant would do some trifling matter not connected with the business. The witness then says " that was
the way the matter was left." After this statement he testifies to no agreement whatever between the parties, but
expressly states that he did not understand or remember
certain terms or conditions called to his attention. His evidence cannot be regarded as showing the terms or conditions

of any contract. His evidence, which we have above referred to, may be understood as showing that there was an agreement to be expressed on the receipt to be afterwards given, but certainly not its conditions or terms. There is not one word in his testimony which tends to show the terms of a contract. The instruction, therefore, was rightly refused. It may be that some parts of his evidence were objectionable, but no part was upon the ground set out in the instruction. But the record fails to show that any objections were made to the evidence when it was introduced. We can consider none except the one raised by the instruction asked by plaintiffs.

IV. It is insisted that the verdict should have been set aside by the court below, for the reason that it is not suffi-
3. VERDICT: evidence to support on appeal.
ciently supported by the evidence. All that can be said on this point is that the evidence is conflicting. We cannot, therefore, disturb the verdict.

We have considered all questions presented in this case.

AFFIRMED.

THE STATE v. GRIFFIN.

1. **Larceny**: PROPERTY FOUND ON DEFENDANT'S PREMISES: IDENTITY: PRESUMPTION: INSTRUCTION. Where there was evidence that certain money found secreted in defendant's place of business, of which, however, there were other inmates, was a portion of the stolen property, and defendant admitted that he had placed the money where it was found, but claimed that it was his own money, *held* that the court properly submitted the question of identity to the jury, and therewith properly instructed them that, if the defendant had the stolen property, or some part of it, in his possession soon after the larceny, and such possession was not explained, it was presumptive evidence of his guilt.

2. **Jury**: RIGHT TO MINUTES OF EVIDENCE: DUTY OF BAILIFF. A bailiff in charge of a jury has no authority, when requested by the jury, to bring in the minutes of the testimony, in order that they may use them in settling a disputed point in the evidence.

3. ———: SICK JUROR: TEMPORARY ABSENCE WITH BAILIFF. During the deliberation of the jury, one of the jurors was taken sick, and was per-

mitted to separate himself from the others for a time, and to take a walk in the open air with an officer, but was not permitted to communicate with any person about the case. *Held* irregular, but not prejudical, and no ground for reversal.

4. ——: JUROR DISCLAIMING VERDICT. A juror who has consented to a verdict cannot afterwards be heard to say that it does not express his honest judgment on the facts of the case, but that he assented to it because he was sick, and desired to be released.

Appeal from Dubuque District Court.

MONDAY, MARCH 14.

THE defendant was convicted of the larceny of a sum of money, and sentenced to a term of imprisonment in the penitentiary.

H. T. McNulty, for defendant.

A. J. Baker, *Attorney-general*, for the State.

REED, J.—I. The evidence against the defendant was purely circumstantial. He kept a saloon in the city of Dubuque,

1. LARCENY: property found on defendant's premises: identity: presumption: instruction.

and the evidence on which he was convicted tends strongly to prove that the alleged larceny was committed in his saloon. The money is alleged to have been stolen from one Frank C. Harmon, on the evening of September 22, 1884. On that evening Harmon went to the saloon, and, after taking a number of drinks of intoxicating liquors, engaged in a game of dice with the defendant. He had been drinking before he went there, and was intoxicated while in the saloon. He had in his possession money to the amount of about $200, which he exhibited to defendant. Other persons were in the saloon at the time, and the exhibition of the money was made in their presence. Soon afterwards Harmon left the saloon, and, in a short time thereafter, discovered that he had lost his money. He immediately informed a police officer of his loss, and defendant and his bar-tender were arrested and kept in custody during that night. The next morning the city marshal, in company with Harmon, searched the

saloon, and, in an ice-chest in the saloon, they found $25 in
gold coin, which Harmon swore on the trial was a part of the
money which was stolen from him. He testified that he
was able to identify it by certain marks which he had placed
upon it the day before the larceny, and which he pointed out
to the jury. Some time afterwards a pocket-book was found
in the water-closet connected with the saloon, and he also
identified it as the one in which the money was when stolen.

The district court instructed the jury that, if defendant
had the stolen property, or some portion of it, in his possession soon after the larceny, and such posession was not
explained, it was presumptive evidence of his guilt. It was
urged by counsel that the court was not warranted in giving
this instruction, for the reason that the evidence did not
show that the money found in the saloon was in the actual
or exclusive possession of defendant. If the question rested
alone on the facts detailed above, this point would probably
be well taken. The fact that the stolen property was found
in defendant's place of business would not alone raise a presumption that he is guilty, there being other inmates of the
place. Rosc. Crim. Ev. 18; 2 Starkie, Ev. 450. But the
case does not rest on that fact alone. Defendant testified
in his own behalf, and he admitted that he had placed the
$25 in the ice-box where the marshal found it; but he claimed
that it was his own money, and that he had placed it there a day
or two before the larceny is alleged to have been committed. The
court was fully warranted on this evidence in submitting the
question as to the identity of the money found in the saloon, with
that stolen from Harmon, to the jury, as was done, and, in
telling them that the fact of the possession by defendant of
the stolen property, if it was proven, was, in the absence of any
reasonable explanation of the possession, presumptive evidence of his guilt. It was shown by his own testimony that
he had had the money found by the marshal in his actual
possession. If it was part of the stolen money, as the jury
may well have found it was, his statement as to the owner-

ship of the money, and the time of placing it in the ice-box, was necessarily false. Objections have been urged to other of the instructions given. Without setting out the instructions objected to or the grounds of objection, we deem it sufficient to say that they appear to us to be correct.

II. While the jury was deliberating, a question arose as to what a witness had testified to on a certain point, and they 2. JURY: right requested the officer in charge to bring the min-
to miuutes
of evidence: utes of the witness's testimony to the jury-room,
duty of
bailiff. that the question of difference might be settled by an examination of them; but the officer refused to do this, and this was one of the grounds of the motion for a new trial. The action of the officer in refusing to take the minutes of the testimony to the jury-room was clearly right. If the jury regarded the question about which they differed as an important one, they should have required the officer to conduct them before the court, where the desired information could have been communicated to them. Code, § 4454. As this course was not taken, but they afterwards agreed upon a verdict, it must be assumed, either that the question as to which the difference arose was not regarded as of importance, or that they were able to determine the question without recourse to the evidence.

III. During the deliberation of the jury, one of their number was taken sick, and was permitted to separate him-
3. ——: sick self from the others, and take a walk in the open
juror: tem-
porary ab- air. He was accompanied, however, by an officer,
sence with
bailiff. and was not permitted to communicate with any person about the case. This action, although it was not strictly regular, affords no ground for disturbing the judgment. Defendant was in no manner prejudiced by it.

IV. It was sought to be shown, in support of the motion for a new trial, that the juror who was taken sick assented to
4. ——: juror the verdict, not because he was convinced by the
disclaiming
verdict. evidence that defendant was guilty, but because of his desire, owing to his sickness, to get released from the

jury room.   But, having consented to the verdict, he cannot afterwards be permitted to say that it is not his honest judgment on the facts of the case.

We have not deemed it necessary to discuss all of the objections to the verdict urged in the motion for a new trial. We have, however, examined the whole record with care, and we find no grounds for disturbing the judgment pronounced by the district court, and it will be

Affirmed.

Quinn v. Brown et al.

1. **Conveyance:** FRAUD: EVIDENCE. Plaintiff's claim, that she was induced by her husband to sign a deed under a belief that it was a mortgage for a small amount, is not supported by the evidence.

2. ——: BLANK AS TO CONSIDERATION AND GRANTEE: SIGNATURE BY WIFE: INNOCENT PURCHASER. Where a wife joins her husband in executing and acknowledging a deed to land, with the consideration and grantee left blank, and leaves it with her husband, and he sells the land to an innocent purchaser for value, and inserts the consideration and the name of the purchaser in the deed, and delivers it to him, *held* that the wife cannot assail the title of the purchaser on the ground that she did not know what she was signing; and that the land may have included a part of her homestead is immaterial.

Appeal from Dallas Circuit Court.

Monday, March 14.

Action in equity to set aside a conveyance of real estate. The relief asked was denied, and the plaintiff appeals.

John R. Hunter, for appellant.

Cardell & Shortley, for appellees.

Seevers, J.—The undisputed facts are that on the twenty-ninth day of May, 1884, the plaintiff and defendant John Quinn were husband and wife, and that said defendant owned the southeast quarter of section seventeen, in township eighty-one, range twenty-nine, in Dallas county. They resided with their family on said premises as their homestead, which had never been platted, set apart, or in any way designated. But the house occupied by them, and the barn and out buildings, were all situate on the northeast quarter of the quarter section above referred to. On the day above stated, the defendant John Quinn conveyed the latter tract of land to the plaintiff, and on the same day said Quinn and the plaintiff executed and acknowledged a warrantee deed, in which the remainder of the quarter section was described, which was perfect in every respect as a conveyance, except that the name of the grantee and the consideration were blank. It was purposely so executed for reasons hereafter stated, as the defendants claim, and left in the hands of the defendant Quinn.

Sometime afterwards, and prior to September 10, 1884, a consideration of $2,400, and the name of the defendant Brown as grantee, were inserted in said deed by direction of the defendant Quinn, the same delivered to Brown, and duly recorded. This is the conveyance which the plaintiff asks to have set aside, on the grounds that it was procured by fraud; that she signed it under the belief, caused by the representations of her husband, that it was a mortgage for a comparatively small amount; and that the conveyance in blank, executed under the circumstances, is invalid.

It is apparent from the evidence that the plaintiff and her husband did not live happily together, and, shortly after the execution of the conveyances, the plaintiff applied for a divorce. As we understand, such action was dismissed.

The defendants claim that at the time the conveyances were made a separation and divorce were contemplated, and that the first conveyance was made by the defendant Quinn to the plaintiff as her proper share of the real estate, and that the deed in blank was executed for the express purpose of enabling said defendant to sell the land for the purpose of paying his debts. That he was indebted, clearly appears. This theory is supported by the fact that said defendant executed what may be designated as a bill of sale to the plaintiff of certain personal property.

The plaintiff's theory is that she believed she was signing a mortgage only; she so testifies; and that she has no recollection of the conveyances, and that the same were obtained by fraudulent representations.

We find the fact to be that the plaintiff signed and acknowledged the blank deed with knowledge of the purpose for which it was executed. The plaintiff admits that about that time she was in great trouble, nervous and excited, and we may therefore well suppose that she is honestly of the belief that she signed the conveyance under the belief that it was a mortgage. But in our opinion the preponderance of the evidence is that she at the time had knowledge of what she signed, and the object and purpose of the conveyance, and why blanks were left for the insertion of the name of the grantee and the consideration. It was merely a part of a family arrangement, made necessary, as the parties thought, because of the unfortunate and unhappy relations existing between them. It may be possible that the plaintiff was to some extent deceived by her husband, but the pivotal question is, did she execute the deed in blank, and leave it with her husband? and as to this there is no doubt. She may not possibly have known the character of the instrument, but we think she did; and, as Brown had no knowledge that it had been fraudulently procured, and as we find he is a purchaser for value, he should be protected. *Swartz v. Ballou*, 47 Iowa, 188.

The fact that the homestead had not been platted or designated is immaterial, for the reason that the homestead character was divested by the conveyance to Brown. In fact, it was a sale and conveyance of that portion of the land; and, if it had included the whole quarter section, it would have been valid as a conveyance of the homestead.

AFFIRMED.

McCormick v. McCormick et al.

1. **Conveyance**: DELIVERY: WHAT IS. Where one brother sold land to another, and executed a deed therefor, and left it in the hands of a sister, and received from the grantee the purchase price, *held* that the possession of the deed by the sister must be regarded as the possession of the grantee, and that the claim that the deed never was delivered could not be sustained.

Appeal from Cass Circuit Court.

MONDAY, MARCH 14.

THE plaintiff is the widow of S. I. McCormick, deceased, who died in September, 1883, and left no children surviving him. Plaintiff claims that her said husband died seized in fee of eighty acres of land, which he had purchased from the defendant George McCormick, and that he took possession of said land and paid the purchase money in full; that George McCormick executed a deed for said land and delivered it to the decedent, and said deed was not recorded, but was lost or destroyed. She claims that, as widow of the decedent, she is the absolute owner of an undivided half of said land, and that the defendant Nancy McCormick, the mother of decedent, is the owner of the other half thereof. Plaintiff asks that her title to the undivided half of the land be quieted in her against both of the defendants.

The defendant George McCormick answered the petition by denying that S. I. McCormick had any interest in said land at the the time of his death. He denied the alleged purchase by decedent, admitted that he (defendant) made a deed for the land in question, but denied that the same was ever delivered to the deceased, or to any one for him.

Upon a full hearing, the circuit court entered a decree for the plaintiff as prayed. Defendants appeal.

Temple & Phelps, for appellants.

L. L. DeLano, for appellee.

ROTHROCK, J.—The land in question was a present from

the defendant Nancy McCormick, who is the mother of the defendant George McCormick. It adjoins a large farm which was owned by the deceased for some time before his death. When George McCormick became the owner, the land was unbroken prairie. S. I. McCormick entered into possession of the land, had· it broken up, and was in full possession thereof, cultivating it up to the time of his death. After George McCormick became the owner of the land, he entered the Iowa State University as a student, where he remained for some time. He stated to a number of persons that he had sold the land to his brother, S. I. McCormick. In the spring of 1882 he executed a deed to the deceased, and left it in the possesssion of his sister. This deed was never actually in the possession of the deceased. But we think the evidence shows that he was entitled to the possession of it before his death, because, in our opinion, it very satisfactorily appears that deceased made full payment for the land, and the possession of the deed by his sister should be regarded as his possession. And we reach this conclusion upon the testimony of the defendant George McCormick, and his admissions made to a number of persons who testified as witnesses in the case. We do not propose to set out his evidence, nor that of the other witnesses. It is enough to say that his explanation of the fact that he made the deed, and the reasons he gives for making it, are such as to convince us that he made it in pursuance of a sale of the property, and we are satisfied from the evidence that the deceased paid him $1,081.50 on the twenty-third day of May, 1883, and that said payment was made upon the contract for the purchase of the land.

It appears to us that the decree of the circuit court is correct.

AFFIRMED.

BROWN v. McLEISH ET AL.

1. **Master and Servant**: NEGLIGENCE OF SERVANT: LIABILITY OF MASTER. Where an employer has no control over an employe, but the latter may alone direct his own acts and the manner of doing the work, the employer is not liable for his negligence;—following cases cited in opinion;—and an instruction given in this case is *held* erroneous as not recognizing this rule. ADAMS, CH. J., from his view of the evidence, dissenting.

2. **Verdict**: DAMAGES: POWER OF COURT TO REDUCE. The court has no power to reduce the amount of damages found by the jury, and to render judgment for the reduced sum.

71
87

7
7
71
96

7
12
61

71
126

71
A128

Appeal from Buchanan Circuit Court.

WEDNESDAY, MARCH 15.

ACTION to recover damages for personal injuries sustained by plaintiff by falling into a ditch dug by defendants in a public street. There was a judgment upon a verdict for plaintiff. Both parties appeal.

E. E. Hasner, for plaintiff.

H. Boies and *Lake & Harmon*, for defendants.

BECK, J.—I. The petition alleges, in substance, that defendants, without right or authority, dug a ditch in a public street of a village, and with gross negligence left it open and without guards, or any protection to prevent persons using the street from falling into it, and that plaintiff, while passing along the street, in the exercise of proper care, fell into the ditch, and was permanently injured. The answer denies the allegations of the petition.

II. Evidence was introduced on behalf of defendants tending to prove that the persons employed by defendants had exclusive control of the work, and that

1. MASTER and servant: negligence of servant: liability of master.

defendants reserved and retained no authority to direct the manner of its execution. Applicable to the evidence, the court gave the following instruction: "(7) As to the liability of the employer for

the act of his servant or employe, you are instructed that if
the act complained of be within the scope and in the course
of the employment,—that is, if it is a thing necessary to be
done to carry out or complete the work about which the
servant was employed,—then the employer is responsible for
any damages resulting from any negligence on the part of the
servant or his employe; and it.would make no difference, as
to the responsibility of the master or employer, that he did
not authorize the particular act complained of, or did not
know of the act or neglect of the servant or employe." This
instruction is clearly erroneous. It extends the rule *respond-
eat superior* to the act of a servant or employe when the master or employer, by the terms of the employment, has no
authority to control and direct the manner of the execution
of the work. The instruction is based upon the thought
that, if the act done be necessary to complete the work which
the workmen was employed to do, the employer is liable for
his negligence or improper conduct in doing the act. If an
act be necessary to accomplish work, as the throwing of earth
from the ditch into the public street, or the leaving of the
unfinished ditch open during the night, it may be carefully
done, or it may be done with negligence. Now, if the employer has no control over the workmen, if they alone may
direct their own acts, and the manner of doing work, he is
not liable for their negligence. An essential element in the
rule *respondent superior,* is the control of the master or
employer over the servant or employe. See *Callahan v.
Burlington & M. R. R'y Co.,* 23 Iowa, 562; *Kellogg v.
Payne,* 21 Id., 575; *Cunningham v. International R'y Co.,*
51 Tex., 503; *Moore v. Sanborne,* 2 Mich., 519. We need
not consider the questions of fact arising in the consideration
of the evidence, which, it is claimed by plaintiff, brings this
case within the rule just stated. It was for determination
by the jury.

III. The defendants, after the evidence was submitted,
and during the argument of the cause, asked permission to

file an amendment to their answer, which was denied. Of this they now complain. We need not consider the question thus raised, as the cause must be, for the error just pointed out, reversed and remanded for a new trial. The defendants, before the next trial, will have the opportunity and right to amend their answer in order to present whatever defense they may plead.

Other questions raised upon plaintiff's appeal, involving mainly rulings upon the admission of evidence, do not now demand consideration, for the reason that they may not arise upon the new trial.

IV. The verdict was for $1,500. This the district court reduced to $1,200, and rendered judgment for that sum. From this ruling the plaintiff appeals. It is plainly erroneous, the district court having no authority to render judgment for a less amount than the verdict.

2. VERDICT: damages: power of court to reduce.

The judgment is reversed upon both appeals, and is remanded to the court below for a new trial.

REVERSED.

ADAMS, CH. J., (*dissenting*.) In the view which I take of the evidence, the instruction in question is applicable to it, and correct.

PUMPHREY v. WALKER.

1. **Practice**: WAIVER OF ERROR BY PROCEEDING. Where plaintiff's petition had been dismissed, and he filed an amended petition, which defendant moved to strike from the files, but his motion was overruled, *held* that he waived the error, if any, in the overruling of the motion, by filing an answer to the amended petition and going to trial on the issues thus raised.

2. **Verdict**: EVIDENCE: PRIVATE KNOWLEDGE OF JURORS EXCLUDED. Where the uncontradicted and unimpeached testimony of defendant established a good defense pleaded by him to the note in suit, a verdict for plaintiff should not have been allowed to stand on the ground that the jury was justified in rejecting defendant's testimony upon their personal knowledge of his unsavory reputation for truth and veracity.

Appeal from O'Brien District Court.

TUESDAY, MARCH 15.

ACTION upon a promissory note. There was a judgment upon a verdict for plaintiff. Defendant appeals.

Alfred Morton, for appellant.

P. R. Baily, for appellee.

BECK, J.—I.   The defendant moved the court to strike the petition from the files, and for judgment for costs. It is not necessary to state the grounds of the motion, as no exception was taken to the ruling thereon. The motion was sustained, and the following record of the ruling was made: "Now, to-wit, December 1, 1884, this cause coming on in regular order, the plaintiff appearing by Harley Day, her attorney, and defendant appearing for himself, defendant files motion to dismiss. Motion confessed, and sustained by the court." Afterwards plaintiff filed a substituted petition, which defendant moved to strike. He asked, in his motion, for judgment. It was overruled, and defendant excepts. Had defendant stopped here, he probably would have ground for reversing the action of the court in permitting a substituted petition to be filed in an action which had been dismissed; but he filed his answer to this substituted petition, and proceeded to the trial of the issues raised thereon. He cannot now insist that no action was pending when the substituted petition was filed, for he has recognized the existence of the action by appearing and pleading therein.

1. PRACTICE: waiver of error by proceeding.

II.   The answer set up as a defense to the action, was that the note was given for a span of horses purchased by defendant from the payee, who warranted the horses to be " sound, free from blemish, and true to work," that they were unsound, and one of them was balky and untrue, and that they wholly failed to comply with the warranty; and therefore defendant received

2. VERDICT: evidence: private knowledge of jurors excluded.

no consideration for the note.   Other defenses pleaded need
not be recited in the view we take of the case.   The note
was transferred by the payee after maturity.

The defense first stated was fully supported by the evidence of defendant, who testified positively, directly and
clearly to the contract of the warranty, and the failure of the
horses to comply therewith, and that the difference of their
value in the condition they were in when he purchased them,
and what it would have been if they had been sound, was
more than the amount of the note.   There is not one word
in the evidence contradicting defendant's testimony.   The
fact that the note was held for about seven years after it was
due without any effort to enforce its collection, and no
attempt to explain the delay, in some measure justifies the
conclusion that there was a defense to it.   There is an
indorsement showing payment of a part of the note before
maturity.   Defendant testifies that this payment was made
by him as a compromise or settlement, and that the payee
agreed that he would hold the note, and not "bother"
defendant any further in regard to it.   The evidence of
plaintiff as well as of defendant shows that, when requested
by plaintiff to pay the note, defendant stated that he had a
defense to it.   There is no evidence in conflict with defendant's testimony, and no attempt is made in any manner to
impeach him, or in any way to impair his testimony.   But
counsel for plaintiff, while admitting this, claim that the
jury were justified in rejecting defendant's evidence upon
their personal knowledge of his "unsavory reputation for
truth and veracity."   Surely we ought not to be required to
say, what is known to every citizen, that cases are tried in
our courts upon the evidence adduced by the parties, and not
upon the private knowledge or prejudice of the jurors; and
that, when a witness whose sufficient intelligence is manifest
testifies, his evidence must be accepted, unless he be contradicted or impeached by evidence in the case, or his statements

are improbable in view of other testimony in the case, or are impossible in the nature of things.

In our opinion, the district court erred in overruling defendant's motion to set aside the verdict on the ground that the defense to the note was established without any conflicting evidence.

REVERSED.

THE STATE v. STERRETT.

1. **Criminal Evidence**: GOOD CHARACTER OF DEFENDANT: REBUTTAL. Where the defendant has introduced evidence of his good character, the state, in rebuttal, is confined to general evidence that his character is not good in the particular in question, and evidence of particular acts indicative of bad character must be excluded. (*State v. Gordon*, 3 Iowa, 410, followed.)

2. ———: MURDER: OTHER MURDERS IN THE NEIGHBORHOOD. On a trial for murder, it was error to allow the district attorney, on the cross-examination of a witness, to inquire whether there had not been other murders committed in defendant's neighborhood.

3. ———: DEFENDANT'S OWN TESTIMONY: INTEREST: INSTRUCTION. A defendant who testifies on his own behalf, when on trial on a criminal charge, is necessarily an interested witness, and there can be no error in directing the jury to consider that fact in determining the weight which should be given to his testimony.

Appeal from Louisa District Court.

TUESDAY, MARCH 15.

THE defendant was convicted of the crime of manslaughter, and sentenced to a term of imprisonment in the penitentiary.

Newman & Blake, for defendant.

A. J. Baker, Attorney-general, for the State.

REED, J.—This case has once before been in this court. See 68 Iowa, 76. The circumstances of the occurrence in question, as shown by the evidence given on the first trial, are set out in the opinion. The evidence on the second trial was not materially different, and there is no necessity for a restatement of the facts.

I. The defendant introduced evidence which tended to prove that his character as a peaceable, orderly and law-abid-

1. CRIMINAL evidence: good charac- ter of defend- ant: rebuttal. ing person, before the occurrence, had been good. The state, in rebuttal, was permitted, against defendant's objection, to introduce evidence tending to prove that he had previously been involved in personal difficulties, and that on one occasion he had threatened to shoot a person with whom he had had a difficulty. The court erred in admitting this evidence. *State v. Gordon*, 3 Iowa, 410. The reasons of the rule which excludes evidence of this character are fully stated in that case, and need not be repeated.

II. The district attorney was permitted, on the cross-examination of a witness, to ask him whether there had not

2. ——: mur- der : other murders in the neighbor- hood. been a number of murders committed in the neighborhood in which defendant lived, and he inquired particularly whether the witness did not know of the murder of a Swede in that neighborhood a short time before the occurrence in question. The testimony of the witness, as set out in the abstract, is very brief, and the connection in which these questions were asked is not shown, and we are not able to determine what object the district attorney had in view when he asked them; but we cannot conceive of any state of the case in which they would be competent. The defendant had the right to have the case tried and determined upon the evidence which related to the occurrence upon which the charge in the indictment was based. The question related to occurrences having no relation to that, and the evidence elicited could hardly fail to be prejudicial to him.

III. Defendant was a witness in his own behalf, and the

court gave the following instruction, to which exception is
taken: "Under our law, a person charged with
a crime may testify in his own behalf, and
defendant has availed himself of this privilege;
and, in determining the question of his guilt or innocence,
you must consider his testimony. He testifies as an interested witness, and from an interested stand-point, and as such
you should consider his testimony; and when you do this,
with all the surrounding circumstances developed by the evidence, give the testimony such weight, in connection with
other evidence in the case, as you think it entitled to, and no
more." The objection urged by counsel against this instruction is, that it throws discredit on the testimony of the witness. Their argument is that, as defendant is a competent
witness, his testimony is to be weighed and tested by the
same rules that are applied to the testimony of other witnesses, and that it was for the jury, and not the court, to say
whether its weight and credit was impaired by the fact of
his interest. We admit the correctness of the premises.
There are no rules specially applicable to a witness in that
position, but his testimony is to be tested by the general
rules which are applicable to all witnesses; and it is always
the province of the jury to determine what weight and credit
should be given to the testimony. But the instruction does
not invade that province of the jury. It leaves it to them
to determine what credit should be given to his testimony
after considering the fact of his interest. But the fact that
some interest of the witness is at stake may always be considered in weighing his testimony. If there is a question as
to whether he is an interested witness, that question should
be submitted to the jury; but, if there is no question as to
the facts, the court may properly instruct the jury on the
assumption that the interest exists, and may tell them that
it should be considered in weighing the testimony. Now,
the defendant in a criminal case who testifies in his own
behalf is always an interested witness. It is impossible that

Marginal note: 3. ——: defendant's own
testimony: in-
terest: in-
struction.

it should be otherwise, and there can be no case in which it would not be proper for the jury to consider that fact in weighing his testimony. The court, therefore, properly assumed the existence of the fact, and directed the jury to consider it in determining the weight which should be given to defendant's testimony.

Exceptions are taken also to certain instructions given by the district court on the right of self-defense. These instructions, however, are in accord with the views expressed by this court on the former appeal, and the questions demand no fur- ther discussion.

REVERSED.

BALDWIN v. FOSS.

1. **Payment:** OF FRAUDULENT NOTE: RECOVERY: PLEADING. One who seeks to recover money paid by him on a note, on the ground that the note was fraudulent, must plead and show that the payment was made under a mistake of fact, or that he did not have knowledge of the fraud at the time the payment was made. (*Murphy v Creighton*, 45 Iowa, 179, and *City of Muscatine v. Keokuk, etc., Packet Co.*, Id., 85, followed.)

2. **Appeal:** FROM ORDER REFUSING NEW TRIAL. Under § 3164, of the Code, an appeal may be taken where the court refuses a new trial, whether jugment has been rendered on the verdict or not.

3. **Practice on Appeal:** PROLIX RECORD: COSTS. Where the appellant prints and files the evidence without abstracting it, the costs of the superfluous printing will be taxed to him, even though he prevails on the appeal.

Appeal from Shelby District Court.

TUESDAY, MARCH 15.

ACTION AT LAW. The facts are stated in the opinion.

P. Wicks, for appellant.

John Wallace, for appellee.

SEEVERS, J.--I. The petition states, in substance, that the

defendant undertook and agreed to procure a loan for the

1. PAYMENT: of fraudulent note: recovery: pleading. plaintiff, to be secured by mortgage on real estate, for a consideration agreed upon; that said real estate was incumbered by liens and judgments, and that the loan to be so procured was not sufficient to pay the same; that the defendant undertook and agreed, for a sufficient consideration, to effect a settlement of said liens and judgments, and to advance and loan the plaintiff sufficient money, in addition to the loan, to accomplish such purpose; that defendant procured the loan, and represented that, in addition thereto, he had advanced, for the purpose of paying said liens, the sum of $367.66, for which the plaintiff executed his note to the defendant; that said representations were false, and made with the intent to cheat and defraud the plaintiff, and that the defendant well knew such representations to be false and fraudulent; that the defendant in truth and in fact only advanced for the plaintiff $165.95; that the plaintiff has fully paid said note, and therefore he asks to recover the difference between the amount actually advanced and the amount paid. There was a denial of the allegations of the petition. Upon the coming in of the verdict for the plaintiff, the defendant moved for a new trial upon several grounds, and afterwards moved to arrest the judgment, upon the ground that no cause of action was stated in the petition,

It will be observed that the petition fails to state that the note was paid under a mistake of fact, or that the plaintiff did not have knowledge of the fraud at the time the note was paid. For aught that is alleged in the petition, the plaintiff may have paid the note with full knowledge of the facts, and it is upon this ground the motion in arrest of judgment is based. No objection was made to the sufficiency of the petition by motion, demurrer or answer, and it is possible the objection now urged should be deemed waived. Code, §§ 2648, 2650. For the purposes of this case, this will be conceded, and therefore the motion in arrest of judgment, it will be conceded, was properly overruled. While this is true, it is also true that plaintiff's right to recover must depend on the question whether the note was paid under a mistake of fact. The note, it may be conceded, was fraudulently procured, but the plaintiff was in no respect damaged by such fraud until he paid the note. If the note was voluntarily paid, with full knowledge of all the facts, then the plaintiff is not entitled to recover. *Murphy v. Creighton*, 45 Iowa, 179; *City of Muscatine v. Keokuk Northern Line Packet Co.*, Id., 185.

The defendant asked the court to instruct the jury as follows: "When one pays money on an alleged claim against him, he is forever precluded from saying he did not owe it, if he paid it under no mistake of fact, and if the party receiving it made use of no illegal means to coerce the payment. In such case, if a party would resist such unjust demand, he must do so at the threshold. The parties treat with each other on equal terms; and, if litigation is intended by the party of whom the money is demanded, it should precede the payment. A party cannot voluntarily pay money in satisfaction or discharge of a demand unjustly made on him, and afterwards recover back the money, even though he should at the time protest that he was not bound to pay the same." This instruction was refused. It, or one substantially like it, should have been given, and the cases above cited so hold. There was evidence upon which the instruction could be based. Therefore, the court erred in overruling the motion for a new trial.

II. Although no such motion has been filed, counsel for the appellee insist in argument that the appeal should be dismissed, for the reason, as we infer, that no appeal

2. APPEAL: from order refusing new trial.

lies from the refusal of the court to grant a new trial where the abstract fails to show that any judgment has been rendered on the verdict. But the statute expressly provides that an appeal may be taken where the court refuses a new trial. Code, § 3164. Such refusal must, under the statute, be regarded as prejudicial error, if the refusal is erroneous.

III. The abstract contains 135 printed pages, and the evidence is not abstracted, but is set out in the abstract in full, as the questions were asked and answered.

3. PRACTICE on appeal: prolix record: costs. Much of the evidence is immaterial, and consists of mere repetitions. Such an abstract cannot be regarded as a compliance with the rules of this court. One hundred and fourteen pages of the abstract contain the evidence as thus set out. The appellee moves the court to tax the costs of the abstract to the appellant. The motion must be sustained, to the extent of taxing the cost of printing 114 pages of the abstract to the appellant.

REVERSED.

---

1 392
490
392
350

MILLER v. SEAL ET AL.

1. **Mechanic's Lien**: PRIOR MORTGAGE: SEPARATE SALE OF IMPROVE-MENT: APPORTIONMENT OF PROCEEDS. Where there was a prior mortgage on the farm on which a new dwelling house was erected, for the materials for which plaintiff claimed the establishment of a mechanic's lien, and the house was securely built on a stone foundation, and covered a cellar suitable for its purpose, and it was stipulated that the land was not worth enough to pay both plaintiff and the mortgagee, but it did not appear what the land and improvement together were worth. *held* that the court below did not abuse the discretion vested in it by Chap. 100, § 9, par. 4, Laws of 1876, in refusing to order the sep-arate sale and removal of the dwelling for the satisfaction of plaintiff's lien; and that, under the doctrine of *German Bank v. Schloth*, 59 Iowa, 316, and *Curtis v. Broadwell*, 66 Id., 662, the court properly decreed the mortgage to be a first lien on the whole property, and ordered a fore-closure sale accordingly.

Appeal from Black Hawk District Court.

TUESDAY, MARCH 15.

ACTION to foreclose a mechanic's lien for lumber fur-nished in the erection of a dwelling-house. From a time prior to that when the lumber was furnished, the defendant Lydia G. Seal had a recorded mortgage upon the land. The court decreed her mortgage to be paramount to the plaintiff's lien, not only as to the land, but as to the building for which the lumber was furnished. The plaintiff appeals.

Platt & Hoff, for appellant.

Alford & Gates, for appellees.

ADAMS, CH. J.—The defendant Seal filed a cross-petition asking for the foreclosure of her mortgage. The court granted a decree of foreclosure, and directed that the property be sold upon execution. The plaintiff insists that the court should have allowed the building for which the lumber was furnished to be sold and removed, and the proceeds to be applied first in payment of his debt. The statute upon which he relies may be found in Miller's Code, 577, and is as follows: "If such material was furnished, or labor performed, in the erection or construction of an original and independent building, erection or other improvement, commenced since the attaching or execution of such prior lien, incumbrance or mortgage, the court may, in its discretion, order and direct such building, erection or improvement to be separately sold under execution, and the purchaser may remove the same within such reasonable time as the court may fix."

The case seems to have been submitted upon a stipulation as to the facts. That part of the stipulation upon which the plaintiff relies, to show his right to a sale and removal of the house, is as follows: "After the execution and filing of said mortgage, the defendant Azza Brown (the owner of the land) purchased of Miller & Jackson, lumber merchants, certain material with which to erect an independent structure upon the first described property, which said structure consists of a dwelling-house securely builded upon a stone foundation, and covering a cellar suitable for its purpose; said house being so fastened upon and to the realty as to constitute a fixture thereupon."

It is evident that a sale and removal of a building would often, if not ordinarily, result in a sacrifice of property.

The house in question appears to have been newly built, and we may assume, in the absence of evidence to the contrary, that it was prudently built, and adapted to the needs of the farm.   Such a building could not ordinarily bɔ sold and removed without a loss, and this would be especially so if the building was built of brick, as this may have been, so far as the evidence shows.   The court could not properly have made the order for which the plaintiff contends without due regard to the loss, if any, which would be involved, and without it was necessary to enable the holder of a mechanic's lien to obtain payment of his claim.   If the land and improvements are of such value that the sale of them together would yield enough to pay both the plaintiff and mortgagee, they should manifestly be sold together.   As to the value of the land and improvements, there is no evidence.   It is stipulated that the land is not worth enough to pay both plaintiff and mortgagee, and that is all we know.   The burden is upon the plaintiff to adduce sufficient evidence to show that the sale and removal of the building would be proper, in view of all the circumstances of the case.   The evidence fails to satisfy us.   We do not discover from it that the discretion vested in the court below was not wisely exercised.

Whether there should have been a decree that, upon the sale of the property, there should be an apportionment and distribution of the proceeds between the plaintiff and mortgagee, is a question upon which there might be some doubt. if we could regard the question as an open one.   But we do not think that we can.   It appears to us to have been settled in *German Bank v. Scholth*, 59 Iowa, 316, and *Curtis v. Broadwell*, 66 Id., 662.   The construction adopted in those cases is assailed; but where the different parts of a statute, like the one in question, are inconsistent with each other, no ruling can be made that will not be open to objection.   The court evidently attempted to follow the ruling in those cases, and we think that the judgment must be

AFFIRMED.

POLK ET AL. V. STURGEON ET AL.

1. **Practice on Appeal**: TRIAL DE NOVO: CERTIFICATION OF EVIDENCE.
A trial *de novo* cannot be had in this court unless it affirmatively appears by the certificate of the trial judge, in some form, that the evidence set out in the abstract is all the evidence which was offered or introduced on the trial.

Appeal from Carroll Circuit Court.

TUESDAY, MARCH 15.

THIS is an action in equity by which the plaintiffs seek to redeem certain land from a tax sale. There was a decree in the circuit court for the plaintiffs. Defendants appeal.

Geo. W. Paine, for appellants.

Whiting S. Clark and *Joseph H. Call*, for appellees.

ROTHROCK, J.—The case is here for trial *de novo*, if triable at all. Counsel for appellees insist that the appeal cannot be entertained because the evidence has not been certified to as required by section 2742 of the Code. The abstract recites that the action " came on for trial, and was submitted to the court on the pleadings and the following written stipulation of the parties." Certain stipulations, signed by counsel for the parties, are set out in the abstract immediately following the above recital. It is not stated in the abstract that the stipulation was filed. The decree recites that the cause was " submitted on the petition and answers filed herein, and the exhibits attached thereto, and the agreed statement of facts filed therein." The decree was signed by the judge, and, if it contained the proper recitals to identify all of the evidence which was introduced or offered on the trial, it may be that no other certificate would be necessary. But it does not recite affirmatively that the stipulation was all the evidence which was offered or introduced on the trial. We have frequently held that such a certificate is necessary in order to entitle the appellant to a new trial in this court.

We think the appeal must be　　　　　　　　　DISMISSED.

LAUB v. TROWBRIDGE, ADM'R.

1. **Estoppel**: CLAIM AGAINST INSOLVENT ESTATE: ACTS OF ADMINISTRA-
TOR. Plaintiff was a creditor of defendant's intestate, who died leaving no property except such as was exempt to his widow. Defendant,
however, sold some of the widow's property, and carelessly took a note
therefor to himself as administrator, on which he afterwards recovered
judgment in his own name, as administrator, which he afterwards collected. Afterwards defendant filed a report,—the first record made by
him in the case,—showing that the decedent left no property with which
to pay debts, and asking to be discharged. Plaintiff, however, knowing
of the said judgment in favor of the administrator, appeared by counsel
and filed objections to the report, and there was a trial of the issues
raised, and judgment was rendered against defendant and the sureties
on his bond for the amount of plaintiff's claim against the estate, and
this was done upon the ground that defendant, by taking said note and
judgment in his own name, misled plaintiff into the expense of employing counsel, etc., in the belief that there were assets of the estate, and
that defendant was thereby estopped from denying the existence of assets
to the extent of the value of the judgment. But *held* that this conduct
did not constitute an estoppel.

Appeal from Ida Circuit Court.

TUESDAY, MARCH 15.

THE defendant was appointed administrator of the estate
of James Dunham, deceased, on the eleventh day of January, 1875. On the twentieth day of September, 1882, he
filed a report as administrator, and asked that it be approved,
and that he be discharged. The plaintiff is a creditor of the
estate, and he filed objections to the report. The defendant
was cited to appear for examination touching his administration of the estate. The examination was had, further
pleadings were filed, witnesses were called and examined,
and a judgment was rendered against the defendant and the
sureties on his bond for the amount of the plaintiff's claim
against the estate. Defendant appeals.

Smith & Cullison, for appellant.

Shaw & Kuehnle and *Rollins & Frink*, for appellee.

ROTHROCK, J.—The circuit court made a written statement of the facts found, and the conclusions of law upon
which the judgment against the defendant was founded
That part of the statement necessary to be considered is as
follows:

"And the court further finds that the said administrator
never made and filed an inventory of the property belonging
to said estate, and that he never filed any report of his doings
therein, other than the one of date September 20, 1882
The court further finds that there is and was no property
belonging to said estate, except such as was exempt from
execution, and as belonging to the widow of the deceased.
But the court finds that the administrator should pay the
notes of the plaintiff for the reason, principally, as follows:
The court finds that the administrator was negligent in failing to file an inventory and report, and that he carelessly
took a note in his name as administrator, and had the same
put in judgment in Crawford county in the name of E. J.
Trowbridge, administrator; and, there being no records and
reports of his doings as administrator of said estate, whereby
the plaintiff could ascertain the condition of said estate, and
it further appearing that the plaintiff ascertained the existence of the judgment in question, and the payment of same
to the administrator by the judgment defendant, and believing therefrom that the administrator had funds in his hands
with which he should pay plaintiff's claim, and the plaintiff
believing, and, as the court thinks, having reason to believe,
that there were funds with which to pay the plaintiff's
claim, the plaintiff went to the expense of employing attorneys at an expense, and at an expense of his own time, to
compel the administrator to pay the claim as required of
him by law.

"Now, upon the plaintiff causing the defendant to make a
report of his doings, and as to the condition of said estate,
the court finds that the administrator took a team of horses
of the widow, which was hers by virtue of the statute, as

belonging to the widow of the deceased, and sold the said horses, taking a note in the name of E. J. Trowbridge, administrator, for $300, and caused the said note to be put in judgment in the name of E. J. Trowbridge, administrator, and collected said judgment, and paid the same to the widow.

"The court finds that the plaintiff had no knowledge of the interest of the widow in said judgment until after he had been to the trouble and expense in the manner and form as before stated. Wherefore, the court finds, as a matter of law, under the circumstances of this case, as shown in evidence, that the administrator is estopped, so far as the claim of the plaintiff is concerned, from claiming that the $300 and interest received on said judgment does not belong to the estate."

It will be observed that the court held that the defendant was liable on the ground of estoppel. It is apparent that there would be no liability on any other ground, for, if the defendant must pay this claim, it is clear gain to the plaintiff, and a personal loss to the defendant. When Dunham died, this claim against the estate was absolutely worthless. The question to be determined is, did the fact that defendant took the note for the property of the widow in his name as administrator, and collected it as administrator, so mislead the plaintiff that the defendant should be precluded from showing the real facts of the transaction? It is not claimed that the defendant made any personal representation or statement to the plaintiff in regard to the assets of the estate. The plaintiff claims that he was misled by the record of the judgment, showing that the administrator had collected assets of the estate which should be applied to the payment of his claim, and that, relying on that fact, he was induced to change his situation by employing counsel to compel the defendant to pay his claim. What was done by his attorneys to procure the defendant to file the report does not very clearly appear, more than that a citation was issued. The report as filed, which is 'the first record in this case, sets forth, in terms which are so plain as to be incapable of being misunderstood, that the decedent left no property except such as was exempt to the widow. It is true, the report did not set forth the reason why the defendant took the note payable to himself as administrator, and took judgment thereon in his name as administrator. But the plaintiff was fully advised by the report that there never had been any assets of the estate with which to pay his claim. He could not after that incur expense, change his situation by litigation, and make such acts the ground of an estoppel, because, if he had made inquiry, he would have learned the real facts. The evidence shows that one of his attorneys knew all about the facts when he employed him. Whether this knowledge should be imputed to the plaintiff we need not determine, because we think that the other established facts in the case do not estop the defendant from showing the real condition of the estate.

It will be observed that the plaintiff's only act, based upon the taking of the note by the defendant, was to employ counsel to collect his debt. He was not induced by any act of the defendant to purchase a claim against the estate. He did not in any manner change his situation, further than to procure the defendant to make a report, and from that time forward he had notice that there were no assets with which to pay his claim. If he had been induced by an examination of the judgment to purchase a claim against the estate, there might be some ground for holding that the defendant should be estopped from showing that the proceeds of the judgment belonged to the widow. It is not shown that because of this judgment, and in reliance thereon, plaintiff refrained or neglected to prosecute his claim against other property, or to avail himself of other means to collect the same. So far as his original claim is concerned, he is in no worse position than he would be if the defendant had not taken and collected the note for the exempt property. The most that can be claimed from the facts is that the plaintiff, when he ascertained that the note had been taken and judgment rendered in the name of the defendant, conceived the idea that the defendant had made himself liable to pay the debts of the estate, and he employed counsel to collect what was, before that, a worthless claim.

We think that a little attention to the law of estoppel by the acts of the parties will demonstrate that the plaintiff is in no position to be profited by any act of the defendant. It is a fundamental rule of the law of estoppel *in pais*, as expressed in *Lucas v. Hart*, 5 Iowa, 419, that, " the estoppel is allowed to prevent fraud and injustice, and exists wherever a party cannot, in good conscience, gainsay his own acts or assertions." In other words, the acts and admissions of a party operate against him where, in good conscience and honest dealing, he ought not to be permitted to gainsay them. The facts in cases of this kind, to be sufficient to authorize the application of the law of estoppel, always involve bad faith on the part of the party sought to be estopped from showing the truth.

In Bigelow on Estoppel, 543, in speaking of estoppel by conduct, or equitable estoppel, it is said: " In its most common phase, this estoppel is founded on deceit, and has its justification in the duty of courts to prevent the accomplishment of fraud. The same rule applies whether the application of the doctrine be sought in a court of chancery or of law." Applying this fundamental principle to the facts of this case, it strikes the mind at once that the defendant ought not to be compelled to pay this claim. It may be said that he ought not to have taken the note and judgment in his own name as administrator. But there is no evidence that any creditor of the estate was prejudiced thereby, further than that the plaintiff believed that by that act the defendant's mouth was closed, and he could not be permitted to show that there were no assets of the estate, and a claim against the estate which was absolutely worthless had become collectible.   The facts do not authorize the conclusion that justice, good conscience and the prevention of fraud require that the defendant should pay this debt.

REVERSED.

71   401
102   309
71   ·401
108   389

HARLE, HAAS & CO. ET AL. V. THE COUNCIL BLUFFS INS. CO.

1. **Fire Insurance:** FAILURE TO PAY PREMIUM NOTE: FORFEITURE: WAIVER: AGENCY: FRAUD. The policy in question provided that the company should not be liable for any loss accruing while any premium note remained overdue and unpaid. The policy would be forfeited unless a premium note was paid by May 15. The insured lived at K., and was postmaster there, but the company did not know that he was postmaster. There being no bank at K., the company, according to its custom in such cases, sent the note, on the 7th of May, to the postmaster for collection. On the 25th of May, the postmaster, in the presence of two witnesses, took the note out of the safe and destroyed it, and put in its place the amount of money necessary to pay it. On the next day the loss occurred. On the 3d of the following June he wrote to the company enclosing the identical money which he had deposited in the safe, which the company received and retained in payment of the note. He did not sign his name to the letter, but subscribed himself simply "Postmaster, K, Iowa." The company did not at this time know that a loss had occurred. *Held—*

> (1) That the policy was forfeited on the 15th of May by the non-payment of the note at that time.

> (2) That, although the company sent the note to the postmaster for collection, yet, since the postmaster and the insured were identical, the law will not regard him as the agent of the company to make a collection from himself; and that his act in taking payment from himself after the forfeiture of the policy was not binding on the company, and was not a waiver by the company of the forfeiture.

> (3) That the conduct of the insured amounted to a fraud, from which the law will not allow him to reap a benefit.

Appeal from Pottawattamie District Court.

TUESDAY, MARCH 15.

ACTION on a policy of insurance against loss by fire, issued by the defendant to one French, who, after the loss, assigned

VOL. LXXI—26

his right of action to the plaintiffs.   The defendant pleaded
that the premium was not paid in cash, but that the insured
gave two notes therefor, and that the policy provides " that
no insurance, whether original or continued, shall be considered as binding until the actual payment of the premiums;
nor shall this company be liable for any loss under this policy occurring when any note, or any part thereof, given for
a part or whole of the premium, shall be due and unpaid.'
The defendant further pleaded that the note first falling due
had been paid, and that the defendant had given the notice
required by statute, but that said French had failed to pay
the second note, and that the same was due and unpaid at
the time the loss occurred.   Trial to the court, judgment for
the plaintiffs, and the defendant appeals.

   Sapp & Pusey, for appellant.

   Wright, Baldwin & Haldane, for appellees.

   SEEVERS, J.—This action was submitted to the court upon
an agreed statement of facts, the material portions of which
are as follows: The note was due on the first day of April,
1884.   On the first day of March, 1884, the defendant notified French in writing that the note would fall due at the
time above stated, and that, unless it was paid in thirty days,
said policy would be suspended.   On the fourteenth day of
April, 1884, the defendant notified French that "said note
had become due April 1, 1884; that, unless it was paid
within thirty days from the date of said notice, said policy
would be suspended; and in said notice also informed him
of the customary short rate and expenses of said policy up
to the maturity of said note;" which notice "was received
by French on the fifteenth day of April, 1884."   The notice
is attached to and made a part of the statement of facts.

   The property insured was in Kirkman, and French resided
there, and was postmaster.   There was no bank at Kirkman, and it was the custom and usage of the defendant in

such case to send notes for collection to the postmaster. On May 7, 1884, the defendant forwarded the note to the post-master at Kirkman for collection, with instructions to collect the same, and to explain to the party holding the policy that it was suspended. At said time French was such postmaster, (but the defendant did not know this fact,) and as such received the note. The loss occurred on May 26, 1884, and on the preceding day French took the note out of his safe in his store in which he had deposited it for safe-keeping, and "can-celed the same, and tore off his signature thereto, and in place thereof deposited in said safe, in the same compartment where he kept said note, and separate and apart from his other money, the exact amount in money necessary to pay his said note which he had canceled." This was done in the presence of two witnesses, to whom, at the time of so doing, French said: "Well, there is another note paid."

On the third day of June, 1884, French, "in a letter written by him to the defendant, forwarded the identical money which he had deposited in his safe to the defendant in payment of his note, which the defendant received in pay-ment thereof, and has since retained;" but defendant did not know that the property insured had been destroyed, or of the acts and declarations of French, made when the note was canceled. A copy of the letter inclosing the money is attached to and made a part of the statement of facts.

I. The first question discussed by counsel is, whether the defendant, in sending the note for collection, made French its agent, so that it is bound by his acts, declarations and pay-ment made to himself. It will be observed that the note was sent to the postmaster, and a large discretion was reposed in him, for he was directed to employ the same means to col-lect the note "you would if it were your own." French being such postmaster, the note came into his possession, and the plaintiffs claim that he paid it to himself prior to the loss. It is a fundamental rule that, where a discretion is reposed in one person by another, the former cannot, at the same time, perform the duty incumbent on him as the agent of the latter, and act for himself as principal. In such case he has antagonistic duties to fulfill, and the rights of his principal must necessarily conflict with his individual rights. In this case he might well conclude, as agent, to postpone all efforts to enforce payment of the note until he, as the maker, became insolvent. The thirty days' notice required by the statute expired on May 15th, and the claimed payment was made on the twenty-fifth of the same month. Between these dates the policy was suspended, and, if a loss had occurred, it must be conceded, we think, that there could not have been a recovery. The payment, if such it is conceded to be, would amount to a waiver. If French was the agent of the defendant, we are not prepared to say that he would not have such power.

The law will not permit a man to occupy such inconsistent positions, or represent such antagonistic rights, or perform such duties. Story, Ag. §§ 210, 212: French had no authority to determine that he would waive the suspension of the policy. He, in fact, could not do so. For this purpose he was not the agent of defendant. Therefore, the defendant is not bound by the payment made by French to himself, or by his acts and declarations at that time. The inquiry, it seems to us, is pertinent, why French did not at that time do what he afterwards did,—forward the money to the defendant.

II. The condition in the policy upon which the defendant relies is valid, and cannot be disregarded except as provided by statute. *Watrous v. Mississippi Valley Ins. Co.*, 35 Iowa, 582; *Garlick v. Same*, 44 Id., 553. The statute simply provides that the condition shall not take effect until thirty days after a specified notice has been served. Chapter 210, Laws Eighteenth Gen. Assem.

To our minds, several exceedingly technical objections are made as to the sufficiency of the notice under the statute. We shall not stop to discuss them; deeming it sufficient to say that the notice is, in all respects, sufficient, and is clearly, in our opinion, a substantial compliance with the statute.

III. Eight days after the loss French forwarded money sufficient to pay the note to the defendant, which it received. At that time defendant had no knowledge of the loss, nor did it know that the money was forwarded by French. The letter inclosing it was signed " POSTMASTER, Kirkman, Iowa." Because of the non-payment of the note on or before May 15, 1884, the policy was suspended after that date. It is perfectly clear, we think, that the receipt of .the money, and its retention under the circumstances, could not amount to a waiver, or reinstate the policy in force as a binding contract of insurance. The policy had lapsed solely through the fault and neglect of French. The property had been destroyed. The subject matter of the contract was not in existence. This French knew, but the defendant did not. It received the money under a mistake of fact. Good faith and fair dealing on the part of French required that he should have notified the defendant that the property had been destroyed, and we think his suppression of such fact amounted to a fraud; and, as no one can be permitted to reap a benefit through or by means of a fraud perpetrated by him, therefore plaintiffs cannot recover. But the failure of French to pay the premium had the effect to render the policy void, so far as the right to recover thereon is concerned. The defendant has done nothing to avoid the contract, but has been ready at all times to perform it. In principle this case is like *Harris v. Royal Canadian Ins. Co.*, 53 Iowa, 236. See, also, *Pritchard v. Merchants' & Tradesman's Mut. Life Assur. Soc.*, 3 O. B. (N. S.) 622.

It may be proper to say that at least a portion of the premium had been earned, and whether the plaintiffs are entitled to recover any portion thereof is not an issue in this case.

The district court erred in rendering judgment for the plaintiffs upon the facts as stipulated. The judgment should have been for the defendant. REVERSED.

SAX & BROS. v. DAVIS.

1. **Agency:** EVIDENCE OF: DECLARATIONS OF AGENT. The fact of agency cannot be established by the declarations of the alleged agent, whether made to the person seeking to establish the agency, or to a third party; and where the question of agency is the point in issue, such declarations are inadmissible for any purpose, even when the trial is to the court, in an ordinary action.

2. **Deposition:** OF WITNESS IN COUNTY: ABILITY TO ATTEND COURT: SHOWING. Where the deposition of a witness for plaintiff, residing in the county, was taken only a short time before the term at which it was expected the case would be tried, on the ground that he would not be able to attend at that term on account of sickness, but defendant then objected to the taking of the deposition, and the case was not in fact tried till a year later, *held* that it was error to allow the deposition to be read at the trial, against defendant's objection, without a showing that the witness was then unable to be present in court. (*Nevan v. Roup*, 8 Iowa, 207, and *Cook v. Blair*, 50 Id., 128, distinguished.)

Appeal from Van Buren District Court.

TUESDAY, MARCH 15.

THIS is an action upon an account for goods and merchandise alleged to have been sold by the plaintiffs to the defendant. The defendant denied that the plaintiffs sold any goods to him, or on his credit. There was a trial by the circuit court without a jury, and a judgment was rendered for the plaintiffs. The defendant appeals.

S. S. Caruthers, for appellant.

Sloan, Work & Brown, for appellees.

ROTHROOK, J.—I. It appears from the evidence that the defendant is the owner of a large farm, situated partly in Van Buren county. He is a non-resident of the state, and seldom visits his farm, and it has been managed and conducted by others. The plaintiffs are merchants in business at the city of Ottumwa. They claim that one T. J. Davis was the agent of the defendant in the management of the farm, and that they

delivered the goods which make up their account to
said agent, and that they are properly chargeable to the
defendant. In order to sustain the action, it was necessary
for the plaintiffs to prove that T. J. Davis was authorized by
the defendant to purchase the goods on the defendant's credit.
The books of the plaintiffs were introduced in evidence. It
appeared therefrom that the items of the account were charged
to T. J. Davis, and not to the defendant. So far, then, as
appeared from the face of the account in the books, credit
was not given to the defendant. But the plaintiffs sought to
prove that the credit was actually given to the defendant,
notwithstanding the manner in which the books were kept.
It appears that one Isaac Nelson managed the farm for several years for the defendant. The defendant claimed that
Nelson was manager at the time the account accrued. The
plaintiffs contended that T. J. Davis was manager at that time.

The following is part of the testimony of one of the
plaintiffs, and the rulings of the court thereon: "*Question
14.* You may state what was said to you about this time by
Isaac Nelson as to what you should do in letting him [T. J.
Davis] have such goods as he desired when he came to your
store. [Objected to by defendant as incompetent, immaterial,
and hearsay.] *Court.* The objections are overruled, and the
testimony is received, not as showing liability on the part of
defendant, but to show under what circumstances plaintiffs
furnished T. J. Davis with goods. [The ruling of the court
excepted to by defendant.] *Answer.* Mr. Nelson said that
anything that T. J. Davis wanted would be all right; that he
[Nelson] was getting too old; and that T. J. Davis' father
was going to let T. J. Davis act as his agent on the farm.
Q. 15. I will ask you what T. J. Davis said to you at any
time about who he was getting the goods for, and who was to
finally pay for them. [Defendant makes the same objections
to this question as made to last preceding one. Same ruling
thereon by the court as made on said objection, and defendant excepted to said ruling.] *A.* Why, he got some goods

for himself, and at different times he got goods for hands that he said were working on his father's place; and in regard to payments he told me several times that he had spent so much money on the place, and that he had incurred expenditure ordered by his father; and at other times he said he had money coming from his father, and he wanted to pay when he got the money from him."

We think this evidence should have been excluded. It is true, the cause was tried to the court without a jury, but the consideration by the court of incompetent evidence in determining the case is as objectionable as if submitted to a jury. The fact that the court received the evidence, not as showing liability on the part of the defendant, but to show under what circumstances the goods were furnished to T. J. Davis, does not, in our judgment, cure the error. The witness was not confined to the circumstances under which the goods were furnished, but he was permitted to state that which, if competent, proved, not only the agency of T. J. Davis, but his authority to purchase the goods on the credit of the defendant. It is scarcely necessary to say that the evidence as to the statements of Nelson is the merest hearsay, and it was not competent to prove the agency by the declarations of the alleged agent. It was, perhaps, competent for the witness to state that T. J. Davis was residing on the farm when the goods were furnished, and the capacity in which he appeared to be acting; but his statements, and the statements of Nelson showing his authority to purchase goods on the defendant's account, are more than the mere circumstances under which the goods were bought.

II. The cause was tried in the court below in the month of February, 1886. The deposition of Isaac Nelson was taken by the plaintiff in January, 1885. The witness is a resident of Van Buren county. He stated in his deposition that he was seventy-four years old, was diseased, and had fallen from a load of hay three weeks before that, and was so injured that

2. DEPOSITON: of witness in county : ability to attend court : showing.

he was unable to leave his room until the day his deposition was taken, and that he did not expect to be able to attend the ne:.- term of court as a witness. The cause was not tried at the next term, and the plaintiffs offered the deposition in evidence at the trial. The defendant objected to the reading of the deposition, on the ground that it was taken about a year before, and that the witness was a resident of Van Buren county. The objection was overruled, and the deposition read in evidence without any showing of the inability of the witness to attend the term of court at which the trial was had. It appears from the deposition that on the day it was taken the witness was able to leave his house, and travel three miles to a village to have his deposition taken, and to visit the store in the village, and return to his house the same day, and the defendant at the time objected to the taking of the deposition. We think the plaintiff should have been required to show some reason why the witness was not present at the trial. It is true that a deposition of a witness residing in the county may be taken when, from any cause, it is expected that he may be unable to attend at the time of the trial. Code, § 3721. In this case, however, it was expected that the trial would take place in February, 1885, a very short time after the deposition was taken; and it does not appear from the deposition, nor elsewhere in the record, that any one expected the witness would not be able to attend court in a year after that time.

The plaintiffs' counsel cite us to the cases of *Nevan v. Roup*, 8 Iowa, 207, and *Cook v. Blair*, 50 Id., 128, as sustaining the ruling of the court below in admitting the deposition to be read in evidence. In the former case the witness was a non-resident of the state. This authorized the deposition to be taken. The objection to the deposition was that the witness stated therein that he expected to be in attendance at the next term of the court; but he was not in attendance. In the last named case the deposition was admitted in evidence because no objection was made to the deposition when it was taken. It appears to us that neither of the cited cases sustain the ruling of the district court in permitting this deposition to be read in evidence.

For the errors above pointed out, the judgment will be

REVERSED.

THE STATE v. THE CENTRAL IOWA R'Y CO. ET AL.

1. **Railroads**: RECEIVING AID BY TAXATION: OBLIGATION TO OPERATE WHOLE LINE: DUTY OF PURCHASER AT FORECLOSURE SALE. The Central Railroad of Iowa was a corporation organized for the purpose of building and operating a line of railway from the south line of the State of Iowa to the north line thereof. The proposed line terminated at Northwood, near the north line of the state. The township in which Northwood was situated was induced to vote a tax in aid of the construction of said road, which tax was collected and paid to said company. The road was afterwards constructed and operated by said company from Albia, in Monroe county, to Northwood, aforesaid. Afterwards the company became insolvent, and its property and franchises were sold under mortgage to the Central Iowa Railway Company, one of the defendants herein. Subsequently the Burlington, Cedar Rapids & Northern Railway Company, the other defendant herein, and which owned and operated a road to Manly Junction, a point on the road first above mentioned, about eleven miles south of Northwood, leased the line of said first named road from Manly Junction to Northwood, and thereafter the Central Iowa Railway Company ceased to operate that portion of its road, but made Manly Junction its northern *terminus*. Upon complaint of the people of Northwood to the railroad commissioners, said commissioners ordered and adjudged that the Central Iowa Railway Company was under legal obligations to equip, maintain and operate its road from Manly Junction to Northwood, and to do so as a part of, and in connection with, its continuous line between Albia and Northwood; and that a failure so to do was a violation of its charter duties and obligations, and contrary to law. *Held* that such order was reasonable and just, and should be enforced, on the grounds, (1) that, by accepting the tax from the township in which Northwood was situated, the original company incurred an obligation to operate its whole road to that place as one continuous line. (2) That such obligation inhered in the franchise, and that the company which took the franchise at the foreclosure sale took it burdened with that obligation. SEEVERS, J., *dissenting*.

Appeal from Cerro Gordo District Court.

TUESDAY, MARCH 15.

THIS is a proceeding to compel the defendant, the Central
Iowa Railway Company, to equip, maintain and operate that
part of its line of road from Manly Junction to Northwood, in Worth county. A mandatory injunction was
ordered by the district court in accord with the prayer of
the petition. The defendants appeal.

J. H. Blair and *Anthony C. Daly*, for Central Iowa Railway Company, appellant.

S. K. Tracy, for Burlington, C. R. & N. R'y Co., appellant.

A. J. Baker, Attorney-general, A. R. Anderson and
Smith McPherson, for appellee.

ROTHROCK, J.—The material facts in the case are not in
dispute. They are as follows:

The Central Railroad of Iowa was organized as a corporation on the twenty-third day of June, 1869. The object of
the corporation, as declared in its charter or articles of incor-
ation, was "to acquire, construct, maintain and operate a
railroad, from the south to the north line of the state of.
Iowa, beginning at the state line of Missouri, at or near the
terminus of the North Missouri Railroad, and running thence
north, on the sixteenth meridian of longitude west from
Washington, or as near thereto as practicable." A railroad
was constructed from Albia, in Monroe county, north, through
the cities of Oskaloosa, Grinnell, Marshalltown, Eldora, and
Mason City, to Northwood, the county seat of Worth county,
which last-named place is within a few miles of the north
line of the state. The road was constructed. and the cars
running thereon, to Northwood, in October, 1871. The said
railroad company became insolvent, and its creditors placed

its road and other property in the hands of a receiver, and
in May, 1879, the road and its franchises were sold upon a
decree of foreclosure. The defendant, the Central Iowa Railway Company, was the purchaser at the foreclosure sale
This company was organized in May, 1879. In its articles
of incorporation the object of the corporation was declared
to be "to acquire, construct, equip, maintain and operate a
railway from the north to the south line of the state of Iowa.
embracing the road and property, both real and personal, of
the Central Railroad Company of Iowa."

The road of the Burlington, Cedar Rapids & Northern Railroad Company, successor to the Burlington, Cedar Rapids &
Minnesota Railroad Company, is a line of railroad constructed
and operated from the city of Burlington, in a northerly
direction, through the cities of Cedar Rapids, Vinton, Waterloo, and Cedar Falls, to a junction with the line of the Central Iowa Railroad at Manly Junction, about eleven miles
south of Northwood. In the year 1877, and while the Central road was under the management of the receiver, he made
a contract with the Burlington, Cedar Rapids & Northern
Company, by which both of said companies run their trains
over the line from Manly Junction to Northwood, to the
same depot. The Burlington, Cedar Rapids & Northern
Company constructed a road from Northwood to the north
line of the state, and on to Albert Lea, there connecting with
another line to St. Paul, Minnesota. The last named company, by this joint running arrangement, was thus enabled
to operate through trains from Burlington to St. Paul. It
has ever since that time operated through trains between the
points named, using the road from Manly Junction to Northwood as part of the line. Both roads continued to use and
operate that part of the line between the points last named
until the year 1881, when they entered into a written agreement by which the Burlington, Cedar Rapids & Northern
Company took full possession of the road from Manly Junction to Northwood, as lessee of the Central Iowa Railway

Company. By the terms of this lease the lessee agreed to pay $14,000 per year to the lessor as rent, and to keep the road in repair, pay all taxes and assessments upon that part of the road, and to have the exclusive use of the same for twenty-five years. Exclusive possession was taken by the lessee under this agreement, and since it was executed such possession has been retained, and the Central Iowa Company has not since that time run its trains north of Manly Junction.

In the year 1870, at a special election held in the township in which Northwood is situated, a tax of five per cent upon the taxable property was voted to aid the Central Railroad Company in constructing its railroad through said township. The tax, amounting to $12,608, was collected and paid to the company. There were also certain lands at Northwood conveyed to the company for depot purposes, by private parties, for which no money consideration was paid. A conveyance of certain alleged swamp lands was made by the county to the company, but, as the company took no lands of any value by the conveyance, this alleged aid to the road demands no consideration.

The proceedings in the case at bar originated before the railroad commissioners of this state, under chapter 133 of the Laws of 1884. The people of Northwood made complaint to the commissioners, and the defendants herein were cited to appear, and such proceedings were had that on the thirteenth day of February, 1883, the said commissioners ordered and adjudged "that the Central Iowa Railway is under legal obligations to equip, maintain and operate its road from Manly Junction to Northwood, and to do so as a part of, and in connection with, its entire and continuous line between Albia and Northwood; and that a failure to so equip, maintain and operate the portion of the road between Manly Junction and Northwood, and its entire road, is a violation of its charter duties and obligations, and contrary to law." The Central Railroad Company refused to comply with this order, and this action was brought to compel obedience thereto.

The statute above cited provides that the rulings, orders and regulations of the railroad commissioners, for the direction and guidance of railroad companies in this state, may be enforced by proper decrees, injunctions and orders in the district court, and that the proceedings therefor shall be instituted by the attorney-general in the name of the state. Said act further provides that "if the court shall find that such rule, regulation or order is reasonable and just, and that, in refusing compliance therewith, said railway company is failing and omitting the performance of any public duty or obligation, the court shall decree a mandatory and perpetual injunction, compelling obedience to and compliance with such rule, order or regulation.　　*　　*　　*"

The ultimate question to be determined in the case is this: Has the Central Iowa Railway Company the legal right to lease that part of its road from Manly Junction to Northwood, and surrender the exclusive use of it to another company, and cease to operate its line north of Manly Junction? It is not claimed in behalf of the plaintiff that the defendant had no legal right to lease its line of road, and we fail to discover why such a lease would not be valid. If the whole line were leased and operated by another company, the integrity of the line would be preserved, and the people of Northwood would have the same means and facilities for transportation from one end of the line to the other as if the owner of the road should retain possession of it and operate it. But the complaint is that by the lease and surrender of part of the line, Northwood is practically deprived of the use of the whole line of road, because it is, in effect, situated some eleven miles north of its northern terminus. The question to be determined is one of very great importance. It involves the rights of railroad companies to lease parts of their roads, and thus destroy or break up a continuous road, and deprive localities of the benefit of competing lines; and whether a sale of a railroad under a decree of foreclosure releases the purchasing company from the obligations and liabilities which its predecessors owed to the public, and what are the rights of the public in such cases.

Railroad companies have the undoubted power to mortgage their property, (*Dunham v. Isett*, 15 Iowa, 284,) and, as we have said, the power of a railroad company to lease its whole line of road is not questioned. Indeed, the power to lease is expressly given by section 1300 of the Code. We come, then, to the question whether the Central Iowa Railway Company had the power to lease the part of its line involved in this controversy. And it is proper, at the outset, that some general principles applicable to the relation between the state or sovereignty and corporations be stated. A corporation is created by legislative power. It can have no power to do any corporate acts without legislative authority, and its power and authority are limited to such acts as are expressly given to it by its charter, or such as are necessarily implied from the powers expressed. Formerly, corporations were chartered by special act of the legislature. Now, they are incorporated under general laws, which, with the articles of incorporation adopted by the incorporators, create the same relation between the state and the corporation which would exist if the general laws applicable to the corporation and the articles of incorporation were embodied in a special act of the legislature creating the corporation, and defining its powers. A railroad corporation differs in some important respects from private corporations in general. It cannot acquire the right to construct its road over private property, against the will of the owner, without an exercise of sovereign power. Eminent domain is an attribute of sovereignty, and, when a railroad company condemns land for right of way upon which to construct its road, it is not the act of an individual. It is the exercise of sovereign authority, and the corporation is the agency through which the state executes the power. And this state authorized towns, cities, and townships to vote taxes to railroad companies to aid in the construction of their roads. This also was an exercise of sovereign power. It is true, the power was not exercised by railroad corporations. But the law authorized taxes to be voted by the legal voters upon all the property in their towns and townships; and those who voted against the tax, and the owners of property who were not voters, were required to pay the tax voted upon them.

The people of Northwood voted the tax, collected and paid it to the railroad company, to the end that they might secure the benefits of the line of road then being constructed by the Central Railroad Company. They did not extend this aid for the building of a line through their township alone. It cannot be admitted that they would have been willing to aid in the construction of a railroad having its beginning and ending in their township without any connection with any other railroad. It is claimed, however, that this is a mere private controversy between the people of Northwood and the railroad company; that no public right is involved; and that the voting of a tax did not create any contractual relations between the tax-payers and the railroad company; and we are cited to *Railway Co. v. Horton*, 38 Iowa, 33; *Trust Co. v. Davis County*, 6 Kan., 257; *Railway Co. v. Kenton*, 12 B. Mon., 144 (150); and other cases. But these were all cases brought to enforce the levy or payment of taxes, or the issue of bonds in pursuance of a vote of the people. It may be admitted that no contract exists between the people and the railroad company; but when taxes are voted, collected and paid to the company, and it has thus availed itself of public aid from taxation, it assumes a relation to the public of a higher and more sacred character than a mere contract between private individuals. It would be at war with every principle of natural justice to hold that it might avail itself of this public aid, and then violate its obligations to the public incurred by reason of the aid thus received.

It is insisted by counsel for appellants that the authority

given by section 1300 of the Code to any railroad company, to sell or lease "its railway property and franchises," includes the power to lease any part of the line, upon the principle that the power to lease the whole includes the power to lease a part. We think this does not follow. If a lease of a part of the line is a breach of a just and binding obligation to the public, the lease would be illegal. It may be assumed that the Central Railroad Company was not bound to construct the road. A railroad corporation is under no legal obligation to construct a railroad because of its articles of incorporation. Its charter is not a contract with the state to build a railroad. *People v. Albany & Vt. R. Co.*, 24 N. Y., 261. But, having constructed and put in operation its road, in part at least, by public aid in the way of taxation, the right to abandon or rather turn over part of its line to another company, to the injury of any locality on the line, is quite another question. We do not undertake to determine the question whether, under the mere charter rights of the corporation to build and operate its road, the corporation may abandon part of its line, or lease it to another company, so as to destroy competition at points on the line. There appears to be a conflict of authority upon this question. See *Black v. Canal Co.*, 22 N. J. Eq. 410; *Com. v. Fitchburg R'y Co.*, 12 Gray, 180; *State v. Hartford & N. H. R'y Co.*, 29 Conn., 538; *Peoria & R. I. R'y Co. v. Coal V. M. Co.*, 68 Ill., 489. It would seem from some of these authorities, and others cited by counsel, that a corporation may abandon its line, and cease to operate it for good and sufficient cause; and, in the case where the business of a railroad will not pay operating expenses, it would be a most unjust rule to require it to be operated by proceedings in *mandamus*. But that question is not necessarily in this case. The Central Railroad Company was the recipient of more from the public than the mere right of invoking the power of the state to condemn land for a right of way. It received taxes from the public, levied and collected to aid in the construction of the road.

Its relation and obligation to the public are therefore different from that of a company not having received any such
aid. It appears from chapter 118, of the Laws of 1876, that
it was contemplated by the legislature that the obligation to
operate a railroad is incurred by accepting taxes in aid of its
construction. That act in effect provides that, upon a proper
proceeding, a railway line may be changed or removed, but
upon the condition that all such taxes shall be repaid. It is
true, the act applies to such railroads only as were constructed
prior to the year 1866, and probably is not applicable to the
road in question. But the act indicates that the legislature
regarded the obligation to operate the road, as contemplated
by the company when it accepted the aid, as binding upon it.

II. We come now to another question in the case, and
that is, whether this obligation to operate the road passed
with the foreclosure sale, and became binding upon the
defendant to the same extent as against its predecessor. In
other words, did the Central Iowa Railway Company take
the road by its purchase charged with the duty of operating
it to Northwood? Counsel for the defendants strenuonsly
insist that by the purchase the defendant acquired the road
clear and free from any such claim. It is to be remembered
that when the decree of foreclosure was entered, and the road
sold, and the sale approved, and the property conveyed,
the old company was, for all practicable purposes, wiped out
of existence. With the sale of its road, right of way, depot
buildings, side tracks, and all the appliances necessary to
operate the road, the franchise, or right to operate the
road, passed with the sale. It is true, the purchaser
took the road unincumbered by the debts of the old
company. But the obligation to operate the road to Northwood was more than a debt. It inhered in the franchise, so
to speak, and pertained to the right to operate the road. It
did not pass by an assignment proper; it passed to the grantee
as a burden or limitation upon the right to operate the road.
Campbell v. Marietta & C. R. Co., 23 Ohio St. 168.

Without further elaboration, our conclusion is that the Central Iowa Railway Company had no power to execute the lease, and thus abandon the part of its line in controversy, and compel its former patrons at Northwood to transport passengers and freight some eleven miles to reach the terminus of a railroad which the defendant was bound to maintain at Northwood. We think that the order of the railroad commissioners, which was approved by the district court, was "reasonable and just," and should be complied with. It will be understood that we do not determine that a contract providing for a joint running arrangement over that part of the line from Manly Junction to Northwood would be illegal. It is the surrender by the Central Railway Company of any right to operate the line, and giving the exclusive right to the Burlington, Cedar Rapids & Northern Railway Company to operate it, that we hold to be unauthorized by law.

AFFIRMED.

SEEVERS, J., (*dissenting.*) When the state granted to railroad corporations the right to mortgage their incorporate property, it clearly was contemplated that the mortgages might be foreclosed, the property sold, and purchased either by a natural person or another corporation. This being so, what does the purchaser obtain at the sale? Without doubt, I think, he gets the mortgaged property, and the right to operate the road. Unless he obtains the latter, the property would be comparatively valueless, and the right to mortgage a barren, instead of a substantial, right. In my judgment, the purchaser obtains a perfect and absolute title to the mortgaged property, except against valid and existing liens of record, or of which the purchaser has express notice.

It is not claimed, in the foregoing opinion, that the tax, or any right or obligation growing out of it, constituted a lien on the mortgaged property. Nor is it claimed that the acceptance of the tax created a contract of any kind between the corporation executing the mortgage and the state, or any citizen thereof. In my judgment, the right to mortgage not only exists, but may be exercised freely by the corporation, as its interest may dictate. The corporation may execute a mortgage on a part of the road at one time, and afterwards upon another part. Upon the foreclosure of such mortgages, the road may be severed, and thereafter adversely operated. This was the case with the Des Moines Valley road. When the purchaser obtains a railroad under a foreclosure and sale under a mortgage, he may use and control it as he sees proper, unless he is prohibited from so doing by some statute, and I do not understand that it is claimed there is such a statute. On the contrary, the statute provides that the owner may lease the road. This necessarily includes the power to lease the whole or a part, unless the owner has entered into some contract or assumed some obligation to the public or individuals which prevents him from so doing. In this case the existing corporation entered into no such contract or obligation. It is a separate and distinct corporation, organized under the statute, and exists independently of the prior corporation. It therefore cannot be said to have assumed an obligation of the prior corporation, of which it had neither express nor constructive notice. This, it seems to me, must be true, in the absence of a statute which either expressly or by necessary implication so provides. In my judgment, the district court erred in entering the decree it did.

JORDAN v. BROWN.

1. **Jurisdiction**: MUST BE INVOKED BY PROPER PETITION: PETITION
ADDRESSED TO WRONG COURT. Where a petition for the foreclosure
of a mortgage was filed in the circuit court, and was by the clerk placed
in a wrapper, on which were written the usual indorsements, but the
cause was afterwards dismissed, and subsequently the plaintiff in that
case gave notice of an action for the foreclosure of the same mortgage
in the district court, but filed no new petition, but simply took the old
petition, and changed the indorsements on the wrapper so as to make it
appear to be a petition in the district court, and on such petition
obtained judgment and decree of foreclosure upon default. *Held*—
   (1) That the wrapper was no part of the petition, and that the
   changes in the indorsements thereon did not change the petition to
   the district court.
   (2) That, there being no petition invoking the jurisdiction of the district court in the case, that court had no jurisdiction of the
   subject-matter, and that the judgment and decree were void, and
   that a sale of the land thereunder, and the title acquired by such
   sale, were also void.

Appeal from Madison Circuit Court.

TUESDAY, MARCH 15.

ACTION to recover possession of real estate. The facts are
stated in the opinion. The plaintiff appeals.

V. Wainwright, for appellant.

Ruby & Wilkin, for appellee.

SEEVERS, J.—The petition states that the plaintiff is the
owner of the real estate in controversy, and is entitled to its
possession. The defendant admits the plaintiff's ownership
in 1876, but pleaded that in that year the plaintiff mortgaged the same to one McClure, and that the mortgage had
been duly foreclosed in 1878, and the real estate sold on
special execution to McClure, and the same conveyed to him
in 1879 by the sheriff, and the defendant claims under
McClure. In a reply, the plaintiff pleaded that the decree
of foreclosure, and the sale and conveyance were void, because

the court had no jurisdiction of the subject-matter, for the reason that no petition had been filed by the clerk which invoked the jurisdiction of the court. A demurrer to the reply was sustained. It is well settled that a demurrer admits all facts well pleaded. The averment that no petition was on file as above stated is in the nature of a legal conclusion. It therefore becomes material to ascertain what facts were pleaded. In March, 1878, an action was commenced in the circuit court by the service of the requisite notice, and filing a proper and sufficient petition. It does not appear that any pleadings other than the petition were filed, but the court caused the following judgment to be entered: "Now, on this day, this cause comes on for hearing, and, the court being fully advised in the premises, this cause is dismissed at plaintiff's costs," and a judgment therefor was rendered against him.

The plaintiff insists that the action was dismissed on the merits, and therefore this action on the same mortgage is barred by reason of such adjudication. We are not prepared to say that such prior adjudication, conceding it to be on the merits, is so pleaded that we are required to pass on such question. The petition filed in the circuit court is entitled in the caption as follows: "In the circuit court of Iowa, in and for Marion county. Petition in equity." It was marked "Filed" by the clerk, and attached to a wrapper, on which were written the following words and figures: "Term No. 119. Case 1252. Chancery, Marion circuit court. Petition foreclosure. Filed February 28, 1878. ALLEN HAMRICK, Clerk. Dismissed, Appearance Docket 3, p. 88." After the dismissal of said action, the plaintiff therein caused a notice to be served on the present plaintiff, stating that on a named day a petition would be on file in the district court asking a foreclosure of said mortgage. The attorney for the plaintiff in such action took from the files of the circuit court the petition which had been filed therein, "drew an ink-mark" through the figures "1252" on the wrapper, and placed the figures "976" above the former figures; "drew a line" through the word circuit, and wrote "district." The date of filing was also changed. After this was done, the indorsements on the wrapper were as follows: "Term No. 119, Case No. ~~1252~~ 976, Chancery, Marion ~~circuit~~ district court. Petition, foreclosure. Filed ~~February~~ May 2 28, 1878. Allen Hamrick, Clerk. Dismissed, Appearance Docket 3, p. 88." The petition on its face remained entitled in the caption as above stated. Afterwards, the district court caused the following entry to be made of record: "Plaintiff appears by his attorneys; and defendants, being duly served with notice, failing to appear, default is entered against them. Cause comes on for hearing upon the petition and evidence adduced by the plaintiff." And then follows a judgment foreclosing the mortgage. It is evident from the journal entry that the district court found that there was a petition on file; but, as the facts pleaded are admitted by the demurrer, such petition was not addressed to the district, but was addressed to the circuit court, and that such petition had been taken from the files of the circuit court and placed among the files of the district court. That the judgment was obtained on such petition, and is irregular, at least, must be conceded. But the question is, whether it is absolutely void.

It is provided by statute that the "petition must contain the name of the court and county in which the action is brought." Code, § 2646. The petition in question did so; that is, it contained the name of, and was entitled in, the circuit court, and thereby the jurisdiction of that court was invoked. The words and figures on the wrapper, no matter by whom they were written, do not constitute a part of the petition. The petition constitutes a part of the record of the case; and, as it appeared on its face that it was addressed to the circuit court, it appeared of record that there was no petition on file that invoked the action of the district court, and therefore the "latter court had no power to act upon it." *Garretson v. Hays*, 70 Iowa, 19.

In *Morrow v. Small*, 33 Iowa, 118, the petition was entitled in the caption, "In the circuit court." The clerk indorsed on the back thereof, "Change to the district court." and placed the cause on the calendar of the latter court, and it was held there was no petition on file in the district court. It must therefore follow that such court did not have jurisdiction.

It is true, this is a collateral attack; but, if there was no jurisdiction of the subject matter, the judgment is void. It must be conceded that the district court has jurisdiction of the foreclosure of mortgages. But it did not have jurisdiction or power to render a judgment foreclosing the mortgage in question, unless there was a petition invoking such action.

In *Morrow v. Weed*, 4 Iowa, 89, it is said: "What gives jurisdiction? The answer is—*First*, the law; *second*, a petition, (or what stands in its place.)"

In *Smith v. Watson*, 28 Iowa, 218, there was on file a petition addressed "to the judge of the district court of Polk county, Iowa," but the names of the parties were not stated "at the head thereof, nor was it headed with the word petition." It was held that these defects were merely formal. In that case the petition did invoke the jurisdiction of the court in an informal manner.

We think the court erred in sustaining the demurrer.

                                                    REVERSED.

SAAR v. FULLER ET AL.

1. **Instructions**: SUBMITTING QUESTIONS OF DOUBTFUL PROOF. A fact is not proved because there is uncontradicted testimony which tends to prove it; and when there are other circumstances shown by the evidence which have a bearing upon the weight and credit which should be given to such uncontradicted testimony, the question as to whether the fact is proved should be submitted to the jury. (See opinion for illustration.)

2. ———: NO EVIDENCE TO WARRANT. An instruction directing the jury to inquire into a matter of which there is no evidence is erroneous. (See opinion for illustration.)

Appeal from Mills Circuit Court.

WEDNESDAY, MARCH 16.

PLAINTIFF instituted an action at law on a money demand, and sued out a writ of attachment, which was levied on certain personal property as the property of the defendant John Finkin. Thomas J. Finkin filed a petition of intervention, claiming to be the owner of the attached property, and asking that the same be released from the levy. Plaintiff answered this petition, denying that intervenor was the owner of the property, and alleging that his only claim thereto was based on a pretended sale by defendant John Finkin, and that such sale was made for the purpose of hindering and delaying the creditors of defendant in the collection of their debts. There was a verdict and judgment for plaintiff. Intervenor appeals.

Stone & Gilliland, for appellant.

Flickinger Bros. and *Watkins & Williams*, for appellee.

REED, J.—I. Intervenor is the son of defendant John Finkin. At the time of the alleged sale of the property to him, he was about twenty-eight years old. He

1. INSTRUC-
TIONS: submitting ques-
tions of doubtful
proof.

had lived in his father's family continuously since he attained his majority, and had rendered service for him during all that time, and had been boarded and clothed and treated in other respects as a member of the family. He and his father testified that soon after he became twenty-one years old, an agreement was entered into between them that he should continue to work for his father until such time as he should conclude to engage in business for himself, and that he should be compensated for his services. They were not contradicted by any direct evidence as to the making of such contract. He claims that part of the consideration for the transfer of the property in question to him was the value of the services rendered by him under that agreement. In addition to that, he claims to have assumed the payment of certain debts his father was owing. The circuit court instructed the jury that if such agreement was entered into, and he performed services under it, the value of such services would constitute a good consideration for the sale of the property to him. The court also told the jury, in effect, that if he rendered the services while he lived with and was treated as a member of the family, but without any express agreement that he was to be compensated therefor, the value of the services would not constitute a valid consideration for the sale. The giving of this latter instruction is excepted to. No question is made as to its correctness as an abstract proposition, but it is insisted that it is not based on any evidence in the case.

As stated above, there was no direct evidence tending to contradict the testimony of intervenor and his father as to the making of the contract; but the burden was on him to establish that the sale was supported by a valid consideration. There was no question as to the rendition of the services; but, under the rule as settled in this state, he was required to prove that they were rendered under an agreement that they should be paid for. Now, the court could not assume that the making of the agreement was proven simply because the testimony which tended to prove it was not contradicted by any direct evidence. There were circumstances disclosed by the testimony of intervenor and his father, which were proper to be considered by the jury in determining whether the alleged contract was ever entered into; such as the fact that there never had been an accounting between them, while intervenor had received money from time to time while rendering the services, of which no account was kept, and had been clothed and in other respects treated as a member of the family. It cannot be assumed, in any such case, that a fact is proven because there is testimony which tends to prove it which is not directly contradicted; for there is always a question as to the weight and credit which should be given to the testimony, and that question is for the jury. If the testimony in the present case was not sufficient to convince the jury that the services were rendered under an agreement that they should be paid for, the question covered by the instruction arose in the case. It was therefore proper for the court to instruct on that question.

II. Intervenor's father owned a farm, and for many years before the transaction in question he had been engaged in the business of farming. Some time before that, however, he became the owner of a merchant tailoring establishment in Council Bluffs. The business of this establishment was managed by an agent in his employ. His indebtedness, aside from what had been incurred in that business, was not large. The property sold to intervenor consisted of the stock and farming utensils on his farm. A short time before the sale, he had incurred an indebtedness of about $3,300 for goods for the establishment in Council Bluffs. That was about the extent of his liabilities growing out of that business, and that indebtedness did not fall due for some time after the sale to the intervenor. He was not able to pay the debt when it became due, and his creditors began to press him for payment, and some months afterwards they instituted suits against him, and sued out attachments, on which the goods in the establishment were seized. These facts were proven on the trial. The circuit court instructed the jury that, in determining whether the sale to intervenor was made with the fraudulent intent charged, they might

2. ——: no evidence to warrant.

inquire whether his creditors were then pressing him for payment or security for their debts. This instruction should
not have been given. When the sale was made, the debts
were not due, and none of the creditors were then pressing
him for payment or security. The evidence on that subject,
all related to a time subsequent to the sale. The instruction
could hardly fail to be prejudicial to intervenor.

As we reverse the judgment on this ground, we will not
consider the question whether the verdict is sustained by the
evidence.

REVERSED.

HERRON v. HERRON.

1. **Estates of Decedents**: ADMINISTRATOR: FIDUCIARY RELATION TO
CO·TENANT OF INHERITED LAND. Where the real estate of a decedent
descended in equal shares to his wife and his father, and the wife was
administratrix of the estate, *held* that she did not on that account hold
a fiduciary relation to the father, so as to cast suspicion upon a purchase
by her of the father's interest in the real estate.

2. **Fraud**: IN PURCHASE OF LAND: INADEQUATE CONSIDERATION AS
EVIDENCE OF. To warrant a court of equity in presuming fraud in the
purchase of land from the inadequacy of the consideration, and in setting aside a conveyance on the ground thereof, it must be such as to
demonstrate some gross imposition or undue influence; and in this case,
where the consideration paid was only about one-fourth the actual value
of the land, *held* that this fact, taken with the other facts of the case.
(for which see opinion) was not sufficient to justify the court in setting
aside the conveyance.

3. ———: ———: NEGLIGENCE OF COMPLAINANT: RELIEF IN EQUITY.
It is the province of courts of equity to afford relief to those who
have been overreached by the artifice or cunning or deceit of others;
but where a seller of land refuses to resort to sources of information to
which he is referred by the buyer as to the value of the land, but chooses
rather to accept the statements of the buyer, he should be held to have
acted on his own judgment, and no relief should be granted him if it
turns out that the statements of the buyer were false as to the value of
the land.

Appeal from Plymouth Circuit Court. ·

WEDNESDAY, MARCH 16.

ACTION in equity for the cancellation of a deed executed

by plaintiff to defendant, by which he conveyed to her his interest in certain real estate, on the ground that the conveyance was obtained by fraud and false representations. The circuit court dismissed the petition, and plaintiff appeals.

M. B. Kelly, G. W. Argo and *E. F. Augir*, for appellant.

Struble, Rishel & Hart, for appellee.

REED, J.—Plaintiff is the father, and defendant the widow, of John Herron, who died intestate and without issue in April, 1882. At the time of his death, the said John Herron held the title to the real estate in question. Some months after his death, plaintiff, who lived in Ireland, executed a power of attorney, by which he appointed Michael Herron, his son, who also lived in Ireland, his attorney in fact, and empowered him to collect and receive for him any property or interest which had accrued to him, under the laws of Iowa, in the estate of deceased, and to dispose of and give conveyance of the same. Michael came to this country, and entered into a negotiation with defendant, which resulted in the sale to her of his father's interest in all of the real estate of which John died seized, for the consideration of $1,500, which was paid at the time, and executed to her the conveyance which plaintiff seeks in this action to have canceled and set aside. The allegations of fraud in the petition, which are relied on, are that defendant concealed from Michael the true condition of the estate, and the amount of property of which her husband had died seized, and falsely represented that the value of the property did not exceed $3,000, whereas its value was much greater than that, and procured relations and acquaintances of his residing in the vicinity, on whom he had a right to rely for information, to make the same false representations, and that he, being a stranger in the country, and ignorant of its laws and usages, and of the value of the property in the country, relied on the statements made to him, and made the sale and conveyance in the belief induced thereby that he was receiving the fair value of the interest of his principal in the property.

I. Defendant had been appointed administratrix of the estate of her husband before the transaction in question. It

1. ESTATES of decedents: administratrix: fiduciary relation to co-tenant of inherited land.

is urged that her position with reference to the estate created a fiduciary relation between the parties; and, as she acquired an interest in the property of the estate in the transaction, it is presumptively fraudulent. But, clearly, this position is not tenable. Defendant did not occupy a position of trust or special confidence towards plaintiff. She did not deal with his attorney in her capacity as administratrix of the estate. On the death of John Herron, the real estate of which he was seized descended in equal shares to plaintiff and defendant. Her interest in the property was a personal interest. In her representative capacity she had no interest whatever. It was a case of tenants in common dealing with each other with reference to the common estate. Neither of the parties was charged with the duty of protecting the rights or guarding the interests of the other in the property. They stood upon an equality, and clearly there can be no presumption of unfairness or fraud in the transaction.

II. It is next urged that the consideration paid by defendant for the conveyance was so grossly inadequate as

2. FRAUD: in purchase of land: inadequate consideration as evidence of.

to raise a presumption of fraud. There is some conflict in the evidence as to the value of the property, but we think the preponderance of the evidence shows that the value was from $20,000 to $22,000. Defendant claims that a portion of the property had been purchased with money which belonged to her, and which she had given to her husband for investment. She made this claim at the time of the transaction, and the parties appear to have proceeded on the theory that it was valid. At least, Michael Herron did not question it; nor did he make any investigation of it, but accepted defendant's statement as true. She testified on the trial that she furnished the money, and that it was invested in the property, and the title taken in her husband, for reasons of conveyance. Her testimony in this respect is uncontradicted. Indeed, she is corroborated, to some extent, by the testimony of other witnesses. It may be that she is not, under the statute, (Code, § 3639,) a competent witness to the transactions between herself and her husband, although no question as to her competency was made by counsel. But it is not necessary in this proceeding to go into the question whether her claim in that respect is valid. The parties, as we have said, dealt upon the theory that she had a valid claim to some portion of the property on account of moneys advanced by her to her husband, and invested by him in the property, and the transaction has not been attacked on the ground that there was any fraud or mistake as to that claim; and it will be assumed, for the purposes of the case, that her claim in that respect is valid. Deducting that portion of the property, the value of the balance is shown to have been from $12,-000 to $14,000; so that in the transaction plaintiff received $1,500 for an interest worth at the time from $6,000 to $7,000. Mere inadequacy of consideration is not a ground for the rescission of an executed contract. Story Eq. Jur. § 245; Kerr, Fraud & M. 186, 187. Cases have arisen, however, in which the inadequacy was so gross as to be regarded as satisfactory evidence of fraud. In such cases, relief is given, not because of the inadequacy of the price paid, but because of the fraud of which it is an evidence. To warrant a court, however, in presuming fraud from the inadequacy of the consideration, it must be such as to demonstaate some gross imposition or undue influence. Story, Eq. § 246. The facts of the present case do not bring it within the rule. The amount received by plaintiff was from one-fourth to one-fifth of the actual value of his interest in the property. The evidence shows, without any conflict, that his attorney thought that his interest would be best served by selling the land. He was not favorably impressed with the country, and he did not regard it as either desirable or to the interest of his principal to retain the ownership of the property. Plaintiff was nearly eighty years old at the time, and his home was in another country. The presumption from the circumstances is that he preferred to accept the comparatively small amount paid him for the interest, rather than that he was cheated and overreached in the transaction.

III. We come now to the question whether actual fraud by defendant in the transaction is proven. Michael Herron

3. —: —; testified that the defendant represented to him, negligence of complaluant: during the negotiations, that the only real estate relief in equity. owned by John at the time of his death was the farm on which she then lived, which, as we understand, is a half section, and another farm of about 150 acres, and that she stated that the value of his father's interest in the property did not exceed $1,500 or $2,000; also that the same statement was made to him by two other persons, one of whom is a relation of his, and the other a nephew of defendant. One of these parties was examined as a witness, and he testified that he had made the statement attributed to him at the request of defendant. We attach but little weight, however, to his testimony. He is positively contradicted by defendant, and his own testimony shows that he has but a low sense of honor. Defendant denied positively that she ever made the statement to Michael which he attributed to her. She also testified that she advised him to take the advice of counsel, and recommended to him one of the attorneys who are appearing for plaintiff, and that she told him that he could acquire accurate information as to the property owned by his brother at the time of his death, at the county recorder's office, and advised him to consult some real estate agent as to the value of the property, but that he declined to make any inquiry on the subject. She also testified that she told him that, rather than pay more than $1,500 for his father's interest, she would permit the matter of the interest

of the parties and the divison of the property to be taken
into the courts for settlement. Her testimony as to these
statements is in no manner contradicted; neither is she
shown to be unworthy of belief. If it should be conceded,
then, that she made the representations attributed to her as
to the extent and value of the property, the fact remains that
she advised him in effect not to rely upon those statements,
but to seek information for his guidance from other sources,
which she pointed out, where accurate and reliable information could be obtained. In addition to this, is the fact that
the deed which he executed contains the description of
more than fifty tracts or parcels of real estate, and this deed
was carefully read over to him before he signed it. Some
of the descriptions in the deed were of lands, but much the
greater number of them were of lots in the city of Le Mars
and the town of Plymouth City. It is true, he was ignorant
of our manner of describing real property, but it seems to
us impossible that he did not know, when he executed the
deed, that he was conveying other property than the two
farms, or that he should have believed that they were the only
property in which his father had an interest. Surely a court
of equity will not interfere, on this state of facts, to rescind
an executed agreement.

If plaintiff's attorney was deceived or misled by the
information communicated to him, it was because he chose
to accept the naked statement of the one he was dealing with,
rather than seek reliable information from the sources
pointed out to him, where it could have been obtained. It
is the province of courts of equity to afford relief to those
who have been overreached by the artifice or cunning or
deceit of others; but where one voluntarily refuses to resort to
the sources of information to which he is referred, but chooses
rather to accept the statements of the person with whom he
is dealing, as to matters material to the trade, he should be
held to have acted on his own judgment, and no relief should

be granted him if it turns out that the statements were false.

The judgment of the circuit court is right, and it will be

AFFIRMED.

GOODALE, ADM'R, v. CASE ET AL.

1. **Reference**: TIME FOR REPORT: LIMITED BY ORDER. Where an order submitting the accounts of an administrator to a referee required him to report at the next term, his authority was limited as to time by the order, and his report ought not to have been received at a later term.

2. ——: ——: WAIVER: ESTOPPEL. The fact that an interested party appeared before the referee after the time when his report should have been filed, and when his authority was at an end, did not confer upon him authority to proceed, and did not estop such party from afterwards objecting to the referee's authority.

3. ——: PRACTICE: REPORTING EVIDENCE. Conflicting claims, on which there is conflicting evidence, ought never to be sent to a referee without requiring him to preserve and report the evidence, unless there be some controlling reason for proceeding differently,—such, for example, as the agreement of the parties that the evidence shall not be reported.

Appeal from Cass Circuit Court.

WEDNESDAY, MARCH 16.

THIS is a proceeding in the court of probate to charge the plaintiff, an administrator, on account of certain indebtedness to the estate. There was an order entered to the effect that he should charge himself in his report and account with such alleged indebtedness. From this order he appeals.

Willard & Fletcher and *D. F. Harding,* for appellant.

L. L. DeLano, for appellee.

BECK, J.—I. The plaintiff filed a report, showing his account of moneys received and paid by him as administrator. At the May term, 1884, the circuit court entered an order referring this report, with the report of a preceding special administrator, to a referee, requiring him to report thereon at the next term of court. Certain heirs of the estate filed objections to several credits in the plaintiff's account, and claimed that he should be charged with $1,000, on account of money borrowed of the decedent in his life-time. At the term following the succeeding term of court, the referee filed his report, which rejects the items of credit, or some of them, objected to by the heirs,—at least, we do not find them in the account stated by the referee,—and charged him with $1,150 on account of money borrowed of the decedent, as alleged by the heirs. The heirs who had made objections to the plaintiff's report filed an objection to the report, on the ground of a written agreement entered into between them and the plaintiff settling the matter in controversy. The plaintiff's name appears in this paper as one of the heirs, which he is in fact. It is stated in the objection that the finding in the report of the indebtedness of the plaintiff to the estate in the sum of $1,150 is not supported by the evidence, and is not in accord with the agreement just referred to. The circuit court entered an order confirming the report of the referee, and requiring the plaintiff to correct his report accordingly. Various objections are made to this action, only one of which will be considered.

II. The order of submission required the referee to report at the next term of the court. This he did not do.

1. REFER-ENCE: time for report: limited by order. We think that the report ought not to have been received after that term. The order has the effect to prescribe the time in which he should discharge the duties required of him by the court. After that time expired, he ceased to have authority as a referee. A referee ought not to be permitted to prolong the settle-ment of matters submitted to him, and parties ought not to be required to watch and wait for his action after the time expires limiting his authority. See *DeLong v. Stahl*, 13 Kan., 558, and authorities cited; *Knipe v. Harrington*, 1 Blackf., 79.

III. But it is insisted that, as the plaintiff had knowl-

edge of the proceeding had by the referee after the term to
which he was to report, and appeared therein

2. ——: ——:
walver: estop-
pel.

and gave his testimony, he ought not now to be
heard to object to the action of the referee after that term.
And it is also insisted that, as the plaintiff appeared and
objected to the report of the referee after it was filed, he is
precluded from complaining of the action of the court in
approving the report. As the referee's authority expired
with the term to which he was to report, his subsequent
proceedings were as the acts of one not a referee, and
authority as such was not conferred by the presumed assent
of plaintiff. The authority could not be conferred by the
court. But, in our opinion, the evidence submitted on
this point shows that he did not appear and object to the
report. He so testifies, and the attorney making the objections corroborates his statements. It is our conclusion that
the report of the referee ought to have been set aside, and
the questions in dispute arising upon the plaintiff's report
ought to have been heard and determined by the circuit court.

IV. We may properly suggest that matters of this kind,
wherein there are conflicting claims upon which there is
conflicting evidence, ought never to be sent to a

3. ——: prac-
tice: report-
ing evidence.

referee, without requiring him to preserve and
report the evidence. The court ought not to delegate its
powers to a referee, so as to cut off all opportunity and
means to review his actions. It is an unsatisfactory and
unsafe way to administer justice. Doubtless, the parties
may waive the taking and reporting of the evidence by the
referee, or it need not be done unless one of the parties
requires it; but, unless there be some controlling reasons for
different proceedings, the court should require the referee to
preserve and report the evidence with his findings of facts
and conclusions of law.

The order and judgment of the circuit court is reversed,
and the cause is remanded for proceedings in harmony with
this opinion. REVERSED.

BYSON v. McPHERSON.

1. **Removal of Causes to Federal Courts**: CONTROVERTING PETI-
TION. The facts stated as grounds for removal, in a petition for the
removal of a cause to the federal court, cannot be controverted in
determining the question of removal. (*Van Horn v. Litchfield*, 70 Iowa,
11, followed.)

Appeal from Kossuth District Court.

WEDNESDAY, MARCH 16.

ACTION to recover forty acres of land in Kossuth county.
The defendant filed a petition for a removal of the case to
the circuit court of the United States, and the petition was
denied. From the order denying the petition the defendant
appeals.

Geo. E. Clarke, for appellant.

R. J. Danson and *J. C. Cook,* for appellee.

ADAMS, CH. J.—The defendant filed-an answer setting up
a defense under certain grants of congress. His application
for a removal was based upon the allegation that the controversy involves the title to the real estate described, and that
the question necessary to the determination of the cause is
one arising under the laws of the United States, and involves
a construction of the grants and laws of the United States,
and that the real estate exceeds in value the sum of
$500. The plaintiff filed an affidavit to the effect that
the value of the property was less than $500. The
court overruled the petition for a removal, and retained
and tried the case, and rendered a decree for the plaintiff.
The defendant insists that the facts stated in the petition for
removal, as a ground of removal, cannot be controverted in
determining the question of removal, and we have to say
that we think that he must be sustained. *Van Horn v.
Litchfield,* 70 Iowa, 11.

REVERSED.

438|
560|
438
242

POLLARD v. DICKINSON COUNTY.

1. **Highway**: VACATION AND ESTABLISHMENT: DAMAGES: APPEAL CLAIM INCREASED BY AMENDMENT. Upon a proceeding to vacate one road and establish another in lieu thereof, plaintiff claimed $100 damages for land taken of him for the new road, which sum was allowed him. His claim was made upon the supposition that the old road was to be vacated upon the establishment of the new one; but after the supervisors had ordered the new one established and allowed plaintiff's claim, they refused to vacate the old one, whereby plaintiff's damages were much in excess of $100. Plaintiff appealed to the circuit court. The defendant moved to dismiss the appeal on the ground that the establishment of the new road and the vacation of the old one were separate proceedings, and, on the former, plaintiff had been allowed all the damages he had claimed. *Held* that the motion was properly overruled; also, that plaintiff was properly allowed to amend his claim for damages by increasing it so as to cover the damages sustained by him by the establishment of the new road without the vacation of the old one. ADAMS, CH. J., and SEEVERS, J., *dissenting.*

Appeal from Dickinson Circuit Court.

WEDNESDAY, MARCH 16.

PROCEEDINGS were had before the supervisors of Dickinson county to establish and vacate certain roads. Plaintiff appealed to the circuit court from an order of the supervisors allowing him damages for locating the road over his lands. In the circuit court a motion of defendant to dismiss the appeal was overruled, and a motion of plaintiff to amend his claim for damages, increasing the amount thereof, was sustained. From these rulings defendant appeals.

Baily, Osborne & Peters, for appellant.

Soper & Allen, for appellee.

BECK, J.—I. The petition presented to the board of supervisors asked that one road be established, and another vacated. It appears that the new road to be established was to take the place of the old one asked to be vacated. At least, plaintiff so regarded it. Plaintiff, it appears, was one of the petitioners, and he became the principal in the bond filed in the case before action by the supervisors, as required by the statute. He subsequently filed a claim for damages in the sum of $100, the value of his land which would be appropriated for the road. A remonstrance was filed against the vacation of the other road, and a claim was filed by one land owner for $3,000 damages, which he claimed he would sustain by the vacation. A commission was appointed to appraise the damages, who allowed plaintiff $100 for the new road, and to the other party $3,000 for the vacation of the old one, and so reported. Thereupon the supervisors established the new road, and allowed plaintiff $100 damages. Afterwards, on the same day, by separate action, the supervisors refused to vacate the other road. Thereupon plaintiff appealed to the circuit court. In that court defendant moved to dismiss the appeal on the ground that, as plaintiff recovered the sum claimed by him for damages, he cannot recover more upon the appeal, and that, as the matters of establishing one road and vacating the other were separate, one was not conditioned upon the other, and that the action of the supervisors in these matters cannot be reviewed upon the appeal. Plaintiff asked leave, by motion, to amend his claim for damages, making it $1,000. These motions by the respective parties were supported by affidavits. On the part of the defendant, it was in this manner shown that the only evidence before the supervisors was the report of the commissioners, and that plaintiff was present when his claim was acted upon, and made no claim for more than $100 damages. It was shown that he assented to the new road, and claimed therefor no more than $100, by reason of an arrangement with those interested to the effect that the other road should be vacated, and unless this should be done his farm would be surrounded by highways, and cut off from the water of East Okoboji lake, upon which it is situated, and that, unless the established road was vacated, which was prayed for in the petition, his land would suffer damage to

the extent of $1,000, and with such vacation he would not
suffer more than $100 damages, and that he understood the
proposition to vacate and establish the several roads was one
proposition, to be acted upon together by the supervisors.
Acting upon this understanding, and the arrangement with
the parties interested, he filed his claim for $100 damages;
but the establishing of the new road, and refusal to vacate
the old one, was a violation of this understanding, and an
injustice to him.

II.   In our opinion, the circuit court, upon these showings,
rightly overruled defendant's motion to dismiss the appeal,
and correctly sustained plaintiff's motion to allow him to
amend his claim for damages.   It must be remembered that
the appeal brought up nothing for determination except
plaintiff's claim for damages.   The action of the supervisors
in establishing one road, and in refusing to vacate the other,
could not be reversed upon the appeal.   Code, § 962, provides that, upon the appeal, "the amount of damages the
claimant is entitled to shall be ascertained by said circuit
court in the same manner as in actions by ordinary proceedings."   Of course, the damages in this case must be ascertained upon the appeal, in view of the rights of the parties,
as settled by the action of the supervisors.   When they
allowed him damages to the amount of $100, the question as
to the vacation of the old road had not been acted upon.
Plaintiff, therefore, in view of the arrangement to vacate the
old road, was authorized to believe that the arrangement
would be carried out.   He was, therefore, not required to
object to the allowance for damage made to him.   By refusing to vacate the old road, the matter was wholly changed,
and plaintiff's rights were changed to correspond with this
action.   When the case came up on the appeal, his rights
stood as they were left by the action of the supervisors.   In
the circuit court his damages were to be determined according to his rights as they were left by the final action of the
supervisors.   They are to be determined, not by the plead-

ings and claims filed before the supervisors, but "in the same manner as in actions by ordinary proceedings." Code, § 962. They were not so determined by the supervisors. In order that the damages should be so determined, and to secure his rights, he is permitted to plead as in an action by ordinary proceedings. He could, therefore, show by pleading, by an amended claim, what his rights are, and what damages he ought to recover. The county could not be prejudiced by the recovery by plaintiff upon the appeal of damages greater than were allowed by the supervisors, as the road could not be established until the trial of the case upon the appeal. The supervisors were authorized to make an establishment of the road conditioned upon the payment of the damages. If they were not paid, they could refuse to establish the road. Code, §§ 946, 947, 962.

These views, which we think cannot be disputed, applied to the peculiar facts of the case, lead us to the conclusion that plaintiff could prosecute his appeal, and that the law authorized him to file an amended claim in accord with his rights. We must not be understood as holding that in ordinary cases, wherein there is absence of facts of the character found in this, the claim for damages could not be increased upon the appeal. The circuit court, therefore, rightly overruled defendant's motion to dismiss the appeal, and rightly sustained plaintiff's motion to amend his claim for damages.

AFFIRMED.

ADAMS, CH. J., and SEEVERS, J., dissenting.

EISFIELD & Co. v. DILL ET AL.

DILL v. SCHOENEMAN BROS. & Co. ET AL.

1. **Fraudulent Conveyance:** BURDEN OF PROOF: EVIDENCE. Where
conveyances of property purport to have been made for a sufficient consideration, the burden is on creditors seeking to subject the property to
the payment of their claims to show a want of consideration; (*Wolf
v. Chandler*, 58 Iowa, 569; *Allen v. Wegstein*, 69 Id., 593;) but it is
wholly immaterial whether the evidence is introduced by the plaintiff
or the defendant. Accordingly, where the conveyances were made by a
husband to his wife at a time when he was likely to be called on to pay
debts as surety for a son, and the wife, to show the consideration for
the transfers to her, introduced a written contract, signed by herself and
her husband, and which bore date of thirty years previous, at which
time they both testified it was executed; which contract was an agreement on the part of the wife to furnish the husband with certain money,
and an agreement on his part to repay it, which money, so furnished,
they testified was the consideration of the conveyances; but the paper
appeared on its face to have been recently written, and experts testified
that it had been recently written, *held* that the conveyances were properly set aside as being without consideration and in fraud of creditors.

2. **Evidence:** AGE OF WRITING: EXPERTS: QUALIFICATION. A county
auditor, a teacher of penmanship, and attorneys at law, all of whom
stated that they were familiar with old papers and writings, and thought
they were able to give an opinion on the age of the writing in question,
were properly allowed to testify as experts in relation thereto.

Appeal from Louisa Circuit Court.

WEDNESDAY, MARCH 16.

THESE are equitable actions, and involve the validity of a
conveyance of a farm of 160 acres, and a chattel mortgage
upon the personal property upon the farm. Charlotte Dill,
the plaintiff in one action and a defendant in the other, is .
the wife of David W. Dill. Eisfield and Schoeneman Bros
& Co. are creditors of David W. Dill. The conveyance of
the farm and the chattel mortgage were executed by David
W. Dill to Charlotte Dill. The creditors claim that said
instruments are void as to them, because they were made and
executed in fraud of their rights as creditors of David W.

Dill. There was a trial upon this issue, and a decree declaring the deed and chattel mortgage to be void as to the cred
itors. Charlotte Dill appeals.

Basset & Wharton and *Hurley & Hale,* for appellant.

Newman & Blake and *Poor & Baldwin,* for appellees.

ROTHROCK, J.—It appears from the evidence that Charlotte
Dill and her husband, David W. Dill, are past sixty years of

1. FRAUDU-
LENT convey-
ance: burden
of proof: evi-
dence.

age. They were married prior to 1856, and
resided in the city of Philadelphia. They
removed to this state some thirty years ago, and
have been living on the farm in question for more than
twenty years. The title to the farm was in the husband.
One of their sons embarked in the mercantile business, and
after a time it became necessary for his father to become
security for him upon certain promissory notes given to the
creditors of the son. It became apparent that the father
would be compelled to pay the security debts. Thereupon
the conveyance of the farm, and all the personal property,
except such as was exempt from execution, was made to Charlotte Dill. It was therefore a material question in the case
whether the transfers were founded upon a sufficient consideration. The evidence upon this vital question consisted in
part of a written agreement between the husband and wife,
of which the following is a copy:

"Contract of agreement, made and entered into by and
between Charlotte Dill, party of the first part, and David
W. Dill, party of the second part, all of Philadelphia, Pa.,
witnesseth, that said party of the first part agrees to furnish
to the said party of the second part the sum of six hundred
dollars; said party of the second part agreeing to return to
the said party of the first part, her heirs or assigns, the said
six hundred dollars, together with five hundred dollars borrowed at a previous date, all of which is to bear interest at
the rate of eight per cent per annum, money payable on

demand; said money to bear interest from this twenty-fifth day of December, 1856. In witness whereof we have set our hands the day and year above mentioned.

her

"CHARLOTTE X DILL.

mark.

DAVID W. DILL.

Appellant claims that this contract was written and signed in the city of Philadelphia, in the year 1856, and she and her husband so testified as witnesses upon the trial. The creditors claimed that the contract was written and signed quite recently, and relied for proof thereof upon the appearance of the paper itself, and the testimony of several experts who united in the opinion that the instrument could not have been written thirty years ago, and that it was written very recently. The original paper was examined by the court, and the learned judge reached the conclusion that the writing was of recent origin; and, this finding being in direct conflict with the claim founded upon the writing, a decree was entered against appellant.

The original instrument has been certified to this court for our examination, and we think that the finding of the circuit court was in accord with the preponderance of the evidence. It is correct, as claimed by counsel for appellant, that, as the transfers show that they were made upon a sufficient consideration, the burden is on the creditors to show that the conveyances of the property were void for fraud. *Wolf v. Chandler*, 58 Iowa, 569; *Allen v. Wegstein*, 69 Id., 598. But it is wholly immaterial whether the evidence to establish the fraud is introduced by the plaintiff or the defendant.

The written instrument above set out was introduced in evidence by the appellant, and she sought to establish its genuineness by her own testimony and that of her husband. If it appears upon its face, and by the opinion of experts, that it was very recently written and signed, it completely overthrows, not only the instrument as evidence, but the testimony of the parties to it, and rebuts the presumption that the conveyances were founded upon a sufficient consideration. When taken in connection with the fact that the title to the property was retained by the husband for many years, and until both he and his wife knew that these security debts were being pressed for payment, we can arrive at no other conclusion than that the alleged indebtedness to the wife was an afterthought,—that it was not regarded by the husband and wife as an indebtedness until it became necessary to pro: tect the property against the claims of creditors.

'It is insisted that the witnesses who testified that the instrument was of recent origin were not experts, and their

2. EVIDENCE: age of writing: experts: qualification. opinions on that question were therefore not competent evidence, and we are cited to an article on scientific investigation of handwriting, volume 20, p. 273, of the American Law Register, *People v. Brotherton*, 47 Cal., 388, (395), and other cases, in support of the proposition contended for. We do not discover anything in the authorities cited which would authorize us to disregard the evidence in question. One of the witnesses had been a county auditor; another had been a teacher of penmanship for twenty-five or thirty years; the others were attorneys, one of them of long practice,—and all of these witnesses stated that they were familiar with old papers and writings, and thought they were capable of giving an opinion upon the question. We do not think it was necessary, to qualify a witness to testify upon the question, that he should be a chemist, and have knowledge of the chemical composition of ink. There can be no doubt that the question was one proper for expert evidence. See Lawson, Exp. & Opin. Ev. 418, and notes; *Fulton v. Hood*, 34 Pa. St. 365.

We think the decree of the circuit court must be

AFFIRMED.

HALLAM v. CORLETT.

1. **Contract: MISTAKE: REFORMATION.** The evidence in this case (see opinion) *held* to establish that there was a mutual mistake in the reduc-
· tion to writing of the contract between the parties for an exchange of lands; and the decree of the court below, reforming and enforcing the contract, is affirmed.

Appeal from Ida Circuit Court.

WEDNESDAY, MARCH 16.

THIS is an action in equity, by which the plaintiff seeks to reform a written contract between the parties, and to enforce a specific performance thereof. There was a decree in the court below for the plaintiff. Defendant appeals.

L. A. Berry and *Cole, McVey & Clark*, for appellant.

Gray, Warren & Buchanan, for appellee.

ROTHROCK, J.—It appears from the pleadings and evidence that the plaintiff was the owner of a farm of 160 acres, and a fractional tract of land of about forty acres adjoining the farm. His land was clear of incumbrance. The defendant was the owner of a farm of 160 acres, which was incumbered by a mortgage of $1,200. These lands were exchanged by the parties. A contract in writing was executed between them, by which each was to convey his said land to the other. The contract recited that the plaintiff was to assume and pay the mortgage on defendant's land, and the defendant was to pay plaintiff twenty-five dollars an acre for the fractional forty-acre tract. The plaintiff claims there was a mistake in the contract as reduced to writing, and that it did not express the agreement of the parties, in that it should have recited that the defendant should pay to the plaintiff, in money, an amount equal to the mortgage, in addition to the twenty-five dollars an acre for the fractional forty-acre tract.

The defendant denies that there was any mistake in the contract, and this is the issue between the parties.

The plaintiff was represented in the making of the contract by his agent, A. Hallam. The defendant acted for himself. There is some conflict in the evidence as to whether the contract was agreed upon orally before it was reduced to writing. We think a very decided preponderance of the evidence is with the plaintiff in this question. His agent testified that the terms concluded upon really were, that defendant was to pay the plaintiff the $1,200 in dispute. It is true, the defendant testified that the terms of the trade were not agreed upon orally; but it is conceded that the defendant went alone to an attorney and procured him to prepare the written contract, and gave him the information necessary to reduce the contract to writing. He directed the scrivener to insert therein an obligation upon defendant to pay plaintiff $2,200. This evidently included the $1,200 in dispute, and twenty-five dollars an acre for the land aside from the quarter section. While the defendant denies that any terms were agreed upon before he employed the scrivener to reduce the contract to writing, he makes no satisfactory explanation why he employed an attorney to write out what he in effect now claims was a mere offer to the plaintiff, and why he should propose to pay the $1,200 in dispute by causing it to be inserted in the contract, if that was not the oral agreement between the parties. Besides, it is a very rare occurrence that persons should exchange farms and have no oral agreement as to the terms of the trade before they set themselves about to bind themselves by a written contract.

When the agent of the plaintiff came to examine the written contract, the defendant being then absent, he claimed that there was more than forty acres in the fractional tract, and that, as the defendant was to pay twenty-five dollars per acre therefor, he directed that an erasure be made in the writing so that the defendant should pay twenty-five dollars per acre. In making this change, by some means, the clause providing for the payment of $2,200 was stricken out, and, as the contract was signed, it omitted the obligation of defendant to pay the $1,200 which he had directed to be inserted in the writing. That this was a mistake is very clearly shown. The agent of plaintiff was mistaken as to the terms of the written contract, and it would be an imputation upon the honesty of the defendant to say that the mistake was not mutual, because he directed the scrivener to insert the obligation to pay the $1,200 in the writing.

That the decree of the circuit court is correct, see *Stafford v. Fetters*, 55 Iowa, 487; *Courtright v. Courtright*, 63 Id., 358, and many other cases determined by this court.

AFFIRMED.

HORTON v. THE ESTATE OF HORTON.

1. **Promissory Note**: MATERIAL ALTERATION: WHAT IS NOT: PLACE OF PAYMENT: INSTRUCTION. For the administratrix of an estate, who is the payee and holder of a promissory note executed by the decedent, to write upon the back of the note, after her appointment as administratrix, "Payable at K.,"—no place of payment being named in the note,—*held* not to be a material alteration, since the payee would in any event pay herself, after the allowance of the note as a claim against the estate, by simply crediting herself with the amount in her account as administratrix; and in such case it was error to submit to the jury any question as to such alteration.

2. ———: ———: AMOUNT: ERRONEOUS INSTRUCTION. Where, in an action on a promissory note, it was alleged that the amount of the note had been materially altered, but the amount was plainly written in the body of the note, and there was no alteration therein, and the only fact relied on as an alteration was that one of the figures expressing the amount at the upper left hand corner of the note was blotted, *held* that there was no ground for submitting to the jury any question as to such alleged alteration.

3. ———: ———: NAME OF PAYEE: EVIDENCE TO BE CONSIDERED: INSTRUCTION. Where the defense to an action on a promissory note was that it had been materially altered, and the body of the note was in the handwriting of the plaintiff, and. she testified that she

had never at any time made any alteration of the note, and there was evidence tending to show that the note had been blotted after it had passed out of the hands of plaintiff, *held* that it was error to instruct the jury to determine, from a mere inspection of the instrument, whether it had been materially altered or not, but that they should have been instructed to make such determination from a consideration of all the evidence.

4. ———: ———: EVIDENCE: INSTRUCTION. In such case, where plaint'ff claimed, as well she might from the appearance of the paper, that no alterations had been made therein, unless a blot was an alteration, and that she did not make the blot, it was error to remind the jury that she had not introduced evidence that the maker of the note had consented to the alleged alterations, nor that they were innocently made, or made by a stranger.

Appeal from Van Buren Circuit Court.

WEDNESDAY, MARCH 16.

THIS is a proceeding to establish a claim against the estate of John Horton, deceased. The claim is in the form of a promissory note for $2,900. The plaintiff is the widow of the decedent, and was appointed administratrix of the estate. When this claim was presented, a special administrator was appointed to act in the premises. He approved the claim, and filed a report to that effect. J. M. Horton and J. O. Horton, sons and heirs at law of decedent, appeared and filed objections to the report and allowance of the claim. These objections were based upon three grounds: "(1) That the note was not executed by John Horton, deceased; (2) that it was without consideration; and (3) that the material alterations have been made in said note without consent of the payor, and that, by reason thereof, said note has become null and void, and the payor is released from any liability thereon." There was a trial by jury, which resulted in a verdict and judgment for the defendant. Plaintiff appeals.

Sloan, Work & Brown, for appellant.

H. C. Raney and *Johnston & Topping,* for appellee.

ROTHROCK, J.—I. The evidence shows conclusively that the note was executed by John Horton, deceased. The court so instructed the jury. There can be no question made as to the consideration for the note. It is plainly shown by the evidence. The case was tried upon the theory that the note was void on account of four material alterations made therein: (1) That the words "payable at Kilbourne," were written across the back of the note; (2) that the name of the original payee has been erased, and an endeavor made to cover it up with an ink-blot; (3) that the time of payment has been changed; (4) that the amount of the note has been changed and increased. Upon these questions the court instructed the jury as follows:

"(6) On the back of said note is a written statement as follows, to-wit: 'Payable at Kilbourne.' The heirs at law claim that this writing was placed on said note since the death of John Horton, and since said note first went into the hands of the special administrator, and said heirs also claim that said writing constitutes a material alteration of said note, and renders the same void. There is no presumption that said writing on the back of said note was placed there since the note was executed, but the burden of proof is on the heirs at law to establish by the weight of the evidence that the writing on the back of said note was placed there since the note was executed, and, if said heirs have failed to do so, then you should find for the plaintiff as to this point. The writing on the back of said note, even if placed there by plaintiff, if done for an innocent purpose, or as a mere memorandum, would not render the note void. But it is proper to remind the jury that there is no evidence that plaintiff placed said writing on the back of said note for an innocent purpose or as a memorandum. Plaintiff denies ever having made said indorsement on said note since its execution, and the burden of proof is on the heirs to show, by the weight of the evidence, that plaintiff placed said indorsement on the back of said note since its execution. If said indorsement was made by a stranger, without the procurement of plaintiff, then it would not render the note void. But if said written indorsement was placed on the back of said note by plaintiff, with the view to make it a part of said note, since the execution of said note, and without the knowledge of John Horton, then you would be justified in rejecting plaintiff's claim, and in that event should do so. But the burden of proof is on the heirs at law who are resisting this claim to establish by the weight of the evidence that said writing on the back of said note was placed there by plaintiff since the execution of said note, and if they have failed to do so, then you should find for the plaintiff as to this question. If the writing on the back of said note was placed there at the time it was executed, then, of course, said note would not thereby be rendered void.

"(7) The heirs at law who resist this claim also claim that the note in question has been altered in the following particulars: That the name of the original payee has been erased, and an endeavor made to cover it up with an ink-blot, and that the time of the payment of said note has been changed, and the amount of the note has been changed and increased; and said heirs claim that these alleged alterations in the note are apparent from an inspection of the note itself, and they ask the jury to inspect said note with the magnifying glass that has been used on the trial, for the purpose of ascertaining the truth as to this contention. The burden of proof is on the heirs to establish, by the weight of the evidence, that these alleged alterations, or some of them, have been made since said note was executed; and, if they have failed to do so, then you should find for plaintiff as to this contention. That is, unless it appears with reasonable certainty, from an inspection of said note, that it has been altered on its face, in some of the particulars claimed, since its execution; then, as to this question, you should find for plaintiff. But, if you find that the note in question has been altered since its execution by erasing the name of the original payee, or by changing the time of payment of said note, or by changing the amount of said note, then these would be material alterations, and would render the note void, because plaintiff denies that any alterations have been made, and plaintiff does not claim, nor has she introduced any evidence to show, that John Horton consented to any alterations (if any were made) in the note since its execution, nor does plaintiff claim that the alleged alterations were innocently made or made by a stranger. But the court once more reminds the jury that the burden of proof is on the heirs at law to show, by the weight of the evidence, facts and circumstances, that the alleged alterations, or some of them, have been made since the note was executed. Of course, it makes no difference what erasures, alterations, or changes were made in said note before or at the time it was signed and delivered."

Counsel for the respective parties have argued at length the question whether the words indorsed on the note, if made since its execution by the holder of the note, and without the knowledge and consent of the maker, are a material alteration. If the body of the note had been altered by inserting these words therein, there is no doubt it would be a material alteration. It would change the place of payment, and be a contract not entered into by the maker. It is contended on behalf of the appellee that the words upon the back are part of the instrument the same as if written upon the face. Counsel for appellant claim that the indorsement should be considered a mere memorandum, not a part of the note.

1. PROMIS-
SORY note:
material al-
teration:
what is not:
place of
payment:
Instruction.

These questions as to the material alterations of commercial paper are frequently attended with no little difficulty, arising from the fact that it rarely occurs that two alterations are exactly similar in words as well as in form. We think we have no occasion in this case to go into an examination of the very many authorities to be found in the books and cited by counsel, bearing upon this question. Whatever rule may be applicable to this indorsement, as an abstract proposition, we do not think that, under the facts of this case, the alleged alteration was material. It will be observed that the defend-ant claims that the alteration was made after the death of

John Horton, and the court states in the instructions to the jury that the defendant claims that the act in question was done after the note first went into the hands of the special administrator. If altered at all, it was therefore done after the plaintiff was appointed administratrix of the estate. The alteration did not, then, change the obligation of John Horton. It did not affect the integrity of his contract. The law imposed the duty on his administrator to pay his debts, and a special administrator was only necessary to adjudicate the claim. When that is done, if the claim be established against the estate, it is to be paid by the plaintiff crediting herself in her account as administratrix with the amount of the claim. It seems to us that it is apparent that the writing of an undertaking on the back of the note, (if this should be regarded as a part of the note,) obligating Mina Horton, administratrix of John Horton, to pay the note to Mina Horton at Kilbourne, is no material alteration. And this is the effect of the writing if made after the plaintiff was appointed administratrix. The sixth instruction was therefore erroneous. We think the question as to that alteration should not have been submitted to the jury. And we may further say that, if the alleged alteration was not made after the death of John Horton, there is no evidence that it was not on the paper when the note was written and signed.

II. We now come to the consideration of the other alleged alterations in the note. The original instrument has been certified to this court, and is as follows:

"$2,900. MARCH 21, 1877.

"(10 years) ten years after date I promise to pay to Mina Horton,—— value received, two thousand nine hundred dollars at ten per ct.; int. to draw int. if not paid. Value received annually. JOHN HORTON."

We have thought it necessary to set out a copy of the note, in view of the seventh paragraph of the charge given by the court to the jury. It is there recited that it is claimed that the alleged alterations are apparent from an inspection of the note. It is impossible to describe the appearance of the original instrument. It was written upon a printed blank. The greater part of the paper is stained, the stain being of a yellowish color. The evidence shows, and this fact is undisputed, that it became stained by reason of having been in a pocket-book in plaintiff's pocket during a rain, in which her clothing and the contents of her pocket were thoroughly saturated with water. It is claimed by the plaintiff that the water caused the heavy lines of ink on the paper to spread, which makes some of the words appear to have been written with a heavier hand. This may be correct, but we do not attach any importance to this fact. It cannot be claimed that the appearance of the note indicates that any alteration has been made in the words which appear to have heavier lines than the others. Indeed, there is no ground for the conclusion that the note has been altered in the amount. The words, "Two thousand nine hundred dollars," are plainly written; they are not effaced; no other words have been erased to make place for them; and they appear the same as other parts of the paper not claimed to have been altered. It is true that one of the figures in the sum written in the left hand upper corner of the note appears to be blotted over. Whether this is a blot, or the mere spreading of the ink, it is difficult to determine. But it is immaterial, so long as the body of the note plainly expresses the amount in writing. It was, therefore, erroneous to submit this alleged alteration to the consideration of the jury. We think the same may said of the alleged alteration in the time of payment.

2. ——: ——: amount: erroneous instruction.

In regard to the alteration as to the name of the payee, it appears from an inspection of the note that immediately after the name "Mina Horton," in the second line, there is a large blot covering that line nearly to the end of the paper, and extending above so as to cover some of the words in the upper line. This blot does not obscure the words in the

3. ——: ——: name of payee: evidence to be considered: instruction.

upper line so that they cannot be read without the aid of a magnifying glass. The blot is most dense at the place where we have left blank in the copy, but, notwithstanding this fact, the word "value" is plainly to be seen without a glass. Whether any other word was ever written therein, cannot be determined. The words "Mina Horton," which appear to be the name of the payee, are plainly written, and do not have the appearance of having been written since the note was executed.

It was upon this appearance of the note, which of necessity we have imperfectly explained, that the court, in the seventh paragraph of the instructions, charged the jury to determine from a mere inspection of the instrument whether it had been materially altered. This, we think, was erroneous. We do not say that under the issues it was not proper to submit the note to the jury for inspection as an item of evidence upon the question of alteration; but to allow them to determine that question upon an inspection of the note alone was clearly erroneous, in view of the fact that the body of the instrument was in the handwriting of the plaintiff, and she testified that she never at any time made any alteration in the note. There was evidence in the case which tended to show that the note was blotted after it passed out of the hands of the plaintiff, and the jury should have been plainly instructed that they should determine the question of alteration from all the evidence. It was also error to remind the jury that the plaintiff had not introduced evidence that John Horton, the maker of the note, consented to the alterations, and that she did not claim that the alleged alterations were innocently made or made by a stranger. 4. ——: ——: Of course, plaintiff made no such claim. She evidence: instruction. could well claim that no alleged alterations were made unless the defacing of the paper by the large blot was an alteration, and as to that, she claimed that it was not done by her. The jury should not have been allowed to consider the question whether she sought to introduce evidence that the maker of the note consented to the alterations, or that the alterations were innocently made or made by a stranger.

For the errors in the instructions above set out, the judgment will be

REVERSED.

FLEMING v. THE TOWN OF SHENANDOAH.

1. **Evidence**: ABSENT WITNESS: NOTES OF TESTIMONY ON FORMER TRIAL: NOTICE. Where a witness properly subpœnaed by plaintiff was out of the state at the time of the trial, without the consent or fault of plaintiff, and three or four days previous to the trial, and in term time, plaintiff learned that the witness would be so absent, and duly notified defendant that the transcript of the reporter's notes of his testimony on a former trial would be offered in evidence, *held* that such transcript was admissible, under § 3777 of the Code as amended, (see Miller's Code,) and that, if any notice was necessary in the case, that given was sufficient.

2. **Instructions**: STATEMENT OF ISSUES: FOLLOWING PLEADINGS. There can be no valid objection to a statement of the issues to the jury in the form in which they are made by the pleadings, even though an issue is thus presented on which, as a matter of law, there can be no recovery.

3. **Damages**: NEGLIGENCE: MENTAL PAIN: INSTRUCTION. In an action for an injury caused by a defective sidewalk, an instruction that plaintiff was entitled to recover "for pain and suffering undergone by her and occasioned by the injury," was not erroneous as authorizing the jury to allow her damages for mental pain.

4. ———: INJURY ON SIDEWALK: AMOUNT. It appearing that plaintiff, who was a woman forty-five years old, was so injured on defendant's defective sidewalk that she was disabled three or four months, and that her injuries are permanent, *held* that a verdict in her favor for $1,000 was not excessive.

Appeal from Page District Court.

WEDNESDAY, MARCH 16.

THIS is an action to recover damages for a personal injury which the plaintiff alleges she received by a fall upon a defective sidewalk upon one of the streets of the town of

Shenandoah, defendant. There was a trial by jury, and a verdict and judgment for the plaintiff. Defendant appeals.

James McCabe, for appellant.

Stockton & Keenan, for appellee.

ROTHROCK, J.—I. This is the second appeal by the defendant in this case. See 67 Iowa, 505. At the former trial one

1. EVIDENCE: absent witness: notes of testimony on former trial: notice.

De Barron was a witness in behalf of the plaintiff. He was not present at the last trial. The plaintiff offered the reporter's notes of his testimony, taken upon the former trial, in evidence. Objection was made by the defendant, and the objection was overruled. It is claimed that this ruling was erroneous, because there was no sufficient showing that the plaintiff could not have secured the attendance of the witness, and the notice that it was intended to introduce the notes in evidence was insufficient. It is provided by section 3777 of Miller's Code that "said notes, or any transcript thereof duly certified by the reporter of said court, shall be admissible, in any case in which the same are material and competent to the issue therein, with the same force and effect as depositions, and subject to the same objections, so far as applicable." It appears that the witness was regularly subpœnaed as a witness to attend the trial, and that plaintiff's counsel learned that he was about to go beyond the state. An interview was sought with the witness, in which he expressed his determination to absent himself on important business, which he claimed must have his attention. Plaintiff's counsel did not consent to the absence, but insisted that the witness should attend the trial. Thereupon counsel for the plaintiff entered a notice on the notice book to the effect that the transcript of the testimony of the witness would be offered in evidence upon the trial. This notice was entered in term time, and some three or four days before the trial was commenced.

We think that the showing made as to the absence of the witness was sufficient. It is not disputed that he was out of the state, and without the fault of the plaintiff or her counsel. And, in our opinion, if any notice is required that the transcript will be used as evidence, the notice given was sufficient. It is true, it is not a five days' notice, and it was given in term time, and it would not have been sufficient notice to have taken a deposition. But the rule with reference to notice for taking depositions has no application to the transcript. It is like a deposition which has been taken with both parties present, and the witness examined, cross-examined and re-examined. The ruling of the court was clearly correct.

II.   Next, it is claimed that the court erred in its statement of the issues in the case in the instructions to the jury.

2. INSTRUC-
TIONS : state-
ment of is-
sues: follow-
ing pleading. The statement of the issues was a mere recital of the allegations of the pleadings. There was a clause in the petition in which plaintiff claims that she suffered " great mental and physical pain " by reason of the alleged injury. It is contended that damages for mental pain are not recoverable in an action grounded upon mere negligence. We think the defendant is precluded by the record in this case from making that question. The petition was not attacked by motion or otherwise. It was answered by a general denial. If the court had neglected to state all of the issues, there might be ground of complaint. But there can be no valid objection to a statement of the issues in the form presented by the parties. It is true that the

3. DAMAGES :
negligence :
mental pain:
instruction. court, in directing the jury as to the elements of damages, stated that plaintiff was entitled to recover " for pain and suffering undergone by her and occasioned by the injury." This is not a direction to the jury to enter into an investigation of that metaphysical element of damages denominated " mental pain." It is a plain statement, having reference to physical pain and suffering.

III. The other errors assigned and argued have reference to alleged errors in the instructions as to the notice to the officers of the defendant that the sidewalk in question was out of repair, and the care requisite to be exercised by the plaintiff to avoid the injury. These instructions are in the usual form, and appear to us to be unobjectionable. It is also insisted that the verdict is not sustained by the evidence, which, it is claimed, shows contributory negligence on the part of the plaintiff. We cannot interfere with the verdict on this ground. We are satisfied that the jury were fully warranted in finding from the evidence that the plaintiff exercised the requisite care, and that the walk was defective, and that the officers of the defendant should have discovered the defects and repaired them before the plaintiff was injured.

IV. Lastly, it is claimed that the damages awarded by the jury are excessive. We cannot concur in this proposition. The verdict was $1,000. The plaintiff is

4. ——:
injury on
sidewalk:
amount.

a woman aged forty-five years. She was disabled by the injury for some three or four months, and the evidence tends to show that her injuries are permanent. It appears to us that the amount of the recovery is fully sustained by the evidence.

AFFIRMED.

WINANS v. HUYCK.

71 459
98 333

71 459
119 108

1. **Contract:** FRAUD AND MISTAKE: REFORMATION. Plaintiff purchased of defendant a certain hotel property, which defendant showed to her, but she did not know the width of the lot, and he, with the intent to defraud her, executed and offered her a deed describing only a portion of the lot, which deed she accepted, and took possession thereunder, supposing that it properly described the premises which she had purchased. These facts being established by clear and satisfactory evidence, *held* that she was entitled to a decree for a reformation of the deed, so as to describe the whole of the lot.

Appeal from Wright District Court.

THURSDAY, MARCH 17.

ACTION in chancery to enforce a specific performance of a contract .to convey lands. There was a decree granting the relief prayed for by plaintiff. Defendant appeals.

Weaver & Baker, for appellant.

Nagle & Birdsall, for appellee.

BECK, J.—I. The petition alleges that plaintiff purchased of defendant a lot in the town of Goldfield, whereon a building used as a hotel was situated. In payment thereof, she conveyed to defendant certain real estate in Iowa Falls, and entered into the possession of the hotel and lot purchased of defendant, who delivered to her a deed for the property, which, however, does not cover all of the lot, conveying only the south forty-four feet; the whole lot being sixty-six feet broad. It is alleged that plaintiff was not acquainted with the boundaries of the lot, and that, when the purchase was made, defendant pointed out to her the whole lot, and certain buildings upon the part not conveyed, as being the property sold, but fraudulently caused the deed to describe but a part of the lot, plaintiff believing that it covered the whole. In the original petition, plaintiff prays that defendant be required to specifically perform the contract, and convey the whole lot, and, in an amended petition, that the deed be reformed in accord with the contract of sale. The defendant in his answer denies the allegations of the petition.

II. The evidence, in our opinion, establishes, in a manner clear, satisfactory and free from reasonable doubt, that plaintiff bought all of the lot. The defendant described and pointed out the whole of it, and the buildings thereon, as the property he sold, and in no way indicated that he reserved any part of it. The description of the lot as shown by the town plat, or its breadth, was in no way referred to in order to identify the property sold. He must have known that plaintiff understood that she was purchasing the whole, and by his language and acts he expressed his own understanding of the sale as including the whole. She was ignorant of the dimensions of the lot. Of this ignorance he fraudulently took advantage, and executed a deed describing but a part of the lot. This deed was accepted by plaintiff through mistake. She took possession of the whole lot, and did not discover her mistake and plaintiff's fraud until afterwards. The sale of the whole property, the fraud of defendant in excepting a part of it in the deed, and the mistake of plaintiff in accepting it, are shown by evidence, clear, satisfactory and free from reasonable doubt. Upon this evidence, in accord with authorities cited by defendant's counsel, plaintiff is entitled to relief. In support of this conclusion, see the following cases: *James v. Cutler*, 54 Wis., 172; *Dane v. Derber*, 28 Wis., 216; *Bryce v. Insurance Co.*, 55 N. Y., 240; *De Peyster v. Hasbrouck*, 11 N. Y., 582; *Rider v. Powell*, 28 N. Y., 310; *Wiswall v. Hall*, 3 Paige, 313; *Goodenow v. Curtis*, 18 Mich., 298.

The decree of the district court is AFFIRMED.

CUNNINGHAM v. McGOWAN ET AL.

1. **Promissory Note:** PAYMENT BY NEW NOTE: EVIDENCE ON APPEAL. As there was evidence (see opinion) which raised a presumption that the notes sued on had been paid by the giving of new notes, *held* that the finding of the trial court in accord with such presumption could not be set aside on appeal.

Appeal from Madison Circuit Court.

THURSDAY, MARCH 17.

ACTION on two promissory notes. The answer admits the execution of the notes, and pleads payment. The cause was tried to the court without the intervention of a jury, and judgment was entered for the defendants. Plaintiff appeals.

Ruby & Wilkin, for appellant.

T. C. Gilpin, for appellees.

REED, J.—One of the notes sued on was executed in 1874, and was made payable to plaintiff or bearer. The other was executed in 1877, and was payable to plaintiff or order. The defense pleaded in the answer is that in 1879, after the maturity of these notes, the defendant McGowan, who is the principal maker, executed to plaintiff two other notes for $1,000 each, which he secured by chattel mortgage, and which he subsequently paid, and that part of the consideration of those notes was the indebtedness evidenced by the notes in suit.

The only question in the case is whether the finding of the circuit court, that this defense was established, is sustained by the evidence. The evidence shows, without any conflict, that the notes which were executed in 1879 were given in settlement of a pre-existing indebtedness. But it was not shown by any direct or positive evidence just what matters were covered by the settlement. It was also proven that, after the payment of those notes, defendant McGowan instituted an action in equity for their cancellation. In that action he alleged that he had made a number of payments in cash on the notes; also that he had made a number of sales of stock to plaintiff, the price of which should be credited on the notes, and that he had sold him a farm for $3,680, and that it was agreed between the parties that so much of said amount as should be necessary for the extinguishment of the debt evidenced by the notes should be applied thereon, and the balance should be paid in cash, and the notes surrendered. Plaintiff pleaded a counter-claim in the action, in which he claimed to recover on certain promissory notes executed by defendant after 1879. He was also required to, and did, set out in his answer all the notes he then claimed to hold against defendant. But neither the answer nor the counter-claim made any reference to the notes in suit. The notes sued on have not been produced in this court for our inspection, but it has not been claimed in argument that either of them bears any evidence of having been negotiated by plaintiff, and there was no evidence that either of them was ever out of his possession.

On this state of the evidence it cannot be said that the finding of the circuit court is without support. The facts proven tend to support the defense pleaded in the answer. The reasonable presumption, from the facts that the notes executed in 1879 were given for a pre-existing indebtedness, and that plaintiff made no claim upon them in the equity action, is that they were included in the settlement, and that plaintiff did not set them up in his counter-claim, for the reason that they had been satisfied. If he was not then the owner of them, that was a fact peculiarly within his knowledge, and he should have proven it. The case in this court, however, is governed by the well-settled rule that the verdict of a jury, or the finding of the trial court on a question of fact in an ordinary action, will be disturbed only when it is clearly without support in the evidence.

AFFIRMED.

LAMBERT v. SHETLER ET AL.

1. **Surety:** DISCHARGE OF BY EXTENSION OF TIME: KNOWLEDGE AND CONSENT. Granting an extension of time to the principal on a note will discharge the surety, unless he consents to such extension; but a mere knowledge of the extension, without more, is not equivalent to a consent.

2. ———: ———: EVIDENCE ON APPEAL. Inasmuch as there was evidence (see opinion) before the trial court tending to show that plaintiff had agreed to an extension of time upon the note in suit, and that the appellee, a surety thereon, did not consent to such extension, *held* that a judgment discharging the surety could not be interfered with on appeal.

Appeal from Johnson District Court.

THURSDAY, MARCH 17.

ACTION at law on a promissory note. Trial to the court. Judgment for the defendant Joseph Shetler, and the plaintiff appeals.

S.·H. Fairall and *Remley & Remley*, for appellant.

Boal & Jackson, for appellees.

SEEVERS, J.—This case was before the court at a former term, and is reported in 62 Iowa, 72. When it was redocketed in the district court, the plaintiff filed a reply to the answer, and therein pleaded that Joseph Shetler consented to the extension of time given the principal on the note, and other defenses which will be hereafter sufficiently referred to.

I. That Joseph Shetler had knowledge of the agreement set out in the opinion in 62 Iowa, 72, is conceded, as we understand, by counsel for the defendant; but it is contended that there is no sufficient evidence that he ever consented thereto. The district court must have found the fact to be as claimed by counsel for the appellee, and we cannot say that such finding is not sustained by the evidence. It is undoubtedly true, we think, that, if an extension of time is granted the principal, the surety is discharged unless he consents thereto. Mere knowledge of such extension, without more, is immaterial. A careful consideration of the record satisfies us that the only evidence which tends to show such knowledge is a certain paper signed by the appellee and two others, wherein they agreed to pay certain sums of money for the purpose of "ascertaining what can be done towards raising the amount necessary to pay off or assume the indebtedness in full discharge of Christian Shetler and his sureties;   *   *   *   this paper not to be used until a committee of the subscribers hereto shall have determined that enough is raised to pay off said debts or discount, and in full discharge of said Shetler and his sureties." This paper is dated on the ninth day of April, 1877, and thereby the appellee agreed to pay a certain amount for the purpose stated. It is insisted by counsel for the appellant that this paper recognizes the existence of, and refers to, the agreement set out in 62 Iowa, 72. This latter paper is dated in May, 1877. The appellee testifies that, when he executed the former paper, he had no knowledge of the latter. There is some evidence tending to show that he may have been mistaken in this respect. An answer sworn to by him in another action is relied on by appellant, but it is not so decidedly clear that it should be so construed as to warrant us in disturbing the finding of the court. Upon a careful consideration of the whole record, and being mindful of the fact that the district court had the opportunity of seeing and hearing the appellee when on the stand as a witness, we cannot say that the finding of the court is not sufficiently sustained by the evidence. It is by no means certain that, at the time the defendant signed the April agreement, he had knowledge of the one subsequently dated. It may be true that there had been some discussion among the creditors prior to April in relation to the matter, but we are unable to say that it had resulted in an agreement which had been reduced to writing, or even that its terms and conditions had been certainly agreed upon. The paper signed by the appellee clearly contemplates that he and other sureties were to be absolutely discharged. We therefore are unable to concede that the finding of the court as to the consent of the appellee is not sustained by the evidence.

II. The only other question we deem material is, whether John Lambert was bound by the May agreement. It is contended that he was not, because it was to be signed by all the creditors, and that this was not done. By reference to the agreement as set out in full in 62 Iowa, 72, we think it will clearly appear that it is not so provided on the face of such instrument. The expression, "We, the subscribers, creditors," it seems to us, should be construed as meaning that it is an agreement between all creditors who may sign the agreement, and is binding on them, whether all sign it or not. We do not understand that counsel for the appellant claims otherwise; but it is said Mr. Coldren testified that the understanding was that it was to be signed by all the creditors. The evidence of Mr. Coldren, however, when read all together, is not entirely clear. To an extent, it is somewhat qualified, and it clearly appears, we think, that the appellee had no knowledge of such condition; nor does it appear that all the other persons who signed the agreement had knowledge thereof. There are some other circumstances relied on by the appellant in support of the proposition above stated; but, upon the whole record, we think the district court was fully warranted in finding that it was understood that the May agreement was not to be signed by all the creditors before it should be regarded as binding on those who did execute it, and therefore the judgment must be

AFFIRMED.

ASHLEY ET AL. v. THE TOWN OF CALLIOPE.

1   466|
    317|
1   466
9   53

1. **Cities and Towns**: RIVAL VILLAGES IN ONE CORPORATION: SEVER-ANCE. Where a small village became incorporated, and included territory two miles long and one mile wide, and a rival village afterwards sprang up in another portion of the territory so included, and the interests of the villages, whose centres were about a mile apart, were antagonistic, and the land lying between them was not platted or used for town purposes, *held* that a petition by the people of the new village, under §§ 440–446 of the Code, for a severance of their territory from the corporation, was properly granted.

Appeal from Sioux Circuit Court.

THURSDAY, MARCH 17.

THIS is a special proceeding, by which it is sought to strike out or sever from the incorporated town of Calliope certain territory on which the plaintiffs reside. There was a trial by jury, and a verdict was returned directing the territory in question to be severed from the incorporation. Upon this verdict an order was made appointing commissioners to adjust the terms upon which the severance should be made Defendant appeals.

Wm. Hutchinson and *Argo & McDuffie*, for appellant.

Finley Burke and *George W. Hewitt*, for appellees.

Rothrock, J.—Numerous objections are urged by counsel for the defendant to the proceedings. They involve the sufficiency of the petition in the matter of whether it was signed by a majority of the resident property holders of that part of the town sought to be severed; whether the proper notice of the filing of the petition was given; and other alleged defects in the proceedings. We have examined the record and evidence with care, and our conclusion is that the jury was warranted in finding that the statute was in these respects fully complied with. It will be observed that the statute (Code, §§ 440–446, inclusive) provides a method for the trial of the question which is somewhat novel in its character. It authorizes evidence in the form of affidadits to be introduced on the trial. Affidavits were introduced by both parties, and the defendant was permitted to cross-examine the plaintiffs' affiants as to the statements of fact in their affidavits. Complaint is made by the appellant of the statute, in that it authorizes the use of affidavits as evidence. We know of no reason why this may not be done in this peculiar proceeding. It is a mere preliminary inquiry as to the propriety of maintaining the corporate limits of a town to its present proportions. If, in the discretion of the court or jury, the municipal corporation ought not to include within its lines the territory sought to be severed, commissioners are appointed to adjust and determine the terms of the separation.

It appears to us that the only question proper to be considered in the appeal from the order appointing the commissioners is, whether the court and jury abused the discretion reposed in them by the statute. If, from the record and evidence, it is manifest that the territory in question ought not to be severed and stricken from the corporate limits, then the order should be reversed. We find no just cause for interfering with the action of the court and jury in this case; and here we may say, in answer to objections to the evidence, that evidence on the question involved necessarily takes a very wide range. The inquiry is, ought the residents of the territory proposed to be severed be required to remain under the municipal control of the corporation? This involves, not only the proximity of the property to the improved part of the territory incorporated, but involves other questions, such as school privileges, municipal control, rivalries in business enterprises, and the like.

The principal facts in this case are that the town of Calliope was incorporated in October, 1882. It is a station and village on the line of the Chicago, Milwaukee & St. Paul Railroad. Before the town was incorporated, the Chicago & Northwestern Railroad Company constructed a railroad which crosses the Chicago, Milwaukee & St. Paul line about a mile from the village of Calliope. At or near the crossing a town was laid out, platted, and named Hawarden. The village of Calliope incorporated a tract of territory two miles in length by nearly a mile in width, and includes therein the plat of the town of Hawarden. Calliope was then a village of several hundred inhabitants. Hawarden has now become a village of some pretensions. Each village has a post-office and railroad depot, and it is about a mile from the business center of one village to the other. The land between the villages is not platted into lots, nor used as town property. There has been some contention and litigation about the erection of a school-house in the corporation, which by law constitutes an independent school district. It will thus be seen that these two villages are rivals, each striving for the business of the surrounding country, and they are of necessity antagonistic to each other. It appears to us that the order directing a severance ought not to be disturbed. There is no evidence warranting the claim made that the intervening territory will soon be necessary for residence and business purposes so as to make a compact city. The fact is that each village has its own post-office, its merchants, lawyers, doctors, "butchers, and bakers;" and if the village of Hawarden desires to throw off municipal control, we think the jury was warranted in finding that it ought to be allowed to "go in peace."

AFFIRMED.

COLBY v. McOMBER ET AL.

1. **Acknowledgment**: CERTIFICATE: TITLE OF OFFICER. Where the title of the officer taking an acknowledgment appears in the body of the certificate, this is sufficient, under § 1958 of the Code, and such title need not be again written after the officer's signature.

2. **Pleading**: ISSUE WITHOUT REPLY. Where, in an action to foreclose a mortgage, plaintiff alleged that his mortgage was superior to defendant's judgment. and defendant, in what he called a counter-claim. alleged that his judgment was superior to the mortgage, *held* that no reply was necessary to put in issue such allegation of the counter-claim.

3. **Mortgage**: FORECLOSURE BY PLEDGEE BEFORE HIS CLAIM IS DUE: OBJECTION BY JUNIOR LIEN-HOLDER. A mortgage assigned as collateral security for a much smaller debt may be foreclosed, when due, by the holder, at least as against a defendant who is merely a junior lien-holder, for the whole amount thereof, and before the last secured debt is due.

4. ————: FORECLOSURE: PRIORITY: EVIDENCE. Where, on the face of the record, plaintiff's mortgage was superior to defendant's judgment, defendant could not claim that a decree declaring the mortgage superior was not warranted by the evidence, when he failed to introduce any evidence to impeach the records.

Appeal from O'Brien Circuit Court.

THURSDAY, MARCH 17.

THIS is an action in equity for the foreclosure of a mort
gage. There was a judgment and decree for the plaintiff.
Defendant Warren Walker appeals.

Warren Walker, for himself.

E. C. Hughes, for appellee.

ROTHROCK, J.—I. The petition is in the usual form. It
is based upon certain promissory notes made by the defendant McOmber to one McAndrews, and a mortgage upon certain real estate, executed by McOmber and wife, to secure
the payment of the notes. It also sets forth an assignment
of the mortgage by McAndrews to the plaintiff. McOmber
and wife were made defendants, and a judgment on the notes
and decree of foreclosure were demanded against them. H.
O. Stanton, Bowles & Newcomb and Warren Walker were
also made defendants upon the ground, as stated in the peti.
tion, that they had or claimed some interest in the mortgaged
property, and it was averred that whatever lien or interest
they had was junior and inferior to the mortgage. None of
the defendants made any appearance to the action, excepting
Warren Walker. A default was entered against all of the
defendants who failed to appear, and a judgment and decree
of foreclosure were entered against them. Walker filed an
answer, in which he claimed a lien on the mortgaged property by virtue of a judgment against McOmber and his wife,
rendered on the twenty-fifth day of September, 1884. He
also averred that the plaintiff was not the real party in interest, because McOmber and wife had conveyed the mortgaged
property to McAndrews, and that he was therefore the proper
party plaintiff. He also averred that his judgment lien was
superior to the lien of the mortgage.

The mortgage was recorded some time before the judgment

was rendered; and the answer, which is denominated a counterclaim, does not state why the judgment should be the
superior lien, unless the pleader meant it to be understood
that the mortgage was extinguished because the mortgagor
had conveyed the land to the original mortgagee. This, however, does not appear to have been claimed on the trial, and, of
course, it could not be so claimed, because the mortgagee
would have the right to use the mortgage as a protection
against subsequent liens, even if the land was conveyed to
him.

The plaintiff offered the mortgage and assignment thereof
as evidence. Walker objected because the instruments were
not properly acknowledged. The acknowledgments appear to have been taken before Frank
Patch, a notary public of O'Brien county. They
are signed "FRANK PATCH, Notary Public." Appellant contends that the acknowledgments are defective because the
notary did not write the words, "for O'Brien county," after
his name. This was not necessary. The body of the certificates recite in plain and unmistakable language that Frank
Patch was a notary public in and for O'Brien county, and
this was sufficient. Section 1958 of the Code requires that
the certificate of acknowledgment shall set forth the title of
the court or person before whom the acknowledgment was
taken. The proper place to make the recital is in the body
of the certificate, and the law does not require a repetition of
it after the signature. The decisions of this court cited by
appellant are not inconsistent with this ruling. This is so
apparent that we cannot take the time to cite them and com-
ment upon them. If they did so hold, they would be in
plain conflict with the statute above cited.

1. ACKNOWL-EDGMENT: certificate: title of officer.

II. It is claimed that the counter-claim should have been
regarded as admitted, because the plaintiff did not reply
thereto. No reply was necessary. The plaintiff
had already set forth in the petition that the
mortgage was the superior lien, and the defendant set forth

2. PLEADING: issue without reply.

in general terms that the judgment was a lien prior to the mortgage. This made an issue between the parties.

III. The assignment of the mortgage was made as collateral security for a note of $600. The mortgage secured

3. MORTGAGE: foreclosure by pledgee before his claim is due: objection by junior lien-holder.

about $1,300. Appellant insists that, as the note for $600 is not yet due, the plaintiff could not maintain the action, and in any event the judgment should not have been rendered for more than the $600 and interest. It may be that, if the makers of the mortgage had defended the action, they would have had the right to raise these questions. But the appellant is in no position to defend for them. Besides, the mortgage was due, and the assignment authorized the plaintiff to collect it. The rights of priority claimed by appellant do not depend on the fact that the note held by plaintiff upon McAndrews is not due.

IV. There are other questions urged by appellant, which we do not think it necessary to discuss. They appear to be

4. ——: foreclosure: priority : evidence.

founded on the idea that the decree is against the evidence. The sum of the whole matter is that the records show that the appellant's judgment is junior to the mortgage. It was incumbent on him to show that, notwithstanding this fact, he was entitled to the superior equity. The plaintiff might well stand upon the mortgage and its assignment, because appellant offered no evidence that invalidated them in any way. It is true, it appears that the mortgagors had made a quitclaim deed of the mortgaged property to McAndrews, and perhaps it would have been wise for the plaintiff to have made him a party defendant, and foreclosed whatever right he had. But we need not determine whether or not he was a necessary party. Appellant has had his judgment lien adjudicated, and he ought to be content.

AFFIRMED.

THE FARMERS' & TRADERS' BANK OF LEON v. COHEN ET AL.

1. **Venue:** ACTION IN WRONG COUNTY: MISJOINDER: CHANGE OF VENUE: COSTS. Y. & P., residents of Decatur county, drew in their own favor a draft on C., a resident of Polk county, and indorsed it to the plaintiff. C. refused to honor the draft, and plaintiff brought suit thereon against the drawers and the drawee in Decatur county. *Held*—

(1) That C. was improperly joined with Y. & P., and that as to C. Decatur was as essentially the wrong county as if he had been sued alone.

(2) That C. was entitled to have the cause as to him removed to the county of his residence, and to an allowance for his expenses in attending in the wrong county to secure such removal.

(3) That, after his motion for such relief had been overruled, and he had filed an answer, and the plaintiff had dismissed the cause without prejudice as to him, he was yet entitled to his expenses for appearing in the wrong county.

Appeal from Decatur District Court.

THURSDAY, MARCH 17.

THIS action was brought against the defendant Cohen on an account for attorney's fees, and against the defendants Young & Parrish, on a draft. The defendant Cohen appeared, and filed a motion for the removal of the case as to him from the district court of Decatur county to the district court of Polk county, and for an allowance of his expenses; the motion being based upon the ground that he was a resident of Polk county. The court overruled the motion, to which he excepted. He then filed an answer. Afterwards, the plaintiff dismissed the action as to Cohen, and took judgment against the other defendants. From the order overruling the defendant Cohen's motion for a removal, and for an allowance for expenses, he appeals.

Read, Hutchinson & Read, for appellant.

Stephen Varga, for appellee.

ADAMS, CH. J.—The case comes to us upon a certificate,

the amount involved being less than $100, and the questions certified are as follows:

"*First.* When action is commenced in Decatur county by a resident thereof against another resident, also joining with such resident defendant a resident of Polk county, Iowa, and where the plaintiff alleges as cause of action that defendant Cohen, who was a resident of Polk county, was indebted to the other defendants in the sum of seventy-five dollars for professional services; that defendants Young & Parrish drew a sight draft upon said Cohen for seventy-five dollars, stated in said draft to be for said professional services, in favor of themselves, and indorsed the same to the plaintiff; and that said Cohen refused to accept said draft, and refused payment thereof; and that, by reason of the premises, defendants are indebted to the plaintiff in said sum of seventy-five dollars, —a copy of said draft being set out in the petition showing the indorsement to plaintiff by Young & Parrish; and when, before answer, such non-resident defendant appeared and moved the court to change the place of trial of said cause, so far as the same related to him, to Polk county, the county of his residence, on the ground of his residence in Polk county; and that the action of plaintiff as to him was improperly brought in Decatur county, and to award him his costs and compensation for attending at the wrong county,—did the court err in overruling said motion, and in refusing to grant such change of place of trial, and to award costs and compensation as asked?

"*Second.* When action is brought as above stated, reference being made to the statements above contained, and they being made a part hereof, and, in addition thereto, when, after judgment is rendered by default against such resident defendants upon said draft as the drawers and indorsers thereof, and where, after the overruling of such non-resident's motion to change the place of trial to the county of his residence as above stated, such non-resident defendant answers, denying any indebtedness, and setting up a misjoinder of causes of action and of defendants, and want of jurisdiction over him by reason thereof, and of his residence in Polk county, Iowa; and where, when such cause is called for trial on the issues between plaintiff and such defendant on motion of plaintiff, the action is dismissed without prejudice, and the said defendant thereupon moves the court to award him, against plaintiff, his costs and compensation and expenses incurred by reason of being compelled to attend at the wrong county for the trial of said cause, on the ground of his residence in Polk county, his improper joinder in said action, the bringing of said action against him in Decatur county, and the failure to obtain judgment against such non-resident defendant on the alleged cause of action against such non-resident defendant, and to award him his costs, compensation and expenses,—did the court err in overruling said motion, and refusing to award such costs, compensation and expenses?"

It is manifest that the liability of Young and Parrish was solely upon the draft, and in no way dependent upon the question of Cohen's liability. The two causes of action were distinct. There was, therefore, an improper joinder, and Decatur county was, as to Cohen, as essentially the wrong county as if he had been sued alone. He had, then, a right to have the case sent to Polk county, and, after he had been put to the expense of filing a motion for that purpose, we think that he was entitled to an allowance for expenses. It was, of course, the plaintiff's right to dismiss as to him; but we do not think that the dismissal should affect Cohen's rights to an allowance for expenses. Such allowance, it appears to us, was in the nature of costs, and a defendant, though the action be dismissed as to him, is still in court for the determination of any question of costs. The case, we think, must be reversed, and remanded for such order in respect to an allowance for expenses as would have been proper if the motion for a removal had been sustained.

REVERSED.

476|
481|

SIGERSON v. SIGERSON ET AL.

1. **Homestead**: JUDICIAL SALE: SALE OF OTHER PROPERTY FIRST: COMPLIANCE WITH STATUTE. C. held a mortgage on eighty acres of land owned by S., one forty of which was his homestead. C. also held a judgment against S., which was a lien on the forty other than the homestead. Each forty was worth $1,000. At a judicial sale under a foreclosure of the mortgage, C. bought the forty other than the homestead for $100, and he bought the homestead forty for $647. On the same day, at an execution sale under his judgment, he bought the forty other than the homestead for $867. He was the only bidder. In due time a sheriff's deed was made for the whole tract to C.'s assignee of the certificates. About six months later, S.'s wife began this action to set aside the foreclosure sale, on the ground that the land other than the homestead had not been first exhausted before the sale of the homestead, as required by statute, and that it was sold for a grossly inadequate price; but *held* that, in the absence of a showing that the sale had not been fairly conducted, equity could not grant her petition.

6
8

Appeal from Dallas Circuit Court.

THURSDAY, MARCH 17.

THIS is an action in equity, by which it is sought to set aside and cancel a sheriff's sale of eighty acres of land, part of which is claimed to be the homestead of the plaintiff. There was a demurrer to the petition, which was sustained, and plaintiff appeals.

. *H. S. Wilcox*, for appellant.

Kauffman & Guernsey, for appellee.

ROTHROCK, J.—It is averred in the petition that the plaintiff and James Sigerson were husband and wife, and that the defendant L. L. Collins was the assignee of a mortgage upon the eighty acres of land in controversy. One forty of the land was the homestead of the plaintiff and her husband. The title to the land was in the husband, and the mortgage was a lien upon the whole tract. Collins also held a judgment against James Sigerson, which was a lien upon the forty acres other than the homestead. The mortgage was foreclosed, and, at the sheriff's sale of the land upon special execution, which sale took place on the twentieth day of April, 1884, Collins bid on the land other than the homestead the sum of $100, and, that being the only bid therefor, the same was struck off and sold to him for that sum. At the same sale Collins purchased the homestead forty acres for the sum of $647. The sheriff issued to Collins the usual certificates of purchase, and a few days after the sale Collins assigned the certificates to the defendant M. E. Collins. A general execution was issued on the judgment of Collins against James Sigerson; and, on the same day of the sale for the mortgage lien, the forty acres other than the homestead was sold to Collins on the general execution for the sum of $867, and a sheriff's certificate of sale was issued to him, which was also assigned to the defendant M. E. Collins. On the twenty-ninth day of April, 1885, the sheriff executed a deed of the land to M. E. Collins in accordance with said sales.

This action was commenced in October, 1885. The ground upon which it is claimed that the sale under the mortgage foreclosure should be set aside is, that each of the forty acre tracts was worth $1,000, and that, when the property was offered for sale, there was no one to bid upon it but L. L. Collins, and that he bid $100 for the forty other than the homestead, as a pretended compliance with the statute, which requires that the real estate other than the homestead shall be first exhausted, and he bid the nominal sum of $100 so as to collect the mortgage lien from the homestead as far as possible, and thus have a large margin in value of the other forty acres from which to collect his judgment, which was not a lien upon the homestead. It is not charged that Collins practiced any fraud at the sales of the land, nor that he in any manner prevented others from being present and bidding at the sales. It is claimed, however, that the sale of the forty acres other than the homestead was for a grossly inadequate price, and that it and the sale of the homestead should be set aside for that reason.   We do not think that under the facts of the case a court of equity can afford any relief to the plaintiff.   So far as appears from the averments of the petition, the sale was fairly conducted, and the property other than the homestead was exhausted before the homestead was offered for sale.   It is true, the bid of $100 was grossly less than the alleged value of the land other than the homestead; but it was a public judicial sale, there was the right of redemption for a year after the sale, and there was the right to move to set aside the sale upon the return of the execution, before a deed was made to an assignee of the purchaser.   If it be allowable for defendants in execution sales to institute original actions in chancery at any time within the statute of limitations, to set aside sales and deeds made in pursuance thereof, upon the ground of inadequacy of consideration, much of the real property in the state would be held by a very uncertain tenure.

We think the demurrer to the petition was correctly sustained.

AFFIRMED.

LONES v. HARRIS ET AL.

1. **Township:** ORGANIZATION: IRREGULARITY AT FIRST ELECTION: SUBSEQUENT ELECTIONS NOT AFFECTED.   The board of supervisors has power, under § 379 of the Code, to divide townships and create new ones whenever the public convenience requires it, and the question of the political existence of a new township so created is in no manner affected by any irregularity in the first election of its officers; nor does such irregularity in any way affect the validity of subsequent elections of officers, or of the acts of officers subsequently elected.

Appeal from O'Brien Circuit Court.

THURSDAY, MARCH 17.

THIS is an action for recovery of damages caused by an

alleged trespass to personal property. There was a verdict and judgment for plaintiff, and defendants appealed.

Broadstreet & Boies and *E. C. Hughes*, for appellants.

Emmes & Bailey, for appellee.

REED, J.—The facts alleged as constituting the trespass complained of were the removal of the stays and braces in a stable or shed in which plaintiff stabled a flock of sheep, whereby the building was caused to fall, injuring and destroying the material of which it was constructed, and killing a number of the sheep, and injuring others. The defendants answered that the building, owing to the filthy condition in which it was maintained, was a nuisance, and that the board of health of the township in which it was situated ordered the abatement of said nuisance, and whatever they did in the premises was done in the execution of such order. Plaintiff, in his reply, denied that the township had ever been legally organized, or that the persons who assumed to make the order for the abatement of the alleged nuisance were ever legally constituted as a board of health. The proof showed that the board of supervisors of the county, at its session in April, 1878, entered an order creating the civil township of Lincoln, including therein the congressional township in which the building was situated. This territory was formerly included in Carroll township. The order provided that the first election in the new township should be held on the day of the general election in that year, and designated the place at which it should be held. It also directed the county auditor to issue a warrant for the election, as required by section 386 of the Code, but there was no proof that such warrant was ever issued or served in the manner prescribed by statute. It was shown, however, that an election was held in the township at the time and place designated in the order, and that due return thereof was made by the persons who assumed to act as judges and clerks. The transaction in question occurred in 1885. The circuit court instructed the jury that the burden of proof, on the question whether the township was legally organized, was on the defendants and, in making out their defense, it was incumbent on them to show the legal organization of the township, and that, to establish that fact, it was essential that they should prove that a warrant for the election, in 1878, was issued by the auditor, and served in the manner prescribed in the statute.

We do not deem it important to enter into the question whether the legality of the organization of the township can be questioned in an ordinary action between private parties, which is brought for the enforcement of a mere private right; for, conceding that the question can be raised in this character of proceedings, we are of the opinion that the question did not properly arise on the evidence in the case. The township was legally constituted by the order of the board of supervisors. That body has the power, and it is its duty, to divide the county into townships, and it has the power to divide townships, and create new ones when the public convenience requires that that be done. Code, § 379. The provisions of sections 386 and 387, with reference to the issuance and service of the warrant, relate solely to the first election in the new township. The question of the existence of the township as a political organization is not at all affected by them. If it should be conceded that the election in 1878 was irregular, or even illegal, it would not follow that those for subsequent years were invalid; for they were held under the general provisions of the statute relating to elections. The persons who assumed to act as a board of health, and who made the order, are presumed to have been elected at subsequent elections. The office of township trustee existed in the township under the statute, and could be filled by the electors at the subsequent elections, whether it had been legally filled before or not. It cannot be essential to the validity of the action of a public officer to prove that his predecessor in the office was legally elected.

Other questions have been argued by counsel, but we do not deem them sufficiently important to demand consideration.

REVERSED.

SEARS v. ALLEN ET AL.

1. **Mortgage**: PAYMENT: CANCELLATION: EVIDENCE. Action to secure the cancellation of a mortgage on the ground that it had been paid by the delivery of property to third parties, pursuant to an agreement with the mortgagee. Upon consideration of the evidence, (see opinion,) *held* that a decree was properly entered according to the prayer of plaintiff's petition.

Appeal from Marshall Circuit Court.

THURSDAY, MARCH 17.

ACTION in equity to obtain a decree declaring a certain mortgage on real estate, executed by the plaintiff to the principal defendant, satisfied of record, on the ground that it had been paid. The relief asked was granted, and the defendant, Josephine J. Allen, appeals.

Caswell & Meeker, for appellant.

Henry Stone and *J. H. Blair*, for appellee.

SEEVERS, J.—There is no material question of law presented in the record. The pivotal question to be determined is one of fact. Almost every proposition affirmed by either party is controverted by the other; but, for the purposes of this opinion, it will be conceded that the appellant, who is the wife of E. W. Allen, owned certain real estate in Marshalltown, which she, either with or without consultation with her husband, sold and conveyed to the plaintiff. A part of the consideration was paid in cash and by the assumption of a mortgage, and for the residue the plaintiff executed a promissory note to the appellant, dated August 14, 1882, for $3,400, with six per cent interest, due January the 1st, 1884. Upon the note was endorsed an agreement to accept in payment a car load of barbed fence wire at a named price; and the plaintiff claims that there was an oral agreement to take another car of such wire in payment of the note, and that he delivered the wire in accordance with the contract. If there was such a contract, and the plaintiff has performed the same, then the note is paid.

At the time of the sale and contract in relation thereto, including the delivery of both cars of wire, E. W. Allen resided in Portland, Oregon, and the contract was made in Marshalltown by Mrs. Allen, as the plaintiff claims, with the knowledge, consent and approval of her husband, and he so testifies. The appellant denies that her husband had any knowledge of the sale or agreements in relation thereto, and in substance they so testify. At the time the sale was made, and until after the second car of wire is claimed to have been delivered, E. W. Allen was the general manager of Seymour, Sabin & Co., dealers to some extent in barbed wire. Under the directions of E. W. Allen, the first car load of wire was shipped to Seymour, Sabin & Co., who paid the appellant therefor, as she claims and concedes.

The first material question we conceive to be is, whether there was a subsequent contract to take in payment of the note a second car of wire. The plaintiff testifies positively that the appellant so agreed. There is no doubt or uncertainty in his evidence in this respect. Mrs. Allen testifies that "this conversation as to selling more wire was had with Dr. Sears while riding with him in his buggy, after we had been to transact some business. I rode home with Dr. Sears soon after the execution of the mortgage. I suppose we talked on the way, but I do not remember the particulars of the conversation. I never stated to Dr. Sears that any arrangement he could make with E. W. Allen about taking a second car of wire on said note would be satisfactory to me, nor did I say that in substance. Sears said he would like to introduce his wire in that part of the country. I told him that perhaps Allen would order more from him for the use of the firm there." Taking this denial altogether, and all the circumstances in the case, we do not regard it as sufficient to overcome the positive evidence of the appellant. That there was some conversation about more wire must be conceded, and also that it took place substantially as the plaintiff testifies. Now, the only dispute is as to its purport. While the appellant testifies with some degree of positiveness and certainty, yet she admits that she did not remember the particulars of the conversation, and therefore we think the preponderance of the evidence as to the agreement to take the second car of wire is with the plaintiff. In accordance with what he believed was the understanding, the plaintiff wrote to E. W. Allen, and, in substance, stated that if he would send him the order of Seymour, Sabin & Co. for the same, he would send him another car of wire, and he could take out of it the balance due him on the house. The original letter was not introduced, but a letter-press copy was. Whether such copy was admissible is doubtful, but we do not understand the appellant to make any objection on this ground in this court. If mistaken in this, the copy may be regarded as excluded. It is certain, however, that E. W. Allen wrote to the plaintiff, and acknowledged the receipt of a letter from him, and stated: "You may ship us a car load of wire," on certain stated terms and conditions. This letter was signed, "E. W. Allen." What he meant by the word "us" is not entirely clear. The order, regarding it as one, did not purport on its face to be given by "Seymour, Sabin & Co.," although Allen was general manager of the business.

The plaintiff, however, shipped a car load of wire to Seymour, Sabin & Co., which was received by them, and the

amount due on the note credited on their books to Allen.
But, as we understand, a credit was first placed on such
books for the price of the wire to a barbed wire company by
whom the shipment was made under the directions of the
plaintiff. It, however, was charged to him on the books of
said company. Allen testifies that the credit made on the
books to him was without his knowledge or consent, but in
this we think he is mistaken. The preponderance of the
evidence is otherwise. Mrs. Allen testifies that she had no
knowledge of such credit, and that her husband was not her
agent; but we think the plaintiff had the right to believe that
he was, and to deal with him accordingly, because we find that
she agreed after the sale that any arrangement made with
her husband would be satisfactory to her. This agreement
had not been in any respect changed or modified. We deem
it immaterial whether Seymour, Sabin & Co. have paid for the
wire, except as above stated, or not, for, as between the plaintiff and defendant, it must be so regarded. There is other
evidence which we think supports the conclusion reached, to
which we have not referred.   AFFIRMED.

THE WISCONSIN, IOWA & NEBRASKA R'Y CO. v. BRAHAM ET AL.

1. **Appeal**: TRIAL DE NOVO: EVIDENCE CERTIFIED TOO LATE. Where, in
an equity case, the evidence is not certified within six months from the
date of the judgment appealed from, it is too late to secure a trial *de
novo* in this court. (See Code, § 2742, and *Mitchell v. Laub*, 59 Iowa, 36.)

2. **Contract**: TO CONVEY RIGHT OF WAY: MUTUALITY. Defendant
agreed in writing to convey to plaintiff a right of way for a named consideration when its road should be located over the land. *Held* that
the location of the road was a condition precedent to the liability of
either party, but that, when that was done, both became liable, and
either might enforce the contract as against the other.

Appeal from Jasper District Court.

FRIDAY, MARCH 18.

THE plaintiff and defendant Michael Braham entered into

a written contract by which the latter agreed to sell to plaintiff, for a specified consideration, the right of way for its railway over certain premises, and to execute and deliver a conveyance of the same when the road should be located, and the consideration paid. He subsequently denied the validity of the contract, and refused to permit the plaintiff's contractor and engineer to enter upon the premises for the purpose of constructing the road. It thereupon instituted this suit, alleging in its petition that it had tendered the agreed consideration to defendant, and its readiness to perform all of its undertakings in the contract, and praying that he and the other defendants, who it charged were aiding and abetting him, be restrained from in any manner interfering with the work of constructing the road. A temporary writ of injunction was issued on the order of the district judge, and on a final hearing the injunction was made perpetual. Defendants appeal.

George W. Wilson, for appellants.

Hubbard, Clark & Dawley and *Cook, Clements & Ogg*, for appellee.

REED, J.—I. The final judgment in the cause was entered on the nineteenth of March, 1885, and the evidence was certified by the trial judge on the eleventh

1. APPEAL: trial de novo: evidence certified too late.

of the following December. These facts are shown by appellants' abstract. On that state of the record, the cause cannot be tried *de novo* in this court. Code, § 2742; *Mitchell v. Laub*, 59 Iowa, 36.

II. Defendants demurred to the petition, and they assign error in the overruling of their demurrer. The petition

2. CONTRACT: to convey right of way: mutuality.

alleges the making of the contract, the tender by plaintiff of the amount of the price agreed upon, its readiness to perform, and the refusal of defendant to permit it to enter upon the premises, and a copy of the contract is set out as an exhibit. It is an undertaking by defendant that he will convey the right of way when the line of the road is definitely located and the consideration is paid. It contains no express agreement by plaintiff to construct its road through the premises, but it bound it to pay the stipulated price in case the road should be located upon the land. The point urged is that the undertakings were not mutual, and that the writing was a mere offer by defendant to sell and convey the right of way, which could be withdrawn at any time before acceptance. The position cannot be maintained. The undertakings of the parties · were dependent upon the happening of a future event, viz., the location of the road through the land. That was a condition precedent to the liability of either of the parties. But, when that condition was performed, the agreement, assuming that it was fairly entered into, was enforceable by either. The petition alleged that the condition had been performed. Very clearly, we think, it stated a cause of action.

AFFIRMED.

THE FIRST NAT. BANK OF NEWTON v. THE JASPER COUNTY
BANK.

1. **Attachment:** LEVY: WHAT NECESSARY: PRIORITY OVER MORTGAGE: NOTICE. In order to perfect a levy of an attachment upon lands in possession of the attachment defendant, it is necessary to notify the defendant thereof, (Code, § 2967,) and to make return of the writ; and a return is not made until signed by the officer. An entry in the incumbrance book is not sufficient, and is not even evidence or notice of a levy, where a levy has not in fact been perfected, as above indicated. Accordingly, a mortgage executed and filed for record before a levy was perfected, as above explained, had priority over the attachment lien.

2. ———: INTERVENTION: WHEN NOT APPLICABLE: SALE OF REAL ESTATE. When attached real estate has been sold under the attachment, a third party claiming a superior lien by virtue of a prior mortgage cannot proceed by intervention, under § 3016 of the Code, but may proceed in equity to restrain the consummation of the sale.

3. **Priority of Liens:** ACTION TO DETERMINE: QUESTIONS NOT INVOLVED: PARTIES. Where the only question made by the pleadings

was as to the priority of liens, *held* that questions as to the validity of the indebtedness on which the liens were based could not be considered, —especially as the debtor was not a party to the action.

Appeal from Jasper District Court.

FRIDAY, MARCH 18.

ACTION in chancery to determine the question of priority between two conflicting liens upon lands. The prayer of plaintiff's petition was granted by the decree, from which defendant appeals.

Alanson Clark and *S. C. Cook*, for appellant.

Winslow & Varnum, for appellee.

BECK, J.—I. The petition shows that plaintiff holds a mortgage upon certain lands, and that the defendant recov-

1. ATTACH-
MENT: levy:
what neces-
sary: priority
over mort-
gage: notice.

ered judgments against the mortgagor rendered in actions in which attachments were issued and levied upon the same lands. Special executions were issued upon the judgments, and the lands have been sold thereon, and a certificate of sale issued by the sheriff to defendant, upon which it will, if permitted, take a sheriff's deed, which will be a cloud upon the title of the land covered by plaintiff's mortgage. The plaintiff prays that a decree be entered declaring that plaintiff's mortgage is a lien paramount to defendant's attachments and judgments, and that defendant be restrained from assigning the sheriff's certificate, and from obtaining a sheriff's deed. The answer of defendant put in issue the facts upon which plaintiff bases its rights to recover. The pleadings need not be more particularly referred to here.

The facts upon which the decision of the case turns are these: Defendant's attachments, as claimed by it, were levied on the first day of May. Plaintiff's mortgage was executed and filed for record on the day following. But the sheriff evying the attachments gave no notice thereof to the defend-

ant, who was in possession of the lands, nor did he make
return of his writs before plaintiff's mortgage was filed for
record, nor do any other act amounting to the levy of the
writs. It may be admitted that he entered his return upon
the writs before that day, but the evidence on this point is
not clear. Certain it is, he did not sign the return until
several days after. The returns, *i. e.*, the statements showing
the service of the writs, were not, therefore, completed before
plaintiff's mortgage was executed and filed for record. On
the first day of May the sheriff made an entry in the incumbrance book of the levy of the attachments upon the lands.

II.   Were the writs levied before plaintiff's mortgage was
filed for record?   The entry in the incumbrance book is no
part of the levy, and, if no levy was made, is not to be regarded
as evidence establishing it.   See *Collier v. French*, 64 Iowa,
577.   The purpose of the entry of the levy in the incumbrance book is to give notice of the levy.   Code, §§ 197,
(par. 6,) 3022.   Of course, if there was no levy, no notice
would be imparted, for the levy did not in fact exist.   Code,
§ 2967, provides that " the mode of attachment must be as
follows: (1) By giving the defendant in the action, if found
within the county, and also the persons occupying and in possession of the property, if it be in the hands of a third person,
notice of attachment."   The punctuation of this statute,
which is clearly incorrect, may, without consideration, lead
to the erroneous conclusion that it applied exclusively to
levies upon stock in corporations, debts due the defendant,
and property owned by him and held by a third party.   But,
upon considering the language of the section and the con-
text, the conclusion is irresistible that the direction extends
to the levies upon all property subject to attachment.   At
least, the sheriff should have made return of the writs, which
would have given notice to the world of the levies.   See
Crawford v. Newell, 23 Iowa, 453; *Clymore v. Williams*,
77 Ill., 618; *Sharp v. Baird*, 43 Cal., 577; *Main v. Tap-
pener*, Id., 206.

III. Defendant insists that plaintiff should have proceeded under Code, § 3016, which authorizes persons other
than the defendant, before sale of attached prop-
2. ——: in-
tervention:
when not
applicable:
sale of real
estate.
erty, to dispute the validity of the attachment,
claim the property attached, etc., by petition
filed in a special proceeding, which shall be
determined in a summary manner. This section authorizes
such proceedings before a sale under an attachment. In
reply to defendant's position, it is sufficient to say that the
property attached had been sold upon an execution issued
upon the judgment rendered in the case. Plaintiff could not
have pursued the special proceedings.

IV. The plaintiff insists that there was no ground for the
attachment, and the defendant, on the other hand, claims that
3. PRIORITY
of liens :
action to
determine :
questions not
involved :
parties.
plaintiff's mortgage was void, for the reason that
it was given by the mortgagor in order to suppress the evidence of a forgery. These matters
are not involved in this action, which is to settle
the priority of liens, and not to assail the validity of the judgments and mortgage upon which the respective liens were based.
They could not have been determined for another reason: The
debtor would be a necessary party to an action involving these
questions. He is not a party in this case.

V. These conclusions upon the merits of the case, leading to the affirmance of the decree of the court below, render it unnecessary for us to pass upon the motions, amendments and other papers filed in the case,— a wilderness as
to numbers and obscurity, all intended to settle the contents
of the records. We find there is no dispute as to its contents, so far as it presents the facts we have found, as stated
above. The controversy carried on by the motions and
amendments involve facts and questions which we do not
find it necessary to determine.

VI. The decree of the court below should simply declare
that, as between plaintiff's mortgage and defendant's attachment, the mortgage is the paramount lien. It cannot affect

the validity of either as to the other matters. There is language in the decree that may bear a different interpretation. In this respect it must be regarded as modified by this opinion.

AFFIRMED.

CONNERS, ADM'R, v. THE BURLINGTON, C. R. & N. R'Y CO.

1. **Judgment on Special Verdict:** WHEN ALLOWABLE. A judgment on special findings, and against a general verdict, is justifiable only when the special findings are inconsistent with the general verdict, and are of themselves, or when taken in connection with facts admitted by the pleadings, sufficient to establish or defeat the right of recovery. (See authorities cited in opinion.)

2. **Railroads:** INJURY TO BRAKEMAN OUT OF PLACE OF DUTY: CONTRIBUTORY NEGLIGENCE. Where the immediate cause of the injury was the derailing of the train, and that was caused by the manner in which it was being run and the condition of the track, *held* that the mere fact that the brakeman who was injured was, at the time of the accident, in the engineer's cab, instead of at the brakes, which was his place of duty, was not such contributory negligence on his part as to defeat a recovery for his injuries, where it did not appear that his absence from the brakes contributed to the accident, nor that he exposed himself to any greater known danger by going into the cab than by remaining at the brakes, even though it happened that no one was in fact injured except those who were on the engine. (*Player v. Burlington, C. R. & N. R'y Co*, 62 Iowa, 723, distinguished.) SEEVERS and ROTHROOK, J J., *dissenting*.

3. **Survival of Actions:** PERSONAL INJURY: IMMEDIATE DEATH. While at common law an action could not be maintained for a personal injury resulting in immediate death, yet the reasons for that rule are abrogated by §§ 2525–2527 of the Code, and now an action by the administrator may be maintained in such a case.

4. **Practice on Appeal:** RECORD: HOW MUCH NECESSARY. In ordinary actions, the parties are required to print only so much of the record as is necessary for the presentation and determination of the questions brought up by the appeal for review. Accordingly, where the only question was whether a judgment for the defendant on special findings, and against the general verdict, was justifiable, it was not necessary to bring up the evidence and the instructions of the court.

Appeal from Cedar Rapids Superior Court.

FRIDAY, MARCH 18.

PLAINTIFF'S intestate was killed while in the employ of defendant as a brakeman on one of its trains, and this action was brought for the recovery of the damages sustained by his estate in consequence of his death. There was a general verdict for plaintiff for $2,000. There were also certain special findings. Defendant filed a motion for judgment on the special findings, on the alleged ground that they were manifestly inconsistent with the general verdict, and that upon the facts found, it was entitled to judgment. The superior court sustained the motion, and entered judgment for defendant, and from that order plaintiff appeals.

Bowman & Swisher, for appellant.

S. K. Tracy and *J. C. Leonard,* for appellee.

REED, J.—It is alleged in the petition that the train on which the intestate was employed was thrown from the track as it approached the station of Northwood, at a point where a switch or side track connects with the main track, and that he was killed in the wreck; also that there is a sharp curve in the track at that point. It is charged that the track was rendered dangerous by the curve and the connection of the switch at that point, and that the company was guilty of negligence in constructing and maintaining it in that condition; also, that the engine drawing the train was new and stiff, and difficult to control when making a curve, and that this was known to the engineer in charge, but that he was running it at a dangerous rate of speed at the time, and at a much higher rate of speed than was allowed by the rules of the company. And it is alleged that the injury was caused by these acts of negligence.

The jury found specially that the accident was caused partially by the curve in the track, and partially by the rate

of speed at which the train was being run at the time, and
that the engine had frequently passed over the curve; also,
that the deceased had been running as a brakeman over the
part of the road where the accident occurred for one month;
that his place of duty at the time of the accident was at the
brakes, but that he was riding in the cab; and that no one
on the train, except those who were riding on the engine,
was injured in the accident; also that he was instantly
killed.

I. To entitle a party to a judgment on special findings
against a general verdict in favor of his adversary, the
special findings must be inconsistent with the
general verdict, and must of themselves, or
when taken in connection with the facts admit-
ted by the pleadings, be sufficient to establish or defeat the
right of recovery. *Lamb v. First Presbyterian Soc.*, 20
Iowa, 127; *Hardin v. Branner*, 25 Id., 364; *Bills v.
Ottumwa*, 35 Id., 107; *Crouch v. Deremore*, 59 Id., 43;
Hammer v. Railroad Co., 61 Id., 56.

*1. JUDGMENT
on special
verdict: when
allowable.*

Under this rule, defendant would be entitled to judgment
notwithstanding the general verdict for plaintiff, if it
appeared by the special findings either that
plaintiff had failed to establish some fact essential to his right of recovery, or that some fact
was established which defeated such right. The
facts which plaintiff was required to prove to establish a
right of recovery are (1) that the injury complained of was
caused by the negligence of defendant or its employes; and
(2) that the intestate was not himself guilty of any negligence which directly contributed to the injury.

*2. RAILROADS:
injury to
brakeman
out of place
of duty: con-
tributory neg-
ligence.*

The general verdict is a finding of each of these facts by
the jury. It is not claimed that there is any inconsistency
between the general and special finding as to the first of
these facts. But it is insisted that the facts specially found
are inconsistent with the general finding that the deceased
was not guilty of contributory negligence, and that they

show conclusively that plaintiff is not entitled to recover. The facts found are that deceased was riding in the cab at the time of the accident, while his place of duty was at the brakes, and no person on the train was injured except those who were riding on the engine. It will be observed that the findings do not determine that the accident would have been prevented if the deceased had been at his post of duty, and had applied the brakes. Neither do they determine that he would not have been injured if he had been at the brakes instead of on the cab; nor that the position in the cab was ordinarily more dangerous than the one at the brakes. All that is determined is that he was away from his post of duty, and that he was injured while in that position by an accident which was caused by the negligent manner in which the train was being run over a defective or dangerous track, and that no person on the train was injured except those who were at the said place.

The question to be determined is whether these facts defeat the right of recovery. We think they do not. It cannot be said, as matter of law, that he was negligent. If he had, by going upon the cab, exposed himself to a known or obvious danger, and had been injured in consequence of such exposure, the case would have been very different. But it does not appear that he was exposed while in the cab to any known danger which he would not have been exposed to if he had remained at the brakes; or if his presence at the brakes had been necessary for the proper government of the train, and the accident had been occasioned by his absence from his post of duty, a different question would arise. But that does not appear. Very clearly, we think, it cannot be said that his act was negligent, unless some consideration of duty or prudence demanded that he should have been at some other place than the one in which he was when the accident occurred. Neither did the act contribute to the injury. The immediate cause of the injury was the derailing of the train, and that was caused by the manner in which it was being run, and the condition of the track. His presence in the cab neither caused nor contributed to the result.

The case differs from *Player v. Burlington, C. R. & N. R'y Co.*, 62 Iowa, 723. The plaintiff in that case was a passenger on a freight train. His proper position was in the " caboose; " but, instead of going into it, he got upon a box car, and, while in that position, the car was thrown from the track by the negligence of the defendant, as was alleged, and he was injured, and it was held that he could not recover. As the company had furnished a safe and convenient car for the passenger to ride in, but he chose, for purposes of his own, to ride on another part of the train, the injury was the result of his own act. He could very properly be said to be guilty of contributory negligence. But the facts of this case do not bring it within that rule.

II. It is next contended that, as the intestate was instantly killed, a civil action cannot be maintained for the injury. The position is that, under the common law, there is no civil remedy for an injury which produces the death of a human being, and, while this rule is modified to some extent in this state by statute, yet the statute goes no further than to afford a right of action to the one who sustains the injury if he survives it, which survives, and may be brought or maintained by his representatives after his death.

3. SURVIVAL of actions: personal injury : immediate death.

The statutes bearing on the questions are sections 2525, 2526 and 2527 of the Code, which are as follows: "All causes of action shall survive, and may be brought, notwithstanding the death of the person entitled or liable to the same." "The right of civil remedy is not merged in a public offense, but may in all cases be enforced independently of and in addition to the punishment of the latter. When a wrongful act produces death, the damages shall be disposed of as personal property belonging to the estate of the deceased, except that, if the deceased leaves a husband, wife, or child, or parent, it shall not be liable for the payment of debts." "The actions contemplated in the two preceding sections may be brought, or the court on motion may allow the action to be continued, by or against the legal represent- atives or successors in interest of the deceased. Such action shall be deemed a continuing one, and to have accrued to such representatives, or successors, at the same time it did to the deceased, if he had survived. If such is continued against the legal representatives of the defendant, a notice shall be served on him as provided for service of original notice."

We will concede that the rule of the common law is as claimed by counsel. We are of the opinion, however, that the rule has been entirely abrogated by our statute. For many years before the enactment of the present Code, a statute was in force in this state which provided, in express terms, that, "when a wrongful act produces death, the per- petrator is civilly liable for the injury." Revision 1860, § 4111; Code 1851, § 2501. When the present Code was enacted, the section in which that provision was contained was repealed, and the sections quoted above were enacted in lieu thereof. As appears, the language of this provision is not contained in any of them. But we think the effect of these provisions is the same as though that express language had been retained. The doctrine that, "in a civil court, the death of a human being could not be complained of as an injury," appears to have been first laid down by Lord ELLEN- BOROUGH in *Baker v. Bolton*, 1 Camp., 493. That was a *nisi prius* case, but the doctrine was adhered to by the English courts until it was abrogated by statute. It has also been followed quite generally by the courts of this country. See *Carey v. Berkshire R'y Co.* and *Skinner v. Housatonic R'y Co.*, 1 Cush., 475; *Green v. Railway Co.*, 2 Keyes, 294; *Eden v. Railway Co.*, 14 B. Mon., 165.

It has been denied, however, by at least one distinguished American judge, that it is capable of vindication, or that it

is so deeply rooted in the common law as to be binding on
the courts of this country. *Sullivan v. Union Pac. R'y
Co.*, 3 Dill., 334. When we look into the cases, however, in
which the doctrine has been held, to ascertain the ground of
the holding, we find that the reasons for the rule are (1) that
the right of civil remedy, when the wrongful act amounts to
a felony, is merged in the public offense; and (2) that the
injury to the person being a personal tort, the right of action
determines with his death. Relief was denied, then, in this
class of cases, upon grounds of supposed public policy,
rather than upon considerations as to the rights and liabilities of the parties. The provisions of the statute quoted
above expressly abrogate both of these reasons. Section
2525 provides that the cause of action shall survive notwithstanding the death of the party, and section 2526 enacts
that the right of civil remedy does not merge in the public
offense, but may be enforced independently of, and in addition to, the punishment of the latter. This express abroga-
tion of the reasons of the rule necessarily carries with it the
rule itself. The case on its actual merits stands as it always
did. A wrongful act has been committed, which was
injurious to another. But the grounds upon which a civil
remedy was denied have been abrogated, and there now
exists no reason for a denial of that right.

III. The abstract does not contain the evidence or the
instructions of the court, and it is insisted that, on this state

4. PRACTICE
on appeal:
record : how
much neces-
sary.

of the record, we cannot review the case. But
the single ground upon which the superior court
entered the judgment for the defendant was that,
upon the facts specially found by the jury, plaintiff was not
entitled to recover, and it is not necessary for the presentation and determination of that question that we have the
instructions or evidence before us. If we had them before
us, we would not look into them in considering it. The
instructions are presumed to be correct, and no question is
made as to the sufficiency of the evidence to sustain both the

general verdict and the special findings. In ordinary actions, the parties are required to print only so much of the record as is necessary for the presentation and determination of the questions brought up by the appeal for review.

REVERSED.

SEEVERS, J.—Being unable to distinguish this from the *Player Case*, I dissent from the foregoing opinion. ROTHROOK, J., concurs in this dissent.

HERD v. HERD.

1. **Administrator**: TAKING WIDOW'S PROPERTY: REPLEVIN: CAPACITY OF DEFENDANT. An administrator who takes the property of the widow is a tresspasser, and is personally liable, and cannot, in an action to recover the property, insist that he shall be substituted in his capacity as administrator.

2. **Continuance**. ABSENT WITNESS: DISMISSAL OF ISSUE. A continuance asked by defendant on the ground of the absence of a witness is properly refused when the plaintiff dismisses the only issue to which his testimony would relate.

3. **Practice on Appeal**; VERDICT: WEIGHT OF EVIDENCE. There being some evidence tending to support the verdict, it is not the province of this court to say that the evidence was not sufficient.

Appeal from Wright Circuit Court.

FRIDAY, MARCH 18.

ACTION to recover the possession of two horses. As to one of them, the plaintiff claimed possession on the ground that the horse was her property, and she claimed possession of the other because she was the widow of W. W. Herd. The cause of the detention of the horses was stated in the petition to be that the defendant was administrator of the estate of W. W. Herd, and as such took possession of the horses. Trial by jury, judgment for the plaintiff, and defendant appeals.

E. M. Sharon and *C. F. Peterson*, for appellant.

Nagle & Birdsall, for appellee.

SEEVERS, J.—The defendant moved the court to substitute him as defendant in his representative capacity as adminis-

1. ADMINIS-
TRATOR:
taking wid-
ow's proper-
ty: replevin:
capacity of
defendant.

trator. This motion was overruled, and the court did not err in so ruling. The theory of the petition—and thereon the plaintiff asked to recover —is that the defendant was a trespasser. This being so, he is personally liable therefor, as is a sheriff who levies on and takes possession of property which the process in his hands does not justify him in doing. The defendant had no right to take the plaintiff's property because he was the administrator of her husband's estate.

II. The defendant moved the court for a continuance because of the absence of a witness. Thereupon the plaint-

2. CONTINU-
ANCE: absent
witness: dis-
missal of is-
sue.

iff dismissed her claim or right to recover for the horse claimed by her as widow. Thereupon the motion to continue was overruled. This ruling was correct, for the reason that it was shown that the evidence of the absent witness related only to such horse, and had no tendency to establish the remaining issue.

III. It is contended that the verdict is not sustained by the evidence. But we think it is. The jury were war-

3. PRACTICE
on appeal:
verdict:
weight of evi-
dence.

ranted in finding that the plaintiff had purchased the horse of her husband during his life-time, if the evidence of the plaintiff and her witnesses was true, and this was a question for the jury. We cannot say that there is any such improbability in their evidence as will warrant us in concluding that the jury should have found otherwise.

Complaint is made of an instruction asked and refused in relation to the weight the jury should give to declarations of

a party, in possession of personal property, in disparagement
of his title.   Conceding that no well-grounded objection can
be made to the instruction, we are clearly of the opinion,
under the evidence, that its refusal does not constitute reversible error.

AFFIRMED.

PERKINS V. HINCKLEY, ADM'R.

1. **Estates of Decedents**: ASSETS: PENSION MONEY. Upon the death
of a married man leaving money derived from a pension received from
the United States, the money goes to his administrator, and not to his
widow.

Appeal from Johnson Circuit Court.

FRIDAY, MARCH 18.

THE defendant is administrator of the estate of E. S. Perkins.   At the time of the latter's death, he owned a certificate of deposit issued by a bank for $1,000, which money
had been received from the United States government as and
for a pension granted him.   The plaintiff is the widow of
said E. S. Perkins, and she in her petition asked the circuit
court to order the defendant to deliver the said certificate to
her, upon the ground that the money was exempt from execution, and that she, as widow, was entitled thereto.   This
was denied by the defendant, and he claimed that the money
belonged to him as administrator.   The court found for the
defendant, and denied the relief asked. The plaintiff appeals.

Remley & Remley, for appellant.

S. H. Fairall, for appellee.

SEEVERS, J.—It is provided by statute that "all money
received by any person   *   *   *   as a pension
*   *   *   shall be exempt from execution,   *
*   *   whether such pensioner shall be the head of a

family or not." Chapter 23, Laws Twentieth General Assembly. It is obvious that under this statute the money in question was not exempt from execution because E. L. Perkins was the head of a family. If he had never been married, the money was just as clearly exempt. The Code provides that, "when the deceased leaves a widow, all personal property which, in his hands, as the head of a family, would be exempt from execution,   *   *   *   shall be exempt in her hands as in the hands of the decedent." Code, § 2371. Under this statute, the widow is entitled to all personal property which is exempt from execution, for the reason or because her deceased husband was the *head of a family*. But we have seen that the money in question was not so exempt, and therefore she is not entitled thereto. As we read the statute, the words, "as the head of a family," define and limit the rights of the plaintiff. There is no rule of construction which authorizes the elimination of such words, and therefore the judgment of the circuit court is

AFFIRMED.

500
442
500
661
500
106
500
194

DAVIS v. THE CITY OF DES MOINES.

1. **Cities and Towns**: DEBT OF: WHAT CONSTITUTES: CONSTITUTIONAL LIMIT: SEWER TAX. A contract entered into by a city for the building of a sewer, whereby the contractor agrees to accept, in full satisfaction for the whole work, certificates of assessment made upon the property adjacent to the sewer, *held* not to create a debt against the city within the meaning of article 11, § 3, of the constitution, limiting the lawful indebtedness of a city to five per cent of the value of its taxable property.

Appeal from Polk Circuit Court.

FRIDAY, MARCH 18.

THE petition sets forth that the defendant is already indebted to the full constitutional limit; that the plaintiff is the owner of certain land fronting on one of the streets of

the city, and that the city, by its officers, entered into a contract with one McCauley to construct a sewer in said street,
and to pay him therefor by assessing the contract price
thereof against the adjacent property; that the municipal
authorities are about to make said assessment, and charge the
same upon the lots, and proceed to collect the same of said
owner. It is prayed that the said contract be canceled and
declared void, and the defendant be enjoined from in any
manner attempting to enforce said contract. The defendant,
by its answer; denies that it has contracted; or proposes to
contract, an indebtedness for the construction of said sewer.
There was a demurrer to the answer, which was overruled,
and the plaintiff appeals.

Henry S. Wilcox, for appellant.

James H. Dietrick and *Hugh Brennan*, for appellee.

ROTHROCK, J.—The question to be determined is, did the
contract in question create an indebtedness against the city?
A copy of said contract is exhibited with the answer. So
far as the said contract purports to create an obligation
against the city, it is as follows: "The said P. H. McCauley
agrees and hereby undertakes to do and perform said work
in accordance with the plans and specifications, at the following rate or price, to-wit: one dollar and seventy-four cents
per lineal foot or square yard, which price shall cover the cost
of the entire work. The said cost is, under the law and
ordinances of said city, to be assessed against the private
property adjacent to or fronting on the street upon which
said improvement is made, and a part thereof, to-wit: in seven
annual installments, as provided by the law and ordinances
of the city, with six per cent interest. Said assessment is
payable as follows: When such assessment is made, and any
portion of the work completed and accepted by the city, certificates thereof shall be made out showing the amount levied
against each piece of property, and the same shall be delivered
to said P. H. McCauley, and the same shall be received by

him in full payment for said work or improvement for the payment of which a special assessment is required by the law and ordinances of said city, and delivered to said P. H. McCauley or order. Said P. H. McCauley agrees to accept said certificates in full payment for any and all work performed by him under his contract, and to collect the same by any of the methods provided by law, and at his own cost and expense; and it is expressly agreed, by and between the parties to this contract, that, upon the issuing of certificates to said P. H. McCauley for any and all work done under this contract, the same shall be received by him in full payment therefor, without recourse to the city of Des Moines, Iowa."

It is provided by section 3, article 11, of the constitution, that "no county or other political or municipal corporation shall be allowed to become indebted in any manner, for any purpose, to an amount in the aggregate exceeding five per centum on the value of the taxable property within such county or corporation, to be ascertained by the last state and county tax-lists previous to the incurring of said indebtedness."

It seems to us that the contract in question does not create an indebtedness against the city. There is no doubt that the city is authorized by law to make special assessments for improvements of this character upon property adjacent to the improvements. Such are the plain provisions of our statute. See chapter 162, Laws 1878, and section 16, c. 168, Laws 1886. The contract involved in this case expressly provides that the certificates issued by the city shall be accepted by the contractor in full payment for his work, without recourse on the city. The city can never be held liable to any action for the construction of the sewer. Its resources cannot be affected thereby. Its contract is fully and completely performed by ascertaining the amount properly chargeable to the adjacent property, and the issuance of assessment certificates to the contractor.

We think the demurrer to the answer was properly overruled.   AFFIRMED.

THE STATE v. THOMPSON.

1. **Homicide:** EVIDENCE JUSTIFYING: SELF-DEFENSE. Defendant, a man of fifty-three years, was the owner of a tract of land over which there was a wagon way which had been used by the public by permission of the owner, but not by any right. Defendant, in fencing his land, was in the act of building the fence across this wagon way, when the decedent, a young, vigorous and bullying man, came up with a wagon and insisted on going through, and over the land. To this defendant objected. Decedent jumped from his wagon, went upon defendant's land, threatened to tear the fence down, and began to do so, and declared that he would go through or do defendant serious injury. When first approached, defendant had his axe in his hand, but he laid it down and picked up a club. After parleying with decedent, and fearing injury from him, defendant stooped to lay down the club and pick up the axe, intending to go away to his house in order to avoid further trouble and probable danger. As he was stooping, decedent punched him with a fence stake, and was raising the stake as if to strike him, when defendant picked up another club lying near and struck decedent a blow from which he afterwards died. Decedent had threatened that if defendant fenced up that road he (decedent) would go through or kill defendant, and defendant had knowledge of these threats. *Held* that the act of defendant was justifiable on the ground of self-defense, and that a verdict of manslaughter could not be sustained under the evidence,—which is fully set out in the opinion.

Appeal from Jasper District Court.

FRIDAY, MARCH 18.

THE defendant was indicted for the crime of murder in the second degree. He was tried and convicted of manslaughter, and sentenced to imprisonment in the penitentiary for one year. He appeals.

Winslow & Varnum, for appellant.

A. J. Baker, Attorney-general, for the State.

ROTHROCK, J.—It appears from the evidence that the defendant is the owner of a small tract of land, consisting of twenty-three acres. He purchased it some time prior to July 19, 1884. The land was covered with brush and timber. For some years before defendant acquired the land, a way had been used for travel over the same. The defendant commenced to improve his land by removing the brush and timber. He built a cabin, and removed his family into it He built fences, and, in order to inclose the land, it became necessary to fence across the said way. He did not build a solid fence across the way, but constructed bars, which could be removed to allow teams and wagons to pass through, if it became necessary to do so. It was thought this necessity might arise in case of teams drawing loaded wagons, as the way around the land was not so good as that through it. It is conceded, and the court instructed the jury, that there was no lawful highway through the defendant's land, and that he had the right to inclose the same and stop travel thereon. It was known through the neighborhood that the defendant intended to build a fence across the way. No one appears to have made any marked opposition to it, except one Isaiah Fenderson, who was a tenant upon land in the neighborhood, but who intended to move away in a short time. Fenderson was violently opposed to having the way closed up. He made threats among the neighbors that, if the defendant did fence across the way, he (Fenderson) would go through or he would "riddle him," and that he would "wade in blood up to his knees" to go through, etc. Some of these threats were communicated to the defendant before he put the bars across the way. On the same day that the bars were erected, and while the defendant was at work near the bars, Fenderson approached with a team and an empty wagon, and demanded his right to go through and over the defendant's land. The defendant directed him to drive around the land. Fenderson became very angry, and leaped from his wagon, attempted to tear down the bars, and crossed over upon the defendant's land inside the inclosure, and an altercation ensued, in which the defendant struck Fenderson upon the head with a club, and fractured his skull, from which injury he died in two or three days thereafter. There was no eye-witness to the final struggle between the parties. A young man named Joseph Thompson was with the deceased in the wagon, and he testified as a witness on the trial that when Fenderson stopped at the bars the defendant was standing near by, and, to Fenderson's statement to defendant that he.was shutting up the road, the defendant directed him to go around his land; that Fenderson jumped out of his wagon, and approached the fence, and said he would go through there, and defendant told him he would not go through, and to go away; that he did not want any trouble with him. The witness took hold of Fenderson and pulled him, and tried to persuade him to drive around,—that they could do so as well as others. Fenderson persisted, and jumped over the fence, took hold of the fence stakes, and spread them apart. When deceased jumped the fence the defendant had an axe in his hand, and said, "I will not draw the axe on you," and he picked up a club, and held the same in his hands, and told the deceased not to touch the fence. Fenderson was spreading the stakes of the fence apart, and the parties were cursing each other, and about six feet apart, when the young man turned away and walked off, for the reason, as he stated, that he believed there would be trouble, and he did not want to see it.

There is no doubt that the death of the deceased was caused by a blow from a club or stick, and that the blow was inflicted by the defendant. The defendant insists, however, that all of his acts in the unfortunate affray were excusable on the ground that they were done strictly in defense of his person. And, as we believe that his claim is well founded, it appears to be necessary to set out further facts in the case quite fully, and these facts are so fully detailed in the testimony given by the defendant as a witness upon the trial that we here insert it in full. It is as follows:

"I am the defendant, and am fifty-three years old past. I reside on twenty-three acres of land that has been described by the various witnesses. Moved there a year ago the twenty-first of April. I improved the piece myself. I cleared out about three acres of ground, and put it into corn and potatoes and beans and small vegetables. I moved the house on the land, and moved the family in the same day. The neighbors helped me move the house, and I put it up and the family in at the same time, and this last summer have continued to improve the place. I built outside fences to inclose the land. Started to fence on the south side with a pole and brush fence. I commenced at the east end, cutting the brush out west along the line, or what I supposed to be the line, and cut up until I got to the hog lot. Then I went back, and commenced to fence on the east line. The fence was made of poles with crotches, and poles set on the crotches. The pole fence was on the east end. I saw Isaiah Fenderson on or about the nineteenth day of July, 1884.

"The first I saw him was in the morning, passing down through the timber where I was at work on the west line, when I was going to get some sticks that I was splitting out of some limbs. I was on the west side of the traveled way, cutting sticks. He went south-east towards his house, down along the traveled way. Joseph Thompson was with him. I kept on with my work, got my sticks out that I needed, and fetched them back, and went to work at the fence. When Fenderson came back it was all finished up to putting on the riders about, but the bars. I was putting up a pair of bars for teams to pass through the field if they found it necessary. Taking down the bars, and putting them up again, and driving through, it was all right, and I was driving some stakes in by these bars. Fenderson came back. He had a team and empty wagon so far as I could see. They drove within about twenty feet, I should judge, of where I was at work. Fenderson said, 'You are fencing up the road.' I said, 'No; there is the road; travel it.' And he commenced cursing me. He said he would tear it down and go through there. He was then in the wagon. He jumped out of the wagon when he said that, off on the east side,—that would be on the left side of the wagon. He came to the fence to me on the north side of it. It was inside of my own field. He came up to the fence and said he was going to tear it down. I told him not to. He said he was going through there or 'I will come and pound the G—d d—d —— out of you.' I had my axe in my hand, and he says, 'Don't strike me with the axe.' I said, 'No, I would not strike any one with the axe.' Then he jumped the fence and came over to me, and I said, 'Go away. I don't want to bother with you.' And Joseph came and pulled him by the coat-tail, and said, 'We can travel that road if any one can.' And he says, 'No, by G—d, I am going through there;' and then Joseph went away up through the woods. I tried to reason with him about the road,—that, if I was violating the law, I told him, to take the law on me; we would not quarrel about it; he had no interest there much,—there was no use of bothering himself about it. He had told me he was going to move away. He said, 'By G—d, he had an interest in there; he was going through there;' and I said, 'Isaiah, there is no use talking;' and he swore some, and I swore some, and I said, 'I will not bother with you,' and I made one step.

. "We was, I should judge, six or seven feet apart at the time this parleying went on, and we were on the north side of my own land, and on the east side of the traveled track. My back would be to the north-east, and he was facing me. He was then standing right close to the east fork of the bars. He kind of stepped back after he made that advance on me, and put his hand on the fence stakes, that way. [The witness here showed movement made in the attempt to pull the stakes apart.] He spead them apart. The one on the south side was driven in pretty firm, and the other one I hadn't driven in yet. I wanted them to hold up the heavy poles I was putting on for riders. I said, 'Isaiah, I won't bother with you. I will go on with my work.' And I made a turn of the hand to pick up my axe, and I spied a club on the ground, and I dropped the club on the ground that I had in my hand to pick up my axe, and just with that he grabbed the stake and gave me a jab, this way. [Witness here showed movement made by Fenderson in punching him with the stake, withdrawing the club, and raising it as if to strike him.] I just picked up the stick, and gave him an underhanded lick, that way, with my right hand. I hit him that way. [Witness here shows by his movements that he struck him with an upward blow as he rose from the ground in picking up the stick, so that he struck upward, being under and lower than the deceased.] I never struck him but once. He says, 'Don't strike me again;' and I says, 'No Isaiah, you provoked me to this. You was trying to punch my guts out, and then you tried to knock my brains out.' He says, 'I will have your heart's blood for that.' I never made any reply to that; and he wheeled short, turned the wheels right to the buggy, and started away to where he lived as fast as he could go, and I heard the wagon stop, and then I started home as fast as I could go. Before this occurrence I had been told by neighbors that Fenderson had made threats against me. William Bullock told me, and Mr. Crews told me. This was told me the day before the trouble."

"*Cross-Examination.* Bullock met me in the road, and said, 'I understand you are going to fence this road up, Aleck.' I told him I was; but I would have bars there so the people could pass through that wanted to. 'Well,' says he, 'you had better not fence it up.' I said, 'Why?' He said that he and Fenderson had a big row about that road. Fenderson threatened him pretty hard, he said, and he said he came pretty near knocking his head off, or something to that effect. And he says, 'You will have trouble with Fenderson.' In that same conversation I had, he said that Fenderson said he would go through there or riddle me, or something to that effect. That is as near as I can tell it. Crews said to me one day, 'Ain't you afraid to work in here?' I asked him 'What will make me afraid?' He says, 'Fenderson has threatened you hard, and he is drinking, too.' I said, ' I guess he will not hurt me.' He says, ' Why, you had better look out;' and I asked him what he said about fencing the road up. He says, ' He says all he wants is one good clip at you.'

" I said Fenderson jabbed me with a stick. It was quite a good sized-stick. May be two and a half inches at the butt, and perhaps somewhere in the neighborhood of six feet long. That was one of the sticks I was using to build the fence with,—one of the stakes I drove in the ground. It was a round stick, and had been part way driven in the ground. He loosened it up before he jerked it out. At this time I had thrown down the axe. He jerked the stick out as I was going to pick up the axe. I was going to pick up the axe and leave him. I told him not to bother me; I didn't want to bother with him at all. I had a club in my hands, and was just stooping down to pick up my axe and go away. I kept my eye on him, for I thought he would get away with me anyway. When I dropped the club out of my hand I had no idea he was going to strike till he came up; I thought if I would go away he would quit and let me alone, and I thought I would drop the weapon I had in my hand and get away. Before I dropped my club he had his hand on the stake. I then thought it was best to drop the stick and go away. I thought it was the best thing for me to go away and take my axe home. He was mad, furious and excited. Before I picked up the axe, as I told you, I seen he was going to get away with me. I was going to run, because I said I would have no fuss with him.

" *Question.* Why did you not run with the stick instead of the axe? *Answer.* I wanted to take my axe home with me. I wanted to go up near the house and chop. I wanted to work with the axe, and not to use it on him by any means. As soon as I stooped down, he prodded me. I made a movement, and dropped the club down and took the axe, and I seen him coming, and I dropped the axe and took the club,

and hit him an under-handed lick. I had stooped down to
pick up the axe, and, as I raised up, I took him that way,
by striking him as I raised up. *Q.* Had he the club
raised? *A.* He had it raised this way, [showing manner.
Witness here showed that he had the club raised as if to strike
him over the head.] I struck him with the club as I raised
up. As I raised up I let it flicker, after I seen that, if I did
not, I was a goner. He fell onto his knees. He said,
‘Don’t hit me again,’ and I said I would not if he would let
me alone. He hurt me considerably when he jabbed me,—
gave me a pretty good jab with it. He struck me here in
the side. I expect he would have put it pretty nearly into
me if he had been a little closer. He was too far off to
have good force at me. When he was down on his knees he
got up just as quick as he could. Was not more than down
till he was up. I expect we was both excited. I was not
very angry, because I had my mind made up that I would
not quarrel with him. He jabbed me with the stick just as
I stooped down. He was next the fence, facing me. When
he jabbed me he must have just grabbed the stick, and then
jabbed me with it, and then when he did not get me down, he
raised it up this way in his hand; I cannot tell you whether the
right hand or left hand in advance; but the stick was raised up
in this way, coming onto me; I would not say whether the right
or left hand. When he jabbed me I could not tell which hand
was in advance. I was stooping down picking up the axe to get
off, when he gave me a jab, and I picked up the stick, as I
have said. He pulled the stake loose out of the fence. It
was a stick that I was using,—driving in,—as I told you
before, when he came up to me. The stake that he pulled
out of the fence was one he used during the difficulty; and
when he was struck he dropped the stick down. I did not
do anything with it at that time. After the difficulty, a
little spell, I took the little boy and girl to fix up the fence,
and I done so, and used the same stick. I would not say
whether I put the stake in the same place or not. When I

struck him I did not see any blood, not till I went back to the fence. I noticed no blood when he traveled off. There was a few drops of blood on some chips back next to the fence. This was in the neighborhood where he fell, and I believe there was one or two little. drops of blood on the stick that he had. I think there was. When he dropped the stake it was near where the chips were, and it was there when I picked it up and put it back in the fence. I am right-handed. Don't very often use my left hand. I struck him with one hand,— my right hand."

It should further be stated that it appeared from the evidence that the deceased was a young, active and vigorous man. We have examined the record with great care, and we fail to find any evidence in any way impeaching or contradictory to the testimony of the defendant. Indeed, so far as the previous threats of the deceased are involved, the defendant's testimony was fully corroborated. And the young man who witnessed part of the affray also fairly corroborates the account of it given by the defendant. He is also corroborated by the fact that he received quite a severe injury in the side during the affray. In our opinion, the evidence in the case shows without conflict every legal requirement to constitute a complete self-defense. We are aware that human life should be regarded by courts and juries with jealous care, and criminal homicides should surely be punished. But the right of self-defense should also be protected and guarded. It does not necessarily follow that the person who kills his assailant is a criminal. It plainly appears from the evidence in this case that the defendant did not intend to kill the deceased. If such had been his intention, he would not have laid down his axe, and stood six feet away from the deceased, as when last seen by the young man named Thompson. The deceased had then crossed over the fence upon the defendant's premises. It must be remembered that the defendant had the legal right to fence up this way. It cannot be claimed that, because he knew the deceased had threatened him with violence, he should be required, to appease the wrath of a bully, to leave his land uninclosed. The law would be no protection to him if he could not be allowed to improve and inclose his humble home in his own way. And he had the right to stand by his fence and contend that his premises should not be invaded; and, when assaulted and wounded as he was, he had the right to strike back, if it appeared to him as a reasonable man to be necessary to protect himself from further great bodily injury. That the necessity existed, there can be no doubt, if the case is considered upon the evidence.

In our opinion, a new trial should have been granted, upon the ground that the evidence did not warrant the verdict found by the jury.

REVERSED.

McCONNELL ET AL. v. HUTCHINSON ET AL.

1. **Intervention:** BY COUNTY: ACTION TO ANNUL SALE OF POOR-FARM. In an action by tax-payers against the purchasers of a poor-farm from the county, to set aside the sale on account of the inadequacy of the price, and other alleged illegalities, *held* that the county was entitled, under § 2683 of the Code, to intervene and join the defendants in sustaining the sale, on the ground that it was advantageous to the county.

Appeal from Davis District Court.

FRIDAY, MARCH 18.

ACTION to set aside a conveyance made to the defendant M. E. Hutchinson of a farm in Davis county. The petition avers, in substance, that at one time the farm was owned by Davis county, and was occupied by it as a poor-farm; that the county sold and conveyed the farm to the defendant M. E. Hutchinson; that the supervisors of the county, in making the sale and conveyance for the county, sold the farm without appraisement, and for a grossly inadequate price;

and that all the matters pertaining to the sale were illegal and void. The county filed a petition in intervention, setting up the unsuitableness of the farm for a poor-farm, and various reasons why the same was properly sold; and averred that the sale was well advertised, and was made for all the farm was worth; and prayed that the sale be approved. The plaintiff moved to strike from the files the petition of intervention. The court sustained the motion, and the intervenor appeals.

Payne & Eichelberger, for appellant.

H. B. Hendershott and *M. H. Jones*, for appellees.

ADAMS, CH. J.—This action was brought by the plaintiff McConnell and one or more others, who aver that they are tax-payers of Davis county, and they ask that they may be heard in behalf of all the inhabitants and tax-payers of the county. The right of the county to intervene is based upon section 2683 of the Code, which provides that any person who has an interest in the matter in litigation, in the success of either of the parties to the action, or against both, may become a party to an action between other persons, either by joining the plaintiff in claiming what is sought by the petition, or by uniting with the defendant in resisting the claim of the plaintiff. In this case the county joined with the defendant Hutchinson in resisting the claim of the plaintiffs. The motion to strike from the files the petition for intervention was based upon the ground that the county had no interest in the action. It might be conceded that the county has no interest in the action if the conveyance could be set aside, and the county be allowed to keep the farm and purchase-money also. But, if the trade should be rescinded by reason of inadequacy of price, or other illegality, the purchaser would be entitled to a refund of the purchase-money. Now, the county avers that the farm did not meet its requirements;

that it was well sold; and that the county needed the purchase-money to aid in purchasing another farm. If the sale was advantageous to the county, as we must assume from the averments of the petition of intervention, and the county would be deprived of the advantage of the sale if the plaintiff should be successful, it follows that the county had an interest in the action.

In our opinion, the motion to strike from the files the petition of intervention should have been overruled.

REVERSED.

Orcutt v. Hanson, Ex'x, et al.

1. **Place of Suit:** FORECLOSURE OF MORTGAGE AGAINST EXECUTOR AND HEIRS OF MORTGAGOR. H., a resident of Greene county, died there, leaving a wife and children, who continued to reside there. Before his death, and prior to the enactment of chap. 126, Laws of 1884, providing that actions to foreclose mortgages *must* be brought in the county where the land lies, he had mortgaged his land in Greene county to secure notes payable in Cedar county. His widow was appointed executrix of his estate, which was in process of settlement in Greene county. This action was brought in Cedar county, where the notes were payable, against the executrix and heirs, to foreclose the mortgage. *Held* that the action was maintainable only in Greene county, and that the court of Cedar county had no jurisdiction of the subject matter. This conclusion is concurred in by all the members of the court, but the argument of the opinion, based on the theory that the action was strictly *in rem*, is not concurred in.

2. **Jurisdiction:** WANT OF: WAIVER. Want of jurisdiction of the subject matter cannot be waived, even by consent of the parties, and the objection may be raised at any time. (*Dicks v. Hatch*, 10 Iowa, 380, and *Cerro Gordo Co. v. Wright Co.*, 59 Id., 485, followed.)

3. **Place of Suit:** WRONG COUNTY: CHANGE TO PROPER COUNTY: NO JURISDICTION. When an action which should be brought in the county of the defendant's residence is brought in another county, but the court has no jurisdiction of the subject matter, the defendant does not waive the want of jurisdiction by failing to move for a change to the proper county, under Code, § 2589. That section is not applicable to such a case; for the court in such a case has no jurisdiction to make any order except to dismiss the case, or strike it from the files.

Appeal from Cedar Circuit Court.

FRIDAY, MARCH 18.

ACTION in chancery to foreclose a mortgage. There was a decree granting the relief prayed for by plaintiff. Defendant Hannah Hanson, executrix, appeals.

R. S. Irvin, for appellant.

Piatt & Carr, for appellee.

BECK, J.—I. The mortgage in suit conveys lands in Greene county to secure certain promissory notes payable in

1. PLACE of suit: foreclosure of mortgage against executor and heirs of mortgagor.

Cedar county, executed by George F. Hanson, who died in Greene county, where he resided. This action is brought against the executrix of the estate, who is his widow, and against his heirs and devisees. All reside in Greene county; and his estate is in process of settlement by the proper probate court of that county, which issued the letters of administration to the widow. There was personal service made upon all of the defendants. All of these facts are not clearly and directly stated in the abstract, but, with what is found therein, together with statements of plaintiff's counsel, the facts as just stated satisfactorily appear. The petition prays for the foreclosure of the mortgage, and for a judgment against the executrix, and that the heirs' interest in the land be declared subject to the mortgage. Relief in accord with this prayer was given by the decree. It does not appear whether the heirs appeared in the case; no default against them was declared.

II. In our opinion, the circuit court of Cedar county had no jurisdiction of the case, the statutes, as interpreted by this court, prescribing that plaintiff should have pursued his remedies in Greene county, where the land is situated, and where the estate of the mortgagor is in process of settlement in the probate court. Code, § 2578, before its amendment by chapter 126, Acts Twentieth General Assembly, as inter-

preted by this court in *Equitable Life Ins. Co. v. Gleason*,
56 Iowa, 47, authorized the foreclosure of a mortgage in the
county wherein the note secured thereby was made payable,
the action being personal, and not *in rem*. The amendment
just referred to, by its express terms, is not applicable to
contracts before existing.

In *Iowa Loan & Trust Co. v. Day*, 63 Iowa, 459, this
court held that an action for foreclosure which is *in rem*, and
not to recover a personal judgment as well as a decree of
foreclosure, must be prosecuted in the county wherein the
land is situated, and not in the county where the note secured
by the mortgage is payable.

III. Is this to be regarded as a personal action, or an action
in rem? Both of the cases just cited teach that, where a personal judgment cannot be rendered in a foreclosure proceeding, it is an action *in rem*. See *Kershaw v. Thompson*, 4
Johns. Ch., 609; *Downing v. Palmateer*, 1 T. B. Mon., 64;
Waples, Proc. in Rem, §§ 563 *et seq.*, 606 *et seq.*

No personal judgment is claimed in the petition against
the heirs, and it is not made to appear in the case that there
were any grounds upon which such a judgment could have
been based. If the decree declaring that they hold their
interest in the lands subject to the mortgage be thought to
be a personal judgment against them, the court had no jurisdiction to enter it, for the reason that, as we shall soon see,
the court below had no jurisdiction to enter the decree of
foreclosure. Of course, if jurisdiction to foreclose the mortgage did not exist, no jurisdiction existed to render a personal
decree against the heirs cutting off their right to redeem.

IV. No personal judgment could have been rendered
against the executrix, for the reason that no personal liability
rested upon her. It is claimed that a judgment was authorized against her in her representative character as executrix.
We need not inquire whether such a judgment may be
regarded as personal, for the reason that, as we understand
the law, the circuit court of Cedar county had no jurisdic-

tion to render such a judgment. The claim for a judgment against the executrix was, in effect and in fact, a claim against the estate. Proceedings to enforce such claim are in the same sense against the estate. It is a proceeding pertaining to the settlement of the estate, and must be prosecuted in the proper probate court which has exclusive jurisdiction of the estate. Code, §§ 2312, 2319; *Shropshire v. Long*, 68 Iowa, 537. *Tillman v. Bowman*, Id., 450.

The question as to the effect of a judgment of foreclosure against an executor, whether it stands as a claim against the estate, etc., need not be considered, for the reason that it does not arise in this case, because no jurisdiction to enter a decree of foreclosure and judgment existed in the court below. It is very plain that, if a judgment against the estate be authorized when a decree is rendered by a court having jurisdiction, it cannot be enforced by execution. It may be filed in the probate court as a claim established against the estate. *Crane v. Guthrie*, 47 Iowa, 542. As bearing on the question under consideration, see Code, §§ 2408, 2416, 2420, 2424, 2427, and *Chadbourne v. Gilman*, 29 Iowa, 181.

V. The executrix attempted to raise the question of jurisdiction we have considered by demurrer to the petition, which was overruled. She afterwards answered. An objection based upon the want of jurisdiction of the court over the subject matter of the action may be raised at any time, and is not even waived by consent. If the law withholds from a court authority to determine a case, jurisdiction cannot be conferred, even by the consent of parties. *Dicks v. Hatch*, 10 Iowa, 380; *Cerro Gordo Co. v. Wright Co.*, 59 Id., 485.

2. JURISDICTION: want of: waiver.

VI. Code, § 2589, contains the following provision: "If a suit be brought in the wrong county, it may then be prosecuted to a termination, unless the defendant before answer demand a change of the place of trial to the proper county, in which case the court shall order the same at the cost of the plaintiff. * * *" If this provision be

3. PLACE of suit: wrong county: change to proper county: no jurisdiction.

applicable to the case before us, defendants, having made no
motion to change the venue as contemplated in the statute
cannot now complain of the judgment rendered in the case
But, in our opinion, the section is not to be applied to the
case, for the reason that the circuit court of Cedar county
had no jurisdiction of the subject matter of the action
which, we think, we have above shown.   To authorize a court
to act in an action *in rem*, it must have jurisdiction of the
subject matter of the suit, and, in an action *in personam*,
it must have jurisdiction of the person of the defendant.
In personal actions, the section just quoted, and those preceding it, give to the court of the " wrong county " jurisdiction of the person of defendants who were served with notice;
but, in actions *in rem*, the court of the " wrong county "
acquires no jurisdiction of the subject matter, under the
statutes and the decisions of this court.   Now, what order
may a court make in an action *in rem* wherein it has no
jurisdiction of the subject matter thereof?   None whatever,
except to dismiss it, or strike it from the docket.   As the
court lacks jurisdiction of the subject matter, it can make
no order whatever affecting the right to the *rem*.   These
views are based upon the most familiar elementary principles,
which demand no authorities in their support in order to
assure the assent of the legal mind.

It will be understood that, where there is jurisdiction of
the subject matter of the action, but no jurisdiction of the
person of the defendant, the court may retain the cause, and
make orders looking to the acquisition of jurisdiction of the
person of defendant, and for some other purposes.   But, as
we have seen, this is not an action *in personam*.   The court
below, having no jurisdiction, could make no order except
to dismiss the case, which ought to have been done.

The other members of the court direct me to say that
they are not prepared to hold that this action of foreclosure
is strictly a proceeding *in rem*.   They reach the conclusion
announced in this opinion upon the other grounds.

REVERSED.

THE STATE INS. CO. v. RICHMOND.

1. **Fire Insurance**: LIABILITY OF AGENT FOR NEGLECT OF DUTY: DAMAGES. An insurance company cannot recover more than nominal damages of its agent, through whose fault, while acting in good faith, it is drawn into a contract of insurance somewhat different from what it supposes it to be, but not less valuable to it; the risk actually taken being such as the company is accustomed to accept. So *held*, where the application falsely represented the insured premises to be an occupied hotel building, when in fact the agent knew it to be unoccupied at the time, but did not communicate that knowledge to the company, but the rate paid was greater than that charged for similar unoccupied hotel buildings, and the building was burned before occupancy, and plaintiff, being charged with the agent's knowledge, was obliged to pay the loss. In such case, even if the premium received had been less than that charged for the risk actually taken, the agent would have been liable only for the difference, and not for the amount paid by the company in adjusting the loss.

2. **Practice on Appeal**: REVERSAL FOR NOMINAL DAMAGES. This court will not reverse a judgment and remand a case for the purpose of allowing the appellant to recover merely nominal damages. (*Watson v. VanMeter*, 43 Iowa, 76 followed.)

Appeal from Kossuth District Court.

FRIDAY, MARCH 18.

THIS action is brought by a principal against its agent, to recover damages alleged to have been sustained by reason of neglect of duty by the agent. The plaintiff demurred to the fourth division of the defendant's answer. The court overruled the demurrer. The plaintiff elected to stand upon its demurrer, and judgment was rendered against it for costs. The plaintiff appeals.

Cummins & Wright, for appellant.

J. C. Cook and *J. H. Call*, for appellee.

ADAMS, CH. J.—The defendant was the plaintiff's soliciting agent in Kossuth county. As such he solicited and obtained from one Jordan an application for insurance upon a building erected for a hotel, but not quite completed. At the date of application and issuance of the policy, the building was not occupied as a hotel, but it was expected that it would be in a short time. In the application, however, the building was described as occupied as a hotel. The defendant knew the facts, but did not inform the plaintiff, and the policy was issued, as may be presumed, in reliance upon the statements as contained in the application. Before the building became occupied as a hotel, it was destroyed by fire. Action was brought upon the policy. The company set up as a defense the false statement in the application; but the defense proved unavailing because of the agent's knowledge that the building was not occupied as a hotel, and the insured was allowed to recover. This action is brought to recover of the agent the amount which the plaintiff was compelled to pay on the policy.

The division of the answer demurred to is as follows: "And as and for a separate and distinct, full and complete defense, defendant says that when the policy was sent by the plaintiff to the defendant it was with instructions to deliver the same to Jordan, and collect the premium; that while it is true that at the time the building was not occupied as a hotel, with sleeping rooms in the second and third stories, and was then in an unfinished condition or completion, preparatory to being soon occupied, and was not occupied by a tenant, and it was also true that there were no stoves in the building, and no kerosene was used for lights, nor were any lights of any kind used, and no coal or other fuel was used for fire, nor were any fires therein used, and there was in fact no furniture therein, all of which in a general way the defendant knew and did not communicate to the plaintiff,—yet he avers and says that each and all of said several matters were wholly immaterial, and none of them in any manner or degree increased the risk or hazard or danger; that in truth and in fact the absence of such matter only decreased the risk, hazard and danger; that the matters and conditions aforesaid, and the true condition of said building, was less hazardous than as represented in the application and policy; that the regular premium which plaintiff, and insurance companies generally, would have charged for insuring said building in its true condition was less than had it been as represented and described in the application for insurance, and that plaintiff would have taken the risk at the same rate had defendant informed it to the fullest extent of his knowledge; that defendant had no instructions or directions except as contained in a written appointment and bond set out and attached to the petition, and in the entire matter acted in good faith and without any fraudulent intent; and defendant says that he has at all times duly performed his duties as such agent of plaintiff, except as herein set forth, which defendant insists is and was neither a violation of his contract with plaintiff, nor any instruction."

In the argument of the appellant's counsel, considerable is said which has nothing to do with the question as to whether the appellant's demurrer to the appellee's answer ought to have been sustained. The appellant's counsel say that "the conduct of the agent was as flagitious as can be conceived." But the answer demurred to contains an averment that "the defendant in the entire matter acted in good faith, and without any fraudulent intent;" and this must be taken as true, unless there are other admitted facts which show otherwise, and we do not see any. The application should, of course, have contained a statement that the building was soon to be occupied as a hotel; but if the agent had reason to suppose that it would be thus occupied before the policy would be issued, or so soon thereafter as to make no material difference, his conduct might be attributed to a misconception of his duty rather than a fraudulent intent; and, if it *might be* thus attributed, then we are bound to take the averment of the answer as true.

Considerable is said in the argument of appellant's counsel about the appellant being drawn wrongfully into an insurance of a carpenter's risk; but there is no good reason for this. It is true that it is averred in the petition that the building was in process of construction, and it appears to be admitted that the building was in an unfinished condition. but to what extent does not appear, and we can easily conceive of things remaining to be done which would manifestly involve no additional hazard. Besides, it is not material to the question before us that the building was unfinished, even if something remained to be done which involved additional hazard. There was no statement in the application that the building was finished, nor warranty in the policy to that effect, nor is it. claimed in the appellant's petition that the appellant was precluded from a successful defense predicated upon such ground. The building might have been occupied as a hotel, and warmed and lighted as represented, without being entirely finished; and, if it had been done, there would have been nothing to complain of.

The untrue statements in the application, which the appellant sets up as a defense against the insured, and which it now sets up as ground for recovery against the appellee, are three in number, and are as follows: That the building was occupied as a hotel; that kerosene was used for light, and that coal was used for fuel. The facts, as shown by the pleadings, are that the building was not occupied at all, and that it was not lighted nor warmed in any way. There is no pretense, so far as the pleadings show, that the unfinished condition of the building has any materiality. This fact is made to do service nowhere except in the argument of appellant's counsel.

We have said this much for the purpose of eliminating extraneous matters. We may go a little further, and say that we do not understand the appellant as seriously complaining of the absence of kerosene or fire in the building. We are virtually, we think, reduced to the complaint that the building was not occupied as a hotel. How precisely it was occupied we do not know, nor is it material to inquire. The case before us, then, is this: The appellant, through a misconception by its agent of his duty while acting in good faith, (as the answer avers,) was drawn into the insurance of a building at a rate of premium fixed for the insurance of a building occupied as a hotel, which in fact had not commenced to be thus occupied, but was expected to be soon, and the agent knew it was not yet occupied in that way. The property was burned before occupancy. The company retained the premium, viz., $80, paid the loss, viz., $3,000 and some interest, and sues its agent to recover of him the whole amount paid. The actual risk was not greater than it was represented to the company to be when it issued the policy, and the premium received and retained was greater than the premium charged for an unoccupied hotel building with neither lights nor fires in it. We state these as the facts, because, upon the question raised by the demurrer to the answer, they must be assumed to be true.

The legal question presented is as to whether an insurance company can recover damages of its agent through whose fault, while acting in good faith, it is drawn into a contract of insurance somewhat different from what it supposed it to be, but not less valuable to it. In answer, we have to say that we do do not think it entitled to recover substantial damages. Whether it should be allowed nominal damages we need not determine, because, if we should conclude that it might, we could not reverse for the mere purpose of allowing such recovery. *Watson v. Van Meter*, 43 Iowa, 76.

We are not prepared to say that the insurance of an unoccupied building is not in fact regarded by insurance men as involving a greater risk than the insurance of an occupied building, even though it be occupied as a hotel, and is three stories high, and lighted with kerosene lamps; but, for the purpose of this case, it must be assumed to be the reverse. The case, then, is not different from what it would have been if the false statement relied upon had been simply that the building was lighted with kerosene lamps, when in fact it was lighted with candles or gas, or that coal was used for fuel, when in fact it was heated by steam transmitted from other premises. It is possible that in such case, if the condition had been warranted, there would have been a breach of warranty; but there would have been no ground for recovery of more than nominal damages against the agent.

It is a very important consideration that the company was not drawn into a contract of insurance against a risk which it does not insure against. There is no pretense that the insurance of unoccupied buildings is not a part of the business of the company upon which it makes its profits. It is a matter of common knowledge that insurance companies do such business, and the fair inference from the pleadings in this case is that the appellant did such business, charging such rates as are usual for such risks, or as it deemed proper. It is a question, then, of rates, and nothing more, so far as any question of substantial damages is concerned. The appellant received $80 as a premium on a policy of $4,000, and on the supposition, formed from the broad experience of insurance companies generally, that less than one in fifty of such risks would result in loss. According to the averment of the answer demurred to, the risk was actually less than the company was paid for. If it had had enough such risks it would have made more than its usual profits. This is not a mere matter of uncertainty and speculation. While there is nothing more uncertain than whether a given building will be destroyed by fire or not within the life of a given policy, the average of losses is such that the business of insurance is, we believe, regarded as about as reliable as most others. At all events, premiums are charged upon the theory that they can be relied upon, and the business be safely done. We are justified, then, in saying that, upon a question of damages for the fault of an agent, it is a question of rates, in any matter which is covered by the company's rates. The cases cited by the appellee (*McDermid v. Cotton*, 2 Bradw., 297, and *Davis v. Garrett*, 6 Bing., 716) involve a different principle

If a merchant's clerk should sell goods on credit, which he is employed to sell in that way, and to a person to whom he might properly sell, but for a price less than he was expressly required to obtain, the measure of the merchant's recovery against the clerk in an action for damages would unquestionably not be greater than the difference between the two prices, and that, too, even if the buyer should become insolvent, and not pay anything. If, on the other hand, the clerk should sell property of his employer of a kind which he was not employed to sell at all, he probably would be held responsible for the whole value. A principle would be involved not very unlike that in the cases cited.

Having, then, reached the conclusion that the risk assumed was within the appellant's business, and that it is only a question of rates, the appellant should have shown, before it could recover more than nominal damages, that it was damaged in the matter of rates. With this view, the judgment must be

AFFIRMED.

OPPENHEIMER & CO. v. BARR ET AL.

71 525
104 691

1. Appeal: TAKEN TOO LATE: QUESTION NOT RAISED BELOW. The right of appeal is lost if not exercised within the time prescribed by statute; nor can a right be insisted on in this court which was not urged in the court below. See opinion for illustrations.

2. Evidence: OF GOOD CHARACTER TO REBUT CHARGE OF FRAUD. Evidence that the character for honesty and integrity of one charged with fraud is good, and that his business standing and credit are good. is not competent to rebut the charge of fraud. (*Stone v. Hawkeye Ins. Co.*, 68 Iowa, 737, followed.)

3. ———: PRACTICE: OBJECTING TO A CERTAIN CLASS OF EVIDENCE. Where it is apparent from the record that defendants all through the trial objected to a certain class of evidence as being incompetent, the question of the competency of such evidence may be raised on appeal, even though each question and answer was not objected to. The rule that the admission of incompetent evidence, tending to prove a fact established by other evidence not objected to, is error without prejudice, does not apply.

Appeal from Jasper Circuit Court.

FRIDAY, MARCH 18.

THIS is an action of replevin, involving the ownership of a stock of boots and shoes. The plaintiffs claim to be the absolute owners thereof, as purchasers from a partnership known as B. Oppenheimer & Co. The defendant Barr is sheriff of Mahaska county, and as such sheriff he levied certain writs of attachment upon the goods at the suits of creditors of B. Oppenheimer & Co. These creditors, who were by order of the court made parties defendant, claim that the alleged purchase of the goods by the plaintiffs was fraudulent as to the creditors of B. Oppenheimer & Co., because the purchase was made with the intent to hinder, delay and defraud said creditors. There was a trial by jury, which resulted in a verdict and judgment for the plaintiffs. Defendants appeal.

Bolton & McCoy and *John F. Lacey*, for appellants.

G. W. Lafferty, O. C. G. Phillips and *L. C. Blanchard*, for appellees.

ROTHROCK, J.—I. The action was brought in the district court of Mahaska county. A trial was had in that court in

1. APPEAL: taken too late: question not raised below.

June, 1883. It was admitted by the pleadings, as they then were, that the goods in question were of the value of $10,000, and the fact, as appears on both trials, was that the plaintiffs made two purchases of the goods. One purchase was made of goods at Oskaloosa, and the other purchase was effected at Ottumwa. The jury in the first trial returned the following verdict: "We, the jury, find for the defendant, and fix the value of the goods replevied at three thousand five hundred dollars, *for goods bought at Ottumwa.*" Thereupon the defendants moved the court to fix the value of the property at the amount admitted in the pleadings, and for judgment for the return of the property, or for a judgment for $10,000, or so much as might be necessary to pay off the writs of attachment, with interest·and costs. On the same day the plaintiffs filed a motion for a new trial, because the verdict was contrary to the evidence, and for various other causes, including alleged errors in instructions to the jury and in rulings upon the admission and exclusion of evidence. On the same day the court overruled the defendants' motion, and sustained the plaintiffs' motion, and granted a new trial. The record entry of this ruling does not show the reason for the rulings of the court.

After the adjournment of the term, the judge signed a bill of exceptions, in which it was stated "that the court sustained the motion of the plaintiffs for a new trial, on the sole and only ground that, under the state of the pleadings, the defendants cannot recover separately for the part of the goods in controversy sold at Ottumwa, and the defendants at the time excepted. The said motion was held by the court insufficient on each and all the other points made therein, and sustained wholly and entirely upon the said point mentioned above; that if the said pleadings are sufficient to justify a verdict in defendants' favor as to the said $3,500 worth of goods sold at Ottumwa, then defendants would be entitled to a judgment on the verdict of not less than $3,500, and costs." Appellants insist that these rulings of the court on the first trial are reversible upon this appeal, and that they are at least entitled to a judgment for $3,500.

It will be observed that the order granting a new trial was not limited to any particular question or claim in the case. It was an order for a trial anew of all the questions in controversy in the case. It was made several years before any appeal was taken or attempted to be taken from it. It would appear that the right of appeal was lost by not exercising the right within the time allowed by law. But a conclusive reason why appellants should not be allowed to present the question now is, they did not ask for a judgment for the $3,500 named in the verdict. They demanded.

in effect, that the verdict should be reformed so as to give them a judgment for $10,000; and it was to the overruling of this motion that they excepted, and from which they should have taken their appeal within the proper time.

II.   It appears from the evidence that B. Oppenheimer & Co. were iu the boot and shoe business at Ottumwa and Oskaloosa.   N. Oppenheimer was a resident of Baltimore, Maryland, and was for years engaged in the mercantile business in that city.   He came to Oskaloosa in the year 1880, and made the alleged purchase of the goods in controversy. B. Oppenheimer was associated with a partner named Kuhn. There ought to be no dispute that this firm made the sale to the plaintiffs with intent to defraud creditors.   In fact, they organized and carried out a stupendous fraud upon wholesale dealers by buying large quantities of goods on credit, and, after receiving them at their store in Ottumwa, they shipped them to St. Louis, and sold them, and pocketed the proceeds; and, before their frauds were discovered, they absconded and escaped from the just consequences of their villainy.   The sale of the goods to the plaintiffs was part of the same general plan.   We would not allude to these facts here if it would in any way prejudice the plaintiffs upon a retrial; but as the main and really the only question in dispute in the case is whether the plaintiffs were participants in the fraud, or had such knowledge thereof as to charge them with its consequences, the fact that the firm from which the purchases were made were actuated by a fraudulent design is an important one to consider in connection with the question we are now about to discuss.

The plaintiff N. Oppenheimer being a stranger in Iowa, it was important for him to show that he was possessed of means to make the alleged purchases.   He associated with him one Lehman in making the purchase.   But it is not claimed that Lehman furnished any of the money to pay for the goods.   A large number of witnesses, residents of Baltimore, testified in behalf of the plaintiffs.   Some of their evidence tended to show that N. Oppenheimer was possessed of considerable property. This evidence was competent. It was his right to show that he was possessed of money sufficient to make the purchases. Quite a number of these witnesses, as well as other witnesses resident at Oskaloosa, were allowed to testify that the character of Oppenheimer for

1. EVIDENCE: of good character to rebut charge of fraud.

honesty and integrity, and his business standing and credit, were good. The defendants objected to this evidence. And this is the principal question in the case as presented to us. It is claimed by counsel for appellees that the defendants are in no position to urge this objection, because they allowed part of this evidence to go to the jury without objection. That the evidence was incompetent must be conceded. *Stone v. Hawkeye Ins. Co.*, 68 Iowa, 737.

We have, then, to determine whether the appellants waived objections to this evidence by allowing it to be intro-

2. ——: practice: objecting to a certain class of evidence.

duced without making objection at the time. It is difficult to determine what the ruling of the court was upon the question of the competency of the evidence. It would appear from a ruling made at one time that the court excluded the evidence from the jury. But the court instructed the jury upon the question as follows: "Evidence of the character and reputation of the plaintiff for honesty has been introduced, and you are instructed that you will not consider such testimony, in so far as it may relate to such character or reputation since the purchase of the goods in controversy." It seems to us this is a direction to the jury that they should consider that class of testimony so far as it related to character or reputation before the purchase of the goods. It is true, the direction to so consider it is implied; but it is as plain a direction as it would have been if given in express words; and one ground of the motion for a new trial is based upon the admission of this evidence. We think it is quite apparent from the whole record that the defendants resisted the intro-

duction of this evidence clear through the trial, and afterwards, and that their objections were only sustained by the
court so far as the evidence related to character after the
purchase of the goods, as set forth in the instruction to
which we have referred.

As has been said, there were quite a number of witnesses
who testified upon this subject. It is true, as claimed by
counsel for appellees, that objection was not made to every
question and answer upon the subject of the plaintiff's
character, and it is claimed that, because this was not done,
appellants cannot be allowed to complain of the evidence
now. The ground of the contention is that the admission
of incompetent evidence, tending to prove a fact established
by other evidence not objected to, constitutes error without
prejudice, and we are cited to the case of *Weitz v. Ewen*,
50 Iowa, 34. That was an action by a wife, to recover damages for intoxicating liquors sold to her husband. Evidence
was introduced, by which it was shown that the plaintiff was
the mother of eight children, and their ages were given by
the witness. This evidence was allowed to go to the jury
without objection. Afterwards, evidence was introduced as
to the age of one of the children, which was objected to,
and the objection overruled. It was held that this was not
prejudicial error, even although it was probable the evidence
was immaterial, but that no substantial prejudice resulted to
the defendant by allowing the proof of the age of one of the
children, as the defendant made no objection as to proof of
the ages of the others.

We are also cited to the case of *White v. Savery*, 50
Iowa, 515. In that case complaint was made of the admission in evidence of certain books of account to prove the
loan of money. It was held that, if this was error, it was
without prejudice, because there was other positive evidence
of the loan which was not contradicted, and the fact sought
to be shown was established independently of the books;
and we are referred to the case of *Iowa Homestead Co. v.*

Duncombe, 51 Iowa, 525.   In that case the defendant was allowed to testify generally as to the value of a certain contract held by him.   It was held that the overruling of an objection to this evidence was not prejudicial, because, if erroneous, the error was cured by the subsequent specific evidence of value, as stated by the witness.

It appears to us that these cases do not justify us in holding that the admission of the incompetent evidence in this case was not prejudicial because some of it was not objected to.   It is apparent that the two last cases do not bear upon the question.   The facts sought to be proved in both of them were material to the cases, and they were proved by other competent evidence.   In the first case the ages of the children were single facts.   The evidence of each witness to the age was evidence of a distinct fact, which could as well be established by the testimony of one uncontradicted witness as that of a great number.   The evidence now under consideration was very different.   It has never been thought that character, reputation, or good business standing could be established by one witness.   It is something of a more general nature than the existence of a physical or known fact.   In the case at bar it was the class of evidence which was objected to, and we do not think that it should be required that the defendants should object to every question and answer, and that, if there was any omission in this respect, they should be held to have waived objections.   If that course had been pursued in this case, the time of the court would have been largely taken up in unseemly interruptions, and in making and repeating rulings which would have the appearance of vain repetition.   We think that the whole record shows that the court understood that the defendants waived nothing as to this evidence.   The instruction to the jury above cited can bear no other construction.

For the error in admitting this evidence the judgment is reversed, and the case remanded for a new trial.

REVERSED.

DAVIDSON v. THE HAWKEYE INS CO.

1. **Fire Insurance:** FORFEITURE BY SALE: FACTS CONSTITUTING SALE. The policy sued on provided that it should immediately be void upon a sale of the premises without the consent of the company. The insured entered into a contract with L., whereby L. agreed to pay him a certain sum for the property,—a small portion in cash, and the rest in deferred payments, and the insured agreed to convey the property to him upon his making all the payments as agreed. But it was also stipulated that if L. should fail to make any payment at the time stipulated the contract should be void, and any payments made should be forfeited. L. took possession under the contract. *Held* that this was a sale which forfeited the insurance. (*Kempton v. State Ins. Co.*, 62 Iowa, 83, distinguished.) REED, J., *dissenting.*

2. **Vendor and Vendee:** CONTRACT FOR SALE: FORFEITURE WAIVED. A vendor of land who has the right to declare the contract forfeited upon the vendee's failure to make payment as stipulated, cannot accept part of a payment and then declare a forfeiture. He must first make demand for the balance of that payment.

3. **Fire Insurance:** FORFEITURE BY CONTRACT OF SALE: RESCISSION OF CONTRACT. A fire insurance policy which has been forfeited by a sale of the premises in violation of its conditions, is not restored by an abandonment of the contract of sale.

Appeal from Polk Circuit Court.

SATURDAY, MARCH 19.

ACTION upon a policy of fire insurance. There was a trial to a jury, and verdict and judgment were rendered for the defendant. The plaintiff appeals.

Guthrie & Maley, for appellant.

Phillips & Day, for appellee.

ADAMS, CH. J.—I. The court gave a peremptory instruction to render a verdict for the defendant. The plaintiff assigns as error the giving of such instruction.

1. FIRE Insurance: forfeiture by sale: facts constituting sale.

The instruction was given upon the theory that the pleadings and evidence showed conclusively that the plaintiff had violated the policy, and forfeited his rights thereunder, before the loss. The policy contained a condition against selling, conveying or incumbering the property. The defendant contended that the plaintiff violated the condition by entering into a contract of sale, by which contract the purchaser took possession, and the plaintiff received a part of the purchase-money, and retained the legal title, which was to be conveyed upon the payment of the balance. The making of such contract is not denied. The plaintiff, however, denies that the contract was of such a character as to constitute a completed sale.

The building insured was a dwelling house situated upon a small farm in Polk county. After the policy was issued, to-wit, in March, 1885, the plaintiff and one Lint entered into a written contract whereby Lint was to pay the plaintiff for the same $400, of which $50 was to be paid down, and the balance in six payments, the first one of which was to be made January 1, 1886. Lint took possession under the contract, and leased the farm to his son, who cultivated it, and occupied the house as a dwelling until it was destroyed by fire. The contract of sale provided that, if Lint should promptly make all the payments called for by the contract, the plaintiff would execute to him a deed of warranty to the land, but that time should be regarded as of the essence of the contract, and that, if Lint should fail to make any payment at the time stipulated, the contract should be void, and any payments made should be forfeited. Before the first deferred payment became due, the insured property was destroyed.

The precise language of that portion of the policy which is alleged to have been violated is in these words: "In case any such property shall be sold, conveyed or incumbered * * * without the written consent of this company is obtained, * * * this policy shall immediately thereafter be null and void." It is manifest from the above that the policy contemplated that there might be a sale without a conveyance. The provision is the same as if the word "or" had been expressed between the words "sold" and "conveyed," and as if the policy read: "In case any such property shall be sold or conveyed," etc. In either case the policy would be void. We come, then, to the question as to whether, where one party binds himself unconditionally to pay a certain price for a piece of real estate, and takes possession under the contract, and the other party binds himself to convey the real estate upon the payments being made, and nothing remains to be done but for the party taking possession to make the payments, and for the other to make the deed, such contract constitutes a sale of the real estate, within the meaning of the policy. In answer to this question we have to say that we think it does. Lint was the real owner of the house that was burned. The loss was his loss. The plaintiff lost nothing, unless he needed the house for security. If Lint is responsible, or the property, without the house, is sufficient security for the balance of the purchase-money, the plaintiff's claim can be collected, and he will have all that he would have had if the house had not been burned. If he is allowed to collect the insurance and the purchase-money both, he will profit by the destruction of the property. That the insured shall, by his own voluntary act, come to have an interest in the destruction of the insured property is forbidden, not only by public policy, but by all the maxims of insurance, and is precisely what this defendant attempted to guard against. If the contract had been of that nature that the loss of the house fell upon the plaintiff as owner, and not upon Lint, the case would be entirely different. We can suppose a case where the owner of insured property makes a contract for the sale of it, but has not made a conveyance of the property, nor delivery of possession, but has retained control, and, while under his control and care, the property is destroyed by fire, and the seller cannot complete the contract by making such delivery as the contract contemplates; then the loss of the property would fall upon him, notwithstanding his contract, and for the reason that he is not able to carry it out;

and it might well be said in such case that there was no sale within the meaning of the policy.

The plaintiff relies, in part, upon the fact that in the contract time was made of the essence of the contract. But' that was a mere provision for its termination. The seller might elect to reclaim the property if the buyer failed to pay promptly as he stipulated; but, while the contract subsisted, it appears to us that the relation which each party sustained to the property was not different from what it would have been if the contract had been drawn without the provision as to forfeiture if the payments were not made upon the day they fell due. Until forfeiture, Lint was the owner of the property, in the sense that the loss of the house must fall upon him.

The plaintiff cites *Kempton v. State Ins. Co.*, 62 Iowa, 83, and several other cases. But those cases all differ from the case at bar. In those cases something yet remained to be done by the vendor in addition to the execution of the deed.

We are aware that reasoning is used in some of the cases which might seem to support the plaintiff's position. Take the case of *Turnbull v. Portage Mut. Ins. Co.*, 12 Ohio, 305, (314.) In that case the court said: "This case turns mainly on the question as to whether the plaintiffs had an insurable interest in the premises insured at the time the loss occurred." Now, it is not to be denied that any vendor of real estate who has not received full payment, and retains the legal title for security, has an insurable interest. But it does not follow, we think, that there cannot be a sale of real estate where the legal title has not been conveyed, and a part of the purchase-money remains unpaid. The very theory that the vendor who retains the legal title, with a right to enforce the payments of the purchase-money, holds the legal title for security, is based upon the idea that there has been a sale; and in such cases it is manifest that a loss by fire must fall upon the purchaser *as owner*, and affects the seller only as it impairs his security. The seller may, indeed, have an insurable interest, but his interest is substantially that of a mortgagee, which is quite different from a proprietary interest. Different rates are charged; and in case of the insurance of a mortgage interest, and payment to the mortgagee of a loss, a right of subrogation accrues to the company to the extent of the amount paid. The law will not allow an insured mortgagee to be subjected to the temptation that he would be subjected to if he had a right to collect his insurance, and at the same time to collect and hold his whole mortgage debt besides.

There is a fundamental and vicious error in the doctrine contended for by the plaintiff. He would collect the insurance upon the theory that there has been no sale, and would collect his purchase-money upon a theory which is just the reverse. If the doctrine for which he contends is correct, he would be able to collect the full amount of his policy, though only a single dollar of the purchase-money remained unpaid.

II. The plaintiff assigns as error the exclusion of certain evidence. He offered to prove that only a part of the payment was made, which, by the terms of the contract, was to be paid at the time it should take effect. The court excluded the evidence as immaterial. It was, of course, the right of the plaintiff to insist upon the whole of that payment, or that the contract should not take effect. But the contract provided that time was of the essence of the agreement, and that all payments made might be forfeited if the buyer made any default. Now, the plaintiff could not be allowed to accept partial payment, and say at the same time that, the payment being partial, the contract is void, and the partial payment thus made is forfeited. The very act of accepting partial payment was a waiver of strict performance as to the balance of that payment. No other theory would consist with good faith. The acceptance, to be sure, was not a waiver of the payment of the balance, and the plaintiff, unless there was an agreement to the contrary, might prob-

2. VENDOR and vendee: contract for sale: forfeiture waived.

ably demand it at any time. But, after accepting partial payment, we think that the plaintiff should have demanded the balance before he could properly claim that Lint was in default. We think that the contract took effect, and that the contract, together with the delivery of possession, constituted a sale.

III. The plaintiff assigned as error the exclusion of other evidence. He offered to show that before the loss the parties had abandoned the contract, but the court excluded the evidence as immaterial. If the policy had been forfeited by the making of the contract, we do not think that we could hold that it would be waived by an abandonment of the contract. Suppose that the plaintiff had forfeited the policy by a sale and conveyance; no one would, we think, claim that the policy would be revived by a repurchase and reconveyance. Yet the principle involved would be the same.

3. FIRE Insurance: forfeiture by contract of sale: rescission of contract.

We see no error in the ruling of the circuit court.

AFFIRMED.

REED, J., (*dissenting.*) The contract between plaintiff and Lint was an executory agreement for the sale and conveyance of the property. Plaintiff was bound, upon the strict performance by Lint of his undertaking, to convey the land. But a failure by the latter to pay any installment of the purchase-price at the stipulated time would work a forfeiture of all interest in the land, as well as of all sums paid under the contract; and the agreement provided that upon such failure the vendee would surrender possession of the premises. What was the extent of the right and interest acquired by Lint under this contract? I think he did not acquire the ownership of the property, but the right acquired was the right to be invested with the ownership when he performed his undertakings in the contract. Until that was done, both the title and ownership remained in plaintiff; for, by the terms of the agreement, Lint would be entitled to be invested with the property only upon a strict performance of its condition, and, upon his failure to perform any of them, nothing further was required to be done for the establishment of a perfect right in plaintiff. Now, what the parties provided against by the clause in the policy quoted in the majority opinion, was such disposition of the property as would divest the plaintiff of the title and ownership of it; and the uniform holding of the authorities is that the policy is not defeated, under a provision to that effect, by an executory contract for the sale of the property. *Hill v. Cumberland Valley M. P. Co.*, 59 Pa. St., 474; *Insurance Co v. Updegraff*, 21 Id., 513; *Insurance Co v. Stewart*, 19 Id., 45; *Trumbull v. Insurance Co.*, 12 Ohio, 305; *Browning v. Insurance Co.*, 71 N. Y., 508; *Washington Ins. Co. v Kelley*, 32 Md., 421; *Kempton v. State Ins. Co.*, 62 Iowa. 83; Wood Ins., § 329; May Ins., § 267.

In *Kempton v. State Ins. Co.*, it was held that the policy which contained a provision similar to that in question was not defeated by a contract for the sale of the property. The only difference between that case and this lies in the fact that the purchaser in that was not entitled to the possession of the property until certain payments were made, and the vendor was in possession at the time of the loss, while in this the purchaser was in possession when the fire occurred. But this is not material. The ground of the holding in that case is that the insured was not divested of the ownership of the property by the contract, and that is the case here.

In my judgment, the holding of the majority is in conflict with that case, as well as with the current of authorities on the subject.

MILLER v. WOLBERT ET AL.

1. **Mortgage of Homestead**: FRAUD OF HUSBAND TO SECURE WIFE'S SIGNATURE. Where nothing was done to prevent a wife from reading a mortgage on her homestead, or to mislead her in regard to its contents, and it is certain that she intended to sign the paper which was presented to her for her signature, the fact that the husband made a false representation to her as to the nature of the debt to be secured thereby will not invalidate the mortgage in the hands of the mortgagee, if he was innocent of the fraud.

2. **Parties to Actions**: PARTY IN INTEREST: OWNERSHIP OF NOTE SUED ON. Where plaintiff's attorneys, in settling a claim, took the two notes in suit, payable to themselves, and it was agreed that they were to have the amount of the smaller note as their fees, but it was not agreed that they should have the note itself, and they indorsed both notes to plaintiff, *held* that this did not show that one of the notes was owned by the attorneys, nor that plaintiff was not the real party in interest in the action to collect the notes.

Appeal from Adair Circuit Court.

SATURDAY, MARCH 19

ACTION upon two promissory notes, and to foreclose a mortgage executed by the defendant Harry Wolbert, and his wife, Melissa Wolbert, upon their homestead. There was a decree for the plaintiff, and the defendants appeal.

Gow & Hager, for appellants.

Grass & Storey, for appellee.

ADAMS, CH. J.—The defendants admitted the execution of the notes and mortgage, but averred that the signature of Melissa Wolbert to the mortgage was obtained by fraud; that the mortgage, being executed upon the defendants' homestead, had no validity.

1. MORTGAGE of homestead: fraud of husband to secure wife's signature.

The facts appear to be that the defendant Harry Wolbert was charged with being the father of a bastard child born to Martha Miller, for whose benefit this action is brought. Grass & Storey, attorneys at law, were employed by her father, Nelson Miller, to obtain a settlement with the defendant Harry Wolbert of his liability for the support of the child. They did obtain such settlement, and in pursuance of it, the defendant Harry executed the notes and mortgage in question. Mrs. Wolbert was not told what the nature of the claim made against her husband was. She was told in a general way, by her husband, that it was an old claim which had come against him, and, while he had supposed that it was settled, he had not taken a receipt, and he had the claim to pay over again. She avers that these representations were made at the instigation of Mr. Grass, of the firm of Grass & Storey; that they were not true; that she was misled by them, and induced to sign the mortgage in reliance upon them. But, in our opinion, the evidence shows that, whatever may have been said to Mrs. Wolbert by her husband, Mr. Grass was not guilty of instigating any false representations. According to Mr. Grass' testimony, he said to Wolbert that he might say to his wife that the claim was one which Grass & Storey had against him, and that it had to be fixed up, or it would make him some trouble. We see no reason to doubt the correctness of this testimony. It is true that he is contradicted to some extent by Wolbert, but Wolbert's honesty and credibility are more or less impeached by his own testimony. He sets up his own fraud upon his wife to defeat the mortgage, and endeavors to make Grass a party to it. The presumption is that Grass was not a party to it, and we cannot hold that he was, without something more to contradict his testimony than the evidence discloses. Now, it is not material what fraud Wolbert may have perpetrated upon his wife. Such fraud, if any, did not affect the mortgage in the hands of the payee of the notes, if he was innocent of the fraud. It was in just reliance upon her signature that the settlement was made, and the claim adjusted.

There was some evidence tending to show that she did not know what she signed, and it is claimed that the mortgage is void for that reason. But it is certain that she intended to sign the paper which was presented to her for her signature, and there is no pretense that anything was done to prevent her from reading it, or to mislead her in regard to its contents.

We think that the judgment of the circuit court must be

AFFIRMED.

SUPPLEMENTAL OPINION ON PETITION FOR REHEARING.

ADAMS, CH. J.—The defendants in their answer denied that the plaintiff was the owner of the notes in question. In a petition for a rehearing, it is insisted that the evidence shows that at least one of the notes was owned by Grass & Storey, the plaintiff's attorneys. The fact appears to be that the notes were taken in the name of Grass & Story, and it was agreed that they should have the amount of the smaller for fees, and both notes, we infer, were retained in their possession. But the notes were given in settlement of a claim due the plaintiff, and were her property. They were made payable to Grass & Storey at the request of the maker. They were soon afterwards properly indorsed by the payees, not for the purpose of transferring any property in the notes, but because they belonged already to the plaintiff, and it was her right to have them indorsed for that reason. If they remained in Grass & Storey's possession, they were simply held by them as her attorneys. While it is true they were to have the amount of the smaller note, it does not appear to have been understood that they were to have the note itself as their property. That was indorsed, as well as the larger one, and both were treated in the same way. It may be that Grass & Storey had the right to hold the smaller note until they should be paid their fees. But we see nothing more. The plaintiff, then, we think, is the real party in interest, so far as both notes are concerned, and we see no evidence tending to show otherwise. We did not notice the question in our opinion, because it is a mere question of fact, and the evidence seemed so clear as to afford no ground for controversy.

The petition for a rehearing must be OVERRULED.

2. PARTIES to actions: party in interest: ownership of note sued on.

THE STATE v. PAYSON.

1. **Seduction**: EVIDENCE: "KEEPING COMPANY" WITH ANOTHER MAN. In a prosecution for seduction, evidence that the prosecuting witness had frequently been seen going home with another man was not material,—not even to contradict her testimony that she had never "kept company" with any other man than the defendant.

2. ———: EVIDENCE OF PRIOR UNCHASTITY: QUESTION FOR JURY. In such case it was for the jury to weigh the evidence as to the prior chastity of the prosecuting witness, and this court cannot disturb their finding in that regard.

Appeal from Carroll District Court.

SATURDAY, MARCH 19.

INDICTMENT charging that the defendant seduced one Dina Granhoff. Trial by jury. Verdict, guilty, and judgment. The defendant appeals.

Bowen & Cloud and *McDuffie & Howard*, for appellant.

A. J. Baker, Attorney general, for the State.

SEEVERS, J.—The defendant sought to prove by one Jacobson that he frequently saw a person other than the defendant going home with her. We are unable to see the

1. SEDUCTION: evidence: "keeping company" with another man.

materiality of this evidence. Counsel, however, say that the prosecutrix denied that any one kept company with her other than the defendant, and therefore the refusal of the court to admit the evidence was prejudicial error. But this, we think, cannot be so. Merely going home with the prosecutrix, without more, certainly cannot be regarded as a material circumstance. The prosecutrix may have understood "keeping company" as something materially different from walking home with a gentleman. Besides this, the evidence in relation to "keeping company" was elicited on cross-examination.

A small portion of the fifth instruction is singled out, and is said to be erroneous. We think the instruction is in no respect objectionable. We deem it unnecessary to set it out

It is also said that the evidence does not sustain the verdict, for the reason that it appears that the prosecutrix was not of chaste character. There is some evidence which

——: evidence of prior unchastity: question for jury. tends to establish that she was not of chaste character. It, however, is not so clear and cer tain as to warrant us in disturbing the verdict This question was fairly submitted to the jury, and we cannot see that there is any prejudicial error in the record.

AFFIRMED.

THE STATE, EX REL. HINKLEY, V. MARTLAND ET AL.

1. **Intoxicating Liquors:** FAILURE TO MAKE RETURN OF SALES: PEN ALTY: WHO MAY SUE FOR. Under § 1538 of the Code, any citizen of the county may maintain an action in the name of the state, on the bond of one authorized to sell intoxicating liquors, for the penalty for failure to make report of sales. The authority given by § 1532 to the district attorney to bring such action is not exclusive.

2. **Appeal:** WAIVER BY SATISFYING JUDGMENT. One whose action has been dismissed does not waive his right to appeal by paying to the clerk on demand, his fees in the case.

Appeal from Plymouth Circuit Court.

SATURDAY, MARCH 19.

THIS is an action upon a bond given by the defendants for a permit to sell intoxicating liquors. The petition was dismissed upon the motion of defendants. The plaintiff appeals.

Zink & Gosselin and *Cole, McVey & Clark*, for appellant

Curtis & Durley, for appellees.

ROTHROCK, J.—It is averred in the petition that the defendants obtained from the board of supervisors of Ply-

1. INTOXICAT- ING liquors: failure to make return of sales: penalty : who may sue for. mouth county a permit to sell intoxicating liq uors, and gave the bond required by law, and that, for the month of July, 1884, they failed. neglected and refused to file the reports required by the statute. The relator, a citizen of Plymouth county, claims to sue in behalf of himself, as well as for the benefit of the school fund, and he demands judgment for the county, for the use of the school fund, for $50, and judgment for himself for a like amount. The action is founded upon section 1538 of the Code, as amended by chapter 143, Acts of the Twentieth General Assembly, and which is as follows: "Any person having such permit, who shall sell intoxicating liquors at a greater profit than is herein allowed, shall be liable to treble damages, to be recovered by civil action in favor of the party injured; and any person holding a permit, either to manufacture or sell, who shall fail to make monthly returns as herein required, or within five days thereafter, or who shall make false returns, shall forfeit for each offense the sum of one hundred dollars, to be recovered in the name of the state of Iowa, upon the relation of any citizen of the county, by civil action on his bond, with costs; and one-half of the sum recovered shall go to the informer, and one-half shall go to the school fund of the county."

The defendants claimed, by their motion to dismiss, that the plaintiff was not authorized by law to maintain the action upon his own motion, and that an action can only be brought at the instance of the district attorney of the proper judicial district. They rely upon section 1532 of the Code, which is as follows: "The bond shall be deposited with the county auditor, and suit shall be brought thereon at any time by the district attorney, in case the conditions thereof, or any of them, shall be broken. The principal and sureties therein shall also be jointly and severally liable for all civil damages, costs and judgments that may be obtained against the principal in any civil action brought by a wife, child, parent, guardian, or other person, under the provisions of sections fifteen hundred and fifty-six, fifteen hundred and fifty-seven, and fifteen hundred and fifty-eight, of this chapter. All other moneys collected on such bonds shall go to the school fund of the county."

We think that the position of counsel for the defendants

cannot be sustained. Section 1538 plainly authorizes a suit to be brought in the name of the state, on *the relation of any citizen of the county.* It is true that section 1532 has not been repealed, and a district or county attorney may, under the authority given by that statute, bring the action. But, since the enactment of section 1538, his right to do so is not exclusive, because any citizen of the county may bring the action, and prosecute it, without the aid of the district attorney. This appears to us to be so plain as to require no more than this mere reference to the two sections of the statute. All of the discussion of counsel upon other provisions of the statute does not appear to us to have any bearing upon the proper construction of these two sections.

II. A motion was submitted to us demanding the dismissal of the appeal, upon the ground that the plaintiff per-

2. APPEAL: waiver by satisfying judgment. formed the judgment of the court below by paying the costs of the action, and therefore he has no right to prosecute the appeal. The facts are that, after the motion to dismiss was sustained, the clerk of the circuit court demanded of plaintiff's counsel a payment of seventy-five cents as clerk's fees. That amount was paid to him. It is scarcely necessary to say that the mere payment of the fees of an officer for his services in the action does not estop the unsuccessful party from prosecuting an appeal in this court.

For the error in sustaining the motion to dismiss the action the judgment will be

REVERSED.

NICKELSON v. NEGLEY & SHERWIN.

1. **Landlord's Lien**: ACTION AGAINST PURCHASER OF CROPS: LIMITA-
TION AS TO TIME. One who purchases from a tenant, and converts to
his own use, crops on which the landlord has a lien for rent, is liable to
the landlord in damages to the amount of his lien, but the action to
recover such damages must be brought within six months after the
expiration of the term of the lease, that is, before the expiration of the
· lien, (See Code, § 2017,) or it will be too late. REED, J., *dissenting*.

Appeal from Shelby Circuit Court.

SATURDAY, MARCH 19.

THE facts are stated in the opinion.   .

Smith & Culleson, for appellant.

Wright, Baldwin & Haldane, for appellees.

SEEVERS, J.—The petition states that the plaintiff leased
certain premises to one Monroe, for one year from the first
day of March, 1884, and that said Monroe agreed to pay the
rent in April, 1884, and on January 1, 1885; that said
Monroe raised on the leased premises 1,000 bushels of
wheat, which he sold and delivered to the defendants in
August and September, 1884, which they converted to their
own use; that plaintiff had a landlord's lien on said wheat,
and in February, 1885, he commenced an action to enforce
his lien, and sued out a landlord's attachment, but the same
was not levied on said wheat for the reason that the same
could not be found. In March, 1885, he recovered a judgment against Monroe for the amount due under the lease.
It is stated that defendants have sold said wheat, and the
same is not in their possession. The relief asked is that
plaintiff recover of the defendants to the extent or amount
of the judgment against Monroe. This action was commenced on the first day of October, 1885. The defendants
demurred to the petition on the ground that, at the time this

action was commenced, the plaintiff's lien had ceased to exist.

It is provided by statute that a landlord has a lien upon all crops grown on the demised premises during the term, and which are not exempt from execution, " but such lien shall not continue more than six months after the expiration of the term." Code, § 2017. The term ended on the first day of March, 1885, and this action was not commenced until more than six months thereafter, and therefore it is contended that the lien had ceased to exist, and that the plaintiff cannot recover. On the other hand, the plaintiff contends that, when the defendants purchased the wheat in August and September, 1884, his lien did exist, and the defendants purchased subject thereto, and must now account to the plaintiff, for the reason that they have converted to their own use property on which he had a valid lien. It seems to us the plaintiff's position cannot be sustained. The defendants did not become absolutely liable to the plaintiff when they purchased the wheat. It is true, they purchased subject to the lien, and became liable to the plaintiff if an action was commenced to enforce it within the time provided by statute. If no such action was commenced within that time, the lien cannot be enforced.

But it is urged that an action was commenced within that time. The defendants, however, were not parties to such action. As to them, it has no force and effect, and was not in fact commenced. But it is contended that the statute provides that "the lien may be effected by the commencement of an action within the period above prescribed, * * * in which action the landlord shall be entitled to a writ of attachment, * * *" Code, § 2018. Counsel for the appellant contend that, as the action was commenced against the tenant within the statutory period, the lien was "effected," for the reason that the statute so provides. The word "effected" certainly was not well chosen to express what clearly, it seems to us, must have been the legislative thought. The meaning of the word as used in the statute, it seems to us, must be regarded the same as enforced; for it does not require an action to effectuate the lien. It exists for and during the statutory period, although no action is brought to enforce it. If, however, it is desired to enforce the lien, then an action is required. Now, this is precisely the object of this action,—that is, to enforce the lien; but, as it was not brought within the statutory period, the plaintiff cannot recover. The statute, in effect, is a limitation on the right of action. The demurrer was therefore correctly sustained.

                                                    AFFIRMED.

REED, J., (*dissenting*.)—The error of the majority, as I conceive, is in the assumption that the action is for the enforcement of the landlord's lien. The material fact alleged in the petition is that defendants received and converted to their own use the property on which plaintiff had a lien for the security of his rent. The action is for the recovery of the damages sustained by plaintiff in consequence of the conversion of the property, whereby his lien was defeated; and, upon the facts stated, I think he has a right of recovery. If defendants by force or stealth have taken possession of the property, and made such disposition of it as defeated plaintiff's lien, it would hardly be claimed that he could not recover for the injury. And I know of no statute or principle that would require him to bring his action within the time allowed for bringing an action for the enforcement of the lien. Yet, wherein is the present case different from that? The act complained of had precisely the same effect upon his rights. It defeated his lien. It was no less a wrong to him, and it as effectively destroyed his right as a conversion by force or stealth or fraud would have done. For this reason I respectfully dissent from the holding of the majority.

REYNOLDS v. SUTLIFF.

1. **Appeal:** DIMINUTION OF RECORD: CORRECTION: PRACTICE. When it is discovered on appeal that the record in the court below is deficient, a continuance of the appeal may be had, in a proper case, for the purpose of procuring a correction of the record in the lower court, but no order of this court is necessary to give the party leave to move for a correction in the trial court, nor to confer on that court authority to make the correction.

2. **Former Adjudication:** HOW PROVED. Where a party relies upon an estoppel by a judgment upon a verdict, he should introduce the verdict and judgment in evidence, and where he neither introduces nor proposes to introduce these, an instruction given by the court in the former case is properly rejected as evidence on that issue.

Appeal from Linn District Court.

SATURDAY, MARCH 19.

THIS is an action upon a promissory note. There was a trial by jury, and a verdict and judgment for the defendant. Plaintiff appeals.

Blake & Hormel, for appellant.

Henry Rickel, for appellee.

ROTHROCK, J.—I. The defendant admitted the execution of the note, and pleaded the following defenses thereto: (1)

1. APPEAL: diminution of record: correction: practice.

That the note was executed on Sunday; (2) that it was usurious; (3) that it was without consideration, for that it arose out of a pretended settlement of partnership transactions between the plaintiff and the defendant, in which settlement the defendant was induced by the false representations and deceit of the plaintiff to execute the note when nothing was due to the plaintiff; (4) that the note had been fully paid.

The plaintiff, by his reply, denied the averments of the answer, and pleaded that the alleged payments were made upon another note, given by the defendant to the plaintiff, upon which an action was brought and a trial had, in which it was adjudged that the alleged payments had been made upon the prior note. The defendant filed an additional abstract, in which he set forth many pages of evidence which he claimed were omitted from appellant's abstract, and, in addition thereto, he presents certain evidence which he claims was introduced on the trial, but which was omitted from the bill of exceptions by mistake. He also filed an additional transcript, from which it appears that, after the appeal was taken, appellee filed a motion in the district court to correct the record, and the motion was heard, and an order made correcting the record, so as to show that part of the evidence claimed to have been omitted was introduced on the trial, and read to the jury. The plaintiff's attorneys appeared to the motion in the court below, and filed affidavits in resistance thereof. It is now claimed by appellant that there was no authority in law for correcting the record, and that the order was erroneously made by the district court, and he filed a motion asking that the additional transcript be expunged from the record.

The motion for the correction of the record was properly made in the district court. There was no necessity for an application to this court for leave to move in the court below for the correction. It frequently occurs that causes are continued in this court for the purpose of giving parties time to procure corrections of the record by motion in the court below, but no order is made in this court for leave to do so. The right exists without an order of this court. The mistake frequently made is that parties come into this court with motions to correct the record. This cannot be done. We are compelled to take the records in appeals as they are made by the trial courts. That the order was not erroneously made, upon the facts presented, appear to us to be very plain.

II. There was a conflict in the evidence as to whether the note was executed on Sunday, and upon the question of usury. We do not understand that this is seriously questioned by the plaintiff. Upon the question of former adjudication as to the alleged payments,

2. FORMER adjudication: how proved.

the plaintiff introduced the petition and answer in the former case. He offered in evidence an instruction given by the court to the jury in that case. This was objected to by the defendant. The objection was sustained. One ground of the objection was that it had not been shown what the verdict of the jury was in that case. The plaintiff did not offer the verdict nor judgment in evidence, nor state, when he offered the instruction objected to, that he would proceed to offer the whole record. We think that the ruling of the court was correct. If the plaintiff relied upon an estoppel by judgment, he should have introduced the verdict and judgment in evidence.

III. The principal contest upon the trial was as to the consideration for the note,—whether it was void by reason of the alleged fraud of the plaintiff in procuring the defendant to execute it. The investigation involved the business of a partnership between the parties for several years in dealing in, and feeding live-stock. The parties kept no regular partnership books. The plaintiff claimed to keep the accounts of the partnership. He also kept a diary of his every-day transactions, parts of which were introduced in evidence. Many other collateral facts were presented to the jury. Complaint is made that the court erred in certain rulings made upon the admission and exclusion of evidence. Our examination of these rulings has led us to the conclusion that they were not erroneous. It would be wholly unnecessary to set out these different exceptions. It would require an attempt to explain about all the evidence in the case in order to make our rulings intelligible.

Objections were made to certain instructions given by the court to the jury, and to the refusal to give instructions requested by the plaintiff. These objections are urged in argument. They are, for the most part, founded upon the thought that, while they do not state incorrect propositions of law, they are given upon a state of facts of which there is no evidence. Most of the instructions asked and refused were, in substance, embodied in the instructions given. We may say, generally, that we find no error in the instructions given, nor in the refusal to give those requested to be given. Our examination of these questions has required us to give the whole evidence in the case a very careful consideration. This has been no slight undertaking. It is very voluminous. The disagreement in the abstract has compelled us to examine the transcript. This also has been made necessary by the fact that it is claimed with great confidence that the verdict is directly contrary to the evidence, so far as the question of fraud is involved. Counsel for plaintiff denounces the judgment as a "piece of legal robbery that arbitrarily, and without the shadow of an excuse, deprived the plaintiff of as valid a claim as was ever evidenced by a promissory note." On the other hand, counsel for the defendant claims that it is "clear and perfectly manifest that there should have been a verdict for the defendant." We cannot set out and discuss the evidence. We deem it sufficient to say that, under the rules so often applied in considering the sufficiency of evidence, the verdict ought not to be disturbed.

AFFIRMED.

JENKINS v. CLARK.

1. **Guardian:** APPOINTMENT: JURISDICTION: DOMICILE. The probate court of the county in which a minor child has its domicile is the court which has jurisdiction to appoint a guardian of its person, though it be not at the time a resident of such county. (Compare *Lore v. Cherry*, 24 Iowa, 204.)

2. **Domicile:** OF MINOR CHILD: WHAT IS CHANGE OF. The domicile of a minor child is the domicile of its parents, and after the death of its parents its domicile continues the same until another is lawfully acquired. But where the father was dead, and the mother, shortly before her death, in her will requested a sister residing out of the state to take and raise the child, and the sister accordingly took the child out of the state, but assumed no legal obligation toward it, *held* that the domicile of the child was not changed.

3. **Guardian:** RIGHT TO CUSTODY OF WARD: EFFECT OF PARENT'S REQUEST. Under § 2249 of the Code, a guardian of the person of a child has the same right to its custody as if he were its parent. And where he is not shown to be an unfit person to have such custody, the child will not be taken from him and given to an aunt, though its mother in her will has requested that the aunt take and raise the child.

4. **Habeas Corpus:** CUSTODY OF CHILD: PRIME CONSIDERATION: EVIDENCE ON APPEAL. Where the right to the custody of a minor child is involved in a *habeas corpus* proceeding, the best interest of the child is the first consideration; but the action is regarded as an ordinary one, and, on an appeal to this court, the judgment of the lower court cannot be disturbed unless it is clearly contrary to the evidence as to the best interest of the child.

Appeal from Cass District Court.

SATURDAY, MARCH 19.

THIS is a proceeding by *habeas corpus* to determine the right to the custody of May Jenkins, who is a minor and an orphan. The controversy is between the guardian and the defendant, who is an aunt of the minor. The district court awarded the custody of the child to the guardian. The defendant appeals.

R. G. Phelps, for appellant.

L. L. DeLano, for appellee.

REED, J.—When this proceeding was instituted, May Jenkins was about six years old. Her parents were Benjamin F. and Josephine Jenkins. Her father died in December, 1882, and her mother in the following October. They had resided for many years in Audubon county, and she was born in that county. They left surviving them six children, all of whom are minors. Benjamin F. Jenkins left an estate consisting of a valuable farm, and personal property of the value of $10,000. John T. Jenkins, the present guardian, is a brother of Benjamin F., and he was administrator of his estate, and the administration has been fully closed. Josephine Jenkins executed a will before her death, by which she devised all of her property to her children. In this will she nominated John T. Jenkins as executor; and, when the will was admitted to probate, he qualified and entered upon the duties of the trust. The will contains the following clause: "It is my further desire that John T. Jenkins take Olive Jenkins, Charles W. Jenkins and Hayden Jenkins; Mary Sheer take my daughter Maggie Jenkins; Eliza Clark take May Jenkins; Laura Gilbert take my daughter Pearl Jenkins,—and raise and care for each and all of said children as if they were their own." The defendant is the Eliza Clark mentioned in the clause, and she and Mary Sheer and Laura Gilbert are sisters of Mrs. Jenkins. The will was executed but a few days before Mrs. Jenkins died. At that time, Mrs. Clark resided in Dakota territory, but during the last sickness of Mrs. Jenkins she was present with her, and assisted in nursing and caring for her. Soon after the death of Mrs. Jenkins she returned to her home, taking May with her. Some time after that, John T. Jenkins was appointed guardian of the property and persons of all the children by the circuit court of Audubon county. A short time before this proceeding was instituted, Mrs. Clark came to Iowa on a visit, bringing May with her. It appears that a doubt had arisen as to the validity of the action of the court in appointing a guardian of her person, such doubt arising out of the fact that she was absent from the state when the appointment was made, and the guardian, accordingly, after she was brought back to the state, applied for and obtained a second appointment as guardian of her person, the appointment being made by the same court. At the time this order was made, however, the child was in Cass county, and she had not been in Audubon county since her return to the state.

The first question which arises in the case is whether the guardian, by virtue of his appointment, is entitled to the custody of the child as against the defendant. In determining this question, it is necessary to consider the relation which each of the parties bears to the child. It is insisted that the action of the circuit court of Audubon county in making the appointment of a guardian of the person is invalid, for the reason that the child was not within the jurisdiction of the court

1. GUARDIAN: appointment: jurisdiction: domicile.

when either of the orders was made. But we think this position cannot be sustained. The law undoubtedly is that the proper court at the place of domicile of the child has jurisdiction of the matter of the guardianship of his person. A person may have a domicile at one place, while he is a resident of another. *Love v. Cherry*, 24 Iowa, 204. Now, the domicile of a child is to be determined by the domicile of the parent; and, when a domicile is once fixed, it remains until another is lawfully acquired. Schouler, Dom. Rel. § 230. If the

2. DOMICILE: of minor child: what is change of.

parent change his own domicile, that of the minor child is thereby changed. The domicile of May Jenkins at the time of the death of her parents was in Audubon county. They had done nothing which in law could have the effect of changing it. Mrs. Clark could not change it, for she bore no legal relation to the child. True, she was requested by the mother, by the will, to raise and care for her, and had taken charge of her in obedience to that request. But she was under no legal obligation to do that; nor could she have been compelled to continue to care for her for a single day, but might have terminated her relation to her at pleasure. The child could not change its own domicile, for it was not *sui juris*. The domicile of the child, then, remained at Audubon county, notwithstanding the fact that she was personally in another jurisdiction, and the circuit court of that county had jurisdiction of the guardianship of her person.

It is provided by statute (Code, § 2249) that "guardians of the persons of minors have the same power and control over them that parents would have if living."

3. GUARDIAN: right to custody of ward: effect of parent's request.

We think there can be no doubt as to the effect of this provision. By his appointment, the guardian is vested with the same right to the custody of the ward as the parent has of his own child. This express provision cannot be defeated by the clause in the will; for, as we have seen, that created no legal relation between defendant and the child. Nor did it impose any legal obligation upon defendant. What she had done in the premises had been done in obedience to the expressed wish of the mother of the child, and her natural affection for it, and not because she was under any legal obligation in the matter. It will readily be conceded that the right of the guardian to the custody of the ward is not absolute. If he were shown to be an unfit person to have the custody of it, the courts would not hesitate to award the custody to another. But no question of that character is made in the case. Neither of the parties make any question as to the personal fitness of the other; and we have no doubt that in the personal custody of either the child would have the same care and kindness of treatment that a loving and kind parent bestows upon his own child. But, aside from any question as to the best interest of the ward, we think the intent of the statute is that the guardian shall have the custody of it.

If, however, the case depended upon consideration of the best interests of the child, which, after all, is the matter of 4. HABEAS cor- prime consideration in cases of this kind, we pus: custody of child: would not be warranted in disturbing the judg- prime consid- eration: evi- ment of the district court. The court might dence on appeal. well have determined, from the evidence as to the financial condition of defendant and her husband, and the disadvantages of their place of residence and other circumstances, that the interest of the child would be best served by placing it in the custody of the guardian. The proceeding is regarded as an ordinary action in which the finding of the trial court in questions of fact, unless clearly contrary to the evidence, is conclusive. *Kline v. Kline,* 57 Iowa, 386; *Fouts v. Pierce,* 64 Id., 71.

AFFIRMED.

THE STATE v. VATTER.

1. **Jurors**: COMPETENCY: OPINIONS FORMED. Where a juror in a criminal case admitted that he had formed an opinion as to the prisoner's guilt, and even stated, in answer to a question, that it was an unqualified opinion, yet, where he insisted all through his examination that it was not such an opinion as would disqualify him from rendering a true verdict upon the evidence, *held* that the court did not err in overruling a challenge for cause based on the ground of such opinion. (Compare Code, § 4405, subd. 11.)

2. **Arson**: EVIDENCE: STOLEN PROPERTY IN DEFENDANT'S POSSESSION. On a trial for the burning of a farm house, evidence that certain goods claimed by the state to have been taken from the burned house on the day of the fire, and other goods claimed to be the property of the owner of the house, but not taken therefrom, were found together, locked up in trunks in the defendant's possession, was properly admitted.

Appeal from Cedar District Court.

SATURDAY, MARCH 19.

THE defendant was indicted, tried and convicted of the crime of arson, and he appeals.

W. A. Foster and *C. E. Wheeler*, for appellant.

A. J. Baker, Attorney-general, for the State.

ROTHROCK, J.—I.   On the fourth day of July, 1885, the dwelling house of one Alexander Spear, situated on his farm in Cedar county, was totally destroyed by fire. The house was a large and valuable farm dwelling, and nearly new. No one was in the building when the fire was discovered. Spear and his family had closed it up, fastened the windows and window shutters, and locked the doors, and gone away to a public picnic about three miles distant. There is no question but that the fire was incendiary. That fact appears to have been conceded on the trial, and it is established by the evidence beyond any reasonable doubt. On the eleventh day of the same month, some out buildings or sheds on the farm were fired, but the fire was extinguished. A few days afterwards, a large quantity of hay and oats, which was in stacks on the farm, was consumed by fire. None of these fires were accidental. They were without doubt the work of an incendiary. The trial from which this appeal was taken was upon an indictment for burning the dwelling house.

The first claim made by counsel for appellant is that the court erred in overruling a number of challenges for cause to

1. JURORS: competency: opinions formed.

persons who were called as jurors in the case. These challenges were interposed as to five of the jurors, and the ground of the challenges was that the persons challenged were disqualified by reason of having formed opinions as to the guilt or innocence of the prisoner. It is provided by subd. 11 of section 4405 of the Code that a person who has "formed or expressed such an opinion as to the guilt or innocence of the prisoner as would prevent him from rendering a true verdict upon the evidence submitted on the trial" may be challenged for cause. Each one of the five persons who it is claimed were disqualified by reason of having formed opinions was examined under oath by the district attorney, and cross examined by counsel for the defendant, touching his knowledge of the case, and any opinions he might have formed regarding the guilt or innocence of the accused. In response to the district attorney, they all answered, in substance, that they had neither formed nor expressed such opinions as would prevent them from rendering a true verdict; in other words, they answered that they did not have such opinions as disqualified them under the statute. The question was put to them by the district attorney in very nearly the language of the statute. It is true that, on cross-examination, they stated that they had opinions on the subject; and one or more of them, in answer to the question whether such opinions were unqualified, stated that they were, but all through their examination they appeared to adhere to the belief that they had no opinion which would prevent them from rendering a true verdict according to the evidence. It is a very rare thing that a person called as a

.juror, who has heard the facts connected with the case, and has formed some kind of an opinion in reference thereto, maintains entire consistency in his examination as to his qualifications as a juror. The difficulty arises from the fact that many of them do not understand the difference between a qualified and an unqualified opinion, and, the questions being put to them in a leading form, there is often an apparent contradiction in the answers given. We think, when the whole examination of the jurors in question is considered, the court did not err in overruling the challenges for cause.

II. The defendant was a farm hand in the employ of Spear, the owner of the building which was burned, and, with his wife and one child, lived in a tenant

2. ARSON: evidence: stolen property in defendant's possession.

house across a public road, and but a short distance from the building which was burned. Two other men who were laborers on the farm had gone in another direction to a public celebration. When Spear and his family locked up their house and went off to the picnic, the defendant and his wife and child were the only persons left upon the farm. Some time after the fire the defendant was suspected of the crime, and a search-warrant was taken out, and his house was searched by the sheriff of the county. There were two trunks in the house which were locked, and, upon being opened, there were found therein an old hat, a towel, a pair of stockings, a piece of dress goods, and other articles which the state claimed were in the building which was burned on the morning of the fire, and that they were taken from the building before the fire was discovered. In the same trunks certain other articles were found, such as a monkey-wrench, a screw-driver, a knife, etc., which were claimed to be the property of Spear, but it was not claimed that the last named articles were taken from the house which was burned. The defendant objected to all the evidence as to these last-named articles, because it was proof of a petit larceny in no way connected with the crime charged in the indictment. The objection was overruled, and this ruling is claimed to be erroneous. We think the ruling was correct. The evidence was not introduced as tending to prove a crime other than that charged. The goods were all found together, and it was competent for the witness to point out and distinguish those claimed to have been taken from the house on the day of the fire from those taken before that time.

III. It is strenuously contended that the verdict is the result of prejudice, passion and excitement, and is without support in the evidence. The evidence has been presented to us without an abstract. It is a full transcript of the short-hand notes taken by question and answer, and we have therefore examined the testimony in the very words of the witnesses. We have thought it proper to give it a most patient and careful examination. We know that the series of fires of which this was the beginning must have created a great excitement in the community; and, if we thought the claim that the defendant was convicted upon mere suspicion, without evidence, was well founded, we would have no hesitancy in reversing and remanding the cause. But our examination of the case leads us to think that there is abundant evidence to sustain the verdict. The facts inculpating the defendant are so numerous that we cannot set them out and review them in an opinion. Taken altogether, they show with reasonable certainty that the defendant was guilty.

AFFIRMED.

PERSHING v. THE CHICAGO, BURLINGTON & QUINCY RAILWAY COMPANY.

71
121
123

1. **Railroads**: INJURY TO PASSENGER: PRESUMPTION OF NEGLIGENCE: BURDEN OF PROOF. In an action against a railroad company for injury to a passenger caused by the derailment of a train and the breaking down of a bridge, the jury was properly instructed that the burden was on plaintiff to show that the injury was caused by the negligence of the defendant; but that, if he had established that the accident was attended by circumstances showing that it was caused by defective construction of the roadway, bridge, track, or the fastenings of the rails, at the point where the derailment occurred, or its train, or cars, or by the management or running of the train, this would raise a presumption of negligence, and would cast upon defendant the burden of proving that it was not caused by any negligence or want of skill on its part, either in the construction or maintenance of its roadway, track, or bridge, or in the management of its train, or the condition of its cars; but that this presumption extended only to those portions of the track, machinery or bridge which the circumstances of the accident indicated were possibly defective; and that it was not required to prove that nothing about its entire train and roadway was defective. In other words, the defendant in such case is not required to show how the accident occurred, and that it was free from *all* negligence in the matter, but it is sufficient if it shows its freedom from negligence as to the matter which the circumstances indicate to have been the cause of the accident and injury.

2. ———: DUTY TO PASSENGERS: DEGREE OF CARE REQUIRED. The rule which has been uniformly recognized and enforced in this state is, that the carrier, in the conduct and management of his business, is bound to exercise the highest degree of care and diligence for the convenience and safety of his passengers; and he is held liable for the slightest neglect. But there are certain dangers that are necessarily incident to travel by railway, and these the passenger assumes when he elects to adopt it; and in the application of the rule to railway companies, all that is meant is that they should use the highest degree of care that is reasonably consistent with the practical conduct of the business. (See opinion for authorities.)

3. ———: ———: SELECTION OF PLANS AND MATERIALS. In an action against a railroad company for an injury to a passenger caused by the derailment of a train and the breaking of a bridge, the court instructed the jury, in effect, that the degree of care required of defendant in the selection of plans and materials for its roadway, bridges and appliances was such as was exercised by the best and most skillfully and carefully managed railroads in the country, under like circumstances. *Held that,* if this instruction was vulnerable to the objection that it makes the very

practices which are called in question the law of the case, the objection was obviated by another instruction, drawn with special reference to the facts of the case, in which the jury were told, in effect, that defendant was bound, not only to select such plans and materials for the construction of its road and appliances as were in use by the best and most skillfully conducted roads of the country, but that such materials and plans must have been found sufficient by the other roads.

4. ——: ——: CONSTRUCTION OF BRIDGES. In such case, the jury was told that defendant "was not required to so construct its bridge that it would resist the unusual and extraordinary shock of a derailed train, running at regular speed, and striking it with great force." *Held* that this instruction afforded plaintiff no ground of complaint, when taken in connection with another, to the effect that defendant was required to take into account, in constructing and maintaining its bridges, the fact that accidents might occur in the operation of its road, and to construct its bridges with reference thereto; and that it was held to a very high degree of care in this respect.

Appeal from Polk Circuit Court.

SATURDAY, MARCH 19.

ON the eighth day of February, 1885, a passenger train on defendant's railway was derailed, as is supposed, by a broken rail, at a point near a bridge over a gully or ravine. When the train went upon the bridge, the wheels on one side passed outside of the guard-rail, and the bridge was broken down, and the car in which plaintiff's intestate was riding as a passenger was thrown into the gully or ravine, and she received injuries which caused her death. This action was brought for the recovery of the damages sustained by her estate. There was a verdict and judgment for defendant, and plaintiff appeals.

Parsons, Perry & Sherman, for appellant.

J. W. Blythe, H. H. Trimble and *Runnells & Walker*, for appellee.

REED, J.—It is alleged in the petition that the injury was caused by the negligence of the defendant, and that its negligence consisted (1) in the manner in which its track and bridge were constructed and maintained, the latter being insufficient; and (2) in the manner in which the train was being run at the time of the accident. The evidence is not contained in the abstract, but it is recited in the "bill of exceptions" that plaintiff introduced evidence tending to prove the occurrence of the accident and injury, and that the deceased was not guilty of any contributory negligence, and that the accident was caused by the negligent manner in which the track and bridge were constructed and maintained, and the negligent manner in which the train was being run at the time, and by the insufficiency of the bridge, and that he then rested his cause; that the defendant thereupon introduced evidence tending to prove that its road, and said bridge, and its rolling stock, and its servants and agents, were in all respects such as were accepted by, and were in general use, and found to be sufficient and approved by, the best and most skillfully managed railroads of the country, doing a like business under like circumstances with it; and the selection of its materials, and the plan and construction of its roadway, track, bridges and rolling stock, and the selection of its employes, servants and agents, and the inspection and repairs of its road and machinery, and appliances connected with the operation of the road, were such as the best, most carefully, prudently and skillfully managed railroads in the country exercise and require, doing a like business, and under like circumstances; and that the bridge went down, and that the car in which the intestate was riding was thrown into the ravine, by reason of the derailment of the train, at a point 378 feet from the bridge; that the ties, rails and fastenings, and the ballast thereunder at that point, and between there and the bridge, were in all respects such as had been found sufficient by the most skillfully and prudently managed railroads of the country, doing a like business, under similar circumstances; that the same were, from time to time, and as frequently as by other railroads, inspected in the usual way of inspecting such appliances by the most carefully and prudently managed railroads of the country, by an employe of competent skill and experience in such matters; and that the rails and joint fastenings appeared sound, and all their supports sound and secure; and that there were no flaws or defects visible that could have been discovered by such inspection; and that the shock or blow which caused the bridge to fall was of unusual and extraordinary violence, and that the bridge would not otherwise have gone down, and that the guard-rails on the bridge were such as were usually and customarily used by the most skillfully managed railroads of the country, under like circumstances.

In rebuttal, plaintiff introduced evidence tending to prove that the bridge was not sufficient, either in plan or construction; that the guard-rails were not of sufficient size, and were not properly placed or fastened; that the joint fastenings at the point at which the derailment occurred were insufficient, and were broken prior to the occurrence of the derailment; and that the break might have been discovered, by a careful and proper inspection, before the passage of the train.

The errors assigned all relate to the instructions given by the court to the jury.

I. In the seventh, eighth and thirteenth instructions, the jury were told, in effect, that the burden was on plaintiff to show that the injury was caused by the negligence of the defendant; but that, if he had established that the accident was attended by circumstances showing that it was caused by the defective construction of the roadway, bridge, track, or the fastenings of the rail at the point where the derailment occurred, or its train or cars, or by the management or running of the train, this would raise a presumption of negligence, and would cast upon defendant the burden of proving that it was not caused by any negligence or want of skill on its part, either in the construction or maintenance of its roadway,

1. RAILROADS: injury to passenger: presumption of negligence: burden of proof.

track or bridge, or in the management of the train, or the condition of the cars, but that this presumption extended only to those portions of the track, machinery or bridge which the circumstances of the accident indicated were possibly defective, and it was not required to prove that nothing about its entire train and roadway were defective; and that the burden cast upon it by proof of the happening of the accident, and the attending circumstances, only required it to show that, as to the matters which the circumstances indicated were the cause of the accident and injury, it had exercised due care; and that it was not required to satisfactorily explain the reason of the breaking of the rail, and the derailment of the train, and the breaking down of the bridge, but was only required to prove that these things did not occur through any negligence on its part.

The point urged by counsel for appellant is that the instructions are erroneous, in that they limit the burden imposed upon defendant by the evidence of the occurrence of the accident, and the attendant circumstances, to proof merely that it had not been negligent in respect to those matters which the circumstances indicated were the cause of the injury. Their position is that the presumption which arises upon proof of the happening of the accident is not a mere presumption of negligence as to some specific matter, but is a presumption of general negligence on the part of the carrier; or, in other words, they insist that the presumption is that he is legally liable for the injury, and that this presumption can be overcome only by proof that it was caused by inevitable accident, and that it follows necessarily from this that he must account for the accident, and show that he was free from all negligence in the matter.

The rule which casts the burden of proof on the carrier is a rule of evidence having its foundation in considerations of policy. It prescribes the quantum of proof which the passenger is required to produce in making out his case originally, and he is entitled to recover on that proof, unless the carrier can overcome the presumption which arises under the rule from the facts proven. *Caldwell v. Steamboat Co.*, 47 N Y., 282; Thomp. Carr., 209.

The rule undoubtedly requires the carrier to prove his own freedom from negligence as to the cause of the injury. But that, it appears to us, is the doctrine of the instructions The immediate cause of the injury to plaintiff's intestate was the breaking down of the bridge, and the consequent precipitation of the car into the ravine, and this was occasioned by the blow or concussion by the derailed train. In seeking for the cause of the injury, then, it became necessary to inquire as to the cause of the derailment of the train, and whether there was any defect in the track or roadway or bridge, or in the cars or machinery of the train, or any negligence in the management of it at the time; for the circumstances indicated unmistakably that the cause of the accident was to be found in some of these matters. They constituted the subject of the inquiry as to this branch of the case, and defendant very properly confined its proof, as to the diligence and care it had exercised, to that subject.

As there was nothing to indicate that any other matter could have contributed to the accident, it could not be required to show that it had been careful as to other matters. Such evidence would clearly have been immaterial, and the holding of the instructions is that it was not required to go beyond the cause of the inquiry in making proof of care and diligence. The holding that it was not required to give a satisfactory explanation of the cause of the breaking of the rail and bridge is supported by *Tuttle v. Chicago, R. I. & P. R'y Co.*, 48 Iowa, 236.

II. The following instructions were given by the circuit court: "It is a duty of a railway company, employed in

2. ——: duty to passengers: degree of care required.

transporting passengers, to do all that human care, vigilance and foresight can *reasonably* do, consistent with the mode of conveyance and the practical operation of the road, in providing safe coaches, machinery, tracks, rails, angle-bars, or splices, bridges and roadway, and in the conduct and management of its trains for the safety of its passengers, and to keep the same in good repair. The utmost degree of care which the human mind is capable of inventing or producing is not required, but the highest degree of care, vigilance and foresight that is reasonably practicable in the conduct and management of its road and business is required. * * * Common carriers of passengers are held to the very highest degree of care and prudence that human care, vigilance and foresight could *reasonably* do, which is consistent with the practical operation of their road, and the transaction of their business; yet they are not absolute insurers of the safety of their passengers; and if you find that the defendant exercised all reasonably practical care, diligence and skill in the construction, preservation, inspection and repairs of its road-bed, bridges, track, rails, . angle-bars or splices, in the management and operation of its road, and of the train, at the time of the accident alleged and shown to have occurred, and that the accident could not have been prevented by the use of the utmost practical care, diligence and skill consistent with the practical operation of its road, and the transaction of its business, then plaintiff cannot recover in this action."

The rule which has been uniformly recognized and enforced in this state is that the carrier, in the conduct and manage- of his business, and as to all the appliances made use of in the business, is bound to crercise the highest degree of care and diligence for the convenience and safety of his passengers, and he is held liable for the slightest neglect. *Frink v. Coe*, 4 G. Green, 555; *Sales v. Western Stage Co.*, 4 Iowa, 547; *Bonce v. Dubuque St. R'y Co.*, 53 Id., 278; *Kellow v. Central Iowa R'y Co.*, 68 Id., 470. It is insisted that the instructions are in conflict with this rule. The position of counsel is that, by the use of the words *reasonable, reasonably practicable,* and *reasonably practical* in the instructions,

the care for the safety of the passenger required of the carrier is lowered, and he is required to exercise reasonable or
ordinary care only. It will be observed, however, that these
words, as they are used in the instructions, while they to
some extent limit the degree of care required of the carrier,
have special reference to the practical operation of the railroad, and the conduct of the business. When the instructions are scrutinized, it will be found that the doctrine
announced by them is that defendant was bound to exercise
the highest degree of care and diligence which was reasonably consistent with the practical operation of its railroad,
and the conducting of its business; and this is right. It is
doubtless true that precautions could be used in the construction and operation of railroads that would prevent many of
the accidents which occur as they are constructed and operated.

It sometimes happens that a derailed train is precipitated
from a high embankment, and the lives of its passengers
endangered or destroyed. Accidents of that character could
be avoided by constructing all railroad embankments of
such a width that a derailed train or car would come to a
stop before reaching the declivity. But this would add
immensely to the cost of constructing such improvements,
and, if required, would in many cases prevent their construction entirely. If passenger trains were run at the rate of
ten miles per hour, instead of from twenty-five to forty
miles, it is probable that all danger of derailment would be
avoided. But railroad companies could not reasonably be
required to adopt that rate of speed. Their roads are constructed with a view to rapid transit, and the traveling public
would not tolerate the running of trains at that low speed.
When it is said that they are held to the highest degree of
care and diligence for the safety of their passengers, it is not
meant that they are required to use every possible precau-
tion, for that, in many instances, would defeat the very
objects of their employment. There are certain dangers

that are necessarily incident to that mode of travel, and these the passenger assumes when he elects to adopt it. But all that is meant is that they should use the highest degree of care that is reasonably consistent with the practical conduct of the business, and that is the doctrine of the instructions, and it is abundantly sustained by the authorities. *Indianapolis & St. L. R'y Co. v. Horst*, 93 U. S., 291; *Dunn v. Grand Trunk R. R.*, 58 Me., 187; *Hegeman v. Western R. R.*, 13 N. Y., 9; *Kansas Pacific R. R. v. Miller*, 2 Colo., 442; Wood, R. R., 1049–1054.

III. The eleventh, twelfth and fourteenth instructions given by the court are as follows:

— : —:
selection of
plans and materials.
"The degree of care required of defendant in the selection of its materials, the plan and construction of its roadway, track, bridges and rolling stock, in the selection of its employes, servants and agents, and in the inspection and repairs of its road, and the machinery and appliances connected with the operation of the same, is such as the best, most carefully, prudently and skillfully managed railroads of the country exercise and require, doing a like business, and under like circumstances.

"The high degree of care hereinbefore referred to, and required of defendant, embraces its roadway, track, bridges and rolling stock, and the selection of its employes, servants and agents. In supplying materials for and in constructing its roadway, track, bridges and rolling stock, it was required to exercise that high degree of care to see that materials used were amply sufficient, and of such quality, size, pattern, as were accepted by and in general use, *and found to be sufficient, and approved* by the best and most skillfully managed railroads of the country, doing a like business with defendant. In the selection of train-men, and in the management of its train, it was bound to exercise that high degree of care, and to provide men of sufficient experience, skill and prudence to run such train safely, as far as was practicable; and it was bound, also, in like manner, to see that, in the actual management of the train at the time of the accident, the train-men exercised a like degree of care and skill in managing and running the train safely in all respects, so as to avoid injury to the passengers. If defendant failed in any of these respects, and such failure was the cause of the injury complained of, it was negligent, and is liable.

"If you find that the rails which were broken were made by a manufacturer of good repute, were made upon the approved method of manufacturing rails, were properly tested by the proper known and usually applied tests then in praccical use, and had been on the track for several years, and had successfully stood the strain of numerous passing trains without in any manner affecting their quality or strength, so far as could be seen by proper examination, carefully and skilfully made; if, at the time of the accident, they were placed and lying securely on sound ties, with good angle-bars or splices at the ends, with sufficient ballast under the ties, with all their connections and supports well adjusted; if they had been subjected to a daily inspection in the most approved and customary way of inspecting such appliances by the most careful and best managed railroads in the country, by some servant of competent skill and experience in such matters, and said rails appeared then sound, and all these connections and supports sound and secure; and if there were no flaws or defects visible, or that could have been discovered by such approved and customary inspection, made in the manner hereinbefore explained,—then the defendant was not negligent with reference to said rails."

Some of the members of the court think that the eleventh instruction is erroneous, but we unite in the conclusion that, if it should be conceded to be erroneous, the plaintiff could not have been prejudiced by it. The doctrine of the instruction is that the degree of care required of defendant in the selection of plans and materials for its roadway, bridges and appliances was such as was exercised by the best and most skillfully and carefully managed railroads in the country, under like circumstances. The objection urged against it is that it treats the practices of the class of railroads named, in the matters in question, as affording an absolute standard of duty as to those matters, thus, in effect, making the very practices which are called in question the law of the case. We admit the force of the objection. But the twelfth instruction was drawn with special reference to the facts of the case, and in it the jury were told, in effect, that defendant was bound, not only to select such plans and material for the construction of its road and appliances as were in use by the best and most skillfully conducted roads of the country, but that such materials and plans must have been found sufficient by the other roads. This is clearly right. When a plan of construction, and the materials made use of, have been found by actual experience to be sufficient and safe, other roads, whose business is to be carried on under like circumstances, are warranted in adopting them. To hold otherwise would be to hold that railroad companies, in the construction and operation of their roads, could not avail themselves of the experience of others, and that the construction and operation of every road must, to a great extent, be a matter of experiment. With this rule distinctly laid down as applicable to the facts of the case, we think the jury could not have been misled by the eleventh instruction, conceding that it is erroneous. This concession, however, must be understood as being made only for the purpose of the argument, for a majority of the court are of the opinion that the instruction is not erroneous. We think, also, that the fourteenth instruction is correct.

IV. In another instruction the jury were told that defendant " was not required to so construct its bridge that

construction of bridges. it would resist an unusual and extraordinary shock of a derailed train, running at regular speed, and striking it with great force." After the jury had been considering the case for some time, they were again brought into court, and the court gave them further instructions on that subject, which very materially modified the one quoted above. In the additional instructions they were told, in effect, that the defendant was required to take into account, in constructing and maintaining its bridges, the fact that accidents might occur in the operation of its road, and to construct its bridges with reference thereto; and that it was held to a very high degree of care in that respect. As thus modified, the instruction quoted affords plaintiff no just ground of complaint.

We have found no ground in the record upon which we think we ought to disturb the judgment, and it well be

AFFIRMED.

ARNOLD v. GOTSHALL ET AL.

1. **Homestead**: USED FOR UNLAWFUL SALE OF LIQUORS: EXEMPTION FORFEITED. Where a house and lot owned by the wife was occupied by the family as a homestead, but the front room of the house was used by the husband for a saloon, *held* that, under § 1558 of the Code, the part used for a saloon was subject to execution for the satisfaction of a judgment obtained against the husband for damages caused by the unlawful sale of liquors by him in said saloon.

Appeal from Tama District Court.

MONDAY, MARCH 21.

THE plaintiff is the wife of A. B. Arnold, and the petition in substance states that the defendant D. H. Gotshall unlawfully sold to her husband intoxicating liquors, thereby causing her said husband to become intoxicated, whereby she was greatly damaged; that such unlawful sales were made in certain described premises occupied as a saloon, the legal title to which real estate was in the wife of the defendant, who is also a party to the action. The relief asked is that the plaintiff may recover a judgment, and that the same be made a lien on the premises. The defendants denied the allegations of the petition, and pleaded that the premise

described in the petition were occupied by them as their
homestead, and therefore could not be subjected to such lien.
It was stipulated that the question as to whether the premises constituted the homestead should be determined by the
court. The plaintiff recovered a judgment, but the court
found the plaintiff was not entitled to a lien because of the
homestead right. From this finding and judgment of the
court the plaintiff appeals.

Brown & Carney, for appellant.

C. B. Bradshaw, for appellees.

BECK, J.—It is conceded that this action was tried in the
district court as an equitable action; and, as all the evidence is
before us, it will be so tried in this court. There is no material dispute as to the facts. The defendants are husband and
wife, and as such are entitled, under the statute, to a homestead; and the single question to be determined is whether
the premises in question are of that character. The premises in question are situate in the town of Gladbrook, and
consist of a lot about twenty-four feet wide, by 120 feet long,
on which is situate a one-story building, which is of about
the same width as the lot, and about sixty feet long. The
front or north forty feet, at the time the petition was filed,
and when the unlawful acts charged were done, was used as
a saloon. The defendants occupied the balance of the building as a kitchen, sitting and bed-room, between which and
the saloon there was a partition, in which was a door which
opened into the saloon. There was a walk of some kind,
probably plank, from the front to the rear, on both sides of
the building. There was a cellar under the saloon, in which
was kept beer; but the evidence fails to show that there was
anything else. The only way of going into the cellar was
through or from the saloon. The wife of the defendant, the
keeper of the saloon, who is a defendant also, owned the
property, which was conveyed to her by the husband before
the suit was commenced. We are authorized to infer from

the evidence that she knew the saloon was kept by her husband, and consented thereto. The plaintiff claims upon
these facts that the part of the premises used for the purpose
of the saloon does not constitute a part of the homestead.

A part of the premises and building upon and in which a
family reside, which is not used for the purposes of a homestead, is not exempt from a judgment against the owner;
that is, a building and the lot on which it is situated may be
partly a homestead, and partly subject to execution, depend-
ing upon the purposes for which the respective parts are
used. *Rhodes v. McCormick*, 4 Iowa, 368; *Wright v. Ditz-
ler*, 54 Iowa, 620; *Mayfield v. Maasden*, 59 Iowa, 517. A
part of a building, or an independent building upon a homestead, used as a shop wherein the owner prosecutes his ordinary business, is exempt, as a part of the homestead. Code, §
1997.

Unless the north or front forty feet of the house and lot in
question be exempt as a shop or a place of business, it is
clearly liable for plaintiff's judgment, under the decision
cited. Is it exempt on the ground that it was used by
defendant in the prosecution of the business of keeping a
saloon? We think not. Code, § 1988, declares that, "where
there is no special declaration of the statute to the contrary,
the homestead of every family, whether owned by the husband or wife, is exempt from judicial sale." In our opinion,
Code, § 1558, is a "special declaration of the statute" to the
effect that a homestead, or a part of a homestead, used as a
saloon, is subject to judgments obtained for violation of the
laws against the sale of intoxicating liquors. It is in the
following language: "For all costs assessed or judgments
rendered of any kind, for any violation of the provisions of
this chapter, the personal and real property, except the homestead, as now provided by law, of such person, as well as the
premises and property, personal and real, occupied and used
for that purpose with the consent and knowledge of the owner
thereof, or his agent, by the person manufacturing or selling

intoxicating liquors, contrary to the provisions of this chapter, shall be liable   *   *   *."

This section provides that the homestead, when not used for the purpose of the violation of the law, shall be exempt from judgments therefor; but, when occupied or used for the purpose of the violation of the law, with the consent of the owner, shall be subject to such judgments. The language will admit of no other construction. The condition upon which the homestead is made liable is that it was used for the violation of the law, with the knowledge and consent of the owner. Surely, if defendant had leased the part of the homestead in question for the express purpose of its use as a saloon, it would be liable. If they use it themselves, it surely would not be exempt. It would be absurd to say that the law will deal more tenderly with defendants when they violate the law themselves, than it would if they simply consent to or have knowledge of its violation by others.

The interpretation we put upon the section doubtless expresses the legislative intention, and is in accord with the policy of all legislation for the suppression of crimes. The law will recognize no business which it forbids and declares to be criminal, as entitling the criminal, and those who aid and abet him, to rights and protection based upon such business. It will not recognize the keeping of a saloon, or a house of ill fame, or the manufacture of counterfeiters' supplies and implements, or other like employment carried on in violation of the criminal laws of the state, as a business upon which the criminal can have a claim for protection or exemption. The courts will not hear a violator of law base a claim of right upon his crimes.

In our opinion, the north or front forty feet of the premises in question are subject to plaintiff's lien.

The judgment of the court below is reversed, and the cause is remanded for a decree in harmony with this opinion; or, at plaintiff's option, such a decree may be rendered here.

REVERSED.

VORWALD V. MARSHALL.

1. **Appeal:** FROM JUSTICE'S COURT: AMOUNT IN CONTROVERSY: JURIS-
DICTION. In an action in justice's court $100 was claimed by plaintiff, but
he recovered judgment for only $10, whereupon he remitted all claims for
damages over and above $24.90. Afterwards the defendant appealed to
the circuit court. *Held* that the amount in controversy was less than
$25, and that therefore an appeal would not lie. (*Milner v. Gross*, 66
Iowa, 252, followed.)

Appeal from Delaware Circuit Court.

MONDAY, MARCH 21.

THE facts are stated in the opinion.

J. D. Alsop, for appellant.

L. B. Lane, for appellee.

SEEVERS, J.—This action was commenced before a justice
of the peace, and the plaintiff claimed to recover $100.
There was a trial, and judgment was rendered for the plaintiff for $10, whereupon the plaintiff remitted "all claims for
damages over and above twenty-four dollars and ninety cents."
At that time the right of appeal existed, but had not been
exercised by either party. If the plaintiff had appealed, it
is perfectly clear that he could not have recovered more than
$24.90, and the pleadings in the circuit court would have so
shown. The plaintiff did not appeal, but the defendant did,
fifteen days after the rendition of the judgment and filing
of the *remittitur*. The plaintiff moved the court to dismiss the
appeal on the ground that the amount in controversy was less
than $25. This motion was sustained, and we are asked
whether the court erred in so doing. We think not; for the
amount in controversy, when the appeal was taken, was less
than $25. This case is not distinguishable from *Milner v.
Gross*, 66 Iowa, 252.

As this is the only question argued by counsel for appellant, the judgment must be   AFFIRMED.

GARDNER v. LIGHTFOOT.

· 1. **Contract:** UNDUE INFLUENCE: RELATIONS OF TRUST: SETTING ASIDE. When persons who sustain relations of confidence and trust enter into a contract, and the stronger obtains an advantage over the weaker mind, the contract will be set aside, unless the beneficiary shows that it was fairly obtained. (*Spargur v. Hall*, 62 Iowa, 498.) But no unfair advantage can be said to be taken where the stronger mind does nothing but accept the terms proposed by the weaker.

2. **Conveyance:** CONSIDERATION: PAROL TO VARY WRITING. Although parol testimony is admissible to show that the consideration of a conveyance is other or different than that stated in the writing, such testimony is not admissible, in the absence of fraud, to prove that a conveyance purporting to have been made for a consideration is in fact without consideration, for the purpose of rendering it invalid.

3. ———: ———: WHAT CONSTITUTES. An agreement by the grantee in a conveyance of land to perform certain sevices for the grantors during their lives and the life of the survivor, and an executed life lease of the land to the grantors, constitute a good consideration for the conveyance. (*Johnson v. Johnson*, 52 Iowa, 586, and *Mercer v. Mercer*, 29 Id., 557, followed.)

4. ———: CONDITION SUBSEQUENT: PARTIAL PERFORMANCE: SETTING ASIDE. An executed conveyance will not be set aside for the failure to perform a condition subsequent, where there has been a partial performance, accepted as such, and the parties cannot be placed in *statu quo*.

Appeal from Jasper District Court.

MONDAY, MARCH 21.

THE petition states that the plaintiff is the widow of Henry Gardner, who died in July, 1883, and who at that time was the owner of certain real estate described in the petition; that the plaintiff is sixty-seven years old, and her husband, when he died, was seventy-two years of age; that, for seven months preceding his death, Henry Gardner had been confined to his bed, and greatly prostrated; that the defendant is thirty-one years old, and had been brought up in the family of the Gardners, was regarded as one of the family, and dependent on them for his living for some years; that in June, 1883, the said Henry and the plaintiff conveyed the said real estate to the defendant; that said Henry was at that time very weak, physically and mentally, owing to his advanced age and exhaustion from sickness; and that plaintiff, when she signed said conveyance, was weak and feeble, both in mind and body, due to old age and long continued watching at the bedside of her sick husband; that defendant took advantage of their weakened and incompetent condition to obtain said conveyance by false pretenses, undue influence, and by fraudulently promising the said Henry that he would keep, provide, maintain and care for the plaintiff during her life, and that there was no consideration for such conveyance; that prior to the execution of said conveyance the said Henry had executed his last will, devising all his property, both real and personal, to the plaintiff, and the same has been duly admitted to probate; that the defendant has failed to " perform any proper and rightful services due the plaintiff, and has refused to care for, provide, protect and maintain her, and demanded an exorbitant price for labor performed, and is especially disagreeable, harsh and mercenary." The relief asked is that the said conveyance be adjudged fraudulent, and the same canceled and set aside, and such other relief as the plaintiff may be entitled to. The defendant denied the material statements of the petition, but admitted the execution of the conveyance in consideration of a lease for life, executed by the defendant to the plaintiff, of said real estate, and an oral agreement with plaintiff and her husband by which the defendant agreed to furnish them with all such provisions as would be produced on the land, and gather and deliver the same in the house and cellar occupied by plaintiff and her said husband, and also cut and haul all fire-wood for them, and take care of the stock as long as either of them should live. In a reply the plaintiff admitted the oral agreement to be correctly stated in the answer. There are other statements therein which may be omitted

There was a trial to the court, judgment for the defendant, and the plaintiff appeals.

Harrah & Myers, for appellant.

Winslow & Varnum, for appellees.

SEEVERS, J.—I. We have read the evidence with great care, and fail to find any which tends to show that the defendant obtained the conveyance by undue influence, or that he made any fraudulent representations whatever, and thereby obtained such conveyance. The evidence fails to show that the defendant even asked for such conveyance, or that it was made in consequence of any representations made by him. On the contrary, the evidence shows that the plaintiff and her husband executed it on their own motion; and, if the fact is otherwise, the plaintiff has wholly failed to introduce any evidence so showing. It will be conceded that the rule is that when persons who sustain relations of trust and confidence enter into a contract, and the stronger obtains an advantage over the weaker mind, the same will be set aside, unless the beneficiary shows the contract to have been fairly obtained. *Spargur v. Hall*, 62 Iowa, 498. But there must be something done by the stronger to influence the weaker mind. If the former is passive, it cannot be said that there is either undue influence or fraud. Now, in the present case, we assert with confidence that the evidence fails to show that the defendant did anything to obtain the conveyance, unless it was his agreement to execute the lease for life, and this he did, and his promise to provide and care for the plaintiff and her husband. As to the latter, as we read the evidence, the defendant simply agreed to the proposition as made by the plaintiff and her husband. They fixed the terms and conditions of the contract upon which the conveyance was made. The defendant did not even make a suggestion in relation thereto. It is impossible, therefore, to say that the conveyance was obtained fraudulently, or by

[margin note: 1. CONTRACT: undue influence: relations of trust: setting aside.]

undue influence, or that the contract was not entered into by the defendant in good faith.

II. It is said there was no consideration for the conveyance. The only consideration named in the conveyance is one dollar. This, it will be conceded, is only nominal. That parol evidence is admissible to show that the consideration named in a conveyance is other or different will be conceded; but a very different question is presented when it is proposed to show by parol that there was no consideration whatever, for the purpose of renderering the conveyance invalid. In the absence of fraud, we think the authorities are substantially in accord that such evidence is not admissible. But, in addition to this, the defendant agreed to provide, care for and maintain, or rather perform certain services for, the plaintiff and her husband during their lives, and during the life of the survivor. If the value of the real estate has been shown, we have overlooked such evidence. We cannot say, therefore, that the consideration is inadequate, —much less that there was none. It must not be forgotten that the plaintiff has a lease on the premises for and during her natural life. That the matters above stated constitute a sufficient consideration has been held in *Johnson v. Johnson*, 52 Iowa, 586; *Mercer v. Mercer*, 29 Iowa, 557.

1. CONVEYANCE : consideration: parol to vary writing.

2. ——: ——: what constitutes.

III. The evidence is conflicting as to whether the defendant in good faith did what he agreed to do. It is not entirely certain that he did not substantially do so. As to this we feel uncertain. But his agreement must be regarded as a condition subsequent; and, as the conveyance has been fully executed and delivered, the rule is that it will not be set aside when, at least, there has been partial performance, and the parties cannot be placed in the same position they were in at the time the conveyance was made. That there was such performance the evidence clearly shows, and that what was done was accepted as such clearly appears. There is no evidence which

3. ——: condition subsequent: partial performance: setting aside.

tends to show that the conveyance was made to the defendant in trust.

We are of the opinion that the decree of the district court must be   AFFIRMED.

COBURN v. THE OMEGA LODGE A. F. & A. M. ET AL.

1. **Promissory Note:** SIGNED BY MAKERS AS TRUSTEES: PERSONAL LIABILITY. A note which reads, "We promise to pay," etc., was signed, "C. F. Clark, M. Samuels, Trustees Omega Lodge." *Held* that Clark and Samuels were personally liable as makers. (*Heffner v. Brownell,* 70 Iowa, 591, followed.)

Appeal from Fremont Circuit Court.

MONDAY, MARCH 21.

ACTION AT LAW. The facts are stated in the opinion.

Anderson & Eaton, for appellants.

Stockton & Keenan, for appellee.

SEEVERS, J.—This is an action on a promissory note in these words:

"$166.66.   RIVERTON, IOWA, November 10, 1880.

" Four years after date we promise to pay to the order of E. Coburn one hundred and sixty-six 66-100 dollars, value received, with ten per cent interest per annum.

                              " C. F. CLARK,
                              " M. SAMUELS,
                    "Trustees Omega Lodge."

In the second count in the petition the plaintiff sought to recover a personal judgment against Clark *et al.* To such count there was a demurrer, which was overruled, and Clark *et al.* appeal, and the question we are called on to determine is whether the court erred in so holding. We are unable to see any distinction between this case and *Heffner v. Brownell,* 70 Iowa, 591, and, following that case, the result is that the judgment of the circuit court must be   AFFIRMED.

BARTEMEYER ET AL. v. ROHLFS ET AL.

1. **Railroads:** TAX IN AID OF: CITIES UNDER SPECIAL CHARTERS:
APPLICABILITY OF STATUTE. Although it is provided by chapter 116,
Laws of 1876, that "no general laws as to powers of cities organized
under the general incorporation act shall in any manner be construed to
affect the charters or laws of cities organized under special charters,
while they continue to act under such charters, unless the same shall
have special reference to such cities," yet the statute authorizing taxation in aid of railroads cannot be held to be a law affecting the chartered powers of cities; and a city acting under a special charter may,
under the provisions of such statute, lawfully vote a tax in aid of a
railroad. (*State v. Finger,* 46 Iowa, 25, distinguished.)

2. ——: ——: NOTICE OF ELECTION: DESIGNATION OF TERMINI.
Where the notice of an election in the city of Davenport, upon the
question of aiding a railroad company in the construction of a road,
stated that the proposed road was to begin at a definitely described
point within that city, and to run "thence westward along the Mississippi river to the western boundary of the city of Davenport; thence
westwardly to Anamosa, in Jones county, Iowa, or to a point nearer, to
connect with a railroad not now running to Davenport aforesaid," *held*
that the notice sufficiently designated the *termini* of the road to satisfy
the requirement of chapter 159, Laws of 1884.

3. ——: ——: ——: DESIGNATION OF TIME WHEN WORK IS TO BE
DONE. It is not necessary that a notice of an election upon the question
of voting a tax in aid of a railroad should state the date upon which
the work shall be done, in order to entitle the company to the tax. It
is sufficient if it provides, as in this case, that the tax shall be payable
when a specified amount of the work is done.

4. ——: ——: PETITION AND NOTICE: VARIANCE: BASIS OF LEVY.
In view of the fact that taxes in aid of railroads must be levied by the
county supervisors, and the further fact that the city of Davenport is
coterminous with the civil township in which it is situated, *held* that a
variance between the *petition* for an election upon the question of
voting a tax in aid of a railroad, and the *notice* of such election—the
petition being for a tax on the "*assessed value of the property in said
city,*" and the notice being of a tax "*upon the assessed value according
to the county valuation,*"—was immaterial, since the supervisors could
not be presumed to know anything of any valuation except the county
valuation.

5. ——: ——: ——: ——: ROUTE OF ROAD. Where in such case
the petition for the election described the route of the proposed railroad
to be from a certain point "*northwestwardly* to Anamosa, or to a point
nearer," and the notice described it to be from the same point "*westwardly* to Anamosa, or to a point nearer," *held* that the variance was
immaterial.

6. ——: ——: NOTICE: TIME OF LEVY AND COLLECTION. Where the notice in such case provided: "One-half of said tax to be levied and collected in the year 1887, and the other half in the year 1888," and the election was held on the 25th of September, 1886, and the levy made on the 29th of the same month, *held* that the levy was valid, and that the notice should be construed, not as requiring the tax to be levied and collected the same year, which the law does not permit, but to be so levied that it might be lawfully collected—one-half in the year 1887, and the other half in the year 1888.

7. ——: ——: CERTIFICATE OF CLERK: ORDER OF SUPERVISORS: IMMATERIAL OMISSION. Where in such case the clerk of the election has, as required by the statute, certified to the county auditor the result of the election, the rate per centum of the tax voted, and the time, terms and conditions upon which the same, when collected, is to be paid to the railroad company, together with an exact copy of the notice under which the election was held, and the same has been recorded in the office of the recorder of deeds; and the order of the board of supervisors by which the levy was made shows that, when the levy was made it had before it the certificate of the clerk of the election, and the levy was made in accordance with the notice of the election, but the order did not set out the conditions on which the taxes were to be paid to the company, as the statute directs, *held* that this omission in the order did not invalidate the tax.

Appeal from Scott District Court.

WEDNESDAY, APRIL 20.

THIS is an action in equity by which the plaintiffs, who are tax-payers of the city of Davenport, seek to enjoin the collection of a tax voted by the legal voters of said city to aid in the construction of a railroad projected by the Davenport, Iowa & Dakota Railroad Company, defendant. The cause was submitted to the court below upon a petition, answer and reply, and upon certain exhibits and affidavits. Upon the record thus made, the plaintiffs moved the court to grant a temporary injunction restraining the defendant Rohlfs, who is treasurer of the county, from proceeding to collect said tax. The motion for an injunction was overruled. From this order the plaintiffs appeal.

Cook & Dodge, for appellants.

Davison & Lane and *Bills & Block*, for appellees.

ROTHROCK, J.—I. The material facts in the case are not

in dispute. The plaintiffs concede that an election was held, in pursuance of a petition for that purpose, signed by the requisite number of the legal voters of the city, and that at said election a majority of those who voted cast their ballots for the tax. It is contended, however, that the tax is illegal and void for a number of reasons, which we will proceed to consider.

The city of Davenport is organized under a special charter. By virtue of its charter, all city taxes are assessed, levied and collected by officers and agents of the city, independently of the agencies and officers provided for the assessment, levy and collection of taxes for state, county and other purposes. The city comprises a township called the township of the city of Davenport, and the municipality and the township embrace precisely the same territory. They are bounded by the same lines, and all taxes other than city taxes are assessed, levied and collected by township and county officers, independently of the city authorities. There are some four or five cities in this state which are organized in the same way. Their charters are not to be found in the general laws. They are, in effect, a law unto themselves, and, by reason of this want of uniformity in the laws governing incorporated towns and cities, many vexatious questions arise in the courts in determining the applicability of legislation pertaining to the powers of cities and towns. It is not easy to perceive why the people of cities organized under special charters do not organize under the general incorporation law, and thus avoid the expense of keeping up all the machinery necessary to collect taxes for city purposes, and also prevent much unnecessary litigation.

It is claimed by counsel for appellants in this case that the tax in question is void, because chapter 159 of the Acts 1. RAILROADS: tax in aid of: cit.es under special charters: applica- bility of stat- ute. of the Twentieth General Assembly, which authorizes taxes to be voted and levied on the assessed value of any township, incorporated town or city, to aid in the construction of railroads, has no application to a city organized and existing under a special charter.   It is true that the act authorizing the voting and levy of the tax does not specially refer to cities existing under special charters.   And chapter 116 of the Laws of the Sixteenth General Assembly provides as follows: "No general laws as to powers of cities organized under the general incorporation act shall in any manner be construed to affect the charter or laws of cities organized under special charters, while they continue to act under such charters, unless the same shall have special reference to such cities."   Before the enactment of this statute, it· had been determined by this court that any statute which, by its general scope and intent, might be applicable to cities acting under special charters, should be construed as applying to them.   *Grant v. City of Davenport*, 36 Iowa, 396.   The act of the Sixteenth General Assembly limited this rule of construction, by providing that general laws, "as *to powers of cities*," shall not affect the charter or laws of cities existing under special charters, unless special reference is made in the law to such cities.

If the law authorizing taxation in aid of railroads were a law "as to powers of cities," the position of counsel would be correct.   It is claimed that the case of *State v. Finger*, 46 Iowa, 25, construed this statute, and that, under the construction there adopted, the law authorizing taxation in aid of railroads must be held inapplicable to cities under special charters.   That was a contest between two persons for the office of assessor in the city of Davenport.   It was held that section 390 of the Code, as amended, and section 829, materially affect the powers of cities incorporated under the general law.   The manner in which the power of cities is affected is pointed out in the opinion in that case.   Among other things, it is said that "it confers upon them power to choose the officer who shall make the assessment upon which their city revenue is to be raised;" and by section 829 the city council is given the power to equalize the assessments of taxpayers.   In other words, it is held that the application of the law in question in that case to a city acting under a special charter would require the election of an officer at the city election who is not recognized by the city charter, or by any ordinance of the city, and it would require the city council to act as a board of equalization.

In our opinion, the law authorizing taxation in aid of rail-roads cannot be held to be a law affecting the chartered powers of a city. It seems to us that this is quite apparent from an examination of the whole act. In the first place, the tax voted under the law is not a city tax. It is not levied by the city council. It is required to be levied by the board of supervisors. It is true, certain officers of the city are required to determine whether a majority of the tax-payers have signed a petition for an election, and to call the election, and declare the result. But the city, as a corpora-tion, is in no manner affected by the result, and is not liable for anything,—not even for the expenses of holding the election. The officers to whom these duties are assigned are clothed with no discretion. They are mere agents designated by law to determine when the statute has been complied with. If the legislature, instead of designating certain officers of the city to perform this duty, had provided for the appointment of commissioners, or had imposed the duty on some court or judge or other person, the powers of the city would surely not have been affected by the law; and we can-not see that the fact that the law designates certain city officers to perform the duties imposed, affects the powers of the city, any more than the appointment of a person or per-sons not connected with the city government.

II. Next it is urged that the tax in question is void because of fatal defects in the notice of the special election. 2. —— : ——: It is claimed that the notice does not specify to notice of elec-tion: designa-tion of ter-mini. what point said railroad shall be fully completed before said tax, or any part thereof, shall become due, collectible and payable, and does not state "the amount of work required to be done, and when and where the same

shall be done," as required by section 3 of the act authorizing the tax. The notice of election was as follows: "In
pursuance of an ordinance of the city council of the city of
Davenport of August 20, 1886, notice is hereby given that
a special election will be held in said city of Davenport on
the twenty-fifth day of September, 1886, upon the question
of aiding the Davenport, Iowa & Dakota Railroad Company
in the construction of a line of railway from a point on the
levee in the said city of Davenport, Scott county, Iowa,
between Brady and Main streets, where the passenger depot
of said road shall be established, and running thence westward along the Mississippi river to the western boundary of
the city of Davenport; thence westwardly to Anamosa, in
Jones county, Iowa, or to a point nearer, to connect with a
railroad not now running to Davenport aforesaid, as is provided by chapter 159 of the Acts of the Twentieth General
Assembly of the state of Iowa; such aid to be by a tax of
three per centum, to be levied and collected upon the assessed
value, according to the county valuation, of the property of
said city of Davenport; one-half of said tax to be levied
and collected in the year 1887, and the other half in the
year 1888. One-half of the amount of said tax shall be
paid to said company when the first ten miles of said railroad from said point of beginning, in said city of Davenport, shall be graded, bridged and tied, and that part of the
said line within the limits of the city of Davenport shall be
completed for the passage of cars thereon. The other half
of the amount of said tax shall be paid to the said railroad
company when thirty miles of the said railroad shall be
completed for the passage of cars, or a connection be made
by said Davenport, Iowa & Dakota Railroad Company, at a
shorter distance, with some other railroad, constructed and
operated, but not running to said city of Davenport."

The initial point of the proposed road is definitely fixed
in the notice as "a point on the levee in the said city of
Davenport,   *   *   *   between Brady and Main

streets." It is insisted that no particular point is named to which the road shall be completed. It appears from the notice that the general direction of the road shall be towards Anamosa, in Jones county. It is true that the notice does not require that the road shall be built to Anamosa, in Jones county, in order to enforce the collection of the tax. There is the alternative that the road may be built in the direction of Anamosa, to a connection with a railroad not running to Davenport. The record shows that the object of the tax was to secure additional railroad facilities for the city of Davenport; and it is evident that the notice contemplates that, if the object could be attained by making a connection with the Burlington, Cedar Rapids & Northern Railroad, or the Chicago & Northwestern Railroad, by building a line in the direction of Anamosa, constructing the road to such point should be sufficient. There is no uncertainty as to the general direction of the proposed road; and, when the tax was voted, the place to which it was to be constructed was one of two places, but both in the same general direction, and the last half of the tax is to be collectible when thirty miles of the road shall be completed for the passage of cars, or a connection made, at a shorter distance, with some other railroad constructed and operated, but not running to the city of Davenport. In construing the notice as to the line of the proposed road, it must be borne in mind that, to whatever point it may be built, it must be in the direction of Anamosa, in Jones county.

It is claimed that the notice does not state when the work shall be done to entitle the company to the tax. It seems to
2. ——: ——: us that the provision that one-half of the tax
——: desig- shall be paid when the first ten miles from Brady
nation of time
when work is
to be done. street shall be graded, bridged and tied, and that part of the line in the limits of the city of Davenport shall be completed for the passage of cars, and the other half shall be payable when thirty miles shall be completed for the passage of cars, or a connection made with some other road,

sufficiently indicates when the work is to be done by which the tax is to be earned. And we do not think it is necessary that the notice shall give the specific date when the work shall be done. It is sufficient if it provides, as in this case, that the tax shall be payable when a specific amount of work is done.

III. It is next claimed that the tax is void because the stipulation and conditions contained in the notice of the
4. ——: ——: special election do not conform to those set forth
petition and
notice: vari- in the petition asking the election. The facts in
ance: basis of
levy. reference to this alleged irregularity in the proceedings are that the petition asked that there be submitted to the electors in the city of Davenport the question whether or not a tax of three per centum shall be levied and collected on the "*assessed value of the property in said city*," and the notice of election provides that the tax is to be levied "*upon* the assessed value, *according to the county valuation*," of the property in said city. It is claimed that, by the terms of the petition, the tax was to be levied upon the city valuation, while the notice requires that it be levied upon the county valuation. The law authorizing the tax requires that the levy be made by the board of supervisors. This plainly implies that the levy must be made upon the county valuation. The board of supervisors are not supposed to have any knowledge of the city valuation. That assessment or valuation is made for the sole purpose of levying city taxes. Now, it appears to us there is no real conflict between the petition and notice, when construed in the light of the fact that the city and township are co-extensive. The levy of a tax on the "assessed value of the property in said city," as provided in the petition, would be a levy on the property of the township, and, under the law, the basis of the levy would be the assessment made by the township assessor.

IV. The petition for the election described the route of the proposed railroad to be from the western boundary of
5. ——: ——: the city of Davenport; "thence northwestwardly
route of road. to Anamosa, or to a point nearer," etc. The notice described the route from the boundary of the city,

" thence *westwardly* to Anamosa, or to a point nearer," etc.
It is claimed that this variance is fatal to the validity of the tax.
As we have above intimated, there is no uncertainty in any
of these proceedings as to the direction of the proposed
road. It is to be built in the direction of Anamosa, in
Jones county. The fact is that Anamosa is northwest from
Davenport. It is north and west, and the notice is not necessarily repugnant to the petition when it describes the line
as "westwardly" to Anamosa.

V. It will be observed that the notice of election provides: "One-half of said tax to be levied and collected in

6. —: —. the year 1887, and the other half in the year
notice: time
of levy and   1888." The election was held on the twenty-
collection.   fifth day of September, 1886, and the levy of the
tax was made by the board of supervisors on the twenty-
ninth day of the same month. It is claimed that, under the
express conditions of the petition and notice for the election,
no levy could be made before the year 1887. We do not
think this is a fair construction of the notice of election.
It should be construed in the light of the law governing the
levy of taxes. The board of supervisors has no power to
levy and collect taxes in the same year. Taxes levied in one
year are collectible the next year. The clause of the notice
above cited should be held to mean that the levy should be
made within such time as that the tax would be collectible
in the year 1887. The insertion of a comma after the word
"levied," in the clause in question, makes this construction
quite plain.

VI. Chapter 159 of the acts of the Twentieth General
Assembly requires that the clerk of the election shall certify

7. —: —: to the county auditor the result of the election,
certificate of
clerk: order   the rate per centum of the tax voted, and the
of supervis-   time, terms and conditions upon which the same,
ors: immate-
rial omission. when collected, is to be paid to the railroad company, together with an exact copy of the notice under which
the election was held; and the same is to be recorded in the

office of the recorder of deeds. These requirements of the law were fully complied with before the order was made levying the tax. The law further provides that the order of the board of supervisors by which the levy is made shall indicate when and in what proportion the tax is to be collected, and upon what conditions it is to be paid to the railroad company. The order of the board shows that, when the levy was made, it had before it the certificate of the clerk of the election, and the levy was made in accord with the notice of the election, but the order does not set out the conditions upon which the taxes are to be paid to the railroad company. It is claimed that this failure to comply with the statute makes the levy of the tax null and void. We do not think that this defect in the order should be held to vitiate the levy of the tax. If the board had refused to levy the tax by reason of a defect in the certificate of the clerk of the election, as in the case of *Minnesota & I. S. R'y Co. v. Hiams*, 53 Iowa, 501, such refusal would doubtless be approved by the court, as it was in that case. But in this case the tax has been levied, and all the stipulations and · conditions necessary for the protection of the tax-payer are made of record; and we do not think that the failure of the board of supervisors to insert these conditions in the order should be held to vitiate the levy. It is a mere omission to do that which is in no manner of the essence of the thing done, and does not inhere in the proceeding as a jurisdictional prerequisite. If it should be necessary to the protection of the tax-payer, we do not see any valid objection to the board making an amended order for the guidance of the county treasurer in paying the tax to the railroad company. But that would be an act of supererogation, because the county treasurer is charged with notice of the conditions of payment which are now of record.

We think the order overruling the motion for an injunction must be   AFFIRMED.

REPORTS

OF

Cases in Law and Equity,

DETERMINED IN THE

SUPREME COURT

OF

THE STATE OF IOWA,

AT

DES MOINES, JUNE TERM, A. D. 1887,

IN THE FORTY-FIRST YEAR OF THE STATE.

PRESENT:

HON. AUSTIN ADAMS, CHIEF JUSTICE.
" WILLIAM H. SEEVERS,
" JOSEPH R. REED,
" JAMES H. ROTHROCK,
" JOSEPH M. BECK.
} JUDGES.

HYNDS v. WYNN ET AL.

1. **Garnishment:** DETENTION OF EXEMPT PROPERTY: LIABILITY. Plaintiff, who was a judgment debtor of W., had delivered to a railway company for shipment certain household goods which were exempt from execution. W. caused the railway company to be garnished as the supposed debtor of plaintiff, wherefore the company, as required by the the notice of garnishment, did not ship the goods. Neither the company nor the officer who held the execution knew that the goods were exempt, but as soon as the officer learned that they were exempt he released them from the levy and notified the company thereof, when the goods were forwarded to their destination. *Held* that the delay of the goods was no ground of recovery against either W., the officer, or the railway company.

Appeal from Cedar Rapids Superior Court.

TUESDAY, JUNE 7.

THE plaintiff claims damages of the defendant for wrong-fully detaining certain goods and chattels from his possession. He claims that said property consisted of certain household goods which were exempt from execution, and that he deliv-ered the same to the defendant, the Chicago, Milwaukee & St. Paul Railroad Company, at Cedar Rapids, Iowa, to be shipped to Oskaloosa, in this state, and that, while in pos-session of the railroad company, a conspiracy was entered into between said company and the other defendants, by which the railroad company held said goods for some sixteen days, to the great damage of the plaintiff. There was a trial by the court, and a judgment for the defendants. Plaintiff appeals.

Geo. W. Wilson, for appellant.

Mills & Keeler, for appellees.

ROTHROCK, J. The court, at the request of the parties, made the following findings of fact and conclusions of law: "*First.* The defendant Geo. W. Wynn recovered a judg-ment, January 12, 1878, against plaintiff herein, before a ·justice of the peace in Linn county, Iowa. The defendant Wynn caused execution to issue on said judgment, and placed same in hands of the defendant herein, Jos. Renchin, as constable, who levied same by serving a notice of garnish-ment on the defendant herein the C., M. & St. P. R'y Co., a supposed creditor of E. Hynds, and required the garnishee to answer on or before January 15, 1886. The notice of garnishment was in the usual form, and required garnishee to retain possession of all property of said defendant, now or hereafter being in custody, or under its control, in order that the same might be dealt with according to law. The defendant Hynds was at the time a married man, and the head of a family, resident in Iowa, and owned these certain household goods mentioned in his petition, which were exempt from execution, and which are of the value of about $125, and which Hynds delivered to the defendant railway company about December 30, 1885, to be transported over its line to Oskaloosa, and then to be delivered to a connecting line *en route* to destination. The railroad company had knowledge of the character of the goods, but not of the fact that they were either claimed to be, or were in fact, at the time of shipment or notice of garnishment, exempt from execution. It does not appear that Renchin, the constable, nor the plaintiff in execution, Wynn, had actual knowledge that said household goods were exempt from execution, nor what precise property the garnishee had in possession at date of garnishment. In obedience to said notice of garnishment, the defendant railway company held possession of said property until about January 16th, at which time, or a day prior thereto, the plaintiff, Hynds, notified the constable that the property was exempt from execution, and thereupon the defendant railway company, within a reasonable time thereafter, on notice of such claim of exemption by Hynds, and release from levy by the constable, sent this property forward to destination. The property was detained under said proceedings about sixteen days, and under the evidence Hynds suffered nominal damages in consequence of such detention. The plaintiff, Hynds, seeks in this action to recover of each and all of the defendants his damages for such detention. On such state of facts above recited, the court finds, as a conclusion of law, that the plaintiff is not entitled to recover."

The findings of the court are fully sustained by the evidence, and the mere casual reading of the findings is sufficient to show that the plaintiff has no cause of action. The goods were not unreasonably detained by the railroad company, nor by the other defendants, after notice that they were exempt from execution. We must decline to follow the plaintiff's counsel through his argument. We have been required to read the sixty-five pages of his abstract and argument, and find that the appeal is not only without merit, but that there is not even a plausible excuse for burdening this court with its consideration.　　　　　**AFFIRMED.**

SIMPSON CENTENARY COLLEGE v. TUTTLE.

1. **Promissory Note**: GIFT TO COLLEGE: FAILURE OF CONSIDERATION: CONTEMPORANEOUS ORAL AGREEMENT. A promissory note given to a college to aid in the formation of an endowment fund, where no consideration for the note is advanced, is only a written promise to make a gift at a future time, and it cannot be enforced by the donee, unless it has, prior to any revocation, entered into engagements, or made expenditures, based on the promise, so that it must suffer loss or injury if the note is not paid. Neither can it be enforced where the fund to which the gift is promised is diverted from its object, in violation of an *oral* agreement made with the donor at the time the note was executed.

Appeal from Warren Circuit Court.

TUESDAY, JUNE 7.

Plaintiff sues on a promissory note, which is as follows:
" ENDOWMENT NOTE, SIMPSON CENTENARY COLLEGE.
"$500.　　　　　INDIANOLA, IOWA, July 21, 1869.
"Within five years after date, I promise to pay Simpson Centenary College five hundred dollars, for value received, with eight per cent interest, payable semi-annually, at the office of the treasurer of said college, on the first day of January and July of each year.
　　　　　　　　　　　　MARTIN TUTTLE."
It is alleged that the whole amount is due, except that interest was paid up to January 1, 1879. There are no other allegations in the petition, except those in regard to the execution of the note and the amount due thereon, and the venue of the cause. To the petition the defendant answered, *First*, admitting the execution of the note, but denying

indebtedness thereon, and denying each and every other allegation of the petition; *second*, admitting the execution of
the note, but denying the right to recover, on the ground that
the note was only a promise that the defendant, at a subsequent time, would make a gift of $500 to the college, and
that he had received no advantage, benefit, or anything of
value or consideration, for the promise, and that, therefore,
the note was wholly without consideration.

The third paragraph of the answer is as follows: *"Third.*
For further answer the defendant admits the execution of
the note sued on, but says that the plaintiff ought not to
recover thereon, because said note was executed as the evidence of a naked promise of the defendant to plaintiff to
make it a gift of $500 in five years thereafter, to be and
continue, when made, part of a permanent endowment fund,
which the plaintiff then had promised to it in part, and was
endeavoring to procure promises for the remainder, and the
defendant promised said gift to the plaintiff on condition
that the principal of said fund should not be expended in
whole or in part, and that the interest accruing on said fund
should be used solely for the purpose of maintaining a college then in operation at the town of Indianola, Iowa, in
which the academic branches of learning usually taught in
such schools should be taught, and that no part of said fund,
or interest thereon, should be used or expended for the purpose of establishing a professional school anywhere, or any
kind of school or college at any other place than said town
of Indianola. The defendant alleges that plaintiff accepted
said promise coupled with said condition, without which condition and acceptance said promise would not have been
made. The defendant charges that the plaintiff has violated
the said conditions upon which it accepted the defendant's
said promise, by expending large sums of money, obtained
from defendant and others, as interest on said endowment
fund, for the purpose of establishing a law school at the city
of Des Moines, Iowa, twenty miles distant from the said

town of Indianola. The defendant says that, by reason of the premises, he is released from his promise to make said gift, and the note in suit is wholly without consideration."

The fourth paragraph of the petition reiterates the third paragraph in substance, and makes the further charge that plaintiff violated the oral agreement on which the promise was based, "by using a portion of said permanent fund for the payment of its debts, and for other wrongful purposes."

To this answer the plaintiff demurred, on the following grounds: "Because it sets out a contract, or condition in a contract, different from, and conflicting with, the note sued on; *second*, that it sets out a prior or contemporaneous agreement or contract, or condition in a contract, which was not reduced to writing, and which was not made a part of the note sued on; *third*, [this paragraph includes, in substance, the first and second;] *fourth*, because the giving of the note was the promise and obligation of the defendant to pay the amount of said note, and that any condition in the gift, or the use of the appropriation of the said fund, or the proceeds arising therefrom, must be embraced in and form a part of the contract; *fifth*, that the appropriation, or the use of the funds given or contributed by others to the endowment fund, constitute no defense to the note sued on." The seventh and eighth paragraphs of the demurrer are substantially repetitions of some of the foregoing. The demurrer was overruled. Plaintiff excepted and appeals.

W. H. Berry and *Nourse, Kauffman & Guernsey*, for appellant.

P. Gad Bryan, for appellee.

ROTHROCK, J.—The note sued upon is still in the hands of the payee; and, notwithstanding the use of the words "value received," the question of consideration is still open. In the case of *Abbott v. Hendricks*, 1 Man. & G. 791, the consideration recited was "for commissions due to the plaintiff for business transacted for the defendant." The defendant was allowed to show that the note was given for services *to be thereafter* rendered, and that there was failure of consideration because the services had not been rendered. It has long been a settled principle that, as between the maker and the payee of a promissory note, the defense of want of consideration may be interposed. Such a defense does not affect the *terms* of the written agreement or payment, or the parties to whom the same is to be paid. A gift is not complete until the money or property constituting the subject of the gift is actually delivered, and before such delivery the gift may be revoked. A promise to give money cannot be enforced even when put in the form of a promissory note. *Phelps v. Phelps,* 28 Barb. 121; *Fink v. Cox,* 18 Johns. 145. The delivery of the note was simply the delivery of the thing promised. *Starr v. Starr,* 9 Ohio St. 75. To this doctrine, however, there must be added the qualification that the benefits to be derived from founding a school, church, or other institution of similar character, may furnish a good consideration for a promise. It must also be remembered, in the case before us, that such consideration is not advanced by plaintiff, and the only reference to its existence is contained in the paragraphs of the answer assailed by the demurrer; the other paragraph setting up a total want of consideration. Where a note, however, is based on a promise to give for the support of the objects referred to, it may still be open to this defense, unless it shall appear that the donee has, prior to any revocation, entered into engagements or made expenditures based on such promise, so that he must suffer loss or injury if the note is not paid. This is based on the equitable principle that, after allowing the donee to incur obligations on the faith that the note would be paid, the donor should be estopped from pleading want of consideration.

There is nothing in the pleadings to show that the defendant ought to be estopped from setting up want of consideration; and, in the absence of anything of that character, he need not be very particular as to what reasons he shall assign for such defense to a promise to give. The obligations and expenditures on the part of the donee which might prevent the interposition of the defense of want of consideration must be directly in the line of the purpose for which the gift of the note or promise to give was intended. A diversion of the funds to other purposes, contrary to the intent of the donor, would certainly be a good excuse for withholding the consummation of the gift; and, if the plaintiff is diverting the funds created by the donations to purposes not contemplated at the time of the gift, but in violation of the agreement on which the promise was based, in such a manner as to show want of good faith on the part of the donee, the proof of such diversion is a defense to the note in the nature of a *failure* of consideration.

The demurrer to the answer was properly overruled.

AFFIRMED.

THE SANDWICH MANUF'G CO. v. TRINDLE.

1. **Sale of Machine**: WARRANTY: INSTRUCTIONS. In an action for the price of a harvester, where failure of warranty was relied on by the defendant, the court instructed the jury on the oral contract of warranty, as claimed by defendant, and also upon the theory that the printed warranty delivered with the machine was all of the contract, and that it could not be varied by parol. *Held* that, since there was no material variance between these contracts, plaintiff was not prejudiced by the instructions.

2. ———: ———: SUBSTANTIAL COMPLIANCE. It was not error to instruct the jury that a *substantial* compliance with the contract was all that was required of defendant, where his duties under the contract were clearly defined in other instructions.

3. ———: ———: FAILURE: NOTICE: RETURN OF MACHINE. The machine in controversy was sold under a warranty providing that the defendant should have one day to give it a fair trial. and, if it did not work, that written notice, stating wherein it failed, should be given to the agent and to the plaintiff, and that the continued possession of the machine, or a failure to give such notice, should be evidence that the warranty was ful-

filled. The agent sent an expert to set up the machine, and was present on the next morning, when it failed to work, and informed the defendant that he would have an expert there on a subsequent day, which he did, the agent also being present. *Held* that, under these circumstances, no notice of the failure of the machine was necessary, and that defendant's attempt to use the machine for a few days longer was not a forfeiture of his rights under the warranty, provided he returned the machine within a reasonable time.

Appeal from Franklin District Court.

WEDNESDAY, JUNE 8.

ACTION at law to recover $175 for a harvester and binder which the plaintiff claims it sold the defendant. The defendant alleged in his answer that he took the machine from plaintiff's agent on trial, with the agreement that, if it worked satisfactorily, he would buy the same; that said machine failed to work, and defendant returned the same as agreed. The plaintiff in reply alleged that the contract of sale was in writing, and that the machine "was not returned until long after it was taken, and no notice was given plaintiff or its agents of any defect in the machine; that said machine was not defective, and an opportunity was not given plaintiff or his agent to adjust the machine, or put a new one in its place." There was a trial by jury, and a verdict and judgment for the defendant. Plaintiff appeals.

Henley & Heminway, for appellant.

D. W. Dow, for appellee.

ROTHROCK, J.—The printed warranty upon which the plaintiff relies is as follows: "The Reliance self-binding harvester is purchased and sold subject to the following warranty and agreement, and no one has any authority to add to, abridge, or change it in any manner: That it is well made of good material, and with proper management it is capable of doing first-class work; that the purchaser shall have one day to give it a fair trial, and, if it should not work well, written notice, stating wherein it fails, is to be given to the agent from whom it is received, and to the Sandwich Manufacturing Co., at Sandwich, Illinois, and reasonable time allowed to get to it, and remedy the defects, if any, (the purchaser rendering necessary and friendly assistance,) when, if it cannot be made to do good work, it shall be returned to the place where received, and a new machine given in its place, or the notes and money refunded, which, when done, shall be the settlement of the whole transaction. Continued possession of the machine, or failure to give notice as above, shall be evidence that the warranty is fulfilled."

The facts are that the defendant made an oral contract with plaintiff's agent, by which he was to take the machine,

1. SALE of machine: warranty: instructions. and pay $175 for it after trial if it did good work, and if it did not do good work he was to return it. The printed warranty, above set out, was delivered to the defendant by the agents who sold him the machine, after the oral contract was made, and at the time of the delivery of the machine. The court instructed the jury upon the contract as claimed by the defendant, and also upon the theory that the printed warranty was all of the contract, and that it could not be varied by parol. Appellant insists that the evidence conclusively shows that the sale was made under the written warranty, and that it was erroneous to instruct the jury on any other theory. We are unable to discover that there was any material variance between the written warranty and that which the defendant claimed as an oral warranty, or rather oral contract of sale. Moreover, it does not appear that any objection was made by plaintiff to the parol evidence of the sale and warranty. The plaintiff was not prejudiced by the instructions complained of.

It is urged that the court erred in instructing the jury that a substantial compliance with the contract was all that was

2. ——: ——: substantial compliance. required of the defendant. We think there was no error in this, especially as the jury were fully instructed as to what acts the defendant was required to perform to comply with the contract.

It is said that the defendant is liable for the machine because he failed to return it in proper time. The facts are that the defendant took the machine to his farm on Friday. The agents who sold the machine sent an expert with the defendant to set up the machine. On Saturday morning the machine did not work well. One of the agents was present, and informed the defendant that he would have an expert there on Monday. On that day the agents appeared with the expert, and the defendant continued to use the machine until Friday evening, when he laid it aside, and borrowed a machine to finish cutting his harvest. He returned the machine in controversy on Monday following. The jury were warranted from the evidence in finding that the machine would not do good work. The plaintiff's agents and experts were with the defendant when the machine was set up, and for some reason they thought it necessary to be on the ground on the two following days. There was no necessity, therefore, for the defendant to give notice that the machine would not work. And the court correctly instructed the jury that, if the machine would not work properly, the defendant was bound to return it within a reasonable time. This was what was required by the written warranty upon which the plaintiff relies.

We find no error in the case.　　　　AFFIRMED.

(marginal note: failure: notice: retn of machine.)

THE CHICAGO, IOWA & DAKOTA R'Y CO. v. ESTES ET AL.

1. **Agency**: FACTS NOT AMOUNTING TO: CONTRACT FOR RIGHT OF WAY. The plaintiff being about to build its railroad through a certain town, many of the owners of land crossed by the road were disposed to donate the right of way; and some of them, not, however, being agents of the company, visited the defendant, and sought to have her donate the right of way over her land, which she stated to them she would do, but she did not constitute them her agents to tender the right of way to the company. *Held* that a tender by them of the right of way did not bind her, nor prevent her from afterwards recovering compensation, by condemnation proceedings, for the damages to her land.

2. **Procedure**: SETTING ASIDE ORDER: NOTICE. Where a motion to change the record by setting aside an order is made, the party adversely interested should have notice; (*Townsend v. Wisner*, 62 Iowa, 672;) but when the adverse counsel appear in the case, and are heard upon the merits, the failure to give such notice is immaterial.

3. ———: INJUNCTION: DISMISSAL AFTER ADVERSE DETERMINATION. The plaintiff in an injunction suit ought not to be allowed to have it dismissed after it has been tried, submitted, and virtually determined adversely to him.

Appeal from Hardin Circuit Court.

WEDNESDAY, JUNE 8.

THIS action was brought by the Chicago, Iowa & Dakota Railway Company, appellant, for an injunction to restrain the defendants from interfering with the plaintiff's alleged right of way, and also to restrain them from prosecuting proceedings for the assessment of damages under the statute. The court dismissed the plaintiff's petition, and rendered judgment in favor of the defendants for costs. The plaintiff appeals.

John Porter and *Weaver & Baker*, for appellant.

M. W. Anderson and *Nagle & Birdsall*, for appellees.

ADAMS, CH. J.—The defendant, Sarah M. Estes, was the owner of certain land adjacent to the town of Iowa Falls,

1. AGENCY: facts not amounting to: contract for right of way.

through which the plaintiff desired to construct its road. Other land owners in the neighborhood, mostly citizens of Iowa Falls, felt disposed to donate to the company a right of way through their lands. Some of them felt anxious that the defendant, Mrs. Estes, should donate a right of way through her land. Two of the citizens, acting for themselves, and claiming to act as a committee of others, visited Mrs. Estes to ascertain what she would do. According to their testimony, she said that she would donate a right of way, but greatly wished that the company would run north of her barn. According to her testimony, she said that she would donate a right of way if the company would run north of her barn. The fact seems to be that the company ran south of her barn. We do not feel called upon to determine what she said. The persons who visited her were neither her agents, nor those of the company. It is not, indeed, we think, claimed that any contract arose at the time they visited her. One of them, however, testified that he afterwards called upon the company, and tendered the ground in question to the company. This, we understand, is relied upon as constituting the contract; but we do not think that it can be so considered. The alleged tender could, at most, be a mere communication to the company of what had been said by Mrs. Estes. But that was not a communication to the company having the force of an offer, unless the person making the communication was authorized to represent Mrs. Estes in the matter, and there is no evidence that he was. It may be that Mrs. Estes presumed that her words would be communicated to the company. But she had a right to assume that no contract could arise between her and the company until she sent an agent to the company, or the company to her, who had the power to treat in the matter, to the end that her rights might be fully protected, and nothing left to misconstruction as to the location of the road or otherwise. In our opinion, the evidence did not show that the plaintiff acquired the right of way in question.

It is contended by the plaintiff that at the time the court dismissed its petition, and rendered judgment on the merits **2. PROCEDURE: setting aside order: notice.** for the defendants, the action had been withdrawn by the plaintiff. The facts appear to be that the case was tried and submitted and held under advisement from one term to the next. The court then announced the conclusion at which it had arrived, which was adverse to the plaintiff. Thereupon the plaintiff asked leave to withdraw the action without prejudice, which was granted, and an order was entered accordingly. Afterwards the defendants moved to set aside the order, and reinstate

the case, and for a decree on the merits. The court overruled the motion, but afterwards, upon the motion being
renewed, the court sustained it. All this was done at the
same term. No formal notice of the renewal of the defendants' motion appears to have been served upon the plaintiff
or its counsel. The plaintiff assigns the action of the court
in this respect as error. The court has control of its records
during the term, and may, for good cause shown, change an
order made during the term. Where a motion to change the
record by setting aside an order is made, the party adversely
interested should have notice, (*Townsend v. Wisner*, 62
Iowa, 672,) but when the counsel, as in this case, appear to
the motion, and are heard, and no prejudice results from a
want of formal notice, it does not appear to us that such notice
is necessary. The case having been fully tried, submitted,
and virtually determined, we think that the court
should have refused leave to withdraw, and that
the court was not in error in sustaining the
defendants' motion afterwards for the reinstatement of the case, and the rendition of a decree.

3. ——: In-
junction:
dismissal
after adverse
determina-
tion.

AFFIRMED.

HAISCH v. THE KEOKUK & DES MOINES R'Y CO.

1 606
∞
<hr>
1 606
9 476
<hr>

1. **Surface-water**: OBSTRUCTION BY RAILROAD: STATUTE OF LIMITA-
   TIONS. Where a railroad company constructs a passage through its
   embankment to allow the escape of surface-water, it may be that an
   action for damages caused by the insufficiency of the outlet would not
   be barred in five years from the discovery of the insufficiency; (*Drake v.
   Railroad Co.*, 63 Iowa, 302;) but where the opening was designed for a
   cattle-way, and was not practicable for a water-way, the case was the
   same as if the embankment had been solid; that is, the injury was permanent and the damages entire, and the right of action accrued as soon
   as the embankment was made or the injury discovered, and was barred
   in five years from that time. (Compare *Stodghill v. Railroad Co.*, 53
   Iowa, 341, and *Van Orsdol v. Railroad Co.*, 56 Id., 470.)

Appeal from Lee Circuit Court.

WEDNESDAY, JUNE 8.

THIS is an action at law by which the plaintiff seeks to recover damages of the defendant because its railroad embankment obstructs the natural flow of surface-water, whereby the water stands upon part of plaintiff's farm, to his injury. There was a trial by jury, which resulted in a verdict and judgment for the plaintiff. Defendant appeals.

Anderson, Davis & Hagerman, for appellant.

Craig, McCrary & Craig, for appellee.

ROTHROCK, J.—The railway embankment was built in 1875, and has been maintained in substantially the same condition from that time to the present. The line of road at the point opposite the plaintiff's land is near the Des Moines River. The plaintiff's farm does not abut upon the railroad right of way. The nearest point is about forty-five rods away. The land which it is claimed has been injured by the embankment is about six hundred yards distant from the railroad embankment. The evidence shows that the alleged injury to plaintiff's land commenced in the year 1875, and has been practically continuous since that time. This action was commenced in October, 1884. Among other defenses, the defendant pleaded the statute of limitations; and it is claimed in argument that, as the railroad embankment was a permanent structure, which has never been changed, the plaintiff's right of action for damages, and his entire right of recovery, accrued when the embankment was made, or, at the latest, as soon as· it was discovered that the plaintiff's land was injured thereby. We quote the reply of counsel for appellee to this proposition. It is as follows: "(1) If the embankment had been solid throughout, so as to necessarily prevent the passage of the water, then the *injury* would have been permanent, and the damages entire, and would have been done at the time the embank· ment was put in. But the embankment was not solid. An opening was made in the embankment near where the water formerly found its outlet, but the defendant neglected to make and keep it sufficient, when defendant could have made the outlet sufficient at a reasonable expenditure. The injury was the neglect to make the outlet sufficient, and there is no presumption that this neglect would continue. If the defendant had furnished no passage whatever for the water, it would have presented a different question. But the defendant, in constructing its embankment, made a bridge or trestle-work, some fifty feet long, near where the water formerly flowed, but such passage-way proved defective and insufficient, and defendant neglected to make it sufficient, when defendant could have done so by a reasonable expenditure. It was not the embankment which was the cause of the injury, but the defect in the outlet. When this defect can be removed by a reasonable expenditure, the injury cannot be said to be permanent."

Now, this reasoning would be a sufficient answer to the position of appellant if the defendant did in fact attempt to make a water-way through its embankment. If such was the fact, the case would probably be within the rule announced in *Drake v. Chicago, R. I. & P. Railroad Co.*, 63 Iowa, 302. But the evidence shows, without contradiction, that, when the railroad was constructed, one Adam Hine was the owner of the land through which it was built. He owned the land on both sides of the right of way; and at his instance, and by his procurement, the company put in piling, and laid the track upon trestle-work for a sufficient space to allow cattle to pass from one field into the other. It was not designed as an outlet for water, was not adapted to that purpose, and the proof shows that it is not practicaable, by excavation, to make a water-way of it. It appears to us that the undisputed facts of the case bring it fully within the rule of the cases of *Stodghill v. Chicago, R. I. & P. R'y Co.*, 53 Iowa, 341, and *Van Orsdol v. Burlington, C. R. & N. R'y Co.*, 56 Id., 470.

We think the cause of action is barred by the statute of limitations, and that the court should have so instructed the jury, as requested by the defendant. REVERSED.

71
80

JOHNSON v. BROWN.

1. **Tax Sale and Deed:** NOTICE TO REDEEM: PROOF. The holder of a tax-sale certificate, in an affidavit written on the same paper whereon appeared the notice of the expiration of the time for redemption, and the affidavit showing its publication in a newspaper, stated that he was "the holder of the certificate of purchase described in the within notice, and that said notice was served on the within named T. J., in the manner and form as shown by the within and foregoing return." *Held* that this affidavit referred with sufficient explicitness to the affidavit showing publication of the notice, and constituted good proof of service. (Compare *Stull v. Moore*, 70 Iowa, 149.)

Appeal from Ringgold Circuit Court.

WEDNESDAY, JUNE 8.

ACTION to enforce plaintiff's alleged right to redeem from certain tax sales. A decree granting plaintiff the relief prayed for was rendered by the circuit court. Defendant appeals.

T. M. Stuart, for appellant.

J. W. Brocket, for appellee.

BECK, J.—I. Eliza A. Johnson was substituted as plaintiff, and the decree was rendered in her favor. No questions are raised involving plaintiff's title to the land, or the regularity of the tax sales.

II. Plaintiff claims the right to redeem upon the ground that the proof of the service of notice, by publication of the expiration of the time within which redemption from the tax sale is authorized, as prescribed by the statute, was not made. The alleged defect in such proof is in the affidavit of the holder of the certificate, which is in the following language: " I, J. N. Brown, being duly sworn, on oath say that I am the holder of the certificate of purchase described in the within notice, and that said notice was served on the within named Theodore Johnson in the manner and form as shown by the within and foregoing return." This affidavit was written or printed upon the same paper whereon appeared the notice and the affidavit showing its publication in a newspaper. It is insisted that this affidavit fails to refer with sufficient explicitness to the paper stating the facts it verifies. There can be no doubt that the affiant refers to the affidavit showing publication which appears upon the same paper. The affidavit in this regard is more explicit than like proof held good in *Stull v. Moore*, 70 Iowa, 149. Indeed, in our opinion, it refers with absolute certainty to the paper, which by virtue of such reference, becomes a part of it. We conclude that plaintiff fails to show a right to redeem from the tax sale.   REVERSED.

MILLER v. WILSON ET AL.

KINNERSLY V. LEE ET AL.

1. **Property**: REAL OR PERSONAL: MACHINERY FOR MILL: ORDER OF LIEN. The owners of a mill held it subject to a recorded lien for purchase-money, and they purchased certain machinery to be annexed to the mill, and the machinery had been delivered on the ground, and it was their intention to annex it, and they had begun the erection of a building in which the machinery was to be placed, but none of it had been put in place. *Held* that the machinery was as yet personal property, and that a chattel mortgage then placed upon it created a lien which was superior to the vendor's lien on the realty for purchase-money. (Compare *Soweden v. Craig*, 26 Iowa, 156, and *First Nat. Bank of Waterloo v. Elmore*, 52 Id., 541.)

Appeal from Van Buren District Court.

WEDNESDAY, JUNE 8.

IN 1880, J. J. Kennersly was the owner of certain real estate on which was situated a mill, the machinery in which was propelled by water. In December of that year he sold the real estate to A. P. Lee; and, as a large portion of the purchase-money was not paid, Kinnersly and Lee entered into a written contract whereby the former reserved and was entitled to a vendor's lien on the premises as security for the payment of the purchase-money. This contract was duly recorded on the second day of December, 1880. After such purchase, J. W. Wilson became interested therein as a partner with Lee, and it was determined to operate the mill wholly or in part with steam-power. Wilson, for the partnership, purchased of Fowler, in Illinois, a steam-engine and other machinery, partly, at least, on credit, and the same was shipped to Keosanqua for the purpose above stated. Miller claims that Wilson & Lee became indebted to him on or about June 1, 1881, and on the thirteenth of that month they gave him a mortgage on said engine and other machinery to secure such indebtedness. The mortgage was duly recorded on the day it was executed. Miller claims that such engine and machinery, at the time the mortgage was given, was personal property. Afterwards, in July, Wilson & Lee gave Fowler a mortgage on the same machinery as was covered by the Miller mortgage, and Fowler also claims that the same, at the time his mortgage was executed, was personal property.

The first of the above actions was brought to foreclose Miller's mortgage. Fowler and Kinnersly were made defendants. The former, in a cross-petition, asked a foreclosure of his mortgage, and Kinnersly pleaded that such engine and other machinery was attached to and had become a part of the real estate, and therefore his vendor's lien was the prior lien. The second action was brought to foreclose such vendor's lien, and Miller and Fowler were made defendants, and the issues therein were the same, in substance, as in the other action. Evidence was taken in the first action only, which, by agreement, was considered in the second action, and both were submitted together. They, however, were not consolidated, and separate judgments were entered in each. The court found and determined in the first action that the Miller mortgage was a valid lien on the property therein described, and foreclosed the same, and also held that it was prior to the liens of Fowler and Kinnersly. The court foreclosed the Fowler mortgage, and held that it was prior to the lien of Kinnersly. The latter and Fowler appeal. In the second action the court foreclosed Kinnersly's lien on the real estate, and in other respects the judgment is the same as in the first named action. From this judgment Kinnersly and Fowler appeal.

Wherry & Walker, for Kinnersly.

Wm. Moore, for Fowler.

Sloan, Work & Brown, for Miller.

SEEVERS, J.—I.   Counsel for the appellant insists that under the issues it becomes necessary to determine whether there was any consideration for the Miller mortgage, and, if so, whether the indebtedness secured thereby has not been paid. Counsel for the appellee insist that no such defense as a want or a failure of consideration is pleaded, and we incline to think that the position of the appellee must be sustained; but it is not necessary to determine such question, for, after a careful examination of the evidence, we reach the conclusion that appellants have failed to establish such defense, or that any portion of the Miller mortgage has been paid, by a preponderance of the evidence. The burden of proof to establish such defense is on the appellants, and we have reached the conclusion that a preponderance of the evidence is in favor of the plaintiff as to both questions. On the side of the appellee, there are the notes and the mortgage, and the evidence of Miller and Lee, who both testify that there was an actual indebtedness secured by the mortgage, and that it had not been paid; and upon the other side there is little evidence which tends to show that there was no consideration for the mortgage. It is true, counsel for the appellants, in an ingenious argument, insist that Miller and Lee are unworthy of belief because of contradictory and manifestly untrue statements made by them. If this is conceded, there remain the notes and mortgage, and we fail to find sufficient evidence showing a failure of consideration, even if the evidence of Miller and Lee is rejected. But we cannot say that such evidence is unworthy of belief. The matters relied on as being sufficient in this respect, when fairly and impartially considered, fail to satisfy us that the material facts testified to by them are false. There is no evidence tending to show payment, unless the evidence of Fowler can be so regarded. The evidence of Miller, Lee and Brown creates a preponderance in favor of the proposition that Fowler is mistaken as to material facts testified to by him.

II. The next question discussed by counsel is whether, at the time Miller's mortgage was executed, the property therein

1. PROPERTY: real or personal: machinery for mill: order of liens.

described was personal property. We find the fact to be that, at the time the Miller mortgage was executed, Wilson and Lee had commenced a building on the real estate purchased of Kinnersly, and about forty feet distant from the mill, in which the engine and boiler were to be placed, and the former connected by a shaft with the machinery in the mill. We further find that, at the time the mortgage was executed, none of the machinery was attached to the real estate, nor had it been put in place. It seems to us that there is a preponderance of evidence in favor of the proposition just stated. Counsel for appellant have separated the act of annexation into

five parts, and insist—*First*, that the machinery was purchased to be annexed; *second*, it was the intention to annex
it; *third*, it was shipped and delivered on the ground for that
purpose; *fourth*, commencement of the work on its actual
annexation; *fifth*, actually connecting or putting it together.
The first three propositions will be conceded; but the last
two, under the facts, we find cannot be regarded as having
occurred when Miller's mortgage was executed.   That work
had been commenced for the purpose and with the intention
of annexation will be conceded, but the machinery, all of it,
at that time, as we find, was lying on the ground near the
mill, or in it; but none of it, as we have said, was attached
or put in place; and therefore, in accord with the rule
established in *Sowden v. Craig*, 26 Iowa, 156, and *First
Nat. Bank of Waterloo v. Elmore*, 52 Id., 541, the
machinery and property described in the Miller mortgage
must be regarded as personal property, and said mortgage is
the prior lien thereon.   The Fowler mortgage was executed
about twenty days after the one given to Miller; and, while
there had in the mean time been some work done in the
direction of annexing such machinery to the real estate, we
think that, under the cases above cited, and particularly the
first one, such machinery cannot be regarded as real estate,
and therefore the judgment of the district court in giving
Fowler the second lien thereon is correct.

Incidentally, counsel for the appellant Kinnersly insist
that the court erred in directing the taxation of costs; but
we think otherwise.   AFFIRMED.

QUINN v. THE CAPITAL INSURANCE CO.

71 61
79 76

1. **Fire Insurance**: PREMATURE ACTION ON POLICY: STATUTE. Under Chap. 211, Laws of 1880, an action cannot be begun upon a policy of fire insurance within ninety days after notice of loss has been given, even though the company may before that time declare absolutely that it will not pay the loss; the effect of the statute being to declare that the loss is not due until the expiration of that time.

Appeal from Lee Circuit Court.

WEDNESDAY, JUNE 8.

ACTION on a policy of insurance against loss or damage by fire. There was a verdict and judgment for the plaintiff, and the defendant appeals.

Conrad & Campbell, for appellant.

Frank Allyn, for appellee.

SEEVERS, J.—Counsel for the appellant insist that the judgment of the circuit court should be reversed on three grounds. It seems to us that the special findings of the jury preclude us from considering the first two grounds, and the third is that the action was prematurely brought. This ground is based upon the statute which declares that no action on a policy of insurance "shall be begun within ninety days after notice of the loss has been given." Laws 1880, c. 211; Miller's Code 1880, p. 299. It is conceded that this action was commenced before the expiration of ninety days after the notice of the loss was given. The court instructed the jury as follows: "There is a provision of the statute prohibiting suits of this kind until ninety days after the proof of loss; and, in the absence of any excuse for so doing, a suit cannot be maintained within that time; but if a company has absolutely refused to pay a loss, and informs a policy-holder, or its representatives, that it will stand a suit, and will not pay, or the like, then the law does not require a needless delay, and the policy-holder may at once sue, if it is perfectly clear that the company does not intend to pay, and proposes to contest."

It will be observed that the statute is clear and explicit, and contains no exception whatever, and yet the instruction ingrafts on or injects into it a very important exception or qualification; and, in so doing, we think the court erred In a statutory sense, the money was not due on the policy until the expiration of the period named therein. The holder of the policy could not lawfully demand payment until that time had elapsed after the notice had been given. If the maker of a promissory note not due should positively declare and state that he would not pay it when due, this would not authorize the holder to bring an action on it prior to the maturity of the note. The same rule must prevail in the present case. The defendant might conclude to pay, but whether it did or not is immaterial, for the reason that the loss was not due and payable to the plaintiff until the expiration of ninety days after the notice of the loss was given, and therefore the court erred in giving the foregoing instruction.   REVERSED.

GERTH v. ENGLER.

1. **Promissory Note**: PAROL TO VARY: INSTANCE. In an action upon a promissory note made by a husband to his wife's father, *held* that it was not competent for the defendant to show that the note was given merely as evidence of an advancement to the wife, and that it was made by the husband because the wife was insane, and the husband received the money in trust for her use and benefit. (*Dickson v. Harris,* 60 Iowa, 727, followed.) BECK, J., not concurring.

Appeal from Boone Circuit Court.

WEDNESDAY, JUNE 8.

ACTION upon a promissory note. There was a judgment upon a verdict for plaintiff. Defendant appeals.

Hull & Whitaker, for appellant.

Crooks & Jordan, for appellee.

BECK, J.—The action is upon a non-negotiable promissory note indorsed to plaintiff. The answer, among other defenses, shows that the note, which was executed to Christian Tish-hauser, the father of defendant's wife, was executed for cer-tain moneys given by the father to the daughter, which was to be considered and treated as an advancement in the set-tlement of his estate; money having been advanced to other of his children in the same way, and like notes taken, which were not to be repaid in the life-time of the payee, but to be charged to the plaintiff's wife and other heirs, respectively, in the final settlement of the estate of the father, and that, plaintiff's wife being insane, the money was received by defendant in trust for her, and was for her and her children expended and invested, and the note was given by him as evidence of the advancement.

There was evidence introduced on behalf of defendant tending to support this defense, which, on motion of plaint-iff, was stricken out, and a verdict rendered for plaintiff. This ruling presents the question of the sufficiency of this defense. We have nothing to do with the evidence further than to determine whether it tends to support the defense. It is not denied that it does; the ground of the motion being that it does not tend to show want of consideration, but tends to contradict and vary the note. The motion is in effect based upon the ground that the answer pleads no sufficient defense to the action. It is not disputed that any defense good against the payee of the note, were it in his hands, may be pleaded in this action.

A majority of the court think the defense was not good, and the evidence therefore was rightly stricken out. They are of the opinion that the parol evidence tended to vary the note, and is therefore incompetent. They think that *Dick-son v. Harris*, 60 Iowa, 727, is an analogous case, and estab-lishes the applicability to this case of the familiar rule excluding parol evidence when attempted to be introduced to change a written instrument. In my opinion, the facts pleaded go to the consideration of the note. The defendant received the money as a trustee of his wife. He received no money in his individual capacity. He is charged personally in this action, but he personally received no consideration.

II. The evidence also goes to the manner of payment of the note. It was to be paid from the wife's share in the estate of her father. It was, indeed, given as evidence of an advancement. Evidence showing the manner of payment of a note does not vary it. See *Ewing v. Folsom,* 67 Iowa, 65.

I am of the opinion that the judgment ought to be reversed; but, the other members of the court being of the contrary opinion, it is   AFFIRMED.

DAVIS & SONS v. ROBINSON.

1. **Evidence:** PAROL TO VARY WRITTEN CONTRACT. Where a written contract concerning the sale of a new machine to defendant provided that an old machine, which was to be taken in part payment, was to be delivered at the time of receiving the new machine, it was not competent for defendant, in an action to recover the value of the old machine and the amount due on the notes given for the new one, to contradict the written contract by parol evidence that a delivery of the old machine was to be made at a later time.

2. **Procedure:** CAUSE WITHOUT EVIDENCE NOT SUBMITTED TO JURY. Where there was no evidence of the wrongful suing out of the attachment, the court did not err in refusing to submit to the jury a counter-claim for damages on that ground.

Appeal from Buchanan Circuit Court.

WEDNESDAY, JUNE 8.

THIS is an action at law by which the plaintiffs seek to recover of the defendant the value of an old threshing-machine, and the amount due upon certain promissory notes executed by the defendant. There was a trial by jury, and a verdict and judgment for the plaintiffs. The defendant appeals.

H. W. Holman and *E. E. Hasner*, for appellant.

Chas. E. Ransier, for appellee.

ROTHROCK, J.—This is the second appeal in this case. (67 Iowa, 355). The opinion on the former appeal contains

1. EVIDENCE: parol to vary written contract.

a full statement of the facts out of which the cause of action arose. It is unnecessary to repeat the facts here. It is enough to say that, when the case was remanded for a new trial, there was really no defense to the action founded upon the alleged breach of the warranty of the new machine purchased by the defendant of the plaintiffs. In the last point in the opinion, the failure to deliver the old machine was held to be a waiver of the warranty. On the last trial, an attempt was made to change the issues, and to prove that the old machine was not to be delivered until the new one was received and accepted. It was not claimed that there was at any time an actual delivery of the old machine. This was necessary in order to comply with the contract, and hold the plaintiffs to their warranty; and it was clearly incompetent for the defendant to show by parol that the old machine was to be delivered after he had tested, tried and accepted the new machine. The written contract (as we held on the former appeal) required that the old machine should be delivered by the defendant at the time the new one was received. He cannot be allowed to contradict the written contract by parol evidence showing that a delivery was to be made at a later period. This is about all there is of this case. The court below ruled that the evidence was not materially different from what it was on the former trial, and directed the jury to return a verdict for the plaintiffs. We think this was correct.

The plaintiffs caused an attachment to be issued and levied

upon certain property of the defendant.   The defendant filed
a counter-claim, in which he demanded damages'

2. PROCEDURE: cause without evidence not submitted to jury. for an alleged wrongful and malicious suing out
of the attachment.   He claims that his counter-
claim should have been submitted to the jury.
We do not concur in his claim.   As it appears to us, there
was no evidence which would authorize a jury to find that
the attachment was wrongfully sued out.   AFFIRMED.

BULFER v. WILLIGROD.

1. **Will:** BEQUEST OF ALL PROPERTY TO WIDOW: ELECTION. Where a
   testator bequeaths all his property absolutely to his widow, it is not
   necessary, in order that she may take under the will, that she file her
   election so to take, instead of taking her third under the statute. Section 2542 of the Code does not apply to such a case.

2. ———: CONSTRUCTION: ABSOLUTE BEQUEST. A bequest in the following form: "I give and bequeath to my beloved wife   *   *   *
   all my property, to use to her own use and benefit as she shall deem
   best for herself and our beloved daughter," *held* an absolute bequest to
   the wife, and that the daughter had no recoverable interest in the property or the proceeds.

Appeal from Marshall District Court.

THURSDAY, JUNE 9.

PLAINTIFF is the only child, and defendant is the widow,
of George W. Kline, who died in 1875.   Defendant converted to her own use the personal property belonging to the
estate.   She also sold the real estate of which her husband
died seized, and received and converted the proceeds derived
therefrom.   Plaintiff brought this action to recover two-
thirds of the value of the personal property and of the proceeds of the real estate.   Defendant answered that the whole
of the property was devised to her by her husband, and that
the will had been duly admitted to probate.   In her reply,
plaintiff, among other things, alleged that defendant did not,
within six months after the probate of the will, file her election to take under it.   The cause was determined in the dis-

trict court on demurrer to the reply. The judgment was for defendant. Plaintiff appeals.

F. M. Davenport and *O. N. Downs*, for appellant.

Brown & Carney, for appellee.

REED, J.—The bequest to defendant is in the following words: " I give and bequeath to my beloved wife, Caroline Kline, all my property, both real and personal and mixed, and of every kind, manner and nature, to use to her own use and benefit as she shall deem best for herself and our beloved daughter, Anna M. Kline, after paying my just debts and expenses of my last sickness and burial." The questions arising on the record are (1) whether the devise was defeated by the failure of defendant to file her election to take under the will; and, if not, (2) whether, under the will or the law, plaintiff took any interest in the property, or its proceeds, for the recovery of which she can now maintain an action.

I. Section 2452 of the Code is as follows: " The widow's share cannot be affected by any will of her husband, unless she consents thereto within six months after notice to her of the provisions of the will by the other parties interested in the estate, which consent shall be entered on the proper records of the circuit court." It was not alleged in the reply that the notice contemplated by this section was ever given to defendant. But it appears by the pleadings that she took possession of all of the property of the estate, and sold and converted it to her own use, acting on the assumption that the whole of it was given to her by the bequest. As she acted with full knowledge of the provisions of the will, perhaps it can be said that notice of its provisions by the other party in interest was not required. But we do not think it necessary to go into that question. The widow's share, spoken of in the section, is that portion of the real and personal property of the husband which, by the provisions of the statute, descends to the widow. Code, §§ 2436,

(marginal note: I. WILL: bequest of all property to widow : election.*)*

2440. Under the provisions of these sections, one-third of the personal property not necessary for the payment of debts, and "one-third in value of all the legal and equitable estate in real property possessed by the husband at any time during the marriage, which have not been sold on execution or any other judicial sale, and to which the wife has made no relinquishment of her right," descends to her if she survive him. By the provisions of section 2452, the right of the wife to take that portion of the property cannot be affected by the will of the husband, unless she consents thereto in the manner prescribed in the section. Is the right affected by the will in question? Clearly, we think not. By section 2441, the widow has the right to have her distributive share so set off as to include the ordinary dwelling-house given by law as a homestead, or so much thereof as will be equal to the share given her by section 2440. Her share, then, would be affected by any provision of the will which would require her to accept a smaller portion of the property than would descend to her under the statute, or which would bestow upon her other property in lieu of the homestead. But the present bequest is a devise to the widow of all of the property. Under it she took the title to the property, coupled with the power to make absolute disposition of it. Under the settled rule, it must be regarded as an absolute bequest to her. See *In re Will of Burbank*, 69 Iowa, 378, and authorities cited. Her share, then, was not "affected by the will of the husband;" for, under its provisions, she took, not only the portion of the property which would have descended to her under the statute, but the residue of the estate as well.

II.   What we have said substantially disposes of the other questions in the case. The will confers upon plaintiff no

2. ——: construction: absolute bequest.

interest either in the property or its proceeds. But, if it could be said that a trust was created in her favor, she clearly could not now maintain an action for the recovery of any portion of the proceeds;

for the right to use the property "for her own use and benefit" which was conferred upon the widow, has not terminated. There is no provision for its termination in the will.

Upon no possible construction of the devise, then, could it be held that she can now maintain an action for its recovery.

AFFIRMED.

PARCELL v. McREYNOLDS ET AL., EX'RS.

1. **Evidence**: EXCLUSION: NO PREJUDICE. The exclusion of evidence offered as a foundation for the introduction of books of account is no ground for complaint, when the books are in fact admitted.

2. **Witness**: COMPETENCY: WIFE OF DECEDENT AGAINST EXECUTOR. Section 3641 of the Code does not prohibit a widow from testifying for the plaintiff in an action upon an account against her husband's executor. The prohibition of that section applies only to actions brought against the husband or wife personally. BECK, J., *dissenting*.

Appeal from Wapello Circuit Court.

THURSDAY, JUNE 9.

THE plaintiff, as the assignee of W. A. Jordan & Sons, filed an account in the circuit court sitting as a court of probate, and asked that the same be allowed as a claim against the estate of Solomon McReynolds. The relief asked was refused, and the plaintiff appeals.

H. B. Hendershott and *McNett & Tisdale,* for appellant.

W. W. McCory and *Stiles & Beaman,* for appellees.

SEEVERS, J.—I.   Plaintiff introduced as a witness one of the assignors of the account, who gave evidence tending to

1. EVIDENCE: exclusion: no prejudice. show that the account books of the assignors were correct, and that the charges therein were made at or near the time of the transactions, for the purpose of laying the foundation for the introduction of the books

in evidence. Such books were offered by the plaintiff, to
which the defendant objected, but the same were admitted
subject to the objection, and whether they were afterwards
admitted the abstract fails to state. As the books were
admitted, the court did not commit any error of which the
appellant can complain. It is true, the court afterwards held
that the evidence of such assignor was inadmissible; but
this, we infer, was because the witness testified, as the court
thought, to certain personal transactions with the deceased,
and as to such transactions the evidence of the witness was
clearly inadmissible. Code, § 3639.

II. The plaintiff introduced as a witness Eliza McReynolds, who is the widow of Solomon McReynolds, who gave
2. WITNESS: evidence tending to show that the plaintiff was
competency:
wife of deced- entitled to recover. The defendants objected to
ent against
executor. this evidence, on the ground that the witness was
incompetent to testify under sections 3639, 3641 and 3642
of the Code. The court held that the witness was competent under sections 3639 and 3642, but incompetent under
section 3641, and therefore refused to consider such evidence.

It is provided that "every human being of sufficient capacity to understand the obligation of an oath is a competent
witness in all cases, both civil and criminal, except as hereafter provided." Code, § 3636. The exceptions afterwards
provided are as follows: "Neither husband nor wife shall
in any case be a witness against the other, except in criminal
cases prosecuted for a crime committed one against the other,
or in an action or proceeding one against the other; but they
may, in all civil and criminal cases, be witnesses for each
other." Code, § 3641. "Neither husband nor wife can be
examined in any case as to any communication made by the
one to the other while married; nor shall they, after the marriage relation ceases, be permitted to reveal in testimony any
such communication made while the marriage relation subsisted." Code, § 3642.

It cannot be doubted that Mrs. McReynolds, under § 3636, was a competent witness, if there was no other statute bearing on that question. Counsel for the appellee do not claim otherwise. Sections 3641 and 3642 must be read and construed together, and the former provides that neither the husband nor wife shall be a witness against the other in a civil case, unless it be brought by one against the other. This section contemplates that the marriage relation exists at the time the husband or wife is offered as a witness. In this case it did not exist, but had been dissolved by death. This action is not against Solomon McReynolds, but against his estate. In such case, section 3641 has no application, and section 3636 is not in any respect limited. Section 3642 provides that neither husband nor wife can as a witness reveal any communication made by one to the other during the existence of the marriage relation after such relation has ceased to exist. Now, if section 3641 has the force and effect claimed by the appellee, section 3642 is useless, and has no force whatever. We are therefore of the opinion that the circuit court erred in rejecting the evidence of Mrs. McReynolds.   REVERSED.

BECK, J.—(*dissenting.*) The rule of the common law rendering a wife incompetent to testify in a case wherein her husband is a party is repealed by provisions of our Code. But the wife, under section 3641, cannot become a witness in civil cases against the husband. The reasons which support the broader common-law rule doubtless induced the onactment of this statute. Each rule is based upon the ground that the intimate relations and unlimited confidence existing between husband and wife ought not to afford the means of disclosing facts coming to the knowledge of either spouse through such relations and confidence, to the prejudice of the rights and property of the other. And the same reasons exist for keeping each silent, after the death of the other, where the property and rights of the estate of the deceased are involved in the action. The spirit of the section quoted renders a husband or wife incompetent to testify against the estate of his or her deceased spouse. It was a rule of the common law that a wife could not testify in a suit wherein the executor or administrator of the deceased husband was a party. 1 Greenl. Ev., § 337; 1 Phil. Ev. (Cow. & H. and Edwards' notes,) 78.

I reach the conclusion that the circuit court rightly excluded the evidence of the widow of the testator.

WALTEMEYER v. THE WISCONSIN, IOWA & NEBRASKA RAIL-
WAY COMPANY.

1. **Railroads:** APPROPRIATION OF ADJACENT LAND: DAMAGES: EVI-
DENCE OF TITLE. Where the owner of land brings an action against a railroad company for a permanent injury to the freehold, and not for a mere possessory right, on account of an appropriation by the company of portions of the land adjacent to its right of way, it is neces-sary for him to prove a freehold title in himself.

2. ———: ———: ———: PLEADINGS AND PROOF. In such case, where plaintiff alleged damages to 160 acres of land, he could not be allowed to prove damages to 240 acres, at a certain rate per acre.

3. ———: ———: LIABILITY FOR ACTS OF SUBCONTRACTORS. Where sub-contractors, in building the embankment for a railroad, go outside of the right of way to obtain earth for the embankment, the company cannot be held liable for the trespass, unless it be made to appear in some way that it assented thereto, or had such knowledge of it at the time, or before it was done, as that assent might be presumed there-from.

Appeal from Hardin District Court.

THURSDAY, JUNE 9.

The plaintiff averred in his petition that he was the unqualified owner of 160 acres of land, and that the defend-ant railway company condemned 100 feet in width through said land for right of way for its railroad; and that, in con-structing the said railroad, defendant entered upon plaintiff's land on each side of said right of way, and took strips of land, outside the right of way, 50 feet wide by 200 feet long, without any authority from plaintiff, and removed the earth from said strips without condemning the same, and destroyed a spring of water belonging to the plaintiff; and he claimed damages in the sum of $500. The defendant by its answer denied each and every allegation in the petition. There was a trial by jury, and a verdict and judgment for the plaintiff. Defendant appeals.

Hubbard, Clark & Dawley, for appellant.

John H. Bradley and *Sutton & Childs,* for appellees.

ROTHROCK, J.—I. The plaintiff averred in his petition that he was the absolute owner of the land. His action was not brought to recover damages to a mere pos-

1. RAILROADS: appropriation of adjacent land: damages : evidence of title.

sessory right. The court instructed the jury that it was incumbent on him to prove that he was the owner of the land. The appellant insists that there was no proper evidence of ownership, and we think this position must be sustained. It is true, some of the witnesses, in giving their testimony, referred to the land as plaintiff's farm, but this was merely descriptive of the land. Indeed, there was no attempt on the part of the plaintiff to prove title in the ordinary and usual way. The proceedings in condemning the 100 feet in width were introduced in evidence, but were not admitted for the purpose of showing title in the plaintiff. Even if they were introduced for that purpose, they do not show title. The report of the commissioners shows that the damages awarded are to be paid to the owners of the land "as their interests may appear." It is claimed by counsel for plaintiff that, the action being in trespass, possession was sufficient without proof of title. But the instruction given by the court to the jury was the law of the case, and under it the plaintiff was bound to show that he was the owner of the land; and we think this view of the case was correct, because the plaintiff sought a recovery, not for a mere possessory right, but for a permanent

injury to the freehold, and the court instructed the jury,
upon this theory, that the taking of the strips of land on
each side of the right of way was a permanent appropriation
thereof, and the right of the defendant to fence the land thus
appropriated is recognized in the fourth instruction. That
an action of this kind, founded upon the ownership of the
land, may be maintained, see *O'Hagan v. Clinesmith*, 24
Iowa, 249; *Brown v. Bridges*, 31 Id., 145; *McCormick v.
Chicago, R. I. & P. R'y Co.*, 47 Id., 347.

II. The plaintiff described his land in his petition as
being a tract of 160 acres. In his evidence he described it

2. ——: ——:
——: plead-
ings and
proof.

as a farm of 240 acres, and he was permitted,
against the objection of the defendant, to show
that the farm of 240 acres was damaged by the
alleged trespass at a certain rate per acre. This was plainly
erroneous. The plaintiff did not bring his action for damages done to a farm of 240 acres.

III. As the cause must be reversed for these reasons, we
might dispose of the case, so far as this appeal is concerned,

3. ——: ——:
liability for
acts of sub-
contractors.

without further consideration. But, in view of
a new trial, it is proper that we should briefly
consider another alleged error which more nearly
affects the merits of the case. The evidence shows that there
is quite an embankment on the line of road at the point in
question, and that, in constructing this embankment, the
earth outside of the right of way, on both sides thereof, was
dug up and used in making the embankment. The work
was done by subcontractors, and the defendant claims that it
is not liable for the wrongful acts of its contractors, unless
such wrongful acts were done by its direction. Upon this
phase of the case, the court instructed the jury as follows:
"The defendant had the right to condemn extra width of
ground beyond 100 feet, if necessary for excavation or
embankment in making its road-bed, as a part of its right of
way. If it was so necessary to take the additional part of
the plaintiff's land for the purpose of embankment, and it

was taken without condemnation, the act of taking it was a trespass, and it is not material to determine whether the persons who did the act in person were contractors or subcontractors, or the employes of subcontractors; they will in law be considered the agents or servants of the defendant, and it will be liable to the plaintiff for whatever injury was directly caused by the act of taking. In other words, the defendant is liable for whatever injury was directly committed by any one acting in its interest in building the road, for taking whatever ground was reasonably necessary to be used for its right of way which was not condemned for that purpose."

We think this instruction cannot be sustained. It puts a mere subcontractor in the place of the company, and authorizes him to determine the question whether the act complained of was necessary to the construction of the embankment. And the evidence does not show that it was necessary to take the earth from outside the right of way. As we read the evidence, earth could have been obtained, for all the purposes required, without making an unreasonable haul. Now, if the subcontractor had no authority from his principal to trespass outside the right of way, and he willfully did so without the assent of the company, the latter is not liable for his willful trespass. We do not determine the evidence necessary to establish such assent. It appears that stakes were set at the outer edge of the land taken, and these stakes were similar to the grade stakes used on the line, and had marks and figures upon them. If these stakes were set under the direction of an engineer of construction, that fact would be competent evidence upon the question as to the assent of the company. It must be made to appear in some way that the company assented to the trespass, or had such knowledge of it, at the time or before it was done, as that assent might be presumed therefrom. Upon this point, see *Steel v. South-Eastern R'y Co.*, 16 C. B., 549; *Eaton v. European & N. A. R'y Co.*, 59 M. E., 520; *Hughes v. Railway Co.*, 39 Ohio St., 461.   REVERSED.

The State v. Montgomery.

1. **Abortion**: ADMINISTRATION OF DRUG: EVIDENCE TO CONVICT. Prosecution for abortion by the administration of a drug. Upon consideration of the evidence, (see opinion,) *held* that the jury were warranted in finding therefrom that the drug would produce miscarriage, that it was administered to the woman by the defendant, with whom she was with child, for that purpose, and that he was guilty as charged.

2. **Criminal Practice**: NEW TRIAL: TESTIMONY OF DEFENDANT WHILE SICK. The defendant in a prosecution for abortion, though advised by his counsel of his right as a witness, gave testimony damaging to himself, and, after a verdict of guilty, he moved for a new trial on the ground that, when he testified, he was suffering from a nervous headache, which affected his mind and memory. But the record of his testimony gave no evidence of his want of memory, or of the full powers of mind. *Held* that, since the trial court, which had an opportunity to observe his manner and deportment, and all the circumstances of the case, overruled the motion, this court could not, in the absence of convincing evidence of the truth of the grounds of the motion, interfere.

Appeal from Washington District Court.

THURSDAY, JUNE.9.

DEFENDANT was indicted and convicted for the crime of administering to a pregnant woman a substance with intent to produce a miscarriage, which was not necessary to save her life. He now appeals to this court.

Dewey & Eicher, for appellant.

A. J. Baker, Attorney-general, for the State.

BECK, J.—It is urged with great earnestness by defendant's counsel that the evidence fails to sustain the verdict.

1. ABORTION: administration of drug: evidence to convict. In support of the indictment, the woman upon whom the abortion was attempted testified that she was *enciente* by defendant, and upon so informing him he replied that, if she thought so, he would procure for her medicine which "would be sure to bring her all right." He afterwards furnished her with two bottles of a preparation called "Dr. Lyon's Spanish Drops," some of

which she drank, causing her to be "dizzy" and sick. The defendant admitted in his own testimony that he bought and gave to the woman this drug for the purpose of restoring regularity in her monthly periods. He denies that he knew she was *enceinte* at the time. He admits that he had frequent intercourse with her. When this illicit relation commenced, she was a servant in his family, he being a married man. He admitted to more than one witness substantially the same facts stated in his testimony upon this point. It cannot be doubted that plaintiff procured and gave to the woman the medicine for the purpose of causing a miscarriage. It is unreasonable to suppose that he would have taken the interest he did in procuring medicine for the woman, which he doubtless knew and believed would have the effect to cause a miscarriage, had he not intended just that result; and surely he would not have given her the drug had he not known or believed that she was *enceinte*. We think the evidence authorized the jury to find that the drug would cause miscarriage, and that it was administered to the woman to produce that effect. We think the verdict is sufficiently supported by the evidence.

II. As has been stated, the defendant testified that he had connection with the woman, and to other facts which probably weighed against him. He moved for a new trial, on the ground that, when he gave his testimony, he was suffering from a nervous headache, which affected his mind and memory. The motion is supported by the affidavits of defendant and others. The record of defendant's testimony gives no evidence of want of memory, or of the full powers of the mind. It is intelligent and coherent. It is shown that he was instructed by his counsel to plead his privilege should he be asked if he did not have intercourse with the woman. This he failed to do. This fact surely does not show that he was suffering from mental disability when he gave his testimony. The facts upon which the motion is based, as well as the

2. CRIMINAL practice: new trial: testimony of defendant while sick.

deportment and manner of the defendant while testifying, were all considered by the district court. The evidence upon the motion is not of the character to fasten conviction upon the judicial mind of defendant's want of mental capacity, while testifying, if his deportment and manner, together with his testimony, were those of a rational man. Doubtless the district court gave proper weight to these matters. In this regard we have not the opportunity to discover the truth, possessed by the court below. We cannot, therefore, hold that its decision upon the motion is erroneous.

No other questions were raised or argued in the case. The judgment of the district court is   AFFIRMED.

CASE v. BLOOD ET AL.

1. **Statute of Limitations**: AMENDMENT: SAME CAUSE OF ACTION: DIFFERENT RELIEF. Where an action is begun within the time prescribed by the statute, and certain relief is asked, and, after the cause would be barred by the statute, the plaintiff files an amended petition, setting up the same cause of action, but asking different relief, *held* that the amendment is not the beginning of a new action, but a continuance of the old one, and that the action as founded on the amended petition is not barred.

2. **Appeal**: PARTIES AFTER REVERSAL. Parties defendant who do not join in an appeal from a judgment against them must be presumed to be satisfied with it, and to be dissatisfied with a reversal of it, and, after the cause is remanded, they are still parties to the action.

3. **School Directors**: REFUSAL TO ACT: REMEDY. From a decision by school directors an appeal lies to the county superintendent; but, where the directors refuse to act, *mandamus*, and not appeal, is the remedy.

4 **School Districts**: FUNDS: INTEREST OF NON-RESIDENT TAX-PAYER. A tax-payer in a school district, though he be a non-resident, has such an interest in the funds of the district that he may maintain an action in *mandamus* to compel the directors to perform their lawful duty in regard to such funds.

5. **Evidence**: USE OF RECORD ON FORMER TRIAL: FOUNDATION. The record of documentary and oral evidence taken and duly preserved on a former trial is not admissible in a subsequent trial, without any showing of the absence of the witnesses, or of inability to produce the original documents, and without any notice to the adverse party. (Compare *Baldwin v. St. Louis, K. & N. R'y Co.*, 68 Iowa, 37.)

Appeal from Sioux Circuit Court.

FRIDAY, JUNE 10.

MANDAMUS to compel the defendants, a part of whom are directors of the independent district of Rock, and the others directors of the district township of Rock, to appoint arbitrators to make an equitable division of the assets of the district township of Rock, held before the organization of the independent district, which covers a part of the territory of the original district township from which it was separated. A judgment was entered granting the relief sought by plaintiff. The directors of the district of Rock appeal.

Bell & Palmer, for appellants.

Van Wagenen & McMillan, for appellees.

BECK, J.—I. The cause has been before in this court. See 68 Iowa, 486, for facts and pleadings upon which the case was decided. Upon the remanding of the cause, plaintiff filed an amended petition presenting substantially the same facts as alleged in the original petition. The relief asked in this amendment is that defendants be required to appoint arbitrators to make an equitable division of the assets of the district township.

1. STATUTE of limitations: amendment: same cause of action: different relief.

II. Defendants now insist that the action was barred by the statute of limitations, which is pleaded as a defense in the answer to the amended petition filed after the cause was remanded to the circuit court. This position is based upon the claim that the amended petition presents a new cause of action which accrued within the time limited by the statute. We think this position is not supported by the facts. The cause of action, in both the original and amended petitions, is the failure of the defendants to equitably divide the assets of the district township. The relief asked is not identical in these separate pleadings. In the original petition, plaintiff asks that the respective boards of directors be required to meet and make a division of the assets of the district township; and, in case they fail to agree, that the court appoint arbitrators to make such division. The amended petition prays that the respective boards of directors appoint arbitrators to make such division, and the court appoint a time and place for the meeting of the boards for the purpose of making such appointment. It will not be disputed that the remedy sought is not the cause of action, and is no part of it. The cause of action, if valid, entitles the plaintiff to a remedy. In a proper case, he may change his claim for the remedy, without in any manner presenting a new cause of action. This was done by plaintiff in this case. The action after the amendment was simply a continuance of the original action, with a claim for a different remedy. It is not claimed that the cause of action was barred when the suit was originally commenced.

III. The directors of the independent district did not join in the former appeal. It is now insisted that the case 2. APPEAL: as to them is ended, and that they were not before parties after reversal. the court after the cause was remanded from this court. If they were satisfied with the first judgment, they cannot be presumed to have abandoned the cause or to have withdrawn from it when it was reversed. Indeed, they must be presumed to be dissatisfied with the reversal of the judgment, as they were satisfied with the judgment. At all events, the reversal of the judgment left all the parties in the condition they were in before the judgment was rendered. These directors did in fact appear in the case, and were therefore before the court below, as they are in this court.

IV. Defendants insist that plaintiff's remedy was by appeal to the county superintendent. But such appeal is 3. SCHOOL di- authorized from a decision or order of the direc- rectors: refus- tors. Code, § 1829. In this case the directors al to act: remedy. did not decide anything, and made no order. They simply refused or neglected to act. No appeal could be taken from their default in this regard. Plaintiff's proper remedy is *mandamus*.

V. It is urged that, as plaintiff has ceased to be a resident of the independent district, and a patron of its school,

4. SCHOOL districts : funds: interest of nonresident taxpayer. he cannot be aggrieved by the official non-feasance of the appellants. But he is still a taxpayer of the district, and as such he is injured, if funds are withheld from it by the district township. Such funds would probably take the place of money raised by taxes. Plaintiff's taxes, therefore, are liable to be increased by the non-action of the respective boards of directors.

VI. The circuit court, against defendant's objection, permitted the evidence incorporated in the bill of exceptions

5. EVIDENCE: use of record on former trial: foundation. taken upon the former trial to be read from the record, thus dispensing with the oral testimony of the witnesses and the original documents. This was done without any showing of the absence of the witnesses, or of plaintiff's inability to produce the original documents, or any notice to defendants. This is clearly unauthorized by law. In Code, § 3777, it is provided that a transcript of the evidence preserved by the short-hand reporter may be admitted in evidence "with the same force and effect as depositions, and subject to the same objections, so far as applicable." But depositions containing the evidence of witnesses, or copies of documents, cannot be introduced in evidence without excuse for not producing the witness in court, or for not producing the original document. This point we have before ruled. *Baldwin v. St. Louis, K. & N. R'y Co.*, 68 Iowa, 37.

For this error the judgment of the circuit court is reversed, and the cause is remanded for a new trial.

REVERSED.

McCONKEY v. LAMB ET AL.

1. Judgment: MODIFICATION AS TO AMOUNT: GROUNDS OF. A judgment can be modified, as to the amount of recovery, in a court of equity, only upon some of the grounds specified in the third, fourth or seventh subdivisions of § 3154 of the Code, which are for mistake or omission of the clerk, fraud by the successful party in obtaining the judgment, and unavoidable casualty or misfortune preventing the party from prosecuting or defending. Consequently, a judgment cannot be thus modified where the judgment defendant appeared by attorney whose authority is not denied, and consented to the amount for which judgment should be rendered, and it was rendered for that amount, though for more than was actually due, and there was no fraud practiced by the judgment plaintiff.

2. ———: ———: STAYING EXECUTION: GROUND OF. A judgment in the foreclosure of a mortgage, providing for the sale of property under a special execution, will not be modified in equity so as to stay the execution, on the ground that the judgment was for purchase-money of the land, and that plaintiff did not have title to a portion of the land, and that defendant did not know of such fact till after the judgment was rendered,—it not appearing that there was any fraudulent concealment of that fact from the defendant, nor that she could not by diligence have ascertained the fact before the judgment was entered.

3. Mortgage: FORECLOSURE: PARTIAL PAYMENT: SALE FOR WHOLE: REDEMPTION. Where the judgment debtor in a mortgage foreclosure paid a part of the judgment, but credit was not given therefor, and the judgment creditor caused the land to be sold for the whole amount, and bid it in himself, but the judgment debtor did not, within the year allowed by the statute, offer to redeem by paying to the creditor the residue that was justly due him on the judgment, *held* that the debtor could not afterwards invoke the aid of a court of equity to enable her to redeem.

Appeal from Polk Circuit Court.

FRIDAY, JUNE 10.

ACTION in equity to modify a judgment, and set aside a sale of real estate thereunder. The circuit court sustained a demurrer to the petition, and from that order plaintiff appeals.

Cole, McVey & Clark, for appellant.

W. G. Harvison, for appellee.

REED, J.—It is alleged in the petition that plaintiff purchased of defendant a certain tract of real estate, at the agreed price of $1,495.50, a portion of which she paid at the time the contract was entered into, and that defendant gave her a title-bond, by which he obligated himself to convey the premises to her on the payment of the deferred installments of the price, the amounts of which, and the times of payment, were designated in the bond; that she afterwards paid the first installment when it became due, but made default in the payment of an installment subsequently falling due, and that defendant thereupon instituted a suit for the foreclosure of the bond; that he obtained a judgment in such suit, but that the amount of such judgment was largely in excess of the amount which was actually due on the bond; that plaintiff subsequently paid to the defendant, to be applied in satisfaction of said judgment, the sum of $700, but that he neglected to give her credit therefor on the judgment, and that he afterwards caused a special execution to be issued on the judgment for the sale of said real estate, and that he bid the same in at the sale thereunder, and received a certificate of purchase from the sheriff. It is also averred that defendant did not have title to a portion of the real estate, and that this fact was unknown to plaintiff when the judgment was rendered, and did not come to her knowledge until more than one year after that; also that plaintiff did not learn for more than one year after the rendition of the judgment that it was for an amount in excess of what was due upon the bond.

The prayer of the petition is that the judgment be modified by reducing the amount thereof to the sum actually due upon the bond, and by adding thereto a provision that execution shall not issue for its enforcement until defendant procures title to that portion of the real estate to which he does not hold the title, and that the sale of the real estate on the special execution be set aside, and the amount paid by plaintiff subsequent to the rendition of the judgment in satisfaction thereof be credited thereon.

I. The power to vacate or modify a judgment after its.

rendition is conferred on the district and circuit courts by
section 3154 of the Code, and the grounds upon

1. JUDGMENT:
modification
as to amount:
ground of.

which such vacation or modification may be
made are also prescribed in that section. It is
provided by section 3155 that, where the grounds for vacating
or modifying the judgment could not with reasonable diligence have been discovered at the term at which it was
entered, but are afterwards discovered, the application must
be by petition, filed not later than the second term after the
discovery, but that no such petition can be filed after the
expiration of one year from the rendition of the judgment.

The petition in this case was filed after the expiration of one
year, and one of the grounds of the demurrer is that no
relief can be granted against the judgment because of that
fact. It has been held, however, that courts of equity have
jurisdiction to grant relief against judgments, in certain cases.
where the ground of relief is not discovered until after the
expiration of one year from the rendition of the judgment.
Young v. Tucker, 39 Iowa, 596; *District Tp. of Newton
v. White*, 42 Id., 608; *Lumpkin v. Snook*, 63 Id., 515.
It is said in the last case, however, that the extent of the
jurisdiction of the court of equity is to grant relief on the
grounds enumerated in section 3154. The question whether
the judgment can be modified, then, depends upon whether
the facts alleged in the petition bring the case within the
provisions of that section. We are clearly of the opinion
that they do not. The judgment is referred to and made
part of the petition, and the record entry is set out in an
amended abstract filed by the appellee. It is shown by the
judgment that, while the plaintiff did not file an answer in
the cause in which it was entered, an attorney appeared for
her at the hearing, and consented to the judgment, and that
the amount of the indebtedness was agreed upon by the
parties, and the judgment is for that amount. Now, the
authority of the attorney to appear for her and bind her by the
agreement as to the amount of the indebtedness, and to consent

to the entry of judgment, is not denied in the petition. Nor is it averred that defendant was guilty of any fraud or concealment as to the amount of the indebtedness. It is averred, simply, that the judgment is for an amount in excess of what was actually due.

The judgment could be modified, as to the amount of the recovery, only upon some of the grounds specified in the third, fourth or seventh subdivisions of the section, which are for mistake or omission of the clerk, fraud by the successful party in obtaining the judgment, and unavoidable casualty or misfortune preventing the party from prosecuting or defending. None of these grounds is shown to exist, either by general averment, or by statement of facts in the petition.

The petition is equally barren of averments as to the other fact relied on. It is simply alleged that defendant did not
2. ——: ——: have title to a portion of the real estate which
staying exe-
cution: he contracted to sell plaintiff, and that she had
grounds of. no knowledge of that fact for more than one year after the judgment was obtained. It is not averred that there was any fraudulent concealment of the fact from her; nor is it shown that she could not have ascertained the fact by inquiry or examination before the judgment was rendered. Having failed by her own negligence to ascertain it in time to plead it as a defense in the action, she is remitted to such remedy as the law will afford her in an ordinary action for damages. Equity will not now open the judgment in order to give her the advantage of it; but the judgment must be regarded as a final determination of the rights of the parties as to all matters that were involved in the litigation.

It is alleged in the petition that defendant is insolvent. But that is immaterial, as plaintiff might have pleaded the fact before the judgment was rendered, but neglected to do so. She is not now entitled to have it modified for her protection against defendant's insolvency.

II.   If plaintiff had sought to redeem the property from the sale, she would have been entitled to credit for the money paid by her to defendant after the rendition of the judgment, and before the sale, and which was not credited on the judgment.   But she does not seek to redeem.   True, she avers that she is ready and willing to pay any sum that may be found due the defendant, and her petition contains a prayer for general relief.   But the right of redemption can be exercised only within the time and in the manner prescribed by the statute.   When the property was sold, something remained due upon the judgment.   The amount which she alleges she paid was not sufficient to satisfy it.   The property was therefore subject to be sold for the balance due upon the judgment. The amount, in addition to the sum paid, which was necessary to be paid to effect the redemption, was easy to be ascertained.   If that amount had been tendered or brought into court, to be applied in making redemption during the year allowed by the statute within which to make the redemption, judgment could have been entered upon the allegations of the petition, under the prayer for general relief, declaring that the redemption was accomplished.   But she made no tender; neither did she bring any money into court; and the time within which redemption might be made has expired.   It is clear, therefore, that she is not now entitled to redeem.

3. MORTGAGE: foreclosure: partial payment: sale for whole: redemption.

As was stated above, the property was subject to be sold in satisfaction of the balance due on the judgment.   No irregularities or illegalities in the proceedings of the sale are shown.   There is therefore no ground for setting it aside. Plaintiff's remedy was to redeem the property from the sale. But she has failed to exercise that right within the time prescribed by the statute, and she is consequently without remedy.

AFFIRMED.

STOUGH v. THE CHICAGO & NORTHWESTERN R'Y Co.

71
89

WOODWORTH v. THE SAME.

1. **Railroads on Streets**: DAMAGES TO LOT-OWNERS: APPRAISEMENT BY SHERIFF'S JURY. The owners of lots abutting upon a city street on which a railway has been built cannot have their damages ascertained by a sheriff's jury in the method prescribed for the condemnation of right of way. (*Mulholland v. Des Moines, A. & W. R'y Co.*, 60 Iowa, 740, followed.)

2. **Appeal**: QUESTION OF JURISDICTION NOT WAIVED. The claim that a tribunal acted without jurisdiction of the subject-matter in making a certain order is not waived by appealing from the order, but the question of jurisdiction may be determined on the appeal. (Compare *Spray v. Thompson*, 9 Iowa, 40.)

3. **Procedure**: WHEN NO JURISDICTION OF SUBJECT-MATTER. When a court has determined that it has no jurisdiction of the subject-matter of an action, it cannot properly consider any other question raised in the case.

Appeal from Kossuth Circuit Court.

FRIDAY, JUNE 10.

THESE causes involve the same questions, and are submitted upon the same abstract and argument. They are special proceedings by which the plaintiffs seek, by a sheriff's jury, to ascertain the damages to which they claim they are entitled by reason of the construction of a railroad upon certain streets in the city of Algona, upon which streets the plaintiffs own abutting real estate. The damages were assessed by the sheriff's jury, and the railroad company appealed from the assessment to the circuit court. The defendant filed a motion to set aside and cancel the assessment on two grounds, as follows: "(1) The plaintiffs are not entitled to any damages, because defendant's railway merely crosses said streets. (2) Plaintiffs had no right to cause their damages to be assessed by a sheriff's jury." The court overruled the motion on the first ground, and sustained it on the second ground, and dismissed the proceedings at the plaintiffs' cost. Plaintiffs appeal.

Geo. E. Clarke, for appellants.

Hubbard, Clark & Dawley, for appellee.

ROTHROCK, J.—I.   It is provided by section 464 of the Code that cities and towns shall have power "to authorize

1. RAILROADS on streets: damages to lot-owners: appraisement by sheriff's jury. or forbid the location and laying down of tracks for railways and street railways on all streets, alleys and public places, but no railway track can thus be located and laid down until after the injury to property abutting on the street, alley or public places upon which such railway track is proposed to be located and laid down has been ascertained and compensated in the manner provided for taking private property for works of internal improvement in chapter 4, tit. 10, Code 1873."

In the case of *Mulholland v. Des Moines, A. & W. R'y Co.,* 60 Iowa, 740, it was expressly determined that the manner of assessing the damages provided for by section 464 of the Code referred exclusively to the company, and not to the abutting owner. That case was followed in *Wilson v. Des Moines, O. & S. R'y Co.,* 67 Iowa, 509. We cannot regard this as an open question, and must adhere to the construction of the statute already adopted.

But it is claimed that the jury selected by the sheriff was the same as had previously been selected at the instance of the railroad company, and that, under section 1245 of the Code, they were the legally constituted tribunal to assess all damages to the owners of real estate in the county, and that the railroad company, or any land-owner, may have the damages assessed by the jury thus selected, upon proper notice. This section has reference to land taken and appropriated for right of way. Under the construction placed upon section 464 of the Code by the cases above cited, the owner of property abutting on a street has no right to pursue this method of ascertaining his damages.

It is further claimed ·that, if the proceeding was irregular and illegal because the owners of the abutting lots had no power to institute the condemnation proceedings, advantage could not be taken thereof by an appeal. It is said that the remedy, if any, was by *certiorari*. It is a general rule that objections to the jurisdiction of the court over the subject-matter of the action are never waived. They are not waived by an appearance of the defendant, nor by an appeal from a tribunal having no jurisdiction to hear and determine the question presented. The sheriff's jury in this case had no power to act; it was without jurisdiction; and this question, we think, could properly be raised and determined upon an appeal. See *Spray v. Thompson*, 9 Iowa, 40.

2. APPEAL: question of jurisdiction not waived.

II. The defendant appealed because the court did not sustain the motion to dismiss, upon the ground that the railroad merely crossed the streets, and that plaintiffs were therefore not entitled to damages. It is manifest that the court was correct in refusing to entertain this ground of the motion. Having ascertained and determined that it had no jurisdiction of the subject-matter of the proceedings, it would have been improper to have undertaken to determine ·what the right of the parties would be if properly presented to the court for its determination.

3. PROCEDURE: when no jurisdiction of subject-matter.

AFFIRMED.

McGinness v. Barton.

1. **Statute of Frauds:** SALE OF LAND: TRUST. An agreement that the grantee of land shall take, hold and dispose of the same for the benefit of another, is within the statute of frauds, and cannot be established by parol.

Appeal from Shelby District Court.

SATURDAY, JUNE 11.

THIS action was brought to recover certain money alleged to be due the plaintiff, Ida McGinness, as guardian of her minor sister, Ella Barton. There was a trial to a jury, and verdict was rendered for the defendant, and judgment was rendered against the plaintiff for costs. She appeals.

Smith & Culleson, for appellant.

Sapp & Pusey and *J. W. De Silva,* for appellee.

ADAMS, CH. J. —The court gave an imperative instruction to the jury to render a verdict for the defendant, and a verdict was rendered accordingly. The instruction, we think, must have been given upon the theory that no evidence was offered by the plaintiff tending to support any proper issue tendered by the petitioner. The plaintiff sought to recover upon two counts. In the first she averred, in substance, that one Asher Barton, (now deceased,) father of her ward, owned, in his life-time, certain real estate, and conveyed the same to the defendant; that the consideration for the sale and conveyance was the verbal agreement of the defendant to pay off all indebtedness of the decedent which was a lien against the property, and take and hold the same until such time as the defendant should think was the best time to sell the same, and out of the proceeds of the sale reimburse himself for money advanced in discharging the liens, and the remainder he should pay to the decedent's daughter, Ella Barton; that in April, 1881, the defendant sold the property for $1,700, which was more than enough to pay him for money advanced, and that he refused to pay to Ella Barton the remainder, as by his agreement with his grantor he had bound himself to do. In the second count, she averred, in substance, after setting out the property, and the ownership thereof by Asher Barton, that the latter sold and conveyed the property to the defendant for the sum of $1,500, and that the defendant was to pay the same by first paying off the liens on the property, and by paying the balance to Ella Barton, and that he had failed to pay the balance to her, as he had agreed. We do not understand that there is any pretense that any evidence was offered tending to show a sale to the defendant for $1,500, or any other specific sum. The second count, then, may be dismissed from further consideration.

We come next to consider whether any recovery could be had under the first count. That sets up a conveyance by Asher Barton to the defendant in consideration of a verbal agreement that the defendant would take, hold and sell the property and dispose of the proceeds in a certain way. The defendant was not to become the owner of the property in the sense that he was to acquire a beneficial interest in the same, other than possibly as mere security, but the property was to be converted into money, and the entire proceeds paid out as directed by the grantor, and no advantage was to accrue to the defendant from the transaction. Under the agreement, then, the defendant took the property in trust. Such an agreement is within the statute of frauds, and should have been in writing. The petition shows that it was verbal, and the evidence offered was parol evidence. The defendant denied the agreement as set up, and it was not established by the testimony of the defendant.

We think that the court did not err in directing a verdict for the defendant.

AFFIRMED.

FRANK v. FRANK ET AL.

1. **WILL: CONSTRUCTION: GENERAL OR SPECIFIC LEGACIES.** A testator bequeathed to each of four persons $600, and then stated in his will: "This amount is in notes such as the executrix of my will may turn out to them. The rest of my property I devise and bequeath to my wife." *Held* that the $600 bequests were not specific legacies of certain notes which the executrix might turn out in their payment, whether good or bad, but that the testator intended that each legatee should have $600, which the executrix could pay in notes of that value, or which would yield that sum, and that, if there should not be sufficient good notes in the hands of the executrix, the sum should be made up of other property of the estate.

Appeal from Jackson Circuit Court.

SATURDAY, JUNE 11.

ACTION involving the construction of a will. The judgment of the circuit court being adverse to defendants, they appeal.

W. C. Gregory and *Graham & Cady*, for appellants.

Keck & Keck and *L. A. Ellis*, for appellee.

BECK, J.—I. The will involved in this action is in the following language: "MONMOUTH, IA., February 4, 1874. I, Jacob H. Frank, of Monmouth, Jackson county, state of Iowa, make this my last will. I give, devise and bequeath my estate and property, real and personal, as follows: that is to say: To Hiram Frank, six hundred dollars, ($600;) George W. Frank, six hundred dollars, ($600;) Sarah Ann Kimball, six hundred dollars, ($600;) Mary Jane Van Duzen, six hundred dollars, ($600.) This amount is in notes, such as Mary P. Frank, the executrix of my will, may turn out to them. The rest of my property, real and personal, I devise and bequeath to Mary P. Frank, my wife. I appoint Mary P. Frank, Monmouth, Jackson county, Iowa, executrix of this, my will. In witness whereof," etc.

II. The question for decision in the case pertains to the legacies to the four persons first mentioned in the will. Plaintiff insists that they are specific legacies of certain notes owned by the testator when the will was executed, and that, as the notes, except one for $100, were collected by him before his death, the legacies were adeemed, except as to that note, or, if there was no ademption of the legacies, they were specific, being of notes which the executrix should select from those in her hands.

In our opinion, the will is not difficult of interpretation, as its language clearly reveals the intention of the testator. It will be readily seen that the will gives to each legatee six hundred dollars; not $600 in notes, nor notes of the value of $600, but $600. The will then designates the fund from which the legacies shall be paid, namely, notes in the hands of the executrix. It is provided that the executrix may "turn out" to the legatees, in payment of the legacies, these notes. The will clearly expresses the intention of the testator to give each legatee $600. A different intention is not expressed in the clause speaking of the notes, which, as we have said, designates the notes as the source from which may be obtained the money—the dollars—provided for in the bequest. The intention expressed in the two clauses of the will, we must presume, is the same. It is not probable that the testator intended in the first clause to give each legatee the sum of money named, and in the next clause intended to give notes, whether they should be good or bad.

In our opinion, the testator intended that each legatee should have $600, which the executrix could pay in notes of that value, or which would yield that sum. If the notes do not yield the amount of the legacies, or there should not be good notes of that value in the hands of the executrix, the sum is to be made up from other property of the estate.

The judgment of the circuit court is reversed, and the cause remanded for a judgment in harmony with this opinion.

REVERSED.

DeWolfe v. Taylor et al.

8
3
4

1. **Appeal**: FROM CIRCUIT COURT: CORRECTION OF RECORD AFTER ABOLITION OF COURT. Upon the abolition of the circuit court its records were transferred by law to the district court; and where an appellant from the circuit court desires to correct the record in that court, he should apply to the district court for that purpose. *Ex parte* affidavits are not admissible.

2. **Interest**: CONSTRUCTION OF CONTRACT. T. was owing D. $3,000, and one clause of a contract between them stated: "T. is to pay D. $1,000 on or before April 1, 1880," and another clause provided: "The balance of said sum is to be paid by T. to D. on or before April 1, 1881, and interest is to be allowed to D. accordingly on said $1,000; and the remaining balance to be paid April 1, 1881, at the rate of 10 per cent from this date." *Held* that the contract provided for 10 per cent on the last payment only, and that, no rate being named for the first payment, it drew only 6 per cent.

3. ———: STOPPAGE BY OFFER TO PAY. A mere statement by a debtor to his creditor that he is ready to pay is not sufficient to stop the accruing of interest. If an actual tender is not necessary, it must at least appear that he has the money, and is in fact ready to pay according to contract.

Appeal from Henry Circuit Court.

SATURDAY, JUNE 11.

ACTION in equity. Decree for plaintiff, but both parties appeal; the plaintiff having taken the first appeal.

R. Ambler, for plaintiff.

Palmer & Palmer and *Woolson & Babb*, for defendants.

SEEVERS, J.—I. The plaintiff filed a motion to dismiss the defendants' appeal on the ground that it was not taken within six months after the judgment was entered of record. The defendants concede that the appeal was not taken within that time, but they insist that the case was in fact decided in vacation, and the decree entered of record as having been rendered on the last day of the preceding term. It is further insisted that the appeal was taken within six months

1. APPEAL:
from circuit
court: correc-
tion of record
after aboli-
tion of court.

from the time the decision was rendered. This appears from certain *ex parte* affidavits which have been incorporated into the record, and the plaintiff has filed a motion to strike such affidavits, on the ground that they are not and cannot be regarded as part of the record. Counsel for the defendants insist that the motion is not well taken, because the circuit court no longer exists, and that they could not get the record corrected in accordance with the fact by making application to the district court. It is true, the circuit court has been abolished, but its records have been by law transferred to the district court, and we think such court has the same power and jurisdiction over such records as the circuit court had, and therefore application should have been made to the district court to correct the record in accordance with the fact. It is obvious that a record cannot be impeached or contradicted by *ex parte* affidavits. As the record shows that the defendants' appeal was not taken within six months after the judgment was entered, it must be dismissed; and also the motion to strike the affidavits must be sustained.

II. In 1873 the plaintiff sold to one of the defendants certain real estate. The contract was reduced to writing, 2. INTEREST: which afterwards, in 1879, was modified by a construction of contract. subsequent writing, and this action, in substance and fact, was brought for the purpose of determining the amount due the plaintiff under said contract. The plaintiff claims that he is entitled to more than was allowed him by the circuit court. The amount was ascertained and fixed at $3,000, when the contract of 1879 was executed. Said contract contains eight paragraphs or divisions, and the fifth provides: "Taylor is also to pay DeWolfe one thousand dollars on or before April 1, 1880;" and the sixth is as follows: "The balance of said sum now agreed upon is to be paid by Taylor to DeWolfe on or before April 1, 1881, and interest is to be allowed to DeWolfe accordingly on said $1,000; and the remaining balance to be paid April 1, 1881, at the rate of 10 per cent from this date." The court held that, under the contract, interest at 6 per cent only could be computed on the $1,000 to be paid in 1880, and we think this is the correct construction. No rate of interest on such payment is fixed in the contract, and it is the balance due thereon after deducting the $1,000 that bears interest at 10 per cent. The plaintiff, however, contends that, when both contracts are read together, it is clear and apparent that the intention of the parties was that the whole amount of $3,000 should bear 10 per cent interest; but in this view we do not concur.

III.   There was a lien on the property in favor of Mrs. Dewey, which the defendants agreed to pay, and the same was to be deducted from the amount agreed upon and fixed in the contract of 1879. The defendants contend that, under the contract, the amount was upwards of $1,900, but the court determined it to be $1,326, which we understand to be the amount actually paid by the defendants in satisfaction of the lien; and this we think is all the defendants are entitled to. Such, in our opinion, is the meaning and intent of the contract. The court further determined that the defendants were ready to pay the amount of the Dewey lien April 1, 1879, and that it should be regarded as paid at that time, although this in fact was not done until some time afterwards. In this we think the court erred. We do not understand that any tender was made, nor are we able to reach the conclusion, under the evidence, that the defendants had the money and were in fact ready to make the payment. At most, it appears that one of the defendants informed the plaintiff that he was ready to pay, but it does not appear that he had in his possession the requisite amount of money to comply with the contract on his part. We think the defendants should have shown, in order to prevent accruing interest, that they had the money ready, and were willing to pay as provided in the contract. This much, at least, they were bound to do. We are not required to determine whether they were bound to make a tender. The court found and determined that the defendants were entitled to certain payments, made at different dates amounting to $584.03; but, for the purpose of computing interest, the court equalized such payments, and fixed upon the thirtieth of September, 1880, as the time such credit should be made. This we think accomplished substantial justice, and is not, we believe, seriously complained of. There is nothing else in the plaintiff's appeal which requires our attention.

The judgment of the circuit court must be

MODIFIED AND AFFIRMED.

TAGUE v. BENNER ET AL.

1. **Practice on Appeal**: IMPERFECT RECORD: DISMISSAL. An appeal from an order excluding certain affidavits upon the hearing of a commissioner's report must be dismissed, where the abstract does not show what judgment the court rendered in the case, nor what the affidavits contained.

Appeal from Fremont District Court.

SATURDAY, JUNE 11.

THIS is a proceeding, under chapter 8 of the Laws of 1874, for the establishment of disputed corners and boundaries of certain real estate. A commissioner was appointed, who went upon the premises, took testimony and made a survey, and returned his report to the court. The defendants filed objections to the report, and offered to introduce certain affidavits in evidence, on the hearing of the objections to the report. The plaintiffs objected to the affidavits, and the objection was sustained. The defendants excepted, and appeal.

A. R. Brewer, for appellants.

Draper & Thornell, for appellees.

ROTHROCK, J.—The abstract does not show that any ruling was made upon the objections to the report. It does not

appear what the objections were, and the record is silent as
to whether or not the report was approved and confirmed.
It does appear that certain affidavits were offered by the
defendants on the hearing of the motion. These were
excluded, exceptions were taken, and error is assigned upon
the ruling; but it is not shown what the affidavits contained.
It is apparent that we cannot reverse the case upon this
record. It is impossible to determine whether the court
erred in excluding the affidavits unless we are advised of their
contents. They may have been upon facts not pertinent to
any issue in the case, and we cannot entertain an appeal
unless the record presented to us shows that the court below
entered a judgment or order from which an appeal may be
taken. The appeal must be

DISMISSED.

LEWIS v. MARKLE ET AL. (Four cases.)

1. **Practice on Appeal:** AMENDMENT OF JUDGE'S CERTIFICATE: TIME.
   Where the original certificate of the trial judge to the evidence was
   insufficient to entitle the appellant to a trial *de novo* in this court, an
   amendment supplying the defect, but made after the expiration of the
   time for taking an appeal, was no part of the record, and could not be
   considered.

2. ———: CERTIFICATE OF JUDGE TO EXPLAIN RECORD. Where an interlineation amending a judge's certificate to the evidence was apparent on
   the face of the original paper, submitted with the cause in this court,
   it was competent to show by a subsequent certificate of the judge that
   the interlineation was made by him more than six months after the judgment appealed from was rendered. (*Pearson v. Maxfield,* 47 Iowa, 135,
   and *Connor v. Long,* 63 Id., 295, distinguished.)

Appeal from Mills District Court.

SATURDAY, JUNE 11.

ACTIONS in equity to cancel certain conveyances from the
intervenor to the defendants, and to quiet in plaintiff the
title to the real estate included therein. The intervenor
alleged in his petition that the conveyance under which

plaintiff claimed the property was obtained by fraud, and he prayed that the same be canceled and set aside. The district court entered judgment dismissing the intervenor's petition, and granting to plaintiff the relief demanded in his petition. Defendant and intervenor appeal.

Kelly Bros. and *E. B. Woodruff*, for appellants.

Watkins & Williams and *Stone & Gilliland,* for appellee.

REED, J.—The judgments in these causes were entered on the third day of October, 1885. On that day the trial judge signed a certificate to the effect that the tran-

1. PRACTICE on appeal: amendment of judge's certificate: time.

script contained all the evidence introduced on the trial of the causes, together with the objections of the parties to the introduction of evidence, the rulings of the court thereon, and the exceptions of the parties thereto. This certificate was subsequently amended by adding thereto a statement that the transcript contained, also, all the evidence offered by the parties on the trial. This additional statement was interlined in the original certificate by the judge on the twenty-sixth of May, 1886.

The certificate, as originally made, is insufficient, and the causes cannot be tried *de novo* in this court upon it. The requirement of the statute (Code, § 2742) is that all of the evidence offered on the trial shall be taken down in writing, and certified by the judge. See, also, *Taylor v. Kier*, 54 Iowa, 646; *Clinton Lumber Co. v. Mitchell*, 61 Id., 132. The amendment to the certificate was not made until after the expiration of the time allowed for taking the appeal. It cannot, therefore, be considered. (Code, § 2742, as amended by chapter 35, Acts of the Nineteenth General Assembly.)

The fact of the interlineation of the additional statement in the certificate is shown by the original paper, which was

2. ——: certificate of judge to explain record.

submitted to us with the causes. But the date at which the interlineation was made was shown in this court by a certificate of the trial judge, which was signed on the seventh of October, 1886, and the

point is made by appellants that it is not competent to contradict the recitals of the record by the certificate or affidavit
of the judge. But, if the amendment was added to the certificate after the expiration of the time allowed for taking
the appeal, it constitutes no part of the record in the case.
When the time had expired within which the certificate was
required to be made, the judge had no jurisdiction or power
to amend or alter it; and we think it may be shown in this
court, by evidence other than the record, that the interlineation was made after the authority of the judge to sign a certificate had terminated. The case does not fall within the
rule of *Pearson v. Maxfield*, 47 Iowa, 135, and *Connor v.
Long*, 63 Id., 295.

We cannot, therefore, consider the cases on their merits.
The judgment will be   AFFIRMED.

ALLINE v. THE CITY OF LE MARS.

<table>
<tr><td>71</td><td>654</td></tr>
<tr><td>86</td><td>59</td></tr>
<tr><td>71</td><td>654</td></tr>
<tr><td>91</td><td>50</td></tr>
<tr><td>71</td><td>654</td></tr>
<tr><td>99</td><td>702</td></tr>
</table>

1. **Cities and Towns**: STEPPING IN HOLE BY SIDEWALK: CONTRIBU-
TORY NEGLIGENCE. A pedestrian on a sidewalk who voluntarily and
without necessity steps from the walk, without knowing that he can do
so with safety, and steps in a hole near the walk, and is thereby injured,
is guilty of contributory negligence, and cannot recover of the city.
(Compare *McLaury v. City of McGregor*, 54 Iowa, 717.)

2. **Practice on Appeal**: ERRORS WITHOUT PREJUDICE. Where under
the evidence plaintiff could in no event recover, errors not relating to
the evidence could not have been prejudicial to him, and are no ground
of reversal on his appeal.

Appeal from Woodbury District Court.

MONDAY, JUNE 13.

As the plaintiff claims, she stepped into a hole in the
the street near a sidewalk on which she was walking, whereby
she was greatly injured. Trial by jury. Judgment for the
defendant and the plaintiff appeals.

Joy, Wright & Hudson, for appellant.

G. W. Argo and *Ira F. Martin,* for appellee.

SEEVERS, J.—The plaintiff testified that in August, 1883, she was walking on a sidewalk on one of the streets in the city of Le Mars, about 8 o'clock in the evening. "It was dark, but not so dark but I could see. It was not as light as dusk, but it was light enough so that I could see those that passed me.   *   *   ∙ *   I had paused to bid the lady that was with me good evening, and, as I paused, I saw two gentlemen coming, and at first I did not recognize them, and as they passed I just stepped aside to let them pass, and I stepped into this hole. This hole was close up to the sidewalk. There was no earth between the hole and the sidewalk, and the hole ran down under the walk."

Such being the evidence, the question is whether the plaintiff is entitled to recover, and we think she is not. There is some evidence tending to show that the sidewalk was not level, but that it slanted in the direction of the hole. The plaintiff, however, does not claim that this caused her to step from the sidewalk into the hole. She was standing on the walk, and, if she had so remained, it is clear she would not have been injured. She voluntarily, and without necessity for so doing, stepped from the walk without knowing she could do so with safety. She gives no explanation whatever why she stepped from the walk, which was her proper place. We think she was clearly guilty of such negligence as will prevent her from recovering. *McLaury v. City of McGregor*, 54 Iowa, 717.

II. Objections are made to the instructions of the court, and it is is said counsel for the defendant made an improper argument to the jury. We are not by any means sure the objections to the instructions are well taken; on the contrary, we incline to think they are not; but we feel satisfied, conceding that the objections are well taken, that the defendant was not prejudiced thereby, or by what was said by counsel, for the reason that in no event was the plaintiff entitled to recover.

AFFIRMED.

GROSS & HORNUNG v. SCARR.

1. **Intoxicating Liquors:** ILLEGAL SALE NOT PRESUMED: EVIDENCE.
A violation of the law in the sale of intoxicating liquors will not be
presumed, but the contrary; and whoever sets it up must prove it. In
this case, the evidence (see opinion) that a sale was consummated in a
county where plaintiffs had no right to sell is *held* not sufficient to
establish that claim.

Appeal from Cass Circuit Court.

MONDAY, JUNE 13.

ACTION to recover for balance of an account for intoxicating liquors sold and delivered to the defendant. The defendant pleaded certain payments, and also that the contract of
sale of a part of the goods was made in Cass county, and of
part in Montgomery county, and that the plaintiffs had no
permit to sell in those counties, and that the sales were illegal.
He also pleaded a counter-claim for money paid on account
of illegal sales of liquors. The plaintiffs denied that the
sales were illegal, and denied that they were made in Cass or
Montgomery county. There was a trial to the court without
a jury, and judgment was rendered for the defendant, though
for much less than he claimed, and he appeals.

Rockafellow & Scott, for appellant.

W. F. Rightmire and *S. L. Glasgow*, for appellees.

ADAMS, CH. J.—The plaintiffs are merchants doing business in Burlington, Des Moines county, and under a permit
from the board of supervisors of that county to sell intoxicating liquors. The defendant is a registered pharmacist
doing business as a druggist in Cass county, and the liquors
were sold for the purposes of medicine, so far as the plaintiffs
knew. The principal question discussed by counsel is as to
whether the sales were made in Des Moines county, where
the plaintiffs had a permit to sell. The fact appears to be

that the sales were made upon orders taken by one of the plaintiffs in part in Montgomery county, and in part in Cass county. These orders were transmitted to the plaintiffs' house in Burlington, and there filled. The question upon which the parties differ is as to whether there was a completed sale at the time the orders were taken. The evidence as to what was said at the time the orders were taken is very meager and unsatisfactory. Taking the defendant's testimony alone, we ought perhaps to infer that he t̶█̶̶ht that there was a completed sale at the time the orders█̶ taken, but we are unable to find that a word was said which was sufficient to justify him in so thinking. There was some evidence of a payment made at one time, but it is not shown that it was made on the order then taken. On the part of the plaintiffs, we have the testimony of the person who took the orders, and he says that "no sales were considered made until the orders received the approval of the house in Burlington."

We will not presume a violation of the law, but the contrary; and whoever sets it up as the foundation of a right of recovery must prove it. The defendant places stress upon the fact that the person taking the orders was one of the plaintiffs. He insists that this person not only had power to make a contract of sale at the time the orders were taken, but that his testimony that the orders were not to be considered as approved until received by the house in Burlington is improbable. That the plaintiff Gross, who took the orders, had the apparent power to make the sale, may be conceded. But we see no improbability in his testimony tending to show that the orders were not to be approved except by the house in Burlington. It was there alone that the fact could be determined as to whether the house had the goods in stock in sufficient quantity at the time. It was there, probably, that the defendant's previous account could be best examined, and commercial reports consulted, and the defendant's promptness and responsibility determined. But, above all, it was there that a sale could be made which was not in violation of law.

The evidence is not such as to justify us in saying that the court below erred.   AFFIRMED.

WALKER *v.* THE CHICAGO, ROCK ISLAND & PACIFIC R'Y CO.

1. **Railroad: HANDLING DYNAMITE: EXPLOSION: NEGLIGENCE: EVIDENCE.** The defendant, in the regular course of business, had received and hauled to its *terminus* at Council Bluffs, a car loaded with dynamite, billed for a point farther west; but for some reason the Union Pacific Railroad Company refused to receive it for conveyance to its destination, and the defendant placed it on the southernmost of the tracks in its yard, awaiting orders concerning it. It stood there about twenty-four hours, when it was found to be on fire inside from some cause unknown. All reasonable efforts were made to extinguish the fire, but without avail, and it exploded, doing injury to plaintiff's property, half a mile away, for which she seeks to recover. *Held* that the defendant had the right to store the car at some place in its yard; that if plaintiff claimed that there was negligence in storing it where it did, she had the burden to establish that claim, and, there being no evidence of negligence in that respect, nor in any of the points charged in the petition, it was error to submit the question of negligence to the jury.

Appeal from Pottawattamie District Court.

MONDAY, JUNE 13.

ON the twenty-sixth day of September, 1881, a box car standing on a side track in the freight yard of defendant at Council Bluffs took fire, and exploded with such force that it injured certain buildings of the plaintiff, situated about half a mile away from where the explosion occurred. This action was brought to recover damages for the injuries to said building. There was a trial by jury, and a verdict and judgment for the plaintiff. Defendant appeals.

T. S. Wright and *Wright, Baldwin & Haldane,* for appellant.

D. C. Bloomer and *J. H. Keatley,* for appellee.

ROTHROCK, J.—The car in question was received by the defendant from a connecting road at Englewood, Illinois. It was a through shipment billed to some point west of Council Bluffs. It was received in the regular course of business, and transported to Council Bluffs, and tendered to the Union Pacific Railroad Company, to be conveyed to its destination. The last named company, for some reason, refused to receive the car, and the defendant placed it upon a side track in its own yards to await orders from the east as to its future disposition. After remaining on the side track about twenty-four hours, the car was discovered to be on fire. The fire appeared to be inside the car, and two of the employes of the defendant attempted to extinguish the fire with buckets of water. They discovered that the car was loaded with dynamite or giant-powder, and abandoned further efforts to save it. A switch engine was used to push the car to a water-tank which was near by, and about the time it was placed in proper position at the tank it was thought unsafe to remain near the car, and it was abandoned, and in a few minutes it exploded.

The alleged negligence of the defendant is set out in the petition as follows: "That on or about the said day defendant received from some of its connecting lines a freight car filled with dynamite, giant-powder, or some other highly-combustible substance, so known to be to defendant at the time the same was received by defendant at its said yard, and that said car was unprotected by any sheet-iron, or any fire-proof walls or covering, but was wholly exposed to fire from passing engines or other sources; that, while so exposed to fire, defendant negligently allowed it to stand in the freight yards for a great many hours, during which time the said car took fire on the outside from a passing engine, or some other source, which fire communicated to said explosive material, whereby the same, on said day, was exploded, destroying many other cars of defendant, its round-house and freight depot, and the concussion thereof destroyed a large quantity of the glass of the plaintiff in her said buildings, above described, and otherwise greatly injuring and rendering insecure said buildings, all of which was the necessary and natural result of the explosion, and of the said negligence of the defendant, whereby plaintiff has been damaged in the sum of six hundred ($600) dollars, for which judgment is prayed."

The evidence shows quite conclusively that the car was loaded with giant-powder. The plaintiff's counsel in their argument contend that it was· ordinary gunpowder. This claim is not only not supported by the evidence, but is not consistent with the averments of the petition which we have herein set out. The case was tried in the court below upon the theory that the explosive substance was giant-powder.

The freight yard is composed of some eight or ten tracks, and is about 300 feet wide, and a mile and a half long. The car in question stood on the outer track at the south side of the yard. The wind blew from the south during the day of the accident, and there is no evidence that fire was communicated to the car by engines passing on other tracks. It is true, the charge in the petition is that the car took fire from a passing engine, or some other source; but there is no averment and no evidence that the passing engines were in any manner defective in their machinery for protection against fire escaping therefrom. The sole ground of complaint was that the car was negligently permitted to remain in an improper place; that it should have been placed at some point where, if an explosion occurred, adjacent property would not be injured. This question was submitted by the court to the jury in the following instruction:

"The defendant, having a right to receive this car and its contents for transportation, and having a right to so transport them over its line, was under obligation, when the car arrived at Council Bluffs, and at the terminus of its line, to keep the car in its possession until it could be forwarded towards its final destination, or otherwise disposed of, as the owners of the property might direct. If the car was destined for some point further west, and was intended to be forwarded over the Union Pacific Railroad, and the company operating that road refused to receive it from defendant, the defendant could not abandon it or deliver it to a stranger, but was bound to keep it as safely and carefully as could reasonably be done until arrangement was made for forwarding it, or until the owner gave some direction regarding the disposition of it. The defendant was not obliged to unload this car, and place its contents in storage, if the car was a reasonably safe place to keep such contents while it would have to remain here; nor was it under obligation to provide a freight yard outside of the city, or at any other particular place, for the keeping of cars laden as this one was; but it was under this, and no greater, obligation, viz: that it use such care and caution as reasonably prudent persons would use, under like circumstances, to place said car and its contents where it would not be exposed to unnecessary risk, or unnecessarily endanger surrounding property. And the only question in this case, so far as the liability of the defendant is concerned, is whether the defendant did use this degree of care. If it did use the degree of care above indicated, it will not be liable. But if the evidence shows that defendant did not use such degree of care, and its failure to do so caused the explosion which occurred, the defendant will be liable for the injury, if any, caused to the property of others thereby."

We think there was no evidence in the case which authorized the jury to determine that the defendant was negligent in storing the car on the south track in its yard. It could not remove it from its yard, and leave it standing on its main track, without interfering with the passage of trains over its road, and there is no evidence tending to show that the damage to property would have been less if the car had been on any other track, or at any other place in the yard.

The court further instructed the jury as follows: "The

defendant had a right to assume that the contents of said car were properly packed and properly protected against all the ordinary dangers incident to transportation of cars and their contents over railroad lines, and there is no evidence to show that such contents were not so properly packed and pro-tected."

The evidence shows that, while giant-powder is an explo-sive substance of immense disruptive power, yet, if properly packed, the shipment of it by rail is not attended with any more hazard than the transportation of ordinary merchan-dise. Now, in view of this evidence, and of the instruction by the court to the jury, there was no ground for imputing negligence to the defendant. The relation between the par-ties to the action is not such that the law presumes negli-gence in the defendant by the mere fact that the plaintiff's property was injured.) The burden was on the plaintiff to show that the place where the car was stored was an improper place. All the light the jury had on this subject was that the car exploded, and the plaintiff's property was injured.

REVERSED.

BARRETT & BARRETT v. WHEELER & HERALD.

1. **Evidence:** WRITTEN WARRANTY: CONTEMPORANEOUS PAROL WAR-RANTY. Where a written warranty and a contemporaneous parol war-ranty were both pleaded by defendant, and the written warranty was established without conflict, it was error to allow evidence of the parol warranty to go to the jury.

2. **Contract:** GOODS ORDERED FOR SPECIAL PURPOSE: PURPOSE DE-FEATED: LIABILITY. Defendants purchased a large quantity of cider from plaintiffs for the purpose of bottling the same for resale, and at the same time requested plaintiffs to have printed for them show cards and labels to be used in the sale of the cider. The cards and labels were pro-cured and paid for by plaintiffs, and sent with the cider to defendants, but they were useless in defendants' hands on account of their not being able to use the cider—it not being of the quality warranted to them. *Held* that defendants were liable to plaintiffs for the price of the cards and labels, notwithstanding the breach of warranty as to the cider.

3. **Evidence:** WARRANTY: HEARSAY AS TO QUALITY OF GOODS. What the purchaser of goods from a vendee may have said as to the quality of the goods, is mere hearsay on a question of breach of warranty between the vendee and his vendor.

4. ———: CONCLUSION ASKED FOR: FACTS GIVEN. Where a question to a witness calls for his conclusion as to the effect of a contract, but the witness simply states what he claims to be the terms of the contract, there is no prejudice from the erroneous question. •

Appeal from Pottawattamie Circuit Court.

MONDAY, JUNE 13.

ACTION at law on an account for goods sold and delivered, and for money paid for the use and benefit of defendants, and at their request. There was a verdict and judgment for defendants, and plaintiffs appeal.

Smith, Carson & Harl, for appellant.

Geo. A. Holmes and *Sapp & Pusey,* for appellees.

REED, J.—Plaintiffs are manufacturers and dealers in cider at the city of Chicago. Defendants carry on a bottling establishment at Council Bluffs. On the twenty-eighth of March, 1883, defendant sent to plaintiffs an order for ten casks of cider. They also requested them to have printed for them 100 show-cards and 3,000 labels for bottles, and promised to pay for the same. The show-cards were intended to be used for the purpose of advertising the cider, and the labels were designed to be placed upon the bottles in which defendants would put it. Plaintiff shipped the cider as requested, and paid the freight on it to its destination. They also procured and paid for the cards and labels, and sent them to the defendants. This action was brought for the recovery of the value of the cider, and for the money paid out as freight on it, and for the cards and labels. The defendants answered that, by the terms of the contract, plaintiffs were to deliver the cider in Council Bluffs, and consequently they are not answerable for the freight; that the sale was by sample, and that the cider delivered did not correspond with the sample, being greatly inferior in quality and value to it; that the sale was upon a written warranty that the cider would be satisfactory to them; also that, pending the negotiation, plaintiffs gave a parol warranty that the cider would be satisfactory to defendants and their customers, and that there was a breach of both of these warranties, in that the cider delivered was unmerchantable and valueless; also that they tendered the cider back to plaintiffs when they discovered its condition, and that they ordered the cards and labels with special reference to the purchase of said cider, and with the intention of using them in the sale of the same, and that they were of no value for any other use.

I. It was proven on the trial that, pending the negotiation which resulted in the sale, plaintiff gave a written warranty

1. EVIDENCE: written warranty: contemporaneous parol warranty.

of the quality of the cider, and that this was relied on by defendants in making the purchase. Defendants were permitted, against plaintiffs' objection, to give evidence tending to prove that the agent of plaintiffs, who conducted the negotiations for them, gave a verbal warranty of the quality of the goods, somewhat different in its terms and effect from the written warranty, and that this also was relied on by them when they made the purchase. This warranty, if given, was made at the same time that the writing was executed. This evidence should have been excluded. The case, in this respect, falls within the familiar rule that parol evidence is inadmissible to vary or alter the terms of a written contract. Counsel for appellees conceded that they could not rely on the parol warranty if the one in writing was proven; but they contended that, as they had pleaded it, and as there was an issue as to whether any warranty at all was given, they had the right to introduce the evidence with reference to it, and rely upon it in case the proof should be found to be insufficient to

establish the written warranty. This would be true if there had been any conflict in the evidence as to the written warranty. But there was none. The giving of the written warranty was proven without conflict. On this state of the case, the court should have taken from the jury all evidence as to the alleged parol warranty, and confined their consideration to the question whether there had been a failure of the war-
· ranty in writing.

II.   The circuit court instructed the jury, in effect, that if the show-cards and labels were ordered with particular and exclu-
2. CONTRACT: goods ordered for special purpose: purpose defeated: liability. sive reference to the order for the cider, and it was so understood by the parties, and they were of no use or value except for advertising the cider, and there was a breach of the warranty of the cider, so that there could be no recovery for it, plaintiffs were not entitled to recover for them.   We think the court erred in giving this instruction.   Plaintiffs did not undertake, as part of the contract for the sale of the cider, to furnish the cards and labels.   But defendants, when they sent the order for the cider, requested them to procure them for their own use, and they expressly promised to pay plaintiffs whatever expense they might incur in procuring them.   The transaction was not a sale by plaintiffs of the cards and labels to defendants; but, at defendant's request, they procured them to be printed, and sent them to them.   The cost of the printing was an expense incurred by them at defendants' request, and upon there promise to reimburse them therefor. There can be no doubt but defendants are liable to them for the amount so expended.   It may be that defendants are entitled to set off the amount of this expense as an item of damages sustained by them in consequence of the failure of the warranty of the cider.   But we do not determine that question, for the reason that the claim was not pleaded as a counter-claim.   Defendants pleaded the facts merely as a defense to that item of plaintiffs' account; but they do not constitute a defense to it.

C66　　　SUPREME COURT OF IOWA,

The St. Louis, Ottumwa & Cedar Rapids R'y Co. v. Devin et al.

III.　After defendants received the cider, they sold a cask

3 EVIDENCE:
warranty:
hearsay as
to quality of
goods.

of it, and on the trial they were permitted to prove the statements of the vendee as to its quality and condition. The evidence was hearsay, and should have been excluded.

IV.　A member of the defendants' firm who was examined as a witness on the trial was asked the following question: "Under your contract with this Barrett

4. ——: con-
clusion asked
for: facts
given.

[plaintiffs' agent, who conducted the negotiation] that was here, where was the cider to be delivered?" This question was objectionable on the ground that it asked for the conclusion or opinion of the witness as to the effect of the contract; but plaintiffs sustained no prejudice by it, for the witness in his answer stated the terms of the contract as he claimed they were.

Other errors were argued by counsel, but we have considered the material questions in the case, and they do not demand attention.

REVERSED.

THE ST. LOUIS, OTTUMWA & CEDAR RAPIDS R'Y CO. v. DEVIN ET AL.

1. **Conveyance:** DELIVERY: CONDITION: EVIDENCE. Plaintiff sought to quiet its title to land under an alleged lost and unrecorded deed; but it failed to establish the delivery of the deed by a preponderance of the evidence, and it appeared by a clear preponderance of the evidence that the deed was a conditional one, and that, by reason of plaintiff's failure to perform the condition, the title never passed. *Held* that plaintiff could not recover.

Appeal from Wapello Circuit Court.

MONDAY, JUNE 13.

THIS is an action in equity, involving the title to a valuable tract of land in the city of Ottumwa. The plaintiff demands a decree quieting its title to the land. The defendants claim that they are the owners of the property, and that the plaintiff has no interest therein. There was a decree in the circuit court for the defendants. Plaintiff appeals.

Stiles & Beaman and *S. S. Carruthers*, for appellant.

Williams & Jacques and *H. B. Hendershott*, for appellees.

ROTHROCK, J.—The plaintiff claims to be the owner of the land under an alleged conveyance made by one Thomas Devin in the year 1868. The defendants are the heirs and representatives of Devin, who died in the year 1873, and they claim that he was seized in fee of the property at the time of his death. No conveyance of the land from Devin was at any time made of record; and the plaintiff did not upon the trial produce a deed purporting to have been executed by Devin. It was claimed that the deed was lost, and reliance was had upon parol evidence of the existence and contents of a deed. On the other hand, the defendants admit that a deed was signed by Devin; yet they contend that the same was a conditional conveyance of the land, to be void unless a railroad depot should be built thereon in three or five years. They further contend that the deed was never delivered.

The evidence is quite voluminous. There is no dispute that a deed was signed by Devin, and that he intended to donate the land for depot purposes. We are inclined to think that plaintiff does not show, by a preponderance of evidence, that the deed was ever delivered. However this may be, we are quite well satisfied that there is a clear preponderance of evidence that the deed was a conditional one, and that the title never passed, by reason of the failure of the grantee to perform the condition.

We are satisfied that the decree of the court below is correct.

AFFIRMED.

HUBBARD V. HART ET AL.

1. **Surety**: EXTENSION OF TIME PROCURED BY FRAUD: DISCHARGE. Where the principal debtor on a promissory note procures its surrender and an extension of time on the debt by presenting a new note to which he has forged the surety's name, *held* that the extension so procured will not discharge the surety. (*Kirby v. Landis*, 54 Iowa, 150, followed.)

2. ———: LOSS OF LIEN FOR INDEMNITY: ESTOPPEL OF CREDITOR. Where a surety held a chattel mortgage from his principal for indemnity, and he told the holder of a junior mortgage that he might take the chattels, provided the debt for which he was surety had been paid, and referred him to the creditor to ascertain that fact, and the creditor told him, not that the debt had been paid, but that the surety's mortgage was no longer a lien on the chattels, whereupon the second mortgagee took the chattels, but before he had sold them under his mortgage the surety learned that the debt had not been paid, but took no measures to protect himself by the enforcement of his mortgage, *held* that the creditor was not estopped from enforcing his demand against the surety.

Appeal from Cass District Court.

TUESDAY, JUNE 14.

ACTION on a promissory note on which defendant is surety. Verdict and judgment for plaintiff and defendant appeals.

Temple & Phelps, for appellant.

R. G. Phelps, for appellee.

REED, J.—The defenses pleaded are (1) that there had been an extension of the time of payment of the debt by a contract between plaintiff and the principal debtor, without the knowledge or consent of defendant; and (2) that defendant had been induced to relinquish the security of a chattel mortgage given him by the principal debtor, to indemnify him against his liability on the note, by the representation of plaintiff that the note had been satisfied.

I. The note in suit was given on the eighteenth of August,
1882, and became due in six months from that date. When
it matured, Hart, the principal maker, desired
an extension, and he presented to plaintiff a new
note, signed by himself, and to which defendant's
name was also signed, which plaintiff accepted, and he surrendered the former note. At the maturity of this note,
Hart again presented a note to which defendant's name was
signed, and secured a second extension. But it afterwards
transpired that he had forged defendant's signature to both
of these instruments. That fact was not discovered by plaintiff until he sought to collect the third note from defendant
after its maturity. As the surrender of the original note
and the extensions of time were obtained by fraud, the note
was not extinguished by the surrender. Nor was the surety
discharged by the extensions of time. *Kirby v. Landis.* 54
Iowa, 150.

1. SURETY: extension of time procured by fraud: discharge.

II. The following facts were proven under the second
defense pleaded: When defendant signed the note sued on,
Hart gave him a mortgage on certain personal
property to indemnify him against liability on
the note. He subsequently gave a mortgage on
the same property to one Herstein. About the time the
third note given by Hart to plaintiff fell due, Herstein
applied to defendant for information as to whether his mortgage remained unsatisfied. Defendant informed him that he
did not know whether the note for the security of which the
mortgage was given was paid or not, but referred him to
plaintiff, and told him that, if the note had been paid, he
could take possession of the property on his mortgage. At
that time, defendant did not know that the second and third
notes had been given. Herstein then applied to plaintiff,
who, after he had compared the date of the note he then held
with that of the one described in defendant's mortgage,
stated that the mortgage was not a lien on the property.
Herstein thereupon took possession of the property under

2. ———: loss of lien for indemnity: estoppel of creditor.

his mortgage, and subsequently sold it thereunder. When plaintiff made the statement to Herstein, he did not know that defendant's signature to the second and third notes given to him by Hart had been forged, but both he and defendant knew that fact before the property was sold under Herstein's mortgage.

The district court ruled that these facts did not have the effect to discharge defendant from liability on the first note This holding is correct. It is certainly true that if the cred-itor represents to the surety that the debt is paid, and thereby induces him to surrender the security which he holds for his own indemnity, or even to forego the steps necessary for his protection, he will be estopped in the future from asserting the claim against him. *Thornburgh v. Madren*, 33 Iowa. 380. But in the present case no such representation was made. The only representation made by plaintiff was that defendant's mortgage was not a lien on the property. That, however, was but a mere expression of opinion, based, doubt-less, upon the fact that the note secured by the mortgage had been extinguished, as plaintiff supposed, by his accept-ance of the one given in renewal. The opinion was probably erroneous, even upon the hypothesis upon which it was expressed. But that is immaterial. Defendant was not misled by it, for he took no action based upon it. His con-sent that Herstein might take possession of the property under his mortgage was coupled with the condition that his own mortgage had been satisfied. Herstein, in taking pos-session of it, acted upon that consent, and the statement made by plaintiff. But defendant knew, before the property was sold, that his mortgage had not been satisfied. He knew that the debt to plaintiff had not been paid. He knew, also, that plaintiff had been induced by the fraud of Hart to sur-render the note which he had signed, and grant an extension of time. He is conclusively presumed to have known that, upon that state of facts, he remained liable for the debt, and that his mortgage continued a valid security for his indemnity; for that is the law upon that state of facts. As the property had not then been sold, there was nothing to prevent him from seizing it upon his mortgage. He stood, then, in precisely the position he would have occupied if plaintiff had never made the statement to Herstein; and, if he lost his security by the sale of the property under the other mortgage, the injury was caused by his own failure to assert his right in proper time to preserve it. There clearly is no element of estoppel in the case.

Error is assigned on the admission in the trial of letter-press copies of certain letters written by plaintiff to defendant, relating to the matters in dispute. But, if it should be conceded that the court erred in admitting them, defendant sustained no prejudice by the ruling.

The facts upon which the court's ruling was based, and which we hold to be conclusive of the rights of the parties, were all clearly proven independently of the letters.

AFFIRMED.

KENNEDY v. ROSIER.

1. **Instructions**: IGNORING POINT IN ISSUE. An instruction which ignores an issue material to the case, or which assumes as true a material point in dispute, cannot be sustained. For illustrations see opinion.

2. **Pledge**: OF NOTE: DUTY OF PLEDGEE. The holder of a promissory note as collateral security is not charged with the same duty as an indorsee. He is liable for failure to present the note and to give notice of non-payment, only in case damage, loss or prejudice results to the pledgeor therefrom, and then only to the extent of such damage.

3. **Depositions**: NOTICE OF TAKING: CODE, § 3730. In the provision of the Code, § 3730, that a notice to take depositions shall be five days, " when served on the party within the county," the county in which the depositions are to be taken is meant, and not that wherein the court in which they are to be used is held.

4. **Appeal**: DISCREPANCY IN RECORD AS TO DATE OF JUDGMENT. A discrepancy between the notice of appeal and an amended abstract, as to the date of the judgment in the case, is no ground for dismissing the appeal, where it is not shown that the appeal is not from the judgment in the case, or was not taken in time.

Appeal from Delaware Circuit Court.

TUESDAY, JUNE 14.

ACTION upon a promissory note. There was a judgment upon a verdict for plaintiff for a part of his claim, from which he appeals.

Ainsworth & Hobson, for appellant.

E. E. Hasner, for appellee.

BECK, J.—I. As a defense, the answer of defendant pleads that he gave to plaintiff a note, and mortgage securing it, as

1. INSTRUCTIONS: ignoring point in issue.

collateral security upon the notes in suit; that the amount and value of these collaterals exceeded defendant's note; and that, through the fault and negligence of plaintiff, they were not collected, and became lost to defendant, whereby he sustained damage, which is set up as a counter-claim to plaintiff's action. The plaintiff, in reply, pleads, among other matters, that defendant did not deliver to plaintiff the collateral note, and that he has never had it in his possession, but it has been all the time in the possession of defendant.

II. The ninth instruction to the jury is to the effect that, upon plaintiff's acceptance of the assignment of the collateral note, he became bound to use reasonable efforts to collect it. This instruction, in view of the matter pleaded in plaintiff's reply, that he never had possession of the note, was misleading and erroneous. If the instruction had been modified so as to have required the jury to find whether plaintiff had the note in his possession, and if they found he had, that the plaintiff should be held liable for loss resulting from failure to use the diligence stated in the instruction, it would have been correct.

III. So the twelfth instruction is erroneous, for the reason that it also ignores the matter pleaded by plaintiff in his reply, to the effect that he never had the possession of the note. If plaintiff did not have the possession of the note, he could not have exercised care and control over it.

IV. The sixteenth instruction is to the effect that it was plaintiff's duty to present the note for payment within a reasonable time after he received it, and, if not paid, to notify defendant of the fact; and, if he neglected such presentation and notice, he cannot recover in this action. The instruction is, in our opinion, erroneous in these particulars: (1) It assumes that plaintiff did have possession of the note. This was a disputed fact, under the issue, upon which the jury should have been directed to find the fact. (2) The

2. PLEDGE: of note: duty of pledgee. plaintiff's duty was not that of an indorsee, as the instruction seems to hold. He would have been liable only for failure to present the note, and give notice of non-payment, if damage, loss, or prejudice resulted to defendant therefrom; and such liability would only have extended so far as to require him to make good to plaintiff the loss or damage he sustained from such neglect.

V. Depositions were taken by defendant in the county of plaintiff's residence, upon eight days' notice. Plaintiff

3. DEPOSI- TIONS: notice of taking: Code, § 3730. moved to suppress the depositions, on the ground that sufficient notice had not been given. The motion was overruled. The cause was pending in a judicial district other than the one in which plaintiff resides. Counsel insist that under Code, § 3730, plaintiff should have had the notice required in the commencement of actions by Code, § 2601. But we think the section relied upon does not sustain plaintiff's position. It provides that a notice to take depositions shall be five days, "when served on the party within the county." Counsel think the county in which the court is held is referred to in this language. We are of the opinion that the county in which the depositions are taken is meant.

The purpose of the statute in prescribing different times

of service is to so provide that opportunity shall be given the parties to appear before the officer at the time of taking the depositions. A party to a suit might live a great distance from the county in which the suit was pending, yet, in counsel's view, if the deposition should be taken in such county, he would be entitled to no more than five days' notice, while, if the depositions be taken in his own county, at the very place of his residence, he would be entitled to twenty days' notice. We think no such absurd result was intended by the legislature in the enactment of the statute in question.

VI. Defendant files an amended abstract showing that the judgment was rendered June 29th, and the notice of appeal designates the judgment as having been rendered June 9th. He claims that the appeal is not from the judgment in this case. But it is not shown or claimed that the appeal is not from the judgment in this case, or was not taken in time. We think the appeal is properly before us.

4. APPEAL: discrepancy in record as to date of judgment.

VII. Defendant also shows that he excepted to the overruling of a motion for a judgment upon plaintiff's evidence; but, as he has not appealed, he cannot ask us to review this ruling.

Other questions discussed by counsel need not be considered. For the errors in the instructions above pointed out, the judgment of the circuit court is

REVERSED.

THE DES MOINES NAT. BANK v. CHISHOLM ET AL. 71 67S
101

1. **Promissory Note:** CONSIDERATION: SURRENDER OF COLLATERAL SECURITY: INNOCENT HOLDER. Plaintiff made a loan to the M. bank, with the understanding that it was to have collateral security, and it received the collaterals some time after the loan had been made. Subsequently the cashier of the M. bank secured a return of the collaterals by depositing in their stead an accommodation note signed by himself and some others, among whom were S. and C. The signature of S. had been forged to the note, and C., relying on the genuineness of the signatures already obtained, signed last. Afterwards, C., being the only solvent signer to the note, gave the notes and mortgage sued on in this case in lieu of the accommodation note, and for an extension of time. *Held—*

> (1) That the pre-existing debt from the M. bank to plaintiff was a good consideration for the delivery of the collaterals to plaintiff.

> (2) That the return of the collaterals was a good consideration for the accommodation note.

> (3) That plaintiff must be regarded as a purchaser for value of the accommodation note, and, having had no notice of the fraud by which C.'s signature had been obtained thereto, it was in no manner affected thereby.

> (4) That fraud and want of consideration could not be successfully pleaded against the notes and mortgage in suit.

2. ———: IMBECILITY OF MAKER: UNDUE INFLUENCE: EVIDENCE NOT ESTABLISHING. The evidence in this case considered, (see opinion,) and *held* to show that the maker of the notes and mortgage in question was greatly impaired in mental and physical vigor at the time of their execution, but that he was not lacking in judgment or reason, but was in the possession of all his faculties, and was fully competent to enter into the contract. Also, that there was no evidence of any concealment or deceit or undue influence used in obtaining the execution of the contract.

Appeal from Monroe Circuit Court.

TUESDAY, JUNE 14.

THE defendant Alexander Chisholm is administrator of the estate of William Chisholm, deceased. The other defendants are the widow and heirs at law of said William Chisholm. This action is upon three promissory notes, and

for the foreclosure of a mortgage securing the same, executed by William Chisholm in his life-time. The defendants answered that the notes and mortgage were given without consideration, that William Chisholm was *non compos
mentis*, and incapable of contracting, when he executed
them, and that they were procured by fraud. The circuit
court entered judgment for the defendants, and plaintiff
appeals.

Mitchell & Dudley and *Seevers & Sampson*, for appellant.

W. A. Nickols and *T. B. Perry*, for appellees.

REED, J.—The facts out of which this controversy arose
are as follows: On the eighteenth of August, 1882, the
Monroe County Bank, a banking corporation doing business
at Albia, made application to plaintiff, whose place of business is at Des Moines, for a loan of $5,000, for four or six
months, offering to secure the same with collaterals. The
application was by letter. On the next day plaintiff wrote
to the bank advising it that it could loan it $3,000. On the
twenty-first of August an agent of the Monroe County
Bank went to Des Moines, taking with him the promissory
note of the bank for $3,000, which plaintiff received, and
paid him that amount less the discount. In subsequent correspondence plaintiff agreed to advance an additional $2,000,
for which amount, when it received the money, the Monroe
County Bank gave its certificate of deposit. This certificate
was dated on the twenty-third of August, when the $3,000
note was delivered. A list of notes executed by other parties
was also delivered as collateral security, but these plaintiff
returned, stating at the time that, if it desired security in the
future, it would call for it. Soon after the additional $2,000
was advanced by plaintiff, it received as collateral security a
list of notes, amounting in the aggregate to over $11,000.
On the thirtieth of September following, the cashier of the

Monroe County Bank sent to plaintiff a promissory note for
$5,000, to which his own name, and those of Lewis Miller,
D. J. Shields, Hiram Hicks, William Hicks and William
Chisholm, were signed, and asked plaintiff to accept it as
security for the loan in lieu of the securities formerly deposited, and to return the same to him, which plaintiff did on
the thirtieth of September. This $5,000 note was dated
September 26th, and by its terms became due in six months
from that date. It was payable to the Monroe County Bank
or order, and was indorsed by it to plaintiff. The parties
who signed it received no consideration for it, but gave it as
an accommodation to the bank, in which they were stockholders.

The $3,000 note of the Monroe County Bank, and the cer-
tificate of deposit, also became due in six months from their
dates. On the eleventh of October following, the Monroe
County Bank failed. In a few days after this failure, plaintiff's president went to Albia, accompanied by its attorney,
for the purpose of ascertaining whether the security held by
it for the loan was good. They ascertained in their investigation that the cashier of the bank and Lewis Miller, another
signer of the note, were insolvent; also that the signature of
J. D. Shields to the note was a forgery. They had an interview with Chisholm, and Hiram and William Hicks, the
other signers, and the proposition was made to accept the
notes of each of these parties for one-third of the amount,
with the other two in each case as sureties. Chisholm, it
appears, was at first willing to enter into this arrangement,
but the other parties declined to enter into it. The parties
took counsel of their attorneys, and were advised that, inasmuch as they had signed the note after the name of Shields
had been attached to it, and in the belief that his signature
was genuine, and plaintiff had taken it as security for a pre-
existing debt, without extending the time of payment, its
collection could not be enforced against them. At that time
it was not known, either to the parties, or to the attorneys

who gave the advice, that plaintiff, when it accepted the note, had surrendered other collaterals which it held as security for the debt. When they received this advice, the parties agreed among themselves that they would take no further action with reference to the matter, except on the advice of their counsel.

In the following February, Chisholm learned that the Hickses had transferred their property to other parties, and he believed that this was done for the purpose of defrauding their creditors. An action had in the mean time been commenced against them, and the other stockholders of the bank, by creditors of that institution, for the purpose of charging them with a very large amount of its liabilities. On the sixth of March, Chisholm wrote to plaintiff admitting his liability on the note, and stating that he was preparing to pay one-third of the amount; also admitting that, in the interview with its president and attorney in the previous October, he was willing to enter into the arrangement which was proposed, but stating that the other parties refused to make that settlement. He also informed it of what the Hickses had done, and his belief as to their purpose in doing so, and he asked it to deal as leniently as possible with him, and stated that he would be compelled to either borrow money, or procure an extension of time from it.

On the nineteenth of the same month he again wrote to plaintiff, stating that it appeared to him that he would have to meet the whole burden of the liability, and, if so, he would be compelled to ask an extension of time, and suggesting that some person be sent to meet him at Albia, on a certain day, to arrange the matter. An engagement was accordingly made to meet him on the 23d. On that day the attorney of plaintiff went to Albia and met him; he having gone from his home, six miles in the country, for that purpose. In the interview which followed it was agreed that he should give them notes falling due at different times, amounting in the aggregate to $5,250, and secure the same by mortgage on real estate. He accordingly sent for his wife, who was at their home, and when she arrived the notes and mortgage were executed. The $250 which was included in the notes, in addition to the amount of the original indebtedness, was added for the purpose of covering the expenses incurred by plaintiff in connection with the settlement. Chisholm made an effort to induce the Hickses to join with him in the settlement, but they refused. He was in very feeble health at the time, and for some months had been suffering from a disease of the throat and lungs, which caused his death on the fourteenth of April following. He was a depositor in the Monroe County Bank, and lost quite heavily by its failure, and he had been greatly harassed and distressed by the loss, and the attempt to charge him with liability for the debts of the bank.

I. The first defense pleaded is that the notes and mortgage were given without consideration. This defense, it is proper to say, has not been much insisted upon

1. PROMIS-
SORY note:
considera-
tion: surren-
der of collat-
eral security:
innocent
holder.

in this court. The facts pleaded as the basis of the defense are that the signature of Chisholm to the accommodation note was obtained by fraud; the fraud being perpetrated by the cashier of the Monroe County Bank in procuring him to sign it in the belief that the signature of Shields, which had been previously attached, was genuine, while he knew it was a forgery, and that plaintiff accepted it as security for a pre-existing indebtedness, without an agreement for an extension of time or other consideration. But the fact is, as shown by the evidence, without conflict or dispute, that plaintiff accepted the note in lieu of other collaterals which it held, and which it surrendered at the time of accepting it.

On this state of facts, plaintiff is a purchaser of the note for value. It makes no difference that the collateral notes surrendered in the transaction were not delivered to plaintiff until after the loan was made. They were delivered and accepted as security for the debt. The existence of the debt was a sufficient consideration, as between the parties, for the transfer of the property. *Meyer v.' Evans,* 66 Iowa, 179. As plaintiff held those securities under a valid transfer, its surrender of them was a valid consideration for the transfer of the note to it; and, as it was a holder of the note for value, the defense that the maker's signature was obtained by the fraud alleged would not have been available against it in its hands, there being no claim that it had any notice or knowledge of the fraud by which Chisholm's signature to the note was obtained. The contract in question, then, is supported by a valid consideration.

II. The next defense pleaded, and the one principally relied on, is that Chisholm, at the time the contract was

2. ——: im-
becility of
maker: un-
due influence:
evidence not
establishing.

entered into, was in such mental condition that he was incapable of contracting. As stated above, he was, and for some time previously had been, suffering from a disease which was the one that caused his death in about three weeks after the contract was executed. He had previously been a man of great force of character, and had been engaged in business enterprises of considerable magnitude, which he had conducted with success. He had also been a man of great physical energy, and had been active in the pursuit of his business. But at the time of the transaction he was greatly reduced in physical strength, being barely able to walk, and being unable to speak above a whisper; and the evidence leaves no doubt but that his intellectual vigor was greatly impaired. In addition to the weakness caused by his disease, he had been vexed and worried by his losses and the unfortunate complication into which his affairs had fallen.

Twenty-nine witnesses were examined by defendants on the question of his mental condition, four of whom are physicians of learning and long practice in their profession. All of these witnesses had been intimately acquainted with him for many years, and they all testified with reference to their personal knowledge of the man. While none of them

claimed that he was insane or imbecile, they quite uniformly
gave it as their opinion that he was incapable, at the time,
of transacting business which was complicated, or which
involved large interests. They all admitted, however, that
they believed him competent to transact the ordinary business pertaining to his affairs. If we were to look alone at
the evidence of these witnesses, we might concur in the conclusion reached by the circuit court, that he was incapable
of contracting; but other facts are proven which must be
considered in determining the question. It is shown that
he had not ceased to give attention to his ordinary affairs, and
he transacted his business with intelligence and judgment.
His letters to plaintiff, which brought about the meeting at
Albia, at which the contract was entered into, show that his
memory was good, and that he retained a keen sense of his
liability and his obligation. He expressed himself with
clearness and perspicuity. He made an honest and clear
statement of his circumstances and intentions, and applied for
an extension of time, stating the rate of interest which he
would be willing to pay, and asked for a meeting for the purpose of adjusting the matter. These letters were written but
a few days before the accommodation note would fall due,
and were doubtless written in view of that fact. When the
day appointed for the meeting arrived, he went, notwithstanding his weakness, and against the advice of his friends, to
meet his engagement. He appears to have been actuated by
that conscientious desire to perform his undertakings which
had characterized him during all his life. His conduct and
language after the transaction show that he fully understood
what he had done, and that he regarded it as the best thing
he could have done under the circumstances. In a letter
written by him afterwards to the attorney with whom he
made the settlement, he told him that he had been criticised
for what he had done by the Hickses, and the attorneys
whose advice he had formerly taken, but that he was satisfied with the arrangement he had made.

Very shortly before the settlement, and afterwards, he transacted other matters of business which appear to us to have
been quite as complicated, although not involving as large
interests, as that in question, and in the transactions he acted
intelligently and with judgment.

These facts lead us to the conclusion that he was not *non
compos*. His mind lacked the vigor it formerly possessed,
but he was not lacking in judgment or reason, but was in
possession of all his faculties, and was fully competent to
enter into the contract. We will not be understood as unduly
disparaging the testimony of the witnesses whose opinions
on the subject were given in evidence. The four physicians
who were examined appear to be learned in their profession,
and all of the witnesses are men of candor and high character; but testimony of that kind has always been regarded as
of the lowest character of evidence, and in this case it clearly
does not overcome the evidence of the established and conceded facts.

III.   Another defense is that the contract was obtained by
the fraud of the attorney who acted for the plaintiff in making the settlement. We do not deem it necessary to discuss
the evidence relied on to establish this claim. It is sufficient
to say that we find no evidence whatever that any concealment or deceit was practiced by the attorney, or that any
undue influence was exercised to induce Mr. Chisholm to
enter into the contract. The attorney was careful to secure
the interest of his client, but he had the right, and it was
his duty, to do that, if he proceeded by fair means, and we
find no evidence that he resorted to any other.

As we reach the conclusion that the contract is supported
by a valid consideration, that the parties were competent to
enter into it, and that it was fairly entered into, it follows
that it should be enforced.

REVERSED.

HOWARD COUNTY v. STROTHER.

1. **Taxation**: PERSONAL PROPERTY IN HANDS OF RECEIVER. Where the county has acquired no lien for taxes upon personal property which has passed into the hands of a receiver, pending litigation concerning the priority of liens which have already attached sufficient to absorb the property, *held* that the county has no claim on the property, or its proceeds, in the hands of the receiver, for the taxes levied on the property. Chapter 14, Laws of 1876, making taxes a preferred claim in case of assignment for the benefit of the creditors, has no application.

Appeal from Howard Circuit Court.

TUESDAY, JUNE 14.

THE plaintiff, Howard county, made a motion for an order that the clerk of the court be directed to pay over certain money in his hands to the treasurer of the county; the motion being made on the theory that the money in question was due the county for taxes. The court overruled the motion, except as to certain taxes upon real estate. The plaintiff appeals.

Barker Bros., for appellant.

H. T. Reed and *McCartney & McCook*, for appellees.

ADAMS, CH. J.—The money in question had passed into the hands of the clerk of the court as the result of certain litigation growing out of the insolvency of the defendants Strother & Conklin. At one time they were doing business as partners. They had acquired a considerable amount of personal property, and had become largely indebted. To one person, Enoch Strother, they became indebted in the sum of $24,000, the indebtedness being for money borrowed. To other persons they had become indebted for property purchased. Enoch Strother obtained from them a chattel mortgage. Other creditors acquired liens by attachment upon the same property. Litigation arose between the creditors in respect to their liens. The court

in the mean time appointed one McHugh receiver to
take charge of the property. Afterwards he resigned, and
one Peck was appointed. The property, under the order of
the court, was converted into money, and the most of it has
been paid over to creditors who had acquired liens. A small
amount was reserved to await the determination of this
motion in respect to taxes. What was reserved, as we
understand, is awarded as due to Enoch Strother, unless the
county has a superior claim for taxes. It seems to be conceded that no one has paid taxes for this property for several
years. The taxes claimed are for the years 1877 and 1884,
and the years included. During the earlier years, Strother
& Conklin were assessed as owners of the property. For
the year 1882 the receiver McHugh was assessed, and for the
years 1883 and 1884 the receiver Peck, McHugh's successor, was assessed. The attempt is now made to enforce the
county's claim for taxes by motion directly against the property, or proceeds thereof, in the hands of the clerk of the court.

A question is raised by the appellees in regard to the
method adopted. It is contended that, if the county had a
claim which it could enforce against the property, such claim
could not be enforced by a motion. We have not thought
it necessary to determine this question, because it does not
appear to us that the county has a claim, so far as the personal
property is concerned, which it can enforce against the property in any way. It had, in respect to such property, a personal claim against Strother & Conklin, but it did not
acquire a lien for the claim, and other liens have attached
which are sufficient to absorb the property. The assessments
made against the receivers do not appear to us to be enforceable against them as receivers, so as to justify sustaining the
motion as to the taxes so assessed. The receivers did not
own the property. They held the property under the
appointment and order of the court, and merely as custo-
dians. The title was still in Strother & Conklin until disposed of under the order of the court, and the proceeds

decreed to the lienholders entitled thereto. The plaintiff relies upon a statute; (Chapter, 14, Laws of 1876;) but that is a provision for taxes in the case of an assignment. There was no assignment in the case at bar, but a contest between lienholders; and McHugh, and afterwards Peck, was appointed to hold the property to await the issue of that contest.

In our opinion, the statute has no application. We think that the court did not err.

Affirmed.

The State v. McGinnis.

71
118

1. **Criminal Law**: OBTAINING SIGNATURE BY FALSE PRETENSE: DELIVERY OF INSTRUMENT: INDICTMENT. It is essential to the commission of the crime of obtaining a signature by false pretenses to a written instrument, (Code, § 4073,) that the instrument be delivered; and an indictment which fails to charge the delivery of the instrument is insufficient.

Appeal from Webster District Court.

Tuesday, June 14.

Indictment charging that the defendant, by false pretense, obtained the signature of another person to a written instrument. Verdict, guilty; judgment. The defendant appeals.

J. F. Duncombe, for appellant.

A. J. Baker, Attorney-general, for the State.

Seevers, J.—The material portion of the indictment is as follows: That the defendant and one Smith "feloniously, designedly, by false pretense, and with intent to defraud, did falsely represent, pretend, and state to one Mathias Kammers that the said Patrick McGinnis was the owner of a certain piece of land," which he offered to sell said Kammers for a named price, and which offer was accepted; "and therefore said Patrick McGinnis and Frank Smith designedly, and by false pretense, and with intent to defraud said Mathias Kammers, did falsely represent and pretend that a certain instrument in writing, then and there exhibited to said Kammers, to-wit, a chattel mortgage from Mathias Kammers to Patrick McGinnis, for seven hundred dollars, upon certain property, (describing it,) was a contract to purchase said land, * * * and was an agreement to sell said land on the part of Patrick McGinnis, * * * and the said Kammers then and there believed said representation to be true, and was deceived thereby, and was enticed by reason of said false pretenses to sign said written instrument, and then and there did sign the same."

It will be observed that the indictment does not charge that the mortgage was delivered, but that the charge is that the signature of Kammers was obtained thereto, and counsel for the defendant insist that no crime known to the law is charged. It is provided by statute as follows: "If any person designedly, and by false pretense, or by any privy or false token, and with intent to defraud, obtain from another money, goods, or other property, or so obtain the signature of any person to any written instrument the false making of which would be punished as forgery, he shall be punished * * *" . Code, § 4073.

The question to be determined is whether, under the statute, it is essential, in order to constitute the crime, that there should be a delivery of the written instrument to which the signature was obtained by false pretense, with intent to defraud. The attorney-general concedes that if "money, goods or property is so obtained," there must be a delivery, and that the title or possession must vest at least for some time before the offense is complete; and it was so held in *State v. Anderson*, 47 Iowa, 142; but he contends that the offense is complete when the signature to the instrument is obtained. In this proposition we do not concur. It will be observed that the statute provides: "Or so obtain the signature of any person." This refers to what precedes such sentence, and that is in relation to obtaining property. If delivery or possession in one case is essential, it would seem to follow that it must be in the other. To obtain means to "get hold of; to get possession of; to acquire." Now, the statute provides that the signature must be "so obtained;" that is, it must be acquired or come into the possession of some person by means of the false pretense to the same extent as is necessary in order to constitute the offense when money or property is obtained. In such case it has been held that, in order to constitute a crime, the fraud must be accomplished. *People v. Wakely*, 28 N. W. Rep., 871. (Mich.) In *State v. House*, 55 Iowa, 466, the false representations were made in Wright county; but the notes were delivered in Polk county, where the indictment was found, and it was contended that the crime was committed in Wright county; but this court said: "The false pretenses made in Wright county were no crime, and no indictment would lie in that county, simply because the notes were not obtained there."

We are of the opinion that no crime is charged in the indictment, and therefore it follows that the judgment of the district court must be

REVERSED.

SUPPLEMENT.

[The following opinions were retained on petitions for re-hearing, and did not come into my hands in time for insertion in their chronological order.— REPORTER.]

BAILEY ET AL. v. THE MUTUAL BENEFIT ASSOCIATION.

1. **Practice on Appeal:** ABSTRACT: EVIDENCE: PRESUMPTION. Where appellant's abstract purports to be an abstract of all the evidence, this court will, in the absence of an additional abstract by the appellee, assume that the evidence was made of record, and that it is before the court.

2. **Life Insurance:** DELAY IN PAYING ASSESSMENT: FORFEITURE WAIVED. Although defendant had a right to declare the insurance in question forfeited on account of the failure to pay an assessment, yet such forfeiture was waived by afterwards, before the death of the assured, receiving the assessment and retaining it; and it makes no difference that the assessment was demanded and received by mistake, while the intention was to regard the insurance as forfeited.

3. ———: ASSESSMENT PLAN: REMEDY ON CERTIFICATE. Upon a certificate entitling the beneficiary to the net proceeds of one full assessment upon the members of the company in good standing, where it appears that the company has no funds to pay a loss except as it is raised by an assessment specially made for that purpose, *held* that an action at law against the company for what would be realized by such an assessment could not be maintained, without averring and proving that such assessment had been made, and the amount thereof. BECK, J., *dissenting.*

Appeal from Pottawattamie Circuit Court.

WEDNESDAY, APRIL 21, 1886.

ACTION to recover upon a certificate of membership in the defendant company. There was a trial to the court, and judgment was rendered for the plaintiff. The defendant appeals.

Flickinger Bros., for appellant.

M. Remley and *C. H. Scott*, for appellees.

ADAMS, CH. J.—The plaintiffs aver that they are the legal

heirs of Vincent J. Bailey, deceased; that he died intestate; and that at the time of his death his life was insured in the defendant company by a contract by which it agreed to pay his heirs "the net proceeds of one full assessment upon all members in good standing at his death, not to exceed $3,000." The defendant pleaded a general denial, and also that the contract of insurance had lapsed by non-payment of an assessment.

I. Before proceeding to the determination of the other questions involved, it is proper that we should say that the

1. PRACTICE on appeal: abstract: evidence: presumption.

plaintiff filed a motion to strike the evidence from the abstract, because it does not appear that the evidence was incorporated in any bill of exceptions properly signed by the judge. By an amendment to the abstract, the defendant sets out two certificates made by the trial judge, from which it appears that a bill of exceptions was signed. The abstract purports to be an abstract of all the evidence, and, in the absence of an additional abstract of the appellee, we must assume that the evidence was made of record, and that it is before us.

II. As to whether there was a default by the deceased in the payment of an assessment we need not determine.

2. LIFE insurance: delay in paying assessment: forfeiture waived.

There was evidence tending to show that before the death of the deceased the company received the amount of the assessment. The court below, we may presume, so found, and the evidence was sufficient to sustain the finding. It is, to be sure, insisted by the defendant that the money was demanded and received by mistake, the real intention being to regard the certificate as forfeited. But we do not think that such mistake, if made, could be regarded as material. The defendant received and held the money until after the death of the deceased, and he had a right to regard the contract as in force, regardless of any intention of the defendant to the contrary.

III. The contract called for the net proceeds of an assess

ment, not to exceed $3,000. The assessment contemplated, it

3. ——: assessment plan: remedy on certificate. appears, is an assessment made in advance of the death which gives rise to the liability. Article fourteen of the articles of incorporation is as follows: "The amount due and payable under any certificat · of membership by reason of death of the member named therein shall be the net amount collected on the advance assessment previous to the death of a member, and . received at the principal office of the association, which amount shall, in no case, exceed $3,000." There is no pretense that there is any averment in the petition as to what the proceeds of an assessment were, as called for by the certificate, nor what the net amount of an assessment was, as provided in the articles of incorporation, nor that there was an assessment at all. The plaintiffs, indeed, claim that there was no assessment, and their theory is that they are entitled to recover outside of the terms of the contract, to-wit, the gross amount of what an assessment would have been if it had been made. But, in our opinion, their position cannot be sustained. This is a mutual association. It does not appear that it has any funds with which to pay claims except the proceeds of assessments. One assessment, and only one, can be made to pay one claim, and each assessment, when made and collected, becomes a special fund, and this fund is virtually appropriated in advance. In the absence of an assessment made for the payment of the claim in question, it would be impossible to pay it without using a special fund, virtually otherwise appropriated, for the payment of another claim. If it be true, as contended, that no assessment was made to pay the claim in question, the plaintiffs, probably, are not without their remedy. But their remedy is, manifestly, not an action at law to recover what would be the amount of an assessment if made. In an action at law upon the certificate the plaintiffs must bring themselves within the terms of the certificate. They have not done so, either by the averments of their petition, or by evidence introduced. They rely upon

Neskern v. Northwestern Endowment Ass'n, 30 Minn., 406; but the contract appears to have been materially different.

The judgment of the court below must be

REVERSED.

BECK. J., (*dissenting.*)   The policy obligates the defendant to pay to the heirs of the assured "the net proceeds of one full assessment, at schedule rates, upon all the members in good standing at the date of said death, [of assured,] to an amount not to exceed $3,000." Article fourteen of the articles of incorporation provides as follows: " The amount due and payable under any certificate of membership, by reason of the death of the member named therein, shall be the net amount collected on the advance assessment previous to the death of a member, and received at the principal office of said association, which amount shall in no case exceed $3,000." The by-laws of defendant contain the following provisions:

" Sec. 19.   One assessment shall be paid in advance. No assessment will be made when the funds in the treasury are sufficient to pay a matured claim."

" Sec. 21.   Dues and assessments must be paid within thirty days from date of notice. If not paid within the time specified, the certificate will lapse, and all money paid shall be declared forfeit, and the mutual obligations shall cease."

The evidence shows that at the date of the death of the assured the number of members was 1336.   The assessment was one dollar upon each member.   There was evidence showing that each member paid the advance assessment; yet, in the absence of evidence that such assessment had not been paid, it is to be presumed that the laws of the association were obeyed, and that each member paid his assessment in advance of the death of any member, thus keeping in the treasury of the defendant a sum equal to one dollar for each member.   This presumption surely arises, and it was the duty of defendant to show, by proof, that the facts were otherwise. Plaintiff was not required to add proof to this presumption. The circuit court well found that there was in the treasury of the defendant $1,336, which, under the policy, it had contracted to pay to the heirs of the insured. It will be observed that this contract is not conditional upon payment of assessments by the members. It is absolute. A judgment, therefore, was properly rendered against defendant for the sum presumed to be realized from the assessments.

KENYON v. TRAMEL ET AL.

71 693
96 637
71 693
115 445

1. **Chattel Mortgage:** DESCRIPTION OF PROPERTY. The description of the property covered by a chattel mortgage was as follows: "Fifty head of steers about (20) months old, now owned by me, and in my possession on my farm in Independence township, Jasper county, Iowa." *Held* sufficient as against subsequent purchasers from the mortgagor, even though one of the purchasers bought some of the cattle in Clear Creek township, where they were in charge of the mortgagor's agent, on a part of his farm, which lay partly in Independence and partly in Clear Creek township.

2. **Decree:** CLERICAL ERROR: REMEDY ON APPEAL: COSTS. Where a decree is in conflict with the evidence on account of a supposed clerical error in drawing it, but is otherwise correct, it will be modified on appeal so as to correct the error, and then affirmed; but the appellant will be entitled to his costs in this court. The fact that appellant did not move for its correction in the trial court will not deprive him of relief here.

Appeal from Jasper District Court.

FRIDAY, APRIL 23, 1886.

ACTION to foreclose a chattel mortgage. Judgment for the plaintiff, and defendants appeal.

Ryan & McElroy, for appellants.

Alanson Clark, for appellee.

SEEVERS, J.—The defendant Tramel executed to the plaintiff a chattel mortgage on "fifty head of steers about (20)

1. CHATTEL mortgage: description of property. months old, now owned by me, and in my possession on my farm in Independence township, Jasper county, Iowa." The mortgage was executed and filed for record on the seventh day of January, 1884. Afterwards the defendant Baker purchased eleven, and the defendant Wilson sixteen, steers of the mortgagor. It is insisted that the description is fatally defective, and that it cannot be aided by extrinsic evidence. It appears from the evidence that the mortgagor did not have in his possession fifty steers of the age of those described at the time the mortgage was given, but he did have at least twenty-eight steers that he had purchased of one Carr. This evidence, we think, was admissible for the purpose of identifying the cattle. Baker and Wilson had constructive notice of the mortgage. When they purchased the cattle, they were bound to know that plaintiff had a mortgage on fifty head of steers which were owned by the mortgagor, and were in his possession on his farm in Independence township. Now, if they had made inquiry, as they were bound to do, the cattle mortgaged could have been identified with reasonable certainty. *Yant v. Harvey*, 55 Iowa, 421. There is no uncertainty in the mortgage, or, if there is, there is sufficient description of the property to enable an honest inquirer to identify it. *Smith v. McLean*, 24 Iowa, 322. The ownership, possession and location of the cattle all are descriptive, and this distinguishes this case from at least many, if not all, of those cited by counsel for defendant.

The fact that there were only twenty-eight head instead of fifty should not have the effect to destroy the validity of the mortgage. It will still be good as to the cattle sufficiently described.

It is said that when at least one of the defendants purchased the cattle they were not in the possession of the mortgagor on his farm in Independence township, but were in the possession of one Kinty, in Clear Creek township. This is immaterial if the cattle were in the possession of the mortgagor on the Independence farm when the mortgage was executed. The evidence is not entirely clear on this point, but, as we understand, Kinty was in possession as the agent of the mortgagor. In fact he was simply taking care of them, as we understand, on land owned by the mortgagor, or his wife, in Clear Creek township, which was known as a part of the mortgagor's farm, the greater portion of which was in Independence township. Although the farm was in two townships, it could well be regarded as a single farm, for the reason that there was no intervening land owned by others. The mortgagor resided in Independence township, and the farm was sufficiently described as being in that township. Inquiry would have clearly shown that the cattle were on that farm.

The evidence shows that Wilson purchased sixteen steers, but the decree finds that he purchased seventeen of the mortgaged steers. The decree is therefore erroneous.

2. DECREE: clerical error: remedy on appeal: costs. Counsel for the appellee concedes this, but insists that it should have been corrected on motion in the district court, for the reason that it was a clear mistake in drawing the decree. Possibly relief might have been thus obtained, but we are not prepared to say that appellants were bound to proceed in that manner, and, if they did not, would be prevented from recovering costs in this court. The mistake does not appear on the face of the decree, nor does it appear that counsel for the appellants had any knowledge of the mistake during the term.

The appellant Wilson is entitled to his costs in this court. One-half the costs must be taxed to appellee, and the residue to appellant Baker. The decree of the district court will be

MODIFIED AND AFFIRMED.

KING v. THE CHICAGO, BURLINGTON & QUINCY R'Y CO.

1. **Surface Water**: DIVERSION BY MEANS OF A DITCH: ESTOPPEL TO TURN AGAIN INTO NATURAL COURSE. The defendant, in building its railroad, spanned with a trestle a slough, along which surface water flowed, under the trestle, upon plaintiff's land below. Afterwards defendant filled the space covered by the trestle, making a solid embankment, and cut a channel along its embankment to carry the water to the river. The diversion of the water was beneficial to plaintiff. But the channel proved inadequate, and caused some of the adjacent lands to be overflowed, and the abutment of defendant's bridge at the river was in danger of being undermined by the water flowing through the ditch. To avoid these results, defendant was about to construct a culvert in its embankment to allow the water to flow again in its original and natural course. The amount of the water had in the mean time been augmented by the fact that some of the land-owners above the embankment had drained their lands by ditches into the slough. Plaintiff sought to enjoin defendant from again turning the water into its natural course, on the ground that he would thereby be damaged, and that defendant was estopped from so doing on account of its having taken control of the water and directed its course in another way. But, as it does not appear that plaintiff did anything in reliance upon the permanency of the diversion of the water, or that he would, on account of anything done by defendant, be in any worse condition by its return to its natural course than he was before its diversion. *held* that there was no estoppel, and that the injunction was not warranted. BECK, J., *dissenting.*

Appeal from Montgomery District Court.

THURSDAY, OCTOBER 7, 1886.

PLAINTIFF brought this action in equity, to restrain the defendant from constructing a culvert or water-way through an embankment on which the track of its railroad is laid. He alleges that the opening of said culvert or water-way through the embankment would have the effect to throw upon his premises, which are adjacent to the railroad, a large amount of surface water, which is drained onto defendant's right of way from the land lying on the opposite side of the railroad from his farm; also to submerge and render impassable a public highway which is the thoroughfare by which he reaches his market town. The district court entered judgment granting the relief demanded, and defendant appeals.

Smith McPherson and *C. E. Richards*, for appellant.

W. S. Strawn and *Frank M. Davis*, for appellee.

REED, J.—Defendant's railway was constructed in 1869. At the point in question it crosses a slough, or swale, through which the surface water from several hundred acres of land lying on the north side of the track found its way to the Nishnabotna river. In the original construction of the railway, this slough was spanned by a trestle, which permitted the passage through defendant's right of way of all the water which came upon it from the north through the slough. The track was maintained in this condition until 1879, when defendant filled the space covered by the trestle, making a continuous embankment which prevented the passage of the water. It also constructed a ditch on the north side of its track, through which it sought to conduct the water to the river. This ditch was not of sufficient capacity, however, to carry all of the water which came through the slough, and it caused a portion of the lands lying on the north side of the track to be overflowed. It was also found that the abutment of defendant's bridge over the river was in danger of being undermined by the water which flowed through the ditch. The owner of the land which was overflowed by the water from the ditch brought suit against defendant to recover the damages caused thereby, and, in compromise of that suit, defendant agreed that it would either enlarge the ditch, or reopen the passage-way for the water through the embankment. It elected to take the latter course, and was proceeding to open a water-way through the embankment when this suit was instituted.

Between the time of the construction of the railroad and the closing of the water-way, in 1879, there had been a

material increase in the amount of water which flowed
through the slough, caused by ditches which had been constructed by the owners of some of the land which drained
into the slough, for the reclamation or improvement of their
lands. And during the time the water-way was closed there
had also been an increase in the amount of water in the
slough, resulting from like causes. Plaintiff's land is south
of the track. It does not abut on defendant's right of way,
but, if the water-way through the embankment should be
opened, the water which will flow through it, after passing
over the intervening land, will enter upon his premises, and
overflow and render unfit for cultivation a portion of his
land. It will also overflow, and at times render impassable,
a highway which affords plaintiff the most convenient way
of access to the town at which he trades.

The question which arises upon the facts is whether
defendant is bound to maintain the embankment in such
condition as to protect plaintiff's premises and said highway
from the water which comes upon its right of way through
said slough. It has not been claimed that defendant originally owed plaintiff any duty in that respect. Before its
railroad was constructed, the water naturally flowed through
the slough, and found its way onto plaintiff's premises, and
at times portions of his land and the highway were overflowed by it. Very clearly plaintiff had no right originally
to demand that the embankment should be so constructed
and maintained as to form a protection to his premises
against the water. The position urged by counsel, however,
is that, when defendant assumed to take charge of the water,
and undertook to conduct it to the river through another
channel, it relinquished all right to have it conducted away
from its premises by the natural channel, and, as the reopen-
ing of the water-way through the embankment would work
an injury to the lower estate, it is now estopped from opening it.

But it is very clear, we think, that plaintiff is not entitled to recover on the ground that defendant is estopped by its previous acts from opening the water-way. What was done by defendant had the appearance, it is true, of being a permanent work. But it is an essential element of an estoppel *in pais* that the one pleading it, or those under whom he claims, should have relied on the act or representation alleged, and been induced by it to alter his position with reference to the subject to which it related. 2 Pars. Cont. 703; *Lucas v. Hart*, 5 Iowa, 415.

It is not claimed, however, that plaintiff did anything in reliance on the permanency of the work done by defendant. The closing of the water-way had the effect to render arable the portions of his land which before that were subject to overflow, and he cultivated them. He simply availed himself of such benefits as resulted from the act done by defendant, but he did nothing himself which contributed to the result. If the water-way should be opened, he would be placed in precisely the same position he would have occupied if it had never been closed. This essential element of an estoppel is clearly wanting in the case. When defendant constructed its embankment, it had the undoubted right to leave a way for the passage of the water through it. By so doing it neither increased the amount of water, nor otherwise changed the flow upon the lower estate. It simply permitted it to flow through its premises by its natural course.

As the water was mere surface water, it had the right to make provision for the protection of its premises from injury from it. Its act in closing the passage-way through the embankment, and constructing the ditch, was not an invasion of any of plaintiff's rights. Neither did it create any new duty or obligation from it to him. There is no legal principle upon which it can be said that defendant is bound to protect plaintiff's premises for all time from the surface water which would flow upon them, because for a time it maintained a work which had that effect. The work was done originally for the amelioration of defendant's estate. and in that respect it was lawful; but the relative rights and obligations of the parties remained the same after as before it was done.

The fact that a greater quantity of water will flow through the water-way than did before it was closed, does not affect the rights or obligations of these parties. That effect will follow, not from anything which defendant has done or pro-posed to do, but will be the result of what has been done by other parties. We need not inquire whether those acts are unlawful or not, for, if it should be conceded that they are unlawful, defendant is under no obligation to protect plaint-iff from the consequences which will result from them. If the act of the adjacent land-owners in draining their land into the slough was wrongful, defendant has the right, doubtless, to take such action as would protect its own premises from injury by the increased amount of water thrown upon them. But it is not under obligation to pro-tect plaintiff's premises from injury by that cause.

The judgment of the district court will be

REVERSED.

BECK, J., (*dissenting*.) I find it unnecessary to inquire whether the water diverted by defendant was surface water or a stream. That defendant did divert the water, whatever be its character, is admitted. It took control of the water, and directed its course away from the land of plaintiff. Its motive for so doing, doubtless, rested upon benefits, or sup-posed benefits, which it would receive therefrom. Among these benefits was, doubtless, one regarded of importance, namely, the dispensing with the bridge or trestle-work of perishable materials, and the substitution therefor of the more substantial and safer embankment of earth, which in the end would be cheaper. The act of building the embank-ment in place of the bridge was inconsistent with the act of again opening it. It was, in effect, a declaration that the bridge was dispensed with, and an invitation for plaintiff, and all other persons, to so act and to so use and control their lands, which would be affected by the change, as their interests demanded. As plaintiff's land was relieved of water flowing through the bridge, it will be presumed to be beneficial to him, for the reason that all lands, whether cultivated or used for meadow or pasture, of either tame or wild grass, are injured by the overflow of water in excess of the natural rainfall. The law will presume injury from such overflow. Section 1, Phil. Ev., (Cow. & H. & Edw. notes,) 546, marg. p. 656.

But there is direct evidence in the record showing injury which would be sustained by plaintiff from the water. The plaintiff testifies, and the evidence is corroborated by other witnesses, that his lands which would be affected by defend-ant's act in opening the embankment would be worth twice as much with defendant's embankment closed as it would be with it open.

It appears that plaintiff acquiesced in the change in the embankment caused by filling up the space occupied by the bridge, and, as it was to his advantage, it will be presumed that he sanctioned and accepted the beneficial act of defend-ant in filling up the opening originally left in the embank-ment,—$_1$ Phil. Ev., (Cow. & H. & Edw. notes,) 505, marg. p. 609,—and it will be presumed that plaintiff used his land affected by the water, and improved it, with reference to the change in the embankment, for the reason that it appears from the record that he is in the occupation and use of the land, and has been since the change. No farmer could cul-tivate or use land similarly situated without improving it, for its use alone, whether for cultivation or for pasture, would improve it; cultivation and use being a source of great improvement of wet lands, or lands in swales, of the character of plaintiff's land.

It clearly appears that to restore the bridge will result in plaintiff's injury. Defendant is now estopped to take from plaintiff the benefits and rights it bestowed upon him by diverting the water. The facts, as we have just stated them, precisely fill the conditions of an estoppel, as they are tersely and correctly stated by defendant's counsel. The law will not permit defendant, for its own convenience or profit, to change the course of the water of a stream, or surface water, after having established its course, and held out inducements to adjoining owners to believe such a course permanent, and to act accordingly. Such owners would be subject to loss, inconvenience and annoyance, if defendant could, at will, divert the flow of surface water once established by it.

Doubtless the motive of defendant in restoring the bridge, and abandoning the ditch, was to save expense required to sink it deeper, and in securing the embankment from washing, and in protecting the abutments of the bridge at the river. It is not to be doubted that all of this could have been done, but at an expense greater than would have been incurred by removal of the embankment and the reconstruction of the bridge. But these matters should have been considered and weighed before defendant, by the filling up the embankment, conferred rights upon plaintiff. These rights defendant cannot now defeat upon the mere ground that expense will be saved thereby.

In my judgment, the judgment of the district court ought to be affirmed.

KREKEL v. KREICHBAUM ET AL.

1. **Estoppel:** FACTS CONSTITUTING. A. held a first, and B. a second, mortgage on a stock of goods. The sheriff had levied a number of attachments on the stock, all of which were subsequent to A.'s mortgage, but some of which were prior, and some subsequent, to B.'s mortgage. A. replevied the goods from the sheriff, and B. was the surety on his bond. It was agreed between A. and B. that the latter should hold the replevied goods, or their proceeds, for his indemnity as surety. The goods were sold pending the action, and B. held the proceeds. It was determined in the action that A.'s mortgage was fraudulent and of no

effect as against the attaching creditors, and judgment was rendered against him and B., his surety, for the value of the goods, which, by agreement of all the parties, was the amount of the proceeds in B.'s hands. It was also agreed between all the parties that B. should surrender said proceeds to the sheriff in satisfaction of the judgment, which he did. Afterwards, but before the sheriff had disbursed such proceeds, B. brought suit against the sheriff to recover, as a mortgagee, such of the proceeds as were not required to satisfy the attachments which were prior to his mortgage, but *held* that, having purchased immunity from the judgment by the surrender of such proceeds, he was estopped from setting up such claim under his mortgage.

Appeal from Des Moines Circuit Court.

FRIDAY, OCTOBER 8, 1886.

THE defendant Kreichbaum is sheriff of Des Moines county, and the other defendants are sureties on his official bond. Plaintiff brought an action to recover the value of his interest in a stock of goods on which he held a chattel mortgage. There was a trial to the court without the intervention of a jury, and the judgment was for defendants. The facts are stated in the opinion. Plaintiff appeals.

S. L. Glasgow, for appellant.

Newman & Blake, Hall & Huston, Smyth & Sons and *Poor & Baldwin,* for appellees.

REED, J.—On the seventeenth of October, 1882, Erb & Schaefer, a firm of merchants doing business in the city of Burlington, executed to one Henry Schaefer a chattel mortgage on the stock of merchandise owned by them, to secure an alleged indebtedness of $7,384. This mortgage was filed for record on the day on which it was executed, but the mortgagors retained possession of the property. On the twenty-fourth of the same month, a creditor of Erb & Shaefer sued out a writ of attachment in an action then pending in the circuit court of Des Moines county, and the same was placed in the hands of defendant Kreichbaum for service, and on the same day he served the writ by taking

possession of the property covered by said mortgage. On
the next day two other attachments against the property of
Erb & Schaefer were placed in his hands, and he levied them
on the same property, the levies being made subject to that
made on the twenty-fourth. On the same day, but after
said writs had been levied, Erb & Schaefer executed to plaintiff a mortgage on the same property, to secure an indebtedness of $1,600. This mortgage recited that it was given
suject to the mortgage to Henry Schaefer. It was filed for
record on the day on which it was executed, and on the next
day the defendant levied seven other writs of attachment,
which came into his hands for service, on the property. On
the eleventh of the following November the said Henry
Schaefer brought an action against the sheriff to recover
possession of the property. He filed the bond prescribed by
Code, § 3229, and the clerk issued an order for the delivery
of the property to him, and this order was duly executed.
The plaintiff in this action was surety on the bond, and, to
indemnify him against his liability thereon, it was agreed
between him and Henry Schaefer that he should have the
control of the property, or of its proceeds, in case it should
be sold during the pendency of the action. It was sold
before the cause was tried, and the 'money derived from the
sale was placed in plaintiff's hands. The action was removed
to the circuit court of the United States, and was tried in
that court. In the answer filed by the defendant in the
action, it was alleged that the mortgage under which Schaefer
claimed was given without consideration, and was executed
for the purpose of defrauding the creditors of Erb & Schaefer;
and on the trial the mortgage was adjudged to be fraudulent
and void as against the creditors.

The amount realized from the sale of the goods was less
than the amount of the debt due the attaching creditors; but,
after the court found the Schaefer mortgage fraudulent, it was
agreed between the sheriff and attaching creditors on the one
side, and Schaefer and this plaintiff on the other, that the

money derived from the sale of the property which was then
in plaintiff's hands should be paid over to the sheriff, and
should be accepted in full satisfaction of the liability of
Schaefer and the sureties in the replevin bond. A judgment was accordingly entered which determined the right of
the sheriff to the possession of the property, and fixed its
value at the amount which had been realized from its sale,
and, the plaintiff electing to take execution for the value of
the property, it was adjudged that execution issue for that
amount against Schaefer and the sureties on the replevin
bond. The judgment also ordered that the amount, when
collected, should be applied in satisfaction of the debts due
the attaching creditors in the order in which their attachments had been served. Plaintiff thereupon paid over to the
sheriff the money in his hands in satisfaction of the judgment, and the sheriff was proceeding to make the application of the fund directed by the judgment. But before he
had completed the disbursement of the money, plaintiff
served a written notice upon him, notifying him that he
claimed the property from the sale of which the fund was
derived, and he subsequently brought this action for the
enforcement of that claim; his position being that by his
mortgage he acquired a lien upon the property junior to
that acquired by the attaching creditors whose writs were
levied before said mortgage was executed, but superior to all
claims of those whose writs were subsequently levied, and
that this lien attached to the fund derived from the sale of
the property. It is proper to say, in this connection, that
the debt secured by plaintiff's mortgage is now due, and the
amount of the fund which would remain after satisfying the
attachments which were levied before the mortgage was executed would exceed the amount of that debt.

The position chiefly urged by defendants is that plaintiff
is estopped by his agreement that the fund should be applied
in satisfaction of the amount of the judgment rendered
against him in the United States circuit court from asserting

that he has a lien upon it under his mortgage, and it appears to us that there is no satisfactory answer to this position. It may be conceded that plaintiff had a lien upon the property which was junior only to that of the attachments which were levied before his mortgage was executed, and that this lien attached to the fund derived from the sale of the property. The judgment in the circuit court of the United States conclusively determined, however, that he and Schaefer were liable to defendant and the attaching creditors for the value of the goods. For the purpose of relieving himself from that liability, he agreed to pay over the fund, and consented that it should be applied in satisfaction of that judgment. He did pay it over, and it was so applied. His agreement that the fund should be so applied constituted the consideration for his release from liability on the judgment. By this action he seeks, in effect, to appropriate a portion of the fund to his own use, while retaining all the benefits and advantages which he secured by his agreement that it should be applied to another use, and which constituted the consideration for such agreement. That he is not entitled to do this we think is entirely clear. When he consented that the fund should be appropriated to the satisfaction of the judgment, and by that means purchased immunity from further liability thereon, he relinquished all personal claim upon it.

The judgment of the circuit court is clearly right.

AFFIRMED.

THE STATE v. BOLANDER.

1. **Larceny**: APPROPRIATION OF PROPERTY FOUND: EVIDENCE. In this case, *held* that the jury was warranted in finding either that defendant stole the pocket-book from the prosecuting witness' satchel, or else that he found it, and knew whose it was, but appropriated it to his own use, (Code, § 3907,) and that a verdict of guilty was properly rendered.

2. ——: ——: INSTRUCTION. In such case the court instructed the jury that "if one finds goods or property of another, knowing the owner, and takes them or it away, with the intention of converting the

same to his own use, and thereby deprive the owner of them, and he afterwards returns the goods when detected, or for any other reason, such return will not purge the act of the crime of larceny." *Held* not erroneous, when the evidence tended to show that defendant knew the owner of the property found by him, (which was a pocket-book contain- ing money,) and that he destroyed the pocket-book and appropriated most of the money to his own use, but afterwards sent to the owner other money in amount almost equal to the sum contained in the pocket- book when found.

Appeal from Hardin District Court.

FRIDAY, OCTOBER 15, 1886.

INDICTMENT FOR LARCENY. The jury found the defendant guilty, and from the judgment he appeals.

J. H. Scales, for appellant.

A. J. Baker, Attorney-general, for the State.

SEEVERS, J.—Miss Eustice, the prosecuting witness, testi- fied that she was at a hotel in Ackley, and had a pocket-book, which was in a hand-bag or satchel, and that there was in the pocket-book $88 in money, and that she placed the satchel on a chair in a room for a short time to see about her baggage, and when she returned she saw the defendant at or near the door of her room. Shortly afterwards she left the hotel in an omnibus driven by or in charge of the defend- ant, and went to the depot, where she took a train for Hamp- ton. When she left the hotel, she carried the hand-bag in her hand, and took it with her to Hampton, and threw it on a table, which caused it to open, and upon then searching for the pocket-book she found it and the money gone. About two weeks afterwards the defendant returned, or caused to be returned, to her, $86 in money. The defendant was a witness in his own behalf, and testified that he found the pocket-book in the omnibus after the prosecuting witness had left, and prior to leaving the depot to return to the hotel. The defendant testified that some man rode in the omnibus with the prosecuting witness. This she denied. He further testified that two men got in the omnibus after the plaintiff left it, and were there when he picked up the pocket-book; but who they were he did not know, nor was he able to describe them. The defendant testified that he removed the money from the pocket-book, and threw the pocket-book into a privy. There is no evidence tending to show that the defendant made any inquiry for the owner of the money, or that he informed any one but his wife that he had found it. There is evidence which tends to show that, when he was spoken to about it, he did not deny that the money belonged to the plaintiff, and he seemed then entirely willing to return it to her. There is also evidence tending to show that he said he had won the money at poker. Such is the material evidence.

I. Counsel for the appellant say the defendant "ought not to be convicted, and, if the sentence is sustained, it will

1. LARCENY: appropriation of property found: evidence. be an outrage on justice." The verdict, we think, is undoubtedly right. The jury were warranted in finding that defendant took the pocket-book from the prosecuting witness' satchel, and that he did not find the money in the omnibus; but, if he did so find it, the jury were warranted in finding that he knew the owner, and was therefore guilty, under the statute, of larceny.

II. The only criticism of the third paragraph of the charge is in these words: "It is an attempt to draw the minds of the jury to the theory of the prosecution, and indirectly directs them to consider the assumption of the prosecution as proof. There was no proof of any taking, as detailed in the instruction, as an hypothesis of guilt." We deem it sufficient to say that the instruction, in our opinion, is without a doubt correct. It is the usual instruction given where the charge is larceny.

III. The fourth paragraph of the charge is in these words: "If one finds goods or property, and knowing who is

2. ——: ——: instruction. the owner, converts the property to his own use, he is guilty of larceny; and if one finds goods or property of another, knowing the owner, and takes them or it away, with the intention of converting the same to his own

use, and thereby deprive the owner of them, and he afterwards returns the goods when detected, or for any other reason, such return will not purge the act of the crime of larceny." It is provided by statute that, "if any person come, by finding, to the possession of any personal property of which he knows the owner, and unlawfully appropriates the same, or any part therof, to his own use, he is guilty of larceny." (Code, § 3907.) It is said that the instruction is erroneous, because a mere mental appropriation is not sufficient; that the defendant must have known the owner, and, if he returned the property, then he did not in fact appropriate it to his own use. The question whether he knew the owner was for the jury, and, as applied to the evidence, the instruction in relation to the return of the money, in our opinion, is clearly correct. By giving the defendant the benefit of a doubt, it is possibly true that he returned a portion of the money taken or found; but much the larger portion of it was money of the same amount or value, but it was not the identical money of which the prosecuting witness had been deprived, and therefore the defendant did unlawfully appropriate to his own use the greater portion of the money taken or found. The fact that he may have returned other and different money is wholly immaterial. The instruction is not erroneous, and, under the evidence, is favorable to the defendant.

Paragraphs 8, 10, and 11 of the charge are briefly criticized by counsel, and we have, as in duty bound, examined them, and readily conclude that they are not erroneous or in any respect prejudicial.

Instructions were asked by the defendant and refused. In relation thereto, counsel simply say they "should have been given, as they contained the law of the defense, which was not given in the charge of the court." We deem it sufficient to say that the charge of the court covers the whole ground, and is as favorable to the defendant as the evidence justified. There was no error in refusing the instructions asked. AFFIRMED.

SILTZ v. THE HAWKEYE INS. Co.

1. **Evidence:** ADMISSION: ERROR WITHOUT PREJUDICE. The admission of incompetent testimony on a certain point is without prejudice when the same point is conclusively established by other competent testimony.

2. **Fire Insurance:** ACTION ON POLICY: DESIGNATION OF LOST GOODS: EVIDENCE. Where part of the insured property was designated in the policy as "restaurant goods," *held*, in an action to recover on the policy, that it was not error to allow plaintiff to refer to the same property by that name, and ask a witness its value. If the designation was definite enough to be used in the policy, it was definite enough for use on the trial.

3. **Appeal:** POINTS NOT ARGUED. Questions merely stated in the argument, but not argued, are not considered by this court.

4. **Instructions:** METHOD OF PRESENTING ISSUES. It is not necessary that all the issues be presented in the statement of the pleadings and issues preceding the instructions. It is sufficient if they be all fairly and fully presented somewhere in the charge.

5. **Fire Insurance:** ACTION ON POLICY: VALUE OF PROPERTY: EVIDENCE. In an action to recover on a policy of fire insurance, where the plaintiff testified that she paid $3,500 for the property, and its value was stated at that sum in the application, *held* that, in the absence of other evidence, the jury was warranted in finding that it was worth that sum.

6. ——: ——: FRAUD OF INSURED: INSTRUCTIONS. In such case, where the policy provided that "any fraud, or attempt to defraud," on the part of the assured, would defeat a recovery, *held* that it was sufficient for the court to instruct the jury as to the *acts* relied on by defendant to defeat recovery under this clause, without distinguishing the actual frauds from the attempts to defraud.

7. **Verdict:** MAY FOLLOW EVIDENCE WITHOUT INSTRUCTIONS. Where a material fact is stated in the pleadings and is not contradicted, and the evidence fully establishes it, the jury may properly find that the statement is true, without an instruction to that effect.

8. **Fire Insurance:** FORFEITURE OF POLICY: WAIVER: REVIVAL. The forfeiture of a policy on account of a breach of its conditions may be waived, whereupon it will have the same binding force which it originally possessed. (*Viele v. Germania Ins. Co.*, 26 Iowa, 9, followed.)

9. ——: WARRANTY IN APPLICATION: WAIVER. Error in a statement in an application for fire insurance, which is made a warranty by the

policy, cannot be relied on to defeat the policy, where the agent who took the application was fully informed as to the facts: but the error will be regarded as waived. (See opinion for authorities cited.)

Appeal from Decatur District Court.

TUESDAY, OCTOBER 19, 1886.

ACTION at law upon a policy of insurance, to recover the amount insured against loss by fire upon a building and certain contents, owned by plaintiff. There was a judgment upon a verdict for plaintiff. Defendant appeals.

Phillips & Day, for appellant.

E. W. Curry, Bullock & Hoffman and J. B. Johnson, for appellee.

BECK, J.—I. We will, in the consideration of the case, notice the objections to the judgment in the order of their presentation by defendant's counsel, and will state the facts involved in each point in connection with the discussion thereof.

F. S. Siltz, the husband of plaintiff, and a witness in her behalf, testified that, three or four days after the fire, W. C.

1. **EVIDENCE: admission: error without prejudice.** Cole came to the house of the witness, claiming to represent defendant, and that the purpose of his visit was to settle and adjust the loss. He made out proofs of loss. The witness was then permitted to state, over defendant's objection, that Cole said he was the assistant secretary of defendant. The evidence was admitted upon the proposition of plaintiff's counsel to follow it with other evidence showing the official relation of Cole to defendant. Such evidence was afterwards introduced, and shows conclusively that he was the assistant secretary, and a director and stockholder of the company; that he visited the plaintiff as an agent of the company, after the loss, with reference to it; and that he prepared papers, or superintended or assisted in their preparation, pertaining to the proofs of

loss, though he did not complete such proofs. The fact that Cole was assistant secretary of defendant being conclusively established by other testimony, the admission in evidence of his declarations or statements to that effect, if erroneous, is without prejudice to defendant.

II. The policy covered certain personal property, described in it as "restaurant goods." A witness was asked the value of these goods, and in response was permitted, over defendant's objection, to state it. The objection is based upon the ground that the question called upon the witness to construe the language of the policy, and determine what goods were covered by the description. There is no force in the objection. If the goods were so generally known as to be described in the policy by the designation "restaurant goods," it will be presumed that the witness understood the designation. He certainly could refer to the goods by the name used in the policy to designate them. If any question existed as to the goods valued by him belonging to the class covered by the policy, the witness could have been called on, in the cross-examination, to further describe the goods to which he referred in his answer.

2. FIRE insurance: action on policy: designation of lost goods: evidence.

III. Two or three objections to the admission of evidence are referred to in defendant's argument simply by a statement of the points made, without any argument thereon. We are not required to consider points not argued.

3. APPEAL: points not argued.

IV. The policy contains a condition to the effect that, in case of loss, if there be liens or incumbrances on the property, defendant shall be liable for no more than three-fourths of the interest of assured, after deducting from the actual cash value of the property the amount of the liens or incumbrances. The answer alleges that there was a mortgage upon the property, and that its value, determined by the terms of the policy, did not exceed the amount due upon the mortgage. Counsel for

4. INSTRUCTIONS: method of presenting issues.

defendant complain that the court below omitted to present the issues raised by this defense. There is no ground for this complaint. The defense pleaded, and the issues thereon, are fairly and fully presented in an instruction,—the tenth. It is as well presented in that connection as though it had been found in the statement of the pleadings and issues preceding the instructions.

V. The court, in the same instruction, directed the jury, if they found plaintiff entitled to recover, to deduct the amount of the mortgage from the value of the property, and if the sum thus ascertained equaled or exceeded the amount they found for plaintiff, which must not exceed the sum insured on the property, they could render a verdict for the plaintiff in the amount thus found for her. Counsel insist that this instruction should not have been given, for the reason that there was no evidence of the value of the property. Upon this question there was no controversy in the evidence at the trial. Plaintiff testified that she gave $3,500 for the real estate, and its value is stated at that sum in the application for insurance. In the absence of any evidence or claim to the contrary, the jury were authorized, for the purpose of the inquiry, to find its value in that sum.

5. FIRE Insurance: action on policy: value of property: evidence.

VI. The policy contained a condition to the effect that "any fraud, or attempt to defraud, or false oath or declaration, or claim for an amount more than is actually due," shall defeat recovery on the policy. The answer alleges that plaintiff violated this condition by filing her petition in this case, under oath, alleging the value of the property destroyed to be $1,000, and that the amount of the policy ($750) is due her, and did not disclose the existence of the mortgage; that she further violated it in her proofs of loss, by stating the value of the personal property at a sum in excess of its true value; and that she also violated the condition by claiming, in her proofs of loss, a sum largely in excess of what was actually due her. It is

6. ——: ——: fraud of insured: instructions.

insisted that this defense was not fairly and fully presented
by instructions to the jury. The ground of counsel's complaint is that the court did not distinguish between fraud and
attempt to defraud, and direct the jury accordingly. We
think it was needless for the court to burden the jury with
such distinctions and instructions, and that the jury were
sufficiently instructed upon the issue presented by the defense.
The answer alleges certain acts and omissions of the plaintiff which it is claimed, under the condition in question, are
sufficient to defeat recovery. The court below correctly
directed the jury as to the legal effect of the acts of plaintiff
relied upon to support the defense. It was not necessary nor
important that the court should have considered or directed
the jury to consider whether these acts were frauds or
attempts to defraud. Without such an inquiry, the jury
were well prepared to find, as to the facts, in accord with the
instructions of the court.

VII. The defendant, as a defense under a condition of
the policy, set up in its answer the existence of a mortgage.
The plaintiff in her reply alleged that, when the insurance
was effected, she fully explained to defendant's agent all matters connected with the mortgage, the date of its execution,
and amount paid upon it, the date of its maturity, the fact
that she held a valid defense for a partial failure of consideration, which she intended to set up, and that, in order to obtain
an abatement of the amount due upon the face of the mortgage,
she was advised that it would be necessary to permit an
action of foreclosure to be brought upon it, which she
intended to do. She further stated in her reply that any
breaches of the condition of the policy which may have
occurred were waived by the act of the assistant secretary of
defendant in requiring and taking proof of loss, which he
pronounced sufficient, at the same time informing plaintiff
that the loss would be paid.

VIII. It is objected that an instruction (the fifth) directs
the jury that matters may be regarded as raising a waiver of

the breach of conditions which were not pleaded in plaintiff's reply. This objection we find, upon a comparison of the reply and instruction, is not supported by the facts. We find that all matters contemplated in the instruction are pleaded in the reply.

IX. It is urged by counsel, in their discussion of the fifth instruction, that neither in it nor elsewhere did the court direct the jury to find that Cole, who, it is alleged, acted for defendant in making the waiver, was authorized so to do. But the authority of Cole to act for defendant was proved beyond question in the court below. As we have shown, he was proved to be the assistant secretary, and the reply pleading the waiver alleges that he acted for defendant as assistant secretary in doing the things upon which the claim of waiver is based. The allegations of the reply are not denied by the defendant, and the evidence shows, without contradiction, that Cole was assistant secretary, and did act for defendant. Under these circumstances, we think there was no prejudicial error in the failure of the court to direct the jury to find as to Cole's authority to do the acts upon which the claim of waiver is based.

7. VERDICT: may follow evidence without instructions.

X. Counsel for defendant insist that, by the breach of the conditions of the policy, it becomes "null and void," and incapable of being revived or restored by a waiver of the breach. The grounds upon which this view is based are noticed and considered in *Viele v. Germania Ins. Co.*, 26 Iowa, 9; and it is held that the forfeiture of a policy on account of a breach of its conditions may be waived, whereupon it will have the same binding force it originally possessed. This court has not recognized a contrary doctrine.

8. FIRE insurance: forfeiture of policy: waiver: revival.

XI. The application for the insurance states that the mortgage upon the property remains unpaid to the amount of $400, and that the incumbrance was due in 1882. The statements of the application are warranties on the part of the assured. It was shown that there was $440 remaining unpaid upon the mortgage, and

9. ——: warranty in application: waiver.

that it matured in 1881. But the policy was issued in 1883. The court below instructed the jury, substantially, that if they should find that defendant's soliciting agent who took plaintiff's application was truly informed of the facts by plaintiff, and that the mortgage was due, but she did not intend to pay it until it was foreclosed, to enable her to set up a defense as to the partial failure of consideration, the defense of the breach of the warranties cannot be supported. The instruction is assailed by counsel with a good deal of earnestness. The knowledge of the facts possessed by the agent is chargeable to the defendant, and it will be held to have waived objection to the incorrect or false statements of the application. *Jordan v. State Ins. Co.*, 64 Iowa, 216; *Boetcher v. Hawkeye Ins. Co.*, 47 Id., 253; *Miller v. Mut. Benefit Life Ins. Co.*, 31 Id., 216. See, also, *Stone v. Hawkeye Ins. Co.*, 68 Id., 737.

XII. The foregoing discussion disposes of all questions arising upon rulings on instructions discussed by counsel. One or two instructions asked by defendant, which were based upon the evidence as claimed by counsel, were properly refused, as being inapplicable to the proof.

XIII. It is insisted that the verdict lacks the support of the evidence. We think otherwise. Upon some points, as the value of the property insured, and the like, the evidence may be meager, and not wholly satisfactory to us. But it cannot be said that there is such an absence of evidence as requires us, under the familiar rules prevailing here, to reverse the judgment.

In our opinion, the judgment of the district court ought to be

AFFIRMED.

HAWLEY v. THE CHICAGO, BURLINGTON & QUINCY RAILWAY
COMPANY.

71	717
80	243
71	717
83	387
71	717
88	413
71	717
90	
(	
(	
1(	
1(	
71	
103	
71	
125	
71	
131	
71	
144	

1. **Personal Injury**: ACTION BY ASSIGNEE. The assignee of a claim for
damages through a personal injury may maintain an action thereon.
(*Vimont v. Chicago & N. W. R'y Co.*, 69 Iowa, 296, followed.)

2. **Pleading**: PENDENCY OF OTHER ACTION. An answer to an action
brought by an assignee, which states that the assignor, previous to his
assignment to the plaintiff, commenced an action against the defendant
for the same claim in his own name; that said action was removed to
the circuit court of the United States; and that no order had been made
dismissing it, and that the defendant has not stipulated that it should
be dismissed, but which fails to aver that the action is still pending,
held not sufficient as a plea of the pendency of another action.

3. **Special Interrogatories**: NOT DETERMINATIVE: UNNECESSARY:
AMBIGUOUS. Certain special interrogatories asked on the trial of this
case *held* to have been properly refused, because the answers, however
given, would not have been determinative of the case; and, as to one,
there was no dispute as to the evidence, and others were ambiguous.

4. **Railroads**: PERSONAL INJURY: CARE REQUIRED OF EMPLOYE FOR HIS
OWN SAFETY. Plaintiff's assignor was an employe of defendant, and
he was run down by a train, and injured, while riding on a hand car in
the performance of his duty. In an action to recover for the injury, the
court instructed the jury that it was his duty " to be reasonably vigilant
and watchful, in view of what he knew, or might reasonably have
expected, as to the movement of the engine, to exercise his senses of
seeing and hearing as a reasonably prudent man would have done under
the circumstances." *Held* correct, as against the objection that it did
not emphasize sufficiently the perils to which he was exposed.

5. ———: ———: ———. In such case, where the evidence tended to show
that the employe was told by the engineer of the engine which struck
him that it would not start for fifteen minutes, but that it actually struck
him in about seven minutes, he could not be charged with negligence in
not keeping a vigilant watch in his rear up to the time of the accident,
even though, had he done so, he might have been able to get off the
track in time to avoid the injury; for he had a right to repose some confidence in what had been told him.

6. ———: ———: RELIANCE UPON ENGINEER'S STATEMENT AS TO MOVE-
MENT OF TRAIN. In such case, while the engineer was subject to the
orders of the conductor, and the employe had no right to rely upon
what he said as to the time the train would start as being *authoritative*,
yet, where the engineer stated, as a reason why it would not start for
fifteen minutes, that they would have to light up and oil up first, *held*

that the employe might rely upon such statement as *information*, and might with reason expect that, after having been so informed, he would not be run down within half that time; for the engineer was not bound to obey the conductor as to the movement of the train, if by so doing he was likely to run down the hand car, and endanger the lives of those on it.

Appeal from Polk Circuit Court.

TUESDAY, OCTOBER 21, 1886.

ACTION for a personal injury. There was a trial to a jury, and verdict and judgment were rendered for the plaintiff. The defendant appeals.

Runnells & Walker, J. W. Blythe and *H. H. Trimble,* for appellant.

Nourse & Kauffman, for appellee.

ADAMS, CH. J.—One Faught, an employe upon the defendant's road, was, on the night of the twenty-fourth of June, 1882, operating, with others, a hand car on the road, going south from Davis City, and, while so engaged, was injured by reason of an engine upon the road being run against the hand car while following it from behind. Faught's claim for damages he has assigned to the plaintiff.

The questions presented to the jury were, as to whether any of the persons in charge of the engine were guilty of negligence in running upon the hand car, and, if so, whether the plaintiff had shown that he was free from contributory negligence. A large number of errors are assigned. For a proper understanding of them it is necessary to set out a little more in detail the facts connected with the accident. As to some of them there is some dispute; but it is undisputed that, on the night in question, Faught was sent with his hand car from Andover, Missouri, northward, with an important message to one Sullivan, who was at Davis City, in charge, as conductor, of the train which included the engine by which the injury was done. Faught went to

Davis City, and delivered his message to Sullivan, and started
to return home, when he was overtaken by the engine which
was being run by one Southerland, as engineer. Obedience
to the message required that the engine should go southward
over the track upon which Faught had started southward
with his hand car a few minutes before. At the time of the
accident the engine was running around a curve at from
twenty-five to thirty miles an hour. The night was dark,
and the hand car could not be seen more than one hundred
and twenty-five feet ahead, and was, when seen, about that
number of feet distant. At the rate of speed at which the
engine was running, it could not be stopped in that space.
It is not clearly shown that either Sullivan, the conductor, or
Southerland, the engineer, knew for a certainty that Faught,
with his gang, had left Davis City with the hand car, but it
seems to have been distinctly understood that they were
either to precede or follow the engine, and it is shown beyond
controversy that a question was raised as to whether the
engine would be delayed long enough to enable the hand
car to precede it with safety. Faught was told, according to
the engineer's testimony, that the engine would not start for
ten or fifteen minutes, and, according to some of the testimony, that it would not start for fifteen minutes. There was
evidence tending to show that it started in less than ten minutes, and ran at a higher rate of speed than was necessary.
While, as before stated, it is not shown beyond dispute that
either the conductor or engineer knew for a certainty that
Faught had started when the engine left Davis City, it seems
to be indisputable that it could have been ascertained by
slight observation whether he had or not, and there is some
ground for the inference that the engineer, if not the conductor, supposed that he had. The negligence is alleged to
consist in starting so soon, and in running at so high a rate
of speed, and especially around a curve where the head-light
could not reveal the hand car at a very great distance. Some
other facts will be stated in the course of the opinion, but

the foregoing statement is sufficient to enable us to enter properly upon the specific consideration of the errors assigned.

I. Some questions are raised in regard to the right of the plaintiff, as assignee of Faught, to prosecute the action. We 1. PERSONAL regard these questions as substantially disposed injury: action by assignee. of by the previous decisions of this court, and especially by the case of *Vimont v. Chicago & N. W. R'y Co.*, 64 Iowa, 513, and 69 Id., 296.

II. After the cause had been set down for trial upon a day named, the defendant asked leave to file an amendment 2. PLEADING: to its answer, averring that Faught, previous to pendency of other action. his assignment to the plaintiff, commenced an action against the defendant for the same claim in his own name; that said action had been removed to the circuit court of the United States; and that no order had been made dismissing it, and that the defendant had not stipulated that it should be dismissed. The court refused to allow the amendment, and the defendant assigns the refusal as error. The proposed amended answer does not aver that the action brought by Faught was still pending. On the other hand, such averment seems to be ingeniously avoided. We suspect the fact to be that Faught had withdrawn his action, or ordered that the same be dismissed, without any distinct order to that effect being made by the court. If the fact is as we suspect, and as it might be consistently with the averments of the proposed amended answer, the circuit court could not treat the case otherwise than as withdrawn.

III. Before the submission of the cause, the defendant 3. SPECIAL propounded a large number of special inter-interroga- tories: not rogatories, and requested that the court require determina- tive: unneces- the jury to answer them, which the court refused sary: ambigu- ous. to do, and the defendant assigns the refusal as error.

We cannot properly set out the interrogatories in full. They all have the common characteristic that they call for a finding of fact not necessarily determinative of the case. The fourth and fifth questions, for instance, inquired whether the engineer *agreed* with Faught, or only *gave an opinion*, that he would not start his engine in less that ten or fifteen minutes. Under the evidence, the jury might have found that the engineer merely stated that he should not start for ten or fifteen minutes. Whether the jury should regard the statement as an agreement, or a mere statement, or an opinion, their finding upon the question would not be decisive of the case, nor, indeed, one of any great importance, viewed in connection with all the other evidence in the case. If Faught did not start from the immediate presence of the engineer, it was so nearly from his immediate presence, we have not a doubt, that Faught took it for granted that the engineer knew he had gone, and would not start sooner than he had stated, or, if he did, would not run him down upon a curve in a dark night at a speed of from twenty-five to thirty miles an hour. If, then, the answer sought had been most favorable to the defendant, it would have gone but little way towards showing that the defendant was free from negligence, or that the plaintiff was guilty of it. The same may be said of the other interrogatories.

We do not say that a party may not be entitled to have a special interrogatory submitted, even where it is such that an answer most favorable to the party would not entitle such party to a verdict. But we do not think that a party is necessarily entitled to a special finding upon every circumstance which might have some bearing upon the case. If we should hold that he is, it might become a favorite mode of trial for each party, by requiring a special finding, to seek to give prominence to every circumstance which he regarded as more or less favorable to him.

It might seem, at first, that the sixth interrogatory called for a material finding. That interrogatory is in these words: "Did Southerland start his engine south before the expiration of ten minutes?" This interrogatory pertains to the very matter in which the negligence was alleged to consist. There was evidence tending to show that Faught might have expected that the engine would start in ten minutes; and if the jury had believed this evidence, and believed also that the engine did not start in less than ten minutes, they might have found that the defendant was not negligent. But an answer to the interrogatory, to the effect that the engine did not start in less than ten minutes, would not alone have been of any special value to the defendant, because there was evidence tending to show that Faught had reason to expect that the engine would not start for fifteen minutes. The special interrogatory should have been as to whether the engine started sooner than Faught had been told that it would.

Another interrogatory is in these words: "Did he [Faught] start said hand car in disregard of the request of the conductor, Sullivan, to not start said hand car until the return of the engine?" The defendant claims that, if Faught did start in disregard of such request, he was guilty of contributory negligence. But we cannot say that he was, necessarily. This will appear more clearly if we set out some of the evidence upon this point. Faught testified in these words: "Sullivan, the conductor, was there, and he said, 'You had better not go now, as we are going to the Y to turn the engine.' We took hold of the car, and had partly set it off of the track, when the engineer said: 'You need not set it off, for we will not run out for fifteen minutes. We have not lit up nor oiled up.'" This remark by the engineer appears to have been made after Sullivan made his request or gave his advice not to start out with the hand car, and does not appear to have been heard by Sullivan. It was a fair question for the jury as to whether Faught was guilty of contributory negligence in view of what they might have found that the engineer said. Besides, there is no dispute as to what Sullivan said. Faught himself testified substantially as Sullivan did on that point. The defendant, therefore, has the benefit of the fact without a special finding, and is not prejudiced by the refusal to submit the special interrogatory upon that point.

Some of the questions appear to us to be ambiguous. Take the twelfth: "Did Southerland exercise ordinary care in the manner of running his engine after leaving the depot, and prior to the accident?" This question we think the jury would have been obliged to answer in the affirmative, if it excluded the matter of speed. But running thirty miles an hour is not uncommon, and is not of itself negligence. It is doubtful, then, what view the jury would have thought that it ought to take of the meaning of the question. The real question touching this matter the jury understood perfectly without any special interrogatory, and that is: Is it ordinary care to run thirty miles an hour, or at whatever rate the speed was, on a dark night, behind a hand car, if it is known, or should be known, that the hand car is ahead, and has had but a few minute's start, and there are curves in the road which preclude it from being seen, even with a headlight burning, more than one hundred and twenty feet distant? We think that the court did not err in refusing the special interrogatories.

IV. The court instructed the jury that "it was Faught's duty to be reasonably vigilant and watchful, in view of what 4. RAILROADS: he knew, or might reasonably have expected, as personal injury: care to the movement of the engine, to exercise his required of employe for senses of seeing and hearing as a reasonably his own safety. prudent man would have done under the circumstances." The defendant assigns the giving of this instruction as error. The objection made to the instruction is that the language is tame, and not adapted to the case, in view of the hazardous situation in which Faught had placed himself. But, in our opinion, Faught was not bound to exercise any greater degree of care than the instruction prescribed. If he was, he was bound to be more careful than a reasonably prudent man would have been under the circumstances. The fact that Faught's situation was hazardous does not render the instruction inapplicable. The more hazardous the evidence showed it to be, the more care was Faught bound to exercise, and the more he did exercise, if he conducted himself as a reasonably prudent man would have done *in view of the circumstances.*

The real objection which the defendant seems to have to the instruction is that it did not emphasize sufficiently the perils to which Faught was exposed by calling specifically the attention of the jury to them. This is shown by an instruction which the defendant asked, and which was not given. It was in these words: "The degree of diligence required of him depends on the amount and character of the danger. As the danger in this case was very grave and destructive, he was required to exercise corresponding vigilance." All the law contained in this instruction was given by the court. The instruction asked exceeds that given by the court, in that it contains a declaration of fact in regard to the gravity of the danger of which the jury was to judge for itself. We think that the court did not err, either in giving the instruction which it did, or in refusing that which was asked.

V. The defendant asked an instruction in these words: "If, by keeping a vigilant watch while moving his hand car,

6. ——:——: he [Faught] could have ascertained the approach
——. of the engine, and by prompt action in removing his car from the track he could have avoided the collision complained of, and he failed to keep a vigilant watch in his rear while running his car, or failed to remove the same promptly from the track when the engine approached so near as to threaten collision, then he was guilty of contributory negligence, and the plaintiff cannot recover." The court refused to give this instruction, and the defendant assigns the refusal as error. We are inclined to think that Faught might have discovered the approach of the engine in time to remove his car from the track. This, we think, he might have done if he had kept a constant, or very nearly

constant, look towards the rear. We are inclined to think that he did not do this; and perhaps did not keep what could be said to be a "vigilant watch" within the meaning of the instruction asked. But we cannot say, as a matter of law, that he was guilty of contributory negligence in failing to do so. If Faught was told, as he says that he was, and as the evidence tended strongly to show that he was, that the engine would not be ready to start for fifteen minutes, he could hardly be expected to have apprehended the approach of the engine during the first half of that time; and yet there was evidence tending to show that he was run over in about seven minutes from the time he started. If he had had any reasonable ground to suppose that the engine could have been seen approaching during the first seven minutes, it is not probable that he would have gone upon the track at all. We think that the jury might well have believed that a prudent man might have failed, under the assurance given, to keep a lookout during that time. If he had entered upon the track without anything being said as to when the engine would start, and without reasonable ground for supposing that the engineer knew that he was preceding the engine, the case would be very different. Under such circumstances he should, of course, have kept an unremitting watch for the engine. But he was certainly justified in placing some confidence in the assurance given, and the care which he was bound to exercise was to be determined in reference to them. We think that the court did not err in refusing the instruction.

VI. The court gave an instruction in these words: "The acts and omissions of the defendant's employes, which it is claimed caused the accident and injuries complained of, are, briefly stated, as follows: That the said James Faught, at the time stated in the petition, was at Davis City, in obedience to orders from his superior, and in the performance of his duty; that, as he was about to return to his post of duty, he asked the engineer in charge of the train how soon said train would start for Chariton, and said engineer told him

that it would be not less than fifteen minutes; that, in reliance upon said statement, Faught, with his squad of men
and the hand car, started for home over the track over which
the engine would pass when it started; that in less than five
minutes after said statement had been made by said engineer,
said engineer started his engine," etc. The giving of this
instruction is assigned as error. The objection urged to it is
that it is so drawn that the jury might have supposed that
the facts stated had been found to be true, and not merely that
they were what the plaintiff claimed to be true. But, in our
opinion, the objection is not well taken. The court set these
facts out very distinctly, as being the plaintiff's claim, and we
do not think that the jury could have understood it otherwise.

Another objection urged is that the court did not tell the
jury that Faught did not have a right to rely upon the
engineer's statement. To this we think that two answers
may be made. In the first place, the court was merely setting
out the plaintiff's claim. In the second place, while it may
be true that Faught had no right to rely upon the engineer's
statement in regard to the exact length of time mentioned,
we think that he had a right to rely upon his not starting as
soon as some of the evidence tended to show that he did.

VII. The defendant asked an instruction in these words:
"The engineer had no authority to make any agreement with
Faught, binding on the defendant, that he would

6. —: —: not start the engine for ten or fifteen minutes.
reliance upon
engineer's
statement as The engineer was subject to the orders of his
to movement
of train. superior officer in the movement of trains, and
Faught, while assuming to act as an officer of the defendant
company, and in its employ, must be supposed to know this
fact, and to govern himself accordingly." The court refused
this instruction, and the refusal is assigned as error.

There was evidence showing that the engineer started in-
obedience to the order of the conductor, and tending to show
that the conductor gave the order in ignorance of what had
been said by the engineer to Faught. This, we think,

accounts for the start being made so soon, and for the accident. But the engineer was not bound to obey the conductor's orders if he had reason to believe that in doing so he
would run down the hand car, and endanger the lives of
those on it. There is an implied reservation accompanying
every order, that it is not to be executed where it cannot be
done with reasonable regard to the safety of human life.
Perhaps the defendant's counsel would concede this. We
are inclined to think that the instruction was asked more as
affecting the question of the plaintiff's negligence than as
affecting the question of the defendant's. Faught doubtless
knew that the engineer could not properly agree as to how
long he would hold his engine. But what was said was not
so much in the nature of an agreement as in the nature of
information. Some things were to be done before the engine
could start, and the engineer claimed to have knowledge how
long it would be, and Faught acted upon the information
given; and it was a fair question for the jury as to whether he
was guilty of negligence in doing so. If the engine had been
ready to start, and Faught had nothing to rely upon except an
agreement of the engineer that he would hold the engine, the
case would have been different. The instruction asked was,
we think, inapplicable to the case made, and properly refused.

VIII. The defendant complains of an instruction upon
the ground that under it the jury might have found that
there was culpable negligence in starting. The objection is
that the starting, without more, could not have caused the
accident. But this the jury understood perfectly, and they
were not misled. The case is a very simple one, and very
easily understood. It was presented to the jury by a set of
intelligible instructions, and it appears to us to have been
fairly tried. We have not specifically noticed every question
raised, but we think that they are substantially covered by
what we have said.

We think that the case was fairly tried, and that the verdict is supported by the evidence.   AFFIRMED.

DIRKSON v. KNOX ET AL.

1. **Contract**: FRAUD: RESCISSION: EVIDENCE. A court of equity will not annul a contract on the ground that it was procured by fraud, unless the evidence is clear and satisfactory, and preponderates in favor of the party asking the rescission. Accordingly, where there was no special confidence reposed by the plaintiff in the defendant, and no artifice used to prevent plaintiff from making the requisite examination to ascertain the truth, and he had an opportunity to do so, and it did not clearly appear that the alleged false representation was anything more than a guess, or an expression of opinion, *held* that a rescission should not have been decreed.

Appeal from Polk Circuit Court.

SATURDAY, OCTOBER 23, 1886.

ACTION in equity to rescind a contract and set aside a conveyance of real estate. Judgment for plaintiff, and defendants appeal.

C. W. Johnson, Geo. W. Seevers and *P. Gad Bryan*, for appellants.

Phillips & Day, for appellee.

SEEVERS, J.—The appellant J. M. Knox was the owner of twenty-five shares of the capital stock, of the par value of $2,500, of the Hawkeye Seed Company, a corporation existing under the laws of this state, which he transferred to the plaintiff in consideration of the conveyance of certain real estate by the latter to H. M. Knox. The plaintiff claims that the conveyance was obtained by means of the fraudulent representions of J. M. Knox as to the business of the said company, the amount of the indebtedness and value of the stock, and that H. M. Knox is not a *bona fide* purchaser. The material representation which is claimed to be fraudulent, relied on by counsel for appellant, is that Knox represented that the amounts due the seed company were about equal to the indebtedness of the corporation, whereas the evidence shows that the latter exceeded the former in the sum of $730.73.

It must, we think, be true that, before a contract can be rescinded, the evidence must be clear and satisfactory, and preponderate in favor of the party asking the rescission. Possibly the rule is that a mere preponderance is sufficient, but the preponderance must be made to clearly appear. It is also true, if no artifice be used to prevent the party asserting the fraud from making the requisite examination to ascertain the truth, and he has the opportunity to do so, and there was no special confidence between the parties, reposed by the one in the other, that the contract will not be rescinded. *McClanahan v. McKinley*, 52 Iowa, 222, and authorities cited. It quite satisfactorily appears that the amounts due the corporation, as well as the indebtedness, appeared on the books of the company, which the plaintiff had the opportunity to examine, and, as we understand, he did make a slight examination of the books; but it is probably true that he did not understand book-keeping. But he could have got some one to make such examination as well before as he did after the contract was made. It is entirely clear that no special confidence was reposed by the plaintiff in Knox; that is, he had no right to do so from the relations which existed between them. Each of them simply dealt with the other on his own judgment, and no doubt tried to make the best trade he could. But, conceding that the plaintiff had the right to rely on the representations of Knox, and that he was not bound to have the books examined for the purpose of obtaining a knowledge of the standing of the corporation, has he established by a clear preponderance of the evidence that any material false representations were made? In considering this question, it will be conceded that Knox knew, or was bound to know, the amount of the indebtedness.

The evidence of the plaintiff is: "I asked Knox whether they owed any debts, and he represented to me that they were on a secure footing. Everything was cleaned; that they had made a clean sweep in January, and everything was paid, and that there were no debts but what the outstanding accounts would balance. On that condition I concluded to buy in." Knox testifies: "I remember that the plaintiff asked me about the amount of the outstanding indebtedness I did not say to him that the credits due the corporation would about liquidate the outstanding indebtedness. I said they might come in the neighborhood of balancing; I could not say. I said that was simply a guess. He said, ' Guess at it,' and insisted upon a guess; and that was my guess. That was my impression at the time I made the statement."

It seems to us to be quite evident that, if Knox can be believed, he did not make any positive statement on which the plaintiff was authorized to rely, and especially so when he had the opportunity to have an examination of the books made, and thus ascertain certainly for himself. Now, neither the plaintiff nor Knox is materially corroborated, and, so far as we can see, they are equally entitled to credit. There is nothing in the story told by either which will warrant us in disbelieving either of them. All that can be said is that they have understood the transaction differently. Counsel for the appellee claim that he is corroborated by the evidence of Sturgis and Gaston. The latter testifies that "Knox said he did not know the amount of the indebtedness exactly, but he thought the debts and credits would not far from balance, or something to that effect." Sturgis testifies to what the plaintiff told him Knox said. Conceding its competency, it is not more definite and certain than the evidence of Gaston. We think the circuit court erred in rescinding the contract and setting aside the conveyance.

The cause will be remanded, with directions to enter a decree in accordance with this opinion; or, if the defendants so elect, they may take a decree in this court.

REVERSED.

FITZGERALD V. KELSO ET AL.

1. **Execution Sale:** APPEAL: REDEMPTION. Under § 3102 of the Code, an execution sale made after appeal taken is without the right of redemption; but an appeal is not taken by service of a notice on the attorney of the execution plaintiff. It must also· be served on the clerk of the court. (Code, §§ 3178, 3179.)

2. ——: ACTION TO SET ASIDE: OFFER TO REDEEM. One whose land has wrongfully been sold without the right of redemption may maintain an action to set the sale aside, without offering to redeem, where his right to redeem has constantly been denied; for the law does not require a man to do a vain thing.

3. ——: WRONGFUL SALE WITHOUT REDEMPTION: INADEQUATE PRICE: SET ASIDE. When plaintiff's land was sold wrongfully without redemption, and for a grossly inadequate price, and there was a manifest attempt to oppress him by denying his right to redeem, *held* that the sale was properly set aside in equity.

Appeal from Hardin Circuit Court.

SATURDAY, OCTOBER 23, 1886.

ACTION in chancery to set aside a sheriff's sale, and a deed executed thereon. The relief prayed for in the petition was granted by the decree of the circuit court. Defendants appeal.

J. H. Scales, for appellants.

Brown & Carney, for appellee.

BECK, J.—I. The record discloses the following facts. The defendant in this case, Kelso, recovered a judgment against Fitzgerald, who is plaintiff in the action before us. Land of the value of $2,050, subject to a mortgage and taxes amounting to $600, was sold on an execution for $276. Prior to the sale, Fitzgerald had served a notice of appeal to the supreme court upon the attorney of Kelso. After the sale, but on the same day, the notice of appeal was served upon the clerk of the court in which the judgment was rendered, and a *supersedeas* bond was filed. The sale was made without redemption, and on the same day a sheriff's deed was executed to Kelso, who was the purchaser.

II. Defendants claim that the sale was without redemption, for the reason that an appeal had been taken in the 1. EXECUTION case. Code, § 3102. But no appeal is taken sale: appeal: and perfected until the proper notice is served redemption. upon the clerk of the court. Code, §§ 3178, 3179. No notice having been served, the appeal was not taken when the sale was had. · It was not, therefore, within the provision of Code, § 3102, and was made subject to redemption.

III. As the deed was made on the same day of the sale, and defendants claim that it is valid, and that plaintiff has no right to redeem, and rely upon the claim to 2. ——: action to set aside: defeat this action, it was not necessary for plaintiff offer to re- deem. to offer to redeem. His right to do so has been constantly denied since the sale. He loses no right by omitting to do what defendants claim he has no right to do. The law presumes his offer to redeem would not have been accepted, and does not require him to do a vain thing, and will not defeat his right because he did not do it. We conclude that the deed was made without authority, and is void.

IV. The land was sold for less than one-fifth of its value. Under the circumstances of the case, we think the price is inadequate, and, in view of the fact of this inade- 3. ——: wrong- ful sale with- quacy and the clearly-established attempt to out redemp- tion: inade- quate price. oppress plaintiff by the denial of his right to redeem, we think equity requires the sale to be set aside.

The decree of the court setting aside the sale and sheriff's deed is

AFFIRMED.

COWDRY v. CUTHBERT ET AL.

1. **Vendor and Vendee:** BOND FOR DEED: TAX TITLE IN VENDEE TO DEFEAT VENDOR. A vendee in possession of land, under a bond for a deed to be executed when the purchase price is paid, and with an agreement to pay all taxes and assessments lawfully imposed on the premises, cannot defeat the rights of his vendor by purchasing a tax title based upon a sale made prior to his purchase of the vendor, but consummated by a deed made subsequent thereto, where notice of the expiration of the time for redemption was served on him as the one in possession of the land. In such case, it was his duty to redeem the land from the tax sale; (see cases cited in opinion;) and whatever was paid to effect such redemption would have amounted to a payment of so much on the purchase money. His purchase of the tax title, under the facts of the case, amounted simply to a redemption which inured to the benefit of his vendor. (*Alexander v. Sully*, 50 Iowa, 192, distinguished.)

71
87
71
121
71
130
71
137

Appeal from Buena Vista District Court.

TUESDAY, OCTOBER 26, 1886.

ACTION IN EQUITY. Decree for the plaintiff, and the defendants appeal.

Robinson & Milchrist, for appellants.

Sweeley & Slocumb, for appellee.

SEEVERS, J.—No pleadings were filed, but there is an affidavit showing that this is a real controversy, and the case is submitted upon an agreed statement of facts, the material portions of which are as follows: The plaintiff, in 1872, became the owner of the land in controversy, and on the fifteenth day of March, 1880, she sold the same to the defendant Cuthbert for $440, of which sum $70 was paid, and the plaintiff gave said defendant a bond wherein she agreed to convey the premises to said Cuthbert upon the payment of the balance of the purchase money when the same became due, in December, 1885. Cuthbert also agreed to pay all taxes and assessments lawfully imposed upon said premises.

Under said contract, Cuthbert entered into possession of the premises, and so continued to hold such possession, and exercise exclusive acts of ownership thereon, until after the execution of the tax deed hereafter referred to. In October, 1877, the land in controversy was sold to the defendant Simmons for the delinquent taxes of 1876. In August, 1880, the expiration notice required to be served was served on Cuthbert personally, and, as the land was taxed in the name of A. Oaks, a notice was served on him by publication, and in January, 1881, the county treasurer conveyed the premises to Simmons. Within a week after the execution of the tax deed, Simmons went upon the land, and notified the defendant that he owned the land, and claimed possession under the tax deed, and he several times thereafter went over the land with parties for the purpose of selling it to them. The defendant Cuthbert, prior to the execution of the tax deed, notified the plaintiff by letter to pay the taxes, and that no more payments would be made under the contract until full redemption was made. In March, 1881, Simmons sold and conveyed the premises by general warranty deed, in consideration of $180, to Cuthbert. The plaintiff asks that the tax deed be declared to be void, and that the bond be foreclosed, and she have judgment for the amount due thereon, and that a special execution issue for the sale of the premises, and general relief is asked. Cuthbert asks that the plaintiff's action be dismissed, the tax deed confirmed, and that he recover a judgment for $70, and interest, and he asks general relief.

Under the contract the plaintiff and Cuthbert occupied the position of vendor and vendee. The former held the legal, and the latter the equitable, title. We also incline to think they should be regarded as mortgagor and mortgagee, (Code, § 3329;) the plaintiff being the mortgagee, and Cuthbert the mortgagor. We think it is well settled by the authorities that a mortgagor cannot acquire a tax title to the prejudice of the mortgagee. This rule is based possibly on the thought that the mortgagor was bound to pay the taxes. In this case, the most that can be said is that Cuthbert obligated himself to pay all taxes lawfully imposed on the premises after he became the purchaser. He was not bound to pay the prior taxes. But, as vendee or owner of the equitable title in possession, he was authorized to redeem from the prior tax sale; and, when the expiration notice was served on him, we think it was his duty to do so. *Rice v. Nelson*, 27 Iowa, 148; *Hunt v. Rowland*, 22 Id., 53; *Stears v. Hollenbeck*, 38 Id., 550; *Fair v. Brown*, 40 Id., 209. Whatever was paid to effect such redemption would amount to a payment of so much of the purchase money due the plaintiff. Such being the duty of Cuthbert, it follows that he cannot be permitted to set up such tax title as against the plaintiff. His purchase of such title, under the agreed statement of facts, amounted simply to a redemption which inured to the benefit of the plaintiff. Counsel for the defendants cite, and seem to rely greatly on, *Alexander v. Sully*, 50 Iowa, 192; but it is, we think, clearly distinguishable.

The judgment of the district court is

AFFIRMED.

VOORHEES v. THE CHICAGO, ROCK ISLAND & PACIFIC R'Y CO.

1. **Railroads**: BREACH OF CONTRACT TO FURNISH CARS: AUTHORITY OF STATION AGENT. Plaintiff applied to the defendant's station agent at O. for cars to ship hogs the next day. There was no telegraph communication at O., and the agent directed plaintiff to go to L., a station on another branch of defendant's road, where there was a telegraph, and have the agent at L. order the cars for the shipment of the hogs at O. Plaintiff did so, and the agent at L. sent a request for the cars to the train dispatcher of his line of road for the cars to be furnished at O., on the other line. The agent at L. afterwards informed plaintiff that he had received an answer, and that the cars would be at O. the next day. Plaintiff accordingly had his hogs at O. the next day for shipment, but the cars did not come until two days later. Plaintiff sues for his damages caused by the delay. *Held* that he could not recover, because it

' was shown that the agent at L. had no actual authority to bind the defendant by a contract for cars at O., and such contract was not within the apparent scope of his authority as station agent at L. (*Wood v. Chicago, M. & St. P. R'y Co.*, 68 Iowa, 491, distinguished.)

2. **Evidence:** HEARSAY: CONDITION OF MARKET. Plaintiff's testimony as to what his broker told him about the condition of the market on a certain day was mere hearsay, and should have been excluded.

3. **Costs:** CONTINUANCE: PLAINTIFF'S FAULT. Where, after both parties had rested, plaintiff asked and obtained leave to introduce other testimony which he had omitted by inadvertence, and the court then granted a continuance on defendant's motion, on the ground that its witnesses had departed, and it could not then rebut the new evidence, *held* that the costs of the trial were properly taxed to plaintiff, because, by his inadvertence, the trial was rendered useless.

Appeal from Marion District Court.

THURSDAY, OCTOBER 28, 1886.

ACTION for the recovery of damages caused, as plaintiff alleges, by defendant's failure to perform its contract to furnish cars at a specified time for the shipment of a lot of hogs to Chicago. The cause came on for trial at the January term, 1885, of the district court, and, after the parties had each rested, defendant's counsel filed a motion to direct the jury to return a verdict for it. After that motion was argued, and before any order upon it had been entered, the plaintiff asked leave to introduce evidence on a material question which his counsel stated they had overlooked by inadvertence. The court granted leave to introduce the evidence; but, after it had been introduced, defendant's counsel moved the court to continue the cause, alleging, as a ground therefor, that when the parties rested they had discharged their witnesses, who had immediately left the court, and they were consequently not prepared at that term to meet the additional evidence which plaintiff had been permitted to introduce. The court sustained this motion, and taxed the costs of the term to plaintiff. At the same term plaintiff filed a motion to set this order aside, which, at the August term, 1885, was overruled. At that term the cause again came on for trial on the merits, and there was a verdict and judgment for plaintiff. Plaintiff [appeals from the order continuing the cause, and taxing the costs to him, and defendant appeals from the final judgment; its appeal being first perfected.

T. S. Wright and *L. Kinkead*, for appellant.

Bousquet & Earle, for appellee.

REED, J.—On the sixteenth of October, 1882, plaintiff went to Olivet, a station on defendant's road, for the purpose of making arrangements for the shipment, on the next day, of five carloads of hogs from that station to Chicago. There was no telegraph office at Olivet, and the station agent informed plaintiff that an order for the necessary cars could not be forwarded by mail in time to receive them for the next day. Plaintiff claims that the agent requested him to go to Leighton, a station a few miles away, and have an order for the cars telegraphed from there, and stated that the agent there frequently ordered cars for Olivet. Leighton is on the line of road between Keokuk and Des Moines, while Olivet is on what is known as the "Washington & Knoxville Branch." Both lines are operated by defendant, and they cross each other at Knoxville Junction, a few miles from Olivet and Leighton. The Washington & Knoxville branch has a direct Chicago connection, and it was by that line that plaintiff desired to ship his hogs. He went to Leighton, and, as he claims, informed the agent there that the agent at Olivet requested that an order for the cars be telegraphed from there. The agent accordingly sent a dispatch to the train dispatcher on the Keokuk & Des Moines line, requesting him to send the cars to Olivet in time for the shipment the next day. The name of the Olivet agent was signed to the dispatch, and plaintiff saw it before it was sent. He also testified that the agent afterwards told him that he had received an answer to the dispatch, and assured him that the cars would be at Olivet in such time that the shipment could be made on the next day. He claims that, relying on this assurance, he drove his hogs to Olivet, and was ready to ship at the designated time. The cars were not delivered at Olivet, however, until the nineteenth, and the hogs were shipped on that day. If they had been shipped on the seventeenth, they would have arrived at Chicago on the nineteenth. As it was, they reached there on the twenty-first. A material decline occurred in the price of hogs in the Chicago market between the nineteenth and twenty-first. By this action plaintiff seeks to recover the cost of keeping the hogs from the seventeenth to the time they were shipped, and the difference between what he received for them when he sold them and the amount he would have received if he had been able to place them on the market on the nineteenth. The Olivet and Leighton agents were both examined on the trial. The former denied that he requested plaintiff to go to Leighton, and the latter testified that he did not give plaintiff any assurance that the cars would be at Olivet the next day; and it was proven that the agent at Leighton had no express authority to transact business for defendant, except that pertaining to his own station; also that the train-master, to whom said dispatch was sent, had no express authority to send cars to stations on the other line.

I. The district court gave the following instruction to the jury: "If you find from a preponderance of the evidence that plaintiff applied to the station agent

1. RAILROADS: breach of contract to furnish cars: authority of station agent.

of defendant at Olivet for cars in which to ship his hogs to Chicago, such cars to be furnished at a specified time and place, and thereupon such agent informed plaintiff that he could not telegraph from Olivet, and requested him to go to Leighton station, on another branch or division of defendant's railroad, and have the station agent at that station telegraph to the proper authorities for such cars, and you find that plaintiff did request such agent at Leighton to so telegraph, and you find that such agent telegraphed to the train dispatcher of defendant at Keokuk for such cars to be delivered or furnished at Olivet station at a specified time, and thereafter informed plaintiff that he had received a reply to the effect that such cars would be furnished at such specified time and place, and you further find that plaintiff relied in good faith upon 'such information, and, in pursuance thereof, drove his hogs to Olivet, and had them there ready for shipment at said time, and defendant failed to have such cars there at such time, and you find that plaintiff suffered damage in consequence of such failure, then plaintiff would be entitled to recover the damages, if any, resulting therefrom."

If defendant is liable on the hypothesis stated in this instruction, such liability must be upon the ground that its failure to have the cars at Olivet at the time in question was a breach of some contract obligation existing between it and plaintiff. Defendant, being a common carrier, is bound to furnish shippers reasonable facilities for the transportation of their property, and would doubtless be responsible to one who had demanded transportation facilities for any damages he may have sustained in consequence of its failure to afford such facilities within a reasonable time after such demand. Plaintiff, however, is not seeking to recover on the theory that there was an unreasonable delay after demand in furnishing the cars, but his claim is that defendant was under obligation to furnish them at a particular time, and that he has been damaged by its failure to furnish them at that time. The doctrine of the instruction is that if plaintiff, at the request of the agent at Olivet, went to Leighton, and requested the agent there to telegraph to the proper officer or agent for the cars, and that agent, acting upon that request, sent the dispatch, and afterwards stated to plaintiff that he had received an answer to it, and that the cars would be at Olivet on the next day, and plaintiff acted on that assurance, defendant was bound to furnish the cars at the specified time, and was answerable in damages for its failure to do so.

That defendant is bound by such contracts as are entered into in its name, by its agents, within the actual or apparent scope of their authority, is, of course, conceded. It was held in *Wood v. Chicago, M. & St. P. R'y Co.*, 68 Iowa, 491, that a station agent who was authorized to contract for the shipment of property from his station was presumed to be empowered to contract with reference to all the ordinary and necessary details of the business, and that when, from the nature of the property to be shipped, or other circumstances, it was necessary or usual to arrange or contract for the shipment of the property in advance of its delivery, the company was bound by his contract to funish the necessary cars at the specified time, whether he had any express power to make the contract or not. The ground of the holding is that, by placing him in charge of its business at that station, the company held him out as possessing authority to make the contract, and shippers were warranted in dealing with him on the assumption that he had full power in the premises. In the present case, however, the agent by whom it is alleged the contract was made, was not held out by defendant as possessing any power with reference to the subject of the contract. He was not in fact authorized to contract for the shipment of property from Olivet; nor was he held out as possessing such authority. His duties were limited to his own station, and there was nothing in the circumstances which warranted plaintiff in the assumption that he had authority to contract with reference to business at Olivet. The facts of the case do not, therefore, bring it within the principle announced in *Wood v. Chicago, M. & St. P. R'y Co.*, *supra*, and the doctrine of the instruction finds no support in that case.

The fact that the agent at Olivet requested plaintiff to go to Leighton, and procure the agent there to send the order for the cars, is not material; for his authority in the premises was neither actually nor apparently enlarged by that request. If the officer or agent to whom the order was transmitted had directed him to make the agreement for the furnishing of the cars on the next day, defendant would probably have been bound by it; but, under the instruction, plaintiff's right of recovery is not dependent on whether such direction was in fact given, but upon whether the agent represented that it had been given. The declaration of the agent at the time of the transaction is thus made proof of the extent of his powers. The instruction, we think, is clearly erroneous.

II. On the trial, plaintiff was permitted, against defendant's objection, to testify to the statements of the broker

2. EVIDENCE: hearsay: condition of market. who sold his hogs in Chicago, as to the condition of the market on the nineteenth of October, and as to the price at which he would have been able to sell them if they had arrived in Chicago on that day. The evidence was mere hearsay, and should have been excluded.

III. It was within the discretion of the district court to permit plaintiff, on the first trial after the parties had rested,

3. COSTS: continuance: plaintiff's fault. to introduce further testimony. (Code, § 2799.) It was also within the discretion of the court to grant a continuance of the cause, if satisfied that substantial justice would thereby be more nearly obtained. (Section 2749.) The continuance was granted for the reason that plaintiff had asked and obtained leave to introduce evidence material to the case after both parties had rested, and after defendant's witnesses had left the court. The costs of that trial were rendered useless by the continuance, and the continuance was rendered necessary by plaintiff's failure to introduce his evidence at the proper time. The costs were therefore properly taxed to him.

On plaintiff's appeal the judgment will be affirmed.

On defendant's appeal it will be reversed.

LAMB ET AL. v. FEELEY ET EL.

1. **Mortgage**: FORECLOSURE SALE: REDEMPTION: WHAT AMOUNTS TO. Where a junior mortgagee. more than six months and less than nine months after a foreclosure sale under a senior mortgage, paid to the purchaser at such sale the full amount of his bid, with interest, and took an assignment of the certificate of sale, and filed an affidavit with the clerk setting out the amount of his mortgage lien, and stating that he had redeemed as junior lien-holder, *held* that this amounted to a redemption under the statute, though the clerk took no part in the transaction. (Compare *Goode v. Cummings*, 35 Iowa, 67.)

2. ——: ——: REDEMPTION BY JUNIOR MORTGAGEE: CLAIMS EXTIN- GUISHED. A junior mortgagee who redeems from a sale under a senior mortgage more than six and less than nine months after the sale, must, within ten days after the expiration of the nine months, enter upon the sale book the utmost he is willing to credit on his mortgage, and, if he does not, and takes a deed for the land under the sale, his mortgage will be extinguished. (Code, §§ 3113, 3115; *Goode v. Cummings*, 35 Iowa, 67.)

Appeal from Tama District Court.

FRIDAY, DECEMBER 17, 1886.

PLAINTIFF, as assignee of a mortgage executed January 9, 1882, due in one year, filed his petition for foreclosure, February 26th, 1885. Defendants answered that there was a foreclosure of a prior mortgage upon the same land given in 1876, and a sheriff's sale thereunder November 5, 1884; that plaintiff purchased the notes and mortgage sued on, March 12, 1883; that more than six and less than nine months after the sheriff's sale, plaintiff, as junior mortgagee, redeemed from the sheriff's sale by paying to the purchaser thereat the full amount, with interest, and taking an assignment of the certificate of sale, and filing an affidavit with the clerk setting out the amount of his mortgage lien, and stating that he had redeemed as junior lien-holder; and that plaintiff, as holder of said certificate, obtained a deed from the sheriff for the land covered by both mortgages. Defendants claimed that by these proceedings plaintiff became absolute owner of the land, and that the mortgage, and the debt on which it was based, are fully paid and satisfied. Plaintiff demurred to the answer. The demurrer was sustained, and judgment was rendered in favor of plaintiff, and a decree of foreclosure on the junior mortgage. Defendants appeal.

Stivers & Louthan and *J. W. Willett*, for appellants.

Struble, Kinne & Stiger, for appellee.

ROTHROCK, J.—Some question is raised in argument of counsel as to whether the plaintiff, in purchasing the certifi-

1. MORTGAGE: foreclosure: sale : redemption: what amounts to.

cate of sale under the senior mortgage, made a redemption under the statute; but we think the transaction amounted to, and actually was, a redemption. It has been decided that such a redemption, made after six and prior to nine months from the sale, can be made between the parties without the aid of the clerk. *Goode v. Cummings*, 35 Iowa, 67. The parties in this case did just what was in law necessary to effect the redemption of a junior mortgage, and the plaintiff, in addition, declared by affidavit that it was intended as such. The plaintiff, then, was a redemptioner within nine months subsequent to the sale,

2. ——: ——: redemption by junior mortgagee: claim extinguished.

and was entitled to a deed, unless the defendant in the foreclosure proceedings should redeem within the year allowed him. He did not redeem, and the plaintiff received a deed for the premises, and his rights are clearly defined by the following provision of the Code:

"Sec. 3113. Unless the defendant thus redeems, the purchaser, or the creditor who has last redeemed prior to the expiration of nine months aforesaid, will hold the property absolutely.

"Sec. 3114. In case it is thus held by a redeeming creditor, his lien, and the claim out of which it arose, will be held to be extinguished, unless he pursues the course pointed out in the next section.

" Sec. 3115. If he is unwilling to hold the property, and credit the defendant therefor with the amount of his lien, he must, within ten days after the expiration of nine months aforesaid, enter on the sale-book the utmost he is thus willing to credit on his claim."

The plaintiff made his redemption prior to nine months, and failed to file the notice required by section 3115, and, having become the absolute owner of the land as provided in section 3113, his mortgage, which he now seeks to foreclose, and the debt on which it was based, were extinguished, according to section 3114. Therefore, he had no right to recover, and the court below erred in sustaining the demurrer to the answer; for, if the allegations of the answer are sustained by the proof, the plaintiff must fail. The case of *Goode v. Cummings, supra*, sustains this position.

REVERSED.

GUTHRIE, TRUSTEE, v. GUTHRIE ET AL.

1. **Judgment:** IN VACATION: CONSENT. In an application by plaintiff for a discharge as trustee, where the court found that there was due from him a certain sum, an order that he pay the same was such an order as might be made in vacation by the consent of parties.

2. ———: ———: FILED AFTER EXPIRATION OF JUDGE'S TERM OF OFFICE: VALIDITY. Where an order was made by the judge in vacation and reduced to writing, and delivered to the defendants' attorney December 30, 1884, to be filed in the clerk's office, but he did not file it until January, 1, 1885, the day after the judge's term of office had expired, *held* (by a divided court) that the order was nevertheless valid. (Compare *Babcock v. Wolf*, 70 Iowa, 676.)

3. **Appeal:** WHEN IT LIES. An appeal lies to this court from a ruling sustaining a motion to expunge from the record an order for a trustee to pay an amount found due from him, on the ground that the order is invalid; for the effect virtually is to grant a new trial.

Appeal from Jasper Circuit Court.

THURSDAY, DECEMBER 23, 1886.

APPLICATION by plaintiff for discharge as trustee. The case was heard and determined by Hon. J. A. HOFFMAN, as judge of the circuit court. The court held that there was due from the plaintiff, as trustee, the sum of $2,280.87, and ordered that he pay the same. The order was made in vacation; the same being reduced to writing on the thirtieth day of December, 1884, and delivered to the attorney of the defendant to be filed in the office of the clerk of the court. He delivered the same to the clerk on the first day of January, 1885. The term of office of Judge HOFFMAN expired on the day preceding. The clerk recorded the order. The plaintiff moved to expunge the order from the record, and the court sustained the motion. From the order sustaining the motion the defendant appeals.

Alanson Clark, for appellant.

Cook & Patterson, for appellee.

ADAMS, CH. J.—The motion to expunge the order from the record was based upon two grounds. In the first place, it was claimed that there was no consent to a decision of the case in vacation; and, in the second place, that the order was void because not filed in the office of the clerk until the term of office of the judge who made the order had expired.

As to the first point, we have to say that we think that the case was one which, by consent, might be determined in vaca-

1. JUDGMENT: tion, and that the evidence shows that such con-
in vacation:
consent. sent was given. The judge evidently so understood it, and it appears to us that he was justified in so understanding it.

The question as to the validity of an order or decree reduced to writing, but not delivered to the clerk to be filed

2. ———: ———: until the term of office of the judge who made
filed after ex-
piration of the order or decree has expired, is one upon
judge's term
of office: va- which this court has not been agreed. But a
lidity.
majority of the court are of the opinion that the failure to deliver the order or decree to the clerk during the term of office of the judge who made the order or decree

does not render it invalid. *Babcock v.· Wolf*, 70 Iowa, 676. Such being the ruling of the court, it must be held that the court erred in sustaining the plaintiff's motion to expunge the order from the record.

The appellee contends that an appeal does not lie from the order sustaining the motion, but we think otherwise. In

3. APPEAL: sustaining the motion to expunge the order from when it lies. the record, the court virtually granted a new trial. Code, § 3164, subd. 3. REVERSED.

THE STATE v. RAINSBARGER.

1. **Criminal Evidence**: TESTIMONY OF WIFE OF ONE JOINTLY INDICTED. The wife of one indicted for the same offense as that for which defendant was alone on trial, was a competent witness against defendant, where no communication between her and her husband was sought to be elicited. Section 3641 of the Code does not exclude her testimony in such a case.

2. ———: BAD CHARACTER OF DEFENDANT: OTHER CRIMES. Evidence which has no other effect than to show that defendant has been guilty of other crimes than that charged in the indictment, is not admissible on the part of the state; neither is evidence of defendant's bad character, where he has not himself placed his character in issue.

3. ———: OPINIONS OF ORDINARY WITNESSES. The opinions of ordinary witnesses, derived from observation, are admissible in evidence, where, from the nature of the subject under investigation, no better evidence can be obtained, or the facts cannot otherwise be presented to the tribunal. Accordingly, *held* that it was competent for ordinary witnesses to give an opinion that the wheel and shaft of a buggy in which decedent had been riding were broken purposely by force applied thereto in a certain manner, the witnesses having also described the appearance of the wheel and shaft, and the general condition of the buggy, and of the ground in the vicinity.

4. **Murder**: INSTRUCTION: INFERENCE OF MALICE FROM USE OF DEADLY WEAPON. On a trial for murder, an instruction that malice would be implied from the unlawful and intentional use of a dangerous or deadly weapon in such manner as that the natural or necessary consequence of the act would be to destroy the life of another, while not correct as applied to all cases of homicide, *held* not to have been erroneous where there was no evidence that the killing was accidental or upon provocation, and the presumption therefore arose that it was voluntary, and with malice aforethought. (Compare *State v. Gillick*, 7 Iowa, 311.)

Appeal from Marshall District Court.

TUESDAY, MARCH 1, 1887.

THE defendant was convicted of the murder of one Enoch Johnson, and sentenced to imprisonment in the penitentiary for life, and from that judgment he appeals.

C. E. Allbrook and *Brown & Carney*, for defendant.

A. J. Baker, Attorney-general, for the State.

REED, J.—On the morning of the nineteenth of November, 1884, the dead body of Enoch Johnson was found on a public road near the village of Gifford, in Hardin county. The circumstances proven on the trial sustain the finding of the jury that his death was caused by injuries which had been inflicted on his person by another, and that the killing was felonious. There was also evidence which tended to prove that the crime was committed by this defendant and his brother, Frank Rainsbarger. But whether the evidence was sufficient to sustain the verdict of guilty against him, we will not determine on this appeal.

I. The state was permitted to examine the wife of Frank Rainsbarger as a witness on the trial, and her testimony tended to prove facts material to the case. An indictment was pending against her husband, in which he was also accused of the murder of Johnson, although he was not on trial at the time. The objection urged against the admission of her testimony was that, as it necessarily tended to prove that her husband was guilty of the crime for which defendant was being tried, she was not a competent witness. We deem it unnecessary to enter upon any discussion as to what the rule in such cases would be in the absence of statutory regulation; for the whole subject in this state is governed by statute. Section 3636 of the Code provides that "every human being of sufficient capacity to understand the obligation of an oath is a competent witness in all cases, both civil and

1. CRIMINAL evidence: testimony of wife of one jointly indicted.

criminal, except as herein otherwise declared." Sections 3641 and 3642 are as follows: "Neither the husband nor wife shall in any case be a witness against the other, except in a criminal prosecution for a crime committed one against the other, or in a civil action or proceeding one against the other.   *   *   *" "Neither husband nor wife can be examined in any case as to any communication made by the one to the other while married, nor shall they, after the marriage relation ceases, be permitted to reveal in testimony any such communication made while the marriage subsisted." These are the only provisions relating to the subject.

Under section 3636, any person of sufficient capacity to understand the obligations of an oath is a competent witness in any case, unless he is included in some of the exceptions created by other provisions. The exception created by section 3641, with reference to witnesses in criminal cases, is that neither the husband nor wife can be examined as a witness against the other, except in a prosecution for a crime committed by the one against the other; and that created by section 3642 makes the husband and wife incompetent witnesses to prove communications made by one to the other during the existence of the marriage relation. Very clearly, we think, the witness is not included in either of these exceptions. Her husband was not on trial, and her testimony was not against him, and she was not examined as to any communication made by him to her.

II.   The witness Mrs. Rainsbarger was asked by the district attorney whether she had heard a conversation between the defendant and the deceased a short time before the death of the latter, in reference to what defendant was to do for deceased; and she answered that deceased asked defendant and her husband what they were going to do about helping him to get money and clothes to get ready for a trial which he was expecting, and that defendant answered that "he had nothing,—only his threshing-machine and team to help him, and they were

2. ——: bad character of defendant: other crimes.

mortgaged; and if he helped him he would have to go out and steal it; that he had stolen to keep the children from cry-ing, and, if they were going to steal, they might just as well go to work and steal." The questions which elicited these answers were objected to by defendant's counsel. They also moved to exclude the answers after they were given, but the court overruled the objection and the motion. These rulings were erroneous. The testimony objected to did not tend to prove any fact material to the case. It was elicited as part of the evidence of the state in chief. It tended only to prove that defendant had been guilty of other crimes than the one charged in the indictment on which he was being tried, or that he was a reckless bad man, who was willing and ready to engage in any criminal enterprise. The rule that the state is not permitted to introduce evidence of the commis-sion by the accused of crimes entirely distinct from that for which he is being tried, for the purpose of proving him guilty of that crime, and that it cannot show his bad char-acter until he has placed his character in issue, has been so long recognized and is so well settled that there can be no necessity now for citing authorities in its support.

III. When Johnson was killed, he was traveling on the highway in a buggy drawn by a single horse. This buggy

3. ——: opin-
ions of ordi-
nary wit-
nesses.

was found standing about eighty rods from the body, with one of the forward wheels and one of the shafts broken. The evidence tended to prove that the homicide was committed at a point about sixty-four rods from where the buggy was found, and that the body was carried to the point where the buggy was left, on the horse which Johnson had driven, and that it had been dragged from there to the place where it was found. The state sought to establish that the buggy had been pur-posely broken by the application of some force to the wheel and shaft. A number of witnesses who examined it as it stood in the highway the morning after the killing were asked their opinion as to the manner in which the wheel and shaft had been broken, and they gave it as their opinion that a force had been applied at the top of the wheel, by which the upper part was forced outward, and the lower part in the opposite direction, and that the spokes were broken in that manner; also that the shaft appeared to have been broken by being pulled outward by a force applied at the forward end A witness was also permitted to testify that in his opinion the buggy was strong enough to carry two men of ordinary size without breaking. The appearance of the wheel and shaft, and the general condition of the buggy and of the ground in the vicinity, were described by the witnesses. It is insisted that the jurors, having these descriptions before them, were quite as competent to form a correct opinion of the capacity of the buggy, and as to the manner in which the breaking had been accomplished, as were the witnesses, and that the opinions of the witnesses were incompetent. It is true, as a general rule, that ordinary witnesses are not permitted to state their opinions upon questions that are to be determined by the jury, but it is the province of the jurors to draw such deductions and conclusions from the facts proven as appear to them to be reasonable. This rule, however, is not universal.

Mr. Lawson, in his work on Expert and Opinion Evidence, lays down the following as the rule on the subject established by the authorities. "The opinions of ordinary witnesses, derived from observation, are admissible in evidence, where, from the nature of the subject under investigation, no better evidence can be obtained, or the facts cannot otherwise be presented to the tribunal." (Rule 63.) See, also, the cases cited in the note.

The present case falls within this rule. Perhaps one of the most important matters to be considered in determining the manner in which the breaking of the wheel and shaft was accomplished, was the strength of the materials of which they were made, and it would be difficult, or impossible, by any mere verbal description, to give the jurors any definite or certain information on that subject. The witnesses had personally inspected them, and had had an opportunity to see and consider every circumstance which should be considered in forming an opinion; and the opinions given by them were formed from their observation of the facts. It was impossible to place all the material facts before the jury. The witnesses were in a position to form a correct opinion upon the subject, and the jurors could not be placed in that position.

IV. In an instruction defining malice as an element of murder, the jury were told, in effect, that malice would be implied from the unlawful and intentional use of a dangerous or deadly weapon in such manner as that the natural or necessary consequence of the act would be to destroy the life of another.

4. MURDER: instruction: inference of malice from use of deadly weapon.

Cases of homicide might arise in which an instruction in the language of the one in question would be misleading and erroneous. The killing of another may be accomplished by the unlawful and intentional use of a deadly weapon, and yet the one committing the act may be guilty of no higher crime than manslaughter. This might be so in any case where the killing was voluntary, but committed without deliberation, and in the heat of passion, induced by great provocation. In such cases, although the homicide was voluntary, and was committed by the intentional use of a deadly weapon, malice is not imputed to the act. But in the present case there was no evidence that the killing was accidental or upon provocation. The presumption, therefore, is that it was voluntary, and with malice aforethought. *State v. Gillick*, 7 Iowa, 311. As applicable to the evidence in the case, the instruction is correct.

Exception is taken to other instructions given by the court, and to other rulings on the admission and exclusion of testimony. We deem it unnecessary to specially notice the rulings complained of. They appear to us to be correct. For the error pointed out in the second paragraph of this opinion, the judgment must be   REVERSED.

APPENDIX.

NOTES OF CASES NOT OTHERWISE REPORTED.

THE STATE v. ROGERS.

A 753
80 164
71a 753
86 752

APPEAL: NO NOTICE ON CLERK: JUDGMENT AFFIRMED.

Appeal from Shelby District Court.

FIRDAY, MARCH 4, 1887.

THE defendant Sarah J. Rogers was indicted for the crime of resisting an officer. Verdict and judgment were rendered against her. She appeals.

No appearance for appellant.

A. J. Baker, Attorney-general, for the State.

ADAMS, CH. J.—This case is submitted upon the transcript. Notice of appeal seems to have been duly served upon the district attorney, but we are unable to discover that the notice was served upon the clerk of the court. The statute provides for such service, and without it we cannot hold that the appeal was perfected. It follows that we have no jurisdiction of the case, and the appeal must be

DISMISSED.

BURDETT, SMITH & CO. v. WOODWORTH & CO. ET AL.

MICHIGAN STOVE CO. v. THE SAME.

CHATTEL MORTGAGE: FRAUD: EVIDENCE TO SUPPORT FINDING OF COURT.

Appeal from Page Circuit Court.

SATURDAY, MARCH 5, 1887.

THESE are actions at law. They involve the validity of a chattel mortgage upon a stock of hardware. The plaintiffs are creditors of the defendant Woodworth, and levied attachments upon the property. The defendant Mather asserted title to the goods under a chattel·mortgage made by Woodworth to him. Pending the action, Mather assigned the mortgage to the Grinnell Barb Wire Co., and it intervened and assumed the place of Mather

VOL. LXXI—48

as a party to the action. It was alleged by the plaintiffs that the mortgage was fraudulent as to the creditors of Woodworth. This was the issue which was tried. The trial was had to the court without a jury, and judgment was rendered for the defendants. Plaintiffs appeal.

S. C. McPherrin, for appellants.

N. B. Moore, *S. B. Jennings* and *Haines, Lyman & Howell*, for appellees.

ROTHROCK, J.—There is but one error assigned and argued. It presents the question as to the sufficiency of the evidence to support the judgment. We have carefully examined the evidence, and have reached the conclusion that we cannot disturb the judgment. It is not necessary to set out the evidence. It is sufficient to say that, applying the same rule to the judgment which is applied by this court to the verdict of a jury, the judgment finds support in the evidence. It does not appear without conflict that the mortgage was fraudulent. It is to be remembered that we are not required to try the cause anew in this court.

AFFIRMED.

THE STATE v. STEWART. (Six cases.)

CRIMINAL LAW: APPEAL FOR DELAY: NO APPEARANCE NOR ASSIGNMENT OF ERROR: JUDGMENT AFFIRMED.

Appeal from Appanoose District Court.

SATURDAY, MARCH 5, 1887.

No appearance for appellee.

A. J. Baker, Attorney-general, for the State.

BECK, J.—In each case, upon an information filed before a justice of the peace charging defendant with the crime of unlawfully selling intoxicating liquors, he was convicted and committed in default of payment of the fine. Upon appeals to the district court, like judgments were rendered there. He now appeals in each case to this court.

The record before us contains transcripts of the proceedings and instructions to the jury, but no part of the evidence is set out.

There is no appearance or assignment of errors. We have examined the record with care, and find no error therein. It is not our duty to support the judgment of the court below by discussing imaginary errors.

The cases evidently belong to the class, now very numerous, in which delay in the enforcements of the judgments in criminal cases is obtained by appeals to this court. The defendant in these cases has been quite successful in his effort in that direction, having by his appeals delayed punishment for about one year.

The judgment of the district court in each case is affirmed, and a *procedendo* is ordered in each case to be issued as speedily as is authorized by the law and rules of this court, to the end that justice be no longer unlawfully delayed.

AFFIRMED.

McFarland v. Elliott et al.

FRAUDULENT CONVEYANCE: CONSIDERATION: EVIDENCE.

Appeal from Boone Circuit Court.

SATURDAY, MARCH 5, 1887. ·

ACTION in equity to subject certain real estate to the payment of a judgment against Amos Elliott. The petition was dismissed, and the plaintiff appeals.

S. R. Dyer and *J. N. Kidder*, for appellant.

E. L. Green, for appellee.

SEEVERS, J.—In 1879, Amos Elliott became indebted to the plaintiff, and he recovered a judgment on such indebtedness in 1884. In 1883, said Elliott owned an interest in certain real estate. His co-defendants also owned an interest therein to the extent of one-eighth each thereof. They sold all the interests to one Livingston, or rather exchanged farms with him. The agreed difference between the two tracts of land was $2,500, and this was paid by Livingston to Amos Elliott. The farm obtained from Livingston was conveyed by him to Belinda Elliott, the wife of Amos Elliott, and Nancy Pugh, her sister. Appellant contends that this transfer is fraudulent and void, because Belinda Elliott paid no consideration therefor. We think the evidence fairly establishes that the land owned by Amos Elliott, his wife, and her sister, was of the value of about $6,000. The amount received by Amos Elliott was $2,500. The value of the land conveyed by Livingston to Belinda Elliott and Nancy Pugh, did not exceed $3,500. It was probably not worth quite that much. Their interest in the land conveyed to Livingston was $1,500. Now, the question is, whether Amos Elliott was indebted to his wife and Nancy Pugh in the amount of $2,000. That he was indebted to them must be conceded, and, if his evidence can be believed, he was indebted in the amount above stated, if not more. There is no evidence which materially contradicts him. We see no reason for disbelieving him, unless it can be said that the story told by him is improbable. But we do not think this is so, and therefore the judgment is

AFFIRMED.

NEILSON v. MATTOCKS ET AL.

PRACTICE ON APPEAL: CONFLICTING EVIDENCE TO SUPPORT VERDICT.

Appeal from Woodbury Circuit Court.

MONDAY, MARCH 7, 1887.

THE plaintiff's action is in the nature of a suit upon an account for work and labor. The defendants are husband and wife, and they filed separate answers. Joseph Mattocks admitted by his answer that the plaintiff had performed work and labor for him, but denied that he was indebted to him therefor. He also set up a counter-claim, in which he demanded damages by reason of the plaintiff having injured and maltreated certain live stock of the defendant while in his employ. The defendant Prudence Mattocks in her answer, denied each and every averment of the petition. There was a trial by jury, and a verdict and judgment for the plaintiff. Defendants appeal.

Lawrence & Burd, for appellants.

Cooper & Lynn, for appellee.

ROTHROCK, J.—There were three questions of fact between the parties. The first was, whether anything was due the plaintiff for his labor; *second*, whether the defendants were jointly liable to the plaintiff, and, *third*, whether the plaintiff was liable on the counter-claim. All of these questions were determined in favor of the plaintiff. The only question to be determined by the appeal is whether there was sufficient evidence to sustain the verdict. The plaintiff is a foreigner, and we infer from an examination of his evidence that he has a very imperfect knowledge of our language. It is true, as claimed by appellant's counsel, that his testimony was somewhat inconsistent. But taking it all together it fairly supports the verdict, both as to the amount claimed and as to the joint liability of the defendants. It is true, the defendants in their testimony contradict the plaintiff. It was a question for the jury to determine which side was in the right, and it is well known that in such cases this court does not interfere with verdicts. The evidence upon the counter-claim was very much in conflict, and of course, that part of the judgment must stand. Considering the whole case, we think that it should be

AFFIRMED.

McREYNOLDS v. McREYNOLDS ET AL.

WIDOW'S DISTRIBUTIVE SHARE: EVIDENCE TO SUPPORT DECREE.

Appeal from Wapello District Court.

MONDAY, MARCH 7, 1887.

THE plaintiff, as widow of Solomon McReynolds, deceased, brings this action in equity against the heirs of the decedent for the purpose of obtaining her distributive share in certain land of which he died seized, and in certain other land, a part of which stands in the name of the defendant M. M. L. McReynolds, and part in the name of the defendant Marsha Tracy, but which she avers also belongs to the estate of the decedent. The court decreed her a distributive share in the land standing in the name of the decedent at the time of his death, but denied her any share in the land standing in the name of the others. Both the plaintiff and the defendants appeal, the latter perfecting their appeal first.

Stiles & Beaman, and *W. W. Corey,* for appellants.

McNett & Tisdale and *H. B. Hendershott,* for appellee.

ADAMS, CH. J.—In 1862 the plaintiff married the decedent Solomon Mc-Reynolds, the latter being somewhat advanced in years, and both having been married before and having adult children. The defendant M. M. L. McReynolds, son of the decedent, was opposed to the marriage from the beginning, and the union, while it subsisted, appears to have been full of trouble, and has resulted in a large amount of expensive litigation.

At the time of the marriage the parties had entered into an ante-nuptial agreement. It is not necessary to set out the terms of it. It is sufficient to say that it was drawn with the view of giving the plaintiff somewhat less than she would receive as her distributive share in the absence of an agreement. It is not important to inquire with what feeling it was entered into between the parties, but we infer that it was insisted upon by the decedent, and with the view, perhaps, in part, of conciliating his son, M. M. L. McReynolds, but that it was never satisfactory to the plaintiff. The evidence tended to show that it was not contemplated, even in the beginning, as certainly a final arrangement, but that the decedent had in mind that, after he had made some provision for his children, he would destroy the agreement, and have the plaintiff take her distributive share.

Whether it was in fact destroyed is one of the controverted questions in this case. The evidence is conflicting. There is considerable direct and positive testimony that it was destroyed. But a portion of the witnesses are interested, and there is a great variety of circumstances tending in a greater or less degree to show the improbability of its destruction, and some evidence tending to impeach the character of the interested witnesses for truth and veracity. A very large amount of testimony was taken, and the printed abstract presented to us contains nearly three hundred pages. The case has evidently been tried with great thoroughness, and perhaps not without some feeling even, on the part of counsel. The arguments are exhaustive, and display the ability characteristic of the counsel. We may say also that the great variety of facts and circumstances testified to, some having much and some very little bearing upon the case, and the conflict of the testimony, have afforded the counsel a great scope for argument. This being the character of the case, it would not only be contrary to our custom, but impracticable, to set out the evidence relied upon by either party, and adduce the reasoning by which one conclusion is reached rather than the other. The correctness of neither one of the main propositions of fact contended for could be demonstrated in such a way as to satisfy the unsuccessful party.

We have, then, to say that, after the best examination which we have been able to give the evidence and the argument of counsel, we have united in the conclusion that there is a preponderance in support of both branches of the decree, and that on both appeals the case must be

AFFIRMED.

PAYNE v. THE DES MOINES & FORT DODGE R'Y Co.

CONTRACT: SPECIFIC PERFORMANCE: NO EVIDENCE OF PERFORMANCE ON PLAINTIFF'S PART.

Appeal from Polk Circuit Court.

WEDNESDAY, MARCH 9, 1887.

ACTION in chancery to enforce the specific performance of a contract to convey lands. After a trial upon the merits, plaintiff's petition was dismissed. He now appeals to this court.

Baylies & Baylies, for appellant.

Kauffman & Guernsey, for appellee.

BECK, J.—I. The contract which plaintiff seeks to specifically enforce is evidenced by the following correspondence, upon which plaintiff bases his right to recover:

"DES MOINES, IOWA, March 9, 1885.

"CHAS. E. WHITEHEAD, *Pres't D. M. & Ft. Dodge R. R. Co.*, *61 Wall St., N. Y.*:

"DEAR SIR:—I arrived home from New York last Friday. In regard to the lands I was talking to you about, I am on track of some in this county which, I think, if followed up, would inure to your company's benefit, and, if my memory serves me right, are not listed on the book you showed me in your office. You offered me a commission of twenty per cent of the value of any such lands I might cite you to. I thought then and think now that the offer was low, and again the difficulty might arise as to the value of the land; then as to the commission to be paid. I am satisfied that I can find some land, after the years' experience I have had in such matters as title, etc.

"You will please state your best terms, when payment is to be made for finding the land, either commission or per acre. Also give me a statement of the land you have on your book there, that I may not spend time over them. By the way you spoke, when you called on me in 1881, I expected a better offer than twenty per cent of value.

"I believe, in these matters, to have a fair and positive understanding at the start. Trusting to receive an early reply, I am, etc.,

"J. J. PAYNE"

"Office President of D. M. & Ft. Dodge R. R. Co.,
"61 Wall St., N. Y. City, March 12, 1885.

"J. J. Payne, Des Moines:

"Dear Sir:—In reply to your favor of the 9th, I would say that our company will give you twenty-five per cent of any lands you may get certified to it in Polk county. If we do not agree on the value of the lands, it will convey to you that proportion of the land itself. I enclose a list of lands we have had in the county.   Yours, etc.,

"Chas. E. Whitehead."

Plaintiff claims that he accepted the proposition found in the letter of defendant's president just quoted. It may, for the purposes of the case, be admitted that he did.

He then insists that, in compliance with the terms of the contract, he "did get certified" to defendant the lands involved in this action. In our opinion the evidence utterly fails to support plaintiff's claim of performance of the terms of the contract. We fail to find any evidence showing that through his labor, efforts and intelligence, the lands were certified to defendant, or that he rendered any service in the matter of any value whatever to defendant. The truth is that the lands were in process of certification before the correspondence was had between the parties, and very soon thereafter were certified. Plaintiff claims that he wrote a letter to the proper department at Washington upon the subject, and, at his request, the clerk of the secretary of state having land matters in charge wrote a like letter to the same department. But it does not appear that plaintiff's effort in that direction caused the certification of the land.

The correspondence clearly discloses the fact that the contract is applicable to lands as its subject, which were unknown to defendant, and could only be found through the superior skill and knowledge of plaintiff, and not to the lands in question, which must have been known to defendant, and which its officers and agents were using efforts to obtain.

The plaintiff's petition was rightly dismissed.

Affirmed.

Curtis v. Lowman et al.

Verdict: on conflicting evidence: not disturbed on appeal.

Appeal from Cass District Court.

Tuesday, March 15, 1887.

Action upon an alleged contract to pay the plaintiff a debt due from one Fuson. There was a trial to the court without a jury, and judgment was rendered against the plaintiff for costs. She appeals.

H. G. Curtis and *F. B. Huckstep*, for appellant.

L. L. De Lano, for appellee.

Adams, Ch., J.—The defendant took a bill of sale of certain hotel furniture from one J. W. Fuson and Mary E. Fuson. The Fusons at the time were indebted to the plaintiff, and she avers that defendants, in consideration of the conveyance to them of the hotel furniture, agreed to pay the Fusons' debt to the plaintiff. The defendants denied that they made such agreement. The evidence in respect to such agreement is in conflict. The action is at law, and we cannot disturb the judgment.

AFFIRMED.

THE STATE v. KOLL ET AL.

CRIMINAL LAW: INTOXICATING LIQUORS: NO APPEARANCE FOR APPELLANT: NO ERROR FOUND.

Appeal from Webster District Court.

WEDNESDAY, MARCH 9, 1887.

THE defendant was tried upon an indictment charging him with the crime of using a certain building for the purpose of keeping intoxicating liquors therein, with intent to sell the same in violation of law. A verdict of guilty was returned, and a judgment was rendered thereon. The defendant appeals.

No appearance for the appellant.

A. J. Baker, Attorney-general, for the State.

ADAMS, CH J.—The instructions are set out. but no part of the evidence. We have examined the instructions carefully, and the entire record, and find no error.

AFFIRMED.

RYAN v. CAMPBELL ET AL.

1. CORPORATIONS: TRANSFER OF STOCK: ENTRY ON BOOKS: WHEN NECESSARY. (*Fort Madison Lumber Co. v. Batavian Bank et al., ante,* p. 270, followed.)

Appeal from Jones District Court.

SATURDAY, MARCH 12, 1887.

J. W. Jamison, H. N. Ryan and *B. H. Miller,* for appellant.

Sheean & McCarn, for appellees.

SEEVERS, J.—The facts in this case and the questions to be determined are precisely the same as in *Fort Madison Lumber Co. v. Batavian Bank, ante, p. 270,* and, following that case, the judgment of the district court in this case must be

REVERSED.

CRAIG V. FLORANG ET AL.

INTOXICATING LIQUORS: NUISANCE: CONSTITUTIONALITY OF STATUTE.

Appeal from Des Moines District Court.

SATURDAY, MARCH 12.

P. Henry Smyth & Son, for appellants.

No appearance for appellee.

SEEVERS, J.—This case in all respects is like *McLane v. Bonn et al.*, 70 Iowa, 752. Following that case the judgment in this must be

AFFIRMED.

HAWKINS V. WILSON.

PROMISSORY NOTE: FRAUD: HOLDER FOR VALUE, BEFORE DUE, WITHOUT NOTICE. •

Appeal from Mahaska Circuit Court.

WEDNESDAY, MARCH 16, 1887.

ACTION on a negotiable promissory note which the plaintiff claims was transferred to him before maturity for a valuable consideration. The defendant pleaded that the note had been obtained by fraud, and that the plaintiff had full knowledge of such fraud prior to and at the time the note was transferred to him. Trial by jury, verdict and judgment for the defendant. A motion for a new trial was overruled, and the plaintiff appeals.

John O. Malcolm, for appellant.

Bolton & McCoy, for appellee.

SEEVERS, J.—The note is dated April 4th, 1884, and is payable to C. E. Abbey or order, nine months after date, and it was transferred to plaintiff before maturity. It will be conceded there was evidence tending to show that Abbey procured the note through and by means of certain fraudulent representations made by him.

After a careful examination of the answer, we have been unable to find any allegation that the plaintiff did not pay a valuable consideration for the note. This being so, the only remaining issue was, whether the plaintiff had knowledge of the fraud at the time the note became his property. We have carefully read the evidence, and have failed to find any so tending. The defendant himself had no knowledge of the fraud prior to December, 1884, and at that time he knew the plaintiff claimed to be the owner of the note, and defendant agreed to pay it.

The plaintiff testified that he procured the note in November, 1884, and that he had no knowledge, directly or indirectly, that it had been obtained by fraud. There is not a particle of evidence contradictory to this. But defendant claims that the plaintiff made contradictory statements when testifying, and that he had known Abbey for some years; that they jointly owned a horse, and were intimate and conversant with each other's business, and therefore it is assumed the plaintiff must have known of the fraud, and the jury were justified in so finding. Conceding all that is claimed in this respect, we are unable to see how such evidence tends to establish the claimed proposition. Besides this, we are unable to concur with counsel that there is any evidence, fairly considered, which tends to prove the matters claimed, unless a strained, instead of a reasonable and natural, construction is placed on the evidence of the plaintiff, on which the defendant solely relies to establish the requisite knowledge.

The court erred in not sustaining the motion for a new trial.

REVERSED.

THE STATE v. FORTIG.

PRACTICE ON APPEAL: CRIMINAL CASE: NO APPEARANCE FOR APPELLANT: RECORD REVIEWED AND JUDGMENT AFFIRMED.

Appeal from Floyd District Court.

TUESDAY, JUNE 14, 1887.

No appearance for appellant.

A. J. Baker, Attorney-general, for the State.

BECK, J.—The defendant, with another, was jointly indicted for maintaining a nuisance by keeping a place for the unlawful sale of intoxicating liquors, and was convicted, the other defendant being acquitted. Defendant now appeals to this court. The case is submitted to us for decision without an assignment of errors, brief or argument, or any appearance for defendant. We have carefully considered the record in the case, without finding any error or irregularity in the proceedings.

AFFIRMED.

INDEX.

ABORTION.

See CRIMINAL LAW, 1.

ABSTRACT OF RECORD.

See PRACTICE IN SUPREME COURT, *passim.*

ACKNOWLEDGMENT.

1. LEGALIZING ACT: EFFECT OF. Chapter 160, Laws of 1870, legalizing acknowledgments of conveyances made in other states in accordance with the laws thereof, caused a deed so acknowledged, and recorded before said act became a law by publication, to have the same effect as if it had been property acknowledged according to the laws of Iowa. *East v. Pugh*, 162.

2. CERTIFICATE: TITLE OF OFFICER. Where the title of the officer taking an acknowledgment appears in the body of the certificate, this is sufficient, under § 1958 of the Code, and such title need not be again written after the officer's signature. *Colby v. McOmber*, 469.

See TAX SALE AND DEED, 2.

ACTION.

1. SURVIVAL OF. See Personal Injuries, 5.

2. IDENTITY OF AFTER AMENDMENT. See Statute of Limitations, 7.

See PARTIES TO ACTIONS.

ADMINISTRATOR.

1. CONVEYANCE OF LAND BOUGHT IN ON MORTGAGE FORECLOSURE. An administrator who buys in land upon the foreclosure of a mortgage belonging to the estate holds it as personal property, and he may convey it without an order of court. *Stevenson v. Polk*, 278.

2. FIDUCIARY RELATION TO CO-TENANT OF INHERITED LAND. Where the real estate of a decedent descended in equal shares to his wife and his father, and the wife was administratrix of the estate, *held* that she did not on that account hold a fiduciary relation to the father, so as to cast suspicion upon a purchase by her of the father's interest in the real estate. *Herron v. Herron*, 428.

3. TAKING WIDOW'S PROPERTY: REPLEVIN: CAPACITY OF DEFENDANT. An administrator who takes the property of the widow is a trespasser, and is personally liable, and cannot, in an action to recover the property, insist that he shall be substituted in his capacity as administrator. *Herd v. Herd*, 497.

See ESTOPPEL, 1; PARTNERSHIP, 1.

ADULTERY.

See CRIMINAL LAW, 3.

AFFIDAVIT.

1. AFFIANT'S NAME IN JURAT. An affidavit stated, "I, Frank Pierce, do on oath say," etc., and was signed "Frank Pierce." The jurat was as follows: "Subscribed and sworn to by ——, before me," etc. "J. Compton, Notary Public." *Held* sufficient to show that the affidavit was sworn to by Frank Pierce. *Kirby v. Gates*, 100.

AGENCY.

1. AUTHORITY TO SELL LAND: LETTERS CONSTRUED. G., a real estate agent in Iowa, but who had never done any business for S., who resided in New York, wrote to S., asking the price of S.'s land in a certain county, and stating that he would, on learning the price, endeavor to effect a sale. S. replied that, to close out all his lands in that county, he would sell for four dollars per acre. *Held* (1) that this did not confer upon G. authority to bind S. by a contract for the sale of the lands; and (2) that, if it were conceded that the letters did confer such authority on G., still he could sell only unconditionally for cash, and that a contract made by him for the sale of all the lands at four dollars per acre, $500 paid in cash, and the balance to be paid when an abstract of title should be furnished showing perfect title in the grantor, was not binding upon S. *Gilbert v. Baxter*, 327.

2. REPUDIATION OF CONTRACT: GROUNDS ASSIGNED: WAIVER. Where the principal did not know the terms of a contract which one claiming to be his agent had made for him, but he repudiated it on the ground that the person who made it was not his agent, *held* that he was not precluded afterwards from repudiating it on the ground that it was not in accordance with the terms of the letter on which the alleged agent relied for his agency. *Id.*

3. EVIDENCE OF: DECLARATIONS OF AGENT. The fact of agency cannot be established by the declarations of the alleged agent, whether made to the person seeking to establish the agency, or to a third party; and where the question of agency is the point in issue, such declarations are inadmissible for any purpose, even when the trial is to the court, in an ordinary action. *Sax v. Davis*, 406.

4. FACTS NOT AMOUNTING TO: CONTRACT FOR RIGHT OF WAY. The plaintiff being about to build its railroad through a certain town, many of the owners of land crossed by the road were disposed to donate the right of way; and some of them, not, however, being agents of the company, visited the defendant, and sought to have her donate the right of way over her land, which she stated to them she would do, but she did not constitute them her agents to tender the right of way to the company. *Held* that a tender by them of the right of way did not bind her, nor prevent her from afterwards recovering compensation, by condemnation proceedings, for the damages to her land. *C. I. & D. R'y Co. v. Estes*, 603.

See ATTORNEY AT LAW, 3.

AMENDMENT.

See PLEADING, 1, 5.

ANIMALS.

1. TRESPASSING: ASSESSMENT OF DAMAGES BY TOWNSHIP TRUSTEES: ALL MUST BE NOTIFIED. When power is conferred on three or more persons to do an act, and notice to such persons is required, all must be notified, if possible, although, when duly notified, a majority may act. (See cases cited in opinion.) Accordingly, *held* that an appraisement

ment is rendered therefor, the defendant cannot appeal to this court without the certificate of the trial judge. *Cooper v. Wilson*, 204.

10. NO NOTICE ON CLERK: JUDGMENT AFFIRMED. *State v. Rogers*, 753. See, also, EXECUTION, 4.

See REMOVAL OF CAUSES, 1.

(1) From Justices' Courts.

11. AMOUNT IN CONTROVERSY: JURISDICTION. In an action in justice's court $100 was claimed by plaintiff. but he recovered judgment for only $10, whereupon he remitted all claim for damages over and above $24.90. Afterwards the defendant appealed to the circuit court. *Held* that the amount in controversy was less than $25, and that therefore an appeal would not lie. (*Milner v. Gross*, 66 Iowa, 252, followed.) *Vorwald v. Marshall*, 576.

(2) To County Superintendent.

See SCHOOLS, 1.

APPEARANCE.

See PRACTICE AND PROCEDURE, 7; REFERENCE, 2.

ARGUMENT.

See PRACTICE, 12; NEW TRIAL, 2; PRACTICE IN SUPREME COURT, 3.

ARSON.

See CRIMINAL LAW, 4.

ASSIGNMENT.

1. EFFECT OF UNACCEPTED ORDER. An order drawn upon a third person cannot, until accepted, be the basis of an action by the payee against the drawee. (*Roberts r. Corbin*, 26 Iowa, 315, where the action was based on a banker's draft, distinguished.) *Poole r. Carhart*, 37.

2. OF CLAIM FOR TORT: ACTION BY ASSIGNEE. See Parties to Actions, 5.

ASSIGNMENT FOR BENEFIT OF CREDITORS.

1. WHAT IS NOT: PREFERRING CREDITORS. The transfer by an insolvent of all his property, in parcels. by deeds and mortgages, to several of his creditors, in satisfaction or security of their claims. does not constitute an assignment for the benefit of creditors, though all done at one time and as one transaction; and such conveyance cannot be set aside as being in violation of § 2115 of the Code. (See opinion for cases followed and distinguished.) *Aulman v. Aulman*, 124.

ASSIGNMENT OF ERRORS.

See PRACTICE IN SUPREME COURT, 415.

ATTACHMENT.

1. ACTION ON BOND: EVIDENCE. Where an attachment was issued on the ground that defendants were about to dispose of their property with intent to defraud their creditors, and defendants sought to recover on the bond for the wrongful suing out of the attachment, *held* that the testimony of one of them that they had no such intent was irrelevant to the issue. (*Selz v. Belden*, 48 Iowa, 451, followed.) *Charles City Plow Co. v. Jones*, 234.

INDEX. 767

2. **RETURN OF SHERIFF: WHAT IT IS EVIDENCE OF.** A sheriff's return
upon a writ of attachment is evidence only of such of his acts as he
may lawfully do under and by virtue of the writ. And so, where the
sheriff returned not only that he had seized certain chattels under the
writ, but that he had also, at plaintiff's direction, seized, closed up and
held possession of the houses in which the chattels were stored, which
was not necessary for the preservation of the chattels, *held*, in an action
on the attachment bond, that the return was not evidence of such seizure of the buildings, nor of the attachment plaintiff's direction so to
seize them. *Id.*

3. **WRONGFUL SUING OUT: ADVICE OF COUNSEL WHO ARE STOCKHOLDERS
OF THE PLAINTIFF.** In an action on an attachment bond for the
wrongful suing out of the attachment, the attachment plaintiff may
show, for the purpose of rebutting the charge of malice, that it sought
the advice of counsel, and acted under such advice, in suing out the
attachment, even though the counsel consulted were stockholders or
officers of the attachment plaintiff, which was a corporation. *Id.*

4. ———: ———: **EVIDENCE OF CONVERSATION WITH COUNSEL.** In such
case, evidence should have been admitted of the conversation between
the attachment plaintiff's business manager and its attorneys, relative
to the suing out of the attachment. *Id.*

5. ———: **ADVICE OF LAWYER NOT IN PRACTICE.** In such case, the attachment plaintiff may show that it consulted an attorney by profession, but
not in actual practice, and that he advised the suing out of the attachment. *Id.*

6. **ACTION ON BOND: ATTORNEYS' FEES.** Where the whole defense in an
attachment case tended to show the wrongfulness of the attachment, it
was proper, in an action on the bond, to allow attorneys' fees for services in defending the entire case. *Whitney v. Brownewell*, 251.

7. **LEVY: WHAT NECESSARY: PRIORITY OVER MORTGAGE: NOTICE.** In
order to perfect a levy of an attachment upon lands in possession of the
attachment defendant, it is necessary to notify the defendant thereof,
(Code, § 2967,) and to make return of the writ; and a return is not
made until signed by the officer. An entry in the incumbrance book is
not sufficient, and is not even evidence or notice of a levy, where a levy
has not in fact been perfected, as above indicated. Accordingly, a
mortgage executed and filed for record before a levy was perfected, as
above explained, had priority over the attachment lien. *First Nat.
Bank v. Jasper Co. Bank*, 486.

8. **INTERVENTION: WHEN NOT APPLICABLE: SALE OF REAL ESTATE.**
When attached real estate has been sold under the attachment, a third
party claiming a superior lien by virtue of a prior mortgage cannot proceed by intervention, under § 3016 of the Code, but may proceed in
equity to restrain the consummation of the sale. *Id.*

See DAMAGES, 3; PRACTICE AND PROCEDURE, 19.

ATTORNEY AT LAW.

1. **FEES OF: CHAP. 185, LAWS OF 1880: AFFIDAVIT IN CASE OF EXISTING
CONTRACTS.** Chapter 185, Laws of 1880, regulating and limiting the
amount of attorney's fees that may be taxed on written contracts stipulating for attorney's fees, applies wholly to contracts made after the
passage of the act, and it is not necessary to file the affidavit required
by § 3 of the act, in order to recover attorney's fees on a contract antedating the act itself. *Eikenberry v. Edwards*, 82.

2. ———: **NOTICE OF LIEN ENTERED ON JUDGMENT DOCKET: EFFECT OF:
REVERSAL OF JUDGMENT.** Where, after a judgment has been procured for the plaintiff in an action, his attorneys enter upon the ju l

ment docket notice of their claim for a lien for their fees in the case, such notice creates a lien not only upon the judgment, but upon any money due the plaintiff from the defendant in that action. And so, even where the judgment is reversed on appeal, the defendant may not settle with plaintiff and pay him the amount agreed on, and thus defeat the lien of his attorneys. And in this case, where a defendant did so settle and pay, *held* that it was still liable to the attorneys for their fees. *Winslow v. Cent. Iowa R'y Co.*, 197.

3. LIMIT OF AUTHORITY. While an attorney cannot consent to a judgment against his client, nor waive any cause of action or defense in the case, nor settle or compromise it, without his special authority, yet he is authorized by his general employment to do all acts necessary or incidental to the prosecution or defense, which pertain to the *remedy* pursued. And, in the application of this rule, *held* that, where a client was a party to two suits involving substantially the same question, it was competent for his attorney to bind him by an agreement that only one of the cases should be tried, and that the judgment resulting from such trial should determine the kind of judgment to be entered in the other case. *Ohlquest v. Farwell*, 231.

4. ALLOWANCE OF FEES. See Attachment, 6.

See CHAMPERTY, 1.

BILL OF EXCEPTIONS.

See PRACTICE, 1; PRACTICE IN SUPREME COURT, 22.

BILLS AND NOTES.

See PROMISSORY NOTES.

BOARD OF SUPERVISORS.

1. COUNTY NOT BOUND BY STATEMENTS OF WHEN NOT IN SESSION. See County, 2.

BURGLARY.

See CRIMINAL LAW, 5, 7, 9.

CARRIERS.

See RAILROADS, 22-26, 28, 29.

CASES IN THE IOWA REPORTS CITED, FOLLOWED, ETC.

[The figures immediately following the title of the case show the volume and page of the Iowa Reports where the case is found; the words in Roman type indicate the subject under consideration; and the figures following refer to the page in this volume where the citation is made.]

CERTIORARI.

See APPEAL, 3.

CHAMPERTY.

1. WHAT IS NOT: CONTINGENT FEE. A contract between an attorney and his client that the former shall have for his compensation one-third of the amount that may ultimately be recovered in an action, the attorney to pay no costs or expenses, except his own personal expenses, is not champertous. (*McDonald v. Railroad Co.*, 29 Iowa, 174, and *Jewell v. Neidy*, 61 Id., 299, followed.) *Winslow v. Cent. Iowa R'y Co.*, 197.

CHANGE OF VENUE.

See PRACTICE AND PROCEDURE, 4; VENUE, *passim*.

· CHARACTER.

See CRIMINAL LAW, 15, 19; EVIDENCE, 2.

CHATTEL MORTGAGE.

1. OF HORSE AND EARNINGS: FUTURE EARNINGS. A chattel mortgage upon a horse, wh ch provided: "This mortgage to cover all earnings of the horse, whether by premiums or otherwise," *held* not to include premiums earned after the execution of the mortgage. (*Lormer v. Allyn*, 64 Iowa, 725, followed in principle.) *McArthur v. Garman*, 34.

2. RECOVERY OF PROCEEDS: PROOF OF BALANCE DUE. Where an intervenor in a garnishment proceeding claimed the attached fund as the proceeds of the sale of chattel property on which he held a mortgage, but he failed to prove for how much the mortgage was given, and it appeared that $700 had been paid on it, *held* that he could not recover, because it did not appear that the mortgage was not fully paid. *Poole v. Carhart*, 37.

3. DESCRIPTION OF PROPERTY. The description of the property covered by a chattel mortgage was as follows: "Fifty head of steers about (20) months old, now owned by me, and in my possession on my farm in Independence township, Jasper county, Iowa." *Held* sufficient as against subsequent purchasers from the mortgagor, even though one of the purchasers bought some of the cattle in Clear Creek township, where they were in charge of the mortgagor's agent, on a part of his farm, which lay partly in Independence and partly in Clear Creek township. *Kenyon v. Tramel*, 693.

4. FRAUD: EVIDENCE TO SUPPORT FINDING OF COURT. *Burdette v. Woodworth*, 753.

See PERSONAL PROPERTY, 1; SALES, 1, 2; SURETY, 3.

CIRCUIT COURT.

1. JURISDICTION OF APPEAL FROM JUSTICE. See Appeal, 11.

CITIES AND TOWNS.

1. INJURY ON SIDEWALK: NOTICE OF DEFECT: EVIDENCE. If a walk is continuously unsafe for sixty feet, and an injury occurs to a pedestrian at one end of such distance, evidence of the condition of the walk for the whole distance may be introduced, in an action against the town by the person injured, for the purpose of showing that the defendant should have known of its condition. (*Ruggles v. Town of Nevada*, 63 Iowa, 185, distinguished.) *Armstrong v. Town of Ackley*, 76.

2. ————: ACTION TO RECOVER: DEFECTS MUST BE PROVED AS ALLEGED. In an action to recover for an injury occasioned by a defective sidewalk, it is not sufficient to prove that the walk was unsafe at the place of the accident, but plaintiff must prove the specific defects alleged in the petition. *Id.*

3. RESTRAINING DISORDERLY HOUSES. Under the power, given by § 456 of the Code, to "repress and distrain disorderly houses," a city has authority by ordinance to make it an offense to visit such houses. *State v. Botkin*, 87.

4. VACATION OF PLAT: WHO MAY VACATE: "PROPRIETORS:" CODE, §§ 563, 564. Under the provisions of §§ 563 and 564 of the Code, not only the original proprietors of a town plat may vacate the same, or a portion thereof, but persons who have acquired title from such original proprietors may exercise the power conferred by the statute. (Compare

Lorenzen v. Preston, 53 Iowa, 580, and *Conner v. Iowa City*, 66 Id., 419.) *McGrew v. Lettsville*, 150.

5. ——: EFFECT ON CORPORATION BOUNDARIES. The vacation of a portion of a town plat does not have the effect to take the vacated portion out of the corporation. *Id.*

6. RIVAL VILLAGES IN ONE CORPORATION: SEVERANCE. Where a small village became incorporated, and included territory two miles long and one mile wide, and a rival village afterwards sprang up in another portion of the territory so included, and the interests of the villages, whose centers were about a mile apart, were antagonistic, and the land lying between them was not platted or used for town purposes, *held* that a petition by the people of the new village, under §§ 440–446 of the Code, for a severance of their territory from the corporation, was properly granted. *Ashley v. Calliope*, 466.

7. DEBT OF: WHAT CONSTITUTES: CONSTITUTIONAL LIMIT: SEWER TAX. A contract entered into by a city for the building of a sewer, whereby the contractor agrees to accept, in full satisfaction for the whole work, certificates of assessment made upon the property adjacent to the sewer, *held* not to create a debt against the city within the meaning of Article 11, § 3, of the constitution, limiting the lawful indebtedness of a city to five per cent of the value of its taxable property. *Davis v. Des Moines*, 500.

8. STEPPING IN HOLE BY SIDEWALK: CONTRIBUTORY NEGLIGENCE. A pedestrian on a sidewalk who voluntarily and without necessity steps from the walk, without knowing that he can do so with safety, and steps in a hole near the walk, and is thereby injured, is guilty of contributory negligence, and cannot recover of the city. (Compare *McLaury v. City of McGregor*, 54 Iowa, 717.) *Alline v. Le Mars*, 654.

9. INJURY ON WALK: MEASURE OF DAMAGES. See Damages, 6.

See RAILROADS, 6.

CLERK OF COURTS.

1. SALARY AND FEES OF. An officer is entitled to charge and receive only such fees as the statute provides as compensation for the services he may perform. Accordingly, the fees of a clerk of the courts are defined and limited by § 3781 of the Code, and reporter's and jury fees and marriage license fees, collected by him, not being included in said section, are no part of his compensation; neither is he entitled to extra compensation for a necessary rearrangement of the papers and records of his office, nor for issuing jurors' certificates to the auditor for the fees of jurors. *Palo Alto Co. v. Burlingame*, 201 .

2. FEES OF FOR SETTLING ESTATES. See Estates of Decedents, 1.

CODE.

See STATUTES CITED, CONSTRUED, ETC.

COLLATERAL SECURITY.

See MORTGAGE, 7; PROMISSORY NOTE, 9.

COMPENSATION OF OFFICERS.

See CLERK OF COURT, 1; ESTATES OF DECEDENTS, 1.

CONSIDERATION.

See CONVEYANCE, 4, 5; MORTGAGE, 3, 6; PROMISSORY NOTE, 7, 10; SPECIFIC PERFORMANCE, 3.

CONSTITUTIONAL LAW.

1. LIMIT OF DEBT OF MUNICIPAL CORPORATIONS. See Cities and Towns, 7

2. PROHIBITORY LIQUOR LAW. See Intoxicating Liquors, 6.

CONSTRUCTION.

See CONTRACTS, 5; WILL, 2, 3.

CONTINUANCE.

1. ABSENT WITNESS: DISMISSAL OF ISSUE. A continuance asked by defendant on the ground of the absence of a witness is properly refused when the plaintiff dismisses the only issue to which his testimony would relate. *Herd v. Herd*, 497.

See PRACTICE AND PROCEDURE, 11.

CONTRACTS.

1. INCAPACITY AND UNDUE INFLUENCE: RELIEF IN EQUITY. The acts and contracts of persons who are of weak understanding, and who are thereby liable to imposition, will be held void in courts of equity, if the nature of the act or contract justifies the conclusion that the party has not exercised a deliberate judgment, but that he has been imposed upon, circumvented, or overcome by cunning or artifice or undue influence; and *held* that the facts of this case (see opinion) in which plaintiff and her husband were induced to convey their homestead for a patent right, worthless in their hands, bring it clearly within the rule above stated. *Clough v. Adams*, 17.

2. FRAUD: PECULIAR KNOWLEDGE OF ONE PARTY: EVIDENCE. Plaintiff assigned to defendant a contract for the purchase of land, which he knew had been forfeited. Defendant, failing to get the land, had a settlement with plaintiff, wherein plaintiff gave defendant his promissory note. Plaintiff now seeks to recover of defendant on the ground that defendant deceived him by false statements as to what it would be necessary to pay to secure the land and avoid the forfeiture; and that defendant was possessed of knowledge in the matter not possessed by him. *Held* that plaintiff's knowledge of the forfeiture was a complete answer to all his allegations of fraud, and that he could not recover. *King v. Williams*, 74.

3 SIGNING AS TRUSTEE: PAROL TO DISCLOSE CAPACITY: WHO LIABLE. Where one signs a contract as trustee, and there is nothing on the face of the contract to indicate for whom he is trustee, parol evidence is not admissible to show such fact, and he is personally liable. (See cases cited in opinion.) *Stevenson v. Polk*, 278.

4. OFFER TO SELL LAND: ACCEPTANCE. An offer by a resident in New York to sell land in Iowa for four dollars per acre, means four dollars per acre cash, paid in New York, and the offer is not accepted by an agreement to take the land at four dollars per acre payable at Des Moines upon the delivery of the deed. *Gilbert v. Baxter*, 327.

5. CONSTRUCTION: SALE OR SECURITY. B. & G. had contracted to build a court house for the defendant county, and had purchased materials therefor of W., but had not paid for the materials, and nothing was yet due from the defendant on the contract. In order to make a payment on the materials out of the contract price of the building, B. & G. and W. made a bill of sale of the materials to defendant, whereupon defendant paid to W., to be applied on the price of the materials, (which was $1,900,) the sum of $450 of the contract price of the building. After

ward:., defendant made further payments to W. upon orders made by B.
& G., but the materials were never fully paid for. *Held* that the bill of
sale was not a transfer of the title of the materials from W. to the
defendant, because W. had already transferred his title to B. & G., but
that the effect of the writing (for the particulars of which see opinion)
was only to secure the defendant for an advance of $150 of the contract
price before it was due, and that W. could not recover of the defendant
the unpaid portion of the price of the materials. *Wilson v. Palo Alto
Co.*, 351.

6. MISTAKE: REFORMATION. The evidence in this case (see opinion) *held*
to establish that there was a mutual mistake in the reduction to writing
of the contract between the parties for an exchange of lands; and the
decree of the court below, reforming and enforcing the contract, is
affirmed. *Hallam v. Corlett*, 446.

7. FRAUD AND MISTAKE: REFORMATION. Plaintiff purchased of defendant a certain hotel property, which defendant showed to her, but she
did not know the width of the lot, and he, with the intent to defraud
her, executed and offered her a deed describing only a portion of the lot,
which deed she accepted, and took possession thereunder, supposing that
it properly described the premises which she had purchased. These facts
being established by clear and satisfactory evidence, *held* that she was
entitled to a decree for a reformation of the deed, so as to describe the
whole of the lot. *Winans v. Huyck*, 459.

8. TO CONVEY RIGHT OF WAY: MUTUALITY. Defendant agreed in writing
to convey to plaintiff a right of way for a named consideration when its
road should be located over the land. *Held* that the location of the
road was a condition precedent to the liability of either party, but that,
when that was done, both became liable, and either might enforce the
contract as against the other. *W. I. & N. R'y Co. v. Braham*, 434.

9. UNDUE INFLUENCE: RELATIONS OF TRUST: SETTING ASIDE. When
persons who sustain relations of confidence and trust enter into a contract, and the stronger obtains an advantage over the weaker mind, the
contract will be set aside, unless the beneficiary shows that it was fairly
obtained. (*Spargur v. Hall*, 62 Iowa, 498.) But no unfair advantage
can be said to be taken where the stronger mind does nothing but
accept the terms proposed by the weaker. *Gardner v. Lightfoot*, 577.

10. FRAUD: RESCISSION: EVIDENCE. A court of equity will not annul a contract on the ground that it was procured by fraud, unless the evidence is
clear and satisfactory, and preponderates in favor of the party asking
the rescission. Accordingly, where there was no special confidence
reposed by the plaintiff in the defendant, and no artifice used to prevent
plaintiff from making the requisite examination to ascertain the truth,
and he had an opportunity to do so, and it did not clearly appear that
the alleged false representation was anything more than a guess, or an
expression of opinion, *held* that a rescission should not have been
decreed. *Dirkson v. Knox*, 728.

11. SPECIFIC PERFORMANCE: NO EVIDENCE OF PERFORMANCE ON PLAINT-
IFF'S PART. *Payne v. Des M. & Ft. D. R'y Co.*, 758.

12. RESCISSION. See Vendor and Vendee, 7, 8, 11, 12.

13. UNDUE INFLUENCE. See Promissory Notes, 11.

See CHAMPERTY, 1; CONSIDERATION; SPECIFIC PERFORMANCE,

CONTRIBUTORY NEGLIGENCE.

See CITIES AND TOWNS, 8; RAILROADS, 8, 14, 21, 27.

CONVEYANCE.

1. FRAUD: EVIDENCE. Plaintiff's claim, that she was induced by her husband to sign a deed under a belief that it was a mortgage for a small amount, is not supported by the evidence. *Quinn v. Brown*, 376.

2. BLANK AS TO CONSIDERATION AND GRANTEE: SIGNATURE BY WIFE: INNOCENT PURCHASER. Where a wife joins her husband in executing and acknowledging a deed to land, with the consideration and grantee left blank, and leaves it with her husband, and he sells the land to an innocent purchaser for value, and inserts the consideration and the name of the purchaser in the deed, and delivers it to him, *held* that the wife cannot assail the title of the purchaser on the ground that she did not know what she was signing; and that the land may have included a part of her homestead is immaterial. *Id.*

3. DELIVERY: WHAT IS. Where one brother sold land to another, and executed a deed therefor, and left it in the hands of a sister, and received from the grantee the purchase price, *held* that the possession of the deed by the sister must be regarded as the possession of the grantee, and that the claim that the deed had never been delivered could not be sustained. *McCormick v. McCormick*, 379.

4. CONSIDERATION: PAROL TO VARY WRITING. Although parol testimony is admissible to show that the consideration of a conveyance is other or different than that stated in the writing, such testimony is not admissible, in the absence of fraud, to prove that a conveyance purporting to have been made for a consideration is in fact without a consideration, for the purpose of rendering it invalid. *Gardner v. Lightfoot*, 577.

5. ————: WHAT CONSTITUTES. An agreement by the grantee in a conveyance of land to perform certain service for the grantors during their lives and the life of the survivor, and an executed life lease of the land to the grantors, constitute a good consideration for the conveyance. (*Johnson v. Johnson*, 52 Iowa, 586, and *Mercer v. Mercer*, 29 Id., 557, followed.) *Id.*

6. CONDITION SUBSEQUENT: PARTIAL PERFORMANCE: SETTING ASIDE. An executed conveyance will not be set aside for the failure to perform a condition subsequent, where there has been a partial performance, accepted as such, and the parties cannot be placed in *statu quo*. *Id.*

7. DELIVERY: CONDITION: EVIDENCE. Plaintiff sought to quiet its title to land under an alleged lost and unrecorded deed; but it failed to establish the delivery of the deed by a preponderance of the evidence, and it appeared by a clear preponderance of the evidence that the deed was a conditional one, and that, by reason of plaintiff's failure to perform the condition, the title never passed. *Held* that plaintiff could not recover. *St. L., O. & C. R. R'y Co. v. Devin*, 666.

8. EFFECT OF MERE QUITCLAIM. See Vendor and Vendee, 1.

CORPORATIONS.

1. CRIMINAL LIABILITY AS NATURAL PERSONS: SALE OF INTOXICATING LIQUORS. Corporations are to be considered as persons, when the circumstances in which they are placed are identical with those of natural persons expressly included in a statute. (*Wales v. City of Muscatine*, 4 Iowa, 302.) Accordingly, *held* that a corporation which, by a committee, sold beer to a person in the habit of becoming intoxicated, at a ball given under its supervision, was liable, under § 1539 of the Code, the same as a natural person, for the penalty thereby provided to be collected for the benefit of the school fund. *Stewart v. Waterloo Turn Verein*, 226.

2. TRANSFER OF STOCK: ENTRY ON BOOKS: WHEN NECESSARY. A transfer of corporation stock is not valid as against attaching creditors of the assignor without notice, unless the transfer is entered on the books of the company, as provided by § 1078 of the Code. (See opinion for a full discussion of the question on principle and authority by ADAMS, CH. J.) *Fort Madison Lumber Co. v. Batavian Bank*, 270; *Ryan v. Campbell*, 760.

3. SATISFACTION OF MORTGAGE BY. See Vendor and Vendee, 5.

COSTS.

1. CONTINUANCE: PLAINTIFF'S FAULT. Where, after both parties had rested, plaintiff asked and obtained leave to introduce other testimony which he had omitted by inadvertence, and the court then granted a continuance on defendant's motion, on the ground that its witnesses had departed, and it could not then rebut the new evidence, *held* that the costs of the trial were properly taxed to plaintiff, because, by his inadvertence, the trial was rendered useless. *Voorhees v. C., R. I. & P. R'y Co.*, 735.

See PRACTICE IN SUPREME COURT, 10.

COUNTIES.

1. SETTLEMENT WITH CLERK: ESTOPPEL. The fact that the board of supervisors, in making settlement with the clerk, failed to compel the latter to account for certain fees collected by him and belonging to the county, did not estop the county from afterwards demanding and recovering such fees. *Palo Alto Co. v. Burlingame*, 201.

2. ACTS OF SUPERVISORS NOT IN SESSION. A county is not bound by statements made by its supervisors when not in session. *Id.*

COUNTY CLERK.

See CLERK OF COURTS.

COURTS.

See JURISDICTION, 1; JUSTICES AND THEIR COURTS.

CRIMINAL LAW.

1. ABORTION: ADMINISTRATION OF DRUG: EVIDENCE TO CONVICT. Prosecution for abortion by the administration of a drug. Upon consideration of the evidence, (see opinion,) *held* that the jury were warranted in finding therefrom that the drug would produce miscarriage, that it was administered to the woman by the defendant, with whom she was with child, for that purpose, and that he was guilty as charged. *State v. Montgomery*, 630.

2. PRACTICE: NEW TRIAL: TESTIMONY OF DEFENDANT WHILE SICK. The defendant in a prosecution for abortion, though advised by his counsel of his right as a witness, gave testimony damaging to himself, and, after a verdict of guilty, he moved for a new trial on the ground that, when he testified, he was suffering from a nervous headache, which affected his mind and memory. But the record of his testimony gave no evidence of his want of memory, or of the full powers of mind. *Held* that, since the trial court, which had an opportunity to observe his manner and deportment, and all the circumstances of the case, overruled the motion, this court could not, in the absence of convincing evidence of the truth of the grounds of the motion, interfere. *Id.*

DAMAGES.

DECREE.

See JUDGMENT AND DECREE.

DEED.

See ACKNOWLEDGMENT, 1, 2; CONVEYANCE, *passim.*

DEFAULT.

See JUDGMENT AND DECREE, 1, 2.

DELIVERY.

See CONVEYANCE, 3, 7.

DEPOSITIONS.

1. OF WITNESS IN COUNTY: ABILITY TO ATTEND COURT: SHOWING. Where the deposition of a witness for plaintiff, residing in the county, was taken only a short time before the term at which it was expected the case would be tried, on the ground that he would not be able to attend at that term on account of sickness, but defendant then objected to the taking of the deposition, and the case was not in fact tried till a year later; *held* that it was error to allow the deposition to be read at the trial, against defendant's objection, without a showing that the witness was then unable to be present in court. (*Nevan v. Roup,* 8 Iowa, 207, and *Cook v. Blair,* 50 Id., 123, distinguished.) *Sax v. Davis,* 406.

2. NOTICE OF TAKING: CODE, § 3730. In the provision of the Code, § 3730, that a notice to take depositions shall be five days, "when served on the party within the county," the county in which the depositions are to be taken is meant. and not that wherein the court in which they are to be used is held. *Kennedy v. Rosier,* 671.

DESCRIPTION.

See CHATTEL MORTGAGE, 1, 3; SPECIFIC PERFORMANCE, 1, 2.

DISORDERLY HOUSES.

See CITIES AND TOWNS, 3; CRIMINAL LAW, 25.

DOMESTIC RELATIONS.

See DOMICILE, 1; DOWER, 1, 2; HUSBAND AND WIFE: GUARDIAN, 2.

DOMICILE.

1. OF MINOR CHILD: WHAT IS CHANGE OF. The domicile of a minor child is the domicile of its parents, and after the death of its parents its domicile continues the same until another is lawfully acquired. But where the father was dead, and the mother, shortly before her death, in her will requested a sister residing out of the state to take and raise the child, and the sister accordingly took the child out of the state, but assumed no legal obligation toward it, *held* that the domicile of the child was not changed. *Jenkins v Clark,* 552.

DOWER.

1. PARTNERSHIP LAND: TITLE IN TRUSTEE. Where two persons entered into a contract, which was, in effect. a contract of partnership for the purchase and sale of real estate, and the contract provid d th it the real

estate purchased and sold should be conveyed to and by a certain person as trustee, and contemplated a conversion of all lands into cash before a settlement of the partnership, and not a division of any lands between the partners, *held* that lands so purchased were to be regarded as personal property belonging to the firm, and that a purchaser of such land from the trustee held the same free from any claim of dower made by the wife of one of the partners. (Compare *Hewitt v. Rankin*, 41 Iowa 35.) *Mallory v. Russell*, 63.

2. IN EQUITABLE ESTATE: ILLUSTRATION. Where a husband enters into an oral contract for the purchase of land, and takes possession thereunder, and subsequently pays the whole amount of the purchase price, he is the equitable owner of the land, and he cannot, by causing the vendor to execute a deed to his son by a former wife, deprive a wife who survives him of her dower interest in the land, but she may recover the same in an action against the son. (*Beck v. Beck*, 64 Iowa, 155, distinguished.) *Everitt v. Everitt*, 221.

See PARTNERSHIP, 1.

EASEMENT.

See SPECIFIC PERFORMANCE, 4.

ELECTIONS.

See TOWNSHIPS, 1.

EMPLOYER AND EMPLOYE.

See RAILROADS, 10-21; MASTER AND SERVANT, 1.

EQUITY.

1. SUBROGATION: LAND SOLD ON TIME CONTRACT: PAYMENT OF PURCHASE MONEY BY ASSIGNEE. D. and wife owned two forty acre tracts of land under contract of purchase. D., acting for himself, and as agent for his wife, but without her authority, sold the land and assigned the contracts to W., who went into possession. In an action by the vendors to foreclose the contracts, there was judgment against D. and wife for the purchase money, but W. intervened, and it was ordered, among other things, that he pay into court a certain sum, and that upon payment of the same the vendors execute to him a warranty deed for the land. D.'s wife was, for certain reasons, not bound by the judgment and decree. *Held* that she was the owner of the undivided one-half of the land during all the time that W. was in possession, and entitled to rents and profits accordingly; that from the time W. paid his money into court under the decree he was entitled to be subrogated to all the rights of the vendors as against D.'s wife, and that his relation to her was that of a mortgagee in possession, and that a judgment and decree of foreclosure were properly entered against her in favor of W. for one-half of the judgment and costs in the former action, less her share of the rents and profits during the time W. had been in possession. *Dillow v. Warfel*, 106.

2. RELIEF AGAINST FRAUD AND MISTAKE. See Contracts, 1, 6, 7, 9, 10.

3. SETTING ASIDE DEED FOR FAILURE TO PERFORM CONDITION SUBSEQUENT. See Conveyance, 6.

See ATTACHMENT, 8; EXECUTION, 3, 6; MORTGAGE, *passim;* VENDOR AND VENDEE, *passim.*

ESTATES OF DECEDENTS.

1. **FEES OF CLERK.** Under § 3787 of the Code, the clerk is entitled to only three dollars for all services performed by him in the settlement of an estate which does not exceed three thousand dollars in value; all fees taxed by him in excess of that sum in such a case are illegal. *Est. of Parker v. Corlett,* 249.

2. **ASSETS: PENSION MONEY.** Upon the death of a married man leaving money derived from a pension received from the United States, the money goes to his administrator, and not to his widow. *Perkins v. Hinckley,* 499.

3. **WIDOW'S DISTRIBUTIVE SHARE: EVIDENCE TO SUPPORT DECREE.** *McReynolds v. McReynolds,* 756.

See ADMINISTRATOR; ESTOPPEL, 1; PARTNERSHIP, 1.

ESTOPPEL.

1. **CLAIM AGAINST INSOLVENT ESTATE: ACTS OF ADMINISTRATOR.** Plaintiff was a creditor of defendant's intestate, who died leaving no property execept such as was exempt to his widow. Defendant, however, sold some of the widow's property, and carelessly took a note therefor to himself as administrator, on which he afterwards recovered judgment in his own name, as administrator, which he afterwards collected. Afterwards defendant filed a report,—the first record made by him in the case,—showing that the decedent left no property with which to pay debts, and asking to be discharged. Plaintiff, however, knowing of the said judgment in favor of the administrator, appeared by counsel and filed objections to the report, and there was a trial of the issues raised, and judgment was rendered against defendant and the sureties on his bond for the amount of plaintiff's claim against the estate, and this was done upon the ground that defendant, by taking said note and judgment in his own name, misled plaintiff into the expense of employing counsel, etc , in the belief that there were assets of the estate, and that defendant was thereby estopped from denying the existence of assets to the extent of the value of the judgment. But *held* that this conduct did not constitute an estoppel. *Laub v. Trowbridge,* 396.

2. **FACTS CONSTITUTING.** A. held a first, and B. a second, mortgage on a stock of goods. The sheriff had levied a number of attachments on the stock, all of which were subsequent to A.'s mortgage, but some of which were prior, and some subsequent, to B.'s mortgage. A. replevied the goods from the sheriff, and B. was the surety on his bond. It was agreed between A. and B. that the latter should hold the replevied goods, or their proceeds, for his indemnity as surety. The goods were sold pending the action, and B. held the proceeds. It was determined in the action that A.'s mortgage was fraudulent and of no effect as against the attaching creditors, and judgment was rendered against him and B., his surety, for the value of the goods, which, by agreement of all the parties, was the amount of the proceeds in B.'s hands. It was also agreed between all the parties that B. should surrender said proceeds to the sheriff in satisfaction of the judgment, which he did. Afterwards, but before the sheriff had disbursed such proceeds, B. brought suit against the sheriff to recover, as a mortgagee, such of the proceeds as were not required to satisfy the attachments which were prior to his mortgage, but *held* that, having purchased immunity from the judgment by the surrender of such proceeds. he was estopped from setting up such claim under his mortgage. *Krekel v. Kreichbaum,* 702.

See COUNTY, 1; MECHANIC'S LIEN, 2; SURETY, 3; WATER AND WATER-COURSES, 1.

EVIDENCE.

former trial would be offered in evidence, *held* that such transcript was admissible, under § 3777 of the Code as amended, (see Miller's Code.) and that, if any notice was necessary in the case, that given was sufficient. *Fleming v. Shenandoah*, 456.

11. USE OF RECORD ON FORMER TRIAL: FOUNDATION. The record of documentary and oral evidence taken and duly preserved on a former trial is not admissible in a subsequent trial, without any showing of the absence of the witnesses, or of inability to produce the original documents, and without any notice to the adverse party. (Compare *Baldwin v. St. Louis, K. & N. R'y Co.*, 68 Iowa, 37.) *Case v. Blood*, 632.

12. HEARSAY: CONDITION OF MARKET. Plaintiff's testimony as to what his broker told him about the condition of the market on a certain day was mere hearsay, and should have been excluded. *Voorhees v. C., R. I. & P. R'y Co.*, 735.

13. WARRANTY: HEARSAY AS TO QUALITY OF GOODS. What the purchaser of goods from a vendee may have said as to the quality of the goods, is mere hearsay on a question of breach of warranty between the vendee and his vendor. *Barrett v. Wheeler*, 662.

14. CONCLUSION ASKED FOR: FACTS GIVEN. Where a question to a witness calls for his conclusion as to the effect of a contract, but the witness simply states what he claims to be the terms of the contract, there is no prejudice from the erroneous question. *Id.*

15. SECONDARY: CONTENTS OF DEED: FOUNDATION. Where the grantee in a deed and the custodian thereof testified positively that it had been lost, *held* that this was sufficient foundation for the introduction of parol testimony as to its contents, without showing that search had been made for it. (*Horseman v. Todhunter*, 12 Iowa, 230, and *Howe Machine Co. v. Stiles*, 53 Id., 424, distinguished.) *Postel v. Palmer*, 157.

16. LOST RECEIPT: EFFECT OF SECONDARY EVIDENCE. Where a written receipt made by plaintiffs to defendants became material as evidence, but defendants testified that it had been lost, an instruction to the effect that "all questions and disputes as to the language of the written receipt are to be taken strongly against defendants and the claim made by them as to the language and construction of the same," was rightly refused, in the absence of any evidence of bad faith or fault on the part of the defendants in suppressing the receipt. *Davis' Sons v. Cochran*, 369.

17. PAROL TO VARY WRITING: RULE NOT APPLICABLE. The rule that parol testimony is not admissible to vary the terms of a written contract does not apply to evidence that a contract was to be made, but which does not refer to the terms of the contract. *Id.*

18. PAROL TO AID MINUTES OF SCHOOL BOARD. Where the record of the proceedings of a school board showed that a motion was passed, but failed to show what the motion was, it was competent to prove by the secretary who made the record what the motion was. *Morgan v. Wilfley*, 212.

19. PAROL TO VARY WRITTEN CONTRACT. Where a written contract concerning the sale of a new machine to defendant provided that an old machine, which was to be taken in part payment, was to be delivered at the time of receiving the new machine, it was not competent for defendant, in an action to recover the value of the old machine and the amount due on the notes given for the new one, to contradict the written contract by parol evidence that a delivery of the old machine was to be made at a later time. *Davis v. Robinson*, 618.

20. WRITTEN WARRANTY: CONTEMPORANEOUS PAROL WARRANTY. Where a written warranty and a contemporaneous parol warranty were both

pleaded by defendant, and the written warranty was established without conflict, it was error to allow evidence of the parol warranty to go to the jury. *Barrett v. Wheeler*, 662.

21. EXCLUSION: ERROR WITHOUT PREJUDICE. Where, in an action on an attachment bond, the jury found only nominal damages, it was at most error without prejudice to exclude evidence offered in mitigation of damages. *Whitney v. Brownewell*, 251.

22. CUMULATIVE: EXCLUSION OF: ERROR WITHOUT PREJUDICE. The exclusion of evidence on a point which has been sufficiently established by other testimony is not prejudicial to the party offering it, and hence is no ground for reversal. *Morgan v. Wilfley*, 212.

23. EXCLUSION: NO PREJUDICE. The exclusion of evidence offered as a foundation for the introduction of books of account is no ground for complaint, when the books are in fact admitted. *Parcell v. McReynolds*, 623.

24. ADMISSION: ERROR WITHOUT PREJUDICE. The admission of incompetent testimony on a certain point is without prejudice when the same point is conclusively established by other competent testimony. *Silts v. Hawkeye Ins. Co.*, 710.

25. IN ACTION ON ATTACHMENT BOND. See Attachment, 1–5.

26. IN ACTION FOR INJURY ON SIDEWALK. See Cities and Towns, 1, 2.

27. PAROL TO EXPLAIN CAPACITY OF CONTRACTOR. See Contracts, 3.

28. PAROL TO DENY CONSIDERATION NAMED IN DEED. See Conveyance, 4.

29. FOR EVIDENCE IN CRIMINAL CASES. See Criminal Law, *passim*.

40. OF RESULTING TRUST. See Partnership, 1.

31. IN ACTIONS FOR PERSONAL INJURIES. See Personal Injuries, 1–4.

32. JUDICIAL NOTICE. See Practice in Supreme Court, 2.

33. PAROL TO VARY WRITING. See Promissory Note, 8.

34. LIMITED TO ISSUES. See Railroads, 2.

See AGENCY, 3; DEPOSITIONS, 1, 2; MORTGAGE, 1; SALES, 3; TAX SALE AND DEED, 2, 5; USURY, 3, 4; STATUTE OF FRAUDS.

EXCEPTIONS.

See PRACTICE, 1; PRACTICE IN SUPREME COURT, 23–25.

EXECUTION.

1. GROWING CROPS CANNOT BE SOLD UNDER. Immature crops belong to the land on which they are growing, and they cannot be levied upon and sold on execution as personal property; and where such sale is attempted the purchaser acquires no right which he can assert as against one who purchases the realty from the judgment debtor before the maturity of the crops. (See opinion for cases followed and distinguished.) *Ellithorpe v. Reidesil*, 315.

2. EXECUTION SALE: IRREGULAR REDEMPTION: ASSIGNMENT OF CERTIFICATE: SHERIFF'S DEED. Where one who was apparently the owner of a junior judgment redeemed from an execution sale of land, and procured an assignment of the certificate of purchase, *held* that, even if he was not entitled to redeem on account of his having assigned his judg-

ment, yet, in the absence of a redemption from himself, he was entitled to a sheriff's deed as a purchaser of the certificate of purchase. (Compare *Wilson v. Conklin*, 22 Iowa, 452.) *Rush v. Mitchell*, 333.

3. ———: SHERIFF'S DEED MADE TOO LATE: INTERVENING PURCHASER: GOOD FAITH: EVIDENCE: BURDEN OF PROOF. Plaintiff, claiming title to the land in question under a sheriff's deed made more than twenty days after the expiration of the year for redemption, (Code, § 3125,) brought this action to quiet his title against M., who claimed under a deed made by the execution defendant after the expiration of the twenty days, and before the execution and recording of the sheriff's deed. The deed from the execution defendant was a mere quitclaim, made to one R., for the purpose of defrauding plaintiff. M. took by a warranty deed from R., and gave to R. notes secured by mortgage on the land for the purchase money. The petition put M.'s good faith in issue. *Held*—

(1) That, since M. took from a fraudulent grantee, she had the burden of proof to show that she was a good faith purchaser for value.

(2) That the mere recitals in her deed would not show that she paid value for the land. Nor would that fact be established by proof that she executed negotiable notes, secured by mortgage, for the purchase money, unless she also showed that the notes had been negotiated by her grantor. (See opinion for authorities cited on all branches of the case.) *Id.*

4. ———: APPEAL: REDEMPTION. Under § 3102 of the Code, an execution sale made after appeal taken is without the right of redemption; but an appeal is not taken by service of a notice on the attorney of the execution plaintiff. It must also be served on the clerk of the court. (Code, §§ 3178, 3179.) *Fitzgerald v. Kelso*, 731.

5. ———: ACTION TO SET ASIDE: OFFER TO REDEEM. One whose land has wrongfully been sold without the right of redemption may maintain an action to set the sale aside, without offering to redeem, where his right to redeem has constantly been denied; for the law does not require a man to do a vain thing. *Id.*

6. ———: WRONGFUL SALE WITHOUT REDEMPTION: INADEQUATE PRICE: SET ASIDE. When plaintiff's land was sold wrongfully without redemption, and for a grossly inadequate price, and there was a manifest attempt to oppress him by denying his rights to redeem, *held* that the sale was properly set aside in equity. *Id.*

EXECUTOR.

See ADMINISTRATOR.

FALSE PRETENSES.

See CRIMINAL LAW, 22.

FALSE REPRESENTATIONS.

See CONTRACT, 2.

FENCES.

1. DIVISION FENCE: OBLIGATION TO MAINTAIN: HERD LAW. Where at defendant's solicitation, after the herd law had been adopted, the township trustees were called together and apportioned the division fence between him and plaintiff, and both parties acquiesced in the apportionment and erected the fence accordingly, *held* that defendant could not

afterwards, of his own motion, relieve himself of the obligation to keep his portion of the fence in repair. *Barrett v. Dolan*, 94.

See RAILROADS, 6.

FIXTURES.

See PERSONAL PROPERTY, 1.

FORECLOSURE.

1. OF TITLE BOND: TENDER OF DEED. No tender of a deed is necessary by the vendor of real estate in order to the maintenance of an action in equity to foreclose a title bond for the collection of the purchase money. In an action at law for the purchase money a different rule prevails. (See opinion for authorities cited.) *Stevenson v. Polk*, 278.

See MORTGAGE, *passim*.

FORMER ADJUDICATION.

1. SEPARATE TRIALS FOR SEVERAL DEFENDANTS. Where several alleged makers of a promissory note were made defendants in an action on the note, and one of them procured a separate trial for himself, *held* that nothing in the record of the trial as to the others could be relied on as *res adjudicata* on the separate trial of such defendant. *Eikenberry v. Edwards*, 82.

2. WHAT IS NOT: WITHDRAWING OF INTERVENOR. Where the claimant of attached property appeared in the attachment suit and took time to file a petition of intervention, but a few days afterwards withdrew his appearance, and afterwards a judgment was rendered against the attachment defendant, with an order for the sale of the property, *held* that such judgment did not in any way affect the rights of the intervenor, and was not a bar to an action by him to recover the property. *Wilson v. Trowbridge*, 345.

3. VENDOR'S LIEN: SUBROGATION OF SURETY UPON PAYING NOTE FOR PURCHASE-MONEY. The vendor of real estate sued the purchaser and his surety on a purchase-money note, and procured judgment, but the court refused to decree a vendor's lien on the premises. The surety paid the judgment. *Held* that, since he was a party to the action in which the vendor was refused a lien, he was bound by that adjudication, and that he could not afterwards claim to be entitled to such a lien by subrogation to the rights of the vendor. *Blake v. Koons*, 356.

4. HOW PROVED. Where a party relies upon an estoppel by a judgment upon a verdict, he should introduce the verdict and judgment in evidence, and where he neither introduces nor proposes to introduce these, an instruction given by the court in the former case is properly rejected as evidence on that issue. *Reynolds v. Sutliff*, 549.

FRAUD.

1. IN PURCHASE OF LAND: INADEQUATE CONSIDERATION AS EVIDENCE OF. To warrant a court of equity in presuming fraud in the purchase of land from the inadequacy of the consideration, and in setting aside a conveyance on the ground thereof, it must be such as to demonstrate some gross imposition or undue influence; and in this case, where the consideration paid was only about one-fourth the actual value of the land, *held* that this fact, taken with the other facts of the case, (for which see opinion) was not sufficient to justify the court in setting aside the conveyance. *Herron v. Herron*, 428.

2. ———: NEGLIGENCE OF COMPLAINANT: RELIEF IN EQUITY. It is the province of courts of equity to afford relief to those who have been overreached by the artifice or cunning or deceit of others; but where a seller of land refuses to resort to sources of information to which he is referred by the buyer as to the value of the land, but chooses rather to accept the statements of the buyer, he should be held to have acted on his own judgment, and no relief should be granted him if it turns out that the statements of the buyer were false as to the value of the land. *Id.*

See CONTRACTS, *passim*; MORTGAGE, 4, 10; PROMISSORY NOTE, 10, 11, 13; STATUTE OF LIMITATIONS, 1, 2; SURETY, 2.

FRAUDULENT CONVEYANCE.

1. EVIDENCE: CONVERSATION BETWEEN PARTIES. Where it was sought to charge a garnishee with the value of goods alleged to have been transferred to him by the principal defendant in fraud of creditors, *held* that it was proper to allow the defendant to testify to a conversation had between him and the garnishee showing their fraudulent purpose. *Risser v. Rathburn*, 113.

2. SALE BY FRAUDULENT VENDEE: LIABILITY ON GARNISHMENT. A fraudulent vendee of goods may sell the same to an innocent third party, and give a good title, but he may nevertheless be he'd liable for the proceeds on garnishment, in a suit against his vendor by the creditors sought to be defeated by the fraudulent transfer. *Id.*

3. ———: ———: INTEREST ON PROCEEDS. In such case, the garnishee is liable for interest on the proceeds of the goods from the date of their sale by him. *Id.*

4. EVIDENCE: RIGHT OF CREDITOR TO SECURE PREFERENCE A creditor has a right to secure his own claim, even though he knows that there will be nothing left to secure or satisfy other creditors; and, there being no other evidence of a fraudulent intent in the conveyances herein assailed, *held* that they could not be set aside as being in fraud of creditors. *Aulman v. Aulman*, 124.

5. BURDEN OF PROOF: EVIDENCE. Where conveyances of property purport to have been made for a sufficient consideration, the burden is on creditors seeking to subject the property to the payment of their claims to show a want of consideration; (*Wolf v. Chandler*, 58 Iowa, 569; *Allen v. Wegstein*, 69 Id., 598;) but it is wholly immaterial whether the evidence is introduced by the plaintiff or the defendant. Accordingly, where the conveyances were made by a husband to his wife at a time when he was likely to be called on to pay debts as surety for a son, and the wife, to show the consideration for the transfers to her, introduced a written contract, signed by herself and her husband, and which bore date of thirty years previous, at which time they both testified it was executed; which contract was an agreement on the part of the wife to furnish the husband with certain money, and an agreement on his part to repay it, which money, so furnished, they testified was the consideration of the conveyances; but the paper appeared on its face to have been recently written, and experts testified that it had been recently written, *held* that the conveyances were properly set aside as being without consideration and in fraud of creditors. *Eisfield v. Dill*, 442.

6. CONSIDERATION: EVIDENCE. *McFarland v. Elliott*, 755.

See EXECUTION, 3.

GARNISHMENT.

1. DISPUTED FUND: HUSBAND AND WIFE. A wife was the owner of certain horses which her husband entered, in his own name, but with his

wife's money, for premiums at a county fair. These entrance fees were returnable by the rules of the society, but the society did not know that the horses belonged to, and that the fees were paid by, the wife. *Held* that the society might have discharged its obligations by paying these fees to the husband, but that, while they remained unpaid, they could not be appropriated by garnishment on execution against the husband, against the objections of the wife as an intervenor. *McArthur v. Garman*, 84.

2. PROPERTY IN CONSTRUCTIVE POSSESSION OF GARNISHEE: LIABILITY. In order that a garnishee may be holden for property belonging to the debtor, he must have the property in his possession, so that he can surrender it, if the court so directs, in exoneration of his liability as garnishee. If he has only a right of possession, or constructive possession, he may possibly be required to make a demand for the property, but he cannot be required to commence an action to recover it; and an action to recover property, on the sole ground that the plaintiff has been garnished in a suit against the owner of it, cannot be maintained. *Smalley v. Miller*, 90.

3. SURPLUS PROCEEDS OF COLLATERAL SECURITY. Where a bank received from C. certain notes as collateral security for a loan, and collected the notes and paid the loan out of the proceeds, and had money left, and the bank was garnished as the debtor of C., and there was no proof by an intervenor claiming the money of an assignment to him, *held* that it was error to discharge the garnishee on motion of the intervenor. *Nat. Bank of Galena v. Chase*, 120.

4. ON EXECUTION: INTERVENTION: WHEN PERMITTED. So long as money paid into court by a garnishee on execution has not been paid over to the execution plaintiff, a third party claiming the money may intervene in the action for the purpose of asserting his claim to the money. (Code, §§ 3016, 3051.) So *held* where the garnishee had paid over the money and had been discharged, without answering, and without notice to the execution defendant, and where the money had been applied in satisfaction of the judgments on which the executions had been issued, but had not yet been paid over to the judgment creditors. *Edwards v. Cosgro*, 296.

5. DETENTION OF EXEMPT PROPERTY: LIABILITY. Plaintiff, who was a judgment debtor of W., had delivered to a railway company for shipment certain household goods which were exempt from execution. W. caused the railway company to be garnished as the supposed debtor of plaintiff, wherefore the company, as required by the notice of garnishment, did not ship the goods. Neither the company nor the officer who held the execution knew that the goods were exempt, but as soon as the officer learned that they were exempt he released them from the levy and notified the company thereof, when the goods were forwarded to their destination. *Held* that the delay of the goods was no ground of recovery against either W., the officer, or the railway company. *Hynds v. Wynn*, 593.

GIFT.

See PROMISSORY NOTE, 7.

GUARDIAN.

1. APPOINTMENT: JURISDICTION: DOMICILE. The probate court of the county in which a minor child has its domicile is the court which has jurisdiction to appoint a guardian of its person, though it be not at the time a resident of such county. (Compare *Love v. Cherry*, 24 Iowa, 204.) *Jenkins v. Clark*, 552.

2. RIGHT TO CUSTODY OF WARD: EFFECT OF PARENT'S REQUEST. Under § 2249 of the Code, a guardian of the person of a child has the same

right to its custody as if he were its parent. And where he is not shown to be an unfit person to have such custody, the child will not be taken from him and given to an aunt, though its mother in her will has requested that the aunt take and raise the child. *Id.*

HABEAS CORPUS.

1. CUSTODY OF CHILD: PRIME CONSIDERATION: EVIDENCE ON APPEAL. Where the right to the custody of a minor child is involved in a *habeas corpus* proceeding, the best interest of the child is the first consideration; but the action is regarded as an ordinary one, and, on an appeal to this court, the judgment of the lower court cannot be disturbed, unless it is clearly contrary to the evidence as to the best interest of the child. *Jenkins v. Clark*, 552.

HIGHWAY.

1. ESTABLISHMENT: ALLOWANCE OF DAMAGES: APPEAL: WHEN TRIABLE. Where a claimant of damages caused by the establishment of a highway gives notice, twenty-one days prior to the next term of the circuit court, of an appeal from the allowance made by the supervisors, the appeal is triable at that term, and he cannot delay such trial by neglecting to file notice of the appeal in the auditor's office for so long a time that the auditor, taking the ten days allowed him by statute to prepare a transcript, does not get it on file in the clerk's office until after the opening of the term. *Scott v. Lasell*, 180.

2. ———: ———: ———: PAYMENT OF FILING FEE. In such case, the appellant must pay to the clerk the fee for filing the transcript and docketing the case, although the costs of the appeal must, in the end, be paid by the petitioner for the road, or by the county. (Code, § 963.) *Id.*

3. ———: ———: ———: FAILURE TO HAVE CASE DOCKETED. Such an appeal is a " civil case " within the meaning of a rule of practice which provides that in appeals from justices' courts, or other inferior tribunals, in civil cases, if the appellant fails to pay the filing fee and to have the appeal docketed by noon of the first day of the term, the appellee may pay the fee and have it docketed, and may thereupon have the judgment below affirmed. *Id.*

4. ———: ———: ———: WAIVER OF FILING FEE. In such case, where the appellee's right to an affirmance had already accrued, it was of no avail to show that appellant caused the transcript to be filed on the third day of the term, and that the clerk then waived the payment of the filing fee. *Id.*

5. VACATION AND ESTABLISHMENT: DAMAGES: APPEAL: CLAIM INCREASED BY AMENDMENT. Upon a proceeding to vacate one road and establish another in lieu thereof, plaintiff claimed $100 damages for land taken of him for the new road, which sum was allowed him. His claim was made upon the supposition that the old road was to be vacated upon the establishment of the new one; but after the supervisors had ordered the new one established and allowed plaintiff's claim, they refused to vacate the old one, whereby plaintiff's damages were much in excess of $100. Plaintiff appealed to the circuit court. The defendant moved to dismiss the appeal on the ground that the establishment of the new road and the vacation of the old one were separate proceedings, and, on the former, plaintiff had been allowed all the damages he had claimed. *Held* that the motion was properly overruled; also, that plaintiff was properly allowed to amend his claim for damages by increasing it so as to cover the damages sustained by him by the establishment of the new road without the vacation of the old one. [ADAMS, CH. J., and SEEVERS, J., *dissenting.*] *Pollard v. Dickinson Co.*, 438.

HOMESTEAD.

1. JUDICIAL SALE: SALE OF OTHER PROPERTY FIRST: COMPLIANCE WITH
STATUTE. C. held a mortgage on eighty acres of land owned by S., one
forty of which was his homestead. C. also held a judgment against S.,
which was a lien on the forty other than the homestead. Each forty
was worth $1,000. At a judicial sale under a foreclosure of the mort-
gage, C. bought the forty other than the homestead for $100, and he
bought the homestead forty for $647. On the same day, at an execu-
tion sale under his judgment, he bought the forty other than the homestead for $867. He was the only bidder. In due time a sheriff's deed
was made for the whole tract to C.'s assignee of the certificates. About
six months later, S.'s wife began this action to set aside the foreclosure
sale, on the ground that the land other than the homestead had not
been first exhausted before the sale of the homestead, as required by
statute, and that it was sold for a grossly inadequate price; but *held*
that, in the absence of a showing that the sale had not been fairly conducted, equity could not grant her petition. *Sigerson v. Sigerson*, 476.

2. USED FOR UNLAWFUL SALE OF LIQUORS: EXEMPTION FORFEITED.
Where a house and lot owned by the wife was occupied by the family
as a homestead, but the front room of the house was used by the husband for a saloon, *held* that, under § 1558 of the Code, the part used for
a saloon was subject to execution for the satisfaction of a judgment
obtained against the husband for damages caused by the unlawful sale
of liquors by him in said saloon. *Arnold v. Gotshall*, 572.

See SPECIFIC PERFORMANCE, 4.

HOMICIDE.

See CRIMINAL LAW, 10, 16, 21.

HUSBAND AND WIFE.

See CONVEYANCE, 2; CRIMINAL LAW, 3, 18; MORTGAGE, 10.

IMBECILITY.

See CONTRACTS, 1, 9; PROMISSORY NOTE, 11.

INDICTMENT.

See CRIMINAL LAW, 5, 22, 26.

INFANT.

See DOMICILE, 1.

INJUNCTION.

1. GRANTED ONLY IN ABSENCE OF LEGAL REMEDY: ILLUSTRATION.
Injunction is an extraordinary remedy, and it will be granted only when
the party is likely to suffer some irreparable injury against which he has
no other speedy or adequate remedy. Accordingly, where plaintiff had
granted to defendant the privilege to construct and maintain a street
railway on its streets and alleys, providing that the track should conform
to the established grade, but with no provision in regard to the kind of
rail to be used, or the gauge of the road, *held* that it was not entitled to
an injunction to restrain the defendant from using a certain kind of
rail, or from building its road upon a certain gauge, on the ground that
thereby the defendant would cause its track to be a nuisance; because

the plaintiff did not part with its lawful authority over its streets, and, in the exercise of such authority, it had full power to make and enforce all necessary and reasonable regulations as to the manner in which the track should be constructed and maintained, and it had no need of the interference of equity. *City of Waterloo v. Waterloo Street R'y Co.,* 193.

See PRACTICE AND PROCEDURE, 18.

INNOCENT PURCHASER.

See CONVEYANCE, 2; EXECUTION, 3; PROMISSORY NOTE, 2-5; VENDOR AND VENDEE, 2.

INSANITY.

See CONTRACTS, 1, 9; PROMISSORY NOTE, 11.

INSTRUCTIONS.

1. PROVINCE OF JURY: WEIGHING PROBABILITIES. It is the duty of the jury to determine, as best they can, which theory of the case is supported by the evidence, and not which is the more probable; and an instruction directing them to consider the probabilities of the case was properly refused. *Butler r. C. & N. W. R'y Co.,* 206.

2. ERROR WITHOUT PREJUDICE. An erroneous instruction is no ground for the reversal of a judgment which could not have been otherwise had the instruction not been given. *Whitney v. Brownewell,* 251.

3. REPETITION NOT REQUIRED. Instructions asked are properly refused when the thought of each is sufficiently expressed in instructions given by the court on its own motion. *Seekel r. Norman,* 264.

4. CORRECT IN THE ABSTRACT BUT NOT PROPERLY APPLIED: ESTOPPEL. It may sometimes occur that a correct abstract rule of law may mislead the jury, in the absence of directions for its application to the facts in the case. In such a case it will be error, if the court fails on its own motion to give such directions for its application that the jury will not be misled. So *held* in regard to an instruction in which the court rightly stated that, to constitute an estoppel, the party pleading it must have been prejudiced, or sustained injury, by acting upon the representations alleged as ground for the estoppel, but failed to give other necessary instructions for the application of the rule. *Id.*

5. SUBMITTING QUESTIONS OF DOUBTFUL PROOF. A fact is not proved because there is uncontradicted testimony which tends to prove it; and when there are other circumstances shown by the evidence which have a bearing upon the weight and credit which should be given to such uncontradicted testimony, the question as to whether the fact is proved should be submitted to the jury. (See opinion for illustration.) *Saar v. Fuller,* 425.

6. NO EVIDENCE TO WARRANT. An instruction directing the jury to inquire into a matter of which there is no evidence, is erroneous. (See opinion for illustration.) *Id.*

7. STATEMENT OF ISSUES: FOLLOWING PLEADINGS. There can be no valid objection to a statement of the issues to the jury in the form in which they are made by the pleadings, even though an issue is thus presented on which, as a matter of law, there can be no recovery. *Fleming v. Shenandoah,* 456.

8. METHOD OF PRESENTING ISSUES. It is not necessary that all the issues be presented in the statement of the pleadings and issues preceding the

instructions. It is sufficient if they be all fairly and fully presented somewhere in the charge. *Siltz v. Hawkeye Ins. Co.*, 710.

9. IGNORING POINT IN ISSUE. An instruction which ignores an issue material to the case, or which assumes as true a material point in dispute, cannot be sustained. (For illustrations see opinion.) *Kennedy v Rosier*, 671.

10. FOR INSTRUCTIONS IN CRIMINAL CASES. See Criminal Law, *passim.*

11. AS TO SPECIAL INTERROGATORIES. See Practice and Procedure, 8, 21.

See DAMAGES, 2, 4, 5; PRACTICE AND PROCEDURE, 19; SALES, 5.

INSURANCE.

(1) *Fire Insurance.*

1. CONTRACT OF INSURANCE: FACTS NOT CONSTITUTING. Plaintiff executed an application to the defendant company for insurance, and delivered it, with the premium and policy fee, to one who was only a soliciting agent of defendant, with the understanding that it should be sent to the defendant for acceptance, and that, if not accepted, the money should be returned. The application and premium were sent by the agent, but were never received by the company, and no policy was issued, and nothing further done. More than two years afterwards the property was burned. *Held* that the facts did not create a contract of insurance, and that defendant was not liable for the loss. (Compare *Walker v. Farmers' Ins. Co.*, 51 Iowa, 679, and *Armstrong v. State Ins. Co.*, 61 Id., 212.) *Atkinson v. Hawkeye Ins. Co.*, 340.

2. CONDITION AGAINST INCUMBRANCE: VIOLATION. A condition in a fire-insurance policy, issued to a firm, that the property should not afterwards be in any manner incumbered, was violated by the execution of a mortgage by one of the partners on his undivided one-third interest in the property, and by a judgment against him which became a lien on his said interest. *Hicks v. Farmers' Ins. Co.*, 119.

3. CHANGE OF INCUMBRANCE ON PROPERTY: EFFECT: QUESTION OF FACT. Where a fire insurance policy provided that it should be void "if the assured hereafter mortgage or incumber the property," and the land on which the property was situated was mortgaged when the policy was issued, and the assured, by the sale of a portion of the land and the purchase of other land adjacent, paid off the original mortgage and made a new one, *held* that. whether this avoided the policy or not depended upon whether the hazard was increased; that is, whether the incumbrance on the insured property was proportionately increased by the change; and that that was a question for the jury. *Russell v. Cedar Rapids Ins. Co.*, 69.

4. FORFEITURE BY SALE: FACTS CONSTITUTING SALE. The policy sued on provided that it should immediately be void upon a sale of the premises without the consent of the company. The insured entered into a contract with L., whereby L. agreed to pay him a certain sum for the property,—a small portion in cash, and the rest in deferred payments, and the insured agreed to convey the property to him upon his making all the payments as agreed. But it was also stipulated that if L. should fail to make any payment at the time stipulated the contract should be void, and any payments made should be forfeited. L. took possession under the contract. *Held* that this was a sale which forfeited the insurance. (*Kempton v. State Ins. Co.*, 62 Iowa, 83, distinguished.) [REED, J., *dissenting.*] *Davidson v. Hawkeye Ins. Co.*, 532.

5. FORFEITURE BY CONTRACT OF SALE: RESCISSION OF CONTRACT. A fire insurance policy which has been forfeited by a sale of the premises in

violation of its conditions, is not restored by an abandonment of the contract of sale. *Id.*

6. FAILURE TO PAY PREMIUM NOTE: FORFEITURE: WAIVER: AGENCY: FRAUD. The policy in question provided that the company should not be liable for any loss accruing while any premium note remained overdue and unpaid. The policy would be forfeited unless a premium note was paid by May 15. The insured lived at K., and was postmaster there, but the company did not know that he was postmaster. There being no bank at K., the company, according to its custom in such cases, sent the note, on the 7th of May, to the postmaster for collection. On the 25th of May, the postmaster, in the presence of two witnesses, took the note out of the safe and destroyed it, and put in its place the amount of money necessary to pay it. On the next day the loss occurred. On the 3d of the following June he wrote to the company enclosing the identical money which he had deposited in the safe, which the company received and retained in payment of the note. He did not sign his name to the letter, but subscribed himself simply "Postmaster, K., Iowa." The company did not at this time know that a loss had occurred. *Held*—

    (1) That the policy was forfeited on the 15th of May by the non-payment of the note at that time.

    (2) That, although the company sent the note to the postmaster for collection, yet, since the postmaster and the insured were identical, the law will not regard him as the agent of the company to make a collection from himself; and that his act in taking payment from himself after the forfeiture of the policy was not binding on the company, and was not a waiver by the company of the forfeiture.

    (3) That the conduct of the insured amounted to a fraud, from which the law will not allow him to reap a benefit. *Harle v. Council Bluffs Ins. Co.,* 401.

7. FORFEITURE: PREMIUM NOTE UNPAID: COPY OF NOTE NOT ATTACHED TO POLICY. Where a past due premium note was set up to defeat a policy of insurance, *held* that it could not have that effect, since a copy of it was not attached to the policy, as required by statute. *Lewis v. Burlington Ins. Co.,* 97.

8. SURRENDER OF POLICY: LIABILITY FOR OVERDUE PREMIUMS. The holder of a policy of fire insurance cannot avoid liability on a premium note, for an installment already past due, by surrendering the policy to the company. *Amer. Ins. Co. v. Garrett,* 243.

9. ACTION ON POLICY: DESIGNATION OF LOST GOODS: EVIDENCE. Where part of the insured property was designated in the policy as "restaurant goods," *held,* in an action to recover on the policy, that it was not error to allow plaintiff to refer to the same property by that name, and ask a witness its value. If the designation was definite enough to be used in the policy, it was definite enough for use on the trial. *Siltz v. Hawkeye Ins. Co.,* 710.

10. ACTION ON POLICY: VALUE OF PROPERTY: EVIDENCE. In an action to recover on a policy of fire insurance, where the plaintiff testified that she paid $3,500 for the property, and its value was stated at that sum in the application, *held* that, in the absence of other evidence, the jury was warranted in finding that it was worth that sum. *Id.*

11. ———: ———: FRAUD OF INSURED: INSTRUCTIONS. In such case, where the policy provided that "any fraud, or attempt to defraud," on the part of the assured, would defeat recovery, *held* that it was sufficient for the court to instruct the jury as to the *acts* relied on by defendant to defeat recovery under this clause, without distinguishing the actual frauds from the attempts to defraud. *Id.*

12. FORFEITURE OF POLICY: WAIVER: REVIVAL. The forfeiture of a policy on account of a breach of its conditions may be waived, whereupon it will have the same binding force which it originally possessed. (*Viele v. Germania Ins. Co.*, 26 Iowa, 9, followed.) *Id.*

13. WARRANTY IN APPLICATION: WAIVER. Error in a statement in an application for fire insurance, which is made a warranty by the policy, cannot be relied on to defeat the policy, where the agent who took the application was fully informed as to the facts; but the error will be regarded as waived. (See opinion for authorities cited.) *Id.*

14. PREMATURE ACTION ON POLICY: STATUTE. Under Chap. 211, Laws of 1880, an action cannot be begun upon a policy of fire insurance within ninety days after notice of loss has been given, even though the company may before that time declare absolutely that it will not pay the loss; the effect of the statute being to declare that the loss is not due until the expiration of that time. *Quinn v. Capital Ins. Co.*, 615.

15. PROOFS OF LOSS: WHAT NECESSARY. Under § 3, Chap. 211, Laws of 1880, proof of loss under a policy of insurance must be by affidavit, stating the facts as to how the loss occurred, so far as they are within the knowledge of the assured, and the extent of the loss. Therefore, *held* that an unverified certificate of a veterinary surgeon, stating how, in his opinion, a certain cow came to her death, without giving the extent of the loss, and fixing the ownership of the cow in a person other than the insured, was insufficient; and in an action on the policy to recover the value of the cow, evidence that such certificate was sent to the company was inadmissible. *Welch v. Des Moines Ins. Co.*, 337.

16. LIABILITY OF AGENT FOR NEGLECT OF DUTY: DAMAGES. An insurance company cannot recover more than nominal damages of its agent, through whose fault, while acting in good faith, it is drawn into a contract of insurance somewhat different from what it supposes it to be, but not less valuable to it; the risk actually taken being such as the company is accustomed to accept. So *held*, where the application falsely represented the insured premises to be an occupied hotel building, when in fact the agent knew it to be unoccupied at the time, but did not communicate that knowledge to the company, but the rate paid was greater than that charged for similar unoccupied hotel buildings, and the building was burned before occupancy, and plaintiff, being charged with the agent's knowledge, was obliged to pay the loss. In such case, even if the premium received had been less than that charged for the risk actually taken, the agent would have been liable only for the difference, and not for the amount paid by the company in adjusting the loss. *State Ins. Co. v. Richmond*, 519.

(2) Life Insurance.

17. DELAY IN PAYING ASSESSMENT: FORFEITURE WAIVED. Although defendant had a right to declare the insurance in question forfeited on account of the failure to pay an assessment, yet such forfeiture was waived by afterwards, before the death of the assured, receiving the assessment and retaining it; and it makes no difference that the assessment was demanded and received by mistake. while the intention was to regard the insurance as forfeited. *Bailey v Mut. Benefit Asso.*, 689.

18. ASSESSMENT PLAN: REMEDY ON CERTIFICATE. Upon a certificate entitling the beneficiary to the net proceeds of one full assessment upon the members of the company in good standing, where it appears that the company has no funds to pay a loss except as it is raised by an assessment specially made for that purpose, *held* that an action at law against the company for what would be realized by such an assessment could not be maintained, without averring and proving that such assessment had been made, and the amount thereof. [BECK, J., *dissenting.*] *Id.*

INTEREST.

1. ON MONEY WITHHELD AFTER TITLE ADJUDICATED. Where the holder of a fund refuses to pay it after the title thereto has been adjudicated, he must pay interest from the date of such adjudication. *Howe r. Jones*, 92.

2. CONSTRUCTION OF CONTRACT. T. was owing D. $3,000, and one clause of a contract between them stated: "T. is to pay D. $1,000 on or before April 1, 1880," and another clause provided: "The balance of said sum is to be paid by T. to D. on or before April 1, 1881, and interest is to be allowed to D. accordingly on said $1,000; and the remaining balance to be paid April 1, 1881, at the rate of 10 per cent from this date." *Held* that the contract provided for 10 per cent on the last payment only, and that, no rate being named for the first payment, it drew only 6 per cent. *De Wolfe v. Taylor*, 648.

3. STOPPAGE BY OFFER TO PAY. A mere statement by a debtor to his creditor that he is ready to pay is not sufficient to stop the accruing of interest. If an actual tender is not necessary, it must at least appear that he has the money, and is in fact ready to pay according to contract. *Id.*

INTERVENTION.

1. BY COUNTY: ACTION TO ANNUL SALE OF POOR FARM. In an action by tax-payers against the purchasers of a poor-farm from the county, to set aside the sale on account of the inadequacy of the price, and other alleged illegalities, *held* that the county was entitled, under § 2683 of the Code, to intervene and join the defendants in sustaining the sale, on the ground that it was advantageous to the county. *McConnell v. Hutchinson*, 512.

See ATTACHMENT, 8.

INTOXICATING LIQUORS.

1. INJUNCTION: REFORMATION BEFORE HEARING. Where it appeared from the evidence that defendants had been engaged in selling intoxicating liquors contrary to law, and had kept and maintained buildings for that purpose, thus creating and maintaining nuisances, *held* that temporary injunctions should have been granted, notwithstanding defendants testified that, after notice of the hearing for the allowance of temporary injunctions had been served on them, they had reformed and quit the business. (See opinion for authorities cited.) *Judge v. Cribs*, 183.

2. ————: ABATEMENT: VESTED RIGHTS: REMOVAL OF CAUSES TO FEDERAL COURTS. Plaintiff sought to abate as nuisances certain places kept for the unlawful sale of intoxicating liquors. Defendants, by proper petitions, sought to have the causes removed to the federal courts on the ground that, long prior to the passage of the statute under the provisions of which the actions were brought, they had purchased the real estate described in the petitions for the purpose of selling beer thereon, and had procured fixtures and furniture for said business, and placed them on the real estate, and that the same were not fitted for any other business, and would be rendered practically valueless if they should be enjoined from carrying on said business, and thus they would be deprived of their property without compensation and without due process of law. *Held* that no federal question was involved, and that it was error to grant the petitions for removal. (*McLane v. Leicht*, 69 Iowa, 401, followed.) *Judge v. Arlen*, 186.

3. CONDEMNATION: VALUE: JURISDICTION OF JUSTICE OF THE PEACE. An action for the condemnation and destruction of intoxicating liquors kept

ment of that fact from the defendant, nor that she could not by diligence have ascertained the fact before the judgment was entered. *Id*

6. CLERICAL ERROR: REMEDY ON APPEAL: COSTS. Where a decree is in conflict with the evidence on account of a supposed clerical error in drawing it, but is otherwise correct, it will be modified on appeal so as to correct the error, and then affirmed, but the appellant will be entitled to his costs in this court. The fact that appellant did not move for its correction in the trial court will not deprive him of relief here. *Kenyon v. Tramel*, 693.

7. RENDERED IN VACATION: CONSENT. In an application by plaintiff for a discharge as trustee, where the court found that there was due from him a certain sum, an order that he pay the same was such an order as might be made in vacation by the consent of parties. *Guthrie v. Guthrie*, 744.

8. ————: FILED AFTER EXPIRATION OF JUDGE'S TERM OF OFFICE: VALIDITY. Where an order was made by the judge in vacation and reduced to writing, and delivered to the defendants' attorney December 30, 1884, to be filed in the clerk's office, but he did not file it until January 1, 1885, the day after the judge's term of office had expired, *held* (by a divided court) that the order was nevertheless valid. (Compare *Babcock v. Wolf*, 70 Iowa, 676.) *Id*.

9. ON SPECIAL VERDICT. See Practice and Procedure, 14, 16.

See CRIMINAL LAW, 26; PRACTICE AND PROCEDURE, 4–6; SPECIFIC PERFORMANCE, 5; SUPERINTENDENT OF PUBLIC INSTRUCTION; USURY, 4.

JUDICIAL SALE.

See EXECUTION.

JURISDICTION.

1. MUST BE INVOKED BY PROPER PETITION: PETITION ADDRESSED TO WRONG COURT. Where a petition for the foreclosure of a mortgage was filed in the circuit court, and was by the clerk placed in a wrapper, on which were written the usual indorsements, but the cause was afterwards dismissed, and subsequently the plaintiff in that case gave notice of an action for the foreclosure of the same mortgage in the district court, but filed no new petition, but simply took the old petition, and changed the indorsements on the wrapper so as to make it appear to be a petition in the district court, and on such petition obtained judgment and decree of foreclose upon default. *Held*—

   (1) That the wrapper was no part of the petition, and that the changes in the indorsements thereon did not change the petition to the district court.

   (2) That, there being no petition invoking the jurisdiction of the district court in the case, that court had no jurisdiction of the subject-matter, and that the judgment and decree were void, and that a sale of the land thereunder, and the title acquired by such sale, were also void. *Jordan v. Brown*, 421.

2. WANT OF: WAIVER. Want of jurisdiction of the subject-matter cannot be waived, even by consent of the parties, and the objection may be raised at any time. (*Dicks v. Hatch*, 10 Iowa, 380. and *Cerro Gordo Co. v. Wright Co.*. 59 Id., 485, followed.) *Orcutt v. Hanson*, 514.

3. QUESTION OF NOT WAIVED BY APPEALING. The claim that a tribunal acted without jurisdiction of the subject-matter in making a certain order is not waived by appealing from the order, but the question of

jurisdiction may be determined on the appeal. (Compare *Spray v Thompson*, 9 Iowa, 40.) *Stough v. C. & N. W. R'y Co.*, 641.

4. OF TOWNSHIP TRUSTEES. See Animals, 1.

5. OF SUPREME COURT. See Appeal, *passim.*

6. OF APPEAL FROM JUSTICE. See Appeal, 11.

See JUSTICES AND THEIR COURTS, 1, 2; PRACTICE AND PROCEDURE, 20; VENUE, 5.

JURORS AND JURY.

1. RIGHT TO MINUTES OF EVIDENCE: DUTY OF BAILIFF. A bailiff in charge of a jury has no authority, when requested by the jury, to bring in the minutes of the testimony, in order that they may use them in settling a disputed point in the evidence. *State v. Griffin*, 372.

2. SICK JUROR: TEMPORARY ABSENCE WITH BAILIFF. During the deliberation of the jury, one of the jurors was taken sick, and was permitted to separate himself from the others for a time, and to take a walk in the open air with an officer, but was not permitted to communicate with any person about the case. *Held* irregular, but not prejudicial, and no ground for reversal. *Id.*

3. JUROR DISCLAIMING VERDICT. A juror who has consented to a verdict cannot afterwards be heard to say that it does not express his honest judgment on the facts of the case, but that he assented to it because he was sick and desired to be released. *Id.*

4. COMPETENCY: OPINIONS FORMED. Where a juror in a criminal case admitted that he had formed an opinion as to the prisoner's guilt, and even stated, in answer to a question, that it was an unqualified opinion, yet, where he insisted all through his examination that it was not such an opinion as would disqualify him from rendering a true verdict upon the evidence, *held* that the court did not err in overruling a challenge for cause based on the ground of such opinion. (Compare Code, § 4405, subd. 11.) *State v. Vatter*, 557.

See NEW TRIAL, 1.

JUSTICES AND THEIR COURTS.

1. TERRITORIAL JURISDICTION: CONSENT. Where the plaintiff resided in one township of the county, and the defendant in another, in which notice was served on him, but the suit was brought before a justice of the peace in still another township, *held* that, while the justice did not obtain jurisdiction of the person of defendant by such service, (Code, §§ 3509, 3510,) yet, when defendant appeared and, without objecting to the jurisdiction, consented to an order for a continuance, he thereby conferred jurisdiction upon the court. *Auspach v. Ferguson*, 144.

2. JURISDICTION: QUESTION NOT RAISED: APPEAL. Where a cause before a justice of the peace involved more than $100, but the question of jurisdiction was not raised, it could not be raised upon writ of error in the circuit court, nor upon an appeal from the judgment of the circuit court to this court. *Edwards v. Cosgro*, 296.

3. SELECTION OF OFFICER TO SUMMON JURY IN CRIMINAL CASE: INQUIRY AS TO FITNESS. When a justice is about to issue a *venire* for a jury in a criminal case to a certain peace officer, (Code, § 4673,) the prosecutor may properly file a motion, supported by affidavit, showing that such officer is prejudiced against the prosecution, and is likely to select jurors to the prejudice of the state, and asking that the *venire* be issued to

some other peace officer: and in such case it is the duty of the justice to institute an inquiry, and investigate the truth of the charge, and govern his action accordingly. *Rainbow v. Benson*, 301.

4. APPEAL FROM: JURISDICTION. See Appeal, 11.

See STATUTE OF LIMITATIONS, 2.

LAND.

See REAL ESTATE.

LANDLORD AND TENANT.

1. LANDLORD'S LIEN: ACTION AGAINST PURCHASER OF CROPS: LIMITATION AS TO TIME. One who purchases from a tenant, and converts to his own use. crops on which the landlord has a lien for rent, is liable to the landlord in damages to the amount of his lien, but the action to recover such damages must be brought within six months after the expiration of the term of the lease, that is, before the expiration of the lien, (see Code, § 2017,) or it will be too late. [REED, J., *dissenting*.] *Nickelson v. Negley*, 546.

LARCENY.

See CRIMINAL LAW, 11-14.

LESSOR AND LESSEE.

See LANDLORD AND TENANT.

LEVY.

1. WHAT NECESSARY. See Attachment. 7.

LIBEL.

1. PRIVILEGED COMMUNICATION: JUDICIAL PROCEEDINGS: STATEMENTS IN AFFIDAVIT. Whatever is said or written in good faith in the course of judicial proceedings, and which is pertinent and material to the matter in controversy, is privileged. So *held* as to the statements made by a prosecutor of alleged criminals before a justice of the peace, in an affidavit setting forth that the peace officer to whom a *venire* was about to be issued was in collusion with the alleged criminals, and therefore an unfit person to summon a jury for their trial. *Rainbow v. Benson*, 301.

● LIENS.

See MECHANIC'S LIEN; MORTGAGE, *passim*; PERSONAL PROPERTY, 1.

LIFE INSURANCE.

See INSURANCE, 17, 18.

LIMITATION OF ACTIONS.

See STATUTE OF LIMITATIONS.

MANDAMUS.

See SCHOOLS. 1, 2.

MASTER AND SERVANT.

1. NEGLIGENCE OF SERVANT: LIABILITY OF MASTER. Where an employer has no control over an employe, but the latter may alone direct his own acts and the manner of doing the work, the employer is not liable for his negligence;—following cases cited in opinion;—and instruction given in this case is *held* erroneous as not recognizing this rule. ADAMS, CH. J., from his view of the evidence, dissenting. *Brown v. McLeish*, 381.

See RAILROADS, 10-21.

MECHANIC'S LIEN.

1. ENFORCEMENT BY SUB-CONTRACTOR: NECESSARY PARTIES. A sub-contractor who holds an open, liquidated and unsettled account against the principal contractor cannot bring his action against the owner of the building or improvement, and establish a mechanic's lien on the property, without adjudicating the claim, or attempting to adjudicate it in any way, against the principal contractor, who is the person principally liable on the account. *Vreeland v. Ellsworth*, 347.

2. SUBCONTRACTOR: ESTOPPEL. A subcontractor who stands by in silence and sees the owner of a building pay the principal contractor in full, is estopped from afterwards claiming a mechanic's lien on the property. *Id.*

3. ———: PAYMENT TO CONTRACTOR: NOTICE. Where the owner of an improvement knows that subcontractors are furnishing labor and materials, and knows who they are, he cannot defeat them of their rights under the mechanic's lien law by paying to the contractor, or to subsequent subcontractors on his orders, the contract price of the work, in disregard of the claims of the prior subcontractors. *Chicago Lumber Co. v. Woodside*, 359.

4. PRIOR MORTGAGE: SEPARATE SALE OF IMPROVEMENT: APPORTION-MENT OF PROCEEDS. Where there was a prior mortgage on the farm on which a new dwelling house was erected, for the materials for which plaintiff claimed the establishment of a mechanic's lien, and the house was securely built on a stone foundation, and covered a cellar suitable for its purpose, and it was stipulated that the land was not worth enough to pay both plaintiff and the mortgagee, but it did not appear what the land and improvement together were worth, *held* that the court below did not abuse the discretion vested in it by Chap. 100, § 9, par. 4, Laws of 1876, in refusing to order the separate sale and removal of the dwelling for the satisfaction of plaintiff's lien; and that, under the doctrine of *German Bank v. Schloth*, 59 Iowa, 316, and *Curtis v. Broadwell*, 66 Id., 662, the court properly decreed the mortgage to be a first lien on the whole property, and ordered a foreclosure sale accordingly. *Miller v. Seal*, 392. ●

MINORS.

See DOMICILE, 1.

MISTAKE.

See CONTRACTS, 6, 7; PLEADING, 7.

MORTGAGE.

1. FORECLOSURE: NOTICE OF EQUITY: EVIDENCE CONFINED TO ISSUES. In an action to foreclose a mortgage, a general averment that plaintiff's mortgage was superior to a mortgage held by one of the defendants was but a legal conclusion, and did not warrant the admission of

evidence to show that the defendant, when he took his mortgage, had actual notice of plaintiff's equity. Such notice should have been pleaded if plaintiff intended to rely upon it. *Koon v. Tramel*, 132.

2. POSSESSION OF LAND BY MORTGAGEE'S VENDOR: NOTICE OF EQUITIES The rule that the possession of real estate is notice to all the world of the equities of the possessor, does not apply to the vendor in possession after he has conveyed the land to another and the conveyance has been recorded. So *held*, where the vendor in possession sought to have a mortgage for purchase money, made some time after the recording of the deed, declared superior to an intervening mortgage made by the vendee while the vendor was still in possession. (See opinion for cases cited.) *Id.*

3. FOR PRE-EXISTING DEBT: SUBSEQUENT MORTGAGE FOR PURCHASE MONEY: PRIORITY. A mortgage for a pre existing debt, without any additional consideration, is inferior in equity to a subsequent mortgage taken for the purchase money of the land; (*Phelps v. Fockler*, 61 Iowa, 340;) but where the time of payment of the pre-existing debt is extended for a definite period, and the mortgage is taken to secure the debt as thus extended, a new consideration enters in, which gives the mortgage priority according to its date. (Compare *Port v. Embree*, 54 Iowa, 14.) *Id.*

4. PAYMENT TO MORTGAGEE AFTER TRANSFER OF NOTES: SALE OF MORT-GAGED PREMISES: LIABILITY. Where the mortgagee of land transferred the secured notes before maturity, but did not assign the mortgage, and afterwards fraudulently, and without the knowledge of his assignee, received from the mortgagor, who was led to believe that he still owned the notes, a partial payment thereon, taking only a receipt therefor, and the mortgagor afterwards sold the land to another, *held*, in an action by the assignee to foreclose the mortgage, that he was entitled to recover, as against the mortgagor and the land, the who'e amount of the notes, regardless of the partial payment so negligently made by the mortgagor. · *Brayley v. Ellis*, 155.

5. PRIORITY: EQUAL EQUITIES: SIMULTANEOUS DELIVERY AND FILING: PAYMENT PRO RATA. S. bought land of W. for $600, paying $300 in cash, and agreeing to secure the residue by a note and mortgage on the property. But he borrowed of T. the $300 with which to make the cash payment, and agreed to secure T. by a mortgage on the property. Both mortgages were executed on the day of the sale, but neither was delivered until some days afterwards, when S. took them to the record-er's office and delivered them to the recorder to be recorded. He first handed the recorder the mortgage to T., and immediately thereafter the mortgage to W., intending to give priority to the one so first delivered, but not expressing any such intention, and the recorder marked them as filed at the same time. In the mortgage to W. the land was described as being in the wrong county. In an action to foreclose, *held*, —

(1) That S.'s secret intention to give priority to the mortgage to T. could not have that effect.

(2) That the mere act of handing one mortgage to the recorder an instant before the other did not give it priority.

(3) That the fact that W. waived his vendor's lien by taking the mortgage, while T. had no prior interest in the property, did not give to W.'s mortgage any superiority in equity.

(4) That the clerical error in the description of the land in W.'s mort-gage did not render it inferior in equity to the other, since there was no question of notice in the case.

(5) That both mortgages were entitled to be paid *pro rata* out of the proceeds of the sale of the land. *Koevenig v. Schmitz*, 175.

MUNICIPAL CORPORATIONS.

See CITIES AND TOWNS; COUNTIES.

MURDER.

See CRIMINAL LAW, 16, 21.

NEGLIGENCE.

See CITIES AND TOWNS, 1, 8; MASTER AND SERVANT, 1; RAILROADS, 7–30, *passim.*

NEGOTIABLE INSTRUMENTS.

See ASSIGNMENT, 1; PROMISSORY NOTES.

NEW TRIAL.

1. CONSIDERATION BY JURY OF EXTRANEOUS EVIDENCE. Where a paper containing evidence material and pertinent to the issues, and capable of influencing the minds of the jurors, but which had not been introduced as evidence in the case, was, by inadvertence, given to the jury with the proper papers in the case, and the same was read by the jurors, *held* that the court properly set aside the verdict and granted a new trial, even after it had denied a new trial on the ground that the verdict was not supported by the evidence. (See opinion for cases cited.) *McLeod v. H. & S. R'y Co.,* 138.

2. MISCONDUCT OF COUNSEL: DISCRETION OF TRIAL COURT. The decision of the trial court upon a question of the misconduct of counsel in argument to the jury, where the decision was based upon conflicting affidavits and the court's own knowledge of the facts, will not be disturbed on appeal. *Seekel v. Norman,* 264.

See CRIMINAL LAW, 2; PRACTICE AND PROCEDURE, 2, 3.

NOTES AND BILLS.

See PROMISSORY NOTES.

NOTICE.

See MORTGAGE, 2; SALES, 2.

NUISANCE.

See INTOXICATING LIQUORS, 1, 2, 6.

OFFICERS.

See CLERK OF COURTS; BOARD OF SUPERVISORS; TOWNSHIP TRUSTEES.

PARTIES TO ACTIONS.

1. TO ACTION TO QUIET TITLE AGAINST MISDESCRIPTION. The wives and husbands of the descendants of one who has conveyed land by a wrong description are not necessary parties to an action to quiet the title against such imperfection, on the ground that they have a dower interest in the land; for they have no such interest. (Compare *Lea v. Woods,* 67 Iowa, 304.) *Stevenson v. Polk,* 278.

2. WHO ARE NOT. Persons whose names are inserted as parties defendant in a petition, but who are not served with notice and do not appear, are not parties to the action. *Vreeland v. Ellsworth,* 347.

3. PARTY IN INTEREST: OWNERSHIP OF NOTE SUED ON. Where plaintiff's attorneys, in settling a claim, took the two notes in suit, payable to themselves, and it was agreed that they were to have the amount of the smaller note as their fees, but it was not agreed that they should have the note itself, and they indorsed both notes to plaintiff. *held* that this did not show that one of the notes was owned by the attorneys, nor that plaintiff was not the real party in interest in the action to collect the the notes. *Miller v. Wolbert*, 539.

4. AFTER REVERSAL. Parties defendant who do not join in an appeal from a judgment against them must be presumed to be satisfied with it, and to be dissatisfied with a reversal of it, and. after the cause is remanded, they are still parties to the action. *Case v. Blood*, 632.

5. PERSONAL INJURY: ACTION BY ASSIGNEE. The assignee of a claim for damages through a personal injury may maintain an action thereon. (*Vimont v. Chicago & N. W. R'y Co.*, 69 Iowa, 296, followed.) *Hawley v. C., B. & Q. R'y Co.*, 717.

6. MISJOINDER. See Venue, 3.

See APPEAL, 3; MECHANIC'S LIEN, 1; PRIORITY OF LIENS, 1; SCHOOLS, 2.

PARTNERSHIP.

1. FIRM PROPERTY DEEDED TO PARTNERS: RESULTING TRUST: PAROL EVIDENCE: DOWER TO WIDOW OF PARTNER: RIGHTS OF ADMINISTRATOR. Where real estate is purchased by a firm with partnership money, and for use in the partnership business, but is deeded to the partners in their individual names, *held* that the real estate still belongs to the firm; and that the individual partners only hold the title in trust for the firm; and that such trust, being an implied or resulting one, may be shown by parol testimony. Also, that, after the dissolution of the firm by the death of a partner. the firm and the individual partners all being insolvent, the widow of the deceased partner cannot recover a distributive share of the realty: and that the administrator of the deceased partner cannot, while the firm creditors are unsatisfied, appropriate a share of the property to satisfy the creditors of the decedent, even though they may have become creditors on the faith that the decedent had an individual interest in the property. (See opinion for authorities cited.) *Paige v. Paige*, 318.

See DOWER, 1.

PAYMENT.

See MORTGAGE, 4, 7; PLEADING, 7; PROMISSORY NOTE, 1, 12.

PENSIONS.

See ESTATES OF DECEDENTS, 2.

PERSONAL INJURIES.

1. DAMAGES: LIFE TABLES. In an action for injuries received through negligence, and which are of a permanent nature, life tables are admissible to show the plaintiff's expectancy of life, in order to determine the measure of his damages. (*McDonald v. Chicago & N. W. R'y Co.*, 26 Iowa, 124, followed, and *Nelson v. Chicago, R. I. & P. R'y Co.*, 38 Id., 564, overruled.) *Knapp v. S. C. & P. R'y Co.*, 41.

2. EXAMINATION BY PHYSICIAN: TESTIMONY OF PHYSICIAN AND PATIENT: HEARSAY. In an action to recover for personal injury, a physician called upon to examine the plaintiff may state as a witness the complaint

made by plaintiff at the time, (*Gray v. McLaughlin*, 26 Iowa, 279,) and may also give an opinion, based on such examination, as to the extent and probable consequences of the injury and what caused it; but the testimony of the plaintiff as to what the physician said at the examination is mere hearsay, and should be excluded. *Armstrong v. Town of Ackley*, 76.

3. EVIDENCE: CONTEMPORARY STATEMENTS OF ONE PRESENT: HEARSAY. The statements made by one present at the time to a person injured on a defective sidewalk, when offered to be shown by the person injured, in an action against the town, are mere hearsay, and are inadmissible, unless, possibly, in rebuttal, to contradict the testimony of such person as a witness for the defendant. *Id.*

4. ———: TESTIMONY OF PATIENT AS TO SUBSEQUENT ILL HEALTH. In an action to recover for a personal injury, the plaintiff may testify as to the condition of his health, and in relation to the pain suffered after receiving the injury; it being for the jury to say whether the impaired health and pain were caused by the alleged injury. *Id.*

5. IMMEDIATE DEATH: SURVIVAL OF ACTION. While at common law an action could not be maintained for a personal injury resulting in immediate death, yet the reasons for that rule are abrogated by §§ 2525-2527 of the Code, and now an action by the administrator may be maintained in such a case. *Conners v. B., C. R. & N. R'y Co.*, 490.

See CITIES AND TOWNS, 1, 2, 8; RAILROADS, 10-27.

PERSONAL PROPERTY.

1. WHAT IS: MACHINERY FOR MILL: ORDER OF LIEN. The owners of a mill held it subject to a recorded lien for purchase-money, and they purchased certain machinery to be annexed to the mill, and the machinery had been delivered on the ground, and it was their intention to annex it, and they had begun the erection of a building in which the machinery was to be placed, but none of it had been put in place. *Held* that the machinery was as yet personal property, and that a chattel mortgage then placed upon it created a lien which was superior to the vendor's lien on the realty for purchase-money. (Compare *Sowden v. Craig*, 26 Iowa, 156, and *First Nat. Bank of Waterloo v. Elmore*, 52 Id., 541.) *Miller v. Wilson*, 610.

2. WHAT CONSIDERED AS. See Administrator, 1.

See CHATTEL MORTGAGE.

PLACE OF SUIT.

See VENUE.

PLEADING.

1. AMENDMENT DURING ARGUMENT: ALLEGATIONS NOT CONTROVERTED ADMITTED. Where the ground upon which plaintiff sought a rescission of a conveyance of real estate was that it was obtained by fraud and undue influence, and for a grossly inadequate consideration, *held* that an amendment to her petition, in which she alleged that she and her husband were of weak intellect, and were wanting in capacity to engage in important business transactions, and that, at the time of the transaction in question, they were in financial distress, was material to the case, but did not state a new cause of action or ground of relief, and that under Code, § 2689, it was properly allowed to be filed after the evidence was all in, and during the argument of the case; *also,*

that the averments contained in the amendment, not being denied, were to be taken as true, under Code, § 2712, in the further consideration of the case. *Clough v. Adams,* 17.

2. PLEA FILED AFTER SUBMISSION WITHOUT LEAVE. An answer which presents new issues, and which is filed after the submission of the cause without leave of the court, is properly stricken from the files. *Sullivan Sav. Inst. v. Copeland,* 67.

3. CONFESSION AND AVOIDANCE: PLEADING ESTOPPEL IS NOT. Where in an action on a promissory note defendant pleaded that his signature to the note was a forgery, and plaintiff replied, averring that defendant's signature was genuine, and that he was by his acts and conduct estopped from denying it, *held* that this reply was not in the nature of a confession and avoidance of the answer, and did not change the issue as to the genuineness of defendant s signature. *Eikenberry v. Edwards,* 82.

ANSWER TO COUNTER-CLAIM IN INJUNCTION SUIT: TRANSFER TO LAW DOCKET. Plaintiff sued out a preliminary injunction restraining the collection of certain notes on the ground that they had been paid. Defendants answered, denying that the notes had been paid, and, upon proper averments, asking judgment thereon; and on their motion the injunction was dissolved and the cause transferred to the law calendar. *Held* that the case then stood like an action at law for the collection of the notes, and that plaintiff had a right to plead any matter of defense. *Gardner v. Halstead,* 259.

5. AMENDMENT AFTER VERDICT. On an appeal from an award of damages for right of way taken by a railroad company, where the land was in township sixty-seven, and the trial and all the proceedings had reference to that land, but the land was described in the papers as being in township sixty-nine, *held* that plaintiff was properly allowed to amend, after verdict, by substituting sixty-seven for sixty-nine. *Ball v. K. & N. W. R'y Co.,* 306.

6. ANSWER: DENIAL OF AMOUNT DUE: EFFECT. A denial in an answer that defendants are indebted in the amount claimed in the petition does not present an issue of fact, and does not amount to a general denial. (*Stucksleger v. Smith,* 27 Iowa, 286, followed.) *Callanan v. Williams,* 363.

7. PAYMENT OF FRAUDULENT NOTE: RECOVERY. One who seeks to recover money paid by him on a note, on the ground that the note was fraudulent, must plead and show that the payment was made under a mistake of fact, or that he did not have knowledge of the fraud at the time the payment was made. (*Murphy v. Creighton,* 45 Iowa, 179, and *City of Muscatine v. Keokuk, etc, Packet Co,* Id., 85, followed.) *Baldwin v. Foss,* 389.

8. ISSUE WITHOUT REPLY. Where, in an action to foreclose a mortgage, plaintiff alleged that his mortgage was superior to defendant's judgment, and defendant, in what he called a counter-claim, alleged that his judgment was superior to the mortgage, *held* that no reply was necessary to put in issue such allegation of the counter-claim. *Colby v. McOmber,* 469.

9. PENDENCY OF OTHER ACTION. An answer to an action brought by an assignee, which states that the assignor, previous to his assignment to the plaintiff, commenced an action against the defendant for the same claim in his own name; that said action was removed to the circuit court of the United States; and that no order has been made dismissing it, and that the defendant has not stipulated that it should be dismissed, but which fails to aver that the action is still pending, *held* not sufficient as a plea of the pendency of another action. *Hawley v. C., B. & Q. R'y Co.,* 717.

e MORTGAGE, 1; PRACTICE AND PROCEDURE, 15; PRIORITY OF LIENS, 1.

PLEDGE.

See Mortgage, 7.; Promissory Note, 9.

POSSESSION.

1. Of stolen property. See Criminal Law, 4, 12.

2. Of land: notice. See Mortgage, 2.

PRACTICE AND PROCEDURE.

1. Saving exceptions: method and time. An exception can be preserved only by having it embodied in a bill of exceptions, or having it noted in the record of the decision to which it relates. (Code, §§ 2831, 2833.) And a party who would save his exceptions by the first method must have his bill of exceptions signed and filed during the term at which the decision objected to was made, or within such time thereafter as the court may fix; and where the court did not fix any such time, *held* that a bill of exceptions signed and filed at the next term must be disregarded on appeal, even though it embodies the several rulings of the court, and recites that appellant excepted to each of them. *State v. Leach*, 54.

2. New trial: motion for: cause decided on demurrer. Where, pending the trial, plaintiff amended his petition, and a demurrer to the petition as amended was sustained, and judgment was rendered thereon, a motion for retrial, based on the ground that, upon the facts proved, the judgment should have been for plaintiff, was properly overruled, because the judgment was not based on any facts proved. *Id.*

3. Motion in arrest of judgment: office of. A motion in arrest of judgment is provided where the facts stated in the petition do not entitle the plaintiff to any relief; (Code, § 2650;) but such a motion is properly overruled when based on the ground of want of evidence to sustain the verdict. A motion for a new trial is the proper remedy in that case. *Kirk v. Litterst*, 71.

4. On procedendo: entering judgment of supreme court: notice: change of venue. Where in a cause on *procedendo* the judge was charged simply with the duty of rendering a judgment against a receiver, the amount of the judgment being fixed by the decision of this court and the receiver's report, which was a part of the record, *held* that, as there was nothing to try, and nothing left to the discretion of the judge, the receiver could not complain because the case was docketed and disposed of without notice to him, after it had been announced that no civil causes would be tried at that term, nor because the judge who entered the judgment had been of counsel in the case, and did not order a change of venue. *Howe v. Jones*, 92.

5. Striking out order granting leave to answer: effect. A default and judgment thereon were set aside on motion, and leave was given defendant to answer. After defendant had answered, the court, on plaintiff's motion, set aside the former order. so far as it set aside the default and gave defendant leave to answer. *Held* that the effect of the last ruling was to lay the answer out of the case, and with it all issues raised thereby. *Kirby v. Gates*, 100.

6. Setting order aside. A court may, for good reasons shown, set aside a previous order made at the same term. *Id.*

7. Appearance: what constitutes: agreement for continuance. A request or an agreement for the continuance of a cause, whether it be made orally by the party or by his counsel, or by a writing filed in the case, involves an appearance in the case, notwithstanding the record

when the special findings are inconsistent with the general verdict, and are of themselves, or when taken in connection with facts admitted by the pleadings, sufficient to establish or defeat the right of recovery. (See authorities cited in opinion) *Conners v. B., C. R. & N. R'y Co.*, 490.

17. SETTING ASIDE ORDER: NOTICE. Where a motion to change the record by setting aside an order is made, the party adversely interested should have notice; (*Townsend v. Wisner*, 62 Iowa, 672;) but when the adverse counsel appear in the case, and are heard upon the merits, the failure to give such notice is immaterial. *C. I. & D. R'y Co. v. Estes*, 603.

18. INJUNCTION: DISMISSAL AFTER ADVERSE DETERMINATION. The plaintiff in an injunction suit ought not to be allowed to have it dismissed after it has been tried, submitted, and virtually determined adversely to him. *Id.*

19. CAUSE WITHOUT EVIDENCE NOT SUBMITTED TO JURY. Where there was no evidence of the wrongful suing out of the attachment, the court did not err in refusing to submit to the jury a counter-claim for damages on that ground. *Davis v. Robinson*, 61 .

20. PROCEDURE WHEN NO JURISDICTION OF SUBJECT-MATTER. When a court has determined that it has no jurisdiction of the subject-matter of an action, it cannot properly consider any other question raised in the case. *Stough v. C. & N. W. R'y Co.*, 641.

21. SPECIAL INTERROGATORIES NOT DETERMINATIVE: UNNECESSARY: AMBIGUOUS. Certain special interrogatories asked on the trial of this case *held* to have been properly refused, because the answers, however given, would not have been determinative of the case; and, as to one, there was no dispute as to the evidence, and others were ambiguous. *Hawley v. C., B. & Q. R'y Co.*, 717.

22. FOR PRACTICE AND PROCEDURE IN CRIMINAL CASES. See Criminal Law, *passim.*

23. FOR PRACTICE AS TO EVIDENCE. See Evidence, *passim.*

See CONTINUANCE, 1; COSTS, 1; DEPOSITIONS, 1, 2; JURISDICTION, 1; JUSTICES AND THEIR COURTS; PLEADING, *passim*; REFERENCE, 1-3; REMOVAL OF CAUSES, 1, 2.

PRACTICE AND PROCEDURE IN SUPREME COURT.

1. AGREEMENT OF COUNSEL ENFORCED. Where counsel agreed to dispense with a transcript unless one was required, and that in that case appellant should have time to file one, and it became necessary to file one on account of denials made in an amended abstract, and appellant showed by affidavit, submitted with the case, that one of the papers required for a transcript was temporarily lost from the files of the court below, *held* that the denials in the amended abstract should not be taken as true, but that appellant's motion to strike it from the files should be overruled, the submission set aside, and the cause continued with leave to appellant to file a transcript. *Artz v. Culbertson*, 366.

2. JUDICIAL NOTICE OF RULES OF DISTRICT COURT. While this court is required to take judicial notice of the rules of the district court, yet, where the non-existence of a rule as to appearance day is implied in a motion to set aside a default as being premature, and opposing counsel do not in any way, in this court, call attention to any such rule, it will be assumed that none existed. *Huebner v. Farmers' Ins. Co.*, 30.

3. POINTS NOT ARGUED. Questions merely stated in the argument, but not argued, are not considered by this court. *Siltz v. Hawkeye Ins. Co.*, 710.

4 ASSIGNMENT OF ERROR: NOT SUFFICIENTLY SPECIFIC. An assignment of error that the court erred in overruling a motion for a new trial, where the motion was based upon eight grounds, is not sufficiently specific to be considered. *Kirk v. Litterst*, 71.

5. ———: JUDGMENT ON VERDICT. An assignment of error that the court erred in rendering judgment against defendant upon the verdict, in the absence of necessary evidence, raises no question for consideration, where the verdict is not assailed; for judgment follows, of course, if the verdict stands. *Id.*

6. ABSTRACT: EVIDENCE: PRESUMPTION. Where appellant's abstract purports to be an abstract of all the evidence, this court will, in the absence of an additional abstract by the appellee, assume that the evidence was made of record, and that it is before the court. *Bailey v. Mut. Benefit Asso.*, 689.

7. AMENDED ABSTRACT NOT DENIED. An amendment to appellant's abstract filed by appellee, and not denied, is deemed to be true. *Sullivan Sav. Inst. v. Copeland*, 67.

8. IMMATERIAL QUESTION. This court will not determine which of two mechanics' liens is entitled to priority, where it appears that both are sufficiently secured and will be paid. *Chicago Lumber Co. v. Woodside*, 359.

9. RECORD: HOW MUCH NECESSARY. In ordinary actions, the parties are required to print only so much of the record as is necessary for the presentation and determination of the questions brought up by the appeal for review. Accordingly, where the only question was whether a judgment for the defendant on special findings, and against the general verdict, was justifiable, it was not necessary to bring up the evidence and the instructions of the court. *Conflers v. B., C. R. & N. R'y Co.*, 490.

10. PROLIX RECORD: COSTS. Where the appellant prints and files the evidence without abstracting it, the costs of the superfluous printing will be taxed to him, even though he prevails on the appeal. *Baldwin v. Foss*, 389.

11. IMPERFECT RECORD: DISMISSAL. An appeal from an order excluding certain affidavits upon the hearing of a commissioner's report must be dismissed where the abstract does not show what judgment the court rendered in the case, nor what the affidavits contained. *Tague v. Benner*, 651.

12. DISCREPANCY IN RECORD AS TO DATE OF JUDGMENT. A discrepancy between the notice of appeal and an amended abstract, as to the date of the judgment in the case, is no ground for dismissing the appeal, where it is not shown that the appeal is not from the judgment in the case, or was not taken in time. *Kennedy v. Rosser*, 671.

13. DIMINUTION OF RECORD: CORRECTION. When it is discovered on appeal that the record in the court below is deficient, a continuance of the appeal may be held, in a proper case, for the purpose of procuring a correction of the record in the lower court, but no order of this court is necessary to give the party leave to move for a correction in the trial court, nor to confer on that court authority to make the correction. *Reynolds v. Sutliff*, 549.

14. APPEAL FROM CIRCUIT COURT: CORRECTION OF RECORD AFTER ABOLITION OF COURT. Upon the abolition of the circuit court its records were transferred by law to the district court; and where an appellant from the circuit court desires to correct the record in that court, he should apply to the district court for that purpose. *Ex parte* affidavits are not admissible. *De Wolfe v. Taylor*, 648.

PRINCIPAL AND AGENT.

PRINCIPAL AND SURETY.

PRIORITY OF LIENS.

PRISONER.

PROCEDENDO.

See PRACTICE AND PROCEDURE, 4.

PROMISSORY NOTE.

1. PAYMENT: DEPOSIT OF MONEY WITH ONE NOT A BANKER. Where a note is made payable at the office of one not a banker, and not the payee, the deposit of money to pay the note with such person is not a payment of the note, as the holder is not required by law to present the note at that place for payment. (Compare *Lazier v. Horan*, 55 Iowa, 75.) *Callanan v. Williams*, 363.

2. MATERIAL ALTERATION: WHAT IS NOT: PLACE OF PAYMENT: INSTRUCTION. For the administratrix of an estate, who is the payee and holder of a promissory note executed by the decedent, to write upon the back of the note, after her appointment as administratrix, "Payable at K.," —no place of payment being named in the note,—*held* not to be a material alteration, since the payee would in any event pay herself, after the allowance of the note as a claim against the estate, by simply crediting herself with the amount in her account as administratrix; and in such case it was error to submit to the jury any question as to such alteration. *Horton v. Est. of Horton*, 448.

3. ———: AMOUNT: ERRONEOUS INSTRUCTION. Where, in an action on a promissory note, it was alleged that the amount of the note had been materially altered, but the amount was plainly written in the body of the note, and there was no alteration therein, and the only fact relied on as an alteration was that one of the figures expressing the amount at the upper left hand corner of the note was blotted, *held* that there was no ground for submitting to the jury any question as to such alleged alteration. *Id.*

4. ———: NAME OF PAYEE: EVIDENCE TO BE CONSIDERED: INSTRUCTION. Where the defense to an action on a promissory note was that it had been materially altered, and the body of the note was in the handwriting of the plaintiff, and she testified that she had never at any time made any alteration of the note, and there was evidence tending to show that the note had been blotted after it had passed out of the hands of plaintiff, *held* that it was error to instruct the jury to determine, from a mere inspection of the instrument, whether it had been materially altered or not, but that they should have been instructed to make such determination from a consideration of all the evidence. *Id.*

5. ———: EVIDENCE: INSTRUCTION. In such case, where plaintiff claimed, as well she might from the appearance of the paper, that no alterations had been made therein, unless a blot was an alteration, and that she did not make the blot, it was error to remind the jury that she had not introduced evidence that the maker of the note had consented to the alleged alterations, nor that they were innocently made, or made by a stranger. *Id.*

6. SIGNED BY MAKERS AS TRUSTEES: PERSONAL LIABILITY. A note which reads, "We promise to pay," etc., was signed, "C. F. Clark, M. Samuels, Trustees Omega Lodge." *Held* that Clark and Samuels were personally liable as makers. (*Heffner v. Brownell*, 70 Iowa, 591, followed.) *Coburn v. Omega Lodge*, 581.

7. GIFT TO COLLEGE: FAILURE OF CONSIDERATION: CONTEMPORANEOUS ORAL AGREEMENT. A promissory note given to a college to aid in the formation of an endowment fund, where no consideration for the note is advanced, is only a written promise to make a gift at a future time, and it cannot be enforced by the donee, unless it has, prior to any revocation, entered into engagements, or made expenditures, based on the

promise, so that it must suffer loss or injury if the note is not paid. Neither can it be enforced where the fund to which the gift is promised is diverted from its object, in violation of an *oral* agreement made with the donor at the time the note was executed. *Simpson Centenary College v. Tuttle* 596.

8. PAROL TO VARY: INSTANCE. In an action upon a promissory note made by a husband to his wife's father, *held* that it was not competent for the defendant to show that the note was given merely as evidence of an advancement to the wife, and that it was made by the husband because the wife was insane, and the husband received the money in trust for her use and benefit. (*Dickson v. Harris*, 60 Iowa, 727, followed.) [BECK, J., not concurring.] *Gerth v. Engler*, 616.

9. PLEDGE OF: DUTY OF PLEDGEE. The holder of a promissory note as collateral security is not charged with the same duty as an indorsee. He is liable for failure to present the note and to give notice of non-payment, only in case damage, loss or prejudice results to the pledge or therefrom, and then only to the extent of such damage. *Kennedy r. Rosier*, 671.

10. CONSIDERATION: SURRENDER OF COLLATERAL SECURITY: INNOCENT HOLDER. Plaintiff made a loan to the M. bank, with the understanding that it was to have collateral security, and it received the collaterals some time after the loan had been made. Subsequently the cashier of the M. bank secured a return of the collaterals by depositing in their stead an accommodation note signed by himself and some others, among whom were S. and C. The signature of S. had been forged to the note, and C., relying on the genuineness of the signatures already obtained, signed last. Afterwards, C., being the only solvent signer to the note, gave the notes and mortgage sued on in this case in lieu of the accommodation note, and for an extension of time. *Held*—

    (1) That the pre-existing debt from the M. bank to plaintiff was a good consideration for the delivery of the collaterals to plaintiff.

    (2) That the return of the collaterals was a good consideration for the accommodation note.

    (3) That plaintiff must be regarded as a purchaser for value of the accommodation note, and, having had no notice of the fraud by which C.'s signature had been obtained thereto, it was in no manner affected thereby.

    (4) That fraud and want of consideration could not be successfully pleaded against the notes and mortgage in suit. *Des Moines Nat. Bank v. Chisholm*, 675.

11. IMBECILITY OF MAKER: UNDUE INFLUENCE: EVIDENCE NOT ESTABLISHING. The evidence in this case considered, (see opinion,) and *held* to show that the maker of the notes and mortgage in question was greatly impaired in mental and physical vigor at the time of their execution, but that he was not lacking in judgment or reason, but was in the possession of all his faculties, and was fully competent to enter into the contract. Also, that there was no evidence of any concealment or deceit or undue influence used in obtaining the execution of the contract. *Id.*

12. PAYMENT BY NEW NOTE: EVIDENCE ON APPEAL. As there was evidence (see opinion) which raised a presumption that the notes sued on had been paid by the giving of new notes, *held* that the finding of the trial court in accord with such presumption could not be set aside on appeal. *Cunningham v. McGowan*, 461.

13. FRAUD: HOLDER FOR VALUE, BEFORE DUE, WITHOUT NOTICE. *Hawkins v. Wilson*, 761.

PROXIMATE CAUSE.

See RAILROADS, 10, 13.

RAILROADS.

1. APPROPRIATION OF ADJACENT LAND: DAMAGES: EVIDENCE OF TITLE. Where the owner of land brings an action against a railroad company for a permanent injury to the freehold, and not for a mere possessory right, on account of an appropriation by the company of portions of the land adjacent to its right of way, it is necessary for him to prove a freehold title in himself. *Waltemeyer v. W., I. & N. R'y Co.*, 626.

2. ———: ———: PLEADINGS AND PROOF. In such case, where plaintiff alleged damages to 160 acres of land, he could not be allowed to prove damages to 240 acres, at a certain rate per acre. *Id.*

3. ———: LIABILITY FOR ACTS OF SUBCONTRACTORS. Where subcontractors, in building the embankment for a railroad, go outside of the right of way to obtain earth for the embankment, the company cannot be held liable for the trespass, unless it be made to appear in some way that it assented thereto, or had such knowledge of it at the time, or before it was done, as that assent might be presumed therefrom. *Id.*

4. RIGHT OF WAY DAMAGES: EVIDENCE ON APPEAL. On an appeal from an award of damages for land taken for right of way for a railroad, it was error to allow evidence as to the damages per acre to the land from which the right of way was taken, without definite proof as to the number of acres in the several tracts. It was also error to allow evidence of damages to certain tracts indefinitely referred to by counsel, and which were not clearly shown to be crossed by the railroad or involved in the case. *Ball v. K. & N. W. R'y Co.*, 306.

5. ON STREETS: DAMAGES TO LOT-OWNERS: APPRAISEMENT BY SHERIFF'S JURY. The owners of lots abutting upon a city street on which a railway has been built cannot have their damages ascertained by a sheriff's jury in the method prescribed for the condemnation of right of way. (*Mulholland v. Des Moines, A. & W. R'y Co.*, 60 Iowa, 740, followed.) *Stough v. C. & N. W. R'y Co.*, 641.

6. RIGHT TO FENCE TRACK IN CITIES AND TOWNS. A railroad corporation does not have the right to fence its track in cities and towns where it is intersected by streets and alleys; and it is immaterial whether the track crosses a lot or block for a greater or less distance, or whether the lot or block is owned by one or many persons. [BECK and REED, JJ., dissenting.] *Blanford v. M. & St. L. R'y Co.*, 310.

7. KILLING COW ON CROSSING: SPEED OF TRAIN: QUESTION FOR JURY. Where there was a conflict in the evidence as to the speed of the train which killed plaintiff's cow at a highway crossing, and as to the distance from the crossing at which the cow could have been seen by the engineer, and there was a sharp curve in the track as the train, which was a wild one, approached the crossing, *held* that it was a question for the jury whether the train was run at a dangerous rate of speed. *Courson v. C., M. & St. P. R'y Co.*, 28.

8. ———: CONTRIBUTORY NEGLIGENCE: QUESTION FOR JURY. Where plaintiffs' cow was killed by a wild train at a highway crossing, and it appeared that plaintiffs lived near the track, and knew of the crossing, and of the time when regular trains passed, and more than an hour before the time for the first regular train they turned the cow into the highway, intending soon to follow her and drive her to a pasture which lay beyond the track, but she was shortly afterwards killed by the passing wild train, *held* that it could not be said, as a matter of law, that

22. **INJURY TO PASSENGER: PRESUMPTION OF NEGLIGENCE: BURDEN OF PROOF.** In an action against a railroad company for injury to a passenger, caused by the derailment of a train and the breaking down of a bridge, the jury was properly instructed that the burden was on plaintiff to show that the injury was caused by the negligence of the defendant; but that, if he had established that the accident was attended by circumstances showing that it was caused by defective construction of the roadway, bridge, track, or the fastenings of the rails at the point where the derailment occurred, or of its train, or cars, or by the management or running of the train, this would raise a presumption of negligence, and would cast upon defendant the burden of proving that it was not caused by any negligence or want of skill on its part, either in the construction or maintenance of its roadway, track, or bridge, or in the management of its train, or the condition of its cars; but that this presumption extended only to those portions of the track, machinery or bridge which the circumstances of the accident indicated were possibly defective; and that it was not required to prove that nothing about its entire train and roadway was defective. In other words, the defendant in such case is not required to show how the accident occurred, and that it was free from *all* negligence in the matter, but it is sufficient if it shows its freedom from negligence as to the matter which the circumstances indicate to have been the cause of the accident and injury. *Pershing v. C., B. & Q. R'y Co.*, 561.

23. **DUTY TO PASSENGERS: DEGREE OF CARE REQUIRED.** The rule which has been uniformly recognized and enforced in this state is that the carrier, in the conduct and management of his business, is bound to exercise the highest degree of care and diligence for the convenience and safety of his passengers; and he is held liable for the slightest neglect. But there are certain dangers that are necessarily incident to travel by railway, and these the passenger assumes when he elects to adopt it; and, in the application of the rule to railway companies, all that is meant is that they should use the highest degree of care that is reasonably consistent with the practical conduct of the business. (See opinion for authorities.) *Id.*

24. ———: **SELECTION OF PLANS AND MATERIALS.** In an action against a railroad company for an injury to a passenger caused by the derailment of a train and the breaking of a bridge, the court instructed the jury, in effect, that the degree of care required of defendant in the selection of plans and materials for its roadway, bridges and appliances was such as was exercised by the best and most skillfully and carefully managed railroads in the country, under like circumstances. *Held* that, if this instruction was vulnerable to the objection that it makes the very practices which are called in question the law of the case, the objection was obviated by another instruction, drawn with special reference to the facts in the case, in which the jury were told, in effect, that defendant was bound, not only to select such plans and materials for the construction of its road and appliances as were in use by the best and most skillfully conducted roads of the country, but that such materials and plans must have been found sufficient by the other roads. *Id.*

25. ———: **CONSTRUCTION OF BRIDGES.** In such case, the jury was told that the defendant "was not required to so construct its bridge that it would resist the unusual and extraordinary shock of a derailed train, running at regular speed, and striking it with great force." *Held* that this instruction afforded plaintiff no ground of complaint, when taken in connection with another, to the effect that defendant was required to take into account, in constructing and maintaining its bridges, the fact that accidents might occur in the operation of its road, and to construct its bridges with reference thereto; and that it was held to a very high degree of care in this respect. *Id.*

uated was induced to vote a tax in aid of the construction of said road, which tax was collected and paid to said company. The road was afterwards constructed and operated by said company from Albia, in Monroe county, to Northwood, aforesaid. Afterwards the company became in-olvent, and its property and franchises were sold under mortgage to the Central Iowa Railway Company, one of the defendants herein. Subsequently the Burlington, Cedar Rapids & Northern Railway Company, the other defendant herein, and which owned and operated a road to Manly Junction, a point on the road first above mentioned, about eleven miles south of Northwood, leased the line of said first named road from Manly Junction to Northwood, and thereafter the Central Iowa Railway Company ceased to operate that portion of its road, but made Manly Junction its northern *terminus*. Upon complaint of the people of Northwood to the railroad commissioners, said commissioners ordered and adjudged that the Central Iowa Railway Company was under legal obligations to equip, maintain and operate its road from Manly Junction to Northwood, and to do so as a part of, and in connection with, its continuous line between Albia and Northwood; and that a failure so to do was a violation of its charter duties and obligations, and contrary to law. *Held* that such order was reasonable and just, and should be enforced. on the grounds, (1) that, by accepting the tax from the township in which Northwood was situated, the original company incurred an obligation to operate its whole road to that place as one continuous line. (2) That such obligation inhered in the franchise, and that the company which took the franchise at the foreclosure sale took it burdened with that obligation. [SEEVERS, J., *dissenting*.] *State v. Central Iowa R'y Co.*, 410.

31. TAX IN AID OF: CITIES UNDER SPECIAL CHARTERS: APPLICABILITY OF STATUTE. Although it is provided by Chapter 116, Laws of 1876, that "no general laws as to powers of cities organized under the general incorporation act shall in any manner be construed to affect the charters or laws of cities organized under special charters, while they continue to act under such charters, unless the same shall have special reference to such cities," yet the statute authorizing taxation in aid of railroads cannot be held to be a law affecting the chartered powers of cities; and a city acting under a special charter may, under the provisions of such statute, lawfully vote a tax in aid of a railroad. (*State v. Finger*, 46 Iowa, 25, distinguished.) *Bartemeyer v. Rohlfs*, 582.

32. ———: NOTICE OF ELECTION: DESIGNATION OF TERMINI. Where the notice of an election in the city of Davenport, upon the question of aiding a railroad company in the construction of a road, stated that the proposed road was to begin at a definitely described point within that city, and to run "thence westward along the Mississippi river to the western boundary of the city of Davenport; thence westwardly to Anamosa, in Jones county, Iowa, or to a point nearer, to connect with a railroad not now running to Davenport aforesaid," *held* that the notice sufficiently designated the *termini* of the road to satisfy the requirement of chapter 159, Laws of 1884. *Id.*

33. ———: ———: DESIGNATION OF TIME WHEN WORK IS TO BE DONE. It is not necessary that a notice of an election upon the question of voting a tax in aid of a railroad should state the date upon which the work shall be done, in order to entitle the company to the tax. It is sufficient if it provides, as in this case, that the tax shall be payable when a specified amount of the work is done. *Id.*

34. ———: PETITION AND NOTICE: VARIANCE: BASIS OF LEVY. In view of the fact that taxes in aid of railroads must be levied by the county supervisors, and the further fact that the city of Davenport is coterminous with the civil township in which it is situated. *held* that a variance between the *petition* for an election upon the question of voting a tax in

2. ———: WAIVER: ESTOPPEL. The fact that an interested party appeared before the referee after the time when his report should have been filed, and when his authority was at an end, did not confer upon him authority to proceed, and did not estop such party from afterwards objecting to the referee's authority. *Id.*

3. PRACTICE: REPORTING EVIDENCE. Conflicting claims, on which there is conflicting evidence, ought never to be sent to a referee without requiring him to preserve and report the evidence, unless there be some controlling reason for proceeding differently,—such, tor example. as the agreement of the parties that the evidence shall not be reported. *Id.*

RELIGIOUS SOCIETY.

1. ROMAN CATHOLIC CONGREGATION: SPECIAL FUND FOR BUILDING CHURCH: TITLE TO. If it be conceded that, under the laws and rules of the Roman Catholic Church, the bishop of the diocese and the priest of the parish under the direction of the bishop, are invested with the absolute control of the general funds and property of the church, yet a special fund raised by a congregation for the purpose of building a church does not belong to the bishop and priest, but to the congregation itself. And although such fund was placed in the hands of the priest for safe keeping, and the bishop afterwards joined the congregation, without its consent. to the congregation and parish at R., and requested the property to be delivered to the priest at R., and ordered the priest to go to R., which he did, and a part of the congregation went also, but a majority refused to go, and continued to worship, but without a priest, at the old place, *held* that the money so raised still belonged to the congregation, and that trustees appointed by the congregation were entitled to recover it from trustees, previously named by the congregation, to whom it had been committed by the priest when he left the congregation. *Amish v. Gelhaus*, 170.

REMOVAL OF CAUSES TO FEDERAL COURTS.

1. APPEAL: BETTER PRACTICE. Where the petition for the removal of a cause to the federal courts has been granted, and the plaintiff desires to contest the legality of such removal, it is the better practice to move in the federal court to have the case remanded, rather than to appeal to this court, since the decisions of the state courts in such cases are not binding on the federal court. *Judge v. Arlen*, 186.

2. CONTROVERTING PETITION. The facts stated as grounds for removal, in a petition for the removal of a cause to the federal court, cannot be controverted in determining the question of removal. (*Van Horn v. Litchfield*, 70 Iowa, 11, followed.) *Byson v. McPherson*, 437.

RES ADJUDICATA.

See FORMER ADJUDICATION.

RES GESTÆ.

See CRIMINAL LAW, 7.

RESIDENCE.

See DOMICILE, 1.

RIGHT OF WAY.

See RAILROADS, 1-5; SPECIFIC PERFORMANCE. 1-5.

SALE

1. CONDITION: MORTGAGE TO THIRD PARTY WITHOUT NOTICE: CODE. § 1922. Where one had possession of personal property under a conditional sale to him, whereby the title remained in the vendor until payment was made, and the contract under which he held was not acknowledged or recorded, (Code, § 1922,) and he mortgaged the property to a third party who had no actual notice of the condition of the title, *held* that the mortgagee's title was superior to that of the vendor. *Moline Plow Co. v. Braden*, 141.

2. ——: ——: WHAT IS NOTICE. In such case, if the mortgagee had such notice as to put him on inquiry, then he had actual notice. If he did not have such notice, negligence on his part in failing to make inquiry was immaterial unless, possibly, it amounted to fraud. *Id.*

3. WRITTEN WARRANTY: EVIDENCE OF ADDITIONAL PAROL WARRANTY. Where there is a written contract of sale, an oral warranty of the thing sold cannot be shown; and when there is a written warranty, the vendee cannot show an additional parol warranty. (*Mast v. Pearce*, 58 Iowa, 579, and *Shepherd v. Gilroy*, 46 Id., 193, followed.) *Nichols v. Wyman*, 160.

4. CONDITIONAL WARRANTY: FAILURE TO COMPLY. Where the contract of the sale of machinery required the purchaser, in case it failed to satisfy the warranty, to give written notice thereof to the vendors and their agent, and he failed to do so, *held* that he could not set up a failure of the warranty in defense to an action for the purchase-money. *Id.*

5. OF MACHINE: WARRANTY: INSTRUCTIONS. In an action for the price of a harvester, where failure of warranty was relied on by the defendant, the court instructed the jury on the oral contract of warranty, as claimed by defendant, and also upon the theory that the printed warranty delivered with the machine was all of the contract, and that it could not be varied by parol. *Held* that, since there was no material variance between these contracts, plaintiff was not prejudiced by the instructions. *Sandwich Mfg. Co. r. Trindle*, 600.

6. ——: ——: SUBSTANTIAL COMPLIANCE. It was not error to instruct the jury that a *substantial* compliance with the contract was all that was required of defendant, where his duties under the contract were clearly defined in other instructions. *Id.*

7. ——: ——: FAILURE: NOTICE: RETURN OF MACHINE. The machine in controversy was sold under a warranty that the defendant should have one day to give it a fair trial, and, if it did not work, written notice, stating wherein it failed, was to be given to the agent and to the plaintiff, and that the continued possession of the machine, or a failure to give such notice, should be evidence that the warranty was fulfilled. The agent sent an expert to set up the machine, and was present on the next morning, when it failed to work, and informed the defendant that he would have an expert there on a subsequent day, which he did, the agent also being present. *Held* that, under these circumstances, no notice of the failure of the machine was necessary, and that defendant's attempt to use the machine for a few days longer was not a forfeiture of his rights under the warranty, provided he returned the machine within a reasonable time. *Id.*

8. GOODS ORDERED FOR SPECIAL PURPOSE: PURPOSE DEFEATED: LIABILITY. Defendants purchased a large quantity of cider from plaintiffs for the purpose of bottling the same for resale, and at the same time requested plaintiffs to have printed for them show cards and labels to be used in the sale of the cider. The cards and labels were procured and paid for by plaintiffs, and sent with the cider to defendants, but they were useless in defendants' hands, on account of their not being

able to use the cider—it not being of the quality warranted to them. *Held* that defendants were liable to plaintiffs for the price of the cards and labels, notwithstanding the breach of warranty as to the cider. *Barrett v. Wheeler*, 662.

See EVIDENCE, 5.

SCHOOLS.

1. SCHOOL DIRECTORS: REFUSAL TO ACT: REMEDY.   From a decision by school directors an appeal lies to the county superintendent; but, where the directors refuse to act, *mandamus*, and not appeal, is the remedy. *Case v. Blood*, 632.

2. SCHOOL DISTRICTS: FUNDS: INTEREST OF NON-RESIDENT TAX-PAYER. A tax-payer in a school district, though he be a non-resident, has such an interest in the funds of the district that he may maintain an action in *mandamus* to compel the directors to perform their lawful duty in regard to such funds. *Id.*

See SUPERINTENDENT OF PUBLIC INSTRUCTION.

SEDUCTION.

See CRIMINAL LAW, 23, 24.

SELF-DEFENSE.

See CRIMINAL LAW, 10.

SETTLEMENT.

See COUNTY, 1.

SIDEWALKS.

See CITIES AND TOWNS, 1, 2, 8.

SPECIAL INTERROGATORIES.

See PRACTICE AND PROCEDURE, 8, 21.

SPECIFIC PERFORMANCE.

1 CONTRACT TO CONVEY RIGHT OF WAY: SUFFICIENCY OF DESCRIPTION. Plaintiff had surveyed and marked by stakes two lines for its proposed railway across defendant's farm, and the road was afterwards built on one of these lines. Before the building of the road was begun, defendant agreed in writing to convey to plaintiff, by metes and bounds, for its right of way, a strip of ground not less than fifty feet in width on each side of the track of said railway, over and through the land owned by him "in sections 22 and 28, Tp. 79, R. 13, Poweshiek county, Ia."   In an action for specific performance, defendant insisted that the contract was too indefinite and uncertain, as to the description of the land to be conveyed, to be enforced by an action for specific performance; and especially that the letters and figures, "Tp. 79. R. 13, Poweshiek county, Ia.," did not locate the land anywhere. But *held* that this position could not be sustained.—"Tp." being universally understood to mean "township," and "R.," "range," and their location being made otherwise definite by naming the county. *O., C. F. & St. P. R'y Co. v. McWilliams*, 164.

2. ——: INSUFFICIENT DESCRIPTION CURED. Even if the description in such case were liable to the objection made, it ought to be regarded as cured by defendant's putting plaintiff in possession of the land intended to be conveyed. *Id.*

3. ——: ADEQUACY OF CONSIDERATION. Even though the land taken under said contract, which provided for the necessary width for embankments, excavacations, slopes, spoil-banks and borrowing-pits greatly exceeded in value the money consideration named in the contract, yet, since the benefits to be derived from the construction of the road were named in the contract as a part of the consideration, *held* that a specific performance could not be avoided on the ground of inadequacy of consideration. *Id.*

4. ——: WAY THROUGH HOMESTEAD: CONTRACT NOT SIGNED BY WIFE. Although part of the land through which defendant agreed to convey the right of way was his homestead, and his wife did not sign the contract, yet, since a right of way is but an easement, (*Chicago & S. W. R'y Co. v. Swinney*, 38 Iowa, 182,) and since the right of way in this case did not destroy the homestead or defeat the occupancy as such, *held* that the homestead character of the premises would not defeat a specific performance. *Id.*

5. ——: CONTRACT FOR FEE-SIMPLE: DECREE FOR RIGHT OF WAY. In such case, where the contract in one place provided for a deed in fee simple, but the whole object of the contract was to procure a right of way only, *held* that the court properly granted a decree for a right of way deed only. *Id.*

See CONTRACTS, 11.

STATUTES CITED, CONSTRUED, ETC.

[The words in Roman type indicate the subject under consideration, and the figures following refer to the page in this volume where the statute is cited.]

CODE OF 1851.

Sec. 2501. Survival of action: Immediate death. 495.

REVISION OF 1860.

Sec. 4111. Survival of action: Immediate death. 495.

LAWS OF 1872.

Chap. 110. (Miller's Code, Ed. 1880, p. 533.) Acknowledgments: Legalizing act. 163.

CODE OF 1873.

Sec. 45, Subd. 13. Word "person" includes corporations. 228.
" 197, Par. 6. Attachment on land: Entrance in incumbrance book. 483.
" 215. Attorney's liens. 199, 200.
" 820. County auditor as agent of supervisors. 27.
" 879. Division of township: Power of county supervisors. 480.
" 386, 387. Division of township: Warrant for election in new township. 479, 480.
" 390. Assessors in cities under special charters. 585.
" 440-448. Towns: Severance of territory: Procedure. 467.
" 456. Cities: Power over disorderly houses. 90.

Sec. 464. Railways on streets: Damages to lot-owners. 612.
" 563 565, 568. Vacation of town plat. 150, 151, 152.
" 829. Assessors in cities under special charters. 585.
" 889, 890. Tax sales: Redemption: Amount to pay. 247, 248.
" 894. Tax deed: Notice to person in possession. 247.
" 897. Tax title: Who may question. 219, 263.
" 902. Tax deed: Statute of limitations. 216.
" 924, 934, 944, 949, 961. County auditor as agent of supervisors. 27.
" 945, 947, 962. Establishment of highway: Payment of damages. 441.
" 962. Highway: Establishment: Appeal: Proceedings. 440.
" 963. Highway: Establishment: Appeal: Who pays filing fee. 182.
" 1078. Corporation stock: How transferred. 271, 277.
" 1091 *et seq.* Corporation: Turn Verein: Sale of liquors by. 217.
" 1241 *et seq.* Railroads on streets: Damages: Remedy. 612.
" 1268, 1288. Railroads: Duty as to cattle guards. 312.
" 1289. Railroads: Duty to fence track. 312.
" 1300. Railroads: Right to lease property. 413, 417.
" 1454. Trespassing animals: Township trustees: All must be notified. 93.

STATUTE OF FRAUDS.

1. SALE OF LAND: TRUST. An agreement that the grantee of land shall take, hold and dispose of the same for the benefit of another, is within the statute of frauds, and cannot be established by parol. *McGinness v. Barton*, 644.

See PARTNERSHIP, 1.

STATUTE OF LIMITATIONS.

1. WHEN IT BEGINS TO RUN: FRAUDULENT CONCEALMENT. When the party against whom a cause of action in favor of another has accrued, by fraud or actual fraudulent concealment prevents him from obtaining knowledge thereof, the statute of limitations will commence to run only from the time the right of action is discovered, or might, by the use of due diligence, have been discovered. (*Dist. Twp. of Boomer v. French*, 40 Iowa, 601, and *Findley v. Stewart*, 46 Id., 655, followed.) *Bradford v. McCormick*, 129.

2. ——: ——: APPLICATION OF RULE TO JUSTICE OF PEACE AND SURE-
TIES. Accordingly, where a justice of the peace had collected a judg-ment upon his docket in favor of the plaintiff, and, when plaintiff inquired of him from time to time whether anything had been collected thereon, the justice falsely answered that nothing had been collected, *held* that the statute of limitations did not begin to run against plaint-iff's right of action against the justice and his sureties to recover the money so collected, until he had discovered the fraud, notwithstanding the collection was entered on the justice's docket, and plaintiff might have learned of it by consulting the docket. *Id.*

3. LIABILITY OF SURETY. Ordinarily, if the principal is bound, so is the surety; and, in this case, *held* that, where the fraudulent concealment of a justice of the peace prevented the statute of limitations from running in his favor, it also prevented it from running in favor of his sureties. *Id*

4. ACTION BY SURETY AGAINST PRINCIPAL. An action by a surety against a principal, for money paid as such surety, is based on an implied promise, and is barred in five years from the date of the payment. (Code, § 2529, par. 4.) *Miller v. Lesser*, 147.

5. RESIDENCE IN IOWA UNDER ASSUMED NAME: INABILITY TO DISCOVER RESIDENCE. An action upon an unwritten contract against one who had removed to Iowa, and had lived here for five years after the cause of

action had accrued, *held* barred by the statute of limitations, notwith-standing the defendant had lived here under an assumed name, and plaintiff, by the exercise of diligence, was not able sooner to discover his place of residence. *Id.*

6. ACTION FOR WILLFUL TRESPASS. An action for a willful trespass com-mitted by entering upon plaintiff's land, and, by digging a ditch thereon, interfering with his water power, accrues immediately upon the commission of the trespass, and is barred in five years thereafter. (Code, § 2529.) *Williams v. Mills Co.*, 367.

7. AMENDMENT: SAME CAUSE OF ACTION: DIFFERENT RELIEF. Where an action is begun within the time prescribed by the statute, and certain relief is asked, and, after the cause would be barred by the statute, the plaintiff files an amended petition, setting up the same cause of action, but asking different relief, *held* that the amendment is not the begin-ning of a new action, but a continuance of the old one, and that the action as founded on the amended petition is not barred. *Case v. Blood*, 632.

8. SURFACE-WATER: OBSTRUCTION BY RAILROAD. Where a railroad company constructs a passage through its embankment to allow the escape of sur-face-water, it may be that an action for damages caused by the insuffi-ciency of the outlet would not be barred in five years from the discovery of the insufficiency; (*Drake v. Railroad Co.*, 63 Iowa, 302;) but where the opening was designed for a cattle-way, and was not practicable for a water-way, the case was the same as if the embankment had been solid; that is, the injury was permanent and the damages entire, and the right of action accrued as soon as the embankment was made or the injury discovered, and was barred in five years from that time. (Compare *Stodghill v. Railroad Co.*, 53 Iowa, 341, and *Van Orsdol v. Railroad Co.*, 56 Id., 470.) *Haisch v. K. & Des M. R'y Co.*, 606.

See TAX SALE AND DEED, 3.

SUBROGATION.

See EQUITY, 1; FORMER ADJUDICATION, 3.

SUPERINTENDENT OF PUBLIC INSTRUCTION.

1. POWER TO CORRECT DECISIONS. The superintendent of public instruc-tion, in the discharge of his judicial duties, has the power, possessed by all courts and judicial officers, to correct mistakes in his decisions; and if, through mistake, he should announce a decision differing from the one actually rendered, or render a wrong decision, he could, before rights have been acquired under it, and within a proper time, upon dis-covering his mistake, recall it and decide rightly, and in such case the second decision would be the one governing the case. *Desmond v. Ind. Dist. of Glenwood*, 23.

SUPREME COURT.

1. JURISDICTION OF. See Appeal and Practice in Supreme Court, *passim*.

SURETY.

1. DISCHARGE OF BY EXTENSION OF TIME: KNOWLEDGE AND CONSENT. Granting an extension of time to the principal on a note will discharge the surety, unless he consents to such extension; but a mere knowledge of the extension, without more, is not equivalent to a consent. *Lam-bert v. Shetler*, 463.

2. EXTENSION OF TIME PROCURED BY FRAUD: DISCHARGE. Where the principal debtor on a promissory note procures its surrender

and an extension of time on the debt by presenting a new note to which he has forged the surety's name, *held* that the extension so procured will not discharge the surety. (*Kirby v. Landis*, 54 Iowa, 150, followed.) *Hubbard v. Hart*, 668.

3. LOSS OF LIEN FOR INDEMNITY: ESTOPPEL OF CREDITOR. Where a surety held a chattel mortgage from his principal for indemnity, and he told the holder of a junior mortgage that he might take the chattels, provided the debt for which he was surety had been paid, and referred him to the creditor to ascertain that fact, and the creditor told him, not that the debt had been paid, but that the surety's mortgage was no longer a lien on the chattels, whereupon the second mortgagee took the chattels, but before he had sold them under his mortgage the surety learned that the debt had not been paid, but took no measures to protect himself by the enforcement of his mortgage, *held* that the creditor was not estopped from enforcing his demand against the surety. *Id*.

See STATUTE OF LIMITATIONS, 2-4.

TAXATION.

1. PERSONAL PROPERTY IN HANDS OF RECEIVER. Where the county has acquired no lien for taxes upon personal property which has passed into the hands of a receiver, pending litigation concerning the priority of liens which have already attached, sufficient to absorb the property, *held* that the county has no claim on the property, or its proceeds, in the hands of the receiver, for the taxes levied on the property. Chapter 14, Laws of 1876, making taxes a preferred claim in case of assignment for the benefit of the creditors, has no application. *Howard Co. v. Strother*, 683.

2. IN AID OF RAILROADS. See Railroads, 30-37.

TAX SALE AND DEED.

1. DEED: NO NOTICE TO REDEEM: NOT VOID BUT VOIDABLE. A tax deed issued without service of the notice to redeem, as required by the statute, or without filing in the treasurer's office the statutory proof of such service, is not void, but it conveys the title to the land subject to the right to redeem when lawfully established. *Bowers v. Hallock*, 218.

2. WHO MAY QUESTION: PROOF OF TITLE. One cannot question the validity of a tax title unless he, or the person under whom he claims, had title to the land at the time of the tax sale. (Code, § 897.) But such title is not shown by proof that *Porter* C. M. had title from the government, and by the introduction of the record of a deed to such a person made by P. C. M., and acknowledged by *Peter* C. M.; nor by the introduction of the record of the deed alone, without the acknowledgment, for then there would be no proof of the execution of the deed by P. C. M. *Id*.

3. NOTICE TO REDEEM TO WRONG PERSON: STATUTE OF LIMITATIONS. Where the notice to redeem from a tax sale is directed to a person other than the one to whom the land is taxed, it is no notice at all, and does not cut off the right of redemption as against one who takes a tax deed under the sale: and in such case the period of limitation, (Code, § 902,) does not begin to run from the date of the tax deed. (*Trulock v. Bentley*, 67 Iowa, 602, distinguished.) *Slyfield v. Barnum*, 245.

4. REDEMPTION: TERMS OF: FILING DUPLICATE TAX RECEIPTS. Section 889 of the Code, requiring one who pays taxes on lands purchased at tax sale to file a duplicate tax receipt with the county auditor, has nothing to do with the amount which the holder of the patent title

must pay to redeem, when redemption is effected by a suit in equity; but in such case the redemptioner is required to pay the interest and and penalty provided by § 890 of the Code on each installment of taxes which has been paid by the purchaser. *Id.*

5. ACTION TO SET ASIDE: CROSS-PETITION TO QUIET: EVIDENCE: PRAC-TICE. Plaintiffs, claiming to be the patent owners, brought their action to set aside a tax deed to defendant's grantor. Defendant, in a cross-petition, to which there was no reply, sought to have his title quieted. After the introduction of the evidence and the argument, plaintiffs, having failed to show that they or their grantors had title at the time of the tax sale, (Code, § 897,) dismissed their petition. *Held* that defendant had the right to proceed with the trial of the cause made by the cross-bill, and that, upon his showing a tax deed sufficient on its face to convey the title to his grantor, he was entitled to a decree, because the court could not consider any evidence of the invalidity of the tax deed without first finding that plaintiffs were the holders of the patent title. (See *Varnum v. Shuler,* 69 Iowa, 92.) *Foster v. Ellsworth,* 262.

6. NOTICE TO REDEEM: PROOF. The holder of a tax-sale certificate, in an affidavit written on the same paper whereon appeared the notice of the expiration of the time for redemption, and the affidavit showing its publication in a newspaper, stated that he was "the holder of the certificate of purchase described in the within notice, and that said notice was served on the within named T. J. in the manner and form as shown by the within and foregoing return." *Held* that this affidavit referred with sufficient explicitness to the affidavit showing publication of the notice, and constituted good proof of service. (Compare *Stull v. Moore,* 70 Iowa, 149.) *Johnson v. Brown,* 609.

TAX TITLE.

See VENDOR AND VENDEE, 14.

TOWNSHIP.

1. ORGANIZATION: IRREGULARITY AT FIRST ELECTION: SUBSEQUENT ELECTIONS NOT AFFECTED. The board of supervisors has power, under § 679, of the Code, to divide townships and create new ones whenever the public convenience requires it, and the question of the political existence of a new township so created is in no manner affected by any irregularity in the first election of its officers; nor does such irregularity in any way affect the validity of subsequent elections of officers, or of the acts of officers subsequently elected. *Lones v. Harris,* 478.

TOWNSHIP TRUSTEES.

1. JURISDICTION TO ASSESS DAMAGES BY TRESPASSING ANIMALS. See Animals, 1.

TRESPASS.

See ANIMALS, 1; DAMAGES, 4; RAILROADS, 1, 3; STATUTE OF LIMITA-TIONS, 6.

TRUST.

See PARTNERSHIP, 1; STATUTE OF FRAUDS, 1.

USURY.

1. NOTE FOR MONEY TO PAY USURIOUS NOTES. A note is not usurious because given for money advanced by the payee for the maker in payment of usurious notes made to a third party. *Cottrell v. Southwick,* 50.

2. WHO MAY PLEAD: GRANTEE OF MORTGAGOR. The grantee of a mortgagor who assumes the payment of the mortgage cannot plead usury as a defense to the mortgage. (See cases cited in opinion.) *Sullivan Sav. Inst. v. Copeland*, 67.

3. EVIDENCE TO DISCOVER: PAROL TO IMPEACH WRITING. The conditions, covenants and recitals of any and all instruments under which usury is hidden may be contradicted. impeached and assailed by evidence, parol or written, in order to disclose the real facts and uncover the usury. *Seekel v. Norman*, 264.

4. JUDGMENT FOR SCHOOL FUND: PROCEDURE: EVIDENCE. Where in the progress of an action on a promissory note it appears that there should be a judgment for the school fund on account of usury, (Code. § 2030,) it is competent for the court to ascertain by evidence, in addition to what is introduced on the trial, the amount of the forfeiture for which the judgment should be rendered. *Id.*

VENDOR AND VENDEE.

1. QUITCLAIM DEED: OUTSTANDING EQUITIES. The grantee in a mere quitclaim deed can acquire no rights thereby against outstanding equities which are valid against the grantor. (*Watson v. Phelps*, 40 Iowa, 482, and other cited cases, followed.) *Postel v. Palmer*, 157.

2. VENDEE OF INNOCENT PURCHASER TAKES GOOD TITLE. One who, as an innocent purchaser of land for value, has good title against an outstanding equity, may transmit such good title to subsequent purchasers, even though they have notice of such equity. (See authorities cited in opinion.) *East v. Pugh*, 162.

3. ACTION FOR PURCHASE-MONEY: DEFENSE OF DEFECTIVE TITLE: BURDEN OF PROOF. Plaintiffs' intestate sold land to defendant, and gave him a bond for a deed, and put him in possession, and his right of possession had not been questioned. He also furnished him an abstract of title to the land. In an action for the purchase-money and to foreclose the title bond, defendants pleaded, not that there was no title to any portion of the land, but, in general, that the title was defective, as shown by the abstract. Plaintiffs on the trial did not trace their title back to the government, by introducing in evidence deeds from their grantors, but simply showed that the land had been conveyed to the intestate, and that he had been in open, notorious and undisturbed possession for more than ten years. *Held* that this was presumptive evidence of title, and that the burden was on defendants to show wherein the title, as shown by the abstract, was defective. *Stevenson v. Polk*, 278.

4. ————: ————: REMOVAL OF INCUMBRANCE. In such case, a recovery cannot be defeated on the ground that a portion of the land is encumbered, if the incumbrance is removed prior to the trial, unless there has been a rescission, or such an offer to rescind as entitled the party making it to a rescission at the time the offer was made. *Id.*

5. ————: ————: MORTGAGE TO CORPORATION: RELEASE. In such case, it is sufficient for the plaintiff to prove that a mortgage on the premises has been paid, without proving a release of record; but where the mortgage was to a corporation, and it was satisfied of record by the secretary and treasurer of the company, *held* that this was a sufficient release, though not executed in the manner required by the articles of incorporation for instruments affecting the title to real estate. *Id.*

6. ————: ————: MERE POSSIBILITY OF LITIGATION. In such case, a mere possibility that there may be litigation over the title will not defeat a recovery, but there must be a reasonable probability that there will be such litigation. And so, where, after plaintiffs' intestate and his

* to make payment as stipulated, cannot accept part of a payment and then declare a forfeiture. He must first make demand for the balance of that payment. *Davidson v. Hawkeye Ins. Co.*, 532.

14. BOND FOR DEED: TAX TITLE IN VENDEE TO DEFEAT VENDOR. A vendee in possession of land, under a bond for a deed to be executed when the purchase price is paid, and with an agreement to pay all taxes and assessments lawfully imposed on the premises, cannot defeat the rights of his vendor by purchasing a tax title based upon a sale made prior to his purchase of the vendor, but consummated by a deed made subsequent thereto, where notice of the expiration of the time for redemption was served on him as the one in possession of the land. In such case, it was his duty to redeem the land from the tax sale; (see cases cited in opinion;) and whatever was paid to effect such redemption would have amounted to a payment of so much on the purchase-money. His purchase of the tax title, under the facts of the case, amounted simply to a redemption, which inured to the benefit of his vendor. (*Alexander v. Sully*, 50 Iowa, 192, distinguished.) *Cowdry v. Cuthbert*, 733.

See MORTGAGE, *passim.*

VENUE.

1. CHANGE OF: DISCRETION OF JUDGE: CHAP. 94, LAWS OF 1884: APPLICATION TO PENDING ACTIONS. Chapter 94, Laws of 1884, permitting affidavits to be filed in resistance of a motion for a change of venue on account of the prejudice of the judge, and vesting the court with a discretion in the matter, applies to actions which were pending when the statute was enacted, as well as to those since begun. Section 45, Subd. 1, does not prevent such application. *Eikenberry v. Edwards*, 82.

2. ACTION IN WRONG COUNTY: MOTION TO CHANGE: PLEADING. In an action brought in Webster county, against a citizen of Butler county, for coal delivered on the track in Webster county, under a contract contained in letters between the parties, plaintiff's petition alleged that, by the terms of the contract, the coal was to be delivered and paid for in Webster county. Certain of the letters between the parties were attached as exhibits to the petition, and from these it appeared that the coal was to be *delivered* in Webster county, but it did not expressly appear therefrom, as was necessary to maintain the action in Webster county, (See Code, § 2581,) that *payment* was to be made in that county. The petition, however, further averred that certain other letters were lost, in which Webster county was expressly stated as the place of both delivery and payment. *Held* that these averments, which must for the purpose be taken as true, showed a right of action in Webster county, under § 2581 of the Code, and that a motion for a transfer of the cause to the county of defendant's residence, under § 2589 of the Code, was properly overruled. *Fort Dodge Coal Co. v. Willis*, 152.

3. ACTION IN WRONG COUNTY: MISJOINDER: CHANGE OF VENUE: COSTS. Y. & P., residents of Decatur county, drew in their own favor a draft on C., a resident of Polk county, and indorsed it to the plaintiff. C. refused to honor the draft, and plaintiff brought suit thereon against the drawers and the drawee in Decatur county. *Held—*

(1) That C. was improperly joined with Y. & P., and that as to C. Decatur was as essentially the wrong county as if he had been sued alone.

(2) That C. was entitled to have the cause as to him removed to the county of his residence, and to an allowance for his expenses in attending in the wrong county to secure such removal.

(3) That, after his motion for such relief had been overruled, and he had filed an answer, and the plaintiff had dismissed the cause without prejudice as to him, he was yet entitled to his expenses for appearing in the wrong county. *Farmers' and Traders' Bank v Cohen*, 473.

4. FORECLOSURE OF MORTGAGE AGAINST EXECUTOR AND HEIRS OF MORT-GAGOR. H., a resident of Greene county, died there, leaving a wife and children, who continued to reside there. Before his death, and prior to the enactment of chap. 126, Laws of 1884, providing that actions to foreclose mortgages *must* be brought in the county where the land lies, he had mortgaged his land in Greene county to secure notes payable in Cedar county. His widow was appointed executrix of his estate, which was in process of settlement in Greene county. This action was brought in Cedar county, where the notes were payable, against the executrix and heirs, to foreclose the mortgage. *Held* that the action was maintainable only in Greene county, and that the court of Cedar county had no jurisdiction of the subject-matter. This conclusion is concurred in by all the members of the court, but the argument of the opinion, based on the the theory that the action was strictly *in rem*, is not concurred in. *Orcutt v. Hanson*, 514.

5. WRONG COUNTY: CHANGE TO PROPER COUNTY: NO JURISDICTION. When an action which should be brought in the county of the defendant's residence is brought in another county, but the court has no jurisdiction of the subject-matter, the defendant does not waive the want of jurisdiction by failing to move for a change to the proper county, under Code, § 2589. That section is not applicable to such a case; for the court in such a case has no jurisdiction to make any order except to dismiss the case, or strike it from the files. *Id.*

VERDICT.

1. DAMAGES: POWER OF COURT TO REDUCE. The court has no power to reduce the amount of damages found by the jury, and to render judgment for the reduced sum. *Brown v. McLeish*, 381.

2. EVIDENCE: PRIVATE KNOWLEDGE OF JURORS EXCLUDED. Where the uncontradicted and unimpeached testimony of defendant established a good defense pleaded by him to the note in suit, a verdict for plaintiff should not have been allowed to stand on the ground that the jury was justified in rejecting defendant's testimony upon their personal knowledge of his unsavory reputation for truth and veracity. *Pumphrey v. Walker*, 383.

3. MAY FOLLOW EVIDENCE WITHOUT INSTRUCTIONS. Where a material fact is stated in the pleadings and is not contradicted, and the evidence fully establishes it, the jury may properly find that the statement is true, without an instruction to that effect. *Seltz v. Hawkeye Ins. Co.*, 710.

4. SPECIAL FINDINGS: JUDGMENT ON. See Practice and Procedure, 14, 16.

See JURORS AND JURY; PRACTICE AND PROCEDURE, 10.

VOLUNTARY ASSOCIATION.

See RELIGIOUS SOCIETY, 1.

WARRANTY.

See SALE, 3-7.

WATER AND WATERCOURSES.

1. SURFACE WATER: DIVERSION BY MEANS OF A DITCH: ESTOPPEL TO TURN AGAIN INTO NATURAL COURSE. The defendant, in building its railroad, spanned with a trestle a slough, along which surface water

flowed, under the trestle, upon plaintiff's land below. Afterwards defendant filled the space covered by the trestle, making a solid embankment, and cut a channel along its embankment to carry the water to the river. The diversion of the water was beneficial to plaint· iff. But the channel proved inadequate, and caused some of the adjacent lands to be overflowed, and the abutment of defendant's bridge at the river was in danger of being undermined by the water flowing through the ditch. To avoid these results, defendant was about to construct a culvert in its embankment to allow the water to flow again in its original and natural course. The amount of the water had in the mean time been augmented by the fact that some of the land-owners above the embankment had drained their lands by ditches into the slough. Plaintiff sought to enjoin defendant from again turning the water into its natural course, on the ground that he would thereby be damaged, and that defendant was estopped from so doing on account of its having taken control of the water and directed its course in another way. But, as it does not appear that plaintiff did anything in reliance upon the permanency of the diversion of the water. or that he would, on account of anything done by defendant, be in any worse condition by its return to its natural course than he was before its diversion. *held* that there was no estoppel, and that the injunction was not warranted. [BECK, J., *dissenting.*] *King v. C., B. & Q. R'y Co.*, 696.

See STATUTE OF LIMITATIONS, 8.

WILL.

1. BEQUEST OF ALL PROPERTY TO WIDOW: ELECTION. Where a testator bequeaths all his property absolutely to his widow, it is not necessary, in order that she may take under the will, that she file her election so to take, instead of taking her third under the statute. Section 2542 of the Code does not apply to such a case. *Bulfer v. Willigrod*, 620.

2. CONSTRUCTION: ABSOLUTE BEQUEST. A bequest in the following form: "I give and bequeath to my beloved wife * * * all my property, to use to her own use and benefit as she shall deem best for herself and our beloved daughter," *held* an absolute bequest to the wife, and that the daughter had no recoverable interest in the property or the proceeds. *Id.*

3. CONSTRUCTION: GENERAL OR SPECIFIC LEGACIES. A testator bequeathed to each of four persons $600, and then stated in his will: "This amount is in notes such as the executrix of my will may turn out to them. The rest of my property I devise and bequeath to my wife." *Held* that the $600 bequests were not specific legacies of certain notes which the executrix might turn out in their payment, whether good or bad, but that the testator intended that each legatee should have $600, which the executrix could pay in notes of that value, or which would yield that sum, and that, if there should not be sufficient good notes in the hands of the executrix, the sum should be made up of other property of the estate. *Frank v. Frank*, 646.

WITNESS.

1. COMPETENCY: WIFE OF DECEDENT AGAINST EXECUTOR. Section 3641 of the Code does not prohibit a widow from testifying for the plaintiff in an action upon an account against her husband's executor. The prohibition of that section applies only to actions brought against the husband or wife personally. [BECK, J., *dissenting.*] *Parcell v. McReynolds*, 623.

2. EXPERTS. See Criminal Law, 20; Evidence, 8, 9.

See CRIMINAL LAW, 18; DEPOSITIONS, 1; EVIDENCE, 10, 11.

Ex. y. a. a.

Lightning Source UK Ltd.
Milton Keynes UK
UKHW020109231118
332756UK00006B/221/P